Entrepreneurial Development and Innovation in Family Businesses and SMEs

Andreas Masouras
Neapolis University, Cyprus

Georgios Maris
University of the Aegean, Greece

Androniki Kavoura
University of West Attica, Greece

IGI Global
PUBLISHER of TIMELY KNOWLEDGE

A volume in the Advances in Business Strategy and Competitive Advantage (ABSCA) Book Series

Published in the United States of America by
IGI Global
Business Science Reference (an imprint of IGI Global)
701 E. Chocolate Avenue
Hershey PA, USA 17033
Tel: 717-533-8845
Fax: 717-533-8661
E-mail: cust@igi-global.com
Web site: http://www.igi-global.com

Library of Congress Cataloging-in-Publication Data

Library of Congress Cataloging-in-Publication Data

Names: Masouras, Andreas, 1980- editor. | Maris, Georgios, 1979- editor. | Kavoura, Androniki, 1972- editor.
Title: Entrepreneurial development and innovation in family businesses and SMEs / Andreas Masouras, Georgios Maris, and Androniki Kavoura, editors.

Description: Hershey : Business Science Reference, 2020. | Includes bibliographical references and index. | Summary: "This book contributes to the understanding, improving and strengthening of entrepreneurial development, and innovation's role in family businesses and SMEs by providing both theoretical and applied knowledge in order to find how and why entrepreneurship and innovation can produce inefficient and dysfunctional outcomes"-- Provided by publisher.
Identifiers: LCCN 2019057835 (print) | LCCN 2019057836 (ebook) | ISBN 9781799836483 (hardcover) | ISBN 9781799836490 (paperback) | ISBN 9781799836506 (ebook)
Subjects: LCSH: Family-owned business enterprises--Management. | Small business--Management. | Management--Technological innovations. | Business planning.
Classification: LCC HD62.25 .E568 2020 (print) | LCC HD62.25 (ebook) | DDC 658.02/2--dc23
LC record available at https://lccn.loc.gov/2019057835
LC ebook record available at https://lccn.loc.gov/2019057836

This book is published in the IGI Global book series Advances in Business Strategy and Competitive Advantage (ABSCA) (ISSN: 2327-3429; eISSN: 2327-3437)

British Cataloguing in Publication Data
A Cataloguing in Publication record for this book is available from the British Library.

For electronic access to this publication, please contact: eresources@igi-global.com.

Advances in Business Strategy and Competitive Advantage (ABSCA) Book Series

Patricia Ordóñez de Pablos
Universidad de Oviedo, Spain

ISSN:2327-3429
EISSN:2327-3437

Mission

Business entities are constantly seeking new ways through which to gain advantage over their competitors and strengthen their position within the business environment. With competition at an all-time high due to technological advancements allowing for competition on a global scale, firms continue to seek new ways through which to improve and strengthen their business processes, procedures, and profitability.

The **Advances in Business Strategy and Competitive Advantage (ABSCA) Book Series** is a timely series responding to the high demand for state-of-the-art research on how business strategies are created, implemented and re-designed to meet the demands of globalized competitive markets. With a focus on local and global challenges, business opportunities and the needs of society, the **ABSCA** encourages scientific discourse on doing business and managing information technologies for the creation of sustainable competitive advantage.

Coverage

- Entrepreneurship & Innovation
- Tacit Knowledge
- Strategy Performance Management
- Cost Leadership Strategy
- Globalization
- Resource-Based Competition
- Customer-Orientation Strategy
- Foreign Investment Decision Process
- Differentiation Strategy
- Competitive Strategy

IGI Global is currently accepting manuscripts for publication within this series. To submit a proposal for a volume in this series, please contact our Acquisition Editors at Acquisitions@igi-global.com or visit: http://www.igi-global.com/publish/.

The Advances in Business Strategy and Competitive Advantage (ABSCA) Book Series (ISSN 2327-3429) is published by IGI Global, 701 E. Chocolate Avenue, Hershey, PA 17033-1240, USA, www.igi-global.com. This series is composed of titles available for purchase individually; each title is edited to be contextually exclusive from any other title within the series. For pricing and ordering information please visit http://www.igi-global.com/book-series/advances-business-strategy-competitive-advantage/73672. Postmaster: Send all address changes to above address.

Titles in this Series

For a list of additional titles in this series, please visit: http://www.igi-global.com/book-series/advances-business-strategy-competitive-advantage/73672

Principles and Practices of Small-Scale Sport Event Management
Anestis Fotiadis (Zayed University, UAE) and Chris Vassiliadis (University of Macedonia, Greece)
Business Science Reference • © 2020 • 335pp • H/C (ISBN: 9781799847571) • US $215.00

Entrepreneurial Innovation for Securing Long-Term Growth in a Short-Term Economy
Jorge Gamez-Gutierrez (Universitaria Agustiniana, Colombia) and Jose Manuel Saiz-Alvarez (Tecnologico de Monterrey, Spain)
Business Science Reference • © 2020 • 300pp • H/C (ISBN: 9781799835684) • US $215.00

Handbook of Research on Transmedia Storytelling, Audience Engagement, and Business Strategies
Víctor Hernández-Santaolalla (University of Seville, Spain) and Mónica Barrientos-Bueno (University of Seville, Spain)
Business Science Reference • © 2020 • 457pp • H/C (ISBN: 9781799831198) • US $265.00

Developing Creative Economy Through Disruptive Leadership Emerging Research and Opportunities
Kristin Joyce Tardif (University of Arkansas – Fort Smith, USA)
Business Science Reference • © 2020 • 226pp • H/C (ISBN: 9781799834168) • US $185.00

Knowledge Management, Innovation, and Entrepreneurship in a Changing World
Murray Eugene Jennex (San Diego State University, USA)
Business Science Reference • © 2020 • 463pp • H/C (ISBN: 9781799823551) • US $215.00

Developing Entrepreneurial Competencies for Start-Ups and Small Business
Jarmila Šebestová (Silesian University in Opava, Czech Republic)
Business Science Reference • © 2020 • 316pp • H/C (ISBN: 9781799827146) • US $225.00

Leadership and Followership in an Organizational Change Context
Sajjad Nawaz Khan (University Malaysia Sarawak, Malaysia) and Abdul Halim Busari (University Malaysia Sarawak, Malaysia)
Business Science Reference • © 2020 • 300pp • H/C (ISBN: 9781799828075) • US $225.00

Digital Marketing Strategies and Models for Competitive Business
Filipe Mota Pinto (Polytechnic Institute of Leiria, Portugal) and Teresa Guarda (Universidad Peninsula de Santa Elena (UPSE), Ecuador)
Business Science Reference • © 2020 • 240pp • H/C (ISBN: 9781799829638) • US $225.00

IGI Global
PUBLISHER of TIMELY KNOWLEDGE

701 East Chocolate Avenue, Hershey, PA 17033, USA
Tel: 717-533-8845 x100 • Fax: 717-533-8661
E-Mail: cust@igi-global.com • www.igi-global.com

Table of Contents

Detailed Table of Contents

identify if the first impression of a person in the Romanian business context is dissimulated or not. The implications for entrepreneurs consist in the degree of promotion of achieving a good first impression and the manipulative or persuasive value of the negotiation techniques applied in the Romanian business environment.

The study examines the IT Greek start-up ecosystem, analyzing the founders' views, strategy, and current perception regarding their ICT start-ups. The study examines the views and perceptions of 143 founders of Greek IT start ups who participated in exhibitions as start-up companies between September 2018 and May 2019, and had completed at least one accelerator program.

This chapter provides an overview of social skills contributing to SME development in the Russian Federation. Building upon prior research and using the data collected by the most recent World Bank Enterprise Survey, the author summarizes the main social skills demonstrated by Russian SMEs. The indicators published by the 2012 and 2019 Enterprise Survey are further supported by analysis of entrepreneurial "success stories" of entrepreneurs published by Russian web-based media. Social skills required to run a successful SME correspond to those identified from the Enterprise Survey data, and they are evenly distributed among skills comprising the "ways of thinking" and the "ways of working." The chapter concludes with directions for future research and implications for practice.

Online reviews have become a significant source of information for travel planning, influencing consumers purchasing decisions and behaviour. This study aims to explore the impacts of online reviews on hotel booking intentions and its significance for entrepreneurial success. It evaluates features from the content of online reviews to understand their impacts upon customers' online booking intention in hotels. Content analysis findings of relevant literature indicates positive causal relationship between online review volume, valence, quality, and online booking intention. There is a significant negative impact of negative online reviews on online booking intention, whilst positive online reviews can gain positive influence. Consumer tend to be more influenced by negative reviews than positive ones. Social media and online travel agent sites are popular internet platforms used. The influence of online reviews on hotel performance is very significant. Hotel entrepreneurs are recommended to pay close attention to online reviews and its impacts and effectively manage reviews.

One of the major roles of governments is to create a favorable business environment for fostering entrepreneurial activities, including good infrastructure and a culture that encourages the adoption of technologies. In such a policy context, the Greek National Electronic Public Procurement System (ESIDIS) was developed. The use of ESIDIS is mandatory for the employees, and its success depends on users' satisfaction. The chapter investigates the factors influencing employees' satisfaction when using the system. Perceived usefulness, perceived ease-of-use, perceived risk, and willingness to learn were investigated using empirical research. Structural equation modeling was used for the analysis of the data. Perceived usefulness has the most significant role in determining user satisfaction while risks importance is diminished when users understand the usefulness of the system for their job performance. Managers and policymakers should take these factors into consideration in order to improve users' satisfaction and consequently maximize the added value of the system for the entrepreneurs.

Healthcare is one of the most targeted industries by cybercriminals. The healthcare sector is far behind in cybersecurity as compared to other organizations. The vulnerabilities in the system open the door for cybercriminals to exploit it and get unauthorized access into the system or network to do a malicious activity. Healthcare should have to take cyber threats seriously and follow a security framework that detects and mitigates cyber threats. This chapter presents all cyber threat actors that exist in the healthcare sector, common cyber-attacks that can be launched against all actors, and real incidents that took place during the past years. Based on these, the authors propose in a tabular form a set of recommendations that can be used as countermeasures against any type of attack.

The role of innovation as a vital driving force of entrepreneurship and economic development has been widely acknowledged. Especially in an era of economic turbulence, innovation can be seen as the only realistic strategy that can lead enterprises out of the crisis. Based on the innovation taxonomies identified in the Oslo Manual, namely organizational, marketing, process, and product innovation, a survey was

This chapter discusses the evolution, opportunities, succession model, and sustainability challenges of formal and informal family businesses in Nigeria. Using qualitative research method, while relying on content analysed secondary data, the chapter found that the family businesses that evolved in Nigeria laid the foundation for socio-economic development, and they contributed immensely to employment generation, stimulation of indigenous entrepreneurship, mobilization of idle savings, and growth of gross domestic product. Family businesses in Nigeria prefer relay succession planning for transferring control to family members. The major sustainability challenges include poor succession planning, harsh macro-economic environment, conflict of interest, emotional family problems, parochial family vision, absence of mentoring, competition from multinational corporation, poor access to funding, inadequate entrepreneurial knowledge, weak financial management, bad governance, and a host of others. The chapter concludes with research implications, limitations, and suggestions for further research.

Family businesses (FBs) are central to economies: in Portugal the impact of these structures reaches 2/3 of the GDP, 1/2 of the labour force, and 4/5 of the firms in operation, most of them being SMEs. These organisations play a central role in terms of job creation, local development, knowledge transfer, and territorial cohesion. Innovative activities are key factors for competitive economies; yet innovation increases risk exposure and FBs are conservative and risk adverse, resisting change, relying on internal factors rather than opening to the external environment, consequently postponing innovation and thus pledging their future. Their embedded culture reduces innovative propensity; still, the existence loyalty trust and informal networks enhance individual or collective innovation processes. Using a dataset of 110 FBs innovation and internationalization along with other structural characteristics are connected to their economic performance, shedding light on the determinants FB economic efficiency. Given their importance, made-to-measure policy schemes should be designed.

The local authorities' incubator for social enterprises should be supporting the connection of local companies that apply CSR with social enterprises that are trying to succeed social value. The research in this chapter relied on a systematic literature review. After reviewing the literature, a methodology has been developed that describes the process of designing and implementing a local authorities' incubator and the synergies with social enterprises and CSR. The benefit of a local authorities' incubator in the field of social entrepreneurship is the facilitation of new social enterprises to overcome knowledge barriers and implement best business practices. Finally, in this chapter, it is suggested that the cooperation between

Preface

Entrepreneurship is a socio-economic process that is supported by national systems (Mazzarol and Reboud, 2020). Specificities may also play a role; for example, a region's ethnic diversity fosters the establishment of small firms (Boudreaux, 2020), or the personality characteristics through which entrepreneurs act strategically and develop competencies to handle procedures (Asonitou and Kavoura, 2019). In this regard, entrepreneurship constitutes a subject that is topical and timeless, since both institutions and the various institutional processes have always been affecting the development of countries and people. People are, after all, the most essential cell of the entrepreneurial process (Masouras, 2019).

The fourth industrial revolution brings together smart physical and digital systems to harmoniously cooperate, where the main target is on the fusion of technology and innovation (Schwab, 2017). Technological innovation needs to be at the forefront for the creation of a smart ecosystem with all stakeholders being involved (Buhalis, 2019). Companies need to move hand in hand with customers (Buhalis Leung and Law, 2011) with the aim to co-create personalized experiences for them that are outstanding and competitive (Mistilis, Buhalis and Gretzel, 2014). The active role of consumers and their cooperation with companies in new product development allows customers to provide their point of view in real-time so that needs and service requirements can be developed meeting excellence (Buhalis and Sinarta, 2019). Thus, the implementation of automated services and web technologies is also an issue that small firms need to consider in relation to large enterprises. For example, in Poland such discrepancy was illustrated between small and large enterprises (Kavoura and Koziol, 2017). In addition, emerging technologies and other forms of entrepreneurship such as digital and societal in tourism, have a lot to offer and open avenues for further research (Ratten, 2019). It is this use of technological innovation that may boost a region, a territory and inequalities can be created based on entrepreneurship and innovation (Ratten et al., 2020). Entrepreneurship and innovation can be offered by firms of different size. In the present study, the emphasis is on small and family businesses due to their importance in the discussion of entrepreneurship.

Family businesses and Small and Medium Enterprises (SMEs) can be defined as follows:

"A proprietorship, partnership, corporation or any form of business association, which is classified as an SME (less than 250 employees) and where the majority ownership is held by the family and family members are employed in the family business and/or the family is represented on the Board of Directors" (Birdthistle, 2003: 76).

Family businesses and SMEs need to create innovative strategies and products that boost entrepreneurship. Most of the family businesses and SMEs cannot handle an internationalization strategy as they face many limitations (Fernández & Nieto, 2005). According to Fernández & Nieto (2005: 86) family businesses and SMEs are most of the times unable to build competitive advantages at the international level mainly because their inability to access the resources and capabilities. Their strategic orientation may affect the eCommerce adoption due to 'external pressure' and 'perceived benefits' (Wang & Ahmed, 2009). In parallel, these small businesses have the potential to be learning organizations (Birdthistle, 2008). But, according to Birdthistle (2008) size of the family business and the structure imposed on the business affect their learning behaviour.

THE CHALLENGES

Entrepreneurs face challenges in their everyday lives and they may be forced to create their business or extend their already existing business (Constantin and Kavoura, 2019). Furthermore, the last ten years the economic crises affected the political, economic and institutional environment both on the national and regional level, creating severe economic challenges (Sklias & Maris, 2012; Sklias & Maris, 2013; Sklias, Roukanas & Maris 2014). In this regard, there are many challenges that the Family Businesses and the SMEs should tackle.

The first challenge is related to the question of whether family businesses and SMEs can work as learning organizations to tackle with global competitiveness. Indeed, family businesses and SMEs may have the potential to become learning organizations, but at the same time, the size of the family business and the structure imposed on the business play a crucial role that affect their learning behaviour (Birdthistle, 2008). Entrepreneurial learning can take place via university hubs and counselling within the university premises before and after graduation; universities can act as an axe to support entrepreneurial efforts (Kavoura and Andersson, 2016; Makarona and Kavoura, 2019).

Second, there are many organizational and cultural issues that should also be tackle (De Vrande, et al. 2009). Indeed, the organizational and cultural issues in external partnerships create several barriers to SME's open innovation activities like for example venturing, customer involvement, external networking,R&D outsourcing and external participations (De Vrande, et al. 2009: 435). Thus, family and small firms need to establish collaborative support networks and manage resources in order to handle potential risks.

Third, the family businesses and the SMEs need to tackle with the global economic conditions in the era of globalization. In this respect, financial challenges are of great importance for family businesses and SMEs (Tagoe et al., 2005). Thus, the most profound vulnerabilities experienced by SMEs are identified with inflation and interest rates, crime and unemployment, low demand for products, the wrong pricing strategies (Cant & Wiid, 2013). It is clear, that the SMEs should focus on critical success factors in order to build competitive advantage remaining at the same time competitive amidst the challenges from globalization and liberalization (Ramukumba, 2014).

Finally, a methodological challenge is the question of how can we measure entrepreneurship and innovation. A well-known measure is the Global Entrepreneurship Monitor (GEM; Bosma et.al, 2016), which, in effect, comprises many variables that link entrepreneurship and innovation to economic growth. Data collection includes interviews with international market representatives, from a sample of more than 200,000 questionnaires per annum. The interest of this indicator lies in the fact that it does not concentrate only on purely economic data, but also touches upon institutional variables, for example cultural and social norms. Moreover, special emphasis is placed about young entrepreneurship. It also classifies entrepreneurs into various categories, for example early-stage entrepreneurs, established entrepreneurs, and potential entrepreneurs, providing an outline of the features of each category (Cusi and Bernal, 2020). The GEM survey also deals with young entrepreneurship. More specifically, the GEM survey classifies young entrepreneurship under "early-stage entrepreneurial activity" and concludes, "entrepreneurs aged 25-34 and 35-44 are the most active entrepreneurs across all 3 development phases." An interesting fact, however, is that the Latin America and Caribbean region shows the highest young entrepreneurship rate, at 16.5%, followed by North America with 14%. Europe exhibits the lowest rates (Masouras, 2019).

ORGANIZATION OF THE BOOK

This edited volume is consisted of 14 chapters that provide a comprehensive evaluation of the current trends on entrepreneurial development and innovation in family businesses and SMEs from different countries all over the world. The authors follow an interdisciplinary approach based on new theoretical and empirical evaluation of each case separately. More specifically:

Chapter 1 reviews Asian entrepreneurs in tourism, with a focus on accessibility to state support and funds, identifying research areas for future studies. Using systematic literature reviews and country-specific profiling of India, Singapore, Thailand and Vietnam, the study reviews the extent governments support entrepreneurs and the sustainability of their business. This research is intended to trigger insights for both industry practitioners and policy makers and to form an awareness to create a sustainable environment for budding entrepreneurs.

Chapter 2 identifies the notions and the relations between communication and entrepreneurship in the Romanian context and also to present the main results of a research that aimed to identify if the first impression of a person in the Romanian business context is dissimulated or not. The implications for entrepreneurs consist in the degree of promotion of achieving a good first impression and the manipulative or persuasive value of the negotiation techniques applied in the Romanian business environment.

Chapter 3 examines the IT Greek start-up ecosystem, analyzing the founders' views, strategy, and current perception regarding their ICT start-ups. Specifically, the chapter examines the views and perceptions of 143 founders of Greek IT start ups who participated in exhibitions as start-up companies between September 2018 and May 2019 and had completed at least one accelerator program.

Chapter 4 provides an overview of social skills contributing to SME development in the Russian Federation. Building upon prior research and using the data collected by the most recent World Bank Enterprise Survey, the author summarizes the main social skills demonstrated by Russian SMEs. The chapter concludes with directions for future research and implications for practice.

Chapter 5 aims to explore the impacts of online reviews on hotel booking intentions and its significance for entrepreneurial success. It evaluates features from the content of online reviews to understand their impacts upon customers 'online booking intention in hotels.

Chapter 6 investigates the factors influencing employees' satisfaction when using the system. Perceived-usefulness, perceived ease-of-use, perceived risk, and willingness-to learn were investigate, using empirical research. Structural Equation Modeling was used for the analysis of the data. Perceived Usefulness has the most significant role in determining user satisfaction while risks importance is diminished when users understand usefulness the system for their job performance.

Chapter 7 presents all cyber threat actors that exist in the healthcare sector, common cyber-attacks that can be launched against all actors and real incidents that took place during the past years. Based on these, we propose in a tabular form a set of recommendations that can be used as countermeasures against any type of attack.

Chapter 8 analyses the effects of economic recession on the firms' innovativeness and drawing a profile of the entrepreneurship innovation in the region of Western Macedonia, Greece. By applying a strategic group's approach, we come up with some interesting findings concerning the type of SMEs' innovativeness and results of innovation during a period of financial crisis.

Chapter 9 investigates the entrepreneurial intention of university students using the Theory of Planned Behavior (TPB) and parents' occupation. A questionnaire-based survey was employed for the data collection. A total of 1244 students participated in the survey. The sample was a convenience one given that the resources available were limited. The findings of our research showed that perceived behavioral control, subjective norms, attitude and parents' occupation are important variables influencing entrepreneurial intention.

Chapter 10 demonstrates how the orientation to organizational learning affects the innovation and performance of the Colombian micro, small and medium (MSmes), based on a study with 403 Colombian MSMEs, pretending that the results allow the government sector and the academy to design strategies for maintain or improve, as appropriate, innovative and learning practices within these organizations.

Chapter 11 discusses the evolution, opportunities, succession model and sustainability challenges of formal and informal family businesses in Nigeria. Using qualitative research method, while relying on content analysed secondary data, the chapter found that the family businesses, which evolved in Nigeria laid the foundation for socio-economic development, and they contributed immensely to employment generation, stimulation of indigenous entrepreneurship, mobilization of idle savings and growth of gross domestic product.

Chapter 12 discusses the central role of family businesses (FBs) to economies: in Portugal, the impact of these structures reaches 2/3 of the GDP, 1/2 of the labour force and 4/5 of the firms in operation, most of them being SME's. These organisations play a central role in terms of job creation, local development, knowledge transfer and territorial cohesion. Innovative activities are key factors for competitive economies.

Chapter 13 reviews issues ab about the cooperation between local companies that apply CSR and local Social Enterprises under the guidance and support of Local Authorities' Incubator could create synergies and produce new local certified -PGI (Protected Geographical Indication) or P.D.O (Protected Designations of Origin) social/ ethical/ green/fair-trade products and services and promote local economy.

Chapter 14 focuses on the digital state of Greek SMEs and attempts to identify the main problems and opportunities for promoting their development through digital technology, as they appear to be weak in this field especially when comparing to most European countries. These findings enrich the literature on Greek SMEs and their future capabilities.

Andreas Masouras
Neapolis University, Cyprus

Georgios Maris
Aegean University, Greece

Androniki Kavoura
University of West Attica, Greece

REFERENCES

Asonitou, S., & Kavoura, A. (2019). Accounting education, technology and entrepreneurship: Current trends and future outlook. *The Malopolska School of Economics in Tarnow Research Papers Collection, 44*(4), 65–78. doi:10.25944/znmwse.2019.04.6578

Birdthistle, N. (2003). Educating the family business: an investigation into centres of excellence for family businesses and family business educational programmes. In *SMEs in the Knowledge Economy: Proceedings of the 26th ISBA Conference, University of Surrey, Surrey, November 12-13, 2003*, Vol. 2003. Institute for Small Business Affairs.

Birdthistle, N. (2008). Family SMEs in Ireland as learning organizations. *The Learning Organization, 15*(5), 421–436. doi:10.1108/09696470810898393

Bosma, N., Schøtt, T., Terjesen, S. A., & Kew, P. (2016). *Global entrepreneurship monitor 2015 to 2016: special topic report on social entrepreneurship*. Academic Press.

Boudreaux, C. J. (2020). 2020 Ethnic diversity and small business venturing. *Small Business Economics, 54*(1), 25–41. doi:10.100711187-018-0087-4

Buhalis, D. (2019). Technology in tourism-from information communication technologies to eTourism and smart tourism towards ambient intelligence tourism: A perspective article. *Tourism Review, 75*(1), 267–272. doi:10.1108/TR-06-2019-0258

Buhalis, D., Leung, D., & Law, R. (2011). eTourism: critical information and communication technologies for tourism destinations. In Destination marketing and management: Theories and applications. CABI.

Buhalis, D., & Sinarta, Y. (2019). Real-time co-creation and nowness service: Lessons from tourism and hospitality. *Journal of Travel & Tourism Marketing, 36*(5), 563–582. doi:10.1080/10548408.2019.1592059

Cant, M. C., & Wiid, J. A. (2013). Establishing The Challenges Affecting South African SMEs. *International Business & Economics Research Journal, 12*(6), 707–716. doi:10.19030/iber.v12i6.7869

Constantin, F., & Kavoura, A. (2019). Entrepreneur without Intention with Websites as a Communication Tool. Current Trends in Romania. In A. Kavoura, E. Kefallonitis, & A. Giovanis (Eds.), *Strategic Innovative Marketing and Tourism* (pp. 1093–1101). Springer. doi:10.1007/978-3-030-12453-3_126

Cusi, M. L. A., & Bernal, L. D. P. (2020). *Global Entrepreneurship Analytics: Using GEM Data*. Academic Press.

Fernández, Z., & Nieto, M. J. (2005). Internationalization Strategy of Small and Medium-Sized Family Businesses: Some Influential Factors. *Family Business Review, 18*(1), 77–89. doi:10.1111/j.1741-6248.2005.00031.x

Kavoura, A., & Andersson, T. (2016). Applying Delphi method for strategic design of social entrepreneurship. *Library Review, 65*(3), 185–205. doi:10.1108/LR-06-2015-0062

Kavoura, A., & Koziol, L. (2017). *Polish Firms' Innovation Capability for Competitiveness via Information Technologies and Social Media Implementation*. In A. Vlachvei, O. Notta, K. Karantininis, & N. Tsountas (Eds.), *Factors Affecting Firm Competitiveness and Performance in the Modern Business World* (pp. 185–214). IGI Global.

Makarona, E., & Kavoura, A. (2019). Redesigning the Ivory Tower: Academic entrepreneurship as a new calling supporting economic growth. *The Malopolska School of Economics in Tarnow Research Papers Collection*, *42*, 15–26. doi:10.25944/znmwse.2019.02.1526

Masouras, A. (2019). *Entrepreneurship in Small and Medium-Sized Enterprises*. Nova Science Publishers.

Masouras, A. (2019). Young entrepreneurship in Cyprus. *Zeszyty Naukowe Małopolskiej Wyższej Szkoły Ekonomicznej w Tarnowie*, *42*(2), 27–42.

Mazzarol, T., & Reboud, S. (2020). Innovation in Small Firms. In *Entrepreneurship and Innovation. Springer Texts in Business and Economics* (4th ed.). Springer. doi:10.1007/978-981-13-9412-6_5

Mistilis, N., Buhalis, D., & Gretzel, U. (2014). eDestination Marketing of the future: The perspective of an Australian Tourism Stakeholder Network. *Journal of Travel Research*, *53*(6), 778–790. doi:10.1177/0047287514522874

Ramukumba, T. (2014). Overcoming SMEs Challenges through Critical Success Factors: A Case of SMEs in the Western Cape Province. South Africa. *Economic and Business Review*, *16*(1), 19–38.

Ratten, V. (2019). Tourism entrepreneurship research: A perspective article. *Tourism Review*, *75*(1), 122–125. doi:10.1108/TR-06-2019-0204

Ratten, V., Álvarez-García, J., & de la Cruz del Rio-Rama, M. (2020). *Entrepreneurship, Innovation and Inequality: Exploring Territorial Dynamics and Development*. Routledge.

Schwab, K. (2017). *The Fourth Industrial Revolution*. Crown Business.

Sklias, P., & Maris, G. (2012). Reassessment of the OCA criteria in the Euro area: The case of Greece. *International Journal of Monetary Economics and Finance*, *5*(2), 124–138. doi:10.1504/IJMEF.2012.048732

Sklias, P., & Maris, G. (2013). The Political Dimension of the Greek Financial Crisis. *Perspectives on European Politics and Society*, *14*(1), 144–164. doi:10.1080/15705854.2012.732392

Sklias, P., Roukanas, S., & Maris, G. (2014). Keynes and the Eurozone's Crisis: Towards a Fiscal Union? *Procedia Economics and Finance*, *9*, 66–73. doi:10.1016/S2212-5671(14)00008-2

Tagoe, N., Nyarko, E., & Anuwaamarh, E. (2005). Financial Challenges Facing Urban SMEs under Financial Sector Liberalization in Ghana. *Journal of Small Business Management*, *43*(3), 331–343. doi:10.1111/j.1540-627X.2005.00140.x

Van de Vrande, V., de Jong, J. P. J., Vanhaverbeke, W., & de Rochemont, M. (2009). Open innovation in SMEs: Trends, motives and management challenges. *Technovation*, *29*(6), 423–437. doi:10.1016/j.technovation.2008.10.001

Wang, Y., & Ahmed, P. K. (2009). The moderating effect of the business strategic orientation on eCommerce adoption: Evidence from UK family run SMEs. *The Journal of Strategic Information Systems*, *18*(1), 16–30. doi:10.1016/j.jsis.2008.11.001

Chapter 1
Asian Entrepreneurship in Tourism and Hospitality:
Financial Support, Business Sustainability

Yash Bhushan Prabhugaonkar
James Cook University, Singapore

Dam Xuan Minh
Royal Embassy of Saudi Arabia in Hanoi, Vietnam

K. Thirumaran
https://orcid.org/0000-0002-8399-1545
James Cook University, Singapore

Karen S. Sim
James Cook University, Singapore

Sapon Pruhtpahon
Independent Researcher, Thailand

Mohit Raghav
World Lifestyle Pte. Ltd., India

ABSTRACT

Entrepreneurs in tourism constantly find business a challenge, especially when competing with well-established players in the industry who have huge capital and large market shares. More often than not, these entrepreneurs must constantly innovate and come up with new ideas on travel booking and new ways to enhance travel experiences. Focusing on entrepreneurs in Asia, very few countries proactively fund aspiring entrepreneurs who often struggle like their American counterparts with credit card debts and huge loans. This chapter reviews Asian entrepreneurs in tourism, with a focus on accessibility to state support and funds, identifying research areas for future studies. Using systematic literature review and country-specific profiling of India, Singapore, Thailand, and Vietnam, the study examines the extent governments support entrepreneurs and the sustainability of their business. This research is intended to trigger insights for both industry practitioners and policymakers and to form an awareness to create a sustainable environment for budding entrepreneurs in tourism.

DOI: 10.4018/978-1-7998-3648-3.ch001

INTRODUCTION

Entrepreneurship has influenced the tourism industry with innovation, competitiveness, productivity, wealth generation and job creation (Fyall, Buhalis & Parra, 2009; Stojanović, 2018; Istudor, 2019; Fua et al., 2019). Entrepreneurship in tourism has taken new dimensions since the advent of technology in the last 20 to 30 years. Entrepreneurs in the past focused their energies on the retail front where interested customers approached tour companies to discuss – face-to-face – tour packages and make travel arrangements. With the development of the internet, customers can now make all their travel arrangements independently without much reliance on visiting a retail corner. In these regards, entrepreneurs have found the interstitial space between the physical and virtual worlds an opportunity for business.

The Asian tourism landscape is vastly changing and has resulted in the appearance of many entrepreneurs. Since 2005, more than 700 start-up companies in the travel sector have emerged (Coletta & Kapoor, 2019). The United Nations World Tourism Organisation (UNWTO, 2018) also sees entrepreneurship and innovation as key practices in the industry. Several different business models have gained popularity in this age of business disruption. Among these, new business models have developed in the areas of online travel and travel reward schemes in hospitality services such as spa or lodges (Devang et al., 2017; Leisure hospitality startup, 2019).

While acknowledging institutional entrepreneurship can often be a major part of the East Asian economies (Ateljevic & Li, 2009; Gillen, 2010), this chapter is very much interested in the individual entrepreneurs and the support they receive from the government and other private venture capitalists. Even though successful entrepreneurs like Bill Gates or Steve Job have changed people's way of life, history suggests the fact that individual entrepreneurs are the most vulnerable and often face financial issues because of unprecedented events such as in policy changes or disasters, which in most of the cases, could be better managed by governments. Their support levels can vary more or less but contemporary states have started to realize the need to protect and develop their economies by supporting entrepreneurs in key industries.

Through a systematic study of the literature on Asian tourism and entrepreneurship, this chapter aims to provide an insight on scholarships and future research trajectories. A country-profile approach is adopted to understand the degree of government and private support in the tourism sector. The countries profiled are India, Singapore, Thailand and Vietnam. A rationale for the selection of these countries are provided in the methodology section. Suffice to add here, these countries are selected on the basis of different degrees of government policy depth and financial support given to entrepreneurs in the tourism sector. Finally, a discussion on the value of this study and for practitioners will be a key contribution of this chapter. Non-government organizations like the *Enterprise Asia* (www.enterpriseasia.org) strives to create an Asia abound in entrepreneurship as it believes that this is the catalyst towards a sustainable and progressive world. With over 3000 members in the Asia-Pacific region, *Enterprise Asia* recognizes and encourages budding entrepreneurs in the hospitality and tourism trade with annual recognition awards ceremony and facilitates participation in business through innovation (Enterprise Asia, 2019). Governments too, in much of Asia both in developed and emerging tourism economies, recognize, facilitate, regulate and even incentivise entrepreneurship in the sector (Person & Van Beek, 1998; Truong & Le, 2017; OECD, 2019). We examine the scope of the government's role in facilitating entrepreneurship in the tourism sector in each of the four countries selected here, and to understand the opportunities and sustainability issues affeccting prospective entrepreneurs.

LITERATURE ON ASIAN ENTREPRENEURSHIP IN TOURISM

The tourism and hospitality industry is a pivotal engine for economic growth in many countries (Tang & Tan, 2013; Webster & Ivanov, 2014). Consumer preferences are changing towards experience-based services, and new technologies are emerging (Solvoll et al., 2015) to replace traditional forms of products and services with experience-based products (Sundbo et al., 2007). Countries are developing long-term plans by investing in infrastructure to support tourism entrepreneurs as it helps the regeneration of communities (Altinay et al., 2012). The tourism industry is dependent on new firms and innovation for market growth (Sundbo et al., 2007; Solvoll et al., 2015). Tourism and hospitality entrepreneurs can develop destinations by offering new products which enhance traveller experience (Alsos et al., 2014).

A tourism entrepreneur is an individual or a group of individuals creating and managing tourism products (Khanka, 2006). Studies argue that lifestyle and autonomy goals dominate the tourism industry (Getz, & Petersen, 2005), as entrepreneur start a new business to attain a higher quality of life than earn profits (Peters et al., 2009). However, there is some profit- and growth-oriented entrepreneurial goals attached to specific business types in the tourism industry (Getz, & Petersen, 2005). Researchers have argued that tourists increasingly become active participants in the co-production of innovation in the tourism business as they act as pioneers signalling opportunities for tourism business (Verreynne et al., 2019).

The literature on entrepreneurship in Asian tourism economies is emerging and quite varied. A fair number of studies focused on the informal economies where social capital plays an essential role in the success of the business (Çakmak, Lie & Selwyn, 2019). Many of the cities in Asia regard urban development as a pathway to growth, and in this context, tourism plays an essential part in creating spaces for tourist consumption and local entrepreneurship (Gillen, 2010). Rather than a confrontational relationship, state-private enterprises are cooperating and growing with a string of social capital running through the informal economies of Cambodia, Thailand, India and Indonesia (Yeung, 2002; Gillen, 2010, see similarities in African examples, Ngoasong, & Kimbu, 2016).

Entrepreneurship is critical for economies to promote innovation and create employment opportunities (Altinay et al., 2012). Growth- and profit-oriented entrepreneurs are highly valued, from the perspective of economic development and industry competitiveness, as entrepreneurs attract and cultivate businesses that can compete, grow, and create jobs (Getz, & Petersen, 2005). Entrepreneurship also plays a vital role in earlier stages of tourism development, particularly in rural and ethnic communities where multi-national firms and international hotel chains are less likely to invest due to the relatively small size of the potential market (Chang, 2011). Tourism and hospitality entrepreneurs thus have the interest to serve these markets by playing an essential role in innovation and value-creation in the tourism industry (Solvoll et al., 2015).

The tourism industry is primarily made up of Small and Medium Enterprises (SMEs) which increasingly play a prominent role concerning the supply of services, job creation, economic stimulus, image-making and balanced development of destinations (Gurel et al., 2010; Carlisle et al., 2013; Hallak et al., 2015). SMEs have stronger linkages to local businesses, and they add a sense of place and authenticity (Altinay et al., 2012). Most of the SMEs in tourism and hospitality businesses are owned by sole proprietors and families (Getz & Petersen, 2005). According to Shaw and Williams (2013), many owners of these SMEs are "non-entrepreneurs" or "constrained entrepreneurs", and due to a severe constraint of under-capitalization, business failures are high. SME owners are often portrayed as "lifestyle entrepreneurs", and family businesses are frequently assumed to be risk averse as they place family security ahead of potential growth (Getz & Petersen, 2005). In the same study, Shaw and Williams (2013) characterized small-scale entrepreneurs in tourism into four ways: having little or no formal qualifications; using mostly family resources and labour; lacking business planning and growth strategies; doing little, if any, marketing, and possessing non-economic motives.

In Southeast Asia, female entrepreneurs play a crucial role in the tourism sector. Despite the cultural and resource challenges in Bali, women have started small stores and restaurants in key tourist attractions and traveller-frequented sites (Tajeddini et al., 2017). In the case of Aurangabad, a tourist district in India, with the help of the Maharashtra Tourism Development Cooperation, a small number of women have managed to negotiate their way into the handloom and tourist product business (Qureshi & Ahmed, 2012).

Recently there has been a surge in the number of tourism entrepreneurs, whose offerings range from homestays, family-style restaurants and cafes to retail stores that cater to tourists of different demographics (Chang, 2011). However, to Asian businessmen, family cohesiveness and collectivism are of high importance. As such, Asian family-owned and operated businesses have become one indispensable component in tourism, and these are often passed down from one generation to the next (Chang, 2011). In an entrepreneurship mobility study, young Chinese entrepreneurs who venture outwards to seek places to set up their business eventually return to their original place of residence (Sun & Xu, 2017).

In another study on entrepreneurship in Xishuangbanna of the southwestern province of Yunan in China, several non-ethnic entrepreneurs find ways of exploiting ethnic communities at times excluding the ethnic individuals as part of the entrepreneurial leadership (Yang & Wall, 2008). The study advocates more opportunities for cooperative and enabling relationships when it comes to ethnic tourism and entrepreneurship. Close to ethnic entrepreneurship topic is entrepreneurship in night markets. Many countries in Asia have night markets, and often than not, the vendors are individuals unrelated to the employment of a company. Liu & Fang (2016) discovered that night market entrepreneurs from several locations in Taiwan developed heightened risk to innovate their products to face stiff competition from other like-minded entrepreneurs at the same location. These types of studies are essential in the Asian context because both ethnic tourism and night markets are prominent characteristics of the tourism landscape.

STUDY APPROACH

This research utilizes secondary information about entrepreneurs in the Asian tourism and hospitality sector with a primary focus on the financial support they receive. Detailed profiling of the entrepreneurship landscape in India, Singapore, Thailand and Vietnam through cumulative articles from national newspapers, and in-country observations allow for a more nuanced analysis and contextual frameworks.

Four Research Questions (RQ) Addressed:

- RQ1: What are the national government or tourism authority's policies towards entrepreneurs in the tourism and hospitality sector?
- RQ2: How are the entrepreneurs sustaining themselves and receiving support from the government and/or alternative sources?
- RQ3: In what ways are the entrepreneurs overcoming their challenges in financial support?
- RQ4: How do these four countries compare in facilitating entrepreneurship in the hospitality and tourism sector?

The research work was conducted from February 2019 to January 2020. This research work was informed by resources accessed through OneSearch – a search engine located in the James Cook University online library resource. Another two more comprehensive database sources with news articles, scholarly journals and reports were accessed. These were EBESCO and ProQuest. Authors located in each of the countries (India, Singapore, Thailand and Vietnam) profiled in this chapter had also access to local tourism resource centers and daily newspapers that carried feature articles on entrepreneurs and innovations in the tourism and hospitality sector. A number of specific and combination of words were used in online searches. These keywords primarily included but were not limited to: 'Asian entrepreneurs'; 'Government role in tourism and hospitality'; 'Government financial support for entrepreneurs in tourism and hospitality'; Government India Entrepreneurship Support Tourism and Hospitality'; 'Tourism and Hospitality innovations and entrepreneurship in India'. Where there was a phrase with a specific country mentioned in the search, other countries' names were replaced with similar searches.

There is one common denominator: the tourism industry is important to each country's economy. While Thailand is the most advanced of the four countries in terms of tourism development, its inclusion in the mix along with Singapore aims to compare the similarities and differences in entrepreneurship with that of India and Vietnam, both of which are currently on the rise as popular tourist destinations. Tourism in all four destinations contribute significant tourism receipts, huge employment opportunities, rising tourist arrivals and stimulus to economic growth and exchange with the international community.

In 2010, 11.6 million tourists visited Singapore and contributed USD13.38 billion (Singapore Tourism Board, 2011) but by 2019, the arrival numbers had increased to 19.1 million tourists with total tourism receipts reaching USD19.52 billion (Singapore Tourism Board, 2020c). Ranking number 5 in the Mastercard's Global Destination Cities Index, tourism contributes about 4.5% to the Gross Domestic Product (GDP) suggesting a significant part to a US$289 billion economy (Budget Direct, 2020; WorldAtlas, 2020) especially with over 325, 000 residents working in the industry.

Currently, India has 11 private and 350 government-initiated tourism projects worth over USD5.34 billion (Invest India, 2020). These numbers further indicate the active role the state is playing and space for more private stakeholders and entrepreneurs. The importance of the world's eighth largest tourism economy cannot be sufficiently emphasised, which is expected to increase tourism foreign exchange earnings from the USD29 billion in 2018 (Ministry of Tourism, 2019) to $50 billion by 2022 (India Brand Equity Foundation, 2020) with an increase in current tourist arrivals of 10.6 million visitors to an expected 23.6 percent increase in the next five years.

Thailand is the second largest economy in Southeast Asia with a GDP size of USD520 billion (Trading Economics, 2020). In 2010, tourists arrivals was at 15.9 million visitors but dramatically increased to over 39 million international visitors in 2019 (World Tourism Organization, 2020). The government's tourism policy is intent to alleviate poverty and income inequality providing ample employment opportunities. The tourism and related sectors employ over 10 million Thais (Siam Commercial Bank, 2016) suggesting the importance of tourism in the world's top 10 destination (Knoema, 2020).

Vietnam is increasingly the new destination emerging from the communist grid to a capitalist style economy. With this change, a burst of youthful energy and a rapidly expanding tourism sector has offered Triple the number of 2010 arrivals, over 16 million internationals visited Vietnam in 2019 contributing US$27 billion to the economy (Doan, 2020; Das, 2019). In a number of government pronouncements and documents, the Vietnamese government is intent on developing and supporting the tourism sector given that it is a significant driver of economic development and opportunities. One such government pronouncement is the '*Strategy on Vietnam tourism development until 2020, vision to 2030*' in which the government had clear vision to consolidate local resources and present to the travel circuit Vietnam as an attractive destination with culture and natural physical beauty to offer (Das, 2019).

India currently has more than 48 million SME's, which is double the number of the SME's in the United States. According to the data provided by the Indian government, Micro, Small and Medium Enterprises (MSME) contribute nearly 8 percent of the country's GDP (Arora, 2015). Similarly, Singapore's efforts transcend multi option avenues across different funding agencies such as the National Heritage Board, Tourism Promotion Board and the Economic Development Board. Thailand has consistently carried out a number of government schemes that promotes community-based tourism and small enterprises. Vietnam in more recent decades have recognised the role of entrepreneurs and have created a number of funding and loan schemes to stimulate a burgeoning tourism sector. We'll examine some of these national and private sector initiatives in the specific country profiles section.

The study also adopts a multi-disciplinary approach, primarily in the context of the business and political economies (Petrof, 1980) for a critical appraisal and comparative study. This comprehensive method of analysis provides a rich lens of each country's public funding support for entrepreneurs and their (un)sustainability (Busenitz et al., 2000).

ENTREPRENEURSHIP AND SUSTAINABILITY

Tourism-related business are expected to generate around 370 million jobs which is roughly 1 out of 9 jobs globally (Nongsiej & Shimray, 2017). The World Travel and Tourism Council (2016) has predicted that by 2026, South Asia will be the fastest-growing sub-region with 7.1% GDP (Gross Domestic Product) growth, with India's at 7.5% (Nongsiej & Shimray, 2017). Opportunities in Asia for entrepreneurship is available. For example, in the case highlighted by Perez & Bui (2010), in an Asian developing country, a lady and her young family employed their skills and struggled to put together travel services for elites. After a client of elite background used their services as a first customer, the outlook and effort began to take a positive turnaround. The following section presents four Asian countries with a brief description on the extent to which entrepreneurs have access to financial support in the tourism and hospitality sector.

India

In 21st century, Indian government has realised the potential of their largest and youngest population which is known to be the 3rd largest start-up community in the world. In recent decades, Indian start-up have emerged in Travel & Tourism Competitive Index at 34th position as of 2019 (*GKToday*, 2019). There are many government initiatives for entrepreneurs in general but lacks initiative targeting the tourism industry for ideas generation specific to the development of the industry.

There are training programs and support initiatives by central government institutions such as the National Science & Technology Entrepreneurship Development and National Institute for Entrepreneurship and Small Business Development (Ramalingegowda & Khare, 2014). The government encourages young entrepreneurs by providing financial loan under the "Pradhan Mantri MUDRA Yojna" (PMMY) scheme. This scheme offers loans of up to INR1,000,000 (US$14,000) to non-corporate, non-farm small or micro enterprises from commercial banks, Regional Rural Banks (RRB), cooperative banks, Microfinance in India (MFI) and Non-Banking Financial Companies (NBFC) (See also, Ngoasong & Kimbu, 2016). The Mudra loan can be taken up by businesses in the service and retail.

Travel & tourism sector gained directly and indirectly in the launch of successful start-ups though Oyo & Ola innovatively transformed their business models from tourism technology model to finance technology with the launch of their own wallet or membership program to provide finance and hospitality services to their consumers. OYO, an Indian hotel chain, entered the hospitality industry by offering accommodation from small establishments such as lodges, rest houses and hotel chains. This company was started by a college drop-out who ventured into entrepreneurship. As Oyo charts its growth path, there are risks. The SoftBank of Japan pulled out of a deal to carry Oyo brand into the Japanese lodges market, creating almost 2000 jobs loss back home in India (Siegel, 2019). Despite growing success and increase funding, travel technology companies cannot ignore the lack of business incubation ecosystem for start-ups in India (Jacob, 2017).

Entrepreneurs who have successfully set up businesses of various models continue to thrive. In 2006, after working regular blue-collar jobs for many years, Abhishek and Chitra Daga decided to fill a gap in the market and provided their corporate clients with ideas for unusual and exotic places to visit that are off-the-beaten-path. They were toying with this idea, and at the same time, gradually getting investments from personal savings, friends and family while also holding onto to well-paying jobs. Eventually, their company Thrillophilia obtained their first client, Wipro. Soon after, other corporate clients started to engage Thrillophilia for their own employees' incentive travel arrangements (Kumar, 2013).

PayTM, founded by Vijay Shekhar Sharma, cleared its debt of INR7 billion / US$98,000 and without any government help in financing, it entered the growing tourism and hospitality industry in India, and eventually, globally, after getting the support of private investors such as Alibaba, Softbank, Berkshire Hathaway, and SAIF Partners (Kripa & Ghosh, 2019). PayTM connected with over 3 million merchants and 185 million registered mobile wallet service users ("PayTM's journey now a case study at Harvard," 2017).

India is also known for religious tourism. The fine line between yogis (religious preacher believed to possess mystical powers) and their role as entrepreneurs out to make money of tourists is another phenomenon in India. These religious entrepreneurs leverage on their networks and status to promote their services for those seeking solace in life (Shinde, 2010). This is one of the biggest business with large landed ashrams catering to vacationers for the sole purpose of partaking in Hindu religious philosophy and practices.

Despite a large pool of entrepreneurs, India still lacks industry development focused policy and private collaboration. These major limitations places India behind other destinations like Thailand and Singapore, where the state plays an active role in facilitating and seed funding topromising entrepreneurs and stimulate industry collaboration. Evidently, there is a lack of support for start-ups in India as policymakers focus instead on initiatives that aid the general public. Though state and national tourism ministries fund promotional activities, these intuitions lack industry focused policy programs that stimulate entrepreneurship activities and motivate entrepreneurs to innovate or promote tourism and hospitality products and services. Nevertheless, potential start-ups continue to find private investors' support not at the early stage but only after they are able to show an expansion in their operation domestically and internationally, like Zomato, PayTM, Oyo, and the likes of Ola.

India needs a comprehensive and well-resourced business incubator in tourism industry with government support to pool technology and financial resources to boost the travel and hospitality industry. In this progressive strategy, government plays an essential role to nudge private investors with technology and financial resources. A strategy that recognises students and professionals can become the second pillar to innovative ideas and facilitate them with well defined resources. State and private institutions play an interactive third pillar to ensure that creative ideas are transformed into viable business entities through various country-wide schemes.

Singapore

The Singapore tourism and hospitality landscape has both opportunities and limitations for entrepreneurs who wish to create sustainable businesses. The Singapore government's approach towards facilitating and encouraging private enterprise initiatives is immediately evident in the various funding and support schemes and programmes for individuals and organizations (Economic Development Board, 2019). In this regard, there are several government agencies, statutory boards and non-government organisations that engage in a tight-knit grid of financial incentives, awards, recognition and facility provisions for entrepreneurs. Tourism and hospitality entrepreneurs have plenty of opportunities to avail themselves to seed funding and co-shared incentive payments.

To gain access to funding, entrepreneurs in Singapore have several options to help them in their initial years of growth. For example, the Singapore Tourism Board (2019) which created the Singapore Tourism Accelerator launched in June 2019 saw 9 start-up companies come up with various ideas from increasing tourism business operations efficiency to applications that can enhance visitor experience. These start-up companies are undergoing a pilot phase and if proven viable, they can receive up to SG$25,000 / US$18,400 for their business. This competitive seed funding is open to entrepreneurs around the world.

However, there are plenty more grants under the Singapore Tourism Board's (2020b) intention:

STB unveils a new five-year Tourism Development Fund, designed to catalyse the creation of innovative and quality tourism products and experiences, and capability and talent enhancement efforts among tourism-related enterprises.

There are three schemes and 9 different categories where entrepreneurs can find financial support if they have a registered business and their ideas can create value to the Singapore tourism landscape.

The National Heritage Board is another government statutory board that welcomes businesses, entrepreneurs who can contribute to the local heritage scene. Many of these schemes require excellent track records of previous achievements. There are ways an entrepreneur can access some of these and other government funds. One way is to team up with more established firms in the application and eventual project implementation. The Singapore government has also a tax exemption for start-up companies which make less than Singapore Dollars$100,000 (US$73,800) and another 50% off for the next Singapore Dollars$100,000 (EHL Education Group, 2020).

In a private-public joint effort to promote entrepreneurship, there exists the First Mover Framework under the Ministry of Trade and Industry. One entrepreneur by the name of Seah Leng Chiang, proposed the idea of repurposing 50 shipping containers as accommodation rooms redone with kitchen and toilets. The idea is to have these containers located in far-flung sites in Singapore where the rental can be cheap for tourist accommodation (Lau, 2019). Such is Singapore where tourism and hospitality entrepreneurs with salient ideas can always depend on the favourable funding ecosystem to support their enterprise.

Hence, the Singapore government is an active stakeholder with many start-up company schemes and is willing to invest up to 70% and thereafter Singapore Dollars SGD$1 (US$0.74) for every SGD$1 invested by the entrepreneur. A whole government-linked website called *Enterprise Singapore* provides all the information an entrepreneur needs to start his or her journey with an idea into the business world.

Thailand

As a consistently popular destination, Thailand welcomes more than 38 million tourists a year and receives more than US$73 billion in tourism revenue (Bangkok Post-a, 2019). The Thai tourism industry is extremely successful, receiving multiple accolades every year. Among other awards, the country was awarded the third place in the "Best Country" category at the prestigious *Conde Nast Traveller UK* 2018 Readers' Travel Awards, won the award for "Destination of the Year" at the *TTG Asia* Travel Awards 2018, and cliched the "Best Destination" award at the *Travel Weekly UK* (Thaivest, 2018). The largesse of this tourism and hospitality economy means that there are ample stimulus and opportunities for growth in entrepreneurship. In a study conducted on the informal sector, it was identified that cultural and symbolic capital both play significant roles in shaping the way freelancers conduct their business (Çakmak et al., 2019).

The Thai government had created an ideal entrepreneurial environment (Hasnan, 2019). According to the World Economic Forum report (2019), 31.9% of Thailand's young generation is likely to become entrepreneurs. The report also found that new entrepreneurs prefer to establish their businesses in new, high-technology field, rather than in the traditional industries.

As part of an effort to foster the entrepreneurial environment, a start-up fund by the Ministry of Digital Economy and Society worth US$570 million was launched to finance about 2,500 start-ups (Balea, 2016). Besides this fund, the Digital Economy Fund worth US$285 million, set up in 2016 funded by the Ministry of Finance, has been supporting start-ups in various industries such as healthcare, finance, agriculture, tourism and digital technology (Lim, 2018). Moreover, Thailand's Board of Investments in 2017 implemented tax-free incentives, greatly benefitting start-ups in Thailand (Channel News Asia, 2017). New companies can apply for an investment promotion and qualify for the incentives.

Although the government gave Thai start-ups their fullest support, new entrepreneurs in tourism industry still struggled. Lim (2018) believed that Thai tourism companies should expand internationally or innovate to find new markets rather than compete among themselves in an already saturated market.

In 2018, Airbnb, Interior Ministry's Department of Local Administration (DLA) and Government Savings Bank (GSB) jointly aid local homestay nationwide. Airbnb and DLA launched "Empower local tourism entrepreneur" which focuses on educating the entrepreneur and provincial officials in hospitality, hosting and compliance standards. Meanwhile, GSB also launched "GSB Homestays", a flexible-rate loan, to help fund the local homestay owners. These programs focus on rural areas favoring the government's attempt to enhance tourism in the second-tier provinces. Since the launch of the program, over 740 homestays have joined (Bangkok Post-b, 2019). The Tourism Authority of Thailand (TAT) believe that travel technology has the potential to create innovative ways for international travellers to experience Thailand. To make this possible, the TAT and National Innovation Agency (NIA) are cooperating to help start-up and local entrepreneurs with knowledge, ideas and funding ("Thailand lacks 'travel tech'," 2019).

Entrepreneurs themselves are also creative, like those in Mae Kampong's tourism sector. A Community Based Tourism (CBT) group sought agreement from the local community to provide an authentic local experience to tourists. There are also regular meetings between the locals and the CBT group to discuss and prepare in advance of resources, personnel, facilities and profit-sharing among participating residents (Thailand International Development Cooperation Agency, 2010). The "Tuk Tuk Hop" application offers on-demand "hop-on, hop-off" service by the well-recognized iconic Bangkok vehicles, Tuk Tuk. The user can choose from over 60 prominent Bangkok tourist locations for pickup. The App offers travelers with an inexpensive, safe, convenient and alternative transportation (Thapphila, 2019). This application was founded by Mick, Mek, Un+ and Ty, all university graduates with two of them holding PhD from Stanford University ("About Us," 2020). Those innovations via information technology further proved the possibility of applying high technology from small and medium enterprises to contribute to their success(see also, Kavoura & Koziol, 2017).

However, with the many schemes, there appears to be limited access to necessary information among the Thai entrepreneurial community (Guelich, 2018). Guelich's report called *Global Entrepreneurshp Monitor*, informs that the awareness of available funding opportunities among Thai entrepreneurs is low, as many are unaware that the Thai government is able to provide support, be it in the form of tax exemptions or financial loans. This has raised concerns that the Thai government's support schemes and programmes do not actually help most entrepreneurs, and that they may need a new strategy to increase the accessibility and awareness of these support schemes.

Vietnam

As one of the fastest growing markets in South-East Asia, Vietnam has a lot of uncovered potentials. Springer (2019) released a list of best places to visit in Asia and two places are in Vietnam. The country's potential is also seen by the increasing number of international tourist arrivals. Loan (2019) indicated a new record of highest-ever number of international visitors to Vietnam at 16.3 million year-to-date, a 15% increase year-on-year. At the *World Travel Awards*, the country was honoured for the first time as "Asia's Leading Destination" (Khang, 2018). Overall, the Vietnamese tourism industry contributed 6.8% in 2019, a good share to the country's GDP, according to the Nhan Dan Online-a (2019).

The tourism and hospitality industry in Vietnam has been one of the country's priorities since the release of Decree 08-NQ/TW in 2017. In the decree, the government has committed to improving facilities and infrastructure for the tourism industry, running more promotional campaigns and offering more favourable conditions for entrepreneurs and the tourism landscape ("Political bureau decree," 2017). Nationwide, entrepreneurs in the Vietnamese tourism industry realized the importance of branding and destination marketing, and that these require the government's support. Thus, they are now trying to foster a closer relationship with the local authorities. In return, the government supported by introducing more tourism festivals as ways to create new excitement for travellers.

In terms of financial support, the country set up a fund for developing SMEs in July 2019 (Dung, 2019) for a maximum 7 years at an interest rate of 80% of the lowest interest rate from commercial banks in Vietnam. This can solve the challenge of accessing sufficient funding, which has been a long-time difficulty for new entrepreneurs in Vietnam (Dong, 2019).

In recent times, tourism entrepreneurs in Vietnam can be divided into two types: the traditional ones and the new start-up ones. These entrepreneurs are from travel agencies, hotels, resorts, restaurants, theme parks and other attractions. The traditional ones are those who have been working since before 2000. The new start-up ones opened after 2000 and are those who focus on any one of these services: online hotel bookings, transportations or local tours. The traditional entrepreneurs are more focused and consider changers in narrower tourism services. Both traditional ones and new start-ups concentrate only on contracting with hotels to sign for best possible rate for rooms only. At this stage, the market varies much because of the influx in international tourists, thus creating fierce competition among travel agents. The entrepreneurs wish to minimize their risks in this competition by seeking the lowest hotel and attractions rates possible. Another change that they are moving towards is the closer relationship with the Ministry of Tourism, Culture and Sports in running more promotional campaigns and creating new experiences. Having a close relationship with the authorities enables them to create more exciting tour packages.

Besides, homestay resorts and hotels in the context of eco-tourism are mushrooming in Vietnam, providing more places for tourists to gain new experiences and at the same time providing opportunities for Vietnamese individuals and families to participate in the tourism economy. However, this business model accounts for a small part of the pie for the entrepreneurs because most travellers are still going through travel agents because of insurance coverage and stress-free service. As the government plays an important role in the better management of the industry and planning, it is required to conduct a survey to find out exactly how many travellers go through travel agents and how many go on free-and-easy tours. Entrepreneurs have to find ways to reach out through new web-based channels. Entrepreneurs in the tourism industry in Vietnam are always coming up with ways to sustainably develop their business by providing travellers with new and authentic experiences.

In South Vietnam, C2T Media and Tourism Company (C2T) created new experiences for tourists by growing their own unique gardens of rambutans and mangroves with special places for visitors to enjoy (Nhan Dan Online-b, 2019). They also connect with locals to bring visitors to their garden for authentic experiences. Tour guides are requested to learn more local knowledge and cultures to deliver genuine experiences for visitors.

Besides, innovative tours included with cultural shows such as water puppet shows and traditional folk song shows provide tourists with new experiences of theatre and tourism (Vietnam National Administration, 2019). However, such a business model is impulsive and driven by individuals and needs a more comprehensive strategy from the government with support in promoting the new products to international tourists.

Before the internet boom in Vietnam, travel agents' main sources of revenue came from providing full services in the areas of rooms, food and beverage, transportation and ticketing. But now, because of keen competition from online travel agents (OTAs) they can only provide the best possible room rates. Due to open-market competitions, competitors appear in every sector, creating challenges and competition among the traditional travel agents. To do that, travel agents themselves must be financially strong, well connected to local governments and international travel agents, and be quick to seize any business that comes. Failure to do so may very much result in their business failure. This is a big challenge for entrepreneurs in the industry who want to set their foot into the market.

In fact, those newly built resorts and homestays can be successful because of their wide connection with many Online Travel Agents (OTA). However, there is another challenge for domestic online travel agents who want to compete with international online travel agents. According to Nhan Dan Online (2018), 10 major local OTAs (Ivivu.com, Mytour.vn, Chudu24.com, Gotadi.com, Tripi.vn) took 20% of the online travel trading market, while international OTAs (booking.com, agoda.com, expedia.com, etc.) took more than 80% of the share. Thus, it is of great urgency to build a management system on guest insights to understand the new habits of internet users for holiday planning, when the preferred periods of travel are, how they make their bookings, etc. This will help entrepreneurs to better understand the travel market and enable them to compete in the OTA space.

Alongside with the three-fold increase in the number of international tourists from 5 million in 2010 to 15 million in 2018 (Das, 2019), qualified labour is required to grow in line. This is another challenge for entrepreneurs because they need to increase competency in human resource.

Without much support from the government, on a provincial scale, independent small homestays (also known as eco-tourism) are springing up in mountainous areas near big cities to attract international and local tourists from those cities, accounting for a relatively big part of the market share. For example, Ninh Binh province, which is now a new destination near the capital of Hanoi, has lots of small homestays and tiny resorts with maximum capacities of 20 rooms each. Each contains a swimming pool, a nice place for BBQ and sightseeing, and surrounding areas for cycling and mountain-climbing. These small establishments are usually characterised by their small capacities, proximities to the big cities, and are surrounded by mountains, hills, lakes or even beaches. Flamingo Dai Lai Resort is an example. The resort is full most weekends and half-full during weekdays. Amenities attributing to this resort's success include an entertainment complex for family activities, including boating (kayak), outdoor jungle games (quite different from other outdoor games in the cities), a golf club and other services.

Policy Directions and Financial Support

Several distinct similarities and differences can be drawn from the way in which entrepreneurs have access to government financial and explicit policy support. Entrepreneurship is one of the key factors of production often driven by innovation, and success is not guaranteed.

With reference to Table 1, Thailand and Singapore can be grouped as similar and India and Vietnam can be in the other group because of the similarities and differences in tourism landscape, entrepreneurship status and government support.

Due to the many uncovered potentials in tourism industry in Vietnam and India, and also their tourism entrepreneurship connections to the world, these two countries' tourism lifecycle can be grouped as development stage. Singapore and Thailand can be grouped as mature economies because of their advanced marketing campaigns and developed tourism landscape.

Tourism entrepreneurs in Singapore and Thailand have been enjoying abundant government support including financial and policy, while Vietnamese entrepreneurs have limited support from state institutions. Indian start-ups have to independently grow on their own volition with very little government backing. This could be a critical point as to explain why even Vietnam and India have been long time focusing on improving their economies but not their tourism industry.

The table also reveals that Vietnam has the most potential to develop the fastest because their tourism entrepreneurs have started to enjoy many government supports due to recent changes in the country's policy to put their tourism industry a top priority, while there are a lot of undiscovered areas to develop in the tourism industry. The potential to create new tourist destinations are abundant and if tourism entrepreneurs can catch up with new opportunities, the industry will grow even faster.

The main difference between group 1 (Singapore, Thailand) and group 2 (Vietnam, India) is the tourism landscape potential. While Singapore and Thailand have developed most of their country's tourism resources, Vietnam and India still have a lot more to explore and develop. Another difference lies in the government support. While Singapore and Thailand governments have been directing their tourism entrepreneurs toward a particular way (Thailand promoting medicinal, culinary and smart tourism, while Singapore promoting tourism as a center hub for all services and creating experiences with modern technology), Vietnam and India do not have much directional detail for their tourism entrepreneurs to innovate and develop their products. Besides, Vietnam has limited financial support and India's tourism industry does not have much support for their entrepreneurs for now, while Thailand and Singapore have already developed many supporting programmes for their tourism start-ups.

Table 1. Comparisons of government support for entrepreneurship

Table 1: Comparisons of Government Support for Entrepreneurship

Destinations	Tourism Landscape	Entrepreneurship	Government Support for Tourism & Hospitality Entrepreneurs	
			Financial	Policy support
Thailand	Mature Economy with potential innovations in rural community-based tourism. (World Economic Forum report, 2019)	Developed with large government supports. (Hasnan, 2019)	Various sources. (Marketer, 2019, translation)	Various activities and promotion campaigns (Focus direction to medicinal and culinary tourism (Banwell et al., 2013)
Singapore	Mature Economy with opportunities to create unique experiences in urban settings. (Singapore Tourism Board, 2020)	Developed with large government supports. (Personal communication, April 27, 2020)	Various sources. (Economic Development Board, 2019)	Various activities & campaigns.(Economi c Development Board, 2019)
India	Emerging Destination (IBEF, 2020; Sharma, 2020)	Developing with low government support. (Personal communication, April 27, 2020)	Government Limited to General Level support (Ramalingegowda & Khare, 2014; Jacob, 2017); Pradhan Mantri MUDRA Yojna scheme (Ngoasong & Kimbu, 2016) Reduce GST on hotels (Indian Brand Equity Foundation, 2020)	Limited Developments on tourist circuits and 17 Iconic Tourist sites, promotion campaigns (IBEF, 2020) Government Training programs (Ministry of Tourism, 2020.)
Vietnam	Emerging Destination (Springer, 2019)	Developing with various government support. (Dung, 2019)	Limited- Government loans but troublesome paper works (Personal communication, April 27, 2020)	Various license for new tourist destinations with Decree 08-NQ/TW. (Political bureau decree, 2017)

FUTURE RESEARCH TRAJECTORIES AND CONCLUSION

Entrepreneurship in Asia is characterized by nurturing young interested people. The extent to which they receive government support is very much dependent on which state the country's development is and how progressive the government thinking is. Young and aspirational people need some form of financial or physical setting to start with; this has even become one of the must-have points that among different fields such as dentistry which were not well known as an entrepreneur's sight for profit before the Internet boom (Constantin & Kavoura, 2019). While all four governments - India, Singapore, Thailand and Vietnam appear to be interested in allowing individuals with ideas and effort to emerge into the tourism scene, only the latter two countries appear to have a strategy and have continuously found concerted schemes and ways to stimulate participation and interests in entrepreneurship. Emerging economies such as India may have social priorities where the focus is to invest in schemes that benefit the immediate communities rather than a specific industry.

Future research on the topic of Asian entrepreneurship can contribute to the body of knowledge by investigating in the following areas:

- Role of Asian entrepreneurs in the one-belt trading route and how they have capitalized in creating new related thematic tour packages
- Technology offering Asian entrepreneurs opportunities to find and implement their business ideas.
- In emerging economies (cf. entrepreneurship research in Africa, see: Ntshangase & Ezeuduji, 2019; Eijdenberg et al., 2020; Eijdenberg et al., 2019), many of the unknown or undeveloped sites can be a means to achieving entrepreneurial activities in the field of tourism and hospitality. How are entrepreneurs taking advantage of these places?
- To what extent have Airbnb, local homestays and small private companies offer entrepreneurship opportunities?

Studies have highlighted the importance of supporting entrepreneurial activities as a source of revenue for the government (Yusuf, 2014). As more and more entrepreneurs take to creating smart website and mobile application businesses, the initial financial support for such initiatives is critical. Although the success or failure of a start-up business is dependent on the entrepreneurs' own drive, there is always concerns as how to minimise the risk of failure among emerging entrepreneurship. It certainly requires the critical role of government in financial backing. However other stakeholders like academia seemed to be underestimated because they give remarkable contribution to entrepreneur community. In this sense, they do contribute to economic growth to a certain extent (Makarona & Kavoura, 2019; Kavoura & Andersson, 2016). The best way to move toward a sustainable entrepreneurship is to have an active participation by every possible stakeholder.

REFERENCES

AboutUs. (2020). Retrieved from https://www.tuktukhop.com/about

Alsos, G. A., Eide, D., & Madsen, E. L. (2014). Introduction: Innovation in tourism industries. In *Handbook of research on innovation in tourism industries*. Edward Elgar Publishing. doi:10.4337/9781782548416.00006

Altinay, L., Madanoglu, M., Daniele, R., & Lashley, C. (2012). The influence of family tradition and psychological traits on entrepreneurial intention. *International Journal of Hospitality Management, 31*(2), 489–499. doi:10.1016/j.ijhm.2011.07.007

Arora, R. (2015). *Why India Is the Land of Rising Entrepreneurship*. Retrieved 7 April 2020, from https://www.inc.com/rohit-arora/why-india-is-the-land-of-rising-entrepreneurship.html

Ateljevic, J., & Li, L. (2009). Tourism entrepreneurship–concepts and issues. In J. Ateljevic & S. J. Page (Eds.), *Tourism and entrepreneurship: International perspectives* (pp. 9–32). Butterworth-Heinemann. doi:10.1016/B978-0-7506-8635-8.00002-2

Balea, J. (2016). *Thailand plans $570m venture fund for startups*. Retrieved from https://www.techinasia.com/thailand-fund-startups

Bangkok Post. (2019a). *Record 38.27m tourists in 2018; 41m expected in 2019*. Retrieved from https://www.bangkokpost.com/business/1619182/record-38-27m-tourists-in-2018-41m-expected-in-2019

Bangkok Post. (2019b). *Airbnb, state agencies aid homestay operators*. Retrieved from https://www.bangkokpost.com/business/1776619/airbnb-state-agencies-aid-homestay-operators

Banwell, C., Dixon, J., Seubsman, S., Pangsap, S., Kelly, M., & Sleigh, A. (2013). Evolving food retail environments in Thailand and implications for the health and nutrition transition. *Public Health Nutrition, 16*(4), 608–615. doi:10.1017/S1368980012004223 PMID:23021291

Budget Direct. (2020). *Singapore Tourism Statistics 2020*. Retrieved from https://www.budgetdirect.com.sg/travel-insurance/research/singapore-tourism-statistics

Busenitz, L. W., Gómez, C., & Spencer, J. W. (2000). Country institutional profiles: Unlocking entrepreneurial phenomena. *Academy of Management Journal, 43*(5), 994–1003. doi:10.2307/1556423

Çakmak, E., Lie, R., & Selwyn, T. (2019). Informal tourism entrepreneurs' capital usage and conversion. *Current Issues in Tourism, 22*(18), 2250–2265. doi:10.1080/13683500.2018.1448763

Carlisle, S., Kunc, M., Jones, E., & Tiffin, S. (2013). Supporting innovation for tourism development through multi-stakeholder approaches: Experiences from Africa. *Tourism Management, 35*, 59–69. doi:10.1016/j.tourman.2012.05.010

Chang, J. (2011). Introduction: Entrepreneurship in tourism and hospitality: The role of SMEs. *Asia Pacific Journal of Tourism Research, 16*(5), 467–469. doi:10.1080/10941665.2011.597572

Channel News Asia. (2017). *Funding Possibilities for Start-ups in Thailand*. Retrieved from https://www.channelnewsasia.com/news/startup/articles/money-matters/funding-possibilities-for-start-ups-in-thailand-8875136

Coletta, M., & Kapoor, C. (2019). The State of Travel Start Ups Interactive Database. *Phocuswright*. Retrieved from https://www.phocuswright.com/Travel-Research/Technology-Innovation/The-State-of-Travel-Startups-Interactive-Database

Constantin, F., & Kavoura, A. (2019). Entrepreneur without Intention with Websites as a Communication Tool. Current Trends in Romania. In A. Kavoura, E. Kefallonitis, & A. Giovanis (Eds.), *Strategic Innovative Marketing and Tourism* (pp. 1093–1101). Springer. doi:10.1007/978-3-030-12453-3_126

Das, K. (2019). Vietnam's Tourism Industry Continues its. *Growth, 2018*. https://www.vietnam-briefing.com/news/vietnams-tourism-industry-continues-growth-2018.html/

Devang, A., Kruse, C., Parker, A., & Siren, P. (2017). The next wave of business models in asia. *MIT Sloan Management Review, 58*(2), 35–39.

Doan, E. Z. (2020) Number of International Tourist Arrivals (ITA) in Vietnam 2019. *Statista*. Retrieved from https://www.statista.com/statistics/981987/vietnam-number-international-tourist-arrivals/

Dong, P. T. (2019). *Rào cản nào trong tiếp cận vốn tín dụng của Doanh nghiệp nhỏ và vừa ở Việt Nam?* [What barrier small & medium enterprises face when accessing financial credit?]. Retrieved from https://nhadautu.vn/rao-can-nao-trong-tiep-can-von-tin-dung-cua-doanh-nghiep-nho-va-vua-o-viet-nam-d21068.html

Dung, V. (2019). *Từ 01/7/2019, doanh nghiệp nhỏ và vừa được vay vốn tối đa 7 năm* [From 1st July 2019, small and medium enterprises can apply for financial credit for maximum 07 years]. Retrieved from http://tapchitaichinh.vn/co-che-chinh-sach/tu-0172019-doanh-nghiep-nho-va-vua-duoc-vay-von-toi-da-7-nam-306978.html

EHL Education Group. (2020). *Singapore Startup Ecosystem: An Entreprenuers' Paradise?* Retrieved from https://hospitalityinsights.ehl.edu/bridging-valley-death-singapore

Eijdenberg, E.L., Isaga, N.M., Paas, L.J., & Masurel, E. (2020). Fluid entrepreneurial motivations in Tanzania. *Journal of African Business.* doi:10.1080/15228916.2019.1695191

Eijdenberg, E. L., Thompson, N. A., Verduijn, K., & Essers, C. (2019). Entrepreneurial activities in a developing country: An institutional theory perspective. *International Journal of Entrepreneurial Behaviour & Research, 25*(3), 414–432. doi:10.1108/IJEBR-12-2016-0418

Fyall, A., Buhalis, D., & Parra López, E. (2009). Entrepreneurship and innovation in tourism. *Pasos: Revista De Turismo y Patrimonio Cultural, 7*(3), 355–357. doi:10.25145/j.pasos.2009.07.024

Getz, D., & Petersen, T. (2005). Growth and profit-oriented entrepreneurship among family business owners in the tourism and hospitality industry. *International Journal of Hospitality Management, 24*(2), 219–242. doi:10.1016/j.ijhm.2004.06.007

Gillen, J. (2010). Tourism and Entrepreneurialism in Southeast Asian cities. *Geography Compass, 4*(4), 370–382. doi:10.1111/j.1749-8198.2010.00322.x

GKToday. (2019). *India in the Travel & Tourism Competitiveness Index 2019.* Retrieved from https://www.gktoday.in/current-affairs/india-in-the-travel-tourism-competitiveness-index-2019/

Guelich, U. (2018). GEM Thailand Report 2017/2018. *Bangkok University & Global Entrepreneurship Monitor.* Retrieved from https://www.researchgate.net/publication/330105669_2017-18_GEM_Thailand_Report

Gurel, E., Altinay, L., & Daniele, R. (2010). Tourism students' entrepreneurial intentions. *Annals of Tourism Research, 37*(3), 646–669. doi:10.1016/j.annals.2009.12.003

Hallak, R., Assaker, G., & Lee, C. (2015). Tourism entrepreneurship performance: The effects of place identity, self-efficacy, and gender. *Journal of Travel Research, 54*(1), 36–51. doi:10.1177/0047287513513170

IBEF. (2020). *ITourism & Hospitality Industry in India.* Retrieved from https://www.ibef.org/industry/tourism-hospitality-india.aspx

Indian Brand Equity Foundation. (2020). *Indian Tourism and Hospitality Industry Analysis.* Retrieved from https://www.ibef.org/industry/indian-tourism-and-hospitality-industry-analysis-presentation

Istudor, L. G. (2019). Innovation and entrepreneurship in tourism. *Cactus, 1*(1), 6–11.

Jacob, M. (2017). Entrepreneurship and Startup Programs: Opportunities in Travel and Tourism. Atna. *Journal of Tourism Studies*, *12*(2), 51–65. doi:10.12727/ajts.18.3

Kavoura, A., & Andersson, T. (2016). Applying Delphi method for strategic design of social entrepreneurship. *Library Review*, *65*(3), 185–205. doi:10.1108/LR-06-2015-0062

Kavoura, A., & Koziol, L. (2017). *Polish Firms' Innovation Capability for Competitiveness via Information Technologies and Social Media Implementation.* In A. Vlachvei, O. Notta, K. Karantininis, & N. Tsountas (Eds.), *Factors Affecting Firm Competitiveness and Performance in the Modern Business World* (pp. 185–214). IGI Global.

Khang, D. (2018*). Vietnam named Asia's leading destination at World Travel Awards.* Retrieved from https://tuoitrenews.vn/news/business/20180905/vietnam-named-asias-leading-destination-at-world-travel-awards/47032.html

Khanka, S. S. (2006). *Entrepreneurial development* (Vol. S). Chand Publishing.

Knoema. (2020). *Singapore – Contribution of Travel and Tourism to Employment.* Retrieved from https://knoema.com/atlas/Singapore/topics/Tourism/Travel-and-Tourism-Total-Contribution-to-Employment/Contribution-of-travel-and-tourism-to-employment

Kumar, A. (2013). Thrillophilia: Chitra & Abhishek Daga's Rs 2.8 crore travel company. *The Economic Times.* Retrieved on 30 January 2019 from https://economictimes.indiatimes.com/small-biz/entrepreneurship/thrillophilia-chitra-abhishek-dagas-rs-2-8-crore-travel-company/articleshow/25892583.cms?from=mdr

Lau, J. (2019). Entrepreneur's out-of-the-box idea for shipping-container hotel in Singapore. *The Straits Times.* Retrieved from https://www.straitstimes.com/singapore/entrepreneurs-out-of-the-box-idea-for-shipping-container-hotel

Leisure hospitality startup 'V resorts' raises $10M in fresh series A funding. (2019). *Business World.* Retrieved from https://search-proquest-com.elibrary.jcu.edu.au/docview/2205290384?accountid=16285

Liu, C. S., & Fang, Y. (2016). Night markets: Entrepreneurship and achieving competitive advantage. *International Journal of Contemporary Hospitality Management*, *28*(11), 2374–2398. doi:10.1108/IJCHM-03-2015-0114

Loan, D. (2019). *Int'l tourists to Vietnam up 39% y-o-y in Nov*. Retrieved from https://en.thesaigontimes.vn/tinbaichitiet/73166/

Makarona, E., & Kavoura, A. (2019). Redesigning the Ivory Tower: Academic entrepreneurship as a new calling supporting economic growth. *The Malopolska School of Economics in Tarnow Research Papers Collection*, *42*, 15–26. doi:10.25944/znmwse.2019.02.1526

Marketer. (2019). *Thailand lacks 'travel tech', pushing tourism not to end, Tourism Authority of Thailand to solve games, focusing on creating people for innovation.* Retrieved from https://marketeeronline.co/archives/104901

Ministry of Tourism. (2019). India Tourism Statistics at a Glance – 2019. *Government of India*. Retrieved from http://tourism.gov.in/sites/default/files/Other/India%20Tourism%20Statistics%20at%20a%20Glance%202019.pdf

Ministry of Tourism. (2020). Human Resource Development. *Government of India*. Retrieved from http://tourism.gov.in/human-resource-development

Ngoasong, M. Z., & Kimbu, A. N. (2016). Informal microfinance institutions and development-led tourism entrepreneurship. *Tourism Management*, *52*, 430–439. doi:10.1016/j.tourman.2015.07.012

Nhan Dan Online. (2018). *Innovating thinking in tourism*. Retrieved from https://en.nhandan.com.vn/travel/item/6479102-innovating-thinking-in-tourism.html

Nhan Dan Online. (2019a). *World Bank sees Vietnam's economy grow 6.8% in 2019*. Retrieved from https://en.nhandan.org.vn/business/item/8236002-world-bank-sees-vietnam%E2%80%99s-economy-grow-6-8-in-2019.html

Nhan Dan Online. (2019b). *Young tourism start-up provides exciting experience for visitors to Ben Tre*. Retrieved from https://en.nhandan.com.vn/travel/item/8113102-young-tourism-start-up-provides-exciting-experience-for-visitors-to-ben-tre.html)

Ntshangase, S. D., & Ezeuduji, I. O. (2019). The attributes of successful tourism-related entrepreneurs: A case from south africa. *Euroeconomica*, *38*(2), 296–313.

Pay, T. M's journey now a case study at Harvard. (2017). Retrieved from https://www.business-standard.com/article/news-ians/paytm-s-journey-now-a-case-study-at-harvard-117013000774_1.html

Perez, K. T., & Bui, T. L. H. (2010). Closing Doors And Opening Windows: Opportunities For Entrepreneurship In An Emerging Asian Country For A Seasoned Woman Professional. *International Journal of Entrepreneurship*, *14*, 45–49. https://search-proquest-com.elibrary.jcu.edu.au/docview/885013588?accountid=16285

Person, G., & Van Beek, H. H. (1998). Uninvited Guests: Tourists and Environment in Siberut. In V. King (Ed.), *Environmental Challenges in Southeast Asia* (pp. 317–341). Routledge.

Peters, M., Frehse, J., & Buhalis, D. (2009). The importance of lifestyle entrepreneurship: A conceptual study of the tourism industry. *Pasos (El Sauzal)*, *7*(2), 393–405. doi:10.25145/j.pasos.2009.07.028

Petrof, J. V. (1980). Entrepreneurial profile: A discriminant analysis. *Journal of Small Business Management, 18*(4), 13.

Political bureau decree. (2017, January 16). *Nghị Quyết Của Bộ Chính Trị Về Phát Triển Du Lịch Trở Thành Ngành Kinh Tế Mũi Nhọn* [Political bureau: to make tourism industry a top industry to develop]. Retrieved from https://thuvienphapluat.vn/van-ban/thuong-mai/Nghi-quyet-so-08-NQ-TW-phat-trien-du-lich-tro-thanh-nganh-kinh-te-mui-nhon-2017-338542.aspx

Qureshi, D., & Ahmed, M. L. (2012). Strengthening women entrepreneurs through tourism employment and entrepreneurship of the rural women in aurangabad. *Johar*, *7*(1), 54–66.

Ramalingegowda, C., & Khare, S. (2014). *Indian Government Entrepreneurship Programs*. Retrieved 23 December 2019, from https://yourstory.com/2014/08/indian-government-entrepreneurship-programs?utm_pageloadtype=scroll

Sharma, Y. (2019). *Number of Startups in India grew 7X to 50K in a decade: KPMG report*. Retrieved from https://entrackr.com/2019/02/startups-india-grew-50k-2019/

Shaw, G., & Williams, A. M. (2013). From lifestyle consumption to lifestyle production: Changing patterns of tourism entrepreneurship. In *Small firms in tourism* (pp. 109–124). Routledge.

Shinde, K. A. (2010). Entrepreneurship and indigenous entrepreneurs in religious tourism in india. *International Journal of Tourism Research*, *12*(5), 523–535. doi:10.1002/jtr.771

Siam Commercial Bank. (2016). *Insight: Thai Tourism: Sustaining Success*. Retrieved from https://www.scbeic.com/en/detail/file/product/2953/ekn1rppsq7/EIC_Insight_ENG_Tourism_2016.pdf/preview

Siegel, J. A. (2019). Future City newsletter: Struggles at SoftBank's $10B hospitality startup, the death of CediFi & more. *The Real Deal New York Estate News*. Retrieved from https://therealdeal.com/2019/12/27/future-city-newsletter-struggles-at-softbanks-10b-hospitality-startup-the-death-of-credifi-more/

Singapore Tourism Board. (2011). *Fact Sheet: Tourism Perfomance for Jan-Dec 2010*. Retrieved from https://www.stb.gov.sg/content/dam/stb/documents/statistics-marketing-insights/Quarterly-Tourism-Performance-Report/stb-monthly-factsheet-jan-to-dec-2010.pdf

Singapore Tourism Board. (2020a). *Singapore Tourism Accelerator*. Retrieved from https://www.stb.gov.sg/content/stb/en/trade-events-and-resources/Singapore-Tourism-Accelerator.html

Singapore Tourism Board. (2020b). *Grants Overview*. Retrieved from https://www.stb.gov.sg/content/stb/en/assistance-and-licensing/grants-overview.html#

Singapore Tourism Board. (2020c). *Tourism Sector Performance Q4 2019 Report*. Retrieved from https://www.stb.gov.sg/content/dam/stb/documents/statistics-marketing-insights/Quarterly-Tourism-Performance-Report/STB%20Q4%202019_Final.pdf

Solvoll, S., Alsos, G. A., & Bulanova, O. (2015). Tourism entrepreneurship - review and future directions. *Scandinavian Journal of Hospitality and Tourism, 15*(sup1), 120-137. doi:10.1080/15022250.2015.1065592

Springer, K. (2019). *Best places to visit for the ultimate Asia experience*. Retrieved from https://edition.cnn.com/travel/article/asia-best-places-to-visit/index.html

Stojanović, S. (2018). Entrepreneurship innovations in tourism. *Industrija*, *46*(4), 69–83. doi:10.5937/industrija46-18741

Sun, X., & Xu, H. (2017). Lifestyle tourism entrepreneurs' mobility motivations: A case study on Dali and Lijiang, China. *Tourism Management Perspectives*, *24*, 64–71. doi:10.1016/j.tmp.2017.06.004

Sundbo, J., Orfila-Sintes, F., & Sørensen, F. (2007). The innovative behaviour of tourism firms—Comparative studies of Denmark and Spain. *Research Policy*, *36*(1), 88–106. doi:10.1016/j.respol.2006.08.004

Tajeddini, K., Ratten, V., & Denisa, M. (2017). Female tourism entrepreneurs in bali, indonesia. *Journal of Hospitality and Tourism Management*, *31*, 52–58. doi:10.1016/j.jhtm.2016.10.004

Tang, C. F., & Tan, E. C. (2013). How stable is the tourism-led growth hypothesis in Malaysia? Evidence from disaggregated tourism markets. *Tourism Management*, *37*, 52–57. doi:10.1016/j.tourman.2012.12.014

Thaivest. (2018). *Even More Thailand 2018 Tourism Awards Have the Country Hit High Spot*. Retrieved from https://www.thaivest.com/thailand-2018-tourism-awards

Thapphila, S. (2019, March 13). เอ็นไอเอดัน‘ทราเวลเทค’ ผสานท่องเที่ยว-นวัตกรรม [NIA pushes ‘Traveltech’ to combine tourism – innovation]. Retrieved from https://www.bangkokbiznews.com/news/detail/828393

Trading Economics. (2020). *Thailand GDP*. Retrieved from https://tradingeconomics.com/thailand/gdp

Truong, V. D., & Le, A. (2017). The Evolution of Tourism Policy in Vietnam: 1960-2015. In The Routledge Handbook of Tourism in Asia (pp. 191-204). New York: Routledge.

UNWTO. (2018). *UNWTO partners with IE Business School to promote tourism innovation and entrepreneurship*. Retrieved from https://www.unwto.org/global/press-release/2018-06-29/unwto-partners-ie-business-school-promote-tourism-innovation-and-entreprene

Verreynne, M., Williams, A. M., Ritchie, B. W., Gronum, S., & Betts, K. S. (2019). Innovation diversity and uncertainty in small and medium sized tourism firms. *Tourism Management*, *72*, 257–269. doi:10.1016/j.tourman.2018.11.019

Webster, C., & Ivanov, S. (2014). Transforming competitiveness into economic benefits: Does tourism stimulate economic growth in more competitive destinations? *Tourism Management*, *40*, 137–140. doi:10.1016/j.tourman.2013.06.003

World Tourism Organisation. (2020). International Tourism, Number of arrivals. *The World Bank*. Retrieved from https://data.worldbank.org/indicator/ST.INT.ARVL?end=2018&locations=TH&start=2016

WorldAtlas. (2020). *The Economies of Southeast Asian Nations*. Retrieved from https://www.worldatlas.com/articles/the-economy-of-the-southeast-asian-nations.html

Yang, L., & Wall, G. (2008). Ethnic tourism and entrepreneurship: Xishuangbanna, Yunnan, China. *Tourism Geographies*, *10*(4), 522–544. doi:10.1080/14616680802434130

Yeung, H. W. (2002). *Entrepreneurship and the internationalisation of asian firms: An institutional perspective*. Edward Elgar Pub. doi:10.4337/9781843765516

Yusuf, L. (2014). Entrepreneurship, tourism and Malaysian economy. *Journal of Asia Entrepreneurship and Sustainability*, *10*(1), 49–67.

KEY TERMS AND DEFINITIONS

Entrepreneurship Mobility: Entrepreneurs who seek to establish their business activities in a location different from their home city.

Institutional Entrepreneurship: Most often refers to government agencies or organisations that engage in creating a business to promote a specific business initiative.

Micro Enterprise: Small business firm with fewer than 10 employers or not at all other than the owner.

Small and Medium Enterprises (SMEs): Businesses with an annual receipt of less than US$100 million or has less than 1000 employees. In some countries and in some sectors the sales turn-over and number of employees may vary.

Chapter 2
Communication and Entrepreneurship in Romania:
Dissimulation of First Impression in 30 Seconds

Victor-Alexandru Briciu
https://orcid.org/0000-0002-7506-8099
Transilvania University of Braşov, Romania

Ioana-Alexandra Mircea
Transilvania University of Braşov, Romania

Arabela Briciu
Transilvania University of Braşov, Romania

ABSTRACT

The entrepreneurs need to create a good impression in order to act in the business environment. A bad impression affects the communication and implicitly the collaboration that can turn into unintended results. Thus, they access information on how to make a good impression by using several sources: specialty literature, training guides, and courses and online shows promoted by business sites. The main objectives of this chapter are to clarify the notions and the relations between communication and entrepreneurship in the Romanian context and also to present the main results of a research that aimed to identify if the first impression of a person in the Romanian business context is dissimulated or not. The implications for entrepreneurs consist in the degree of promotion of achieving a good first impression and the manipulative or persuasive value of the negotiation techniques applied in the Romanian business environment.

DOI: 10.4018/978-1-7998-3648-3.ch002

INTRODUCTION

Discussing about the concepts of entrepreneurship and communication, different perspectives and definitions associated with these concepts of scholars emerged (Adejimola, 2008, Enuoh and Inyang, 2009, Onetti, Zucchella, Jones and McDougall-Covin, 2010, Constantin and Kavoura, 2019, Sahinidis, Stavroulakis, Kossieri and Varelas, 2019, Makarona and Kavoura, 2019, Masouras, 2019), so in this light the chapter purpose is to examine the literature review about business communication, teaching activities and entrepreneurship. To help the development of the studied field, the authors present the main results of a research that aimed to identify if the first impression of a person in business context from Romania is dissimulated or not.

The point that this chapter approaches is to identify the degree of promotion of achieving a good first impression and to identify the manipulative or persuasive value of the negotiation techniques applied in the Romanian business environment within the specialty literature related to this field; training guides or courses, aimed at educating people in this field; the theme of online shows promoted by business sites. For that, the present research selected ten bibliographic theses in Romania, in the field of business environment, which are also found in the academic year program of the specializations of this field; the first ten training guides that appear in Google's organic search for the phrase "business communication training" and five online programs in Romania promoted by business sites.

Background

At the first glance it can be said that "entrepreneurship is a process whereby firms and individuals in firms (entrepreneurs) explore and exploit opportunities" (Onetti, Zucchella, Jones and McDougall-Covin, 2010, p. 338). Talking about entrepreneurship it can be observed that nowadays innovativeness or an entrepreneurial perspective is imperative for the flexible and proactive management of business activities in a complex and dynamic globalizing world. (Onetti et al., 2010, p. 338).

Another definition says that entrepreneurship is the process through which one company explores and exploits global opportunities, leveraging both local and international relationships, regarding inward and outward business activities (Onetti et al., 2010, p. 339).

The term "entrepreneur" is French in origin and literally translates to mean "one who takes between". (Enuoh and Inyang, 2009, p. 64) or is defined in the ordinary sense as every man (or woman) of business, every entrepreneur who owns or has no capital (Constantin and Kavoura, 2019, p. 1093). The gender related problem is also discussed in literature, as Entrepreneurship has been imbued with the male stereotype, as the entrepreneur has been attributed traits pertaining to masculinity including "competitive", "resolute", "strong-willed", "courageous" (Sahinidis, Stavroulakis, Kossieri and Varelas, 2019, p. 174). At this point, it can be concluded that entrepreneur is someone who exercises initiatives by organizing a venture to take benefit of an opportunity and, as the decision maker, decides what, how, and how much of a good or service will be produced (Makarona and Kavoura, 2019, p. 16-17).

Drucker (1985 in Enuoh and Inyang, 2009, p. 64) considers that the entrepreneur always searches for change, responds to it and exploits it as an opportunity. The American Heritage Dictionary defines an entrepreneur as a person who organizes, operates and assumes the risk of business ventures.

Based on all the definitions presented so far, the term or the idea entrepreneur can be conceptualized as a change agent, "an innovator who is also a risk taker, who exploits business opportunities in his environment and utilize resources effectively to develop new technologies, produces new products and services to maximize his profits and contributing significantly to society's development" (Enuoh and Inyang, 2009, p. 64).

Enuoh and Inyang (2009) concludes that entrepreneurship is a process of organizing, managing an enterprise and assuming the risk involved in the enterprise and the entrepreneur is endowed with three qualities - power, knowledge, will - to accomplish three tasks on a daily basis - manage, predict and anticipate (Constantin and Kavoura, 2019, p. 1093). All in all, entrepreneurship is already established worldwide as a legitimate scholarly research subject, with many existing academic journals, while business schools offer courses on entrepreneurship aiming at innovation, growth, economic progress and the creation of strong bonds with the local community (Makarona and Kavoura, 2019, p. 16).

COMMUNICATION AND ENTREPRENEURSHIP

Teaching and Gaining Skills and Competencies about Entrepreneurship

Sinkovics, Bell and Deans (2004) consider that many researchers claim that the use of web-based learning tools and information and communication technology will revolutionize traditional learning methods in university contexts and fundamentally change the process of how knowledge is gathered and disseminated. Therefore, it becomes clear that in order for the second academic revolution to take shape and bear fruit, it is firstly the very academia that needs to change from the inside following a bottom-up approach (Makarona and Kavoura, 2019, p. 18) It is also stated that the students are increasingly challenged to develop international competence, become globally aware of opportunities and threats and develop strategic knowledge of the global marketplace and because of these reasons entrepreneurship is an integral part of the social and economic process, and this is why it must be incorporated into the various levels of the education system (Masouras, 2019, p. 40). In order to link essential entrepreneurship skills and web based teaching approaches they found four conceptual backgrounds and these are as it follows: the notions of competence and business competence, competence as a prerequisite for competitive advantage, competence as a synonym for 'success factor' and competence as a means of distinguishing between average and high performers.

It is also argued that may be other competencies addressing particular teaching approaches that refer to interpersonal competence as qualitative thinking, intrapersonal competence, organizational competence, awareness/ understanding of e-commerce and electronic transactions.

"Each technology can assist in particular aspects of academic program design and delivery, supporting the acquisition of specific international entrepreneurial competencies in students and play a distinctive role in improving the international competitiveness of entrepreneurial firms" (Sinkovics et al., 2004), as the search for change is an opportunity according to Drucker (2015) that brings innovation and individuals increasingly take responsibility for their own learning and careers and the organization, either the university and/ or the business should be seen as a learning organism (in Makarona and Kavoura, 2019, p. 18).

Today, the entrepreneurship is taught in Europe through four main channels: (1) as a separate subject/ course/ qualification, focused on learning the skills and know-how for setting up and running a business with a more theoretical focus; (2) as an extra-curricular subject, usually voluntary; (3) as a core subject in the curriculum, usually focused on the development of transversal competences related to entrepreneurship such as initiative, confidence and creativity; (4) a non-formal adult education course (public or private) (Martin and Iucu, 2013).

The best way to motivate students from other faculties to learn entrepreneurship is by presenting examples from the field. The emphasis should be placed on essential connections and practicalities, given the target group represented by students. Entrepreneurship education may foster business incubation and may have direct positive impact on entrepreneurial intention of students (Makarona and Kavoura, 2019, p. 16).

At the higher education level, the main purpose of entrepreneurship education should be the development of entrepreneurial skills and attitudes. In this context Martin and Iucu (2013) says that entrepreneurship education programs may have different objectives, such as: a) awareness and motivation; b) training students in terms of starting and running a business; c) developing entrepreneurial skills to identify and exploit opportunities. From this perspective, it is clear that "since skills and ideas are the new currency, academia needs to evolve from a purely epistemological enterprise to a wealth- -generator capitalizing and promoting its main asset, human creativity. Emphasis should be put upon the strengthening of students' competent skills, since they are tomorrow's entrepreneurs, so that economic viability and society return on investment may emerge" (Makarona and Kavoura, 2019, p. 18). "Students from non-business studies have often very interesting ideas. However, they are less trained in sales and marketing.

These students may need courses on intellectual property, sales, marketing and venture capital. In fact, most students from non-business faculties tend to be product-oriented in their business approach and do not understand that it does not matter how innovative the product would be if the market doesn't need it. This should help avoid the mistakes made by most young entrepreneurs who are developing products for the first time and afterwards they look at the potential on the market. The programs and courses should be aimed at acquiring the skills to make students be: more creative, highly motivated, proactive, self-aware, self-confident, open to challenges, to communicate better, to be decision makers, leaders, better negotiators, problem solvers, to work in teams, to think systematically, to be less dependent, able to live with uncertainty, able to identify opportunities" (Martin and Iucu, 2013, p. 4398).

Wei and Guo (2010) consider that teachership is the key factor. As we all known, the weak teachership is the crux of the problem. It shows two aspects for quantity and quality: from the quantity, number of teachers cannot satisfy the requirement of entrepreneurship education and from the quality, the collage lacks of "double teachers" (the specialized theory and practice experience of engineer and economical manager, etc.) and part-time teachers of quality in institutions. The next section will discuss more about the concept of communication in regards to the business environment and the dimensions of the main areas of improvement for defining the business model of entrepreneurship.

Communication and the Business Environment

Human beings naturally are compulsive communicators and also real good ones. "In our daily activities in the society, we communicate with people around us and in far places through face-to-face conversations through telephone, internet, letter and a host of others. The significance of communication is very crucial to our continued understanding, cooperation and development not only in the business circle but also in the society." (Adejimola, 2008, p. 202). It is crucial to mention that an entrepreneur cannot succeed without communicating with his or her human elements in the organization. An entrepreneur needs a communication string that links people together in his or her day-to-day business activities. Without this, he or she cannot succeed. The key point to be emphasized here is that any business organization is made up of socio-technical resources. The social elements are the human beings and interpersonal interactions while the technical elements are the infrastructures put in place to smoothen the effective running of the business. Although it is possible to repair the faults arising from the physical use of the infrastructures, it is not so with the social elements (Adejimola, 2008, p. 203).

The major purpose of communication in any business organization, therefore, are summarized as follows: a. To establish and disseminate the goal of a business enterprise; b. To develop plans for laudable achievements; c. To organize human and other resources in the most effective and efficient way; d. To select, develop and appraise members of the business enterprise; e. To lead, motivate and create a climate in which people want to contribute; f. To control performance; g. To achieve effective communication (Adejimola, 2008).

The next five dimensions were identified by Onetti et al. (2010) as main areas of improvement for defining the business model of entrepreneurship: (1) There is a need for a clear separation between the business model and the strategy concepts. (2) A separation between the business model concept and the financial implications is also required. (3) Business model definitions have to include location decisions that are more and more relevant in the extant competitive scenario. (4) Business model definitions have to integrate and synthesize the earlier work in this area that seems to identify, as building blocks, activities (value chain) and network. (5) Business model conceptualizations must be reasonably simple and generalizable so that they can be applicable to firms of all sorts and sizes (managerial implication).

Business Communication

Adejimola (2008) considers that: "There are ways entrepreneurs can achieve effective communication within and outside their enterprises. These include examining the purpose of communication, clarifying ideas before attempting to communicate, considering the content and overtones of their communication or messages, using simple words and sentences, expressing thoughts logically and in a straight forward way, using short sentences and paragraphs, avoiding unnecessary words, avoiding ambiguous words, phrases and sentences, following up messages with actions and approximating actions with the goals of the organization, understanding the physical and human environment when communicating and above all, developing listening skills, and acquiring knowledge/skills of information and communication technologies."

Considering all the above described characteristics, there are some important components or elements of communication and each of them has their own role. First of all, the stimulus is considered very important, than the source, the receiver, the message, the medium, the channel, the feedback and the noise. The purpose of communication within such groups is to achieve common goals, either of a professional nature or as a result of responding to a social need (Lesenciuc, 2017, p.18).

In business communication many scholars argue that the types of communication are very important, whether we discuss about verbal communication, appearance, posture, gestures, eye contact, speech production, nonverbal communication, writing and information flow. Adejimola (2008) considers that exchanging and sharing of information during business meetings, telephone conversations and interactions on the internet are very crucial in the survival and growth of any business venture. The business partners should have access to correct information and give the same to the public or financial houses. Such information may include the location of a business organization, products, production capacity, prices, interest rates, financial reports, branches, telephone, cable, e-mail address, telegraph, fax etc.

According to Mayo-BPP (1997 in Adejimola, 2008, p. 206), information in business can be analyzed into three levels: (1) Strategic information: this is used to plan the objectives or the goals of the business organization and to assess whether the goals are being met. Such information comprises overall profitability, future market prospect, the availability and cost of funds, local cash needs etc.; (2) Tactical information: this bothers on how to use resources of the business and how to monitor their quality and quantity being produced. Such information comprises productivity measurement, variance analysis report, cash flow forecast, etc.; (3) Operational information: this is concerned with the planning of specific tasks and how they are executed within the business premises or offices. Operational information includes the hours each employee puts in, amount of raw materials being put to the production process etc.

After all, "the importance of language, communication and information flow are no longer doubtful. This declaration, however, needs to be understood better when we consider them as necessary tools that drive or propel business activities within and around any organization or entrepreneurial venture. Business all over the world, therefore, cashes in on the advantage and manipulates language as a tool of communication to achieve organizational goals." (Adejimola, 2008, p. 207)

Online Entrepreneurship, Online Business Communication and Social Media

New phenomena come and go on a frequent basis. But every now and then something with potential to change the business environment comes to the forefront. The business world is not immune to any impact that may arise and the organizations have adopted the internet in an attempt to enjoy economic benefits on the market (Briciu, Briciu and Găitan, 2020, p. 418). Social media is one such phenomenon. Social media which is sometimes referred to as social networking and Web 2.0 refers to collaboratively produced and shared media content and to network communities, representing "the next step of Web 2.0 technology development" (Briciu, Briciu and Găitan, 2019, p. 43), becoming the shift "from a passive and consumer-oriented Internet experience to a decentralized and interactive hype of networking with a more active experience based on cooperation and user-generated content" (Briciu and Briciu, 2020, p. 426). The users of social media have the ability of sharing their views and encounters. This assists in creativity, open communication and sharing of knowledge among users. Facebook, Skype and discussion forums are examples of social media tools (Tapscott and Williams, 2008 in Jagongo and Kinyua, 2013).

Putting the evolution of the behavior of the entrepreneur in the perspective of societal changes, the new challenges facing the entrepreneur today are associated with the new skills, new market opportunities, issues of growth, to better support entrepreneurship and business creation in the twenty-first century in order to adapt to a world in permanent change (Constantin and Kavoura, 2019, p. 1094).

Social networking allows businesses to gain access to resources that might otherwise not be available to them. It can also aid the development of a firm's worthiness, increase the customer and supplier contacts, bring to light where resources and funding are available, promote innovation and help in the cultivation of strategic partnerships (Zontanos and Anderson, 2004 in Jagongo and Kinyua, 2013).

The sky is the limit with social media. Owing to of the flexibility of social networking tools, businesses can realize different benefits. „Many businesses are now turning to social networks as a worthwhile communication tool and, if used adequately, they can significantly improve their online presence, in the form of effective promotion. To achieve success with the online marketing, the marketers need to have a presence in the environment that their customers inhabit. Mark Zukerberg, co-founder of Facebook supports this by saying that advertising is fast changing and businesses need to understand the usage of Internet technologies in order to remain relevant (Maymann, 2008 in Jagongo and Kinyua, 2013, p. 214).

Social marketing (Papademetriou, Masouras & Ioannou, 2020) has taken the idea of price beyond monetary to include psychological, social, geographic and other rewards and punishments for everyday behaviors for the web consumer or the digital users (Masouras & Papademetriou, 2018).

Social networking has led to the introduction of social media marketing and presented new ways of communicating to expanse audiences on various Internet platforms. Marketers can no longer rely on mass media channels alone to communicate with their consumers. They must adopt new strategies if they wish to succeed (Kotler and Armstrong, 2011 in Jagongo and Kinyua, 2013).

To reflect the idea in the next section of the chapter, it is important to mention that constructing and maintaining positive self-images is important to achieving all the above discussed ideas about the on-line self-presentation methods that are becoming more and more difficult to manage nowadays because communication technology limits user control over the information they use to strategically present themselves, and consequently because research shows that unsuccessful self-presentation is often associated with rejection and criticism (Briciu, Briciu & Găitan, 2019, p. 584).

DISSIMULATION OF FIRST IMPRESSION

Research Focus

Modern corporations, businesses and entrepreneurs invest time and resources trying to build a favorable image among customers, using a vast array of communication channels. It is in the interest of companies to manage the impressions and perceptions of individuals in order to create or maintain a strong corporate identity (Briciu et al, 2020). The main purpose of this research is to identify if the first impression of a person in business context from Romania is dissimulated or not. The image of a negotiator, a product or service influences its success in the business environment (Nistor, 2010, p. 20). The "negotiation game" can be won or lost. Everything is depending on the created image. The higher is the stake, the greater is the need and desire to win (Popescu, 2003, p.61). This research begins from the impression management theory developed by Brissett and Edgley in 1990 (in Chiru, 2003, p. 102). Impression management theory is part of the dramaturgical sociology and in the same time it is integrated in the dramatic approach of communication. Impression management is the activity that involves controlling information about a person, object, idea, entity, or event, that is, the art of controlling the impressions of those around us in our favor. As a result, both businesses and individuals try to con-vey messages that will benefit them and contribute to the formation of preferential impressions (Briciu et al., 2020).

This theory embraces the human as a social actor and his life is the scene in which he interprets his chosen roles that depending on the context in which he is. Roles are not largely played out for themselves but to "convince others of the truthfulness of the reality it composes; the actor is condemned to be an interpreter and to invite others, through the „artistry" of his game, to a reality as a sum of these interpretations" (Chiru, 2003, p. 102). The theory starts from the premise that the person is interdependent in his actions manifested against innate strategies, based on a system of action codes, called axioms which develops through practice. Brissett and Edgley (1990) argue that individuals are persuasive and influential in how they create and adapt their behavior toward other persons (in Chiru, 2003).

So, when a person wants to make a certain impression about himself for other people, he plays a role. This assumed role includes all the characteristics of a certain type of behavior that adapts to the respective context. Adopting a role requires study and exercise; otherwise a role is like a mask covering some defining features. That is why it is required that the interpreted role be as close as possible to the real features of the person, in order not to have too high discrepancy. So, any role is actually a dissimulation, this being the mask or camouflage of a particular thing. Dissimulation of an impression can be achieved by assuming roles, manipulation and persuasion. Based on this theory, in order to fulfil the purpose of our research, the objectives are: to identify the degree of promotion of achieving a good first impression and to identify the manipulative or persuasive value of the negotiation techniques applied in the business environment within (i) the Romanian literature sources related to this field; (ii) training guides from Romania, aimed at educating people in this field; (iii) the theme of online shows promoted by business sites in Romania.

Methodology

In order to conduct the research according to the objectives stated above, the researchers have chosen as a research method the content analysis, as the methodology procedure was conducted in May 2018. “Content analysis is a quantitative-qualitative way of studying communication, but not only its manifest content, but also latent content. It is precisely the latent content, which is not immediately noticeable, what is “hidden” is the object of interest of the content analysis technique” (Chelcea, 2001, p. 217). As an analysis procedure to identify the degree of promotion of a good impression, the manipulative or persuasive value of the negotiation techniques applied in the business environment and their impact on the target audience, we will use the frequency analysis, thus determining the frequency of the recording units’ occurrences (Chelcea, 2001).

In order to achieve a most accurate result, the co-product of the present research is limited to ten bibliographic theses in Romania, in the field of business environment, which are also found in the academic year program of the specializations of this field; the first ten training guides that appear in Google’s organic search for the phrase “business communication training” and five online programs in Romania promoted by business sites. Although content analysis in general, and its application to media sources, in particular, has a rich theoretical and methodological content, Web based analysis is a recent framework of research (Briciu, Briciu & Nechita, 2018) and it’s applicability in the online environment is supported by the explanation that content analysis would be “an observational research method used to systematically evaluate the symbolic content of all recorded forms of communication” (Kolbe and Burnett 1991 in Briciu, Briciu & Nechita, 2018, p. 83).

The method of content analysis implies determining the registration units, content units and numbering units as well as establishing the analysis scheme’s categories. The registration unit represents the part of communication which will be characterized and introduced into one of the analysis scheme’s category. The smallest units of registration are the words and symbols (Chelcea, 2001).

In the following research procedure, it was commonly agreed the ideas regarding the determining role of content analysis, as a method for examining the manifest content of messages, while also being an ideal tool for examining online materials. In addition, it must be accepted that content analysis is traditionally considered a quantitative method, but which also requires a qualitative evaluation. In the light of these last clarifications, the analysis will consider the content analysis as a research method, being at the border between the two research models, as a quantitative-qualitative variant of analyzing the content of communication, the frequency analysis the research technique and the grid of categories – the research instrument for coding and quantitative processing the collected data (see the Research grids).

The sampling technique chosen for this study is the non-probability sampling. According to Earl Babbie, this technique implies choosing the sampling units based on the researcher's opinion. These units are the one considered by the researcher the most useful and representative for the study (Babbie, 2010, p.261).

Analysis of the Content of Ten Bibliographic Theses in Romania Aimed at Education in the Field of Business Communication

The researchers choose to analyze the content of ten bibliographic theses from Romania that aim to educate in the field of business communication because they are teaching materials, they form reasoning, attitudes and behaviors. This methodological process is possible as "researchers generally need to develop their own coding scheme for analyzing content, although sometimes researchers can adopt existing coding schemes established by their peers. Human intuition can intervene in the process of developing coding schemes. Although all research is subject to some human intuition, the process of content analysis allows relatively more room for the researcher's intuition than do some methods such as surveys or experimental designs" (Hwang et al., 2013 in Briciu et al, 2018, p. 84).

In this case, the chosen literature sources form the reasoning, attitude and behavior of its target audience in terms of communication in the business environment. The target audience of these open access bibliographic theses is made up of students from this field, professors who study the field of business communication, negotiators and people who work in the business field. The reason for this choice to analyze their content is that it represents the systematization of the first impact of a book, more exactly, the title. The table of contents is an important decision-making factor in choosing a book. Depending on this, it can be observed what kind of topics are treated and in which manner. It was also analyzed how the topic found in the table of contents was approached and corresponding to it.

Thus, it was identified the fact that within the ten bibliographic theses that represent teaching materials in order to educate the target audience in the business environment and in the communication within it, the total percentage of promoting dissimulated, persuasive and manipulative behavior and achievement a favorable impression is 53.3%. In order to see if the authors are promoting or challenging these techniques and attitudes, it was measured the positive attitude they express in relation to these topics. The researchers identified that the promotion of a favorable impression is 80%. From the percentage of 60% of the mention of the word "simulation/ dissimulation" the positive attitude of the authors is only 30%. From the 30% percentage of the word "manipulation" presented in the table, it is confirmed that the percentage of the authors' positive attitude towards it in the text is 60%. Regarding the word "persuasion", the percentage of its presentation in the bibliographic sources is 20% and the attitude of the authors in publications regarding to it is 90% positive.

Thus, it can be observed that although the percentage of promoting the word "simulation/ dissimulation" is 30%, the persuasion and manipulation, the first impression's dissimulation processes are promoted by more than 50%, which denotes education for a favorable image (in 80%). At the same time, it can be seen that the degree of accessibility of these publications, through their price, the highest price being 40 RON (equivalent to 9.5 USD) and the smallest one under 15 RON (equivalent to 3.5 USD), some being free in electronic format. The degree of accessibility is not high, so that a middle-class person can afford to buy a book in this area. The oldest publication analyzed was from 1996, and the most recent from 2011. Thus, it can be concluded that this subject has been dealt with in Romania for at least 22 years. The audience's attitude towards publications is positive because the stock of some of them was exhausted and one of the publications obtained 19,000 views on www.scribd.com, an impressive number for a specialty book.

Table 1. Interpretation of bibliographic sources research data

Research grid	Recording units
-the degree of promotion of achieving a favorable first impression;	-the phrase "first impression" is/is not specified; -the phrase "impression/image good/favorable" is/is not specified; -the word "simulation/dissimulation" is/is not specified; -number of occurrences of the phrase "first impression" in the publication; -number of occurrences of the phrase "impression/image; good/ favorable" in the publication; -the number of occurrences of the word "dissimulation" in the publication; -positive/neutral/negative author's attitude towards simulation/ dissimulation.
-the degree of promotion of the manipulative and persuasive attitudes of the negotiation techniques by the authors;	-the word "manipulation" in the table of contents is/is not specified; -the word "persuasion/conviction" in the table of contents is/is not specified - is/is not specified in the word "success/success/ gain" in the table of contents -the number of occurrences of the word "manipulation" in the table of contents; -the number of occurrences of the word "persuasion/belief" in the table of contents -the number of occurrences of the word "success/gain" in the table of contents -the number of occurrences of the word "manipulation" in the publication; -the number of occurrences of the word "persuasion/belief" in the publication; -the number of occurrences of the word "success/gain" in the publication; -the author's attitude positive/neutral/negative towards manipulation; -the attitude of the author positive/neutral/ negative towards persuasion; -the attitude of the author positive/neutral/ negative towards success.
-from which period the manipulative and persuasive attitudes of the negotiation techniques are promoted;	-year of publication -how many years have been since the publication until now.
-the degree of accessibility of the publication	- the price of the publication
-the attitude of the target audience towards the publication	- number of views on www.scribd.com, www.slideshare.com, www. adevărdivin.com; - number of online purchases; - notes / reviews.

Analysis of Training Guides in Romania Aimed at Education in the Field of Business Communication

In this analysis, the body of our research consists of the first ten training programs that appear in Google's organic search using the keywords combination: "training in business communication".

Table 2. Interpretation of data regarding research of training programs

Research grid	Recording units
-the actuality of the trainings.	- the deadline for registration.
-the degree of promotion of achieving a good first impression.	-the percentage of the study of types of human communication language within the training program; -the roles in communication/interaction are/are not studied; -percent of the study of roles in communication/interaction within the training program.
- the degree of promotion of manipulative and persuasive attitudes of negotiation techniques by trainers.	-the manipulation is/is not studied; -the percentage of the study of the manipulation within the training program; -persuasion is/is not studied; -the percentage of the persuasion study within the training program.
- the degree of accessibility.	-the price of the training.
- the attitude of the target audience towards the manipulative and persuasive negotiation techniques.	-side/ note.

According to the theory of impression management, used as the foundation of our research, the interpretation of some roles implies the concealment of the actual behavior of a person. In this content analysis it was identified the percentage of promoting the interpretation of roles in the business environment and promoting the study of the types of language of hidden behavior, manipulation, persuasion present in the programs of the first ten trainings that appeared in Google's organic search for the phrase "training in business communication". The study of the types of language of human communication facilitates the awareness of one's own behavior, so that it can lead to the control and subsequently to its modification depending on the context, which denotes dissimulation. The total percentage of studying the types of language, roles in communication/interaction, manipulation and persuasion is 67.5%. It was identified that the total percentage of the study of the types of language of human communication within the training programs is 33.83%, the total percentage of the study of manipulation is 25% and that of the persuasion 26%. Also, because the trainings educate specialists already in the field, the price of a session can reach up to 3,000 RON (equivalent to 715 USD), and for people who are still in the first stages in this field it can be observed that the minimum price can reach up to 300 RON (equivalent to 71.4 USD). The audience's attitude towards trainings is a positive one because most of them were sold out. The major disadvantage that these trainings have at first impact is that most of them are not updated. They appear in the first 10 trainings in organic search on Google, but some of them were organized in 2015. Since then are no longer valid, the audience invests more time in searching for current trainings.

Analysis of Online Broadcasts in Romania Aimed at Education in the Field of Business Communication

In this analysis, the body of the research consisted of the programs dedicated exclusively to business communication, which have the most ratings on YouTube.

Table 3. Ranking of business shows

Shows	YouTube Subscribers	Video	TV Channel	Year of appearance
1. *Business la superlative* (in Romanian)	7,161	33	a7tv.ro https://www.youtube.com/channel/UCvXWhITuhnvUyHu4idMrgkA	2017
2. *Business Days*	4,880	1,482	Independent https://www.youtube.com/user/businessdaysro/featured	2011
3. *Etichetă și comunicare în afaceri* (in Romanian)	4,805	54	Canal 33 https://www.youtube.com/channel/UChXVCKn5sa-e-bNXjX47lJw	2015
4. *Bizilive*	485	198	Independent https://www.youtube.com/channel/UCl_5yjNcsPhxDa8H9XbDx3Q	2014
5. *Legile afacerilor* (in Romanian)	71	18	TVR2 https://www.youtube.com/channel/UC_IAoMeqR3pBTdeTGgu0abQ	2016

Following this ranking of online shows, the researchers selected to analyze the issue of *Etichetă și comunicare în afaceri* (*en.*, Label and communication in business), because it is the show dedicated especially to business communication.

Table 4. Research grid for the episodes of the show Label and communication in business

Research grid	Recording units
-frequency of episodes.	-frequency of episodes
-the degree of promotion of achieving a good first impression.	-the percentage of promoting the approach of some roles within the show -the percentage of promoting the first impression within the show.
-the degree of promotion of manipulative and persuasive attitudes of negotiation techniques by authors/trainers/presenters and guests.	-the percentage of promotion of manipulation within the program; -the percentage of promoting persuasion within the program.
-the attitude of the target audience towards the materials that promoted the first impression, the roles, the manipulation, the persuasion.	-total views of materials that promoted the first impression, roles, manipulation, persuasion.

Since one of the functions of the media is to educate the audience, we considered it necessary to analyze such a source. First of all, the media can be accessible to all categories of audience, both from the financial point of view and from the point of view of how the information is transmitted, being structured within the questions: who, what, where, when, how and by what, so that the subject is presented more accurately than in the case of a bibliographic source. The issue of Label and communication in business records in the editions that promote the first impression, the creation of a favorable image, the concealment, manipulation and persuasion, a total of 2,433 views on YouTube. The total percentage of promoting the first impression, roles, manipulation, and persuasion is 83% of all editions of this show. Thus, it can be observed that the percentage of promotion of these subjects is more than 50%, approaching very close to 100%. An edition is made once a week, so that the rate of transmission of information is quite frequent and at the same time this periodicity favors the time needed to prepare the edition. The percentage of promoting the approach of some roles within the show is 20% that of promoting the first impression is 40.7%, the percentage of promoting manipulation is 12.9% and the promotion of persuasion is 10%. We can see that although individually they are below 50%, if we realize their sum, because all have the purpose of concealing the first impression, the percentage exceeds 50%.

SOLUTIONS AND RECOMMENDATIONS

As a result of this research, we identified that the promotion of dissimulation of the first impression in the Romanian business environment is 67.9%.

Thus we can say that in Romania the first impression created in the business environment is hidden above the 50% average. The promotion of dissimulation of the first impression in the business environment is 53.3% within the bibliographic theses in Romania represented in the business field. The first ten training programs that appear in Google's organic search under the phrase "business communication training" promote dissimulation within the first impression by 67.5%. Regarding the online broadcast dedicated to communication in the business environment, the percentage of dissimulation within the first impression is 83%, the highest percentage of the three analyzed environments.

Table 5. Final data of the three researches

The research corpus	The total percentage regarding promoting disguised behavior, manipulation, persuasion
1. ten bibliographic theses from Romania, in the field of business environment, which are also found in the academic year program of the specializations of this field;	53.3%
2. the first ten training programs that appear in Google's organic search for the phrase "business communication training"	67.5%
3. the online show dedicated to business communication	83%
Total percentage of promoting disguised behavior: 67.9%	

The three mediums of education in business communication involve different degrees of accessibility for the target audience. The most accessible medium is the online issue, followed by the bibliographic theses that do not exceed the amount of 40 RON (equivalent to 9.5 USD)/ publication. The most expensive medium of education is the training, which can reach up to 3,000 RON (equivalent to 715 USD), but its advantage is that it is an approved person who can observe the mistakes that each student makes individually and can correct them. So it is up to the audience to choose the education environment according to their needs. The audience's attitude towards these media is a positive one, because the researchers were able to identify the fact that the online stock of some publications was sold out, the places of certain trainings were sold out, and regarding the online broadcast, the number of views on YouTube of the materials they promote the first impression and its concealment is 2,433. The attitude of the authors of the publications, the trainers, the presenter/guest regarding the concealment of the first impression and the techniques for its creation, is on average positive. In this situation, the target audience assimilates the information, interprets them, and creates reasons and then behaviors based on the positive attitude of the issuers of the educational materials for the purpose of the behavior in the business environment in Romania.

FUTURE RESEARCH DIRECTIONS

The business environment in Romania is developing more and more. Business is thriving, and investors from other countries are starting to see more and more opportunities in Romania. Considering that until 1989, respectively the year of ending of the communist regime in Romania, we could not talk about the business environment and the notion of entrepreneurship, it can be stated that the country is beginning to make its first steps in this field. Individuals and organizations interested in this field have approached publications from other countries in order to understand it and to learn how to "survive" within it. Because the interest in winning is very high, a number of techniques have been developed in order to be successful: manipulation, Neurolinguistics' programming and dissimulation.

CONCLUSION

Communication is the key to any field in which interaction is the fundamental element. In the business environment communication can tilt the balance towards a common yes or no or a win-lose situation. Also, through this research the authors wanted to illustrate the importance of communication in the field of business. Through communication the actors involved convey the intentions, the benefits of collaboration and the desire to maintain a relationship or not. The business environment juggles with all types of language. If one of them is dysfunctional, communication itself may become dysfunctional. In conclusion, an entrepreneur must be a catalyst, who loves his mission as an entrepreneur and works tirelessly; capable of accepting and managing uncertainty, risks and opportunities; the entrepreneur must be the demanding client of his own project and always be surrounded by people whose experience and knowledge he must value. We are talking about "entrepreneurial stance" and even about "entrepreneurial ecosystem" (Constantin and Kavoura, 2019, p. 1094).

REFERENCES

Adejimola, A. S. (2008). Language, communication and information flow in entrepreneurship. *African Journal of Business Management*, *2*, 201–208.

Babbie, E. (2010). *The Basis of Social Research*. Wadsworth Cengage Learning Publisher.

Briciu, A., & Briciu, V.-A. (2020). Participatory Culture and Tourist Experience: Promoting Destinations Through YouTube. In A. Kavoura, E. Kefallonitis, & P. Theodoridis (Eds.), *Strategic Innovative Marketing and Tourism. Springer Proceedings in Business and Economics* (pp. 425–433). Springer. doi:10.1007/978-3-030-36126-6_47

Briciu, V.-A., Briciu, A., & Găitan, Ş.-M. (2019). New Media and Organizational Communication. A Multiple Analysis of Romanian Bank Online Environment. In *6th International Multidisciplinary Scientific Conference on Social Sciences and Arts SGEM 2019, Conference Proceedings* (pp. 41-52). Sofia: STEF92 Technology Ltd. 10.5593gemsocial2019V/6.1/S07.006

Briciu, V.-A., Briciu, A., & Găitan, Ş.-M. (2019). The Image Management Strategy through Social Networks. An Analysis of the Banking Environment in Romania. In V. Bevanda (Ed.), *International Scientific Conference EMAN – Economics & Management: How to Cope with Disrupted Times - Conference Proceedings* (pp. 583-588). Belgrade: All in One Print Center Publisher. 10.31410/EMAN.2019.583

Briciu, V.-A., Briciu, A., & Găitan, Ş.-M. (2020). Impression Management Through Websites: An Analysis of the Romanian Banking Industry. In A. Kavoura, E. Kefallonitis, & P. Theodoridis (Eds.), *Strategic Innovative Marketing and Tourism. Springer Proceedings in Business and Economics* (pp. 417–424). Springer. doi:10.1007/978-3-030-36126-6_46

Briciu, V.-A, Briciu, A., & Nechita, F. (2018). Content Analysis Made Simple for Students. An Interactive Online Application Solution. *Cognitive Science – New Media – Education, 5*(2), 77-91.

Chelcea, S. (2001). Tehnici de cercetare sociologică. Academic Press.

Chiru, I. (2003). *Comunicarea interpersonală*. Tritonic Publishing House.

Constantin, F., & Kavoura, A. (2019). Entrepreneur Without Intention with Websites as a Communication Tool: Current Trends in Romania. In A. Kavoura, E. Kefallonitis, & A. Geovanis (Eds.), *Strategic Innovative Marketing and Tourism. Springer Proceedings in Business and Economics* (pp. 1093–1102). Springer. doi:10.1007/978-3-030-12453-3_126

Enuoh, R. O., & Inyang, B. J. (2009). Entrepreneurial Competencies: The Missing Links to Successful Entrepreneurship in Nigeria. *International Business Research*, *2*(2), 62–71.

Jagongo, A., & Kinyua, C. (2013). The Social Media and Entrepreneurship Growth (A New Business Communication Paradigm among SMEs in Nairobi). *International Journal of Humanities and Social Science*, *3*(10), 213–227.

Lesenciuc, A. (2017). Teorii ale comunicării. Braşov: Academia Forţelor Aeriene „Henri Coandă" Publishing House.

Makarona, E., & Kavoura, A. (2019). Redesigning the Ivory Tower: Academic entrepreneurship as a new calling supporting economic growth. *Tarnów Research Papers Collection*, *42*(2), 15–26.

Martin, C., & Iucu, R. (2013). Teaching entrepreneurship to educational sciences students. *Procedia: Social and Behavioral Sciences*, *116*, 4397–4400. doi:10.1016/j.sbspro.2014.01.954

Masouras, A. (2019). Young entrepreneurship in Cyprus: An institutional analysis. *Tarnów Research Papers Collection*, *42*(2), 27–42.

Masouras, A., & Papademetriou, C. (2018). Digital Consumer Behaviour in Cyprus: From Uses and Gratifications Theory to 4C's Online Shopping Approach. *Journal of Advertising and Public Relations*, *1*(1), 1–11.

Nistor, C. (2010). *Comunicare şi negociere în afaceri*. Europlus Publishing House.

Onetti, A., Zucchella, A., Jones, M. V., & McDougall-Covin, P. P. (2010). Internationalization, innovation and entrepreneurship: Business models for new technology-based firms. *The Journal of Management and Governance*, *16*(3), 337–368. doi:10.100710997-010-9154-1

Papademetriou, C., Masouras, A., & Ioannou, A. (2020) Social Networking Sites: The New Era of Effective Online Marketing and Advertising. In A. Kavoura, E. Kefallonitis & P. Theodoridis (Eds.), Strategic Innovative Marketing and Tourism. Springer Proceedings in Business and Economics (pp. 443-448). Cham: Springer.

Popescu, D. (2003). Comunicarea managerială, strategii şi tehnici de negociere. Academic Press.

Sahinidis, A., Stavroulakis, D., Kossieri, E., & Varelas, S. (2019). Entrepreneurial Intention Determinants Among Female Students. The Influence of Role Models, Parents' Occupation and Perceived Behavioral Control on Forming the Desire to Become a Business Owner. In A. Kavoura, E. Kefallonitis, & A. Geovanis (Eds.), *Strategic Innovative Marketing and Tourism. Springer Proceedings in Business and Economics* (pp. 173–178). Springer. doi:10.1007/978-3-030-12453-3_20

Sinkovics, R. R., Bell, J., & Deans, K. R. (2004). Using Information Communication Technology to Develop International Entrepreneurship Competencies. *Journal of International Entrepreneurship*, *2*(1/2), 125–137. doi:10.1023/B:JIEN.0000026909.49686.a5

Wei, Y., & Guo, W. (2010). Construction of the Entrepreneurship Education Teachers Based on the Characteristics of Business Education Level. *International Education Studies*, *3*(2), 91–96. doi:10.5539/ies.v3n2p91

ADDITIONAL READING

Bolino, M. K., Kacmar, K. M., Turnley, W. H., & Gilstrap, J. B. (2008). A Multi-Level Review of Impression Management Motives and Behaviors. *Journal of Management*, *34*(6), 1080–1109. doi:10.1177/0149206308324325

Funk, T. (2011). *Social Media Playbook for Business. Reaching Your Online Community with Twitter, Facebook, LinkedIn, and More*. Praeger.

Goffman, E. (1959). *The presentation of self in everyday life*. Doubleday Anchor.

Guadagno, R. E., & Cialdini, R. B. (2007). Gender Differences in Impression Management in Organizations: A Qualitative Review. *Sex Roles*, *56*(7), 483–494. doi:10.100711199-007-9187-3

Lincoln, S. R. (2009). *Mastering Web 2.0: transform your business using key website and social media tools*. Kogan Page Limited.

Masouras, A. (2019). *Entrepreneurship in Small and Medium-Sized Enterprises*. Nova Science Publishers.

Oosterbeek, H., van Praag, M., & Ijsselstein, A. (2008) The Impact of Entrepreneurship Education on Entrepreneurship Competencies and Intentions: An Evaluation of the Junior Achievement Student Mini-Company Program. *IZA Discussion Paper 3641*, 1-24.

Schlenker, B. R. (1980). *Impression management: The self-concept, social identity, and interpersonal relations*. Brooks/Cole.

Smallbone, D., Leitão, J., Raposo, M., & Welter, F. (Eds.). (2010). *The Theory and Practice of Entrepreneurship Frontiers in European Entrepreneurship Research*. Edward Elgar Publishing, Inc. doi:10.4337/9781849805933

Turner, J., & Shah, R. (2011). *How to make money with social media: an insider's guide on using new and emerging media to grow your business*. Pearson Education, Inc., FT Press.

White, K., & Chapman, E. (1996). *Organizational Communication. An Introduction to Communication and Human Relations Strategies* (1st ed.). Simon & Schuster Custom Publishing.

KEY TERMS AND DEFINITIONS

Business Communication: A form of human communication, a special technique aimed at reaching directly and individually the goals proposed by the seller, determining the potential customer to act and/ or react immediately.

Entrepreneur: Someone who exercises initiatives by organizing a (business) venture to take benefit of an opportunity.

Entrepreneurship: A process whereby organizations and individuals in those organizations explore and exploit opportunities by using proactive management of business activities.

First Impression: Is achieved by framing people, things, events, with which they interact in contrasting categories such as good/bad, beautiful/ugly, etc.

Impression: The effect left in the human consciousness of things or happenings around him with which he comes in contact.

Online Business Communication: A web-based online communication targeted to specific publics used in the organizational and business context.

Organizational Communication: Various communication channels, strategies and techniques through which the corporation interacts with customers and other audiences.

Social Media: A range of different Web 2.0 internet-based tools that increase and enhance the exchange of information.

Chapter 3
Key Challenges for Greek IT Start Ups:
An Analysis of Founder Perceptions

Theocharis Stylianos Spyropoulos
Department of International Business, Perrotis College, Greece

ABSTRACT

The study examines the IT Greek start-up ecosystem, analyzing the founders' views, strategy, and current perception regarding their ICT start-ups. The study examines the views and perceptions of 143 founders of Greek IT start ups who participated in exhibitions as start-up companies between September 2018 and May 2019, and had completed at least one accelerator program.

INTRODUCTION

The study examines the IT Greek start-up ecosystem, analyzing the founders' views, strategy, and current perception regarding their ICT start-ups. The study examines the views and perceptions of 143 founders of Greek IT start ups who participated in exhibitions as start-up companies between September 2018 and May 2019, and had completed at least one accelerator program.

The study highlights the fact that Greek IT Start-Up founders face three main challenges: getting new customer, securing financing and improving their product. The study also examines whether the impact of these challenges can be reduced through actions and planning during the pre-launch phase of the start-up. The study examines the relationships between variables which, are related to these challenges, within the Greek macroeconomic environment, according the start-up founders' perceptions and self evaluations.

The research findings provide a deeper understanding of the dynamics of Greek ICT start-ups, in terms of perceived challenges faced. The findings are useful to entrepreneurs as they strive to increase the success rates of current and future projects as well as to the wider innovation ecosystem, e.g. business angels, venture capital firms, the state etc., to further improve their success rates or design and implement policies for innovation promotion. Finally, key areas for further research are highlighted.

DOI: 10.4018/978-1-7998-3648-3.ch003

BACKGROUND

Recent academic study (Roy, 2019) highlights the economy's and organization's investments on innovation; for start-up companies, commitment to innovation is their very own for existence – and the way they will manage to overcome the challenges they meet will determine their very own survival.

The study examines the Greek start-up ecosystem, with a special focus on companies engaged in information technology solutions (IT sector). The objective is to identify the key challenges and priorities that Greek Start-Up founders are facing, based on their own perceptions. The study examines the IT Greek Start-Ups participating in exhibitions in Greece, in the cities of Athens and Thessaloniki, for the time period between September 2018 and May 2019.

Founders of the start-ups were all participants at least in one start-up boot camp or start-up accelerator program, operating in Greece. To this respect, the founders have received at least basic business and entrepreneurial training regarding the various aspects of establishing and managing a start-up company, such as company formation, product design, market selection, human resources, negotiations, and pitching to potential investors, and therefore can be considered to be trained to a satisfactory degree on the business and managerial aspects of running a start-up company.

Furthermore, the Greek macroeconomic and business environment in which Greek IT start-uppers are trying to develop their business activities and overcome their challenges has to be taken into account. The austerity measures, since 2009 resulted to an economy characterized with high unemployment levels and increased poverty, over taxation and dramatic cuts of income level for the majority of population, as well as corporate investment budgets for IT solutions.

The purpose of this study is to highlight the challenges the Greek IT start-ups are facing, as the actual founders of the start-ups perceive them. Furthermore the study examines the impact of these challenges to the start-ups and finally, provides a better understanding for the start-up ecosystem in Greece.

LITERATURE REVIEW

Previous academic studies identified critical success factors for success of start-up companies.

Aulet (2013), highlights the importance of entrepreneurial education and provides an integrated framework for start-up success factors.

Aulet (2013) highlights the importance of segmentation; apart from the traditional segmentation criteria, such as demographics, cultural, behavioral and transactional, Aulet suggests that once the company identify a potential target market, several key issues are recommended to be evaluated, such as budget availability on behalf of the customers, whether the customer is accessible to the start-up's sales force, whether the value proposition is strong enough to ensure that the customer will actually select the start-up's product to cover the specific need. Gender issues appear to have a significant impact on entrepreneurial behavior; Mustapha et al (2015) summarize previous literature, regarding the importance of the family environment for female entrepreneurs. In addition, Kavoura et al (2016), highlights cultural and gender issues in entrepreneurship.

Further studies (Amit et al, 2012, Aulet 2013) highlight the benefits of business model innovation; in addition Juntunen et al, (2018) highlight the role of business model innovation with a special focus on IT solutions, in addition the same study links business model and business opportunity: "the scalability of the business model fundamentally stems from the synchronization of a business model to the respective business opportunity."(Juntunen 2018 p. 33) and examines flexibility in terms of product features (platform), marketing and financial resources. "A dynamic business model framework allows for entrepreneurs to analyse the main changes in the context of the entrepreneurial endeavor that are required to envision potential logic sequences of or changes in business models over time." (Khodaei & Ortt, 2019, p.10). "The business model should be aligned with strategy, taking into account changes in the external environment and with business processes to ensure continued successful management of people". (Stott et al, 2016, p. 951)

"Entrepreneurial opportunities come in many ways, shapes and forms to those who pursue them." (Muzyca, 1997, p.30). The same study suggests that opportunities are closely related to past knowledge and experience. Previous studies (Konig, 1997) also provide useful highlights for securing financing; such as founder's education, achievements, business plan and successful case studies.

Previous studies also highlight the importance of estimating the sales cycle of the start-up's product, building credibility (Johnson, 1997) and evaluating the costs and time related to the sale process (Aulet, 2013). Additional research (Shankar et al, 1999) examines the options for pioneers and late entrants.

Academic research offered managers a conclusive advice for success: "Innovate incrementally on proven technology through a continued R&D process". This way the firm develops modifications for the basic product and process ''without undertaking major basic research in areas unrelated to the original successful innovation'' (Grosse & Kujava 1999, p. 509). This strategy is served well by offering an improved product to an existing market a market that can easily been identified and analyzed, during the planning phase of the start-up. However this is not always an option for start-ups – in fact, this is exactly what they may need to avoid. Following such a strategy the start-up will just find itself competing with existing companies, which probable have far superior resources, market knowledge and business networks.

Considering the above, the academic literature provides a wide set of frameworks and highlights for start-up founders to examine during the planning phase.

"By a pro-active customer approach the start-up is able to bring to the market, successfully, a radical innovation with enough unique advantages (compared to other existing possibilities) to overcome initial customer and market resistance." (Gelderen et al, 2003, p.11)

Further research, (Hallam et al, 2017, Makarona et al, 2019) examines strategic alliances between start-ups and universities, highlighting the role of organizational culture. Furthermore, establishing strategic alliances is another issue that may help Greek IT Start-ups. Academic study highlights the fact that management controls the firms' alliance activity (Karamanos, 2016) According to Rotsios et al. (2019, p.25), "executives should allocate resources, effort and time in developing and maintaining a trusting relationship with their partners in order to achieve better International Joint Ventures performance and, thus, better benefits for partner firms." In addition, academic studies (Usman et al, 2017) examine the ways start-ups engage with the business ecosystem, in an effort to organize and manage open innovation, dealing with larger companies, while Colombo (2018) highlights the role of academic (spin-off) start-ups. Further studies (Hormiga et al, 2010, Aulet, 2013) also highlight the role of intellectual capital for business success.

Further academic research (Roberts, 2015), that highlight the role of integration of IT systems, resulting lower cost for developing new business opportunities (especially for IT companies) and furthermore enabling engaging on entrepreneurial projects in younger ages. Roberts concludes that reduced need for investment and lower risks were factors that offered entrepreneurs the opportunity to launch ventures with a lower budget and less capital requirements, from a younger age.

"The lean start-up approach divides up the key decisions. A venture starts with relatively imprecise and limited hypotheses about where an opportunity may lie. Multiple stages of information gathering and "pivoting" follow." (Girotra et al, 2014, p.1) Ries (2011) highlights the benefits of lean start up strategy, emphasizing on the fact that enables start-up companies to test fast the two riskier hypotheses of their business plan; the value (the actual value as perceived by the potential customer or user) and growth (ability of the start-up to grow fast enlisting new customers) assumptions. Furthermore, Blank (2013) recommends start-ups to focus on "experimentation over of elaborate planning, customer feedback over intuition, and iterative design over traditional "big design up front" development.

Recent study also highlight the role of the wider start-up ecosystem: "identified the significant impact of grant systems, legal text interpretations, and incubators as a source for a shift in dominant logics in the early entrepreneurial process. Such supporting organizations follow their own logics, which is still dominated by a commercial approach." (Gregori et al, 2019, p. 23)

Additional studies (Santisteban et al, 2017) summarized findings of previous academic literature and identified key success for ICT start-ups, such as experience, governmental support, capital, organizational age, and product innovation. Furthermore Cozzolino et al (2018, p.42) emphasized on the availability of disruptive technological platforms as a prerequisite for disruptive innovation: "Disruptive technologies tend to come first and do not necessarily paralyze incumbents, but rather create opportunities. Disruptive business models tend to emerge after, when entrants find ways to commercialize previous disruptive technologies, and they threaten incumbents' business models."

Finally, academic studies highlight the role of entrepreneurial education and its impact on start-ups survival and success; Spyropoulos (2020b) summarizes conclusions of previous studies (Evers (2003), Morgan & Vorhies (2009), Chesbrough (2010), Gambardella & McGahan (2010), Amit & Zott, (2012), Aulet, (2013), Raj & Srivastasva (2016)) on the impact of entrepreneurial education, as it enables both entrepreneurs and stakeholders of the start-up ecosystems to identify and evaluate business opportunities.

RESEARCH APPROACH & METHODOLOGY

The literature review presented above provides several key factors for entrepreneurial success; based on the topics highlighted by academic literature the research questionnaire was designed.

The actual research was conducting with the use of structured Questionnaires for primary research data collection. The questionnaires were distributed to founders of the ICT start-ups who participated in exhibition events from September 2018 to May 2019. More specifically 143 questionnaires were distributed, on site, during the exhibitions, to the founders of the startups, and were filled-in and collected immediately on site as well. In certain cases brief discussions with the responders took place, in order to clarify certain points and to confirm validity of the data. The study examines a wide range of variables both from the founder's perspective (such as age, education, prior experience and previous ventures) and start-up organizations perspective (key achievements, main challenges, sources of competitive advantage, disruption and degree of innovation introduced).

The data were encoded and advanced statistical analysis software (SPSS) was used in order analyze the correlation between variables, with the use of Spearman Correlation Coefficient.

RESULTS

Part 1 – Descriptive Statistics

There were 143 responders in total, which were the founders of the ICT Start-Ups participating in various exhibitions in Greece, in the cities of Athens and Thessaloniki, as innovative start-up companies, during the time period between September 2018 and May 2019.

Figure 1.

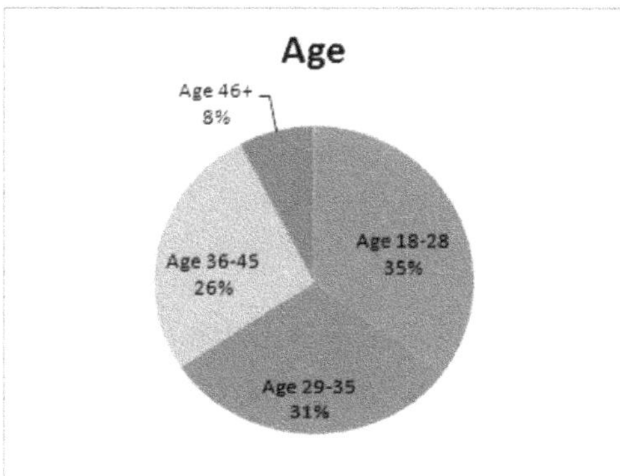

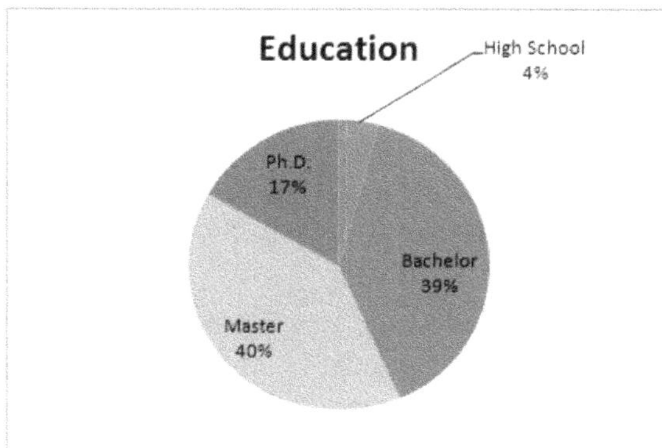

From the respondents, 76% were men and 24% women. A total of 35% were between 18 to 28 years of age; 31% from 29 to 35; 26% from 36-45, and 8% were over 45 years old. Regarding Education, 4% of the respondents were High School Graduates, 39% hold a bachelor Degree, 40% of the responders hold a Master's Degree and 17% hold a Ph.D. Degree.

Figure 2.

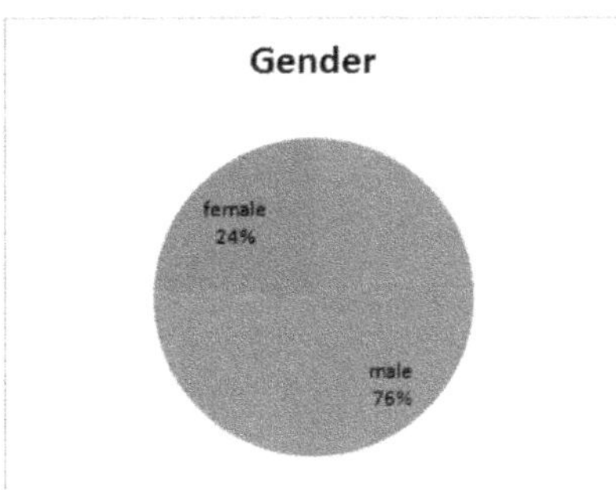

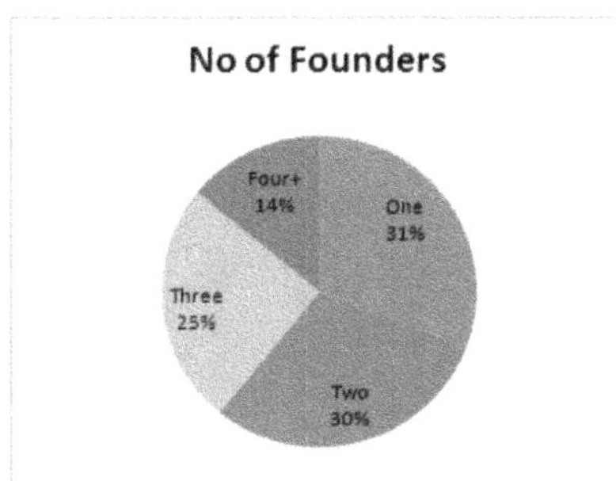

Regarding the Number of Founders per Start-up Company, 31% of the responders were the only founder, 30% responded that their founders team had two members, 25% responded that their founders team had three members and 14% responded that the founders team included four members.

Figure 3.

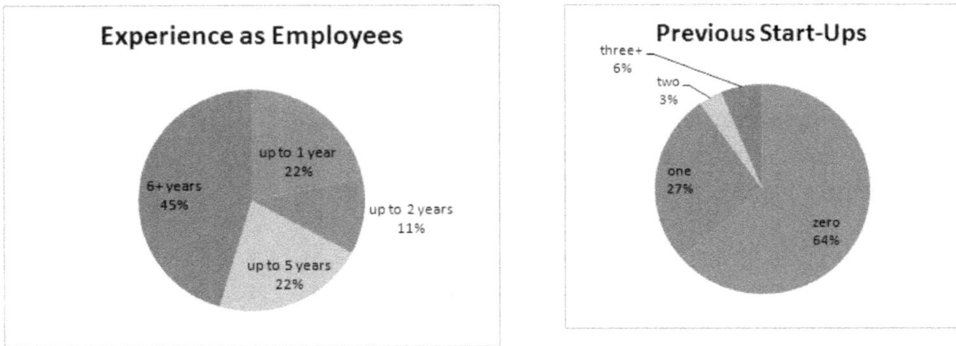

Regarding previous experience as employees, 22% responded that their working experience was up to one year, 11% responded that their working experience was up to two years, 22% responded that their working experience was up to 5 years, while 45% of the responders had 6 years or more working experience.

Regarding previous experience as entrepreneurs, 64% of the responders had not launched a previous venture. 27% of the responders had previous experience of launching one venture. However, there is also a noticeable percentage of serial entrepreneurs among the responders: 3% of the responders had launched three business ventures, while 6% of the responders had launched three or more previous ventures. Furthermore, regarding success rates of previous start-up ventures: 18% of the responders have one venture in the past that is still surviving today, 2% of the responders had two previous ventures that survived, while another 2% had three or more of previous business ventures that survived.

Regarding strategic alliances formed by Start-ups, 53% of the start-Up founders responded that they have no strategic alliances, 8% responded that they have angel investors, 26% responded that they have strategic alliances, while 13% responded that they are spin-offs of other organizations.

Figure 4.

Regarding the main challenges for their start-ups, 25% of the responders consider as primary challenge the need to improve their product, 39% the need to get more customers, 26% the need to secure funding, while 10% of the responders faces different challenges. Furthermore 55% of the responders face one challenge, 11% of the responders face two challenges, 24% of the responders face three challenges and 10% faces all four challenges as mentioned above.

Further examination of the descriptive statistic reveals that 19% of all responders consider as challenges both the need to get more customers and improve their product. In addition, 31% of those who responded that a key challenge is to get more customers also consider as challenge the need for further product improvement. Finally, 54% of those who responded that a key challenge is the need to improve product also consider a challenge the need to get more customers.

As an additional finding, 26% of the responders classify their innovation as "sustaining" while 74% of the responders consider their innovation to be disruptive.

Figure 5.

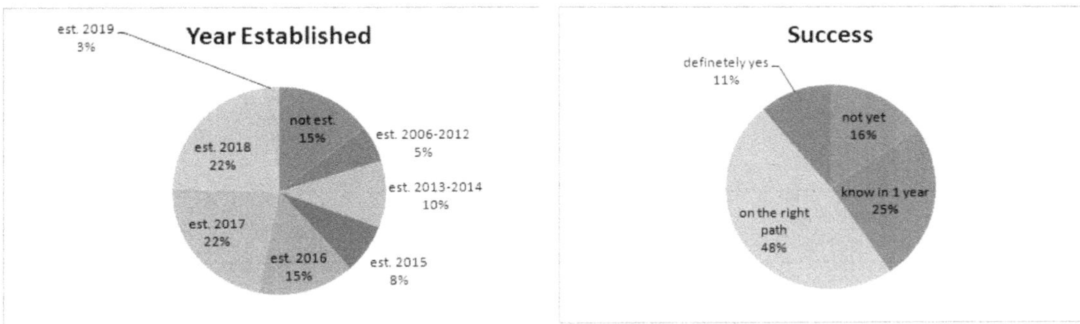

Regarding the year of establishment of their start-up, in terms of having a company officially formatted, 15% of the responders have not yet established their company. 5% of the responders had their companies established during the period 2006-2012, 10% of the responders had their companies established in 2013 or 2014, 8% of the responders had their company established in 2015, 15% of the responders in 2016, 22% of the responders in 2017 22% of the responders established their company in 2018 and 3% of the responders established their company in 2019. In total, 62% of the companies have been established for less than 3 years (Sept. 2018 – May 2019 was the period of data collection).

Regarding their feelings for success of their current start-up, 16% of the responders cannot consider it a success as yet, 25% of the responders feel that they will know after 1 year, 48% of the responders considered that they are on the right path, while 11% already consider their current start up as a success.

Finally, regarding funding requirements, 20% of the responders do not ask for funding, 23% of the responders require funding of 100k Euros, 17% of the responders require funding of up to 250k Euros, and 40% of the responders require funding more than 250k Euros.

Table 1. Statistical significant correlations

No	Variable 1	Variable 2	Relationship	Correlation	Spearman Value	Statistical Significance
1.	Improve Product	Gender	Analogous	Very Weak	0,177	*Correlation is significant at the 0.05 level (2-tailed).
2.	Improve Product	Number of Founders	Analogous	Very Weak	0,183	*Correlation is significant at the 0.05 level (2-tailed).
3.	Get more Customers	Other Challenges	Reverse Analogous	Weak	-0,234	** Correlation is significant at the 0.01 level (2-tailed).
4.	Get more Customers	Prof of Concept	Analogous	Very Weak	0,181	*Correlation is significant at the 0.05 level (2-tailed).
5.	Get more Customers	Amount of Funds Required	Reverse Analogous	Weak	-0,210	*Correlation is significant at the 0.05 level (2-tailed).
6.	Get more Customers	New Approach	Analogous	Very Weak	0,182	*Correlation is significant at the 0.05 level (2-tailed).
7.	Get more Customers	Technology as Competitive Advantage	Reverse Analogous	Weak	-0,209	*Correlation is significant at the 0.05 level (2-tailed).
8.	Get more Customers	Management as Competitive Advantage	Analogous	Weak	0,271	** Correlation is significant at the 0.01 level (2-tailed).
9.	Get more Customers	Business Model as Competitive Advantage	Analogous	Weak	0,259	** Correlation is significant at the 0.01 level (2-tailed).
10.	Get more Customers	Improved Product	Analogous	Weak	0,224	*Correlation is significant at the 0.05 level (2-tailed).
11.	Get Funding	Age	Analogous	Weak	0,235	** Correlation is significant at the 0.01 level (2-tailed).
12.	Get Funding	Education	Analogous	Weak	0,304	** Correlation is significant at the 0.01 level (2-tailed).
13.	Get Funding	Experience	Analogous	Very Weak	0,187	*Correlation is significant at the 0.05 level (2-tailed).
14.	Get Funding	Business to Consumers	Analogous	Weak	0,211	*Correlation is significant at the 0.05 level (2-tailed).
15.	Get Funding	Both Business to Business and Business to Consumers	Analogous	Weak	0,257	** Correlation is significant at the 0.01 level (2-tailed).
16.	Get Funding	Sales of 100k euros	Reverse Analogous	Weak	- 0,275	** Correlation is significant at the 0.01 level (2-tailed).
17.	Get Funding	Amount of Funds Required	Analogous	Weak	0,248	** Correlation is significant at the 0.01 level (2-tailed).
18.	Get Funding	New Approach	Analogous	Weak	0,221	** Correlation is significant at the 0.01 level (2-tailed).
19.	Get Funding	Intellectual Property	Analogous	Very Weak	0,167	*Correlation is significant at the 0.05 level (2-tailed).
20.	Get Funding	New Product	Analogous	Very Weak	0,172	*Correlation is significant at the 0.05 level (2-tailed).

Part 2 – Statistical Analysis

In this study, use of Statistical Analysis has been used to identify relationships between variables. The data were encoded and entered into an advanced statistical analysis software (SPSS) was used in order analyze the correlation between variables, with the use of Spearman Correlation Coefficient. Findings indicate Statistical Significance for the Correlations presented at Table 1 below:

Regarding the Correlations between two Variables, the correlation coefficient (r), is a measure of the strength of the linear relation between the x and y variables." (Isotalo, 2014, p.78). "Positive r indicates positive association between the variables, and negative r indicates negative association. The correlation r always falls between -1 and 1. Correlation measures the strength of only a linear relationship between two variables. Correlation does not describe curved relationships between variables, no matter how strong they are." (Isotalo, 2014, p. 81)

Furthermore the table below (Table 2) provides a list of Variables examined for potential correlation, in which there was no evidence of Correlation Significance, which are worth noted.

Table 2. No evidence of correlation significance

No	Variable 1	Variable 2	Correlation Significance
1.	Previous Start-Ups	Get more customers	No
2.	Previous Start-Ups	Improve Product	No
3.	Previous Start-Ups	Get Funding	No
4.	Previous Start-Ups	Other	No
5.	Previous Start-Ups Surviving Today	Get more customers	No
6.	Previous Start-Ups Surviving Today	Improve Product	No
7.	Previous Start-Ups Surviving Today	Get Funding	No
8.	Previous Start-Ups Surviving Today	Other	No
9.	Success	Get more customers	No
10.	Success	Improve Product	No
11.	Success	Get Funding	No
12.	Success	Other	No
13.	Success	Strategic Partnerships	No
14.	Strategic Partnerships	Get more customers	No
15.	Strategic Partnerships	Improve Product	No
16.	Strategic Partnerships	Get Funding	No
17.	Strategic Partnerships	Other	No

It has to be noted that there was no evidence of correlation between founders that are already successful serial entrepreneurs and any of the challenges examined; furthermore there was no evidence of correlation between feeling of Success and any of the key challenges identified and examined; there is also no evidence of correlation between Strategic Partnerships and any of the key challenges examined.

Table 3.

Challenge	Planning Phase of the Start-Up	During Operation of the Start-Up	Business Functions
Getting New Customers	Market Segmentation and Market Target (Beachhead Selection)	Create an effective sales team Simplify and Automate Customer on-boarding Processes Marketing Efforts to generate leads and secure a healthy sales pipeline Sales Partners & Reseller to extend sales coverage, keep costs under control and increase sales leads and opportunities	Marketing & Sales
Secure Financing	Identify potential investors (Business Angels, Network, Potential Customers) Create Business Plan and Pitch Determine the Deal Structure Evaluate Cash flows and need for Cash	Negotiate and Redefine Deal Structure as necessary Review and re-valuate Cash-flow and the needs for cash for the next 6-18 months.	Finance & Investor Relationships
Improving the Product	Product Design (Minimum Viable Product) Initial Product Requirements Secure Alignment between Product Features and Market Needs (including compliance issues)	Product Management Development of Product Roadmaps Update and Prioritize Product Requirements List in order to Include Customer Feedback and market trends Enhance Product, adding more features, in order to attract / be able to satisfy more customers and improve value proposition.	Marketing

Further research reveals that the 10 most funded Greek Start-Ups in 2018 had their first funding after 5 years, and have a mean of 6,67 years of operations, and 2,9 Funding Rounds. 5 of the 10 have a branch in USA, with offices in 3 countries. They employ between 51-100 people and the mean number of investors is 5,52. (EIT, 2018).

A key problem of the Greek Start-Up ecosystem becomes clear: “The lack of funding at early stages can kill a promising start-up, depriving resources from product development, market research and investments, especially in Intellectual Property.” (Spyropoulos, in-press)

MANAGERIAL IMPLICATIONS

Considering the findings of the descriptive statistics, the main challenge faced by Greek IT Start-Ups is increasing its customer’s base; 41% of the responders highlight this need. The importance of this challenge is evident; more customers’ results sales and profitability required for the survival of the start-up, and for further growth and investments.

The second key challenge is the need to secure funding; 28% of the responders highlight this need. Funding, especially on the early stages is critical for any start-up.

In addition, 24% of the responders highlight the need to improve their product. This can be interpreted both in terms to secure a better product-market fit and meet the needs of the targeted market segment; or proceeding from Minimum Viable Product to a more complete product, which can be offered to more demanding customers. To this respect, product improvement can lead to a better value proposition, and enable the start-ups to target more demanding customers, and the potential to increase their customer base. From this point of view there is some connection between the challenge of getting more customers and improving the product.

Finally, just 10% of the responders identify other needs; their needs vary in this case and include issues such as attracting co-founders and employees, establishing and improving processes, setting up location or legal issues, protecting their Intellectual Property.

Based on the above, the present study examines the implications of the three main issues identified, which are: 1. Gain more Customers (41%), 2. Secure Funding (28%), 3. Improve the Product (24%).

From an operational and business functional point of view, two of the main challenges (getting more sales (41%) and improving the product (24%)) are issues relating to the marketing (and sales) business functions. More specifically, the challenge of getting more sales can be addressed either in advance, during start-up planning phase, or as a business process once the business is running.

At this point it is important to highlight the need of Entrepreneurial Education, with a special focus to marketing, and more specifically market analysis and segmentation and product requirements analysis and product design. This is further highlighted by the fact that for 19% of the responders there is a need for both product improving and more customers. Despite the fact that statistical analysis does not provide causality (e.g. there is no a clear statement that "we need to improve our product in order to have more sales" or an even more concluding statement "by improving our product by X,Y,Z features our sales will increase up to 15%"). There is also no conclusive evidence whether the challenges to improve the product or to improve sales (by getting more customers) are due to the need for careful planning in advance, or for effective management of the sales, marketing and product management processes during operation; after all, increasing sales by getting more customers and improve the basic product may goals and strategies of business in most sectors or the economy regardless of their size and years of operation; for a start-up however this can be a critical prerequisite for its very survival.

Considering the high levels of uncertainty start-ups face, it is recommended that during start-up planning phase founders should give special focus on improving the market segmentation process and product design in the early planning phases of the start-up may reduce risk for start-ups.

Further statistical analysis of the data, seems to provide additional evidence for the need of careful planning in the initial planning phases of the start-up, especially in terms of market segmentation and targeting (selection of a beachhead market, according to Aulet's approach (Aulet, 2013)). Regarding the findings of the statistical analysis, there is a very weak analogous correlation between the variable "Improve Product" challenge and "Gender". This can be interpreted that women founders are more likely to consider "improve product" as a challenge. There is also a positive, analogous, very weak correlation between the variables "Improve Product" and "Number of Founders". One explanation may be that with more founders available, more focus can be given on product management, recording and prioritizing future product specification and creating roadmaps. As a result a better product may be expected in the future and – with the creation of a better value proposition – better sales and overall performance in the future.

There is a reverse analogous, weak correlation between the variables "Get more customers" and "other" as challenges; this may be interpreted that as founders focus on increasing sales and expanding the customer base other challenges become less important – probable been considered less important or already met – on the other hand for start-ups that have additional challenges defined as "other" ("other" refers to several challenges other than secure financing, get more customers or improve product, and just

10% of the founders reported such challenges) it is likewise such challenges to prevent them from actual sales; such cases may be team (founders or employee) issues, actual establishment of the company in order to be in position to have transactions, etc.

There is an analogous, very weak correlation between the variables “Get more customers” and “Prof of Concept”. A positive relationship between these variables is expected, since Prof of Concept is a process where the demonstration of a product proves its claims; to this respect it adds to the credibility of the solution; the weak correlation is harder to be interpreted – it means that despite a successful prove of concept the need to get more customers is still important – such a situation may arise in terms of value proposition issues, where the customer is satisfied with the results of the product demonstration but unwilling to commit with the asking price – another reason may be customer facing budget problems or the solution proposed is not on the customer’s priority list, or longer sales cycles. Such cases may be an indication of a need for better market research during the planning phase, especially in terms of market segmentation and targeting. On a more positive interpretation, could highlight the need to scale sales after a successful Prof of Concept, since this is a common goal for most private companies.

There is a weak, reverse analogous correlation between the variables “Get more customers” and “funds required”. The interpretation for this is that founders that request higher amounts from investors require more customers, either in order to reduce the need for funding or – a much more possible interpretation – to persuade investors for their value proposition in terms of investor / start-up relationship; potential investors may be more willing to invest in a start-up with actual and growing sales.

There is a very weak, analogous correlation between the variables “Get more customers” and “new approach”. This can be interpreted with the fact that founders with a value proposition and a product offering that offers a new approach towards the problem addressed consider as a main challenge their need to get more customers. This is something that was anticipated; new approach to a problem, either in terms of product features, business model or another approach is associated with a higher risk; or from this point of view it is reasonable for founders to consider getting more customers as a critical challenge. In each case however, this reinforces the recommendation for effective market analysis, segmentation and targeting during the planning phase of the start-up.

Another interesting finding is the weak reverse correlation between the variables “Get more customers” and “technology as competitive advantage”. This can be interpreted that start-up founders who consider that technology is their source of competitive advantage consider the challenge to get new customers as - to a relative degree – a less important one. One reason for this is the opportunity for advanced IT solutions to scale, by creating partnerships and alliances with other companies. Open architectures schemes, White Label Software and use of API (sets of functions enable connectivity and execution of software programs) enables IT companies to enter advanced ecosystems and create partner networks that can scale their sales.

There is also an analogous weak correlation between the variables “Get more customers” and “Management as competitive advantage”. The interpretation is that founders who consider management skills to be their company’s competitive advantage consider getting more customers as a key challenge.

A more interesting finding is the analogous weak correlation between the variables “Get more customers” and “Business model as competitive advantage”. The interpretation is that founders who consider their business model to be their start-up’s competitive advantage consider getting more customers as a key challenge. This is consistent with academic literature conclusions; since business model innovation may offer the opportunity for differentiation, however this opportunity comes at a risk; some market segments may find the new business model proposed appealing and become customers of the start-up

– other segments will remain loyal to the existing way of doing business, since they already have optimized their operations accordingly. It is therefore important for start-up founders to evaluate carefully the market in advance, during the planning phase of their start-up and identify the markets or segments where the new model proposed will offer additional value.

There is also an analogous weak correlation between the variables "Get more customers" and "Improved Product". This means that founders of start-ups who offer an improved version of the product in an existing market also consider getting more customers as a main challenge. Offering an improved product to an existing market is considered to be a safer strategy; the main risks in this phase is ability to scale fast and market responsiveness – in many cases, especially B2B markets, an improved products solves a need that is already covered by another competitive product, and existing suppliers may have developed switching costs. Customers may be faced with sunk costs in addition to switching ones, and credibility of the company can be a key factor – especially in B2B markets, managers may prefer investing in well known companies instead of start-ups. The is a well know moto in the Greek IT market "no one was fired for purchasing from IBM", which describes the culture of purchasing managers, at least up to a certain point. Last and not least, a start-up adopting this strategy, may consider two critical issues; the first one is that – especially for IT markets – improved features and functionality of a software product can be easily copied (at least unless protected with relevant copyright or patents) from the existing competitors, especially from those who already serve the customers and have available resources. The second case of course is that the "improved" version of the product that is their proposal needs to address critical issues of the customer needs and pains – small technical improvements may be of little value to the customer, along with non-important or non-required features. Market research at this point is critical in order for start-ups to identify promising segments, where their improved product proposal may gain a considerable share of the specific segment.

There is a weak, analogous correlation between the variables "Get funding" and "Age". There may be several reasons for this behavior; older start-uppers are probable more experienced and have a better understanding of their business needs, including investments for Intellectual Property Rights and potentially a better estimation of sales & marketing effort. Furthermore, additional funds create a feeling of safety net, especially for founders that have families to support. There is also a weak, analogous correlation between the variables "Get funding" and "Education", which can be interpreted that founders with more education tend to consider getting funded as a key challenge; probably for the same reasons as presented above. Similarly, there is a very weak, analogous correlation between "Get funding" and "Experience", which means that founders with more working experience as employees tend to consider getting funding as a key challenge; the same reasons can also apply as well.

There is also a weak, analogous correlation between the variables "Get funding" and "Business to Consumer". This means that founders of companies addressing to Business to Consumer markets (B2C) tend to consider more getting funding as a critical challenge for their start-ups. There can be many reasons for this; business to consumer markets usually involves products sold at a relevant low price, therefore requires many transactions in order to accumulate a substantial amount as income, while one or few business-to-business contracts can provide substantial income; in addition Business to Consumer markets may require additional marketing efforts to attract a large enough number of end-customers – in both cases cash are required to secure survival of the start-up. Furthermore, there is also a weak, analogous correlation between the variables "Get funding" and "Both B2B and B2C", the same interpretation and reasons can also apply, since this involves companies that still need to attract a large number of consumer customers, or at least integrate effectively with them (such cases can be social media or fintech, where network externalities and number of users is critical, even though paying customers may be different types of business entities, such as advertisers or lenders).

What is interesting is a weak, reverse analogous correlation between the variables “Get Funding” and “Sales 100k”; this means that founders of start-ups that achieved sales goals of 100k (euros) consider to a less degree getting funding as a challenge for their organization. Creating income from paying customers is a great achievement, especially since it actually proves that there is an actual need for the product and a market to be conquered; furthermore it proves that the value proposition is accepted and that the offering is considered superior to other competitive offerings. Therefore it is reasonable for founders to feel less stress regarding getting funding, since their success can lead to investors and financing deals far easier and at the same time finance part of their investment plan from actual sales. In this case, apparently a strong focus on sales and marketing efforts is recommended in order for the start-up to scale effectively.

There is also a weak, analogous correlation between the variables “Get Funding” and “Amount of Funds Required”. This means that the more funding requested from the founders of start-ups in order to finance the business, the more important they consider getting these funds as a challenge. This is reasonable, considering the fact that in case large amounts of funds are required, the harder it becomes for the company to collect through actual, organic sales; in many cases these funds are indeed a prerequisite for actual sales, and failure to secure such funds will most likely lead the start-up to terminate operations.

There is also a weak analogous relationship between “Get funding” and “New approach”; founders of start-up that offer a new approach to a problem and offer a different value proposition consider getting funding as a key challenge. The reasons for this can be similar to the reasons discussed earlier regarding the correlation between “Get more customers” and “New approach”; to a large degree due to the risk whether the new proposal will be accepted by the market. What can he recommended here is focus on careful market research during the initial planning phase of the start-ups, in terms of marketing and segmentation.

In addition there is a very weak, analogous correlation between the variables “Get funding” and “Intellectual Property”; founders of start-ups who consider that the competitive advantage of their company is primary their intellectual property also tend to consider getting funding a key challenge for their start-ups. A reason for this can be the high costs associated with the protection of intellectual property, especially in European and Global level, (including of course USA). Protection of intellectual property is a rather expensive (at least for start-ups) and time consuming process; and to this respect having available funds at the right time, early on the start-up life, is a critical value. In addition creation of material worth protecting (such as diagrams and software code, algorithms and specific type of results) is also an expensive process, usually requiring highly skilled employees and therefore relevant high salaries and costs for the start-up company.

Finally there is a very weak, analogous correlation between the variables “Get Funding” and “New Product”; again there is an analogy – and similar managerial implications – with the correlation between “Get more Customers” and “New Product”.

At this stage there are some important conclusions to be drawn; First of all, the correlations examined were all either weak or very weak; to this respect statistical analysis highlights that there is not a single dimensional factor that leads founders to consider a specific key challenge (or more specifically to determine which one of the three more important ones will be their main challenge). On the contrary, it appears that there are 3 main challenges and the founders depend on the impact of several factors when they try to determine their main challenge or challenges.

A second remark is that certain factors have a more decisive impact on more than one challenge; the variable "New Approach", an indication that the start-up proposes a new answer and a new approach to an existing need or problem correlates with both "Get more customers" and "Get funding" variables. In both cases correlation is analogous, therefore founders whose start-ups offer a new proposal consider both challenges as important; this can be interpreted from the additional stress whether the new proposal will finally be accepted by the market. Furthermore, the variable "amount of funds required" has a reverse analogous relationship with "get more customers" challenge and an analogous correlation with "get funding" challenge; both of them have been discussed.

A third remark derives not from the correlations identified, but from the cases where there was no evidence of correlation significance. There is no evidence of correlation significance between any of the challenges identified (Get more customers, Secure Funding, Improve product and other) and variables such as "Previous Start-Ups" and "Previous Start-Ups Surviving today" – to this respect, there is no correlation between founders who have previous experience in start-ups and successful serial entrepreneurs on the IT with a specific challenge. There is also no evidence of correlation significance between any of the challenges examined and the founder's perception of success (whether they consider their start-up a success).

Another point to consider is the fact that the majority (74%) of the IT Start-up founders describe their solutions as "disruptive". From this point of view, the task of analyzing the market and define segments becomes much harder; "Markets that do not exist cannot be analyzed: Suppliers and customers must discover them together. Not only are the market applications for disruptive technologies unknown at the time of their development, they are unknowable." (Christensen, 1997, p. 147).

To make things more complicated, a number of start-ups (45%) face more than one challenge; however at some degree (get new customers and improve product) these challenges are – up to a point – correlated.

However, the main challenge that the Greek IT start-uppers face appears to be the Greek macroeconomic environment. During the last 10 years Greece lost about 25% of GDP, while many organizations bankrupt; migration of professionals lead to brain drain effect, and capital controls were imposed – in this business environment IT investments of established companies were kept to a minimum. A recent report from the European Institute of Technology (EIT) released in 2018 concludes: "Greece is not performing well on "Business dynamism" and "Innovation capability pillars", placing 120th in "Growth of innovative companies" and 126th in "Companies embracing disruptive ideas". Government regulations appear to be holding the country back … as it ranks very low on "Quality of land administration" (135th), "Efficiency of legal framework in challenging regulations" (127th), "Burden of government regulation" (131st), "Efficiency of legal framework in settling disputes" (133rd) and "Future orientation of government" (135th)". (EIT 2018, p. 9)

According to the EU's Digital Transformation Scoreboard for 2018, Greece performs lower than the EU average in six of the seven dimensions. The country ranks significantly lower than the EU average in the areas of "Digital Infrastructure" and "E-leadership". (EIT 2018, p.17)

LIMITATIONS AND SUGGESTIONS FOR FURTHER RESEARCH

The study examined the ICT start-ups founders participating in a number of exhibitions in the cities of Athens and Thessaloniki, for an eight months period, and more specifically from September 2018 to May 2019. The study covered start-up companies from various cities of Greece, with the majority of founders from the cities of Athens and Thessaloniki, Greece. All start-up founders have participated to at least one accelerator program – and to this respect they have the elements of business acumen to run their start-ups. However, it has to be noted that there were significant differences at the maturity level of the participating start-ups; 15% of the responders did not had established a company, while 62% of the start-ups were in fact companies less than 3 years old (2015, 2016, 2018, 2019). Therefore, more focused research in the future is recommended to examine start-ups at similar stages of development, which may highlight new types of relationships and correlations.

Another key point that needs to be highlighted in this study is that responders were the founders of the start-ups – and therefore the study examines perceptions of founders regarding the companies and not actual performance of the company, based on pre-defined standards.

Furthermore the sample size consists of 143 founders of ICT start-ups. Additional research is recommended to take place with an increased sample size, keeping the same key criteria (IT Start-Ups in Greece, having completed one acceleration program).

Finally, during most of the the past decade (2008-2018) the macroeconomic environment in Greece was characterized by economic decline and stagnation, high unemployment rates, capital controls, major cuts in IT investments; brain drain effect, increased taxation, and increased bureaucracy – it is therefore reasonable to assume that the economic and business environment was not friendly for start-up companies as well; to this respect, future research is recommended in more entrepreneurial-friendly business environments.

CONCLUSION

Academic studies and the research findings provide the basis for a better understanding of the challenges the Greek IT start-ups face. First of all Greek IT Start-up founder consider mainly three main challenges; getting new customers, securing funding and improving their product. Despite operating in a very hard macroeconomic environment, Greek IT start-up founders remain focused on overcoming these specific challenges.

An interesting finding is that past entrepreneurship experience, including the launch of successful ventures which survive until today from serial entrepreneurs, appear to have no evidence of correlation with feelings or success or the specific challenges they face on their current venture. The majority of the start-ups founders describe their value propositions as disruptive, however offering new approach to solving a problem is in fact associated with the both challenges of getting new customers and get funding.

The study contributes to academic knowledge as an analysis of the perceptions of the start-up founders regarding the key changes their start-ups face. The same study provides useful insights for all members of the ecosystem, such as policy makers, business angels and venture capital investors and of course for future start-up founders.

REFERENCES

Amit, R., & Zott, C. (2012). Creating Value Through Business Model Innovation. *MIT Sloan Management Review*. http://sloanreview.mit.edu/article/creating-value-through-business-model-innovation/

Aulet, B. (2013). *Disciplined Entrepreneurship, 24 Steps to a Successful Start Up*. John Wiley & Sons, Inc.

Christensen, C. M. (1997). *The Innovator's Dilemma- When New Technologies Cause Great Firms to Fail*. Harvard Business School Press.

Colombo, M. G., & Piva, E. (2008). Strengths and weaknesses of academic startups: A conceptual model. *Engineering Management. IEEE Transactions on*, *55*(1), 37–49.

Cozzolino A., Verona G., Rothaermel F. (2018). Unpacking the Disruption Process: New Technology, Business Models, and Incumbent Adaptation. *Journal Of Management Studies*. doi:10.1111/joms.12352

European Institute of Technology (EIT) Digital - Start-Ups in Greece 2018. (2018). *A maturing ecosystem points to a brighter future EIT Digital in partnership with Velocity Partners*. Author.

Gelderen, M.V., Thurik, R., & Niels Bosma, N. (2003). *Success and Risk factors in the Pre-Start-Up Phase*. EIM – Business & Policy Research, SCALES Scientific Analysis of Entrepreneurship and SMEs – Paper N200314

Girotra, K., & Netessine, S. (2014, July). Four Paths to Business Model Innovation. *Harvard Business Review*. https://hbr.org/2014/07/four-paths-to-business-model-innovation

Gregori, P., Wdowiak, M. A., Schwarz, E. J., & Holzmann, P. (2019). Exploring Value Creation in Sustainable Entrepreneurship: Insights from the Institutional Logics Perspective and the Business Model Lens. *Sustainability*, *11*(9), 2505. doi:10.3390u11092505

Grosse, R., & Kujawa, D. (1995). *International Business, Theory and Management Applications* (3rd ed.). Irwin.

Hallam, C., Novick, D., Gilbert, D. J., Frankwick, G. L., Wenker, O., & Zanella, G. (2017). Academic Entrepreneurship and the Entrepreneurial Ecosystem: The UT transform project. *Academy of Entrepreneurship Journal*, *23*(1), 2017.

Hormiga, E., & Batista-Canino, R.M., & Sánchez-Medina, A. (2010). The role of intellectual capital in the success of new ventures. *Journal of International Enterpreneuship Management*.

Isotalo, J. (2014). *Basics of Statistics*. Available at: http://www.mv.helsinki.fi/home/jmisotal/BoS.pdf

Johnson, R. (1997). Negotiating the start-up obstacle course, Mastering Enterprise. *Financial Times Management*, 126-129.

Juntunen, M., Ahonkangas, P., & Nguyen, A. (2018). Business Model Scalability in the cloud business context. *Journal of Business Models*, *6*(1), 19–39.

Karamanos, A. (2016). Effects of a firm's and their partners' alliance ego–network structure on its innovation output in an era of ferment. *R & D Management*, *46*(S1), 261–276. doi:10.1111/radm.12163

Kavoura, A., & Andersson, T. (2016). Applying Delphi method for strategic design of social entrepreneurship. *Library Review*, *65*(3), 185–205. doi:10.1108/LR-06-2015-0062

Khodaei, H., & Ortt, R. (2019). Capturing Dynamics in Business Model Frameworks, Journal of Open Innovation: Technology. *Market and Complexity*, *5*, 8. doi:10.3390/joitmc5010008

Konig, A. (1997). A business plan to entice backers, Mastering Enterprise. *Financial Times Management*, 116-119.

Makarona, E., & Kavoura, A. (2019). Redesigning the Ivory Tower: Academic entrepreneurship as a new calling supporting economic growth. *The Malopolska School of Economics in Tarnow Research Papers Collection*, *42*, 15–26. doi:10.25944/znmwse.2019.02.1526

Mustapha, M., & Subramaniam, P. (2015). Challenges and Success Factors of Female Entrepreneurs: Evidence from a Developing Country. *International Review of Management and Marketing*.

Muzyca, D. (1997). Spotting the Market Opportunity, Mastering Enterprise. *Financial Times Management*, 28-31.

Ries, E. (2011). *The Lean Start Up*. Crown Publishing Group.

Roberts, E.B., Murray, F., & Kim, J.D. (2015). *Entrepreneurship and innovation at MIT, Continuing Global Growth and Impact*. Martin Trust Center for MIT Entrepreneurship, MIT.

Rotsios, K., Sklavounos, N., & Hajidimitriou, Y. (2019). (in press). Successful Knowledge Transfer in International Joint Ventures: The Role of Trust, Partner Compatibility and Expected Benefits. *European Journal of International Management*. Advance online publication. doi:10.1504/EJIM.2019.10017016

Roy R. (2019). For Innovations That Have no Precedent in Human History It's Time to Ask Disruptive Questions. *Performance Improvement, 58*(6). Doi:10.1002/pfi.21879

Santisteban J., Mauricio D. (2017). Systematic Literature Review of Critical Success Factors of Information Technology Startups. *Academy of Entrepreneurial Journal, 23*(2).

Shankar, V., & Krisnamurti, L. (1999). What are the Options for Later Entrants? Mastering Marketing. *Financial Times*, 172-178.

Spyropoulos, T. (in press a). Start-Ups Ecosystems Comparison: MIT and Greece Experiences. *The Małopolska School of Economics in Tarnów Research Papers Collection*.

Spyropoulos, T. (in press b). MIT Start-Ups Ecosystems and Greek Start-Up Reality – an Ecosystem Comparison. In A. Kavoura, E. Kefallonitis, & P. Theodoridis (Eds.), *Strategic Innovative Marketing and Tourism*. Springer Cham. doi:10.1007/978-3-030-36126-6_102

Stott, R.N., Stone, M., & Fae, J. (2016). Business models in the business-to-business and business-to-consumer worlds – what can each world learn from the other? *Journal of Business & Industrial Marketing, 31*(8), 943–954. DOI doi:10.1108/JBIM-10-2016-267

Usman, M., & Vanhaverbeke, W. (2017). How start-ups successfully organize and manage open innovation with large companies. *European Journal of Innovation Management*, *20*(1), 171–186. doi:10.1108/EJIM-07-2016-0066

ADDITIONAL READING

Chesbrough, H. (2010, April–June). Business Model Innovation: Opportunities and Barriers. *Long Range Planning*, *43*(2–3), 354–363.

Christensen, C., & Overdorf, M. (2000, March-April). Meeting the Challenge of Disruptive Change. *Harvard Business Review*, *78*(2), 67–76.

Davila, A., Foster, G., & Gupta, M. (2003). Venture capital financing and the growth of startup firms. *Journal of Business Venturing*, *18*(6), 689–708.

Maroosis, J. (2001, January). How to Anticipate and Capitalize on Innovation. *Harvard Management Update*, *6*(1), 10.

Milat, A. J., King, L., Bauman, A. E., & Redman, S. (2013, September 1). The concept of scalability: Increasing the scale and potential adoption of health promotion interventions into policy and practice. *Health Promotion International*, *28*(3), 285–298. doi:10.1093/heapro/dar097

Sosna, M., & Trevinyo-Rodríguez, R. N. (2010, April–June). S.R., (2010) Business Model Innovation through Trial-and-Error Learning: The Naturhouse Case. *Long Range Planning*, *43*(2–3), 383–407.

Trott, P. (1998). *Innovation Management & New Product Development*. London, U.K.: Financial Times-Pitman Publishing.

Zhou, K., Yim, C., & Tse, D. (2005). The effects of strategic orientations on technology-and market-based breakthrough innovations. *Journal of Marketing*, *69*(2), 42–60.

Zott C., Amit R., Massa L., (2011) The Business Model: Recent Developments and Future Research, Journal of Management, Volume: 37 issue: 4, page(s): 1019-1042 Article first published online: May 2, 2011; Issue published: July 1, 2011

KEY TERMS AND DEFINITIONS:

Business Model: The way an organization plans its activities and key relationships with customers and suppliers, in order to create and capture value.

Disruptive: A type of innovation which offers some characteristics that offers superior value to specific market segments, but not the mainstream market.

Integration: The ability of software systems to communicate seamlessly, exchanging data and activating processes.

Intellectual Property: A set of company's intangible assets protected by legal means, such as patents, copyrights, trademarks, etc.

Pitch: A presentation of the key characteristics and benefits of the Start-Up, including the problem addressed, market size and growth potential, team and competitive advantage.

Prof of Concept: A demonstration of a product or service aiming to satisfy pre-agreed goals, and prove value to end customer.

Sales Cycle: The time required to turn a lead to an actual sale, according to the sales process

Start-Up: an organization, formally established or not, that aims to launch a new product or service proposal. The main aim of this entity is to test hypotheses, mainly of value to end customer and growth potential.

Chapter 4
Social Skills and Competencies as the Driving Force of SME Development in Russia

Natalya Totskaya
Laurentian University, Canada

ABSTRACT

This chapter provides an overview of social skills contributing to SME development in the Russian Federation. Building upon prior research and using the data collected by the most recent World Bank Enterprise Survey, the author summarizes the main social skills demonstrated by Russian SMEs. The indicators published by the 2012 and 2019 Enterprise Survey are further supported by analysis of entrepreneurial "success stories" of entrepreneurs published by Russian web-based media. Social skills required to run a successful SME correspond to those identified from the Enterprise Survey data, and they are evenly distributed among skills comprising the "ways of thinking" and the "ways of working." The chapter concludes with directions for future research and implications for practice.

INTRODUCTION

Researchers have widely recognized social skills as essential contributors that help individual entrepreneurs to achieve and maintain their business success (Baron & Markham, 2000). In recent years, the universal applicability of these skills and related competencies has become a focus of post-secondary education around the globe. Workplace skills such as communication, collaboration, and problem-solving, as well as the ability to learn and innovate are essential not only in the field of entrepreneurship, but also in various professions, industries, and countries (Griffin & Care, 2015). Specific models and approaches linking academic and practical components of education may vary across academic programs and countries, yet all of them recognize the need to develop the toolkit of skills to enhance the employability and career success of graduates (Abeysekera, 2006; Jackson, 2015; Makarona & Kavoura, 2019; Orrell, 2011).

This chapter will discuss social skills and competencies that are of great importance for owners, managers, and employees of small and medium-size enterprises (SMEs), with particular focus on

DOI: 10.4018/978-1-7998-3648-3.ch004

emerging economy of Russia. First, Russian SMEs represent an under-investigated segment of emerging economies. Countries of former Soviet Bloc, often referred to as transition economies, constitute a small, yet essential part of global economy. Some of transition economies have successfully integrated in the European Union, whereas others still struggle to redesign their socio-economic systems while dealing with obstacles such as economic and political turbulence, crime, and corruption. Second, Russian higher education has been practicing work-integrated learning for over fifty years (Khohlov, 1994; Fedko & Dolgun, 2004). Institutions of higher education have tailored mandatory "placements" to specific academic programs, and they exposed students to real-life workplace environments and experiences. In recent years, Russia has been moving its experiential and work-integrated education towards developing more interdisciplinary skills and "cross-professional" or general competencies required in the modern, innovative, and service-oriented economy (Bogoudinova & Kazakova, 2018; Morozova & Suzdalova, 2014). New educational standards combine traditional placements with multiple elements of experiential learning aimed to build interdisciplinary and general competencies. Therefore, it is reasonable to expect that Russian graduates may have more social skills than previous generations when entering the workforce. Graduates have some professional experience and personal contacts; and perhaps they have faced the need to learn and develop new skills fairly quickly. Therefore, it would be interesting to identify specific social skills and competencies that contribute to success of Russian entrepreneurs and SMEs.

This chapter will continue with brief review of the literature on skills and competencies that are instrumental in advancing entrepreneurship and SME development in emerging markets. The author presents a summary of the recent World Bank Enterprise Survey report highlighting the main characteristics of Russian SMEs, with particular focus on topics related to social skills and competencies. The author further illustrates key social skills by analysis of interview data on SME "success stories." Finally, this chapter will conclude with discussion of findings and implications.

SOCIAL SKILLS CREATE BIG PERSPECTIVES FOR SMALL BUSINESSES

Social skills can be broadly defined as general abilities and personality traits that allow individuals to develop competencies to navigate various social situations, build effective communications, and create positive impressions. Baron and Markham (2000) argue that advanced social skills contribute to an entrepreneur's success by enhancing his or her social capital and providing access to wider range of resources. Generic or cross-professional competencies are built upon social skills; they reflect one's ability to communicate ideas, participate in a teamwork, develop and apply new knowledge, follow good ethics, think critically, etc. Generic competencies representing bundles of social skills, knowledge, and related behaviors are essential in any country, industry, company, or job position.

Social skills are especially important for SME development as they enhance the quality of its human capital. Individual entrepreneurs often act as founders, owners, and managers of small and medium enterprises. Thus, entrepreneurs contribute to SMEs' approach to doing business, including performance, patterns of growth and development, etc. While entrepreneurs play a pivotal role in starting and running their businesses, other employees may make significant contributions into SMEs' long-term success. SMEs often have fewer resources than larger enterprises, and they serve smaller or less attractive market segments. Under these circumstances, the human capital of SMEs becomes their critical asset that can help to sustain and grow the business. Therefore, when discussing the role of social skills in SME development, this study will look at SME human capital (i.e., the various internal stakeholders, including SMEs owners (entrepreneurs), top managers, and employees).

Researchers consider entrepreneurship to be one of the greater contributors to economic growth, innovation, competitiveness, and job creation around the world. Organization for Economic Co-operation and Development (OECD) reports that SMEs and individual entrepreneurs make significant contributions in their national economies providing between 45% and 70% of jobs, up to 30-40% of GDP, and playing an important role in fostering knowledge-sharing and innovations (OECD, 2017). Personal characteristics of entrepreneurs as well as contextual factors are known to influence the state of entrepreneurship in both economically advanced and developing countries. Bosma and Kelley (2019) have highlighted the various types and facets of entrepreneurship in the latest Global Entrepreneurship Monitor 2018/2019 Global Report (GEM). According to 2018/2019 GEM, early stage and micro-entrepreneurship is more evident in emerging and developing countries, as is seen as a job-creation tool. Developed countries encourage long-term, growth oriented entrepreneurial undertakings, as well as organizational development through entrepreneurial activity of employees and managers. Twenty years of GEM research have expanded the range of studied countries and revealed the evolving nature of entrepreneurial activities, motives, and impacts on socioeconomic development. Over the years, emerging economies have demonstrated higher levels of entrepreneurial activity than developed ones. Researchers have analyzed GEM data to look at different aspects of entrepreneurship across the world, and they have found that well-developed professional and social skills are associated with high-impact entrepreneurship (Estrin, Mickiewicz, Stephan, & Wright, 2018). In turn, this kind of entrepreneurship increases the level of innovations and technological advancement that stimulate economic growth (Acs, Estrin, Mickiewicz, & Szerb, 2018). Unfortunately, many emerging economies lag behind on high-impact, innovative entrepreneurial ventures and lean towards traditional small and family business activities. Research suggests that SMEs demonstrate lower levels of productivity than larger firms due to weaker managerial skills, lack of training, limited access to business networking and technological innovations (Gray & Mabey, 2005; Marchese, Giuliani, Salazar-Elena, & Stone, 2019). Marchese et al. (2019) indicate that institutional environment, availability of state support, size of a firm and type of its business affect the bundles of skills developed by SMEs in advanced and emerging economies.

Cross-country analysis of entrepreneurial activities and outcomes provided in the GEM and OECD reports is complemented by country-specific evidence. Entrepreneurs in low-income emerging countries require both better education and supportive institutional environments as main conditions to develop their businesses. For instance, Zamberi and Xavier (2012) argue that nascent entrepreneurs in Malaysia lack proper education and rely on family-centered networks to support their businesses. In mid-income transition economies, such as China and Russia, entrepreneurs are motivated toward success and supported by extensive social networks. Furthermore, they have better education and knowledge of their national business environment (Djankov, Qian, Roland, & Zhuravskaya, 2006; Gudov, 2013). Researchers recognize strong motivation, friendly attitude, and other positive personal characteristics as important contributors to success for Turkish entrepreneurs (Benzing, Chu, & Kara, 2009). However, the use of innovative advanced skills and technologies in emerging economies may be limited, as illustrated by Kavoura and Koziol (2017) for the case of Polish SMEs. Therefore, prior research indicates that both level of knowledge and social skills shape entrepreneurs' abilities to start and develop more impactful and innovative businesses, even in underdeveloped institutional environments.

SMALL AND MEDIUM SIZE FIRMS IN RUSSIA: MAIN OBSTACLES AND KEYS TO SUCCESS

External Environment and SME Development

For a number of years, the Russian Federation undergoes massive changes related to economic liberalization and modernization. Over the period of socio-economic transition, the state has provided support to large projects and key industry players, while maintaining significant control over them; however, the state did not do much for bridging the gaps in cooperation across regions and among small business organizations (Osipov & Skryt, 2016). Russian SMEs face many developmental challenges, including the need for more transparency in registration, employment, reporting practices and access to governmental programs (Velinov & Ponomarev, 2016). As the literature suggests, the Russian institutional environment continues to demonstrate high levels of regulatory uncertainty, hostility, and corruption (Puffer & McCarthy, 2015; Schulze, Sjahrir, & Zakharov, 2016; Wales, Shirokova, Sokolova, & Stein, 2016). The level of entrepreneurial confidence is low, while the overall risk of doing business is quite high (Petrov, Abramov, & Michailov, 2018). The recent Doing Business report (World Bank Group, 2019a) shows some positive trends in rankings and topics related to components of Russian business environment. Policy improvements include easier trading across borders, faster process of getting electricity and construction permits, and higher tax depreciation rates. Russia's overall score for the ease of doing business places it as #28 on the list of 190 countries surveyed. However, specific rankings for trading across borders (#99), paying taxes (#58), resolving insolvency (#57) and protecting minority investors (#72) remain relatively low. These particular indicators reflect access to finance, ease of conducting daily operations and security of business environment (World Bank Group, 2019a). All these aspects are extremely important for resource-constrained SMEs, and they need improvement.

There's no single standard for SME criteria and definition. World Bank Group research applies various definitions when it comes to discussing SMEs and related issues (World Bank Group, 2019d). Specifically, employment thresholds set in the methodology section of the World Bank Enterprise Surveys (World Bank Group, 2019c) define firms with five to 19 employees as "small", and firms with 20 to 99 employees as "medium" firms. These criteria are somewhat close to those stipulated by the Federal Law of July 24, 2007 N° 209-FZ "On the development of small and medium entrepreneurship in the Russian Federation" and by the Government Decree of February 9, 2013 N°101 "On the thresholds of sales revenues for each SME category". Russian law classifies businesses with up to 15 employees as "micro-enterprises", firms with 16 to 100 employees – as "small; firms with 101-250 employees are considered "medium" enterprises. Micro and small businesses in Russia may operate as individual entrepreneurs without legal status, as farmers, or as legal entities. These categories of small firms are subject to different record-keeping and reporting standards. Legal entities are monitored more closely than farmers and individual entrepreneurs operating under simplified tax system. Therefore, Russian entrepreneurship is quite diverse in organizational forms, and statistics on SMEs is somewhat unreliable and inconsistent across different legal forms and industries. The Federal State Statistics Service of the Russian Federation (Rosstat) collects key indicators on Russian SMEs and publishes them annually in a statistical year book. Table 1 provides some indicators of SME development in Russia.

As Table 1 suggests, micro and small enterprises with up to 100 employees constitute the bulk of all Russian SMEs. 90% of all SMEs are "micro" enterprises, 9.5% are small firms, and 0.5% are medium firms (Federal State Statistics Service of the Russian Federation, 2019). This is similar to other emerging countries, even though some microenterprises registered as individual entrepreneurs may have sales revenues placing them under "small firm" category. Over 70% of Russian individual entrepreneurs (SME owners) are located in urban areas, and have completed some post-secondary education. 37% of full-time entrepreneurs are female, 63% are male; but gender balance is more evident in the category of part-time entrepreneurs. About 50% of SME legal entities operated in various service industries, 21.2% were involved in manufacturing and construction, and only 2.1% worked in agriculture, forestry and fishery. Unlike Rosstat and Table 1, the website of Federal Taxation Service (https://rmsp.nalog.ru/statistics.html) presents another view on SME industry structure. Ten "most popular" industry codes for all SME categories in the year 2018 include construction and infrastructure development (39%), agriculture (28%), wholesale (20%), private security services (8%), and shipping (5%). While different from Rosstat information, this data set provides another perspective on entrepreneurial activities conducted by Russian SMEs. The website of Federal Taxation Service also illustrates SME geographical distribution: 25% of SMEs are located in Ural, Siberia, and Far East, and 75% are concentrated in European part of Russia. This proportion holds for both legal entities and individual entrepreneurs. Taken together these pieces of information imply that the level of SME development, as well as specific needs of businesses and entrepreneurs vary across industries, regions and types of Russian SMEs.

Adding to Russian national data, the Enterprise Survey reports (www.enterprisesurveys.org) are conducted by the World Bank. Enterprise Surveys present some of the most comprehensive and reliable indicators of Russian business environment and various categories of firms. Furthermore, the information in these reports is collected in collaboration with the European Bank for Reconstruction and Development. Researchers often refer to the Enterprise Survey for Russian Federation as the Business Environment and Enterprise Performance Survey (BEEPS). Country profile and broader data sets for the Russian Federation are available for the years 2009, 2012, and 2019. Researchers collected the data for the most recent survey between January and July of 2019. In total, 1,323 owners and top managers of Russian enterprises (small, medium, and large) participated in this study, which was published in November, 2019. Main indicators presented in 2019 Russian Federation Country Profile illustrate the various components of the business environment through the average firm-level characteristics for all participated firms (World Bank Group, 2019b). The number of firms surveyed in 2019 was much smaller than the 4,220 firms surveyed in 2012, and several indicators were excluded from the most recent data collection. Therefore, it seems reasonable to complement the Enterprise Survey information for 2019 by downloading the full data file, and using some metrics of the Russian business environment collected in 2012. Enterprise Survey data set provides additional comparison by contrasting the Russian Federation to "all upper-middle income countries" and to the regional group of Europe and Central Asia. Table 2 illustrates some firm characteristics and performance indicators used in Russian Federation 2019 country profile.

In addition to country profile, one can browse or download the full data set (World Bank Group, 2019b), and use country-specific information collected in various time points between 2009 and 2019 to calculate and compare national, regional, and world averages. Based on the abovementioned data set, it is safe to conclude that the Russian business environment has improved between 2009 and 2012, and all three types of surveyed enterprises (i.e., large, medium, and small) demonstrated positive changes. For instance, in 2012 survey data annual sales have increased on average by 4.7% for small-size firms and by 3.2% for medium-size firms. The latest information (see Table 2) presents a very different picture: in 2019, SMEs reported declining sales, with "negative growth" between -1.6% and -2.2% for small and medium enterprises, even though employment trend remained positive.

Table 1. Selected statistical data for various categories of Russian SMEs

Indicators	2017	2018
Number of small enterprises*	2754577	2659943
Number of medium enterprises**	13309	13682
Percent of SMEs (legal entities only) operating in:		
• wholesale, retail and auto repairs	n/a	34.8
• construction	n/a	12.7
• professional services	n/a	9
• manufacturing	n/a	8.5
• real estate services	n/a	7.7
• shipping and logistics	n/a	6.5
• agriculture, forestry and fishery	n/a	2.1
• other industries	n/a	18.7
Percent of full-time female individual entrepreneurs	37.0	37.8
Percent of part-time female individual entrepreneurs	45.9	47.2
Percent of full-time male individual entrepreneurs	63.0	62.2
Percent of part-time male individual entrepreneurs	54.1	52.8
Percent of full-time individual entrepreneurs located in urban areas	71.9	71.9
Percent of part-time individual entrepreneurs located in urban areas	77.4	74.9
Percent of full-time individual entrepreneurs located in rural areas	28.1	28.1
Percent of part-time individual entrepreneurs located in rural areas	22.6	25.1
Percent of individual entrepreneurs by level of education:		
• university	27.9	27.4
• college	42.6	42.7
• high school	24.6	24.7
• middle school/ incomplete	4.9	5.1
Percent of individual entrepreneurs by age groups:		
• under 30 years old	15.5	15
• 30-59 years old	78.3	76.7
• 60+ years old	6.2	8.3

* Including micro-enterprises
** Excluding state-owned or municipal enterprises
Source: Federal State Statistics Service of the Russian Federation (2019)

The average level of bribery in Russia was fluctuating. Percentage of firms involved in at least one bribery incident has decreased from 27.3% in 2009 to 14.2% in 2012, and then it bounced back to 26.8% in 2019. This is much higher than 12.3% of firms reporting bribery in Europe and Central Asia. The practice of "informal gifts and payments" intended to speed-up the access to key public services and infrastructure is persistent, too. Gift giving can be viewed as "hidden bribery", and this practice varies for specific services, industries, regions, and firm sizes (World Bank Group, 2019b). For instance, in 2012, up to 47% of Russian SMEs were involved in gift-giving to get an import license, and in 2019, 61% of medium firms reported giving gifts for obtaining a construction permit. On average, gift giving by all surveyed Russian firms occurs two to three times more often than in its regional group of Europe and Central Asia. This unfortunate practice alone indicates that the owners and managers of Russian SMEs get to use some of their social skills more often than their regional counterparts. Perhaps an increase in gift-giving is related to the economic sanctions that were imposed on Russia since 2014. Restrictions on doing business are most painful for smaller enterprises that have limited resources; the sanctions put SMEs at a greater disadvantage compared to large companies. Therefore, it is possible that extensive gift-giving is used as the way to compensate for decreasing sales and keep SMEs operating in difficult economic conditions.

Table 2. Selected Enterprise Survey indicators used in Russian Federation 2019 country profile

Indicators	Russia 2019 - all firms	Russia 2019 -small firms	Russia 2019 -medium firms	Europe and Central Asia	All upper-middle income countries
Firm characteristics:					
• age of the establishment, years	11.4	10.7	12.6	15.6	17.4
• percent of firms with female participation in ownership	34.0	35.8	29.9	32.9	39.5
• percent of firms with a female top manager	24.3	24.6	24.5	18.3	19.3
• proportion of permanent full-time workers who are female (%)	39.2	40.8	36.7	37.5	35.6
• percent of firms offering formal training	11.8	11.0	11.1	33.8	37.4
Performance and trade:					
• real annual sales growth (%)	-1.6	-1.6	-2.2	2.7	0.3
• annual employment growth (%)	3.4	2.2	6.5	3.6	4.2
• percent of firms importing directly or indirectly (at least 10% of sales)	7.1	3.6	17.8	19.2	14.1
• percent of manufacturing firms using material inputs and/or supplies of foreign origin	54.2	51.2	56.6	65.3	63.5

Source: World Bank Group (2019c, p.11)

Tenacious gift-giving also illustrates the on-gong importance of "who you know" versus "what you know" as one of the key factors driving entrepreneurial activity in the Russian Federation (Afanassieva, 2015; Batjargal, 2007; Totskaya, 2015). Over a number of years, the Russian business environment required that firms of all kinds to be involved in extensive networking to ensure their survival and adequate performance. Most of SME networking in Russia is built upon domestic relations and partnerships. On average, Russian firms are less involved in direct and indirect exporting than firms in Europe and Central Asia. The gap is especially noticeable for small firms that are 2 to 3 times less likely to export their goods or services (World Bank Group, 2019b). This fact may imply that Russian entrepreneurs are cautious about expanding their social capital abroad, or perhaps they lack knowledge and skills required to conduct foreign operations.

In addition to the important aspects of macro-environment discussed above, the Enterprise Survey covers topics directly related to social skills and the level of their development. Table 3 presents numerous indicators covering the situation for "Innovation and Technology." The vast majority of Russian SMEs use the Internet as a way to increase their visibility and to improve their interactions with investors, business partners, and customers. Up to 2/3 of surveyed SMEs have their own websites, and over 90% use email communications. In terms of Research and Development activities (R&D), Russian SMEs lag behind on new product and new process development, but they are very active in R&D spending. Taken together, between 2012 and 2019, Russian SMEs have demonstrated well-developed skills and competencies for building communications, using technological innovations, and developing new products and services.

"Gender" and "workforce" are two other topics that cover issues related to social skills. Both 2012 and 2019 Enterprise Surveys provide an account of gender diversity demonstrated by the Russian workforce. According to 2019 data (World Bank Group, 2019b), half of all full-time workers were female; and SMEs reported having 37% to 40% of female employees. The average for female representation in ownership of all enterprises was 34%, and that statistic is above the 33.2% of female representation reported for Europe and Central Asia. In fact, the subgroup of SMEs' female participation in ownership has also improved, ranging between 30% to 35% for medium and small firms. The percentage of SMEs with a female top manager was also higher in Russia than in the region of Europe and Central Asia (24.5% vs. 16 to 19%). Gender diversity implies more complex relations within and between business organizations, and a need to develop additional adaptive approaches to managing SME workforce and operations.

In terms of workforce assessment, Russian SMEs reported that well over 80% of their workers were qualified for the job. This statistic may imply that the existing system of mandatory industry placements provides the required experience and improves practical knowledge of graduates. Only a small portion of SMEs (11%) provided formal training to their employees. However, this practice indicates that attention is being paid to continuous learning and to development of SME human capital. Researchers widely accept that SMEs have limited access to resources in comparison to large firms. Most SMEs are not able to sustain their internal unit dedicated to on-the-job teaching and learning. Therefore, it is safe to conclude that invited consultants completed all formal training reported by Russian SMEs. Alternatively, employees were sent to short courses, seminars, and other professional development events. In either case, continuous learning in SMEs provides some exposure to a broader professional community and helps professionals practice interpersonal communication skills.

Table 3. Innovation and technology: selected indicators for SME subgroup, (%)

	Small firms				Medium firms			
Innovation and technology	**Russia 2012**	**Russia 2019**	**Europe and Central Asia**	**All upper - middle income countries**	**Russia 2012**	**Russia 2019**	**Europe and Central Asia**	**All upper - middle income countries**
Percent of firms having their own website	55.2	53.8	58	36.7	68.8	67.6	71.4	55.4
Percent of firms using e-mail to interact with clients/ suppliers	92.4	n/a*	86.8**	68.8**	97.5	n/a	86.8**	68.8**
Percent of firms that introduced a new product/ service	17.0	6.8	29.7	33.5	31.8	18.3	34.2	42.5
Percent of firms whose new product/service is also new to the main market	65.8	31.2	63	63.7	73.2	61.1	65.5	67.2
Percent of firms that introduced a process innovation	15.5	7.9	17.4	27	29.3	24.1	23.7	36.6
Percent of firms that spend on R&D	7.5	48.5	32.6	19.2	19.3	60.1	39	28.5

* 2019 data is missing

** for all firms, subgroup information is not available

Source: World Bank Group (2019b)

The summary of recent Enterprise Survey findings allows us to make the following conclusions on social skills demonstrated by Russian SMEs:

- **Effective communication skills** are used for direct and indirect interactions with partners, clients and general public.
    - Emails provide a fast and reliable mode of communication.
    - Websites help to create awareness of SMEs' products and services, maintain a positive image, and demonstrate that SMEs are technology-friendly.
- **Ability to innovate** is evident, but Russian SMEs can develop it further.
    - Products and services "new to the market" indicate that SMEs are able to think outside of the box and find and implement new ideas.
    - Investments in R&D improved between 2012 and 2019.
    - Lower product and process innovation may signal low potential for long-term incremental innovation.
- **Skills in building and managing human capital** need more development.
    - Providing additional training to employees and managers may indicate that SMEs are interested in building strong teams.
    - On-the-job training contributes to professional development and therefore improves the quality of the SME workforce.

  - Training programs and activities may indirectly strengthen problem-solving skills, teamworking, and networking abilities.
  - The percentage of firms offering formal training is three to four times below the regional average for all Russian firms, including SMEs. This useful practice needs to be developed at a much larger scale.
- **Networking skills** need improvement.
  - Lack of institutional support strengthens the role of SME social capital and external networking, and Russian SMEs are actively involved in building and maintaining relations with clients, partners, and government officials.
    - Networking helps to develop competencies and personality traits that would allow individuals to navigate and adapt to various social situations, build effective communications, and create positive impressions.
    - Ethical aspects of networking with government officials and the practice of gift-giving are questionable. This kind of networking undermines formally declared efforts to create a more transparent, fair, and enabling institutional environment.
    - Russian SMEs are focused on domestic activities; their level of internationalization is low. SME social networking may be limited to the Russian Federation only.

Success Stories: What are the Common Themes Across Industries?

While the Enterprise Survey collects information from thousands of firms, the data is mostly quantitative. To illustrate the qualitative aspect of social skills in SME development, this study has reviewed "success stories" of individual entrepreneurs and their SMEs. The authors screened non-governmental web resources aimed to provide various business information for semi-structured interviews featuring successful entrepreneurs. The authors collected the purposeful sample of 102 interviews from two Internet sources: www.openbusiness.ru and www.secretmag.ru. The authors chose these online resources as they target entrepreneurs and SME managers and provide them with on-going updates on macro-environment, taxes, and business regulations. Additionally, they discuss new business ideas. Both OpenBusiness.ru and SecretMag.ru had no formal affiliation with government structures. Therefore, they were not aiming to promote specific programs and SME support opportunities provided by federal or regional grants. They both had on-going projects on collecting and disseminating the stories of entrepreneurial success with no particular focus on industry, region, and type of firm. SMEs featured in success stories were also diverse in terms of their age, size, and scope of operations.

The authors only selected the interviews focused on personal stories of entrepreneurs that discussed success factors and challenges of starting and running an SME. We have calculated the share of male and female representation in research sample. Sixty-three interviewees were male (62%) and 39 were female (38%); this proportion is similar to the average female representation in SME ownership reported in the 2019 Enterprise Survey. The interviews were posted on OpenBusiness and SecretMag websites in 2017-2019 years. Entrepreneurs featured in those success stories were running their businesses from one to 19 years, with an average age of SME in the working sample being between seven and eight years. Eighty-eight SMEs, (i.e., 86% of the sample) represented various types of services (e.g., information technology, retail, consulting, vocational training, entertainment, social services, etc.); fourteen SMEs were in manufacturing (for both business to business and business to consumers segments).

The interviews varied from 1,000 to 2,500 words in length, and in many cases, up to 50% of the content was related to entrepreneurs' personal stories, discussion of specific products or services offered by their SMEs, and general business advise. The researchers coded all interviews manually in the original Russian language. A trained research assistant completed the initial coding, and the leading researcher verified the coding. Building on the ideas of Griffin and Care (2015), the authors arranged the content of interviews into two broad categories: ways of thinking and ways of working. Social skills related to ways of thinking included creativity, innovative and critical thinking, learning, problem-solving, and decision-making. Ways of working included skills for communication and collaboration, networking and team-building. In the process of coding, the researchers identified all individual skills and formulated related competencies. The authors articulated ten broad competencies common for all interviews for the ways of thinking, and they articulated nine categories for the ways of working. Table 4 illustrates the competencies derived from success stories of Russian entrepreneurs and their SMEs.

Table 4. What drives SME success: main interview topics and findings

Topics	Ways of Thinking	Ways of Working
Business Idea and Start-up	• Understand your motivation and professional background for starting a business. • Assess the industry and/or customers.	• Active search for investors. • Engage business partners. • Franchising.
Main Challenges	• Assess seasonality of demand. • Consider flexibility of product / service offerings. • Use the low demand period for revising SME operations, training, team-building, etc. • Be ready to combine traditional media, internet, and direct marketing.	• Build the team of professionals. • Test multiple ways of communication with customers.
Keys to Success	• Understand the needs of customers. • Understand business partners and employees. • Pay attention to emerging industry trends. • Find affordable ways to innovate.	• Find a compromise between one's own ideas and the needs of partners and clients. • Be prepared for digitalization of business interactions: use internet platforms, social networks. • Use extensive networking. • Value continuous learning.

All competencies listed in Table 4 were complex (i.e. they combined several social skills). Furthermore, most competencies related to "ways of working" also required skills related to "ways of thinking." The authors identified critical thinking and learning skills as the most important social skills in both categories; they attributed these skills to 10 competencies in total. Communication skills were present in all nine "ways of working" competencies. Collaboration and decision-making skills were part of seven competencies, and problem-solving skills were present six competencies. Creativity and innovative thinking were less frequent among the skills associated with drivers of SME success. Perhaps the relatively lower importance of creativity and innovation can be attributed to the nature of SMEs featured in success stories. The researchers could only classify 16% of all firms as innovative, high-technology firms. All manufacturing SMEs in the sample represented traditional, low-technology small businesses, even though they have produced quality products. Additionally, over 10% of service SMEs were franchisees and followed a pre-set business model. Other SMEs delivered services such as various types of retail, tourism, event management, vocational training, personal consulting, and personal and social services. Table 5 presents the summary of social skills identified for all nineteen competencies in two categories.

Table 5. Summary of social skills associated with competencies of successful SMEs

List of Social Skills	Count of Skills for Ways of Thinking	Count of Skills for Ways of Working	Total
Collaboration		7	7
Communication		9	9
Creativity	3		3
Critical Thinking	8	2	10
Decision Making	3	4	7
Innovative Thinking	2	3	5
Learning	5	5	10
Problem Solving	5	1	6

In addition to the various skills discussed above, the interviewees specifically named negotiation skills as the most crucial skill in building supply and distribution channels, suggesting that SMEs are successful if their clients achieve their desired outcomes. Finding the right employees and managers, being able to delegate responsibilities, and focusing on the future goals were the second most important factors of success. At the same time, this task of putting together an effective team was among the biggest challenges faced by Russian SMEs. Critical importance of human capital, and challenges in developing it were well aligned with the data presented by the Enterprise Survey.

About 2/3 of the interviewees mentioned the ability to think outside of the box and use innovative approaches in delivering traditional products, or introducing the products and services, but these skills were not very evident in the summarized competencies for success. One of the explanations may refer to the somewhat arbitrary use of "creativity" and "innovation" as popular buzz words without providing specific details on what innovative and creative thinking meant for specific SMEs.

Entrepreneurs gave some additional details on communication and collaboration when they discussed their approaches to industry analysis, and to building their professional networks. In addition, interviewees discussed traditional instruments, such as trade fairs, exhibitions, and business forums, as useful for assessing new market trends and competitors. Entrepreneurs used these instruments selectively as finding the right venue or event was time-consuming and expensive, especially for entrepreneurs who did not have enough professional experience and had started their business in a new industry.

Entrepreneurs and SMEs were actively involved in exporting, which interviewees referred to as building their foreign operations upon ethnic connections (diaspora networks). Entrepreneurs used these networking resources to introduce Russian products and services abroad. SMEs that focused on domestic expansion were more likely to introduce franchising as the way of reproducing successful business models and access new regions and markets within Russia. Moreover, resource-sharing, such as technology and promotional costs, were among factors supporting growth through franchising. On a similar note, entrepreneurs with limited experience in their chosen industry referred to franchising as a viable option to fast-start a business and learn from experiences of their franchisor and fellow franchisees. Female entrepreneurs were more willing to consider social outcomes as part of their SME performance. Overall, in both categories, key success factors were related to critical and creative thinking, high adaptability to changing environment, and willingness to learn.

Analysis of "success stories" supports the findings derived from the aggregate data provided by the Enterprise Survey reports for the Russian Federation. Enterprise Survey data indicates that Russian SMEs demonstrate good skills for building effective communications, being innovative and creative in their activities. Qualitative information collected from successful entrepreneurs supports statistical data, and refers to the same social skills related to both thinking and bringing ideas into practice.

FUTURE RESEARCH DIRECTIONS

This chapter has focused on the importance of social skills in entrepreneurship and SME development. The analysis of open-access quantitative and qualitative data has illustrated the context of entrepreneurial activities in the Russian Federation. The main findings confirm that social skills greatly contribute to successful SME development across different institutional settings. These skills are essential for starting a business, overcoming daily challenges, and building relations with employees, partners, and customers. Country-specific environment may affect the toolkit of skills and competencies. For the Russian Federation, the key social skills are related to building supportive networks, extensive negotiating, and finding effective ways to access industry participants, including customers. These skills are meant to overcome environmental deficiencies, such as access to infrastructure, financing, corruption, and bribery. The Enterprise Survey data and success stories of Russian SMEs identify communication, learning, and innovation as essential factors that stimulate growth and increase competitiveness of any SMEs, from small traditional firms to high-technology ventures. Both ways of thinking and ways of working are critical for building a successful business.

More research is needed to measure specific social skills in real business situations and across multiple countries. Testing the impact of experiential learning on young entrepreneurs is another prominent avenue of research. Research widely supports the importance of high-impact entrepreneurship for economic development, yet recommendations for practice are focused on institutional environment. Further research into the impact of social skills on SME performance would benefit entrepreneurs and managers by providing directions for advancement of their business.

CONCLUSION

At the end of 2018, the Russian government introduced a new national project aiming to support entrepreneurship and boost the contribution of Russian SMEs to economic development. Future Russia web portal (https://futurerussia.gov.ru/) is dedicated to all newly introduced national projects, including the one aimed to support entrepreneurship and SME development. The six-year-long project is very ambitious: with a budget of 481.5 billion roubles, it includes five subprojects and annual targets to be achieved (TASS Russian News Agency, 2019). The subprojects aim to provide SMEs with better access to financial resources, help them to grow faster, advance SMEs in agriculture, build an enabling environment, and promote entrepreneurship through the variety of national media.

Russian SMEs need to close the gap in social skills identified through the Enterprise Survey data. Additionally, SMEs need to move from traditional to high-impact, innovative SMEs recognized by GEM as the prominent avenue for entrepreneurship and SME development. The Doing Business 2019 report (World Bank Group,2019a) has listed the Russian Federation among economies with the most improved score for the ease of doing business. The goals set for the national project attempt to build upon this achievement and increase the number of SMEs, their level of technological advancement, and their export potential, etc. The goals of this project include the creation of SME support system, which will inform and train individual entrepreneurs and SMEs on proper ways of doing and expanding their business.

REFERENCES

Abeysekera, I. (2006). Issues relating to designing a work-integrated learning program in an undergraduate accounting degree program and its implications for the curriculum. *Asia Pacific Journal of Cooperative Education*, *7*(1), 7–15.

Acs, Z. J., Estrin, S., Mickiewicz, T., & Szerb, L. (2018). Entrepreneurship, institutional economics, and economic growth: An ecosystem perspective. *Small Business Economics*, *51*(5), 1–14. doi:10.100711187-018-0013-9

Baron, R., & Markman, G. (2000). Beyond social capital: How social skills can enhance entrepreneurs' success. *The Academy of Management Executive*, *14*(1), 106–116. doi:10.5465/ame.2000.2909843

Benzing, C., Chu, H. M., & Kara, O. (2009). Entrepreneurs in Turkey: A factor analysis of motivations, success factors, and problems. *Journal of Small Business Management*, *47*(1), 58–91. doi:10.1111/j.1540-627X.2008.00262.x

Bogoudinova, R. Z., & Kazakova, W. A. (2018) Engineering pedagogy in the system of formation of professional engineering competences. *Engineering Education*, *24*, 45-50.

Bosma, N., & Kelley, D. (2019). *Global Entrepreneurship Monitor 2018/2019 Global Report*. Retrieved from: https://www.gemconsortium.org/report/gem-2018-2019-global-report

Djankov, S., Qian, Y., Roland, G., & Zhuravskaya, E. (2006). Entrepreneurship in China and Russia compared. *Journal of the European Economic Association*, *4*(2/3), 352–365. doi:10.1162/jeea.2006.4.2-3.352

Estrin, S., Mickiewicz, T., Stephan, U., & Wright, M. (2018). Entrepreneurship in emerging markets. In R. Grosse & K. Meyer (Eds.), *The Oxford handbook of management in emerging markets*. Oxford University Press.

Federal Law of July 24, 2007 N° 209-FZ On the development of small and medium entrepreneurship in the Russian Federation. Retrieved from: https://fzrf.su/zakon/maloe-i-srednee-predprinimatelstvo-209-fz/

Federal State Statistics Service of the Russian Federation. (2019). *Maloe i srednee predprinimatelstvo v Rossii 2019* [Small and medium-sized entrepreneurship in Russia 2019]. Retrieved from: https://gks.ru/storage/mediabank/Mal-pred_2019.pdf

Fedko, V. T., & Dolgun, B. G. (2004) Experience in implementing the integrated training system "HTEI-plant". *Engineering Education*, *2*, 146-155.

Gamble, N., Patrick, C. J., & Peach, D. (2010). Internationalising work-integrated learning: Creating global citizens to meet the economic crisis and the skills shortage. *Higher Education Research & Development*, *29*(5), 535–546. doi:10.1080/07294360.2010.502287

Gray, C., & Mabey, C. (2005). Management development: Key differences between small and large businesses in Europe. *International Small Business Journal, 23*(5), 467–485. doi:10.1177/0266242605055908

Griffin, P., & Care, E. (2015). The ATC21S method. In P. Griffin & E. Care (Eds.), *Assessment and teaching of 21st century skills: Methods and approaches* (pp. 3–33). Springer.

Gudov, A. (2013). Combining formal and informal financial sources. *Journal of Chinese Entrepreneurship, 5*(1), 39–60. doi:10.1108/17561391311297879

Jackson, D. (2015). Employability skill development in work-integrated learning: Barriers and best practice. *Studies in Higher Education, 40*(2), 350–367. doi:10.1080/03075079.2013.842221

Kavoura, A., & Koziol, L. (2017). Polish Firms' Innovation Capability for Competitiveness via Information Technologies and Social Media Implementation. In A. Vlachvei, O. Notta, K. Karantininis, & N. Tsountas (Eds.), *Factors Affecting Firm Competitiveness and Performance in the Modern Business World* (pp. 185–214). IGI Global. doi:10.4018/978-1-5225-0843-4.ch007

Khokhlov, N. G. (1994). Directions and forms of integration of education, science and production. *Higher Education in Russia*, 3, 108-112.

Makarona, E., & Kavoura, A. (2019). Redesigning the Ivory Tower: Academic entrepreneurship as a new calling supporting economic growth. *The Malopolska School of Economics in Tarnow Research Papers Collection, 42*(2), 15–26.

Marchese, M., Giuliani, E., Salazar-Elena, J. C., & Stone, I. (2019). *Enhancing SME productivity: Policy highlights on the role of managerial skills, workforce skills and business linkages. OECD SME and Entrepreneurship Papers, No16*. Paris: OECD Publishing; doi:10.1787/825bd8a8-

Morozova, M. V., & Suzdalova, M. A. (2014). Bachelor's programs in technical colleges inn Russia and abroad (empirical research). *Professional Education in Russia and Abroad, 2*(14), 84-88.

Openbusiness.ru: Encyclopedia of Russian business. Available from: https://www.openbusiness.ru/

Orrell, J. (2011). *ALTC good practice report: Work-integrated learning*. Australian Learning and Teaching Council.

Osipov, V., Skryl, T. (2016). The strategic decisions of the modern Russian economic development. *International Business Management, 10*(6), 710-717.

Petrov, N. A., Abramov, D. V., & Michailov, A. M. (2018). Modern state of the institutional environment of the region as a factor influencing the outcome foreign investments. *RUDN* Journal of Economics, 26(2), 283–295

Phillips, L., & Oliveros, J. (2018). Open innovation as means of building social capital. globalization for traditional SMEs. Journal of Strategic Innovation and Sustainability, 13(3), 115-126.

Puffer, S. M., McCarthy, D. J. (2015). Institution building and institutional voids: Can Poland's experience inform Russia and Brazil? *International Journal of Emerging Markets, 11*(1), 18-41.

Rambler Group. (2019). Sekret firmy [Company's secret: online business magazine]. Available from: https://secretmag.ru/

TASS Russian News Agency. (2019*). Natsionalnyj proekt "Maloe i srednee predprinimatelstvo i podderzhka predprinimatelskoj initsiativy" [Medium and small entrepreneurship: National project information* [PDF document]. Retrieved from: https://cdn.tass.ru/data/files/ru/maloe-i-srednee-predprinimatelstvo.pdf

Totskaya, N. (2015). Relational ties in emerging markets: What is their contribution to SME growth? *New England Journal of Entrepreneurship*, *18*(2), 47–60. doi:10.1108/NEJE-18-02-2015-B004

Wales, W. J., Shirokova, G., Sokolova, L., & Stein, C. (2016). Entrepreneurial orientation in the emerging Russian regulatory context: The criticality of interpersonal relationships. *European* Journal of International Management, 10(3), 359–382.

World Bank Group. (2019a) *Doing business 2019. A World Bank flagship report.* Retrieved from: https://www.doingbusiness.org/content/dam/doingBusiness/media/Annual-Reports/English/DB2019-report_web-version.pdf

World Bank Group. (2019b). *Enterprise surveys data for the Russian* Federation. Available from: https://www.enterprisesurveys.org/en/data/exploreeconomies/2019/russia

World Bank Group. (2019c). *Enterprise surveys: what businesses experience. Russian Federation 2019 Country Profile* [PDF document]. Retrieved from: https://www.enterprisesurveys.org/content/dam/enterprisesurveys/documents/country/Russian-Fedaration-2019.pdf

World Bank Group. (2019d) *World Bank Group support for small and medium enterprises: A synthesis of evaluative findings.* Retrieved from: https://ieg.worldbankgroup.org/evaluations/world-bank-group-support-small-and-medium-enterprises-smes

Zamberi, A. S., & Xavier, S. (2012). Entrepreneurial environments and growth: Evidence from Malaysia GEM data. *Journal of Chinese Entrepreneurship*, *4*(1), 50–69. doi:10.1108/17561391211200939

Chapter 5
The Significance of Online Reviews for Hotel Entrepreneurial Success

Zilmiyah Kamble
https://orcid.org/0000-0002-4506-4804
James Cook University, Singapore

Quoc Toan Doan
James Cook University, Singapore

Hoai Nam Nguyen
James Cook University, Singapore

Zeqi Zeng
James Cook University, Singapore

Liao Liao Zihui
James Cook University, Singapore

ABSTRACT

Online reviews have become a significant source of information for travel planning, influencing consumers purchasing decisions and behaviour. This study aims to explore the impacts of online reviews on hotel booking intentions and its significance for entrepreneurial success. It evaluates features from the content of online reviews to understand their impacts upon customers' online booking intention in hotels. Content analysis findings of relevant literature indicates positive causal relationship between online review volume, valence, quality, and online booking intention. There is a significant negative impact of negative online reviews on online booking intention, whilst positive online reviews can gain positive influence. Consumer tend to be more influenced by negative reviews than positive ones. Social media and online travel agent sites are popular internet platforms used. The influence of online reviews on hotel performance is very significant. Hotel entrepreneurs are recommended to pay close attention to online reviews and its impacts and effectively manage reviews.

DOI: 10.4018/978-1-7998-3648-3.ch005

INTRODUCTION

Online reviews create an outstanding phenomenon for consumers who want to get better experience at making a purchase decision. Electronic word of mouth (e-WOM) is perceived as a marketing tool with significant influences on hospitality industry (Li et al., 2009, Kamble et al., 2020). When customers are planning to travel or make a hotel booking, they usually seek for advice from reviews as a tool in decision-making due to unfamiliarity with new destinations (Sparks & Browning, 2011). Consumers now rely on e-WOM as a tool for seeking information about intangible products as hotels, restaurants and online service (Litvin, Goldsmith & Pan, 2008). Easily accessible internet allows customers to access reviews posted by previous customers which helps in purchase decision making. Internet provides suitable platforms for eWOM to operate such as blog, forum, and travel websites. However, the appearance of social media platforms as Facebook, Twitter, and Instagram have brought about new dimensions for online reviews (Xiang & Gretzel, 2010). Consumer can post their reviews online as a part of their reaction when they feel disappointed by a service or betrayed by a hotel (Gregoire & Fisher, 2008). In addition, the motivation for posting review comes from multitude of reasons but the main reason is the concern for other consumers (Hennig-Thurau et al., 2004). As a result, customers freely discuss and exchange their experiences and comments about hotel quality and service to their peers, family, friends and potential customer. Some review website like TripAdvisor are applying algorithms to make online reviews become more trustworthy and reduce biased negative reviews rate (TripAdvisor, 2018). Therefore, the quality of reviews have improved which could increase the trust and confidence from consumers. In general, customers rely on online platforms like social media, forums, blogs and travel website to make purchase decision (Xiang & Gretzel, 2010). Consumers are sensitive and tend to reduce risk by collecting other's opinion regarding online purchase decision because independent third-party opinion are relatively unbiased and uncontrolled from hoteliers (Sparks & Browning, 2011). In addition, advice and recommendation from other customers raise more influence on service and product choice than any public relation tool from hotels (Chen, 2008).

On the other hand, online reviews are giving both challenges and opportunities for hotel entrepreneurs. Study found that e-WOM can help to develop trust and reputation for hoteliers (Riegelsberger, Sasse & McCarthy, 2005). Positive reviews can build good image and sentiment from the customer, whilst negative reviews can harm hotel booking intention and damage hotel image (Sparks & Browning, 2011). Thus, online reviews influence potential customer perception and actions, despite it being positive or negative (Vermeulan & Seegards, 2009). As a result, it is important to conduct research about e-WOM on consumer decision-making due to its ability to influence decisions (Hennig-Thurau et al., 2004). Few studies have investigated the impact of e-WOM on booking intention of customers (Lee, Park & Han, 2008; Phillips et al., 2017; Tsao et al., 2015). However, it's limited and there is need for more in depth studies. In general, online reviews have a strong impact on customer booking intention, although not all reviews influence on customer purchase decision (Sparks & Browning, 2011). This study intends to highlight the impact of online reviews on booking intention. In order to achieve it, this conceptual paper investigates a range of factors such as online review volume, valence, quality, and usefulness that have potential impact on customer purchase decision. It is important for hotel entrepreneurs to understand the influence of communication and online information on consumer choice and the relationship between the online reviews and business performance. Thus, entrepreneurs need to pay closer attention on what is written online about their product and service (Ye, Law & Gu, 2009).

LITERATURE REVIEW

Customers book a hotel based on if they trust their product. Trust is one of the most important factors in determining whether people will shop online. For hotels, the quality of online reviews will greatly affect consumers' willingness to spend (Masouras & Siakalli, 2016). Negative or mixed reviews (including positive and negative) will have greater impact than only have positive reviews (Siakalli & Masouras, 2020). Bad reviews are trusted more easily than good reviews, due to underlying belief that negative reviews does not entail falsification motive. Negative information also spreads faster than positive. In order to further explore the impact of electronic word-of-mouth on consumer purchasing decisions, it is not only essential to establish the influential relationship between online commentaries related factors and consumers' adopted behaviour (Cheung, 2014). The impact of electronic word-of-mouth adoption behaviour on social networks is high. Consumer reviews found in the travel and hotel online communities provide customers with alternative access to previous service experiences, on which they can build beliefs or trust that the company will provide quality service (Pietraru, 2018). It is also believed that potential consumers use online consumer reviews as a way to reduce the risk and uncertainty of purchases. Comments and suggestions from other customers can help determine if you can trust the hotel you are considering. This study investigated how a series of factors have a causal relationship with two key assessments: the likelihood of purchase and the trust of the target entity (Foroudi, 2019). Due to advancement in technology and communication, people have become accustomed to searching for information in all directions through various channels before consumption, and publishing their experiences and feelings after consumption. Internet or electronic word of mouth plays an increasingly important role in people's lives. In this context, this paper takes discusses the influence of online reviews on customers' purchase intentions and communication intentions through various factors such as valence of online reviews, volume of comments, quality of comments and source credibility.

Valence of Online Reviews

A consumer's awareness of any hotel is increased by exposure to online reviews. Valence of overall online reviews for any products or services can be positive or negative, demonstrating the failure or success of that services or products (Spark & Browning, 2011). Negative messages reflect low-quality products resulting in unpleasant consumer attitude, harming brand reputation. Furthermore, negative information trends quickly than the positive information, and the increase in number of negative reviews results in difficulty for the brand (Spark & Browning, 2011). In contrast, positive valence reviews present novel descriptions and pleasant consumer experiences in using the services or products (Vermeulan & Seegars, 2009). Researchers agree that positive reviews can significantly increase hotel bookings after analyzing hotel data (Philips et al, 2017; Ye, Law & Gu, 2009). However, consumers are more influenced by negative information, which can impact their purchasing decision (Higgin & Bargh, 1987; Kamble et al., 2020). Negative reviews have been observed to have more influence than positive one, in changing consumer perception (Lee, Park & Han, 2008). A study conducted on sales of books on amazon indicates that positive valence increases the sales of books, whilst the negative valence reduces sales volume (Chevalier & Mayzlin, 2006). It has also been observed that consumers tend to respond to text-review valence more than rating valance (Tsang & Prendergast, 2009). Negative reviews are perceived as a reflected image, which has more influence on customer attitude than the positive review, resulting in people believing negative review more than positive reviews (Buttle & Bok, 1996).

Volume of Online Reviews

With the ease and accessibility of internet, different platforms, there is a large volume of online reviews. Consumers who come in contact with all this information are always feeling insecure before they decide to buy something online, especially booking online. To ensure they are making the right decision, they want the correct and reliable information, thus they often rely on items that have greater volume of online reviews (Rrustemi & Jashari, 2018). Likewise, according to Zhao, Wang, Guo & Law (2015), volume plays an important role in the attributes of eWOM. The volume of reviews includes the number of reviewers' comments on a particular product or service, which in this article is an online review of hotels. There is a connection between the number of reviews, consumer behaviour and awareness of the product before they decide to purchase. High volume of online reviews lessens the risks, which impacts customers' booking intention. However, the impact of online review volume will be diminished if consumers narrowed their choices as the number of hotels evaluated was nearly the same. This suggests that the number of online reviews only focuses on the early stages of the customers' decision-making process. In this case, the quantity of online reviews turns to the quality of online reviews instead (Gavilan, Avello & Martinez-Navarro, 2018).

Online Reviews and Consumer Behaviour

Customers want to reduce the uncertainty and potential risks of product quality and service by referring to consumer online reviews. Prior studies found that online reviews and customer behaviour have a close association; thus, online reviews have a positive impact on brand choice and consumer attitude (Goldes & Mayzlin, 2004; Park et al., 2007). The perception of consumers on the usefulness and credibility of review is influenced by attributes of the online reviews (Zhang et al., 2018). In the consumer decision making stages, purchase process happens when consumer observe a demand, i.e. when there is a difference between their expected state and current state (Solomon, 2009). Then, consumer start seeking for the information to assist them to make a reasonable choice. There are many sources of information search: personal information (collecting from friends, family, neighbourhoods), commercial search (collecting from advertisement, salesman, showroom), public search (collecting from social media), and deliberate source (collecting from experience and direct learning). The influence of information source on buying decision will be changed on type of product and consumer characteristic (Solomon, 2009, p. 324). After searching information, consumer moves to the next step - alternative assessment. Consumer categorizes products or services to define alternatives, which are suitable for their satisfaction and demand. Product choice is the next stage, in which consumer choose a service and product after alternatives assessment. Consumer tend to narrow down their alternatives by implementing and applying evaluation criteria, product attributes, product signal, familiar brand, and using internet tool as eWOM, travel agencies website, forum, social media (Solomon, 2009, p. 325). Thereafter, consumers will evaluate their outcome for decision purchasing process to address their demand in the beginning.

Theory of Reasoned Action Model

Ajzen and Fishein (1969) came up with the Theory of reasoned action (TRA), which is a social psychological model, used to determine the relationship between consumer intention and behaviour attitude (Hansen, Moller Jensen, Stubbe Solgaard, 2004). The TRA model can help to predict the behavioral intention based on two determinants - attitude and subjective norm (Yousafzai, Foxall, Pallister, 2010). Attitude is individual's own performance of the behavior. Ajzen and Fishbein (1980) wrote individual attitude towards behavioural conduct will determine his or her intention to conduct a certain behaviour. Moreover, personal beliefs, relating to the outcome of performing the behaviour, will determine personal attitude towards conduct the behaviour. As a result, personal intention to perform the behaviour increase when the personal beliefs also increase in positive way (Ajzen & Fishben, 1980).

Subjective norm is a set of beliefs and personal perception toward a behaviour. Therefore, normative social beliefs which are held by a consumer will influence on behavioural intention. For example, a customer's intention to buy the online product might be impacted by consumer's belief about the rightness and their motivation to follow these normative beliefs. According to the TRA theory, consumers are rational in using available information to them (Belleau, Summers, Xu, Pinel, 2007). Social media provide mass information and suggestion regarding service and product for consumer buying decision. Consumers with less experience will refer to their friends and relatives or social network to make behavioural intention. Previous studies used to observe, explain and demonstrate the relationship between attitude toward behaviour by applying knowledge of normative beliefs, intentions and attitudes (Xu, Summers, Belleau, 2004). Therefore, TRA can help to predict the relationship between online reviews and purchase intention. The relationship between personal attitudes and subjective norms influence on their behavioural intention is also noted in many research (Park, 2000). TRA theory also explains how consumers make their buying decision when they faced with many options (Buttle & Bok, 1996). The above discussions can be noted through the theory of reasoned action model as indicated in Figure 1.

Figure 1. Theory of reasoned action model. Source: Fishbein and Ajzen (1980).

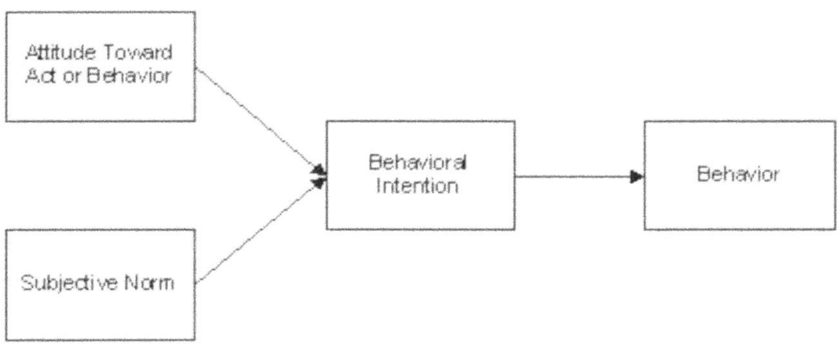

UNDERSTANDING THE NATURE OF INFLUENCE

With the increasing influence of eWOM on their business performance; entrepreneurs should understand eWOM impacts to implement their implication to optimize it as a marketing tools (Tsao et al, 2015). It is clear that online reviews and recommendations can influence potential purchase decision, especially for booking intentions. Furthermore, customers have not yet experienced the intangible service usually seek for review information to reinforce for advance information (Chan et al., 2017). Online reviews can provide massive information about the target hotel which potential customers want to stay. Online review valence has significant impact on hotel booking intention. Positive review can positively influence potential customers' perceptions (Vermeulen & Seegers, 2009). Thus, positive reviews can rise interest and booking intentions in the target hotel (Tsao et al., 2015). When customer reads the positive online reviews, it strongly increases their booking intention regards to the target hotel. Positive reviews can increase potential customers' confidence on their purchase intention. Besides that, young people are mostly positively influenced by positive reviews. Positive comments are conducive to establishing a hotel's social image, establishing a good online reputation, and having a positive impact on consumer booking decisions. Positive comments will create a positive psychological cue for consumers.

In contrast, the negative reviews hurt hotel reputation and image, significantly diminishing booking intentions (Tsao et al., 2015). Therefore, negative reviews damage to hotel booking intentions by discouraging potential customer purchase intentions. Consumers are highly aware of the risks in the booking process, and the decision-making behaviour is cautious and sensitive to the negative information of the hotel. Not all reviews equally influence consumers (Chan et al., 2017; Shan, 2016). The impact of online review valence on booking intention is influenced by different consumer demographic especially their age and job. Not all consumers were affected by negative reviews, especially the middle age group who have their job and frequently travel. Whilst the younger generations who are still studying are more influenced by negative reviews on their booking intentions, making them hesitate to their purchase intentions.

In addition, negative review has stronger negative impact on booking intention than the positive review (Park & Lee, 2009). Potential customers place more emphasis on negative information to their purchase intentions. Therefore, the increasing in negative information will cause unfavourable drawback for hotel business, and spreading quickly on social media. With the gradual popularization of e-commerce, online travel and online hotel bookings have also flourished, and more and more customers tend to browse relevant online reviews before booking online. In the era of such a reputation in the 21st century, online reviews of hotels have gradually become an important indicator for consumers to choose hotels, so the impact of online reviews on hotels cannot be ignored. According to the data, 84% believe that online evaluation is like trusting their friends (Craig, 2017). Since the consumer is unknown to the hotel before booking the hotel, they would like to find more information from all sides to know if the hotel is worthy of trust (Craven, 2016). So, most consumers will assess the online reviews of the hotel and compare the different hotels through comments. It is clear that most people read online reviews because they want to know the hotel's information and previous customer experiences, such as price, location, environment and security. In addition, people tend to be influenced by other people thoughts and opinion. They seek information from other consumers and adapt it to change their purchasing behaviour (Belleau et al., 2007). Thus, other people's opinion influences potential customer decision-making, especially in a community culture. As a special Internet word-of-mouth, online commentary can have a great impact on consumers' consumption behaviour, and it has the characteristics of wide distribution, strong storage, wide range of transmission, variety and influence (Widing, 2003). Customers' spending intentions depend entirely on whether they feel that the conditions of this hotel are suitable for them.

In online reviews, it is evident that detailed and comprehensive reviews will positively impact on hotel booking intention (Cheung, Lee & Rabjohn, 2008). Comprehensiveness and details in online reviews is an important element which engages consumer willingness to read and accept online reviews. Thus, customer tend to need more details and completed information to get specific information to make their booking (Zhao et al., 2015). Therefore, the study of consumer behaviour must adhere to the principle of comprehensiveness (Sparks & Browning, 2011). The higher the quality of the review content, the greater the impact on hotel consumer booking decisions. This indicates that if the content of the review is closely related to the product or service, and the content is authentic and reliable, the language is plain, and the viewpoint is relatively neutral, it will be accepted by consumers (Xu, 2015).

Hotel environmental quality refers to the natural attributes that the hotel provides to meet the needs of guests, usually in terms of meeting the material and spiritual needs of the guests (Zamhury, 2015). Base on this, different services have different quality characteristics, and different quality characteristics meet the different needs of guests. In the same environment, due to the different levels of quality characteristics, the adaptability, that is, the degree of satisfaction of the guests, is not the same. Therefore, whether these natural attributes of the hotel environment can meet the material and spiritual needs of the guests and the degree of satisfaction is the main indicator of the quality of the hotel environment. The so-called satisfaction refers to whether the use value can bring guests physical and mental pleasure and enjoyment. A prime focus was on the clean environment and comfort of the hotel. Service quality, was also a priority in a hotel's service and service attitudes in the online comments before deciding whether to book the hotel. Comments on the Internet was believed to be more relevant, because it was commonly accepted that the more the comments, the more real content it was. Online commentary is a small social collection where people can understand their own perceptions and comments about the same goods and determine their own consumption intentions. In the process of consumption, consumers have various factors that influence their purchasing decisions, such as demand, motivation, attitude, etc. These factors are interrelated and mutually restrictive. Understanding the consumer behaviour, hotel entrepreneurs would be able adopt better strategies.

The volume of reviews for hotel, which is received from customers plays an important role in attribution of a hotel business. Moreover, it indicates the volume of online reviews about that hotel over a certain period and differentiates it amongst other hotels (De Pelsmacker et al, 2018). This study highlights different aspects of customers and that more the online reviews, leads to better business performance, which means that the more the customers are influenced in their booking intentions confirming large volume of online reviews, bring bigger revenue from the big number of customers' bookings (Blal & Sturman, 2014). Online reviews raises customer awareness providing information and hint customers about the number customers, who visited and stay in the hotels (Zhao et al, 2015). Besides, due to the pressure to comply with a peer group, it means that consumers are most likely to follow the opinions of the majority of others. Therefore, the behaviours of customers can obey the crowd's actions as a function of choice. Moreover, this helps them rationalize their decision to buy or make a reservation by telling themselves that there are many people also book a room at the hotels like them.

IMPLICATIONS FOR ENTREPRENEURS

Hotel online reviews provide a simple, effective and convenient way for consumers to better understand hotels, products and services. Although consumer behaviour is a discipline based on observation and measurement of practice, it still needs to be tested in marketing activities, so as to better guide the marketing planning of enterprises (Antonio, 2019. By reading the experiences of other consumers to understand the quality of service and the reputation of the hotel, it is conducive to foster the trust and loyalty of consumers. At the same time, online reviews also provide a lot of information to the hotel itself, becoming an important feedback mechanism for consumers. As an emerging information sharing platform and network communication means, entrepreneurs can use it to effectively disseminate corporate information, collect and organize consumer information from websites at a low cost, and help to manage customer relationships and provide comprehensive services. Technological innovations and social media can support especially small to medium scale enterprises to achieve the needed revenue and competitive edge (Kavoura & Kaziol, 2017). Hotel entrepreneurs hoping to attract customers more seriously, need to arrange some activities that can attract the public during some holiday cycles, and always pay attention to customer feedback. Some people's feedback can help them understand the direction the hotel needs to improve. Entrepreneurs need to achieve more positive reviews, which will attract unknown customers seeking opinions of experience from others. The study found that factors such as review valence, volume of comments, quality of comments, and source credibility can significantly affect consumers' perceptions of the usefulness and credibility of online reviews, which in turn will not only positively influence consumers' online comments. As an effective low cost tool, online platforms need to be closely managed to increase revenue and brand reputation. Hotel entrepreneurs can use diverse methods to increase profitability using technology or create awareness if it is a social enterprise and learn from examples from other fields like the way universities contribute (Kavoura & Anderson, 2016; Makarona & Kavoura, 2019)

CONCLUSION

In general, there is a significant impact of online reviews on booking intention. This paper investigate that consumers usually read online reviews before they book the hotel because they want to get more information and other people experiences prior to make booking decision. In addition, the female customer prefers to read more online review to make sure the information is correct. Studies have shown that the quality of the content of the reviews has a significant positive effect on hotel booking decisions. At the same time, the more volume of comments, the higher the popularity of the hotel, the greater the possibility of consumer booking. Moreover, positive reviews tend to have positive impact to increase booking intentions, whilst negative comments played a negative role to reduce consumer booking decisions. With regards to comparing review valence, negative reviews were more influential than positive reviews. Realizing the impact of online reviews on booking intention is necessary for entrepreneurs to implement suitable implication to mitigate its negative impact and gain competitive advantage. Although e-WOM will bring both advantageous and disadvantageous information for entrepreneurs, they should optimize online reviews as a marketing tool and pay attention to responses and negative reviews online.

REFERENCES

Ajzen, I., & Fishein, M. (1969). The Prediction of Behavioral Intentions in a Choice Situation. *Journal of Experimental Social Psychology*, *5*(4), 400–416. doi:10.1016/0022-1031(69)90033-X

Ajzen, I., & Fishein, M. (1980). *Understanding attitudes and predicting social behavior*. Prentice-Hall.

Antonio, N., de Almeida, A., & Nunes, L. (2019). Hotel booking demand datasets. *Data in Brief*, *22*, 41–49. doi:10.1016/j.dib.2018.11.126 PMID:30581903

Belleau, B. D., Summers, T. A., Xu, Y., & Pinel, R. (2007). Theory of reasoned action: Purchase intention of young consumers. *Clothing & Textiles Research Journal*, *25*(3), 244–257. doi:10.1177/0887302X07302768

Blal, I., & Sturman, M. C. (2014). The differential effects of the quality and quantity of online reviews on hotel room sales. *Cornell Hospitality Quarterly*, *55*(4), 365–375. doi:10.1177/1938965514533419

Buttle, F., & Bok, B. (1996). Hotel marketing strategy and the theory of reasoned action. *International Journal of Contemporary Hospitality Management*, *8*(3), 5–10. doi:10.1108/09596119610115943

Chan, I. C. C., Lam, L. W., Chow, C. W. C., Fong, L. H. N., & Law, R. (2017). The effect of online reviews on hotel booking intention: The role of reader-reviewer similarity. *International Journal of Hospitality Management*, *66*, 54–65. doi:10.1016/j.ijhm.2017.06.007

Chen, Y. (2008). Herd behavior in purchasing books online. *Computers in Human Behavior*, *24*(5), 1977–1992. doi:10.1016/j.chb.2007.08.004

Cheung, C. M., Lee, M. K., & Rabjohn, N. (2008). The impact of electronic word-of-mouth: The adoption of online opinions in online customer communities. *Internet Research*, *18*(3), 229–247. doi:10.1108/10662240810883290

Cheung, R. (2014). The influence of electronic word-of-mouth on information adoption in online customer communities. *Global Economic Review*, *43*(1), 42–57. doi:10.1080/1226508X.2014.884048

Chevalier, J. A., & Mayzlin, D. (2006). The Effect of Word of Mouth on Sales Online Book Reviews. *JMR, Journal of Marketing Research*, *43*(3), 345–354. doi:10.1509/jmkr.43.3.345

Craig, B. (2017). *84 Percent of People Trust Online Reviews As Much As Friends. Here's How to Manage What They See*. Retrieved from https://www.inc.com/craig-bloem/84-percent-of-people-trust-online-reviews-as-much-.html

Craven, M. (2016). *For hotels, online reviews really matter to the bottom line*. Retrieved from https://www.wsj.com/articles/for-hotels-online-reviews-really-matter-to-the-bottom-line-1479477602

De Pelsmacker, P., van Tilburg, S., & Holthof, C. (2018). Digital marketing strategies, online reviews and hotel performance. *International Journal of Hospitality Management*, *72*, 47–55. doi:10.1016/j.ijhm.2018.01.003

Foroudi, P. (2019). Influence of brand signature, brand awareness, brand attitude, brand reputation on hotel industry's brand performance. *International Journal of Hospitality Management*, *76*, 271–285. doi:10.1016/j.ijhm.2018.05.016

Gavilan, D., Avello, M., & Martinez-Navarro, G. (2018). The influence of online ratings and reviews on hotel booking consideration. *Tourism Management*, *66*, 53–61. doi:10.1016/j.tourman.2017.10.018

Godes, D., & Mayzlin, D. (2004). Using online conversations to study word-of-mouth communication. *Marketing Science*, *23*(4), 545–560. doi:10.1287/mksc.1040.0071

Gregoire, Y., & Fisher, R. J. (2008). Customer betrayal and retaliation: When your best customers become your worst enemies. *Journal of the Academy of Marketing Science*, *36*(2), 247–261. doi:10.100711747-007-0054-0

Hansen, T., Møller Jensen, J., & Stubbe Solgaard, H. (2004). Predicting online grocery buying intention: A comparison of the theory of reasoned action and the theory of planned behavior. *International Journal of Information Management*, *24*(6), 539–550. doi:10.1016/j.ijinfomgt.2004.08.004

Hennig-Thurau, T., Gwinner, K. P., Walsh, G., & Gremler, D. D. (2004). Electronic word-of-mouth via consumer-opinion platforms: What motivates consumers to articulate themselves on the internet? *Journal of Interactive Marketing*, *18*(1), 38–52. doi:10.1002/dir.10073

Kamble, Z., Namnuad, S., Phuong, N. H., Tuan, N. D., & Hanh, N. H. (2020). Review of Social Media's Influence on Airbnb Accommodation's Booking Intention. In A. Kavoura, E. Kefallonitis, & P. Theodoridis (Eds.), *Strategic Innovative Marketing and Tourism. Springer Proceedings in Business and Economics*. Springer. doi:10.1007/978-3-030-36126-6_79

Kavoura, A., & Andersson, T. (2016). Applying Delphi method for strategic design of social entrepreneurship. *Library Review*, *65*(3), 185–205. doi:10.1108/LR-06-2015-0062

Kavoura, A., & Koziol, L. (2017). Polish Firms' Innovation Capability for Competitiveness via Information Technologies and Social Media Implementation. In A. Vlachvei, O. Notta, K. Karantininis, & N. Tsountas (Eds.), *Factors Affecting Firm Competitiveness and Performance in the Modern Business World* (pp. 185–214). IGI Global. doi:10.4018/978-1-5225-0843-4.ch007

Lee, J., Park, D., & Han, I. (2008). The effect of negative online consumer reviews on product attitude: An information processing view. *Electronic Commerce Research and Applications*, *7*(3), 341–352. doi:10.1016/j.elerap.2007.05.004

Li, X., Pan, B., Zhang, L., & Smith, W. W. (2009). The effect of online information search on image development: Insights from a mixed-methods study. *Journal of Travel Research*, *48*(1), 45–57. doi:10.1177/0047287508328659

Litvin, S. W., Goldsmith, R. E., & Pan, B. (2008). Electronic word-of-mouth in hospitality and tourism management. *Tourism Management*, *29*(3), 458–468. doi:10.1016/j.tourman.2007.05.011

Makarona, E., & Kavoura, A. (2019). Redesigning the Ivory Tower: Academic entrepreneurship as a new calling supporting economic growth. *The Malopolska School of Economics in Tarnow Research Papers Collection*, *42*, 15–26. doi:10.25944/znmwse.2019.02.1526

Masouras, A., Siakalli, M., & Papademetriou, C. (2016). *E-marketing in the Hotel Industry: Marketing Mix Strategies*. Springer International Publishing.

Park, C., & Lee, T. M. (2009). Information direction, website reputation and eWOM effect: A moderating role of product type. *Journal of Business Research*, *62*(1), 61–67. doi:10.1016/j.jbusres.2007.11.017

Park, D.-H., Lee, J., & Han, I. (2007). The effect of on-line consumer reviews on consumer purchasing intention: The moderating role of involvement. *International Journal of Electronic Commerce*, *11*(4), 125–148. doi:10.2753/JEC1086-4415110405

Park, H. S. (2000). Relationships among attitudes and subjective norms: Testing the theory of reasoned action across cultures. *Communication Studies*, *51*(2), 162–175. doi:10.1080/10510970009388516

Phillips, P., Barnes, S., Zigan, K., & Schegg, R. (2017). Understanding the impact of online reviews on hotel performance: An empirical analysis. *Journal of Travel Research, 56*(2), 235–249. doi:10.1177/0047287516636481

Pietraru, R. N., Banu, A., Mocanu, Ş., & Saru, D. (2018). Low cost technologies for awarness and early warning in conditions of severe weather. *The International Scientific Conference eLearning and Software for Education, 2*, 349-354.

Riegelsberger, J., Sasse, M. A., & McCarthy, J. D. (2005). The mechanics of trust: A framework for research and design. *International Journal of Human-Computer Studies, 62*(3), 381–422. doi:10.1016/j.ijhcs.2005.01.001

Rrustemi, V., & Jashari, F. (2018). Impact of online reviews in online booking – case study capital city of kosovo. *EuroEconomica, 37*(1) Retrieved from https://search-proquest-com.elibrary.jcu.edu.au/docview/2118384814?accountid=16285

Shan, Y. (2016). How credible are online product reviews? The effects of self-generated and system-generated cues on source credibility evaluation. *Computers in Human Behavior, 55*, 633–641. doi:10.1016/j.chb.2015.10.013

Siakalli, M., & Masouras, A. (2020). Factors That Influence Tourist Satisfaction: An Empirical Study in Pafos. In *Strategic Innovative Marketing and Tourism* (pp. 459–466). Springer. doi:10.1007/978-3-030-36126-6_51

Solomon, M. R. (2009). *Consumer behavior: Buying, having, and being* (8th ed.). Pearson Prentice Hall.

Sparks, B. A., & Browning, V. (2011). The impact of online reviews on hotel booking intentions and perception of trust. *Tourism Management, 32*(6), 1310–1323. doi:10.1016/j.tourman.2010.12.011

TripAdvisor. (2018). *How Does TripAdvisor Catch Fake Reviews?* Retrieved from https://www.tripadvisor.com/TripAdvisorInsights/w3688

Tsang, A., & Prendergast, G. (2009). Is a "star" worth a thousand words? *European Journal of Marketing, 43*(11/12), 1269–1280. doi:10.1108/03090560910989876

Tsao, W., Hsieh, M., Shih, L., & Lin, T. M. Y. (2015). Compliance with eWOM: The influence of hotel reviews on booking intention from the perspective of consumer conformity. *International Journal of Hospitality Management, 46*, 99–111. doi:10.1016/j.ijhm.2015.01.008

Vermeulen, I. E., & Seegers, D. (2009). Tried and tested: The impact of online hotel reviews on consumer consideration. *Tourism Management, 30*(1), 123–127. doi:10.1016/j.tourman.2008.04.008

Widing, R. E. (2003). *Customer behaviour: Consumer behaviour and beyond.* Thomson Learning.

Xu, Y., Summers, T., & Belleau, B. (2004). Who buys American alligator? Predicting purchase intention of a controversial product. *Journal of Business Research, 57*(10), 1189–1198. doi:10.1016/S0148-2963(02)00327-2

Xu, Z. (2015). Online comment-based hotel quality automatic assessment using improved fuzzy comprehensive evaluation and fuzzy cognitive map. *IEEE Transactions on Fuzzy Systems*, *23*(1), 72–84. doi:10.1109/TFUZZ.2015.2390226

Ye, Q., Law, R., & Gu, B. (2009). The impact of online user reviews on hotel room sales. *International Journal of Hospitality Management*, *28*(1), 180–182. doi:10.1016/j.ijhm.2008.06.011

Yousafzai, S. Y., Foxall, G. R., & Pallister, J. G. (2010). Explaining internet banking behavior: Theory of reasoned action, theory of planned behavior, or technology acceptance model? *Journal of Applied Social Psychology*, *40*(5), 1172–1202. doi:10.1111/j.1559-1816.2010.00615.x

Zamhury, N. (2015). The praxis of langkawi's sustainable regeneration strategy through eco-tourism. *Procedia: Social and Behavioral Sciences*, *170*, 49–57. doi:10.1016/j.sbspro.2015.01.014

Zhang, K. Z. K., Xu, H., Zhao, S., & Yu, Y. (2018). Online reviews and impulse buying behavior: The role of browsing and impulsiveness. *Internet Research*, *28*(3), 522–543. doi:10.1108/IntR-12-2016-0377

Zhao, X., Wang, L., Guo, X., & Law, R. (2015). The influence of online reviews to online hotel booking intentions. *International Journal of Contemporary Hospitality Management*, *27*(6), 1343–1364. doi:10.1108/IJCHM-12-2013-0542

KEY TERMS AND DEFINITIONS

Behavioural Intention: Determination and willingness to act on a particular behavior.

e-WOM: Electronic word of mouth is a marketing tool that is free and can be widely shared and can be quite useful for SMEs.

Online Booking Intentions: The determination and willingness to book a product or service online.

Online Reviews: Evaluations posted online on diverse platforms by consumers who have used or experienced a product or services.

Subjective Norm: Beliefs or opinions of influences, peer pressures and peer approval to perform or not to perform a specific behavior.

Valence: Mental worthiness allocated by a person to an outcome, task, person, product or service based on its perceived appeal.

Chapter 6
Enhancing Entrepreneurship:
The Greek National Electronic Public Procurement System – Internal Customer Opinions

Nikolaos G. Bitzidis
International Hellenic University, Greece

Sotirios G. Dimitriadis
International Hellenic University, Greece

George I. Karavasilis
International Hellenic University, Greece

Evangelos C. Kehris
International Hellenic University, Greece

Vasiliki G. Vrana
International Hellenic University, Greece

ABSTRACT

One of the major roles of governments is to create a favorable business environment for fostering entrepreneurial activities, including good infrastructure and a culture that encourages the adoption of technologies. In such a policy context, the Greek National Electronic Public Procurement System (ESIDIS) was developed. The use of ESIDIS is mandatory for the employees, and its success depends on users' satisfaction. The chapter investigates the factors influencing employees' satisfaction when using the system. Perceived usefulness, perceived ease-of-use, perceived risk, and willingness to learn were investigated using empirical research. Structural equation modeling was used for the analysis of the data. Perceived usefulness has the most significant role in determining user satisfaction while risks importance is diminished when users understand the usefulness of the system for their job performance. Managers and policymakers should take these factors into consideration in order to improve users' satisfaction and consequently maximize the added value of the system for the entrepreneurs.

DOI: 10.4018/978-1-7998-3648-3.ch006

INTRODUCTION

Public procurement is an internal part of G2B processes (Panayiotou, Gayialis, & Tatsiopoulos, 2004) and can be defined as the "acquisition (through buying or purchasing) of goods and services by government or public organizations" (Hommen & Rolfstam, 2009). The public procurement process requires the contracting authorities -all levels of government and public agencies – to call public tenders, usually when the value of the procurement exceeds a certain threshold and wait for suppliers' responses. After receiving the suppliers' responses, a negotiation process between the contracting authorities and the interested suppliers for the acquisition of goods or services (Kastanioti et al., 2012; Klabi, Mellouli & Rekik, 2014). Governments adopt different regulations for procurement processes and each year spend billions in procurement (Klabi, Mellouli & Rekik, 2014). Governments, on one side aim at minimizing cost through maximum competition, protecting public fund reducing and eliminating corruption and increasing transparency, while suppliers, on the other side, aim at winning the contract and maximizing their profits (Concha, Porrúa, & Pimenta, 2010). Thus, governments are associated with entrepreneurial activity, providing invaluable help to entrepreneurs (Kavoura & Andersson, 2016; Makarona & Kavoura, 2019).

Drucker (1993, p.35) defined entrepreneurship as "...change that always provides the opportunity for the new and different. Systematic innovation therefore consists in the purposeful and organized search for changes, and in the systematic analysis of the opportunities such changes might offer for economic or social innovation". Entrepreneurship is an art of recognizing a business opportunity, mobilizing resources to exploit that opportunity (Mufutau &Ajetomobi, 2016) and is commonly associated with choice-related issues (UN, 2005). Growth and expansion are key goals for entrepreneurs and public procurement may be used as a lever to drive to economic growth and prosperity.

Information technology is a critical enabler of the redefinition of organizations and plays a critical role in procurement process and in improving information flows across supply chains (Handfield, Jeong & Choi, 2018). It is considered as the most feasible and promising path to be followed by public administration in the acquisition of goods and services for the public sector. Using information technology the public sector may create efficient workflows and processes, eliminating the existing procurement inefficiencies without disrupting its primary business activities (Masika, 2013). Information technology supports internal processes and involves business partners while it can offer efficient distribution of information, increased transparency and better control, smoother and faster process flow, shortening the order fulfillment cycle time, decentralization of tasks and decisions, reduction in administrative costs and lowering price paid for products (Praveen & Khaliq, 2018; Tanner, Wölfle & Quacde, 2006). Furthermore, information technology can play an important role to reduce corruption by promoting good governance (Bertot, Jaeger & Grimes, 2010), enhancing relationships between government employees and the other stakeholders in the procurement process, monitoring and controlling activities of the government employees and reducing potentiality of corrupt behaviors. (Neupane et al., 2012). Nowadays many developing and developed countries have focused on e-procurement systems as a key tool to reduce the corruption by opening competition in government procurement processes to the public (Neupane et al., 2012). Many OECD countries engage artificial intelligence and block-chain technology in public procurement process to share transaction information (OECD, 2019a). Block-chain technology in e-procurement may be use to (i) track full-cycle procurement workflows to prevent record tampering; (ii) create interoperable supplier profiles across fragmented e-procurement systems to reduce asymmetry of information in purchasing or pre-tender assessment; and (iii) "decentralize" bid evaluation to disincentivise bribery and biased decision-making" (Yang, 2019 p. 1). Therefore, use of block chain solutions offer immutability and decentralization, single source of truth for all parties in the value chain, security in transactions, more transparency and increased accuracy of supply chain due to diligence information (OECD, 2019a).

E-procurement can be defined as "a comprehensive process in which organizations use IT systems to establish agreements for the acquisition of products or services (contracting) or purchase products or services in exchange for payment (purchasing)" (Gunasekarana & Ngai, 2008). The emergence of Internet technologies and public e-procurement systems facilitate the effective delivery of public goods and services, enhance procurement efficiency, transparency and accountability, cut operational costs all across the supply chain, and also increase non-discrimination, equal treatment, open access and effective competition (Arrowsmith, 2001; Thai, 2009; Vaidyanathan & Devaraj, 2008), making thus easier for enterprises of any size to access public procurement opportunities and to perform better in public procurement markets by removing barriers to their participation (OECD, 2019b). Technological innovation and information technologies that support business and managerial activities are important factors affecting the global competitiveness and profitability of the companies (Kavoura & Koziol, 2017).

Public Procurement is an important part of the economy accounting for 13% of GDP in OECD countries and 1/3 of overall government expenditures. Governments around the world spend $9.5 trillion for procuring (OECD, 2016). Public procurement is also an important part of the European Union economy (CMS, 2019). Every year, over 250,000 public authorities in the European Union spend around €2 trillion per year, accounting for 14% of GDP on the purchase of supplies, services and works (European Union, 2019). However, public procurement is vulnerable to corruption (Yang, 2019) both at the national and sub-national levels (OECD, 2016). Worldwide corruption drains are estimated at 20-25% of national public procurement budgets (OECD, 2016) and within the European Union, corruption is estimated to cost €120 billion per year (European Commission, 2014). Corruption in public procurement damages trust in governments, limits competition and hurts development and public welfare (Yang, 2019). Kochanova et al (2016) using a cross-country data set on e-government systems, investigated whether e-procurement adoption improves public procurement competitiveness, and reduction of corruption. They found that use of e-procurement systems can help improve government capacity, but the impact is stronger in more developed countries. The number of firms attempting to secure a government contract is increasing with e-procurement implementation only in countries with higher levels of development and better quality institutions. According to their findings there is no systematic relationship between e-procurement and bureaucratic corruption. Public procurement in the Western Balkan region is characterized by "deficiencies in planning and tender preparation, and inefficient follow-up and monitoring" (European Court of Auditors, 2018 p.62). Regarding e-procurement in western Balkans and Eastern Europe, in 2016, only three out of thirteen countries had not yet implementing e-Procurement. Countries are mostly moving towards the direction of e-procurement though at different stages (Ferrand, 2019).

The public procurement in Greece is characterized by its singular complexity among both legal and institutional structures (European Commission, 2016), manual activities (Tsagkaris et al. 2010), heavy paperwork, poor service delivery, complicated bureaucracy (Karafoti, 2013), delays in making decisions (Koutsouris & Maglavera, 2006) and lack of transparency and accountability and is thus prone to fraud and corruption (European Commission, 2016; Panagiotidou & Intzesiloglou2016). Within the e-government framework, the General Secretariat of Commerce of the Greek Ministry of Development in cooperation with the section of Industrial Management and Operational Research of the National Technical-University of Athens, implemented an integrated information system, named National Electronic Public Procurement System (ESIDIS), aiming at acquiring direct supplies of goods and services for the public sector (Panayiotou, Gayialis & Tatsiopoulos, 2004).

The introduction of an e-procurement system is an important government decision since it decreases corruption practices and improves transparency, while at the same time it increases the productivity of daily procurement activities, attracts new suppliers to do business with the government and facilitates SMEs access to public procurement (Concha et al., 2012; Hellenic Republic, 2018). Despite the importance of a government e-procurement system this subject seems to be to a large extent understudied by the researchers and thus a knowledge gap has been created (Vaidya et al., 2006). This is especially for Greece where little if any limited research efforts on this issue exist. Platis, Karafyllis & Kaoura (2019) studied the implementation of e-procurement systems in Greek public hospitals. Findings provide evidence that the majority of Greek public hospitals does not conduct their procurement through ESIDIS, thus reducing transparency. Furthermore, ESIDIS is not used in the most efficient way, probably due to technical malfunctions. Savvas (2018) investigated the attitudes of internal (i.e. public employees) and external (i.e. businesses) ESIDIS users. According to his findings the majority of the users (more than 65%) find ESIDIS platform easy to use, although 19% of users find it difficult to use. Most users seem to be concerned with technical problems, since they reported that the system "hangs and/or is slow", "requires reloading quite often", "shut downs frequently". Despite the concerns and difficulties, a very high degree of acceptance and use was recorded.

The success of e-government projects dependents not only on the government support but also on users' willingness to accept and adopt them. Usually, governments do not take into consideration users' opinions and needs and do not examine issues that increase users' willingness to adopt the systems. The design of such information systems and services follow a "top-down" approach, based on their understanding of what users' needs. (Karavasilis et al., 2016). As a result, quite often government information systems fail to consider adequately users' needs. What is more, in public procurement sector, officers lack the appropriate skills and specialized knowledge to provide value for money and take into account strategic considerations (Licenji, 2015).

User satisfaction is the most widely used measure of success for an information system (Tu, Fang and Lin, 2012). Taken all the above into consideration together with the fact that limited research exist on ESIDIS (Klatis, Karafyllis & Kaoura, 2019; Savvas, 2018), this paper aims at contributing at the study of ESIDIS and investigates the factors that affect internal users' satisfaction from ESIDIS. Well established constructs from previous models and studies such as *usefulness, ease-of-use, risk perception* and *willingness-to-learn,* are used in this investigation. The conceptual model is tested using the Structural Equation Modeling (S.E.M.) analysis. The paper is structured as follows: Firstly, the definitions of the constructs and the conceptual model are discussed. Next, the methodology, model estimation and the measurement model are presented. Finally, the conclusions together with the limitations of this work for future research are discussed.

NATIONAL ELECTRONIC PUBLIC PROCUREMENT SYSTEM (ESIDIS)

The National Electronic Public Procurement System (ESIDIS), Supplies and Services is the central electronic website for public procurement in Greece. ESIDIS aims at simplifying the procurement process and supporting stakeholders (contracting authorities, suppliers, supervisors, citizens). ESIDIS was initially introduced in 2013 by Law 4155 which set out its operational framework and its original timetable and was amended by relative legislation in the following year. As of 2016 and according to Law 4412/2016, its use is mandatory by the Contracting Authorities are obliged when the estimated value of contracts is exceeding sixty thousand (60,000) euros, excluding VAT. The legislation introduced aimed at modernizing the tendering process, bring significant economic benefits, streamline public procurement procedures, cause significant changes in the way the administration operates, and influence all Greek government agencies and their suppliers.

ESIDIS is an information system through which all the bodies of the Public Sector, carry out all the steps involved in the entire procurement process. The system supports activities such as the publication of a tender notice, the submission of bids by candidates, the staged assessment of the bids, the award of the contract and the conclusion of the contract. The system also monitors the execution of the contracts and introduces procedures such as electronic ordering, electronic pricing and electronic payment. Finally, the system, allow public authorities to implement new contract award procedures, such as e-auctions, dynamic purchasing systems, competitive dialogues and framework agreements.

A total of 23,625 tenders have been published from 1,242 entities and a total of 66,891 bids have been submitted by 9,928 economic operators since the launch of ESIDIS until the end of 2018. The monthly average number of tenders is 653 and their monthly average value is € 270 million. In 2018, the savings for the public entities was estimated to be 10.2% of the initial budget of the procurements (Ministry of Development and Investments, 2019).

The Contracting Authorities / Contracting Entities registered with the right of access to ESIDIS are a total of 1,495 (Table 1.)

Table 1. Contracting authorities / contracting entities registered with the right of access to ESIDIS

Contracting Authorities / Contracting Entities	Total	Percentage
Central Administration	252	17%
Local Administration	578	39%
Healthcare Providers	217	14%
Other Entities	448	30%

Source: Ministry of Development and Investments, 2019

Regarding Internal Users' Profiles little is known. They are public servants working for the Contracting Authorities / Contracting Entities. Savvas (2018) mentioned that more than 65% of Contracting Authority users are certified users of the system, trained by the National Center for Public Administration and Local Government seminars and/or by Private Training Companies. A significant percentage of 83% of them think they should be better trained by attending more National Center for Public Administration and Local Government seminars.

CONCEPTUAL BACKGROUND AND HYPOTHESIS FORMULATION

Internal User Satisfaction

Government e-procurement is becoming quickly an essential part of national e-government programs in many counties (Concha et al., 2012) and legislation has been introduced according to which it is mandatory for all procurement and finance operations related to acquisition of goods, works and services acquired by public sector to be conducted through online platforms. The implementation of government e-procurement systems requires resources, specialized skills and users' training programs, well-coordinated change management practices and good governance (Rotich & Okello, 2015) as it comes with organizational challenges such as restructuring difficulties and resistance to change (Corsi, 2006). In case of mandatory use of a public e-procurement system, user satisfaction is a very important indicator of success (Braun, 2013). User satisfaction can be defined as the sum of experiences that user acquires from his/her interaction with the technology over time (Au et al. 2008).

Success of information systems depends on user satisfaction and individual performance. In this vein the impact of e-procurement adoption on internal users' perceptions of service quality was investigated by Croom & Johnston (2003). They compared users' perceptions of pre-electronic and post-electronic procurement processes for two categories of supply: computer consumables and stationery. Findings showed that users expressed 'delight' in many aspects of the service provision relating to the design characteristics of the e-procurement system, but dissatisfaction with issues concerning the actual system delivery. Kipkorir & Omwenga (2015) surveyed internal users of the e-procurement system in the County Government of Bomet to investigate the influence of technology on the progress. Their findings indicate that technology, environment, and organizational culture greatly influence the adoption of the e-procurement system. Costs, quality, risks, benefits and success factors were identified as the cornerstones of e-procurement adoption factors by government officials who were dealing with e-procurement activities nationwide in Indonesia (Napsah, 2016). Sharabati et al. (2015) investigated the impact of content, usability and processing on end-user satisfaction and the relationships between end-user satisfaction and individual end-user performance. They gathered data from 432 end-users of the ePerolehan, the Malaysian government e-procurement system. The findings provide strong support that processing, content and usability significantly affect end-user satisfaction, while the higher levels of end-user satisfaction lead to improved individual performance.

Taking into consideration the aforementioned studies, user satisfaction is identified as a critical determinant of the success of information systems, especially in case of mandatory usage of information systems like a public e-procurement system. As such, the paper uses user satisfaction, and investigates factors that influence users' satisfaction.

Usability and Ease of Use

Attitudes and intentions are important factors in the adoption of computer technologies (Bagozzi et al., 1992). The Technology Acceptance Model (TAM) is a parsimonious and robust model (Gao & Bai 2014) with strong behavioral elements (Bagozzi et al., 1992) that attempts to explain user's future behavior after a very brief period of interaction with a system (Han & Jin, 2009). According to TAM, a person's actual system usage is mostly influenced by his/her behavioral intentions toward usage and is influenced by the *perceived usefulness* and *perceived ease-of-use* of the system. *Perceived ease-of-use* is defined as "*the degree to which a person believes that using a particular system would be free of physical and mental effort*" and *perceived usefulness* of the system as "*the degree to which a person believes that using a particular system would enhance his or her job performance*" (Davis 1980, p. 320). *Perceived usefulness* is influenced by *perceived ease-of-use* because the easier a system is to use, the more useful it can be (Davis et al., 1989). In many cases, organizations mandate for employees to use technology systems for specific organizational tasks (Koh et al., 2010). Thus, users rarely have complete volitional control over their decision to use or not use the system (Bhattacherjee et al., 2017). In case that the use of a mandatory system is troublesome, users will probably be disappointed as the effort to use the system would be relatively high (Sharabati et al., 2005). When studying the mandatory use of a system, the dependent variable *use* is not suitable, thus Brown & Massey (2002) recommended replacing it with the *satisfaction* variable. Bias & Mayhew (2005) claimed that *perceived ease-of-use* of a system improves *user-satisfaction.* Past research has also revealed the role of *usefulness* in determining *user-satisfaction* (Brown & Massey, 2002; Rezaei & Amin, 2013). In a mandatory situation, Mather Caputi & Jayasuriya (2002) claimed that *perceived usefulness* is more important than perceived *ease-of-use* for satisfaction. It is expected that *perceived ease-of-use* will have a significant effect on *perceived usefulness* and subsequently *perceived usefulness* will have a significant effect on *user-satisfaction.* Thus, the following hypotheses are formed:

H1: ESIDIS e-procurement system *perceived usefulness* is positively influenced by *perceived ease-of-use*
H2: *User-satisfaction* is positively influenced by ESIDIS e-procurement system *perceived usefulness*

Willingness-to-Learn

Willingness-to-learn is an important behavioral attribute that affects the users' overall performance, reveals the user's motivation power and determines the amount of effort the user makes. *Willingness-to-learn* is usually conceptualized as a task-value construct (Gorges et al., 2013) and according to Tzafikou et al. (2017) it is the users' willingness to try, persist, tinker and even study to learn how to use new technologies. It can be easily detected in the user's behavior such as reading instructions, viewing video tutorials, searching on the web and using new features. Employees' willingness to learn new knowledge and skills can not only improve the organization's competitive advantage but also foster ongoing success (Tsai et al., 2007). Primary determinants of *Willingness-to-learn* are associated with *perceived ease-of-use* and *perceived usefulness* of the system under investigation (Atalatti et al., 2015; Pilcher & Bedford, 2011). Therefore, it is expected that *willingness-to-learn* is positively influenced by *perceived ease-of-use* and *perceived usefulness* and in turn to influence *user-satisfaction.*

H3: *Willingness-to-learn* ESIDIS e-procurement system is positively influenced by *perceived ease-of-use*
H4: *Willingness-to-learn* ESIDIS e-procurement system is positively influenced by *perceived usefulness*
H5: *User-satisfaction* is positively influenced by *willingness-to-learn* ESIDIS e-procurement system

Risk

Perceived Risk is defined as the '*potential for the realization of unwanted, negative consequences of an event*' (Rowe, 1977). In the information technology context, risk is the potential that a system is insufficiently protected from various types of damages (Straub & Welke, 1998). If the system provides an 'advice' component and 'what if' tools that highlight the negative effects of some choices, rendering the user more careful and conscious then decreased users' perceptions of risk may be achieved (Beckwith et al., 2005; Tzafikou et al., 2017) while high risk-perception renders users less likely to make use of unfamiliar features (Tzafikou et al., 2017). In the context of e-government the risk is a main barrier towards acceptance (Karavasilis et al., 2016). Moreover, strong negative correlation has been found between the *risk* and *users' satisfaction* (Ghotbabadi et al., 2016). It is expected that p*erceived* r*isk* will be negatively influenced by *perceived ease-of-use,* that implies that risk is perceived to be lower by users who find use of a system easier. P*erceived* r*isk* is also expected to negatively influence w*illingness-to-learn.* In this vein, the following hypotheses are formed:

H6: *Perceived Risk* is negatively influenced by the *perceived ease-of-use* of ESIDIS e-procurement system
H7: *Willingness-to-learn* ESIDIS e-procurement system is negatively influenced by *perceived risk*

Figure 1. The research model

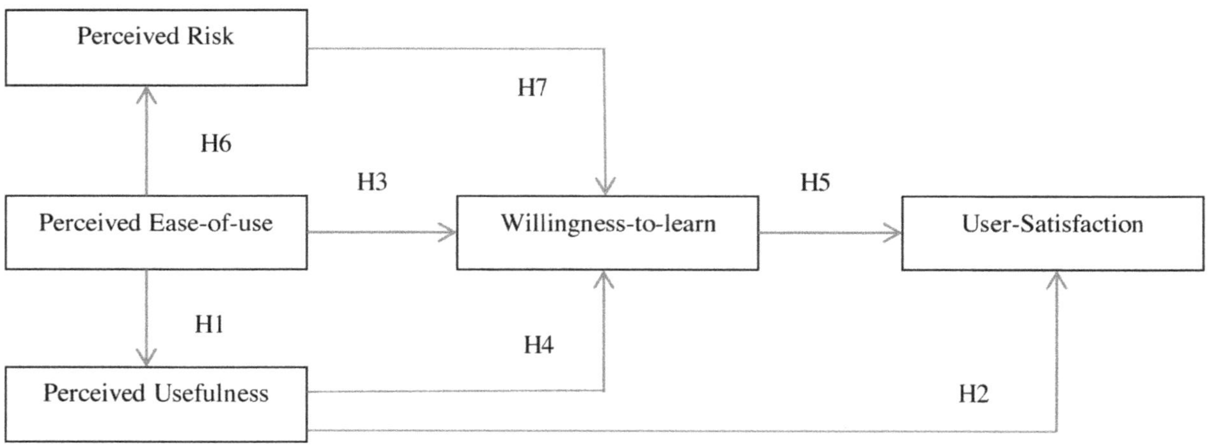

RESEARCH METHODOLOGY

Figure 1 presents the research model and the formulated hypotheses. In order to validate the hypothesized model an empirical research study was conducted using an online survey.

Convenience sampling was used in the study. The target population for this study was limited to certified users of ESIDIS. An email notified users about the online questionnaire website. The questionnaire was written and administered in Greek. Users willing to participate visited a tailor-made website, from 15 January 2019 to 15 April 2019, and responded to the questionnaire. User responses were recorded in a database. In total, 256 completed and usable questionnaires were received.

The questionnaire used in this study was created by adopting or adapting constructs from previous studies (Kassim et al., 2011; Tzafikou et al., 2017). Five-point Likert scales were used ranging from strongly disagree to strongly agree. The questionnaire consists of five parts: (1) Perceived Ease-of -Use, (2) Perceived Usefulness, (3) Perceived risk, (4) Willingness-to-learn (5) User-Satisfaction.

FINDINGS AND RECOMMENDATIONS

Sample Breakdown

The sample consists of 256 civil servants, where the majority 180 (70.30%) are females and 76 (29.70%) are males. The two thirds (67.20%) of the participants are middle aged between 41 and 50 years old while almost all of them (97.70%) have at least intermediate level computer skills. Furthermore, 85.20% of the sample are university graduates or have completed postgraduate studies (MSc or PhD). Over the half of the respondents are highly experienced with ESIDIS because they use it at least for three years but there is also a considerable percentage (41.40%) of users with up to two years of experience.

Table 2.

		Frequency	Percent %
Gender	Male	76	29.70
	Female	180	70.30
Age	21-30	4	1.60
	31-40	32	12.50
	41-50	172	67.15
	51-60	44	17.15
	>=61	4	1.60
Computer skills	Basic	6	2.30
	Intermediate	84	32.80
	Advanced	166	64.90
Education level	Middle/High School graduate	38	14.80
	University graduate	142	55.50
	Postgraduate studies graduate	72	28.10
	Phd degree holder	4	1.60
Experience with ESIDIS	1 year	40	15.60
	2 years	66	25.80
	3 years	48	18.80
	More than 3 years	102	39.80

Model Estimation

In case of ordered categorical data with five or less ordered categories, a robust diagonally weighted least squares (DWLS) estimator should be used to find the model's estimates (Hancock & Mueller, 2012, p. 475). Specifically, the weighted least squares mean and variance adjusted (WLSMV) estimator has been used using the lavaan R package (Rosseel, 2012; Finch & French, 2015).

The Measurement Model

The measurement model was examined for validating and refining the research constructs and Structural Equation Model Analysis was used for testing the research hypotheses.

Confirmatory Factor Analysis was used for model refinement. Before testing the structural relationships, the measurement model was tested by examining convergent validity, discriminant validity, and internal consistency of the constructs. Reliability and convergent validity of the measurements were estimated by the item factor loadings, Composite Reliability, and Average Variance Extracted (Fornell & Larcker, 1981). The Constructs, Items, Factor Loadings, Composite Reliability and Average Variance Extracted are presented in Table 3.

Table 3. Validity and reliability of constructs

Construct	Items	Factor Loadings	Cronbach α	CR*	AVE**
Usefulness	ESIDIS is useful	0.735	0.911	0.959	0.726
	ESIDIS makes me more productive	0.870			
	ESIDIS makes me save time	0.833			
	ESIDIS satisfies my needs and requirements	0.936			
Ease-of-use	ESIDIS is easy to use	0.851	0.862	0.912	0.588
	I do not need to try too hard to use ESIDIS effectively	0.897			
	I can use ESIDIS without written instructions	0.699			
	I can learn how to use ESIDIS easily and fast	0.619			
	I can easily correct my mistakes while I use ESIDIS	0.792			
Willingness-to-learn	I wanted to learn how to use ESIDIS while I was using it	0.901	0.853	0.855	0.651
	I'd like to learn how to use other similar systems too	0.745			
	In general, I enjoy learning new ICT related to ESIDIS	0.780			
Perceived Risk	I felt nervous every time I took an action (e.g. pressed a button)	0.798	0.807	0.805	0.589
	I had no hesitation to take an action	0.805			
	I had no difficulty to try which feature (among others) to use	0.690			
Satisfaction	ESIDIS is effective	0.818	0.899	0.927	0.754
	ESIDIS makes me more efficient	0.901			
	I am completely satisfied with ESIDIS	0.878			

*Composite reliability = (square of the summation of the factor loadings) / [(square of the summation of the factor loadings) + (square of the summation of the error variances)]

**AVE = (summation of squared factor loadings)/(summation of squared factor loadings) (summation of error variances)

For measurement model, all the standardized factor loading of each construct are above 0.690 and thus above the suggested threshold of 0.55 (Teo et al., 2009) ensuring convergent validity. Internal consistency of the model is examined by Cronbach's alpha coefficient and by Composite Reliability (CR). The Cronbach's alpha coefficient is influenced by the number of items and assumes equal weights of all the items of a construct. Composite Reliability, on the other hand, provides a better indicator for measuring internal consistency since it relies on the actual loadings to compute the factor scores (Teo et al., 2009). Cronbach's alpha coefficient for the five constructs is between 0.807 and 0.911 and Composite reliability is between .805 and .959. As it is evident both Cronbach's alpha coefficient and Composite Reliability are higher than 0.7 (see Table 1), ensuring internal consistency for the proposed model. The AVE values are between 0.588 and 0.754, exceeding the cut-off criterion of 0.50 indicating the reliability of the measurement model in measuring the construct (Hair et al., 1998; Teo et al., 2009).

Discriminant validity of the constructs was also assessed: discriminant validity is satisfied as all items loaded more heavily on their corresponding constructs rather than on other constructs (See Table 4).

Table 4. Discriminant validity

	Perceived Usefulness	**Perceived Ease-of-use**	**Willingness-to-learn**	**Perceived Risk**	**User Satisfaction**
Perceived Usefulness	1.000				
Perceived Ease-of-use	0.723	1.000			
Perceived Willingness-to-learn	0.684	0.592	1.000		
Perceived Risk	-0.478	-0.660	-0.320	1.000	
User Satisfaction	0.829	0.727	0.762	-0.468	1.000

Since all the measurements ensure reliability and validity of the measurement items, the model can be further tested for the structural model and hypotheses. Thus, next the Goodness-of-Fit of the research model is estimated. Recommended indices, according to Hair et al. (1988) and Bagozzi & Yi (1988), for evaluating the overall model fitness are: goodness-of-fit index (GFI), normed fit index (NFI), non-normed fit index (NNFI), comparative fit index (CFI) and root-mean-square error of approximation (RMSEA). Chi-square per degrees of freedom (Bagozzi & Yi, 1988) was used to statistically test for the null hypothesis that the model fits the data. All of the fit indexes indicate that the structural model has a good fit (Table 5).

Table 5. Goodness of fit

Fit index compared to the Recommended value	**Measurement model**
Chi-square/d.f. ≤3.0	0.416
GFI ≥0.80	0.990
AGFI ≥0.80	0.987
NFI ≥0.90	0.986
NNFI ≥0.90	0.986
RMSEA ≤0.08	0.000
CFI ≥0.90	1.000

The Validated Model

The study identified three factors that directly or indirectly affect *User-satisfaction*. These factors are *Perceived ease-of-use*, *Perceived Usefulness* and *Willingness-to-learn*.

Figure 2. The validated model

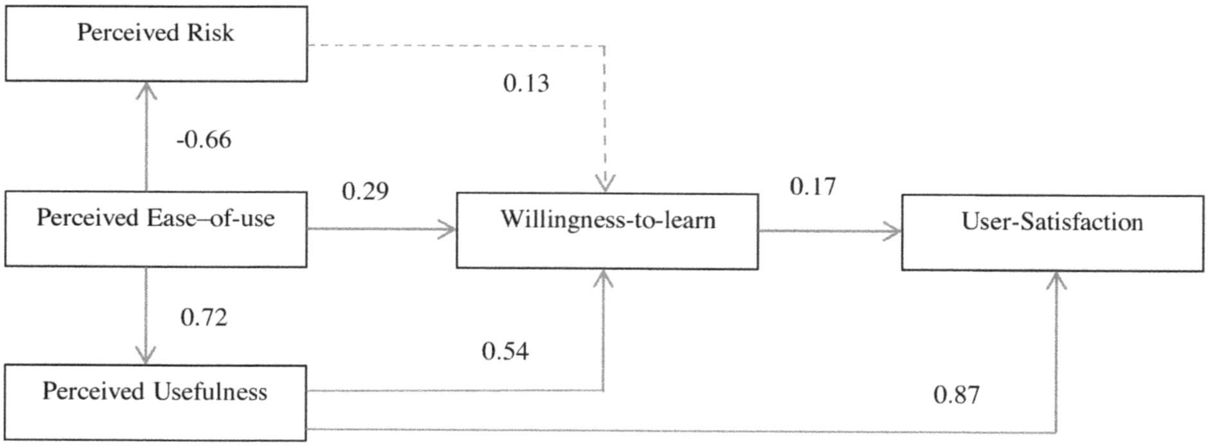

Perceived ease-of-use has significant positive effect on *perceived-usefulness* (γ=0.72, p<0.05). So, H1 is supported. *Perceived usefulness* refers to users' perceptions regarding the outcome of the experience while *perceived ease-of-use* refers to their perceptions regarding the process leading to the final outcome (Monsuwe, Dellaert, & Ruyter, 2004). According to TAM (Davis et al. 1989) the easier a system is to use and less complicated, the more users will find it useful (Chen & Aklikokou, 2019). In this vein, development of easy-to-use functions of ESIDIS will enhance users' perception of its usefulness and, indirectly, their satisfaction.

Research findings highlight the role of *perceived-usefulness* as a key factor in *user-satisfaction* while *perceived ease-of-use* plays a secondary role. Findings are consistent with with the TAM framework (Davis et al. 1989; Mathieson 1991; Schillewaert et al. 2005). *User-satisfaction* is positively influenced by ESIDIS e-procurement system *perceived usefulness* (γ=0.87, p<0.05) thus H2 is also supported. Policy makers should give more emphasis on promoting ESIDIS with a marketing strategy that focuses on the usefulness of the system, the advantages of using ESIDIS and communicate to employees its possible contribution to their productivity. Friendly services meeting international usability standards should enhance user satisfaction; however *perceived ease-of-use* is not the most important factor in determining the user satisfaction.

Both *perceived ease-of-use* and *perceived usefulness* have positive influence on user's *willingness-to-learn* ESIDIS e-procurement system. Thus, H3 (γ=0.29, p<0.05) and H4 (γ=0.54, p<0.05) are supported. Also in this case *perceived usefulness* has more significant effect than *ease-of-use* on *willingness-to-learn* ESIDIS. If employees perceive ESIDIS as more useful for their work they are more willing to learn its functions and capabilities as well as other similar to ESIDIS information systems. H5 is also supported (β=0.17, p<0.05). *User-satisfaction* is positively influenced by *willingness-to-learn* ESIDIS e-procurement system. Users that are more willing to learn ESIDIS are more satisfied with it. May be this is due to the fact that users who are more keen to learn discover more advanced functions of ESIDIS, that have positive impact on the quality of their work. Taken into consideration the fact that users do not read any tutorial or long instructions that the system offers for their assistance, the system should be adapted in way that the user is introduced to the new or more advanced features of the system gradually and be presented with brief but comprehensive explanations (Tzafikou et al., 2017). Animations, colors and tips highlighting 'new' features of the system could be also used to attract users' attention and curiosity and motivate user to explore and use specific features. As of the above, *perceived ease-of-use* has positive indirect effect on *user-satisfaction* through *willingness-to-learn*. The ministry should take steps to educate its workforce about use of ESIDIS especially in advanced functions that make their work easier. Users may not be sufficiently educated to be able to use all functions of ESIDIS confidently unless they receive some level of training. This implies that, if users consider that ESIDIS will be useful and improve their job performance, efficiency and effectiveness then this will result in strengthening their satisfaction. H6 is also supported (γ=-0.66, $p<0.05$). *Perceived risk* is negatively influenced by the *ease-of-use* of ESIDIS e-procurement system. Users who find ESIDIS easier to use feel less risk while using it.

As the users feel more confident with using ESIDIS they do not have doubts and hesitations about their actions, do not need to double check their actions or to reduce their speed due to any confidence-related errors. However, *Perceived risk* has not any effect on *Willingness-to-learn*. H7 is rejected. Therefore, *perceived risk* has no indirect effect on *user-satisfaction*. Weerakkody et al. (2014) who undertook a comprehensive review of the literature to identify the most critical factors that influence user satisfaction in e-government claimed that *perceived risk* was found to be a non-significant one.

Even after more than a decade of intensive research work in the area of electronic government, research related to user's satisfaction is still limited (Weerakkody et al., 2014) especially investigation of employees – internal customers of governments views and attitudes.

FUTURE RESEARCH

The paper reports on satisfaction of the government e-procurement information system in Greece, particularly investigating the views of the Greek public servants who use the system. Given that this research is focused on a specific information systems (EDISIS), the findings may not necessarily apply to other similar systems implemented in other countries. Additional work, surveys and analyses should be conducted using samples of users of government e-procurement systems in order to derive more general conclusions.

Another limitation of the study is about using the particular set of variables which measure satisfaction of the e-procurement information system. The analysis validates a model that describes and measures how these particular variables associate to each other. By including or using other variables, other appropriate models could also be calculated. All these models may describe and measure different aspects of satisfaction and may be equally correct and important. The capacity of incorporating various variables into the model constitutes a major advantage of TAM, which can be extended appropriately when new technologies emerge by using domain-specific constructs. TAM has been used in previous studies in the e-government context but it was found that TAM alone was not able to explain issues related to e-government and it was therefore necessary to be integrated with other models and constructs (Al-adawi et al., 2005; Carter & Belanger, 2005; Colesca & Dobrica, 2008; Karavasilis et al., 2016; Tahinakis et al., 2006; Zafiropoulos et al., 2014), as in this paper.

CONCLUSION

Entrepreneurship is a central force of economic development generating growth and social development and serves as a vehicle for innovation and change (Lordkipanidze, Brezet & Backman, 2005). One of the major roles of governments is to create a conducive and enabling business environment for fostering entrepreneurial activities, motivating and providing opportunities, comfort and support to entrepreneurs. A favourable business environment supporting entrepreneurship includes among others good infrastructure and a culture which encourages application of technologies (Mok, 2005). In such a policy context, the Hellenic Ministry of Development implemented a business-friendly public procurement system, named ESIDIS.

The use of ESIDIS is mandatory for the employees who are the internal customers of the government. Governmental information systems and services are often designed "top-down" and as a result, quite often, fail to adequately consider internal customers' needs. The success of the implementation of the ESIDIS, as all e-government projects, dependents not only on the government support but also on users' willingness to accept and adopt the information system. The paper aims at investigating the factors that influence users' satisfaction from ESIDIS and explain employees' attitudes toward satisfaction using the system. *Perceived usefulness*, *perceived ease-of-use*, *perceived risk* and *willingness-to learn* were investigated. *Perceived ease-of-use has significant positive effect on perceived-usefulness.* These results are in line with Brandon-Jones & Kauppi (2018) who found that p*erceived ease-of-use* has significant positive effect on *perceived-usefulness,* when investigating key antecedents of the Technology Acceptance Model for employees expected to use e-procurement systems in their day-to-day activities.

Perceived Usefulness has a significant role in determining user satisfaction, while *willingness-to-learn* affects to a lesser degree *user-satisfaction* in the mandatory use of ESIDIS. *Perceived Usefulness* relates to the benefits that the system provides to users. The more apparent such usefulness is to the users, the more evident the satisfaction becomes. This finding is in accordance with the findings of Mather Caputi & Jayasuria (2002). *Willingness-to-learn* also serves as a mediator for indirect effects from *perceived ease-of-use* to *user-satisfaction.* Sharabati, Noor & Salleh(2015) found that *Perceived ease-of-use* has significant positive effect on end-user's satisfaction. From a practical viewpoint *Perceived ease-of-use* and *perceived-usefulness are important* factors as systems, can be rejected by users due to the unsuitable interfaces (Autry et al., 2010). To our knowledge the role of *Willingness-to-learn* has not been previously investigated in the e-procurement context.

In practice, the study reveals users' fundamental priorities concerning the satisfaction of an e-procurement system. Managers and policymakers should take these factors into consideration in order to improve internal customers' satisfaction and consequently increase the success of e-government strategic program. However, the primary focus should be the promotion of the usefulness of the system and raising awareness of its capabilities and benefits. What is more is that the risks are diminished when users' understand how useful the system is for their job performance. Thus, the design and deployment of e-procurement systems should put great emphasis on what could be offered to the users to assist them enhance their job performance and on maximizing the added value of the system. Even though the study offers the first piece of evidence on satisfaction from ESIDIS information system, the recommendations would be helpful in developing and implementing new government information systems especially in case of mandatory use.

REFERENCES

Al-adawi, Z., Yousafzai, Z., & Pallister, J. (2005, September). Conceptual Model of citizen adoption of e-government. *Second International Conference on Innovations in Information Technology.*

Arrowsmith, S. (2001). E-Commerce Policy and the EC Procurement Rules. The Clash between Rhetoric and Reality. *Common Market Law Review*, *38*(6), 1447–1477. doi:10.1023/A:1013990310541

Atalatti, A., Lanham, E., & Coldwell-Neilson, J. (2015). Usability in mLearning. In *Proceedings of the 7th International Conference on Computer Supported Education* (pp. 213-219). Lisbon, Portugal: SCITEPRESS.

Au, N., Ngai, W., & Cheng, T. (2008). Extending the understanding of end user information systems satisfaction formation: An equitable needs fulfillment model approach. *Management Information Systems Quarterly*, *32*(1), 43–66. doi:10.2307/25148828

Autry, C., Grawe, S., Daugherty, P., & Richey, G. (2010). The effects of technological turbulence and breadth on supply chain technology acceptance and adoption. *Journal of Operations Management*, *28*(6), 522–536. doi:10.1016/j.jom.2010.03.001

Bagozzi, R., Davis, F., & Warshaw, P. (1992). Development and Test of a Theory of Technological Learning and Usage. *Human Relations*, *45*(7), 659–686. doi:10.1177/001872679204500702

Bagozzi, R., & Yi, Y. (1988). On the Evaluation of Structural Equation Models. *Journal of the Academy of Marketing Science*, *16*(1), 74–94. doi:10.1007/BF02723327

Beckwith, L., Sorte, S., Burnett, M., Wiedenbeck, S., Chintakovid, T., & Cook, C. (2005). Designing Features for Both Genders in End-User Programming Environments. In *Proceedings of the 2005 I.E. Symposium on Visual Languages and Human-Centric Computing* (pp. 153-160). Washington, DC: IEEE Computer Society. 10.1109/VLHCC.2005.31

Bhattacherjee, A., Davis, C. J., Connolly, A. J., & Hikmet, N. (2017). User response to mandatory IT use: A Coping Theory perspective. *European Journal of Information Systems*, 1–21. doi:10.105741303-017-0047-0

Bias, R. G., & Mayhew, D. J. (2005). *Cost-Justifying Usability: An Update for an Internet Age*. Morgan Kaufman. doi:10.1016/B978-012095811-5/50001-8

Brandon-Jones, A., & Kauppi, K. (2018). Examining the antecedents of the technology acceptance model within e-procurement. *International Journal of Operations & Production Management*, *38*(1), 22–42. doi:10.1108/IJOPM-06-2015-0346

Braun, M. T. (2013). Obstacles to social networking website use among older adults. *Computers in Human Behavior*, *29*(3), 673–680. doi:10.1016/j.chb.2012.12.004

Brown, S., Massey, A., Montoya-weiss, M., & Burkman, J. R. (2002). Do I really have to? User acceptance of mandated technology. *European Journal of Information Systems*, *11*(4), 283–295. doi:10.1057/palgrave.ejis.3000438

Carter, L., & Belanger, F. (2005). The Utilization of E-Government Services: Citizen Trust, Innovation and Acceptance Factors. *Information Systems Journal*, *15*(1), 5–25. doi:10.1111/j.1365-2575.2005.00183.x

Chen, L., & Aklikokou, A. K. (2019). Determinants of Egovernment Adoption: Testing the Mediating Effects of Perceived Usefulness and Perceived Ease of Use. *International Journal of Public Administration*, 1–16. Advance online publication. doi:10.1080/01900692.2019.1660989

CMS. (2019). *E-public procurement*. CMS Public Procurement Group. Retrieved from: https://cms.law/en/int/publication/e-public-procurement

Colesca, S. E., & Dobrica, L. (2008). Adoption and use of e-government services: The case of Romania. *Journal of Applied Research and Technology*, *6*(3), 204–217. doi:10.22201/icat.16656423.2008.6.03.526

Concha, G., Astudillo, H., Porrúa, M., & Pimenta, C. (2012). E-Government procurement observatory, maturity model and early measurements. *Government Information Quarterly*, *29*(1), S43–S50. doi:10.1016/j.giq.2011.08.005

Concha, G., Porrúa, M., & Pimenta, C. (2010). E-government procurement observatory model, design and pilot testing. In *Proceedings of the 4th International Conference on Theory and Practice of Electronic Governance ICEGOV '10* (pp. 195–201). New York: ACM. 10.1145/1930321.1930362

Corsi, M. (2006). *Good Governance for Development in Arab Countries Initiative E-Procurement Overview*. Retrieved from: OECD, http://unpan1.un.org/intradoc/groups/public/ documents/caimed/unpan024302.pdf

Croom, S., & Johnston, R. (2003). Examining the contribution of internal customer service to improved e-procurement performance: A Case Study investigation. In *Proceedings of* 3rd *International Conference on Electronic Business (ICEB 2003)*. National University of Singapore. Retrieved from: http://iceb.johogo.com/proceedings/2003/

Davis, F. (1980). Perceived Usefulness, Perceived Ease of Use, and User Acceptance of Information Technology. *Management Information Systems Quarterly*, *13*(3), 318–341.

Davis, F., Bagozzi, R., & Warshaw, P. (1989). User Acceptance of Computer Technology: A Comparison of Two Theoretical Models. *Management Science*, *35*(8), 982–1003. doi:10.1287/mnsc.35.8.982

Drucker, P. (1993). *Innovation and Entrepreneurship: Practice and Principle*. HarperBusiness.

European Commission. (2014). *Report from the Commission to the Council and the European Parliament - EU Anti-Corruption Report*. Retrieved from: https://ec.europa.eu/dgs/home-affairs /e-library/documents/policies/ organized-crime-and-humantrafficking/ corruption/docs/acr_2014_en.pdf

European Commission. (2016). *Public procurement – Study on administrative capacity in the EU Greece Country Profile*. Retrieved from: https://ec.europa.eu/ regional_policy/sources/ policy/how/improving-investment/ public-procurement/study/ country_profile/el.pdf

European Court of Auditors. (2018). *Public Procurement in Western Balkans*. Retrieved from: https://www.eca.europa.eu/ other%20publications/synthesis _w_balkans/synthesis_w_balkans_en.pdf

European Union. (2019). *Public Procurement.* Retrieved from: https://ec.europa.eu/growth/single-market/public-procurement_en

Ferrand, A. (2019). *e-Procurement: lessons from interventions and approaches from Emerging Economies of Eastern Europe and Western Balkans K4D Helpdesk Report.* Brighton, UK: Institute of Development Studies. Retrieved from: https://assets.publishing.service.gov.uk/ media/5dcd797ce5274a07aad0a54b670_eProcurement _lessons_from_interventions_ and_approaches_from_Emerging _Economies_of_Eastern_Europe_ and_Western_Balkans.pdf

Finch, W. H., & French, B. F. (2015). *Latent Variable Modeling with R.* Routledge. doi:10.4324/9781315869797

Fornell, C., & Larcker, D. F. (1981). Evaluating structural equation models with unbearable and measurement error. *JMR, Journal of Marketing Research, 18*(1), 39–50. doi:10.1177/002224378101800104

Gao, L., & Bai, X. (2014). A unified perspective on the factors influencing consumer acceptance of internet of things technology. *Asia Pacific Journal of Marketing and Logistics, 26*(2), 211–231. doi:10.1108/APJML-06-2013-0061

Ghotbabadi, A. L., Feiz, S., & Baharun, R. (2016). The Relationship of Customer Perceived Risk and Customer Satisfaction. *Mediterranean Journal of Social Sciences, 7*(1), S1. doi:10.5901/mjss.2016.v7n1s1p161

Gorges, J., Schwinger, M., & Kandler, C. (2013). Linking University Students' Willingness to Learn to Their Recollections of Motivation at Secondary School. *Europe's Journal of Psychology, 9*(4), 764–782. doi:10.5964/ejop.v9i4.638

Gunasekarana, A., & Ngai, E. (2008). Adoption of e-procurement in Hong Kong: An empirical research. *International Journal of Production Economics, 113*(1), 159–175. doi:10.1016/j.ijpe.2007.04.012

Hair, F. Jr, Anderson, R. E., Tatham, R. L., & Black, W. C. (1998). *Multivariate data analysis* (5th ed.). Prentice Hall.

Han, L., & Jin, Y. (2009). A Review of Technology Acceptance Model in the E-commerce Environment. In *Proceedings of the 2009 International Conference on Management of e-Commerce and e-Government* (pp. 28- 31) IEEE. 10.1109/ICMeCG.2009.64

Hancock, G. R., & Mueller, R. O. (Eds.). (2012). *Structural Equation Modeling: A Second Course* (2nd ed.). IAP.

Handfield, R., Jeong, S., & Choi, T. (2018). Emerging procurement technology: Data analytics and cognitive analytics. *International Journal of Operations & Production Management, 38*(1), 22–42.

Hellenic Republic. (2018). *Greece: A growth strategy for the future.* Retrieved from: http://www.mindev.gov.gr/wp-content/uploads/2018/09/Growth-Strategy.pdf

Hommen, L., & Rolfstam, M. (2009). Public procurement and innovation: Towards a taxonomy. *Journal of Public Procurement, 9*(1), 17–56.

Karafoti, D. (2013). *Bureaucracy and corruption in public administration* (Master thesis). University of Peloponnese. (in Greek)

Karavasilis, I., Vrana, V., & Zafiropoulos, K. (2016). An Extended Model of E-Government Adoption by Civil Servants in Greece. *International Journal of Electronic Government Research*, *12*(1), 1–23. doi:10.4018/IJEGR.2016010101

Kassim, E. S., Jailani, S. F. A. K., Hairuddin, H., & Zamzuri, H. N. (2011). Information System Acceptance and User Satisfaction: The Mediating Role of Trust. *Procedia: Social and Behavioral Sciences*, *57*(9), 412–418.

Kastaniotia, C., Kontodimopoulos, N., Stasinopoulos, D., Kapetaneas, N., & Polyzos, N. (2013). Public procurement of health technologies in Greece in an era of economic crisis. *Health Policy (Amsterdam)*, *109*(1), 7–13. doi:10.1016/j.healthpol.2012.03.015 PMID:22502936

Kavoura, A., & Andersson, T. (2016). Applying Delphi method for strategic design of social entrepreneurship. *Library Review*, *65*(3), 185–205. doi:10.1108/LR-06-2015-0062

Kavoura, A., & Koziol, L. (2017). Polish Firms' Innovation Capability for Competitiveness via Information Technologies and Social Media Implementation. In A. Vlachvei, O. Notta, K. Karantininis, & N. Tsountas (Eds.), *Factors Affecting Firm Competitiveness and Performance in the Modern Business World* (pp. 185–214). IGI Global. doi:10.4018/978-1-5225-0843-4.ch007

Kipkorir, R. N., & Omwenga, J. Q. (2015). Factors Contributing to Adoption of E-Procurement in County Governments: A Case Study of County Government of Bomet. *International Journal of Academic Research in Business and Social Sciences*, *5*. Advance online publication. doi:10.6007/IJARBSS/v5-i10/1871

Klabi, H., Mellouli, S., & Rekik, M. (2018). A reputation based electronic government procurement model. *Government Information Quarterly*, *35*(4), 543–553. doi:10.1016/j.giq.2016.01.001

Kochanova, A., Hasnain, Z., & Larson, B. (2016). *Does e-Government improve government capacity? Evidence from Tax Administration and Public Procurement*. Background Paper to the 2016 World Development Report. Retrieved from: http://documents.worldbank.org/curated/en/334481468193734893/pdf/WPS7657.pdf

Koh, C. E., Prybutok, V. R., Ryan, S. D., & Wu, Y. (2010). A model for mandatory use of software technologies: An integrative approach by applying multiple levels of abstraction. *Informing Science: the International Journal of an Emerging Transdiscipline*, *13*, 177–203. doi:10.28945/1326

Koutsouris, D., & Maglavera, S. (2006). *Public procurement in Healthcare*. Retrieved from: http://www.ebusinessforum.gr/ engine/index.php?op=modload& modname=Downloads& action=downloadsviewfile &ctn=1078&language=el

Licenji, A. (2015). Standards and challenges of public procurement. *European Scientific Journal*, *11*(25), 229–240.

Lordkipanidze, M., Brezet, H., & Backman, M. (2005). The entrepreneurship factor in sustainable tourism development. *Journal of Cleaner Production*, *13*(8), 787–798. doi:10.1016/j.jclepro.2004.02.043

Makarona, E., & Kavoura, A. (2019). Redesigning the Ivory Tower: Academic entrepreneurship as a new calling supporting economic growth. *The Malopolska School of Economics in Tarnow Research Papers Collection*, *42*, 15–26.

Masika, D. (2013). *Challenges and Prospects for using ICT in public procurement in Tanzania. The case of Maryland global initiative Tanzania–head Office* (Master thesis). Mzumbe University

Mather, D., Caputi, P., & Jayasuriya, R. (2002). Is the technology acceptance model a valid model of user satisfaction of information technology in environments where usage is mandatory? In A. Wenn, M. McGrath, & F. Burstein (Eds.), *Enabling organisations and society through information systems* (pp. 1241–1250). Victoria University.

Mathieson, K. (1991). Predicting User Intentions: Comparing the Technology Acceptance Model with the Theory of Planned Behavior. *Information Systems Research*, *2*(3), 173–191. doi:10.1287/isre.2.3.173

Ministry of Development and Investments. (2019). *ESIDIS 2018. Annual Report on statistics of National electronic Public Procurement System*. Retrieved from http://www.eprocurement.gov.gr/webcenter/files/statistics/yearly/ 2018_%CE%95%CF%84%CE% AE%CF%83%CE%B9%CE%BF%CE%94%CE%B5%CE%BB%CF%84% CE%AF%CE%BF%CE%95%CE% A3%CE%97%CE%94%CE%97%CE%A3.pdf

Mok, K. H. (2005). Fostering entrepreneurship: Changing role of government and higher education governance in Hong Kong. *Research Policy*, *34*(4), 537–554. doi:10.1016/j.respol.2005.03.003

Monsuwe, T. P., Dellaert, B. G., & Ruyter, K. D. (2004). What drives consumers to shop online? A literature review. *International Journal of Service Industry Management*, *15*(1), 102–121. doi:10.1108/09564230410523358

Mufutau, G. O., & Ajetomobi, O. S. (2016). Procurement Functions as Tools for Entrepreneurial Success. *IOSR Journal of Business and Management*, *18*(1), 1–8.

Napsah, M. (2016). *The Adoption of E-procurement in the Indonesian Public Sector* (Ph.d Thesis). School of Built Environment Department of Construction Management, Curtin University.

National Electronic Public Procurement System. (2019). *National Electronic Public Procurement System. Supplies and Services*. Retrieved from: http://www.eprocurement.gov.gr/ webcenter/faces/oracle/webcenter/page/ scopedMD/sd0cb90ef _26cf_4703_99d5_1561 ceff660f/Page120. jspx?_afrLoop=17663529742836374

Neupane, A., Soar, J., Vaidya, K., & Yong, J. (2012). Role of public e-procurment technology to reduce corruption in Government Procurement. In *Proceedings of the International Public Procurement Conference* (pp. 304-334). IPPC.

OECD. (2016). *Preventing Corruption in Public Procurement*. Retrieved from: http://www.oecd.org/gov/ethics/Corruption-Public-Procurement-Brochure.pdf

OECD. (2019b). *Productivity in Public Procurement. A case study of Finland: Measuring the effiency and effectiveness of Public Procurement*. Retrieved from: https://www.oecd.org/gov/public-procurement/publications/productivity-public-procurement.pdf

OECD. (2019a). *Is there a role for blockchain in responsible supply chains?* Retrieved from: https://mneguidelines.oecd.org/Is-there-a-role-for-blockchain-in-responsible-supply-chains.pdf

Panagiotidou, E., & Intzesiloglou, N. (2016). The 'morality' of Practices in Public Procurement. Economic and Social Development: Book of Proceedings, 306-316.

Panayiotou, N. A., Gayialis, S. P., & Tatsiopoulos, I. P. (2004). An e-procurement system for governmental purchasing. *International Journal of Production Economics*, *90*(1), 79–102. doi:10.1016/S0925-5273(03)00103-8

Pilcher, J., & Bedford, L. (2011). Willingness and Preferences of Nurses Related to Learning With Technology. *Journal for Nurses in Staff Development*, *27*(3), E10–E16. doi:10.1097/NND.0b013e318217b447 PMID:21602623

Platis, C., Karafyllis, I., & Kaoura, G. (2019). E-Procurement in Public Hospitals in Greece. In Strategic Innovative Marketing and Tourism. Springer doi:10.1007/978-3-030-12453-3_134

Praveen, N., & Khaliq, M. (2018). A General Study for Role of the Quality in the E-Procurement Process. *International Journal of Scientific Research in Computer Science. Engineering and Information Technology*, *3*(1), 102–106.

Rezaei, S., & Amin, M. (2013). Exploring online repurchase behavioural intention of university students in Malaysia. *Journal of Global Business Advancement*, *6*(2), 92–119. doi:10.1504/JGBA.2013.053561

Rosseel, Y. (2012). lavaan: An R Package for Structural Equation Modeling. *Journal of Statistical Software*, *48*(2), 1–36. doi:10.18637/jss.v048.i02

Rotich, G. K., & Okello, B. (2015). Analysis and use of e-procurement on performance of the procurement functions of Country governments in Kenya. *International Journal of Economics. Commerce and Management*, *3*(6), 1381–1396.

Rowe, W. D. (1977). *An Anatomy of Risk*. John Wiley & Sons.

Savvas, A. (2018). *Public Procurement Suplies and services, Use of ESHDHS* (Master Thesis). Technological Education Institute of Epirous.

Schillewaert, N., Ahearne, M., Frambachc, R., & Moenaert, R. (2005). The adoption of information technology in the sales force. *Industrial Marketing Management*, *34*(4), 323–336. doi:10.1016/j.indmarman.2004.09.013

Sharabati, M. M. N., Sulaiman, A., & Salleh, M. N. A. (2015). End User Satisfaction and Individual Performance Assessments in e-Procurement Systems. *International Journal of Computer Theory and Engineering*, *7*(6), 503–509. doi:10.7763/IJCTE.2015.V7.1010

Straub, D., & Welke, R. (1998). Coping With Systems Risk: Security Planning Models for Management Decision Making. *Management Information Systems Quarterly*, *22*(4), 441–469. doi:10.2307/249551

Tahinakis, P., Mylonakis, J., & Protogeros, N. (2006). The contribution of e-government to the modernization of the Hellenic taxation system. *Electronic Government, an International Journal*, *3*(2), 139-157.

Tanner, Wölfle, & Quade, (2006). *The role of information technology in procurement in the Top 200 companies in Switzerland.* Basel: Competence Center E-Business Basel at the University of Applied Sciences Northwestern Switzerland – FHNW.

Teo, T., Srivastava, S., & Jiang, L. (2009). Trust and Electronic Government Success: An Empirical Study. *Journal of Management Information Systems, 25*(3), 99–131. doi:10.2753/MIS0742-1222250303

Thai, K. V. (2009). *International Handbook of Public Procurement: Public Administration and Public Policy*. CRC Press.

Tsagkaris, A., Tzouros, Th., Patelis, A., & Tolis, D. (2010). *The Logistics Operation at the Hellenic Public Hospital.* Myth or Reality; 1st Olympus Internation Conference on Supply Chains, Katerini, Greece. (in Greek)

Tsai, P., Yen, Y., Huang, L. C., & Huang, I. C. (2007). A study on motivating employees' learning commitment in the post-downsizing era: Job satisfaction perspective. *Journal of World Business, 42*(2), 157–169. doi:10.1016/j.jwb.2007.02.002

Tu, C. C., Fang, K., & Lin, C. Y. (2012). Perceived Ease of Use, Trust, and Satisfaction as Determinants of Loyalty in e-Auction Marketplace. *Journal of Computers, 7*(3), 645–652. doi:10.4304/jcp.7.3.645-652

Tzafilkou, K., Protogeros, N., Karagiannidis, C., & Koumpis, A. (2017). Gender-based behavioral analysis for end-user development and the 'RULES' attributes. *Education and Information Technologies, 22*(4), 1853–1894. doi:10.100710639-016-9519-4

UN. (2005). Entrepreneurship and economic development: the empretec showcase. In *United nations conference on trade and Development.* Retrieved from: https://unctad.org/en/Docs/webiteteb20043_en.pdf

Vaidya, K., Sajeev, A. S. M., & Callender, G. (2006). Critical Factors that Influence E Procurement Implementation Success in the Public Sector. *Journal of Public Procurement, 6*(1), 70–99. doi:10.1108/JOPP-06-01-02-2006-B004

Vaidyanathan, G., & Devaraj, S. (2008). The role of quality in e-procurement performance: An empirical analysis. *Journal of Operations Management, 26*(3), 407–425. doi:10.1016/j.jom.2007.08.004

Weerakkody, V., Irani, Z., Lee, H., Hindi, N., & Osman, I. (2014). A Review of the Factors Affecting User Satisfaction in Electronic Government Services. *International Journal of Electronic Government Research, 10*(4), 21–56. doi:10.4018/ijegr.2014100102

Yang, C. (2019). *Is there a role for blockchain for enhancing public Procurement integrity? 2019 OECD Anti-corruption and integrity forum.* Retrieved from: http://www.oecd.org/corruption/integrity-forum/academic-papers/Chan-Yang-blockchain-public-procurement-integrity.pdf

Zafiropoulos, K., Karavasilis, I., & Vrana, V. (2014). Exploring e-governance acceptance by primary and secondary education teachers in Greece. *International Journal of Information Technology and Management, 13*(4), 285–304. doi:10.1504/IJITM.2014.065629

KEY TERMS AND DEFINITIONS

E-Procurement: A comprehensive process in which organizations use IT systems to establish agreements for the acquisition of products or services (contracting) or purchase products or services in exchange for payment (purchasing).

Perceived Ease of Use: The degree to which a person believes that using a particular system would be free of physical and mental effort.

Perceived Risk: The potential for the realization of unwanted, negative consequences of an event.

Perceived Usefulness: The degree to which a person believes that using a particular system would enhance his or her job performance.

Public Procurement: Acquisition (through buying or purchasing) of goods and services by government or public organizations.

User Satisfaction: End-user's overall affective and cognitive evaluation of the pleasurable level of consumption-related fulfillment experienced with IS.

Willingness-to-Learn: The users' willingness to try, persist, tinker and even study to learn how to use new technologies.

Chapter 7
Cyber Threats in the Healthcare Sector and Countermeasures

Muhammad Mashhood Ahmed
https://orcid.org/0000-0001-9825-3476
De Montfort University, UK

Leandros Maglaras
https://orcid.org/0000-0001-5360-9782
De Montfort University, UK

Mohamed Amine Ferrag
https://orcid.org/0000-0002-0632-3172
Guelma University, Algeria

ABSTRACT

Healthcare is one of the most targeted industries by cybercriminals. The healthcare sector is far behind in cybersecurity as compared to other organizations. The vulnerabilities in the system open the door for cybercriminals to exploit it and get unauthorized access into the system or network to do a malicious activity. Healthcare should have to take cyber threats seriously and follow a security framework that detects and mitigates cyber threats. This chapter presents all cyber threat actors that exist in the healthcare sector, common cyber-attacks that can be launched against all actors, and real incidents that took place during the past years. Based on these, the authors propose in a tabular form a set of recommendations that can be used as countermeasures against any type of attack.

INTRODUCTION

A Cyber threat is a malicious act by an individual or organisation to steal the data and damage the computer, systems and networks. The threats include in cyber-attacks are malware, phishing, denial of services and data breaches. In 1971, Bob Thomas was the first person who created the first virus and named Creeper. He just wanted to create a self-duplicating program. Creeper is a worm which replicates

DOI: 10.4018/978-1-7998-3648-3.ch007

itself and spreads from one computer to another computer. It displayed the phrase "I am a creeper, catch me if you can" on the computer screen. It was not like a today modern era virus who cause damage, steal information, encrypt the files or demand for a ransom (Parikka, 2007). In 1986, Clifford Stoll who was the system administration at the Lawrence Berkeley National Laboratory, notice a suspicious activity in accounting data. He Found out that unauthorised person was hacking in to his system. Robert Tappan Morris is the son of cryptographer Robert Morris. He graduated from Cornell University. In 1988, he did the first cyber-attack with good attention but ended with horrible consequences. He wanted to know how big the internet is so he developed the Morris worm virus which travels the web, installs itself automatically on other systems and then counts how many duplicate copies it created (Orman, 2003). The consequences caused by this worm was a horrible nightmare and it damaged approximately 6000 computers and total estimated damage of $98 million. His program was the first type of cyber-attack called "distributed denial of services". Morris was charged fines and three years of trial to violate the Computer Fraud and Abuse Act.

There are different types of cyber threat actors who do cyber-attacks for their own benefits or as a revenge from the company. These actors cause damage to the organisations, steal the data or demand a ransom. Cyber criminals are also targeting the healthcare sector because it is an easier task to do. Healthcare sector is spending very limited budget in IT department to secure their systems or networks so there are few back doors for the hackers to get unauthorized access in to the system and cause damage. The systems are not secure because they are using almost out-dated software and old version of operating systems.

The main reason for targeting the healthcare sector is that the patient sensitive information is valuable and worth a lot of money. It is more valuable than the credit card and provides a decent amount of money to hackers if they sell the information. Cyber criminals also use the information to make fake ID to take full advantage of the healthcare facilities and claim the insurance as well.

There are many cyber-attacks are happening in the healthcare sector which are causing a lot of damages economically and reputation. For example, in UK, USA and many other countries healthcare sector was hacked and the damage it causes was too much. In most cases data breaches and ransomware attacks took place. Common impacts on the healthcare sector when an incident happened were loss of reputation and patient's trust, compromised medical data and risk of patient safety. Newly trends of cyber-attacks are hackers that sell out the medical information on the black market. Ransomware and phishing emails both are the most attack happen in the healthcare sector cause data breach and loss of billions of dollars.

The UK has identified sixteen critical infrastructure sectors including the healthcare and protection of these infrastructures is very important. The UK and every other country must use a security framework in order to detect and mitigate the cyber incidents. NIS directive is the cyber security law implemented across the EU countries. The objective of the directive is to create a common framework that EU countries can use in order to detect and protect the systems and networks from cyber-attacks (Maglaras, 2018).

When people are aware about the cyber threats and know how much damage they cause then they are ready to take action that could mitigate these attacks. There are many different ways to mitigate cyber-attacks which are really helpful in order to secure the systems or networks. In this chapter, different types of countermeasures are discussed and also their advantages and disadvantages as well. Once a healthcare provider is secure the can be more competitive against their competitors (Makarona E, 2019), (Kavoura A. a., 2017) and should incorporated in the strategic design of new co mpanies in the field (Kavoura A. a., 2016).

As stated in the latest report from ENISA (ENISA, 2020) cybersecurity becomes more of a priority for hospitals and it is essential to be integrated holistically inside all processes, components and stages that may influence the healthcare ICT ecosystem. During the coronavirus pandemic a lot of cyber incidents using or targeting the Health sector globally since January 2020 were reported. The Coronavirus (COVID-19) pandemic is used as the vehicle to attack and the vast majority of the incidents are related to cybercrime, using Spearphishing, Malware, Ransomware, DDoS, Misinformation campaign, and even mobile telephony attacks (SMShing). Moreover, in order to showcase the importance of cybersecurity on healthcare the European cyber exercise that ENISA organizes every two years (Cyber Europe 2020) is focused on healthcare and involves national/governmental CSIRTs, Cybersecurity Authorities, Ministries of Health, healthcare organisations (e.g. hospitals/clinics), eHealth service providers, and health insurance providers.

Based on these findings this book chapter presents all cyber threat actors that exist in the healthcare sector, common cyber-attacks that can be launched against all actors and real incidents that took place during the past years. Based on these, the current chapter, proposes in a tabular form a set of recommendations that can be used as countermeasures against any type of attack. These recommendations can be incorporated into a cybersecurity framework or cyber security assessment model that healthcare providers could use in order to perform a gap analysis, assess their security level and take appropriate mitigation actions.

Cyber Threat Actors

Cyber threat Actor can be anyone individual person or group of people from any organisation who just do malicious things for their own benefits and revenges (Ayres, 2016). Some of the cyber threat actors are as follows which include:

- Individual users who are alone and using their own software tools to create an attack.
- Organisations that are running criminal stuff like developing and executing attacks.
- Insider who is unhappy from their bosses.
- Terrorists
- Hackers
- Business competitors (who wants to know new ideas or plans from their competitor)
- Nation State (Countries who want to know other's country secrets)
- Spy

Cybercriminals are targeting the healthcare industry for many years. The main reason behind it is that healthcare data is more valuable than many traditional resources. On dark web, cyber criminals buy and sell patients records for various purposes, like identity theft. Healthcare sector has a vast amount of data such as bank account details, personal information, transaction records, and diagnosis, and these types of data is the main target for the cyber criminals.

From the past few decades until now, healthcare sector remains on a low priority in order to spend the money in IT security as compared to other big organisations. Previously hospitals used to record their health data on paper-based system such as registers and after that when they change their system to electronic system they created more entry points for cyber criminals (Evans, 2019).

The IoT medical devices like the ones used for monitoring heart rate or insulin levels were initially designed without the security aspect in mind. These devices can be used from cyber criminals in order to launch an attack on a hospital server that contains critical and valuable information. Cyber criminals see the medical devices as an easy target as well as other devices like mobile phones and laptops which are not really secure (Ferrag, 2018). These devices are the biggest issue for healthcare sector since they open back doors for attackers to get access into the network and cause damage.

Hospitals store a large amount of patient's data on their server that worth more money than the actual financial data such as credit cards, debit cards. Cyber criminals use the patient information to create the fake ID and buy the medical equipment's or medicines and can claim insurance by using the false patient ID number along with the provider number.

In most of the cases people discover after a long-time when cyber criminals already take benefits of health services from their personal medical ID. If patient data contain sensitive protected health information (PHI) such as sexually transmitted diseases or psychological problems cyber criminals can use this information to blackmail the patients. This is actually a hospital responsibility to secure their patients data (Zhang, 2018). When cyber criminals exploit the vulnerability and get inside the targeted system then they can install a ransomware and block out the user access to the systems and ask for ransom payment in order to unblock the sensitive data.

The healthcare industry is using out dated operating systems such as window XP or window 7 due to their limited budget. The second issue is that staff hesitate to learn new systems. An expert report found out that about "76% of healthcare sectors are using window 7 on their systems and 22% of healthcare customers browse on unsupported versions of internet explorer". The outdated software contains bugs and that is the biggest problem for the healthcare sector while updated versions contain bug fixes in order to secure the systems. Healthcare sector has responsibility to quickly act on any latest threat in order to protect the patient data.

Common Cyber Threats

Cyber-attacks are growing now a days and every organisation in every country including healthcare system are also being targeted by cyber criminals. The worst thing is the impact and damage the cyber-attack caused. The problem is in the systems and networks, which are vulnerable and opens the back door for the attacker to get inside and stole the confidential data.

According to the researcher's report there are common cyber threats that are causing serious damages to the healthcare industry as well. The most common types of cyber threats are as follows:

Malware

Malware is a piece of software which is developed by cyber criminals to gain unauthorized access into the computers or networks to cause damage and steal sensitive data. It consists of executable code, malicious content and scripts. It is sent in the form of file or a link via email. In order to execute the malware, the user has to click on it. There are different types of malware, like viruses, Trojans and worms.

A Virus is the most common type of malware. A Virus is a malicious piece of software that when executed, creates copies of itself by modifying other computer files and programs. Virus can spread too quickly from one computer to another computer and damage core functionality, corrupting software operation and locking users out of the systems. Cyber criminals before writing a virus make use of social engineering techniques and exploit the knowledge they obtain about security vulnerabilities that exist into the networks. Usually viruses mostly target system that are using Microsoft windows and by using a complex anti-detection technique manage to avoid being captured by anti-virus software.

There are different types of viruses which are affecting the systems on daily basis. For example; Resident Virus, Multiple Virus, Direct Action Virus, Overwrite Virus, Browse Hijacker, Web Scripting Virus, Boot Sector Virus, Directory Virus, Macro Virus, Polymorphic Virus, Encrypted Virus, File Infector Virus, Companion Virus, Non resident Virus, Network Virus, Stealth Virus, Space filler Virus, Sparse Infector and FAT Virus. (Subramanya, 2001).

A worm is a common type of malware which has the ability to replicate itself and spread from computer to computer without any human interaction. It does not need to attach itself to any software to cause damage to the systems. A Worm can get into the systems as an attachment file via spamming email or messages. When the user opens the attachment file, he automatically downloads the worm into the system. When it is installed, it goes in the system and infect it without the knowledge of the user. A worm can add other malicious software as well in the computer. Worms have the ability to modify and delete files and give access to the cyber criminals so they can control the system and its settings. There are different types of worms such as email worms, Instant message worms, Internet worms, file-sharing network worms and IRC worms (Weaver 2003).

A Logic bomb is another type of malware that is activated when specific conditions are met such as when the pre-defined date or time is reached. Cyber criminals can add a malicious code of logic bomb in a fake application or with another malware such as spyware so they can steal users' credentials and cause more damage. It is not like virus or worms that spread from one computer to another.

Ransomware is a malicious malware that takes over your system, prevents the users from accessing their data and ask for ransom payment in order to provide access to the data. First ever ransom was developed in 1980's and payment were sent via snail mail but today cyber criminals demand for ransom payment to be sent via cryptocurrency because it is safe and do not leak the information who is the sender and receiver of the payment. Most common way to send ransom is malspam. Cyber criminals deliver ransom via emails by attaching a PDF or Word files. Attackers use social engineering techniques to trick people to open attached files or click specific links by faking friend or trusted institution name. Another way to send ransom is malvertising in which they advertise an attractive ad on an internet. While browsing, user see an ad which seems interesting and clicks on it (Sood, 2011). There are different types of ransomware such as scareware, screen lockers and Encrypting ransomware.

Spyware is a software that can hijack your system. It is installed in the system to track and monitor the user activity on the web. It is not a virus to replicate itself and damage the systems but it is a software which gives access to your computer without your permission. Some organisations intentionally install this software in the systems in order to monitor user activity. There are four types of spyware: adware, system monitors, trojans and tracking cookies.

Adware is a software that pops-up advertisements or banners on your screen within a web browser on a computer screen. Developers add an adware software in their websites or software so it can automatically generate revenue for them. It is also used as a malicious adware software like virus or trojan to steal credentials of the users. For example: adware enter in to your system when user download a peer-to-peer file in which the adware is hidden then the pop-up ads begins to show after the program files are loaded on your system and add tracking cookies, key loggers or hard drive scans so it may transfer passwords, documents, credit card numbers and pictures to the cyber criminals.

MAN IN THE MIDDLE ATTACK

During a Man-in-the-middle attack an attacker secretly intercepts the communication between two parties in order to steal sensitive credentials, corrupt the data or spy on the victims. This attack always has three players: Victim, Man in the middle (who is intercepting the communication) and Third party (to whom victim is communicating).

For example: user gets an email from the bank asking him to log in to the account and confirm the information. The user does not know about the middle of the man in this scenario. The attacker has actually created a fake website and send the email to the user which looks like one that originated from the bank so the user clicks on it and logs in without hesitation. This means that the user itself handed over the credentials to the cybercriminal.

Session Hijacking is a malicious activity also known as a TCP session hijacking. It is a technique in which the attacker hijacks the trusted web user session by secretly getting the session ID. After accessing the User's session ID then attacker can do anything on the network that the legitimate user is authorized to do. To do a session hijacking, hackers use a sniffer application such as wireshark or OWASP Zed to capture the network traffic which has the session ID between website and client. When capturing the string which is known as token the attacker can use the valid token to get the unauthorised access in to the web server.

IP spoofing is a hacking technique in which the attacker creates an internet protocol (IP) with the fake IP address in its header. The purpose of creating the fake IP address is to hide the attacker own identity when attacking a server or any other device. Ip spoofing is not illegal because since users can fake their IP address to hide their internet activities and enjoy online privacy. It is illegal if someone uses the spoofing in order to pretend being someone else and do criminal acts such as identity theft.

A reply attack is a malicious attack in which the attacker secretly intercepts on a secure network communication and fraudulently delays or repeats the valid data transmission. This attack helps the attacker to get the authorised access in a network to steal the information or complete a duplicate transaction.

It is important to note here that humans need to cooperate with start-ups, university hubs and or governments in order to find ways to deal with attacks that may also contribute in other sectors apart from health (Filkins, 2004)

PHISHING ATTACK AND SPEAR PHISHING ATTACK

Phishing attack is a hacking technique in which attacker sends a fake call, email or message in the form of a link or attachment file through any bank or organisation in order to acquire details of a targeted person such as account number, credit or debit card or password for a malicious purpose. The cyber criminals send a fake email or message so the target user click on it, which is similar to any organisation or bank webpage. Phishing emails or messages are send to a very large number of people with the expectation that few will respond to it. Phishing attacks typically rely on a social engineering technique which is applied to emails or other electronic communication such as direct messaging sent over social networks, SMS text messages and other instant messages. Phishers may also use other social engineering and other information gathering techniques in order to get the information from LinkedIn, Twitter or Facebook to gather background information about the targeted personal and work history, interests and activities.

Spear phishing attack works like a phishing attack but the difference is that the attacker carefully design the emails to target to a single user in order to make him replay back. Cyber criminals select individual persons to target in an organisation using social media or other information gathering techniques to get some confidential information and then use them in order to create a fake email or message for the targeted individual.

PASSWORD ATTACK

Password attack or cracking is a technique to recover the passwords which has been forgotten or to gain an unauthorised access to the targeted system. Organisations system administrators usually use this technique to check easily crackable passwords in order to suggest the staff to use a strong password to protect their system from any cyber activity. Cracking a password is not an easy task because most of the services lock down the accounts on repeated login attempts. Once an attacker gets a complete list of cracked passwords then he will try his best to break it. The goal of the attacker is to look for large number of targets so they crack down their target's password one by one rather than just to crack the password of an individual person.

Brute-force attack is a technique to get the information such as username, passwords and PIN. Brute-force can be done by using an automated software which is used to try to guess the combinations of passwords such as administrator password, encryption key or a hash key of the password. This technique is used by cyber criminals to decrypt the encrypted data. Organisations security analyst also used the brute-force to test the network security in order to make it more secure. Brute-force techniques happen in the early stages of attack when attackers are trying to get authorised access in to their targeted systems. Attackers use the brute-force in order to check hidden web pages which are not linked to other web pages and which can be exploited easily. Computers are incredibly fast so cyber criminals can do a brute-force in order to crack the password 8 character long in just 2 hours and decrypt the weak encryption hash in just a month. If the password is longer 8 characters, with a combination of Capital or small alphabets and special characters then it makes brute-force more difficult and takes years to guess it.

Dictionary attack is a technique which is used to crack or recover the password by using an actual dictionary list. The type of passwords includes in dictionary list are common password list such as pet names, famous names of television character and other words. Dictionary attack can be used where password is weak and easy to guess such as words, numbers or just phrases. It does not mean if the password is weak then attacker can easily crack the password, it takes a long time and a many attempt.

SQL INJECTION ATTACK

SQL Injection attack is a technique which is used to hack a website by inserting malicious SQL statements which make some condition give as outcome always true. A website has two important components, one is the html code and the second is database server. The SQL statements control the database server. These database servers contain username and passwords which are the main target for cyber criminals. Cyber criminals use SQL statement in order to add, delete and modify the data or queries from the database to gain the full control of the database server. To do a SQL injection attack, the attacker has to find the vulnerabilities in the web application and then put the malicious SQL code on a user login form in order to get the unauthorised access in to the database.

For example; In the user login page, write the SQL condition in the password field e.g. 1' or '1'='1 then it will show the list of usernames and their passwords if there is a vulnerability in the web application code. This condition 1' or '1'='1 always makes the query 'TRUE' in the database. After getting the username and passwords, hackers easily get access in to the system.

CROSS-SITE SCRIPTING ATTACK

A Cross-site scripting attack is an activity in which the malicious code is injected into trusted websites. Cross-site scripting is known as XSS. XSS attack happen when the cybercriminal uses the website as a vehicle to transport the malicious code to the targeted user in the form of a HTML script. When the user visits the web application then the code executes. Vulnerabilities in the websites allows the attacks to be successfully occur. The most commonly vulnerable vehicle used for the XSS attack are web pages comment section and forums. XSS attack mostly happen in JavaScript. XSS vulnerabilities are less dangerous as compared to the SQL injection vulnerabilities. There are three types of Cross-site scripting attacks: DOM-based XSS, Reflected XSS and Stored XSS.

EAVESDROPPING ATTACK

Eavesdropping attack in which attacker intercepts the communication between the sender and the receiver. In this attack, cybercriminal steals the information that smartphones, computers and other electronic devices send over a network. Eavesdropping attacks are not easy to be detected because they do not cause any abnormal activity in a network transmission.

Cybercriminals can intercept the data which is transmitting between sender and receiver over a network by installing a network monitoring software on their computer or server. Attacker can insert or install a software in the targeted system directly or by malware then come back later in order to check the retrieved data. Data sniffing can be done easily on the local network as well as on the wireless networking. In local networks, data is sent to all ports and sniffer can easily accept all incoming data. In wireless networks, the data is broadcast so if the sniffer is using a proper tool then he can receive the data.

DENIAL OF SERVICES ATTACK AND DISTRIBUTED DENIAL OF SERVICE ATTACK

Denial of service is a cyber-attack in which cybercriminals aims to interrupt the devices normal functioning so that devices are unavailable for the users. Dos Attack is done by flooding the network or servers with requests so it is difficult for the authorised victim to access it. It is difficult to recover from a denial of service attack. When attack crashes the server, sometimes it can be handled by just rebooting the system. A Dos attack can be launch by using a single computer. The US-CERT team provide some guidelines and indications that can be used in order to discover a Dos attack such as difficulties to access the website, higher number of spamming emails than usual and bad network performance. The motive behind this attack is to harm the organisation or the individual target but sometimes cyber criminal demand for the payment from the victim to end the DOS attack.

A Distributed denial of service attack is the most powerful cyber-attack on the internet. Cyber criminals aim is to send too much traffic to make a server or network unavailable for the user by flooding a website. The traffic used to make server unavailable contains fake packets or requests for connections. Botnets plays an important role to launch the DDos attack.

Buffer overflow is a type of Denial of service attack when more data insert in to the limited length of buffer and the extra data start to corrupting or overwriting the data in that limited space which causes the overflow and results in system crash. The malicious overflow data also creates the opportunity for the cyber criminals to run the script in order to do a malicious activity.

Flood attack is a kind of distributed denial of service attack in which it consumes all the available server resources in order to make a server unavailable for the target. Three-way handshake of TCP connection could be exploited by a flood attack. The attacker floods the victim device with the connection requests and when the victim device replies back the attacker the attacker system does not respond back due to which the victim system causes to time out and force the system to crash.

A Smurf Attack is a type of distributed denial of services attack. It uses ICMP request packets and IP spoofing to the targeted system. Smurf attack has a potential to exploit the broadcast networks IP addresses. The ICMP echo requests start from the fake targeted address.

Ping Death is a malicious type of denial of service attack. The attacker aim is to crash or freeze the victim computer or network by sending a large number of packets by using a ping command. POD attack can exploit the vulnerability which is already patched in the targeted system and for the unpatched systems, this attack is very dangerous.

Botnets are systems controlled by the cybercriminal which were infected in a previous stage with a specific malware. These botnets are very difficult to locate because bots are located in different locations in the world. These bots are used to launch an attack on the target system in order to consume the bandwidth and increase the processing tie of the victim's system.

LOT ATTACKS

Internet of things are those advance tech devices which are smart enough to do their tasks and can work wirelessly and do not need to connect to other devices to communicate by wire such as mobile phones, tablets, pagers, wearable tech which measure heart rate and insulin level, cameras, headphones, cars, etc. In modern era, broadband service is growing, gadgets with Wi-Fi capabilities are introudced day by day and processors are more efficient and affordable. The devices makers are creating the devices that can collect, send and shares the data. These gadgets make the life of users a lot easier. In hospitals, modern tech devices are able to monitor the patients more efficiently and make the communication easy between the staff and doctor. Cyber criminals are targeting these devices because these devices are not very secure.

Insider threats

Insiders are those one who know everything about the organisation, such as employees, former employees or business associates. Insider threat may occur by the three different kinds of people:

- **Malicious Insiders:** employees of an organization who take advantage of their rights for harming an organisation for their personal benefits.
- **Negligent Insiders:** employees of an organisation who are not following the policies and take the organisation at risk.
- **Infiltrators:** not part of the organisation but secretly gather information.

CYBER ATTACK INCIDENTS

Singapore

In 2018, a report published stated that Singapore was hit by a major cyber-attack. SingHealth is the largest Singapore healthcare group that was targeted by state-sponsored hackers. They stole the healthcare data of 1.5 million people and approximately 160,000 medical reports including the prime minister Lee Hsien Loong by exploiting an unpatched version of Microsoft outlook. They used a hacking tool which is available publicly and allowed them to install the malware on their vulnerable systems. In the published report, it was explained that the attack campaign lasted more than 10 months and stole the medical data as well as confidential data such as names, address, numbers and National identity card IDs. The main purpose was to target the higher-level individuals from politicians to industrial mangers (Quah, 2014). SingHealth has been fined $250,000 and the IT agency (IHiS) who is responsible for Singapore health sector get financial penalty of $750,000 for failing not to take the security measures to protect the information so the total sum is $1 million fine. Based on the success of the attack we can conclude that the staff of IHiS did not have the proper cyber security awareness and training which was the reason staff did not respond quickly and effectively to the attack. Moreover, there were mis-configurations and vulnerabilities in the SingHealth Network and SCM system that should have been resolved before the attack. Finally, the IT security incident response team of an IHiS failed to take an appropriate or timely action to prevent data stealing.

Based on the findings of the analysis of this incident the recommendations that could be given to the organizations would include the improvement of cyber security policies, the redesign of their incident response plans, the scheduling of appropriate training of key staff of the organization, the installation of IPS and IDS systems and the overall change of the governance model in terms of cyber security.

United Kingdom

The year 2017 was a nightmare in the history of cyber World because of a global cyber-attack known as WannaCry ransomware. A report from the department of health and social care found that NHS is attacked by the cyber criminals which costs NHS a total estimated amount of £92m. The WannaCry attack caused a serious damage to more than 80 trusted hospitals and 8% of GP practices. The total of 200,000 computers were shut down and lock out the users with the error messages demanding the ransom payment through Bitcoins. According to the report, WannaCry attack cancelled a number of total 19,000 appointments which costed the NHS £20 million and £72 million in order to clean up the mess and upgrades the IT systems. After the Investigation the attack is blamed on the North Korea Hackers. When the attack happened, NHS was using outdated operating system and software such as Windows XP which is vulnerable and allowed attackers get unauthorised access in to their systems. NHS had increased the infrastructure investment of £60 millionin 2018 and Government said that they will spend the total of £150 million to upgrade their IT technology over the next three years. The results have shown that organisations have made good progress in implementing data security standards related to people and process, but that those relating to technology continue to be challenging.

One year before the incident, NHS was warned about the cyber-attack because their two local healthcare branches were infected previously by a ransomware attack. One major reason that attack was successful was that NHS was running old operating system (Window XP) in their systems. Based on the findings of the analysis of this incident the recommendations that could be given to the organizations would include the update of the operating systems, the development of appropriate incident response plans, the scheduling of appropriate training of key staff of the organization, the installation of antivirus, antimalware, IPS and IDS systems and the overall change of the governance model in terms of cyber security.

Data Breach:

After the devastating WannaCry attack, NHS was affected by a data breach in 2018. NHS accidentally shared the sensitive data of 150,000 patients. The reason behind is a coding error in the IT system known asSystmOne used by GPs and developed by the TPP. Confidential data were given to the healthcare on the basis that it was used to provide the medical care to the people but it was exploited for research purposes and clinical audit by the NHS without the knowledge of patients. All the GPs and the patients have been informed about this issue. The Software Developer TPP apologised for the fault in the system and working with the NHS digital to resolve the issue. TPP clinical director John Parry said the privacy of patient data "is a key priority for TPP, and we continually make improvements to our system to ensure that patients have optimum control over information". This attack was due to a coding error in the SystmOne software. A correct countermeasure for this attack is the testing of any new software before deployment by the software assurance team.

United States of America

UnityPoint Health data breach was the biggest breach in the history of the US. A total of 1.4 million patient records has been breached. A Phishing attack was used in order to compromise their business system. In 2018, there are two data breaches in UnityPoint health. First breach happened in its Madison campus by a phishing attack on a staff member email account and breached the total of 16,000 patient's confidential data. According to the report, the staff of the UnityPoint health received the attachment file in the email, used to trick them to give the login information which led the hacker get access into their internal email system. According to the forensics investigators and law enforcement research, the purpose of the attack was financially based because the hackers were trying to use the email system of the staff to make changes in the payroll payments.

The unauthorised access to their patient confidential data have happened but there is no misuse of the patient data is still reported. The main focus of the hackers was to divert the business funds of an organisation. This attack exploited the human factor that is responsible for the majority of the cyber attacks. In this instance proper training along with specific technologies that can secure email applications (mail filters, IDS and IPS) along with proper incident response plans are the first recommendations to give to this organization.

On the 18th of March of 2018, another cyber-attack which compromised the confidential data of 500,000 patients of LifeBridge took place. The EMR server of the LifeBridge Health that shared the registration and billing system for the other LifeBridge providers was infected with a malware that compromised the confidential information of patients. According to the investigation report, the hackers first got the access in to the servers on 2016 and compromised the data such as patient name, dates of birth, medical history, treatment information and insurance data of patients. Hackers also compromised the social security number of some patients. This attack exploited a vulnerability in the EMR server of the LifeBridge Health which allowed hackers to install malware in the system. Key recommendations for this incident would be the use of a secure SSL/HTTPS encryption protocol, installation of antivirus, patching and update of software and routers proper configuration.

RECOMMENDATIONS

The table that follows states all recommendations that need to be taken in order to secure a hospital from cyber attacks., based also on the findings from the real incidents that happened during the past years. Other security measures can also be applied (Cook, 2017). Education of employees is an important aspect of cyber security and dedicated cyber ranges can be used (Hallaq, 2018). These recommendations can be used as a basis for building a cyber security framework that can be used from healthcare providers in order to perform a gap analysis and conduct cyber security assessments. These assessments can reveal the security gaps in the organization, help organize the mitigation plans and their immediate actions. A standardized maturity assessment model could be used a trademark for organizations to showcase their increased cyber security level and thus improve their entrepreneurial position.

The proposed countermeasures can be grouped in several categories. Technical measures consider the technological tools (software and hardware) to prevent, detect, mitigate, and respond to cyber-attacks. Organizational measures are important for the proper implementation of any type of national initiative or policy. Capacity building measures aim to enhance knowledge and know-how in order to promote cyber security. Finally, legal measures aim to provide legislations and an implementable regulatory framework to protect the cyber space.

CONCLUSION

In Conclusion, Healthcare is the biggest industry in the world. Every country has its own healthcare system such as hospitals, care centres but they are not secure. The systems in the healthcare sector are vulnerable and software is most of the times outdated. Cyber criminals are targeting the healthcare sector because it is easy to exploit the vulnerabilities and steal the medical data which is valuable and worth a lot of money. Medical Information is a sensitive data of patient such as names, address, medical ID number and diagnosis.

Table 1.

No	Cyber Threats		Recommendations
1	**Malware**	**Virus** **Trojans** **Worms** **Logic bombs** **Ransomware** **Adware** **Spyware**	• Always keep your software updated and apply patches when released • Do not click on links or download files if any untrusted email you get • Always install an antivirus in your systems • Always backup your data if you do not want to lose it. For backup use external hard drives or private cloud storage • Use a strong password which includes Capital and small alphabets, numbers and special characters • Turn on and configure properly firewalls which are built-in in your system • On your browser always use an ad pop-up blocker • Do not download files from untrusted websites.
2	**Ma-in-the-Middle Attack**	**Session Hijacking**	• Use the secure SSL/HTTPS encryption protocol in order to secure your communication • Always install antivirus software in your systems • Always keep your software updated and patch which has a bug fix when release
		IP spoofing	• Use secure encryption protocols like HTTPS • Use a software like network blocker • Configure your routers and switches in a way that they block the packets that are coming from other networks, not from your local network if supported
		Replay	• Encryption: encrypt your messages
3	**Phishing and Spear Phishing attack**		• Use ad pop-up blocker • Install anti-virus software • Always update software • Always turn on firewalls
4	**Password Attack**	**Brute-Force** **Dictionary Attack**	• Use a two-factor authentication method • Use a Multi-factor Authentication which is more secure
5	**SQL Injection**		• Always update and apply patches • Always turn on the web application firewalls • Avoid using dynamic SQL queries • Use encryption and password hashing to secure your data • Install monitoring tools
6	**XSS attack**		• Use SDL standard when you are developing the website • On each page Use the right Meta tag to declare characters in your website • Sanitize the data • Add functions which validate the data
7	**Eavesdropping**		• Encrypt your emails • Use the secure SSL/HTTPS encryption protocol in order to secure your communication • Use VPN's • Use the secure SSL/HTTPS encryption protocol in order to secure your communication
8	**Dos and DDos**	**Buffer overflow**	• Disable the services which are unneeded • Use a firewall • Use an Intrusion prevention system
		Flood overflow	• Use a firewall before servers • increase the connection queue size and decrease the open connection timeout.
		Smurf	• disable the router IP-directed broadcast
		Ping Death	• use a firewall to block the ping death attack
		Botnets	• Use the RFC3704 filtering which blocks the traffic from spoofed addresses • Black-hole filtering which stops the undesirable traffic to enter in the network
9	**IoT Attack**		• Use strong encryption • Strong and unique passwords for the Wi-Fi network • Keep your software updated • Use a two-factor authentication method • Try to avoid public free wi-fi • Update your network devices like routers and switches which are offering strong security
10	**Insider Threat**		• Monitor the activity • Organisation must provide cyber security training to their employees to notice the suspicious activity and benefit of cyber security • Publish a security policy • Apply Physical security • Secure the systems and use a secure authentication finger print scanner in the building

There are many cyber threats which can affect the healthcare system in a second and cause a lot of damage which we cannot imagine. The impact of cyber-attacks is devastating. Millions of patient records were compromised during several attacks that took place in recent years which cost the loss of billions of dollars.

It is always the organisation staff and higher rank officers' fault that they do not take the cyber-attack seriously and do not take the action immediately in order to secure their systems or networks. There are few security solutions that could be applied but healthcare sector should have to follow a proper security framework. There must be set of rules and regulations and policies. There must be an incident response team ready and well trained which immediately can act and try to mitigate an attack once happened. There are security mechanisms like an Intrusion detection system and an intrusion prevention system, that are really helpful in order to detect and block attacks that can be used in order to increase the security level of the healthcare sector.

This book chapter presents major cyber threat actors that exist in the healthcare sector, common cyber-attacks that can be launched against all actors and real incidents that took place during the past years. Based on these, the current chapter, proposes in a tabular form a set of recommendations that can be used as countermeasures against any type of attack. These recommendations can be incorporated into a cybersecurity framework or cyber security assessment model that healthcare providers could use in order to perform a gap analysis, assess their security level and take appropriate mitigation actions. A proper assessment can reveal any security gaps in the organization, help organize the mitigation plans and their immediate actions. A standardized maturity assessment model could be used a trademark for organizations to showcase their increased cyber security level and thus improve their entrepreneurial position.

REFERENCES

Ayres, N., & Maglaras, L. A. (2016). Cyberterrorism targeting the general public through social media. *Security and Communication Networks*, *9*(15), 2864–2875. doi:10.1002ec.1568

Cook, A. J., Janicke, H., Maglaras, L., & Smith, R. (2017). An assessment of the application of IT security mechanisms to industrial control systems. *International Journal of Internet Technology and Secured Transactions*, *7*(2), 144–174. doi:10.1504/IJITST.2017.087163

Evans, M. H., He, Y., Maglaras, L., & Janicke, H. (2019). Heart-is: A novel technique for evaluating human error-related information security incidents. *Computers & Security*, *80*, 74–89. doi:10.1016/j.cose.2018.09.002

Ferrag, M. A. (2018). *Authentication schemes for Smart Mobile Devices: Threat Models, Countermeasures, and Open Research Issues.* arXiv preprint, arXiv:1803.10281

Gozzi, R. (2000). The Trojan horse metaphor. *ETC: A Review of General Semantics, 57*(1), 80-84.

Hallaq, B. N. (2018). CYRAN: a hybrid cyber range for testing security on ICS/SCADA systems. In Cyber Security and Threats: Concepts, Methodologies, Tools, and Applications (pp. 622-637). IGI.

Kavoura, A. a. (2017). Polish Firms' Innovation Capability for Competitiveness via Information Technologies and Social Media Implementation. Factors Affecting Firm Competitiveness and Performance in the Modern Business World. In A. N. Vlachvei (Ed.), Factors Affecting Firm Competitiveness and Performance in the Modern Business World. Academic Press.

Kavoura, A., & Andersson, T. (2016). Applying Delphi method for strategic design of social entrepreneurship. *Library Review*, *65*(3), 185–205. doi:10.1108/LR-06-2015-0062

Kenkre, P. S. (2014). Real time intrusion detection and prevention system. In *3rd International Conference on Frontiers of Intelligent Computing: Theory and Applications (FICTA)* (pp. 405-411). Springer International Publishing.

Kenkre, P. S. (2014). Taxonomy and survey of collaborative intrusion detection. *ACM Computing Surveys, 47*(4), 55.

Maglaras, L. A., Kim, K.-H., Janicke, H., Ferrag, M. A., Rallis, S., Fragkou, P., Maglaras, A., & Cruz, T. J. (2018). Cyber security of critical infrastructures. *ICT Express*, *4*(1), 42–45. doi:10.1016/j.icte.2018.02.001

Makarona, E. K. A. (2019). Redesigning the Ivory Tower: Academic entrepreneurship as a new calling supporting economic growth, The Malopolska School of Economics. *Tarnow Research Papers Collection*, *42*, 15–26.

Orman, H. (2003). The Morris worm: A fifteen-year perspective. *IEEE Security and Privacy*, *1*(5), 35–43. doi:10.1109/MSECP.2003.1236233

Parikka, J. (2007). *Digital contagions: A media archaeology of computer viruses*. Peter Lang.

Quah, J. L., Yap, S., Cheah, S. O., Ng, Y. Y., Goh, E. S., Doctor, N., Leong, B. S.-H., Tiah, L., Chia, M. Y. C., & Ong, M. E. H. (2014). Knowledge of signs and symptoms of heart attack and stroke among Singapore residents. *BioMed Research International*, *2014*, 1–8. doi:10.1155/2014/572425 PMID:24812623

Sadeghi, A. R. (2015). Security and privacy challenges in industrial internet of things. In *52nd Annual Design Automation Conference* (p. 52). ACM. 10.1145/2744769.2747942

Sood, A. K., & Enbody, R. J. (2011). Malvertising–exploiting web advertising. *Computer Fraud & Security*, *2011*(4), 11–16. doi:10.1016/S1361-3723(11)70041-0

Subramanya, S. R., & Lakshminarasimhan, N. (2001). Computer viruses. *IEEE Potentials*, *20*(4), 16–19. doi:10.1109/45.969588

Woo, P. S. (2015). *Towards Cyber Security Risks Assessment in Electric Utility SCADA Systems. Electrical Engineering and Technology*, *10*(3), 888–894.

Zhang, X. L., Liu, S., Chen, X., Wang, L., Gao, B., & Zhu, Q. (2018). Health information privacy concerns, antecedents, and information disclosure intention in online health communities. *Information & Management*, *55*(4), 482–493. doi:10.1016/j.im.2017.11.003

ADDITIONAL READING

Andreasson, K. J. (Ed.). (2011). *Cybersecurity: public sector threats and responses.* CRC Press. doi:10.1201/b11363

Coventry, L., & Branley, D. (2018). Cybersecurity in healthcare: A narrative review of trends, threats and ways forward. *Maturitas*, *113*, 48–52. doi:10.1016/j.maturitas.2018.04.008 PMID:29903648

Maglaras, L., Ferrag, M. A., Derhab, A., Mukherjee, M., Janicke, H., & Rallis, S. (2019). Threats, Protection and Attribution of Cyber Attacks on Critical Infrastructures. *arXiv preprint arXiv:1901.03899.*

Mariani, D. M. R., & Mohammed, S. (2015). Cybersecurity challenges and compliance issues within the US healthcare sector. *International Journal of Business and Social Research*, *5*(02).

Rowe, B. R., & Gallaher, M. P. (2006, March). Private sector cyber security investment strategies: An empirical analysis. In *The fifth workshop on the economics of information security (WEIS06).*

Shackelford, S. J., Proia, A. A., Martell, B., & Craig, A. N. (2015). Toward a global cybersecurity standard of care: Exploring the implications of the 2014 NIST cybersecurity framework on shaping reasonable national and international cybersecurity practices. *Tex. Int'l LJ*, *50*, 305.

KEY TERMS AND DEFINITIONS

CSIRT: Computer security incident response team.
ENISA: European Union Agency for Cyber Security.
ICT: Information and communication technology.
IDS: Intrusion detection system.
IPS: Intrusion prevention system.

Chapter 8
Profiling Small and Medium Enterprises' Innovativeness During Periods of Economic Crisis:
A Case Study From a Greek Region Using Strategic Groups

Ioannis Antoniadis
https://orcid.org/0000-0002-5008-2935
University of Western Macedonia, Greece

Elpida Tryfon Samara
https://orcid.org/0000-0002-2683-1131
University of Western Macedonia, Greece

Thomai Karamitsou
University of Western Macedonia, Greece

ABSTRACT

The role of innovation as a vital driving force of entrepreneurship and economic development has been widely acknowledged. Especially in an era of economic turbulence, innovation can be seen as the only realistic strategy that can lead enterprises out of the crisis. Based on the innovation taxonomies identified in the Oslo Manual, namely organizational, marketing, process, and product innovation, a survey was carried out in a Greek region adapting the fourth Community Innovation Survey questionnaire in 43 SMEs, capturing the effects of economic recession on the firms' innovativeness, and drawing a profile of the entrepreneurship innovation in the region of Western Macedonia, Greece. By applying a strategic group's approach, the authors come up with some interesting findings concerning the type of SME innovativeness and results of innovation during a period of financial crisis.

DOI: 10.4018/978-1-7998-3648-3.ch008

INTRODUCTION

Innovation - being organizational, marketing, process and product - is the engine of competition and industry competitiveness (Ambec et al., 2013; Cegarra-Navarro et al., 2016, Bookis, 2016) and a major drive for entrepreneurship (Masouras 2019b). Companies innovate primarily by introducing new products in the market and innovating is a way of scoring points against competition. Nevertheless, innovation on its own cannot make a business blossom since market success and development is highly influenced by the economic environment (Workman, 1993).

There is a consensus among economists on innovative actions to be taken during an economic recession and crisis (Gulati et al., 2010; Hyytinen and Toivanen, 2005). In that sense, these actions can be seen as the only realistic process that can lead enterprises out of the crisis, and help them build social capital and trust with stakeholders (Antoniadis and Charmantzi, 2016). Moreover, someone should take into consideration Joseph Schumpeter, who famously argued that the process of "creative destruction", while painful, fosters innovation and progress by discarding the old and familiar for the new and better (Schumpeter, 1983). From this perspective, the downturn may be a source of opportunities for innovators and innovation systems. Also, it is particularly relevant to study innovation to understand whether the crisis potentially affected firms' innovation and, in this way, their capacity to improve their competitiveness.

Based on the above, this chapter seeks to examine whether innovative activities can be maintained in a difficult economic situation and if so will they constitute a valid way to cope with crisis and recession periods. To do so, a questionnaire measuring innovativeness is used in a Greek region. The questionnaire was answered by participants for 2 different time periods, the first from 2007-2010 and the second from 2011-2016 in order to study the impact of the economic crisis on the innovative activities of the region. The chapter is organized as follows: In the next section, we put forward the theoretical background of the empirical analysis. Section three presents the data sources and methodology. Section four presents a descriptive analysis and results on the firms' innovativeness in a Greek region, and more specifically the region of Western Macedonia, describing the different profiles of innovative firms using the strategic group methodology and cluster analysis. Finally, the last section contains discussion and conclusions.

THEORETICAL FRAMEWORK

Innovation for Business

As today's global economic landscape is changing rapidly, the ability of businesses to introduce new innovative products to the market faster than their competitors is perhaps their most distinct competitive advantage. This becomes obvious by the significant market share that innovative companies gain while increasing profitability (Cegarra-Navarra, 2016). Extensive research in this field has shown that companies that are constantly innovating normally double their profits compared to others. Therefore, innovation constitutes the foundation and driver of competitiveness worldwide (Carayiannis, et al., 2014). In the context of the green paper on innovation, innovation is taken as being a synonym for the successful production, assimilation, and exploitation of novelty in the economic and social spheres. Innovation, at an aggregate level, represents the successful exploitation of ideas that are new to an adopting organization, into profitable products, processes and / or services (Boukis, 2016).

The term innovation refers to a process that comprises three stages: the conception of a new idea, its evaluation, and, finally, its practical implementation. Thus, innovation is a multidimensional concept constituting an important element of modern entrepreneurship. It includes the element of introducing and implementing innovations as well as the creative imitation of any innovative entrepreneurial endeavor, recognizes and exploits market-generated profit opportunities, seizes opportunities differently from others, and undertakes business initiatives that do not only focusing on the creation of businesses but also on their modernization.

The list of innovation taxonomies is really broad. It starts from architectural, modular, improving and evolutionary innovations, to radical, incremental, really new, discontinuous and imitative innovations (Garcia and Calantone, 2002). In the literature, the two categories of radical and incremental innovations are referred to as the most embedded taxonomies (Chandy and Tellis, 2000; Henderson and Clark, 1990; Myers and Tucker, 1989). Radical innovation refers to major changes in technology/knowledge that stem from the discovery of something new, while incremental innovations are major advances to an established technology/knowledge (Garcia and Calantone, 2002). In Organization for Economic Co-operation and Development (OECD's) Oslo Manual, which provides guidelines for collecting and interpreting innovation data, innovation is defined as the implementation of products or production and delivery of processes with new or significantly improved characteristics. The third edition of the Oslo Manual extends the definition to include new organizational methods in business practices, workplace organization, or external relations (OECD, 2005).

In this research, we use the four types of innovation as identified in this third edition of Oslo Manual for measuring innovation: product innovation; process innovation; marketing innovation and organizational innovation (OECD, 2005).

- **Product Innovation**, *involves a good or service that is new or significantly improved. This includes significant improvements in technical specifications, components, and materials, incorporated software, user-friendliness or other functional characteristics. In the education sector, product innovation can be a new or significantly improved curriculum, a new educational software, etc*" (OECD, 2005).
- **Process Innovation** *involves a new or significantly improved production or delivery method. This includes significant changes in techniques, equipment and / or software. In education, this can, for example, be a new or significantly improved pedagogy*" (OECD, 2005).
- **Marketing Innovation** *involves a new marketing method engaging significant changes in product design or packaging, product placement, product promotion or pricing. In education, this can, for example, be a new way of pricing the education service or a new admission strategy*" (OECD, 2005).
- **Organizational Innovation** *involves introducing a new organizational method in the firm's business practices, workplace organization or external relations. In education, this can, for example, be a new way of organization of work between teachers, or organizational changes in the administrative area*"(OECD, 2005).

Schumpeter considers innovation as a critical dimension of economic change and competitiveness (Hyytinen and Toivanen, 2005). From his point of view, economic change revolves around innovation, entrepreneurship and market power. According to M. Porter (Damanpour, 1992), sustainable competitive advantages are achieved by a firm while performing the same profit with lower costs than its competitors (cost advantage) or get higher profits compared to its competitors on competitive products (differentiation advantage). Taking all the above into consideration, the competitive advantage enables the firm to provide higher value for consumers and also make a higher profit. The competitive advantages are based on a strategic management model that works simultaneously with the innovation process that has to be encouraged, maintained and developed through various business strategies (Garcia and Calantone, 2002, Bookis, 2016).

The Crisis Environment

The economic crisis that started in 2008 has negatively affected business innovation and research and development (R&D) in all countries. It has caused a severe slowdown of global economic growth. This slowdown means the reduction of goods demand, services, and industrial products. In fact, businesses are under strong pressure to adapt to these conditions. Often they have to cut costs, rethink their corporate strategy, investments as well as restructuring their activities (Ulrich, Rogovsky and Lamotte, 2009). A combination of the economic downturn and fiscal austerity are negatively influencing aggregate demand. On the other hand, the banking crisis led to tougher credit conditions. Generally, the problems that businesses face during that period of crisis of relevance to innovation are:

- The lower demand for their products and substantial uncertainties over future trends in consumption (Almunia et al., 2009; Reinhart and Rogoff, 2009).
- The potential challenges that public support for innovation faces, given the priority attached to fiscal consolidation.
- The vulnerabilities of the global financial system (Reinhart, 2011). Fragilities in the banking sector affect innovative businesses' opportunities to obtain external financing. With markets speculating in sovereign default risks, moreover, the banking sector in Europe and beyond remains at risk (IMF, 2011a, 2011b).

So, in this turbulent economic environment of the crisis, businesses are faced with the urgent need to take action to survive. Businesses that act decisively and strategically and respond early to the crisis they usually do better than those who suffer from paralysis or re-act panic-stricken (Branstad, Jackson and Banerji, 2009). Indeed, how fast and effectively someone responds to a business crisis, affects its reputation, its credibility, the integrity of its business and its market performance (Calloway & Keen, 1996).

Although crisis affects all sectors of business activity, Small and Medium-sized Enterprises (SMEs) are considered more vulnerable compared to large enterprises since they lack, in comparison, the management mechanisms, the manpower, the material and the financial resources to deal with such unexpected events. According to Archibugi et al. (2013), small and medium-sized enterprises are generally more vulnerable in times of crisis for many reasons, such as:

- It is more difficult for them to shrink as they are already small enough.
- There are no significant differences between their economic activities.
- They have low capitalization.
- They have a low or no credit rating.
- They are highly dependent on their credit rating.

The global financial crisis did not affect all countries to the same extent and recovery processes were very unequal (EC, 2011a). The intensity of the shock and the differences in countries' innovation systems also produced differential impacts on innovation performance. Moreover, according to international articles the crisis was widely predicted by markets but without predicting the intensity and extent with which it spread (Togni, Cubico and Favretto, 2010). Most businesses have had more or less time to prepare. In addition, businessmen and business executives had already faced different types of crises in previous years and therefore already had implemented and consolidated their strategy to cope with difficult economic times. Taking into consideration that a crisis is never far from business, several of them prepared a plan in case they are faced with high situations of uncertainty. Moreover, some firms will exhibit a persistency in investing in innovation during recessions, but others will not.

The Greek SMEs During the Crisis

The recent economic crisis has significantly influenced businesses in Greece both from the demand and supply side. The Greek economy and especially the Greek SMEs were called upon to operate in an explosive environment. Greece's credibility in international capital markets has been shaken. Private and public investment has been significantly reduced. Over-lending and over-consumption of the public fueled over-consumption of the private sector, maintaining significant deficits in competitiveness and productivity. The government debt as a percentage of GDP has grown significantly and the state is now left in extraordinary lending by official bodies to finance social expenditure, wages, and budget deficit. So the country had to appeal to the IMF, the ECB, and the EU to avoid a halt to payments; and adopted an ambitious and rigorous fiscal adjustment program. Of course, beyond the deficit and debt crisis, the country is facing challenges to its competitiveness and employment prospects, as well as to its human resources (Masouras, 2019a). It falls short of its European partners in critical sizes, such as foreign direct investment, labor productivity and the degree of participation population in the workforce. The Greek economy was unable to provide employment opportunities, especially among young people and women and suffers from low rate mobility of the workforce, which makes it difficult to find a job for new entrants to the market.

According to PwC of Greece, the crisis has led Greek companies to reduce their long-term plans, increase their liquidity, reduce operating costs and adopt a more cautious attitude towards large investments. Coming out of the crisis, however, Greek companies need to choose the strategy to follow, to increase the value of their business, either by accelerating their growth or by improving their profit margins. Many have been forced to close their businesses and switch to foreign markets, migrating to third countries or investing in third countries creating new businesses there. We cite Bulgaria as an example. Moreover, PwC reports that the competitiveness of Greek companies has improved, but only marginally. Of the 8.7 that was the average competitiveness indicator for the 3,000 largest companies, in 2016 it was 10.4. However, this change in the scale of competitiveness from 1 to 27 is not considered a "tectonic" change. Finally, the study concludes: "the crisis is over, but the corporate economy is neither ready nor willing to grow." This is because Greek companies eventually, after a decade of the financial crisis, adapted more to a low-demand environment than to a process of deeper competition.

Taking all the above into consideration, the crisis has made it clear that the pre-existing Greek model of development suffered from structural disadvantages that the country had to face for the Greek economy to recover. Today, the need for adoption in innovative actions is imperative to lead the country gradually out of recession and austerity into one sustainable economic growth.

Numerous surveys have been carried out at a regional and national level, to study the impact of the crisis on small and medium-sized enterprises. The present research focuses on studying the impact of the crisis on the innovativeness of SMEs in a Greek Region, the region of Western Macedonia.

Western Macedonia's regional economy is based heavily on the mining activities, the production of electric power (70% of the country's total electric power is produced in the region) and the fur-leather sector (Samara et al. 2010). The primary sector is significantly underperforming, regarding productivity, although lately, it has developed new directions through niche markets, for example, organic production and high-end wine production. The tertiary sector develops important areas of tourism-related activities and supporting services as well as of the main manufacturing activities. Western Macedonia and Epirus are the two Greek regions that posted the highest unemployment rate (20.3 percent) for 2018 (Samara et al., 2018).

According to the most recent study on the competitiveness of EU regions, out of a total of 262 EU-27 regions, RWM, like all Greek regions, is very low on all indicators (except Attica). More specifically, based on the competitiveness indicators we have (Regional competitiveness statistics):

- Ø On the main pillars, the RWM is particularly low in the quality of institutions (last in the ranking in the Greek regions along with the regions of Central Macedonia and Thessaly) and infrastructure in 6th place out of the 13 Greek Regions. In terms of health, almost all of the Greek regions are in the best position at the European level, with RWM ranking 4th in Greece.
- Ø In the pillars of efficiency, in the Higher Education and Lifelong Learning Index, the RWM is ranked 9th out of 13, 10th in labor market efficiency and 6th in market size. In all three indicators of the pillar of efficiency, the Greek regions are very low in the ranking of European regions.
- Ø In terms of innovation pillars and technological readiness index, RWM is in the 5th position along with the Regions of Eastern Macedonia - Thrace, Central Macedonia, Thessaly, and Epirus while in the innovation index is in 6th place.

Noteworthy is the RWM's position in the index of business culture, which occupies the last position in the Greek regions and two positions before the end in the European regions (260th out of 262 regions). In the sub-category indices, the RWM is in the last positions of the European regions while in the Greek regions it is 8th in the key pillars, 13th in the efficiency pillars and 12th in the innovation pillars. The RCI (Regional Competitiveness Index) 2016 ranks 12th in Greece and 258th out of 262 in Europe. The RWM ranks lower than the European average in all ICT-related indicators, both at the level of public services to the citizen and at the level of businesses. The European Commission has been monitoring Member States' digital competitiveness with the Digital Economy and Society Index (DESI) reports since 2015. Greece ranks 26th out of the 28 EU Member States in the European Commission Digital Economy and Society Index (DESI) 2019 (Digital Economy and Society Index (DESI) 2019 Country Report, 2019). Greece - compared to the other Member States - still ranks low on all indicators related to the Digital Agenda 2020 (European Commission, 2017). Of the few indicators available, it appears that RWM in 2011 is significantly behind the European average frequent use of the Internet (44%, EU27 68%) but also online shopping (15%, EU27 45%). Although it has experienced rapid growth in both categories over the last 2 years (at 54%, and 23% in 2013 respectively) the divergence from the European average remains.

The innovative image of the Region of Western Macedonia is detailed in the Regional Innovation Scoreboard, 2016. Specifically, RWM belongs to the third category of innovation, moderate innovation, while its innovative performance decreased significantly (-12%) compared to the last two years. The graphs of the summary innovation index (Figures 1, 2) show that the relative advantages compared to the EU28 average are in the indicators: non-R&D innovation costs, SMEs with marketing innovation or organizational innovation, as well as tertiary education.

Figure 1. Innovation Summary Index. Source: Regional Innovation Scoreboard, 2016.

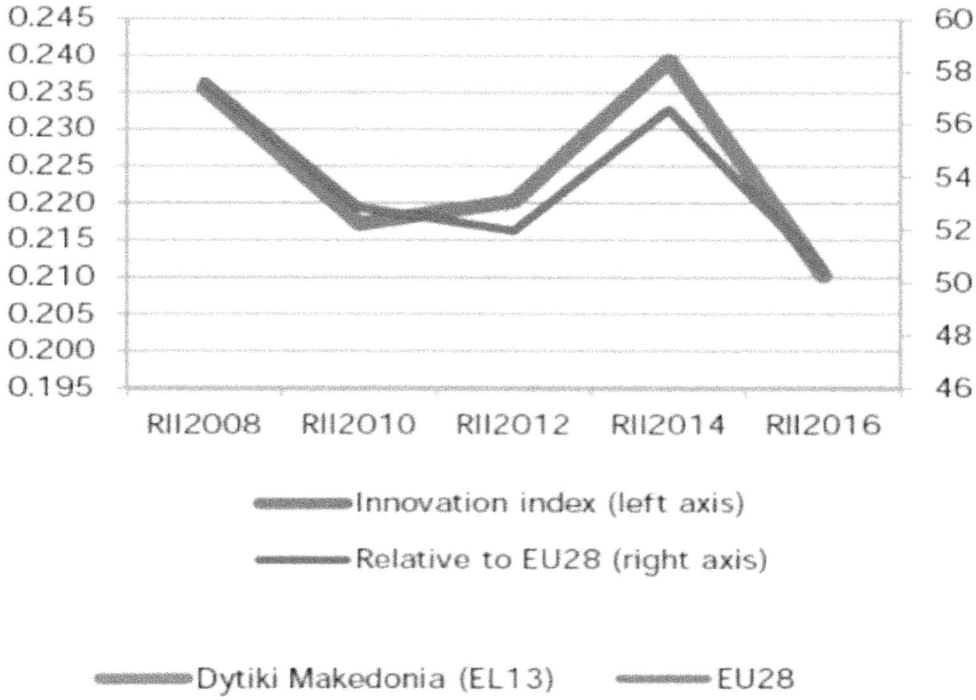

Figure 2. Histogram of innovation subcategories that make up the summary innovation index. Source: Regional Innovation Scoreboard, 2016.

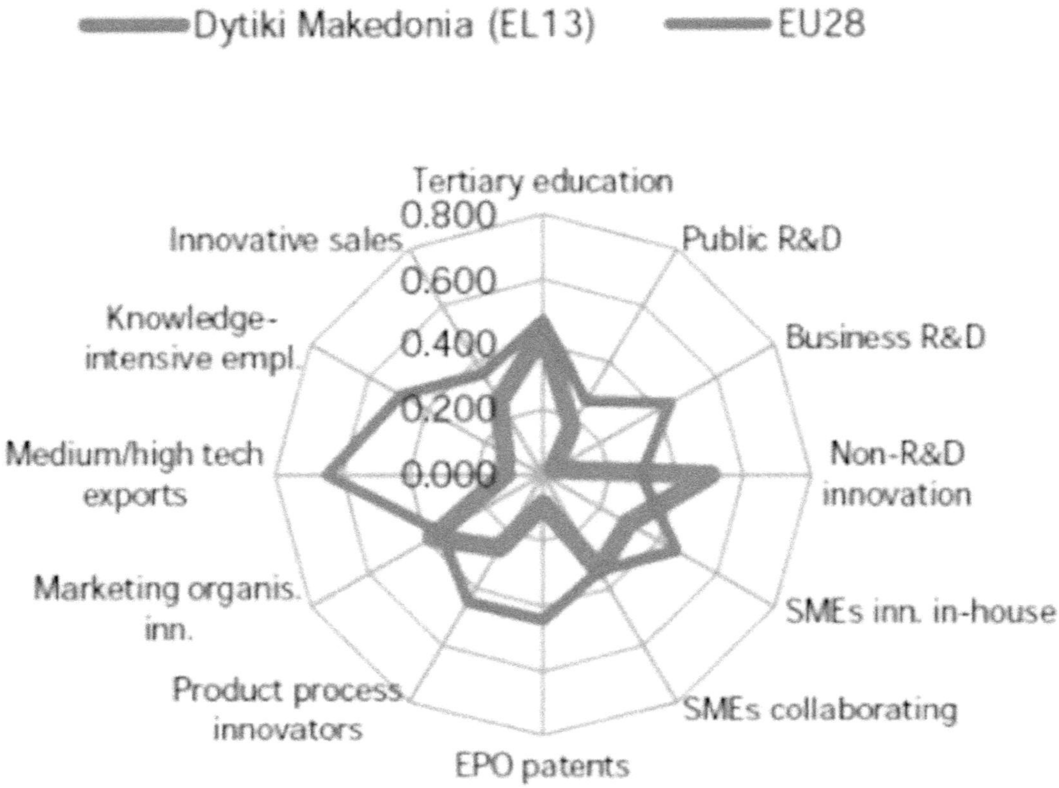

The trend graph (Figure3) below shows that the relative advantages of the Regional Innovation System (i.e. the indicators above the shaded area, reflecting the Regional Innovation Index of the Region) are the non-R&D costs innovation, participation in higher education, and SMEs with marketing or organizational innovation. Weakness appears in business R&D spending, EPO patents and exports of medium and high technology products.

Figure 3. Graphs of innovation subcategories of the innovation summary index. Source: Regional Innovation Scoreboard, 2016.

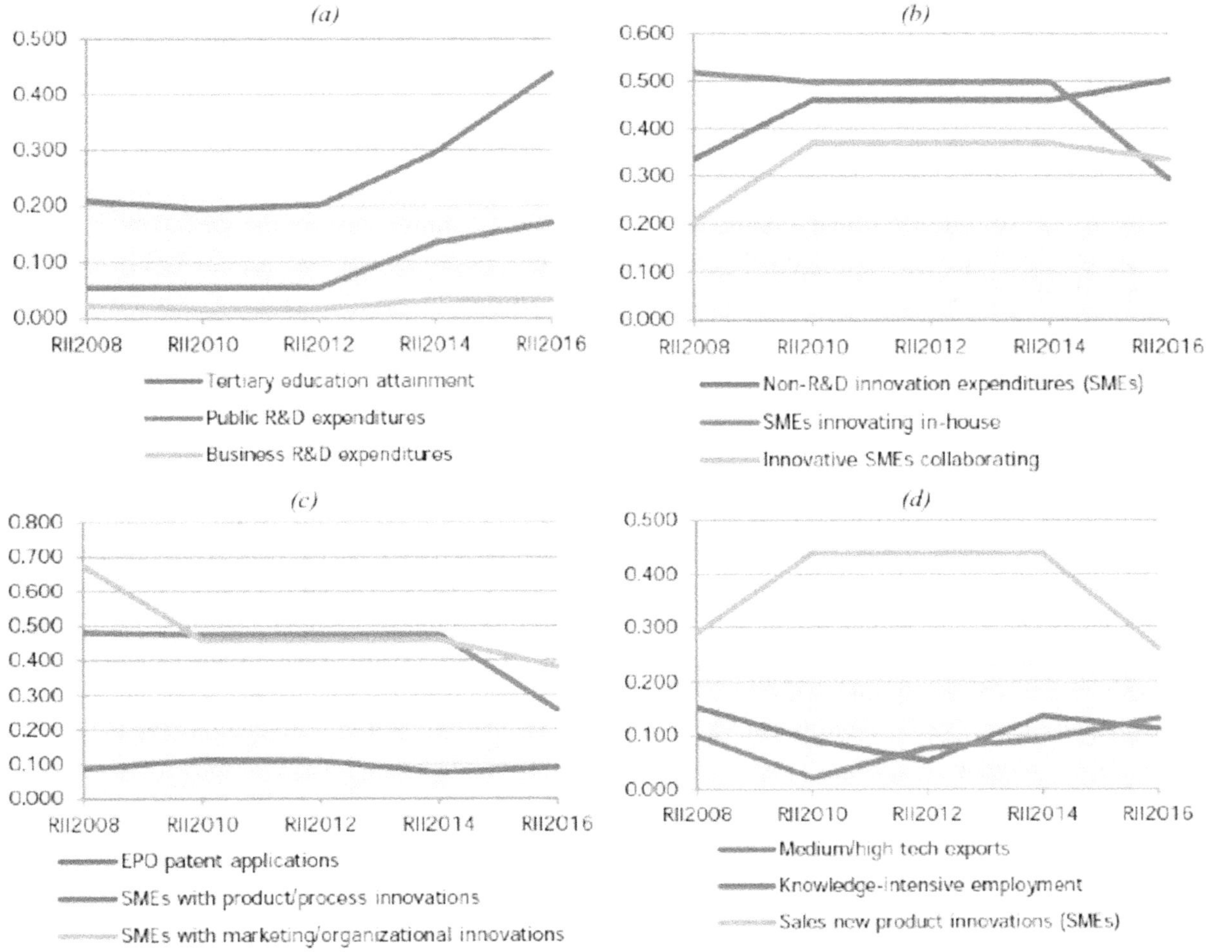

The study of the innovation indicators for the Region of Western Macedonia under the impact of the crisis is the main objective of this research study, using the Community Innovation Survey (CIS) 4 questionnaire. The study horizon of the questionnaires is from 2007-2016 and is the same as the time horizon of indexing the charts above. Therefore, we can identify and confirm the trend of these indicators through our research.

METHODOLOGY

The authors conducted a survey methodology based on the Community Innovation Survey (CIS) 4 questionnaire concept in one Greek region, namely the Region of Western Macedonia, during the first semester of 2016. This research is investigating the four types of innovation in the region, namely, product innovation; process innovation; marketing innovation and organizational innovation, and the attitudes of SMEs towards them, and also the ways they felt it benefited their business, and helped them to tackle the crisis.

The sample used was random, and face to face interviews were used as a method to gather information. In particular, in simple random sampling, all statistical units and all n-size samples have the same probability of being selected. The sampling frame was generated from a database provided by

the chambers of the region. An initial questionnaire, was sent in 300 randomly selected firms from various economic sectors, containing 10 questions concerning basic innovation principles (e.g if the firm has a site, or whether it has filed a patent for a product etc.). The firms that have answered positively in 70% of the questions in the initial questionnaire were then selected for the second stage of our research, that included the extended CIS questionnaire. That questionnaire was sent in 102 firms from the original 300 firms.

To maximise the response rate, the researchers contacted with the targeted SMEs, educate them of the objectives/ benefits of the study and proactively encouraged participation by being a point of contact which respondents could approach if in need of assistance when filling in the questionnaires. 43 completed usable questionnaires were obtained, representing an 28,66% response rate. It is acknowledged that this response rate is relatively low, although not entirely unexpected, taking into consideration the above mentioned numbers and indicators of the RWM regarding innovation culture. It is however satisfactory considering the response rates of similar organizational studies concerning firms (Baruch and Holtom, 2008; Fulton, 2018). In any case, the businesses that accepted and completed the questionnaire, based on the Central Limit Theorem, are a reliable sample that can contribute to the formulation of statistically significant research results. In this context, we can use the table of N (0,1) distribution when n (sample) is greater than 0. Therefore, for the purpose of a questionnaire survey, the sample should be greater than 30 (Chatzinikolaou, 2002). Finally, the value of Cronbach's Alpa for the 29 questions regarding the importance of innovation (process, product organizational and marketing) was 0.859.

From the analysis of the data gathered through face-to-face interviews the following key point areas were assessed:

- the number of staff, since usually small companies in terms of employees very rarely innovate,
- existence of Research and Development (R&D) activity indicating innovative policy and technological development orientation,
- the proportion of workers with tertiary education as a prerequisite for the minimum sufficient level of human resources to manage the innovation process,
- existence of minimum "digital compliance" with the use of computers and internet, since today no business operates without them not to mention an innovative business,
- to date and future intended introduction of a new product, service, technology or organizational innovation, as it highlights an innovative orientation that may have existed or had sound foundation for it to grow in the foreseeable future,
- geographical markets for its products - services, since typically only companies with a supra-range (at least by national and especially international scope) develop or use extensively organizational and technological innovations.

The effort to use a multi-criteria evaluation for each criterion (question) was assessed as inelastic in the sense that it removes the value of empirical knowledge on entrepreneurship and entrepreneurial activity in the region and instead the empirical and synthetic analysis was preferred, taking into account each and every single criterion - questions with special reference to the ones highlighted above.

Figure 4. Process related innovations

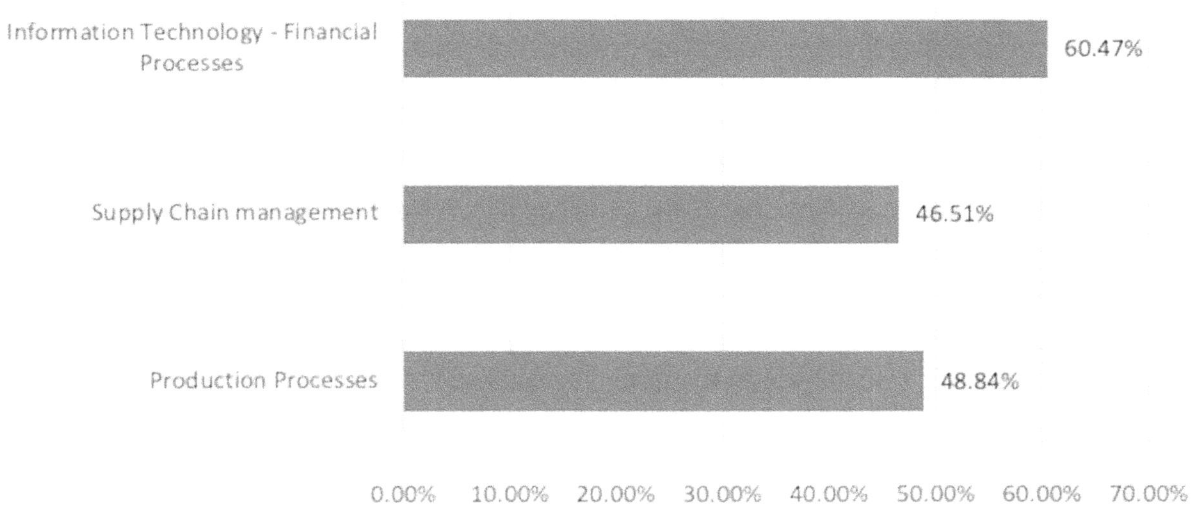

Our analysis is grounded on the CIS 4 questionnaire of 2008 which collects information about product and process innovations as well as organizational and marketing innovation. The questionnaire included eleven sets of questions examining the following:

1. general information about the company;
2. organizational innovation;
3. marketing innovation;
4. process innovation;
5. innovative products and services;
6. abandoned innovation activities;
7. activities (internal, external, etc.);
8. expenditure related to innovation, inventory information sources and collaborative innovation activities;
9. the impact and the extent of innovation outcomes;
10. hampering innovation activities; and
11. requests vesting copyright.

In our research each question had to be answered for 2 time periods, the first from 2007-2010 and the second from 2011-2016 in order to in order to study the impact of the economic crisis on this innovative measure.

Figure 5. Sources of information regarding innovation activities

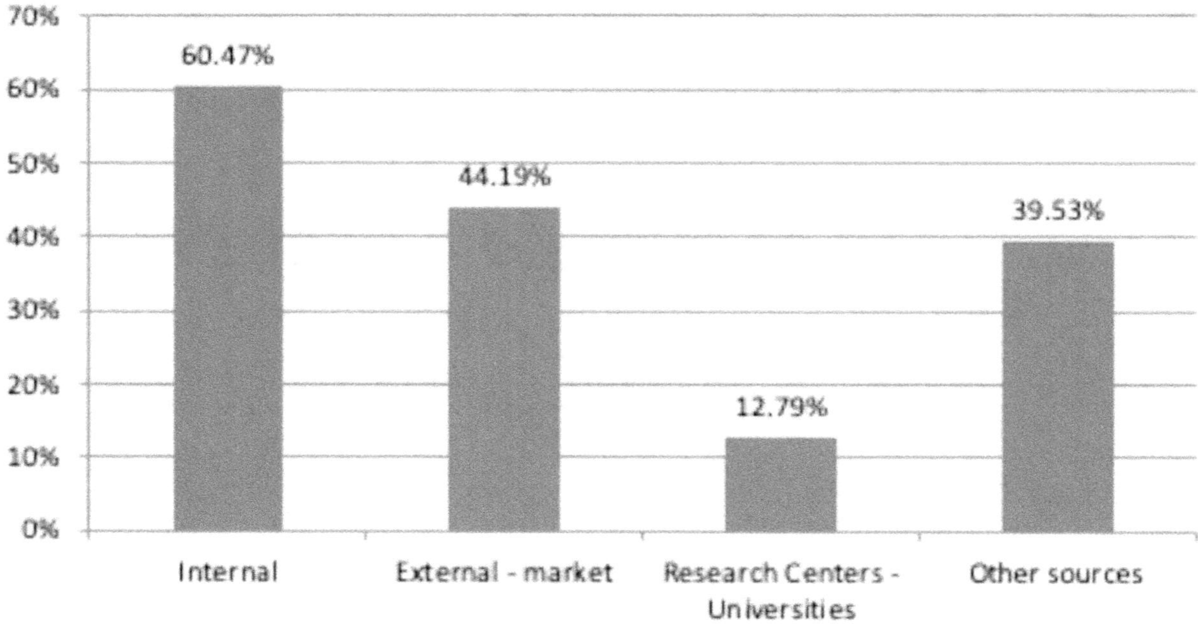

INNOVATION AND STRATEGIC GROUPS IN THE REGION OF WESTERN MACEDONIA.

Innovation Characteristics

The majority of the participating firms have engaged in some form of innovation adoption. The most important one was product-related innovation that was introduced by the 79.07% of the firms of the sample, while some kind of process innovation were implemented only by 3 out of the 4 firms that participated in our survey. The most important process innovations (Figure 4) were the ones concerning information technology and the adoption of information system as they are an important factor for supporting other business processes of a firm and their adoption is an important and difficult decision for SMEs (Antoniadis et al., 2015; Kavoura and Koziol, 2017). Innovations and changes concerning the production of goods or services accounted for 48.84% and supply chain management changes for 46.51% denoting its importance (Serdaris et al., 2014). It is interesting to note that these changes can be related to either the introduction of new products or the need to reduce costs, as a result of the dear economic situation firms had to face because of the reinvigorated financial crisis in 2016.

It is interesting however to note that only 4 out of the 43 firms had a dedicated R&D department, and most of them rely on informal internal sources of innovations, like employees or entrepreneurs' ideas and research (60.47%), or sources from the market (Tödtling and Kaufmann, 2001) like suppliers and business partners, customers, competitors or business consultants (44.19%), as it can be seen in Figure 5.

Other sources of information are also important like business fairs, business associations, and specialized press articles is important for the 39.53% of the respondents, while only 12.79% rely on research and collaborations with universities and research institute that is quite disappointing as it demonstrates a lack of connection between SMEs and universities (Tödtling and Kaufmann, 2001; Masa and Testa, 2008), and demotes the role universities can play in promoting innovation for SMEs and knowledge transfer exchange (Padilla-Meléndez and Garrido-Moreno, 2012; Makaraona and Kavoura, 2019).This is an important issue that should be considered by entrepreneurs, universities, and policymakers, to provide a framework of entrepreneurial education and counseling, that would help entrepreneurs and SMEs in their strategic design process (Kavoura and Andersson, 2016).

Figure 6. Factors obstructing innovation adoption and implementation

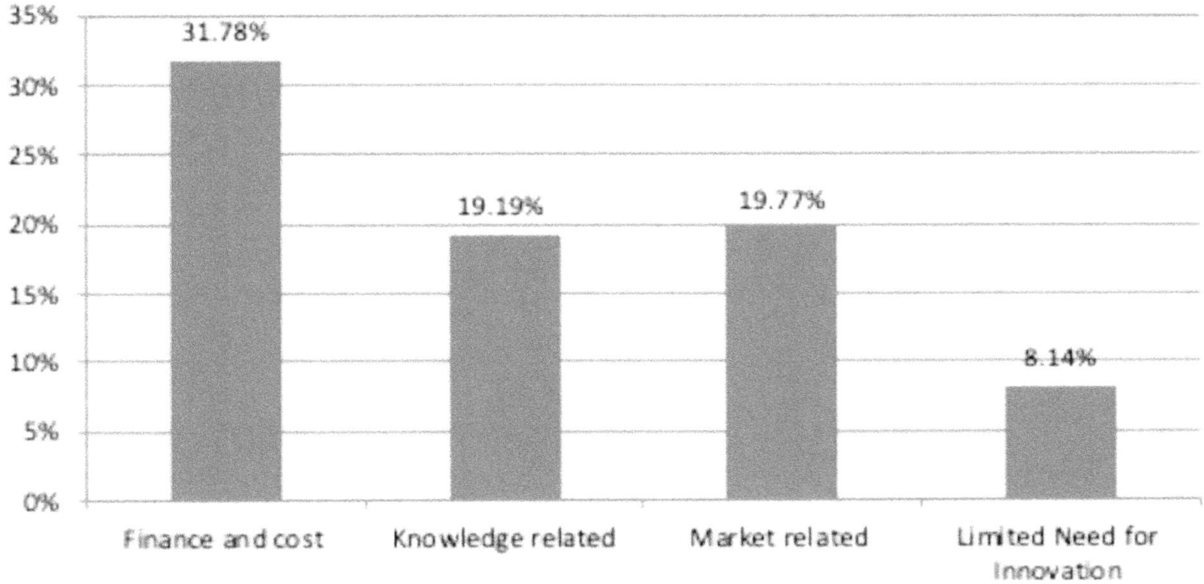

The financial crisis had seemed to only marginally affect the number of money firms spent on innovation. Despite the fact that literature identifies innovation and differentiation as one of the main strategies for firms and entrepreneurs, to tackle financial crises (Makkonen et al., 2014; Peris-Ortiz et al., 2014; Notta and Vlachvei, 2014) only 18.60% of the respondents of the sample stated that they have increased the amount spent on innovation, while the 16.28% decreased their innovation-oriented budget. The rest 37.21% have not made a change, while 20.93% did not spend money on any innovation.

The most important factor that obstructed the adoption and implementation of innovation (Figure 6) was financial and cost-related (31.78%). This comes with no surprise as the financial crisis and capital controls had a severe effect in the ability of firms, and especially small ones, to raise money(Cowling et al., 2012), and have access to finance from banks, or other sources of funds (like state and EU incentive schemes for investments and innovations).

Another important reason that made innovation implementation difficult was the lack of specialized personnel, which was deteriorated by the financial crisis as it was more difficult for firms to hire people with specialized knowledge and skills, and poor access to information concerning technology issues and market needs and demand. These factors can be characterized as knowledge related and were found to be the most important by 19.19% of the respondents. Market-related issues concerning market structure and uncertainty in the market and the economy was also considered to be important (19.77%), while 8.14% responded that they felt there is no demand for innovations by their customers, or they have adopted innovations in the past, and there is no need for innovation for their firms in the present.

As far as the perceived results of the adopted innovations are concerned (Figure 7), the product-related innovations were considered to be the most important ones (52.71%), as these innovations, according to the respondents, increase product and service range of the firm, help market entry in new markets or the expansion of market share in existing markets, and finally it helps improve the quality of products and services. Process related innovation followed with 41.28%, with respondents identifying as production flexibility, an increase of output, but most importantly the reduction of cost both in terms of labor and materials as the most important components. Finally, only 15.12% found that environmental-related results were the most important, including regulatory compliance requirements.

Figure 7. Importance of perceived results of innovation

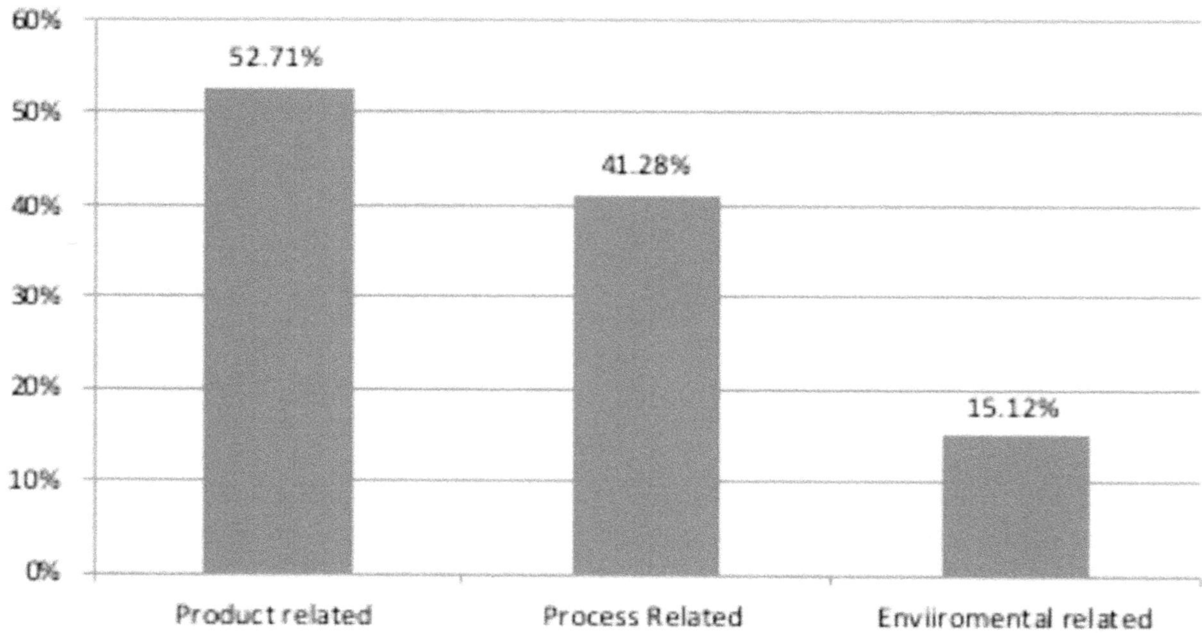

Profiling the Strategic Groups of Innovativeness

Strategic Groups analysis is considered to be one of the most useful analytic tools in terms of strategic management that helps us understand the structure of an industry and its dynamics (Mas-Ruiz et al., 2014). Porter (1980) defined strategic groups as a "group of firms in an industry, following the same of similar strategy along the strategic dimensions". Although it has been used mainly for industry analysis and is a rather "old" technique of analysis it has several advantages that prove her to be relevant even today. For example, it provides a detailed analysis of the strategies applied in an industry categorizing them in an analytic and easy to measure way (Ketchen and Shook, 1996) that is easy to be applied, used and interpreted by managers (Leask and Parker,2006).

Figure 8. Cluster membership

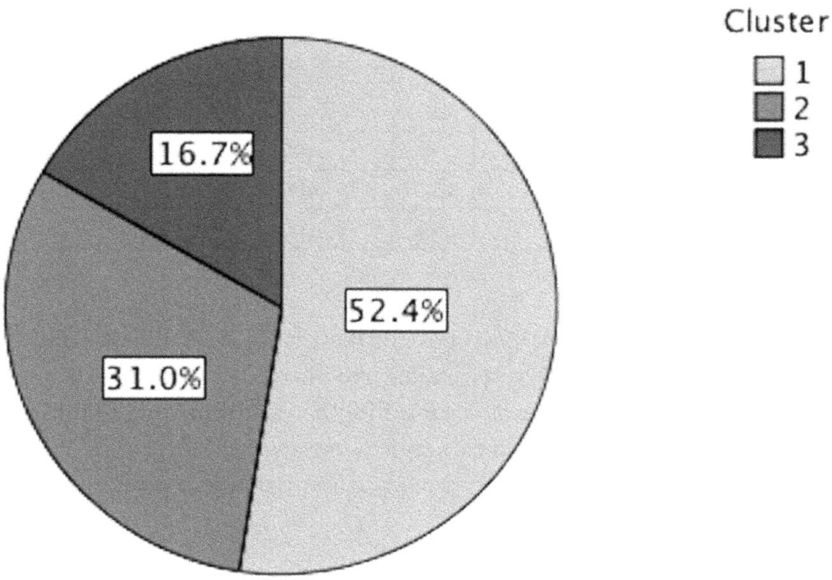

Size of Smallest Cluster	7 (16.7%)
Size of Largest Cluster	22 (52.4%)
Ratio of Sizes: Largest Cluster to Smallest Cluster	3.14

In that way strategic groups' analysis provides an insight into the existing differences between competitors and the ways they are using resources and their capabilities to compete within a market, facilitating the strategic management process (Panayides 2002). A number of studies have attempted to identify strategic groups in various Greek industries (Oustapassidis, 1998; Tsourogiannis et al., 2008 Goulas et al., 2009), but few have attempted to classify firms in terms of their innovation orientation in regional level. Although it is accustomed to perform this analysis only within one industry, it is possible to perform this analysis to create a strategic profile of firms that have a common characteristic as Halkias et al. (2009) did examine entrepreneurship from immigrants in Greece. The common characteristic of the firms in our sample is that they are SMEs from local entrepreneurs that have their main base of operations is in the region of Western Macedonia.

Table 1. Centroids values for the identified strategic groups

		Employees		Product innovation results		Process innovation results		Environmental innovation results	
		Mean	*Std. Deviation*	*Mean*	*Std. Deviation*	*Mean*	*Std. Deviation*	*Mean*	*Std. Deviation*
Cluster	**1**	10.41	17.101	-.3375	1.0968	.0696	1.0658	-.2716	.6623
	2	32.08	55.420	.2135	.7640	-.0185	.8019	.7801	1.2030
	3	28.14	20.062	.6643	.6506	-.1845	1.2300	-.5949	.6329

In order to identify the profile of innovativeness of the firms in the region, and classify them into strategic groups we have used cluster analysis (Ketchen and Shook, 1996) and most specifically the Two-Step method as our data sample and the variables used for the classification of the firms that responded to our questionnaire, had both numerical and categorical variables (Hair et al., 2006).

The variables used to identify the strategic groups of the firms that participated in our survey are the following:

- Innovation importance (based on perceived by the entrepreneur results), for four types of innovation were grouped in three categories namely Process, Product, Environmental related results, measured in a 4 scale level of importance. These factors were identified with the usage of factor analysis of the related components. It is interesting to note that although cost related to the material and energy used was considered to be a process related result and benefit when factor analysis was conducted it scored high on the factor related to environmental results.
- Industry: Manufacturing, Commerce, Services.
- Market orientation, and extroversion, identifying the main markets of the firms, as local, regional, national, and international in case of exporting in counties inside or outside the EU.
- Quality control schemes (like ISO etc.).
- Existence of other kinds of certifications that would be necessary for exports or to comply with customers' standards, and finally
- Total Number of employees.

One company was dropped out due to missing values. Using the Two-Step technique we have identified 3 main strategic groups as shown in Figure 8, with the ration of largest to smallest cluster taking the value of 3.14. The Average Silhouette value of cohesion and separation equals to 0.4 that is considered to be fair (Hair et al., 2006). Although the firms are competing in different industries the strategic groups' approach can provide useful insights on the nature of innovative firms and the strategic characteristics of innovation on a regional level, during an economic crisis, as all firms compete for limited resources, and market share in terms of financing and consumers' income.

In Table 1 the results of the cluster analysis are presented. The values of the centroids are offered for the 4 continuous variables, namely the number of employees, and the three types of perceived innovation results, product, process and environmental. It is interesting to note that the 3 groups present common characteristics in terms of the number of employees that are in line with the European Union classification of SMEs companies according to their size (very small, small, medium sized). As far as the rest of the variables are concerned the three identified groups seem to share same perceptions, concerning their innovation strategies, certification policies and tactics, and market orientation.

The results of Table 1 offer interesting insights for discussion in both terms of the characteristics of entrepreneurs in the region as well as the role of innovation in each firm depending on which group they belong. The first strategic group, that is the biggest one of the three, numbering 22 firms, consists mostly of smaller firms in the commerce sector, from local entrepreneurs, but there are also a few manufacturing firms. The main markets for this group are the regional and national ones, and only a few of them do export, mainly cross-border trade transactions, and more specifically in neighboring Balkan countries. None of the three types of innovation seems to be an important factor of competitive advantage for the firms of this group, but the innovation that is considered to be the most important for the firms of this group, in terms of results is process innovation, despite the fact that the introduction of new products is crucial for their survival and their growth both in the regional and cross-border level (Soninen et al., 2012; Notta and Valchvei, 2015). The small size of the firms of this group, in terms of employees may be responsible for the low levels of perceived results of innovations by entrepreneurs as small firms are more vulnerable in times of recession (Cowling et al., 2012). Certifications do not seem to be very important for this group as their small size, but also their local and regional orientation renders these processes unnecessary for their consumers, and possibly too costly in terms of resources and time (Crals and Vereeck, 2005; Santos et al., 2011), that would be an important factor for not implementing such a scheme, especially in a period of financial crisis. Another interesting characteristic of this group is the low importance of results concerning product-oriented innovations, and the innovations related to the environment. Considering the above, we could characterize this group as the "Small Regional and Cross-Border oriented firms", due to their market orientation and size.

The second group is consisted by13 firms. These firms are bigger in size compared to the ones of the first group, and are mostly manufacturing firms, that invest heavily in quality assurance schemes (ISO) and other certifications. That can also be explained since these firms are the most extroversive of the firms of our sample, as their main markets besides the national level, are mainly EU countries, and other neighboring countries. In this group environmental innovations results are considered to be the most important of the three examined types of innovation followed by product innovations related to environmental results. This is a reasonable finding since most exporting firms need to acquire necessary certifications to get access to foreign markets, especially the one of the EU. These along with environmental-related innovations, help bring down the cost (Santos et al., 2011), that is an important driver during a period of financial crisis, but could also be used as a way of attracting customers and consumers that are sensitive to environmental issues (Ammenberg et al., 2017). Another important issue that should be considered is the strict environmental standards and legislations that manufacturing firms must comply with. For this group, therefore, we can speculate that product and environmental results of innovation provides a competitive advantage not only at a national level but also in international and cross border markets. Another interesting fact is that although these firms are not big ones, they manage to implement complicated and innovative production and management processes, providing some evidence on the flexibility that SMEs and entrepreneurs, have on adopting innovations, and grow even in periods of recession (Antoniadis et al., 2015).The above characteristics lead us to label this group as the "Small Flexible Nationals Exporters".

The third group identified is the smallest of the three, numbering just 7 firms of the sample, that are also medium sized, and operate in the commerce and retail sector, mainly in the regional level. These firms implement quality assurance schemes and have been accredited with other certifications. The main driver of innovation for these companies is product innovations. Process and environmental related results caused by innovations are not considered to be an important driver for differentiation, at a regional level, although customers and consumers become more sensitive concerning environmental issues (Chen and Chai, 2010). The reasons for that should be searched in the regional characteristics of consumers. Since retailers are mainly found in this group, product innovations are focused on keeping the interest and the preference of existing customers, but also on attracting new customers, while process innovations are mainly focused on reducing cost, and the time of responding to consumers' demand and request. These attributes also contribute in an increase in the performance of the personnel that is an important factor for these firms due to their size (in terms of employees), in order not only to survive but also to maintain and increase their competitive advantage, in the regional level during the recession period. These characteristics may have also helped some of them to expand in a regional level, gaining market share in regional level as many firms closed because of the crisis, or even to defend their market shares, creating barriers to entry for other national firms, that would consider entering the regional market. These characteristics may also provide the potential for expansion beyond the regional borders, taking advantage of new distribution channels like e-shops (Mazzarol, 2015). We are going to name this group of firms as the "Regional Retailers".

CONCLUSION AND FUTURE RESEARCH

This study has been motivated by a need to shed some insight into the attitudes of firms and entrepreneurs towards innovation, and the ways they are implementing them in their operations on a regional level and most specifically in the region of Western Macedonia in Greece, by applying a strategic groups' approach. As innovation can provide the most needed dynamic for an economy to pull out of a financial crisis (Hausman and Johnston, 2014), understanding the factors driving innovation and sketching the profile of innovativeness for the SMEs at a regional level are extremely important for any economy and especially for the recovery of the Greek economy (Masouras 2019b).

This research is offering insight for that matter, as it was conducted during a period of extreme financial crisis, in a Greek region that faces significant economic challenges, concerning its future economic growth in conjunction with the importance of established and prospect cross-border transactions and relations with neighboring Balkan countries. Another important aspect to consider is the role entrepreneurship and innovation is going to play in the coming years for the region of West Macedonia, as a main economic driver for the region, namely electricity production from coal, is going to be abandoned.

The findings of this chapter provide evidence on the ways that future entrepreneurs should orient their firm in implementing innovations, by identifying three major strategic groups. Smaller local companies should focus on product innovations pivoting on introducing new and differentiated products that could benefit from sales in neighboring countries' markets taking advantage of cross-border transactions, avoiding thus competition by larger and national or multinational enterprises. If, however, an entrepreneur wishes to create an extroversive company, oriented in EU or other Balkan countries markets, process and environmental results of innovations, along with the necessary certifications could provide the needed competitive advantage. Another strategic implication is the fact that product innovation could be a significant barrier to entry for entrepreneurs and retailers wishing to operate in the market of the region we have investigated, or in neighboring countries, as new firms must introduce innovative products and services that would offer differentiation advantages, and an enhanced value proposal to consumers. On the other hand, process innovations should not be considered as a barrier to entry for entrepreneurs who would wish to create an extroversive firm that would export their products in other countries or in cross-border transactions.

Finally, the limited role of universities and research institutes should be a worrying finding for all stakeholders and entrepreneurs, as it is diminishing entrepreneurship and innovation, for both existing firms but also start-ups in the region. This relationship should be rebuilt in order to enhance the economic growth of the region (Makarona and Kavoura, 2019).

Our research comes with a number of limitations. First of all the size of the sample is very small, rendering it inappropriate for the application of more complex statistical techniques that would provide better insight on the profile and relationship of entrepreneurship and innovation at a regional level. More data should be collected to identify the relationship between entrepreneurship and innovation, and the way it affects the former in a regional and cross-border level. Moreover, the period of time the research was conducted is characterized by extreme economic and social instability that was unprecedented for an EU country. Therefore, more research should be conducted at a regional level to identify the effect the crisis had on entrepreneurship and the ways that innovation helped existing firms to survive and grow, but also to the opportunities that were created in a regional and cross-border level, and how local entrepreneurs took advantage of them.

REFERENCES

Almunia, M., Bénétrix, A., Eichengreen, B., O'Rourke, K., & Rua, G. (2009). *From Great Depression to Great Credit Crisis: Similarities, Differences and Lessons.* NBER Working Paper 15524.

Ambec, S., Cohen, M., Elgie, S., & Lanoie, P. (2013). The Porter Hypothesis at 20: Can Environmental Regulation Enhance Innovation and Competitiveness? *Review of Environmental Economics and Policy*, *7*(1), 2–22. doi:10.1093/reep/res016

Ammenberg, J., Börjesson, B., & Hjelm, O. (2017). Joint EMS and group certification: a cost-effective route for SMEs to achieve ISO 14001. In *ISO 14001* (pp. 58–66). Routledge. doi:10.4324/9781351282765-6

Antoniadis, I., & Charmantzi, A. (2016). Social network analysis and social capital in marketing: Theory and practical implementation. *International Journal of Technology Marketing*, *11*(3), 344–359. doi:10.1504/IJTMKT.2016.077387

Antoniadis, I., Tsiakiris, T., & Tsopogloy, S. (2015). Business Intelligence during times of crisis: Adoption and usage of ERP systems by SMEs. *Procedia: Social and Behavioral Sciences*, *175*, 299–307. doi:10.1016/j.sbspro.2015.01.1204

Archibugi, D., Filippetti, A., & Frenz, M. (2013). Economic crisis and innovation: Is destruction prevailing over accumulation? *Research Policy*, *42*(2), 303–314. doi:10.1016/j.respol.2012.07.002

Baruch, Y., & Holtom, B. C. (2008). Survey response rate levels and trends in organizational research. *Human Relations*, *61*(8), 1139–1160. doi:10.1177/0018726708094863

Bookis, A. (2016). *Managing Innovation within Organizations.* DOI: doi:10.4018/978-1-4666-9607-5.ch012

Branstad, P., Jackson, B., & Banerji, S. (2009). *Rethink Your Strategy An Urgent Memo To the CEO*. Booz & Company Inc.

Calloway, L. J., & Keen, P. G. W. (1996). Organizing for crisis response. *Journal of Information Technology*, *11*(1), 13–27. doi:10.1177/026839629601100102

Carayannis, E., Samara, E., & Bakouros, Y. (2014). *Innovation and Entrepreneurship -"Theory, Policy and Practice*. Springer.

Cegarra-Navarra, J., Reverte, C., Gómez-Melero, E., & Wensley, K. P. (2016). Linking social and economic responsibilities with financial performance: The role of innovation. *European Management Journal*, *34*(5), 530–539. doi:10.1016/j.emj.2016.02.006

Chandy, R. K., & Tellis, G. J. (2000). The incumbent's curse? Incumbency, size, and radical product innovation. *Journal of Marketing*, *64*(3), 1–17. doi:10.1509/jmkg.64.3.1.18033

Chatzinikolaou, D. (2002). Statistics for Economists. Academic Press.

Chen, T. B., & Chai, L. T. (2010). Attitude towards the environment and green products: Consumers' perspective. *Management Science and Engineering*, *4*(2), 27.

Cowling, M., Liu, W., & Ledger, A. (2012). Small business financing in the UK before and during the current financial crisis. *International Small Business Journal*, *30*(7), 778–800. doi:10.1177/0266242611435516

Crals, E., & Vereeck, L. (2005). The affordability of sustainable entrepreneurship certification for SMEs. *International Journal of Sustainable Development and World Ecology*, *12*(2), 173–183. doi:10.1080/13504500509469628

Damanpour, F. (1992). Organizational size and innovation. *Organization Studies*, *13*(3), 375–402. doi:10.1177/017084069201300304

European Commission. (2017). *Digital agenda scoreboard 2017*. Author.

Fulton, B. R. (2018). Organizations and survey research: Implementing response enhancing strategies and conducting nonresponse analyses. *Sociological Methods & Research*, *47*(2), 240–276. doi:10.1177/0049124115626169

Garcia, R., & Calantone, R. (2002). A critical look at technological innovation typology and innovativeness terminology: A literature review. *Journal of Product Innovation Management: An International Publication of the Product Development & Management Association*, *19*(2), 110–132. doi:10.1111/1540-5885.1920110

Goulas, A., Blanas, G., & Gomes, E. (2008). The Formation of Strategic Groups in the Athens Stock Exchange. *MIBES Transactions*, *2*(1), 60–77.

Gulati, R., Nohria, N., & Wohlgezogen, F. (2010). Roaring out of recession. *Harvard Business Review*, *88*(3), 62–69.

Hair, J., Black, W., Babin, B., Anderson, R., & Tatham, R. (2006). *Multivariate data analysis* (6th ed.). Pearson: Prentice Hall.

Halkias, D., Nwajiuba, C., Harkiolakis, N., Clayton, G., Akrivos, P. D., & Caracatsanis, S. (2009). Characteristics and business profiles of immigrant-owned small firms: The case of African immigrant entrepreneurs in Greece. *International Journal of Business Innovation and Research*, *3*(4), 382–401. doi:10.1504/IJBIR.2009.027104

Hausman, A., & Johnston, W. J. (2014). The role of innovation in driving the economy: Lessons from the global financial crisis. *Journal of Business Research*, *67*(1), 2720–2726. doi:10.1016/j.jbusres.2013.03.021

Henderson, R. M., & Clark, K. B. (1990). Architectural innovation: The reconfiguration of existing. *Administrative Science Quarterly*, *35*(1), 9–30. doi:10.2307/2393549

Hyytinen, A., & Toivanen, O. (2005). Do financial constraints hold back innovation and growth?: Evidence on the role of public policy. *Research Policy*, *34*(9), 1385–1403. doi:10.1016/j.respol.2005.06.004

IMF. (2011a). *World Economic Outlook: Slowing Growth, Rising Risks*. IMF.

IMF. (2011b). *Global Financial Stability Report*. IMF.

Kavoura, A., & Andersson, T. (2016). Applying Delphi method for strategic design of social entrepreneurship. *Library Review*, *65*(3), 185–205. doi:10.1108/LR-06-2015-0062

Kavoura, A., & Koziol, L. (2017). Polish Firms' Innovation Capability for Competitiveness via Information Technologies and Social Media Implementation. In A. Vlachvei, O. Notta, K. Karantininis, & N. Tsountas (Eds.), *Factors Affecting Firm Competitiveness and Performance in the Modern Business World* (pp. 185–214). IGI Global. doi:10.4018/978-1-5225-0843-4.ch007

Ketchen, D. J. Jr, & Shook, C. L. (1996). The application of cluster analysis in strategic management research: An analysis and critique. *Strategic Management Journal*, *17*(6), 441–458. doi:10.1002/(SICI)1097-0266(199606)17:6<441::AID-SMJ819>3.0.CO;2-G

Leask, G., & Parker, D. (2006). Strategic group theory: Review, examination, and application in the UK pharmaceutical industry. *Journal of Management Development*, *25*(4), 386–408. doi:10.1108/02621710610655846

Makarona, E., & Kavoura, A. (2019). Redesigning the Ivory Tower: Academic entrepreneurship as a new calling supporting economic growth. *The Malopolska School of Economics in Tarnow Research Papers Collection*, *42*, 15–26. doi:10.25944/znmwse.2019.02.1526

Makkonen, H., Pohjola, M., Olkkonen, R., & Koponen, A. (2014). Dynamic capabilities and firm performance in a financial crisis. *Journal of Business Research*, *67*(1), 2707–2719. doi:10.1016/j.jbusres.2013.03.020

Mas-Ruiz, F. J., Ruiz-Moreno, F., & Ladrón de Guevara Martínez, A. (2014). Asymmetric rivalry within and between strategic groups. *Strategic Management Journal*, *35*(3), 419–439. doi:10.1002mj.2102

Masouras, A. (2019a). Young entrepreneurship in Cyprus. *The Małopolska School of Economics in Tarnów Research Papers Collection*, *42*, 2.

Masouras, A. (2019b). *Entrepreneurship in Small and Medium-Sized Enterprises*. Nova Science Publishers.

Massa, S., & Testa, S. (2008). Innovation and SMEs: Misaligned perspectives and goals among entrepreneurs, academics, and policy makers. *Technovation*, *28*(7), 393–407. doi:10.1016/j.technovation.2008.01.002

Mazzarol, T. (2015). SMEs engagement with e-commerce, e-business and e-marketing. *Small Enterprise Research*, *22*(1), 79–90. doi:10.1080/13215906.2015.1018400

Meyers, P. W., & Tucker, F. G. (1989). Defining roles for logistics during routine and radical technological innovation. *Journal of the Academy of Marketing Science*, *17*(1), 73–82. doi:10.1007/BF02726356

Nelson, R. R. (2009). *An evolutionary theory of economic change*. Harvard University Press.

Notta, O., & Vlachvei, A. (2014). The impact of Financial Crisis on firm performance in case of Greek food manufacturing firms. *Procedia Economics and Finance*, *14*, 454–460. doi:10.1016/S2212-5671(14)00734-5

Notta, O., & Vlachvei, A. (2015). Marketing responses of Greek food manufacturing firms due to economic crisis. *Procedia: Social and Behavioral Sciences*, *175*, 350–357. doi:10.1016/j.sbspro.2015.01.1210

OECD. (2005). *Annual Report 2005*. OECD.

Oustapassidis, K. (1998). Performance of strategic groups in the Greek dairy industry. *European Journal of Marketing*, *32*(11/12), 962–973. doi:10.1108/03090569810243578

Padilla-Meléndez, A., & Garrido-Moreno, A. (2012). Open innovation in universities: What motivates researchers to engage in knowledge transfer exchanges? *International Journal of Entrepreneurial Behaviour & Research*, *18*(4), 417–439. doi:10.1108/13552551211239474

Panayides, P. M. (2002). Identification of strategic groups using relationship marketing criteria: A cluster analytic approach in professional services. *Service Industries Journal*, *22*(2), 149–166. doi:10.1080/714005071

Peris-Ortiz, M., Fuster-Estruch, V., & Devece-Carañana, C. (2014). Entrepreneurship and Innovation in a Context of Crisis. In *Entrepreneurship, Innovation and Economic Crisis* (pp. 1–10). Springer. doi:10.1007/978-3-319-02384-7_1

Porter, M. E. (1980). *Competitive strategy*. Free Press.

Reinhart, C., & Rogoff, K. (2009). *This Time is Different*. Princeton University Press.

Reinhart, V. (2011). A year of living dangerously: The management of the financial crisis in 2008. *The Journal of Economic Perspectives*, *25*(1), 71–90. doi:10.1257/jep.25.1.71

Samara, E., Galanakis, K., Bakouros, I., & Platias, S. (2010). The spin-off chain. *Journal of Technology Management & Innovation*, *5*(3), 51–68.

Samara, E., Galanakis, K., Bakouros, I., & Skalkos, D. (2018). Effectiveness of Regional Innovation Actions: Cases from Small, Low-Innovative Regions. *Journal of the Knowledge Economy*, •••, 1–34. doi:10.100713132-018-0518-0

Santos, G., Mendes, F., & Barbosa, J. (2011). Certification and integration of management systems: The experience of Portuguese small and medium enterprises. *Journal of Cleaner Production*, *19*(17-18), 1965–1974. doi:10.1016/j.jclepro.2011.06.017

Schumpeter, J. A. (1983). *The Theory of Economic Development*. Transaction Publishers.

Serdaris, P., Antoniadis, I., & Tomlekova, N. (2014). Supply chain management: A view of the distribution channel. *Bulgarian Journal of Agricultural Science*, *20*(2), 480–486.

Soininen, J., Puumalainen, K., Sjögrén, H., & Syrjä, P. (2012). The impact of global economic crisis on SMEs: Does entrepreneurial orientation matter? *Management Research Review*, *35*(10), 927–944. doi:10.1108/01409171211272660

Tödtling, F., & Kaufmann, A. (2001). The role of the region for innovation activities of SMEs. *European Urban and Regional Studies*, *8*(3), 203–215. doi:10.1177/096977640100800303

Togni, M., Cubico, S., & Favretto, G. (2010). Owners and managers in an economic crisis: How to exploit the differences. *Procedia: Social and Behavioral Sciences*, *5*, 1312–1316. doi:10.1016/j.sbspro.2010.07.281

Tsourgiannis, L., Errington, A., Eddison, J., Mattas, K. and Tsakiridou, E. (2005). Marketing strategies of agricultural producers in objective one Greek region: the factors affecting the selection of marketing channels of sheep and goat producers. *Cahiers Options Méditerranéennes*, (64), 307-320.

Ulrich, S., Rogovsky, N., & Lamotte, D. (2009). *Promoting Responsible and Sustainable Enterprise-Level Practices at Times of Crisis: A Guide for Policy-Makers 105 and Social Partners*. International Labour Organization. available at: http://www.ilo.org/empent/Publications/WCMS_108420/lang--en/index.htm

Workman, J. P. Jr. (1993). Marketing's limited role in new product development in one computer systems firm. *JMR, Journal of Marketing Research*, *30*(4), 405–421. doi:10.1177/002224379303000402

ADDITIONAL READING

Karlsson, C., Johansson, B., & Stough, R. R. (2010). *Entrepreneurship and regional development*. Edward Elgar Publishing. doi:10.4337/9781781000793

Leskovar-Spacapan, G., & Bastic, M. (2007). Differences in organizations' innovation capability in transition economy: Internal aspect of the organizations' strategic orientation. *Technovation*, *27*(9), 533–546. doi:10.1016/j.technovation.2007.05.012

Masouras, A. (2019). *Entrepreneurship in Small and Medium-Sized Enterprises*. Nova Science Publishers.

Porter, M. E. (1980). *Competitive strategy*. Free Press.

Samara, E., Georgiadis, P., & Bakouros, I. (2012). The impact of innovation policies on the performance of national innovation systems: A system dynamics analysis. *Technovation*, *32*(11), 624–638. doi:10.1016/j.technovation.2012.06.002

Traill, W. B. (2000). Strategic groups of EU food manufacturers. *Journal of Agricultural Economics*, *51*(1), 45–60. doi:10.1111/j.1477-9552.2000.tb01208.x

KEY TERMS AND DEFINITIONS

CIS: The community innovation survey (CIS) is conducted in all European Union (EU) countries, in order to collect data on innovation activities undertaken by enterprises. Questions include a number of indicators concerning innovation activities and spending, sources of information, obstacles for innovation activity, etc.

DESI: The Digital Economy and Society Index is a composite index that summarises relevant indicators on Europe's digital performance and tracks the evolution of EU member states in digital competitiveness.

Innovation: The conception and application of better solutions that meet new requirements, unarticulated needs, or existing market needs, that leads to gaining competitive advantage.

RCI: The Regional Competitiveness Index (RCI) in EU is a composite indicator that provides insight on the competitiveness for the regions of the 27 Member States. It uses the approach suggested by the World Economic Forum (WEF), in calculating the Global Competitiveness Index, helping regions and policymakers to monitor and assess their development over time and in comparison with other regions.

SMEs: Small and Medium Enterprises in the European Union are defined as enterprises that have less than 250 employees, and less than €50m turnover, or €43m of balance sheet total.

Strategic Groups: A group of companies within an industry that have similar business models or similar set of strategies.

Western Macedonia: A region of Northern Greece, with 4 main cities. An important characteristic of the area is the heavy reliance of the local economy from coal mining that is used for electricity production by Public Power Cooperation SA-Hellas (DEI).

Chapter 9
An Investigation of Entrepreneurial Intention Among University Students Using the Theory of Planned Behavior and Parents' Occupation

Panagiotis A. Tsaknis
University of West Attica, Greece, Greece

Alexandros G. Sahinidis
University of West Attica, Greece

ABSTRACT

The purpose of this paper is to investigate the entrepreneurial intention of university students using the Theory of Planned Behavior (TPB) and parents' occupation. A questionnaire based survey was employed for the data collection. A total of 1244 students participated in the survey. The sample was a convenience one given that the resources available were limited. The size of the sample allows us to proceed with reliable statistical analyses and produce valid conclusions. The findings of our research showed that perceived behavioral control, subjective norms, attitude and parents' occupation are important variables influencing entrepreneurial intention. The variable that affects entrepreneurial intention the most is attitude. The findings led support to the theory and the hypotheses proposed. These findings indicate that the recommended model can be used to explain a large part of variation in entrepreneurial intention. This study, contributes to the entrepreneurial intention literature providing empirical evidence to help formulate policies encouraging university students' entrepreneurship practices, attracting the interest of both educators and policy makers. This evidence will become increasingly important, as research in the field of entrepreneurship continues to place models of entrepreneurial intentions at the center of our understanding of the entrepreneurial process. Future studies could investigate the validity of the findings reported here, in different contexts using more variables, not included in this study and inquire the potential existence of latent variables which may be confounding the relationships discussed in this paper.

DOI: 10.4018/978-1-7998-3648-3.ch009

INTRODUCTION

In recent years, the concept of intention and its antecedents have received growing attention in entrepreneurship research for its usefulness in predicting entrepreneurial behavior on the one hand and understanding how intentions are formed on the other. Theory of Planned Behavior (TPB) could be a particularly useful tool for researchers seeking to analyze entrepreneurial intention (Fayolle., and Gailly, 2013). TPB (Ajzen, 2002; Ajzen, 1991) is probably one of the most widely used models of entrepreneurial intention to this day. Numerous research works have used it to improve our understanding of the entrepreneurial intentions of students and of other categories of individuals (Sahinidis, Stavroulakis, Kossieri and Varelas, 2019; Sahinidis, Polychronopoulos, and Kallivokas. 2019; Laguía, Moriano, and Gorgievski, 2019; Gieure, Benavides-Espinosa, and Roig-Dobón, 2019; Al-Jubari, Hassan, and Liñán, F. 2018; Naushad, 2018; Naushad, Faridi, and Syed 2018; Gorgievski, Stephan, Laguna, and Moriano, 2017; Ruiz-Alba, Soares, Rodríguez-Molina, and Banoun, 2019; Liñán, and Chen, 2009; Gird, and Bagraim, 2008; Maes, Leroy, and Sels, 2014; Esfandiar, Sharifi, Pratt, and Altinay, 2019; Santos, Roomi, and Liñán, 2014; Tsai, Chang, and Peng, 2014; Rueda, Moriano, and Liñán, 2015; Wach, and Wojciechowski, 2016; Kautonen, Gelderen, and Tornikoski, 2013; Shook, and Bratianu, 2008; Gird, and Bagraim, 2008; Autio, Keeley, Klofsten, Parker, and Hay, 2001; Veciana, Aponte, and Urbano, 2005; Tkachev, and Kolvereid, 1999; Souitaris, Zerbinati, and AlLaham, 2007; Segal, Borgia, and Schoenfeld, 2005; Fayolle., and Gailly, 2013). These studies have made a substantial contribution to the entrepreneurship literature. Given the socio-economic benefits generally attributed to entrepreneurship, academic, educational and governmental institutions are motivated to investigate the factors that influence entrepreneurial intentions.

The research undertaken here, aims to provide a better understanding of the dynamics involved in the entrepreneurial intention formation process among Greek students, thus contributing to existing knowledge. In this context, this research intends to investigate the entrepreneurial intention of university students using the TPB and parents' occupation variables. According to TPB, a person's intention to participate in the business formation process is shaped by the following three factors: personal attitude, subjective norms and perceived behavioral control. Parents' occupation is an important factor affecting entrepreneurial intention in young people, the models discussed below, explain the importance of the family background in entrepreneurial intention (Sahinidis, et. al., 2019; Liñán, and Santos, 2007; Laspita, Breugst, Heblich, and Patzelt, H. 2012; Heck, Hoy, Poutziouris, and Steier, 2008; Kristiansen, and Indarti, 2004; Wang, and Wong, 2004).

ENTREPRENEURSHIP AS HUMAN BEHAVIOR

Entrepreneurship is perceived a key phenomenon responsible for economic growth and entrepreneurs as the prime agents of economic change, who pull together the factors of production; capital, land, labour and knowledge, to create socioeconomic value responsible for the dynamism of nations (Mwatsika, Patrick, and Levison, 2018). The concept of entrepreneurship has been studied from various scholarly perspectives (economics, sociology, psychology, anthropology, business, marketing, finance, geography, history etc.) in the effort to advance its understanding. Studies of entrepreneurship have focused on the traits/characteristics of the entrepreneur, the motivations and drivers of entrepreneurship, the processes involved in the creation of new (Mwatsika, et.al. 2018).

Entrepreneurs play a key role in turning scarce resources into goods and services. The phenomenon of the production of goods and services, exchange and trade have been studied by scholars from different disciplines. Entrepreneurship is the human action responsible for the production, marketing and exchange of goods and services, the person who practices this activity is called an entrepreneur. So, several years ago, a commonly accepted definition of entrepreneurship was created that is based on the actions of the entrepreneur (Mwatsika, et.al. 2018). An individual is called an entrepreneur because of his or her behavior i.e. the creation of socio-economic value as a result of the outflow of business process. Some definitions have argued that an individual is an entrepreneur, if he successfully establishes a business or an organization even if he has no profit. Through his behavior, the individual recognizes, evaluates and takes advantage of opportunities (Mwatsika, et.al. 2018) to create new goods / services, new organizations, new production methods, and to find new sources of raw materials. Entrepreneurship refers to the behavioral process by which individuals create socio-economic value. Theory of Planned Behavior (Ajzen, 1991) and Entrepreneurial Event Model provide data on the factors that influence entrepreneurial behavior (Mwatsika, et.al. 2018).

The variables involved in the successful creation of a business include self-efficacy, perceived feasibility, and attitude towards the establishing of a business. In the extant literature, two different types of forces that lead individuals to adopt a business behavior (push and pull factors) are described. Push factors force individuals to begin the process of creating value through the creation of a business. They are prompting people into entrepreneurship because of the lack of viable alternatives. Examples of such incentives are unemployment, autonomy and difficulties in finding a job that may be the result of the educational environment, gender, race or economic class (Gonzalez-Gonzalez, Bretones, Zarco, & Rodriguez, 2011). Financial crises and periods of high unemployment can lead individuals to self-employment, due to lack of other opportunities (Dawson and Henley, 2012). Pull factors tempt persons towards the business creation process. They attract entrepreneurs to start-up businesses, taking advantage of market opportunities. As reported in the Global Entrepreneurship Monitor (2002), Reynolds, Bygrave, Autio, Cox and Hay distinguish push and pull factors by introducing the concepts of opportunity motivated entrepreneurship and necessity motivated entrepreneurship (Thurik, Verheul, Hessels, and Zwan, 2010)

Push factors lead to necessity motivated entrepreneurship, while pull factors form the basis of opportunity motivated entrepreneurship. Opportunity motivated entrepreneurship is described at the moment an individual makes an active choice to engage in entrepreneurial behavior and create socio-economic value by identifying the advantage of an unused or underutilized opportunity. Successful people create small businesses in order to innovate and grow (Decker, Haltiwanger, Jarmin, and Miranda, 2014). Necessity motivated entrepreneurship occurs when a person cannot find alternatives to survive. Successful people create small businesses, so as to provide employment for themselves and few other people who are primarily family members (Decker, et.al., 2014). This distinction is important because motivation can influence the way an entrepreneur runs his/her business and therefore can affect the performance of the business (Hessels, van Gelderen, & Thurik, 2008). Studies confirm that opportunity driven entrepreneurs are more successful than necessity driven ones (Vivarelli, 2004). A business purporting to seize an opportunity has a greater growth potential than a business whose founder is motivated by a push factor such as unemployment or dissatisfaction with another job. Recognizing opportunities is influenced by the economy, it is a complex process and is the first fundamental step of the business creation process (Vaghely and Pierre-Andre, 2010). Researchers approach it from different angles and take into account a wide range of factors when studying it. The basis for identifying new opportunities involves continuous search, alertness, prior knowledge of markets, customers and technology (Baron, and Ensley, 2006). A bad economy reduces opportunities and impedes the entrepreneur's ability to exploit them (Mwatsika, et.al. 2018).

In summary, entrepreneurship is a human behavior responsible for creating socio-economic value. People who have a business attitude have all the skills required. However, these skills do not necessarily lead one to adopt a business attitude. Business intention models provide information on the factors that influence business creation behavior. Entrepreneurship encourages both necessity motivated entrepreneurship and opportunity motivated entrepreneurship, both of which are variants of the same concept of entrepreneurship that is based on the creation of socio-economic value through human behavior.

ENTREPRENEURIAL INTENTION

Entrepreneurial intention precedes entrepreneurial behavior and is defined as the recognized belief of a person who intends to undertake a new business venture (Mwatsika 2015). Intentions are the best predictors of planned behaviour. They are influenced by attitudes towards a behavior, subjective norms, perceived behavioral control (Ajzen, 1991), perceived desire for behavior, and one's tendency to act. The required skills of the entrepreneur, the outputs of entrepreneurship, its results, its impact, the external environment (political, economic, social, technological), factors of production, market parameters and stakeholders influence entrepreneurial intention and, thus, entrepreneurial behavior (Mwatsika, et.al. 2018).

A significant number of studies identify and analyze the evolution of entrepreneurial intention over the years. The first research was performed about 38 years ago, but today its study seems to be of greater concern to society than ever before and is a contemporary research topic. The integration of theories from the field of social psychology has contributed to the enrichment of theoretical knowledge and methodologies. Since the early 1990s there has been a strong interest by young researchers, who began to standardize the study of entrepreneurial intention (Mwatsika, et.al. 2018). The increasing number of studies based on the concept of entrepreneurial intention has revealed new ways of implementation and research (Krueger and Day 2010). In the early years of research, studies could not be categorized and, consequently, the development of knowledge in the field was lagging, as each research was almost starting from scratch. In this way there were difficulties in identifying key issues and gaps in the literature (Fayolle and Liñán 2014).

From the study of literature, two separate sections of entrepreneurial intention research emerge. The first derives from social psychology, with the purpose of analyzing behaviors and identifying the process that, through attitudes and beliefs, leads to effective action. The studies of Ajzen and Fishbein (1980) and Bandura (1997) have made a significant contribution to the study of business intention. The Theory of Planned Behavior is a more advanced theory and a more widespread theory in social psychology. The second part focuses exclusively on entrepreneurship (Shapero 1984).

In literature, the theories referring to entrepreneurial intention are Bandura's (1997) theory of self-efficacy and social learning, the theory of planned behavior (Ajzen, 1991), the model of intention in entrepreneurial situations, as well as the theory that combines planned behavior and the model of intention in entrepreneurial situations. Individuals' intentions are a function of the perceptions of feasibility, desire and tendency to act in opportunities (Shapero 1975).

THEORY OF REASONED ACTION

Theory of Reasoned Action (TRA) was developed from the attitude measurement theory based on the notion that an attitude toward an object or an action is determined by the expectations or beliefs concerning attributes of the object or action and evaluation of those characteristics (Edwards, 1954; Rosenberg, 1956; Rotter, 1954). This theory has been applied extensively in psychology (in learning theories, attitude theories and decision-making theories).

Behavioral intention according TRA is the most important determinant of behavior, it lists the motivating factors that influence a behavior, and is an indicator of one's effort to perform it (Ajzen, 2002; Ajzen, 1991). If a person intends to follow a behavior, it is more likely s/he will follow it. Direct determinants of individuals' behavioral intention are their attitudes and subjective norms.

Attitude is determined by individuals' beliefs about outcomes or attributes of performing the behavior (behavioral beliefs), weighted by evaluations of those outcomes or attributes. Thus, a person who has strong beliefs that positive outcomes will result from performing such behavior will have a positive attitude toward it. Conversely, a person who has strong beliefs that the results will be negative will have a negative attitude towards the behavior.

Subjective norms refer to perceived social pressure from society as well as family and friends. A person's subjective norms are determined by his or her normative beliefs (important referent individuals approve or disapprove of performing the behavior) weighted by the person's motivation to comply with those referents. A person who believes that certain referents think that he or she should perform a behavior and who is motivated to meet their expectations will hold a positive subjective norm. Conversely, a person who believes that, these referents think he or she should not perform the behavior, will have a negative subjective norm, and a person who is less motivated to comply with those referents will have a relatively neutral subjective norm (Glanz, Rimer, and Viswanath, 2015).

This model suggests that external factors influence both the individual's attitude and subjective norms. External factors consist of personality characteristics, attitude toward the target, demographic variables and other personal and individual factors such as political influences, organizational structures, etc. There is a strong correlation between attitudes, subjective norms, and behavior (Sheppard, Hartwick, and Warshaw, 1988). The main tenet of the TRA is the assumption that the most important direct determinant of behavior is behavioral intention. The success of the theory for the behavioral explanation depends on the extent to which a particular behavior is under volitional control (individuals may exercise great control over the behavior). The TRA elements may be insufficient concerning the prediction of behaviors in which the volitional control is reduced. Thus, Ajzen (1991) added perceived behavioral control to the TRA, in order to include factors beyond the individual control, which may affect the behavioral intentions and subsequently the behaviors, forming the TPB (Glanz et. al. 2015).

THEORY OF PLANNED BEHAVIOR (TPB)

By adding perceived control to TRA, situations in which someone does not have total control over a behavior are taken into account (control beliefs, perceived power), the theory is revised forming the TPB, which constitutes one of the most popular models on behavioral intention analysis. TPB has been used to predict a wide range of behaviors with respect to health and marketing among other areas (Armitage, and Conner, 2001) and it has been proved that it constitutes a framework which helps in the comprehension and study of entrepreneurial intentions. According to the above mentioned, the following diagram is formed:

Figure 1. Theory of planned behavior (Glanz et. al. 2015)

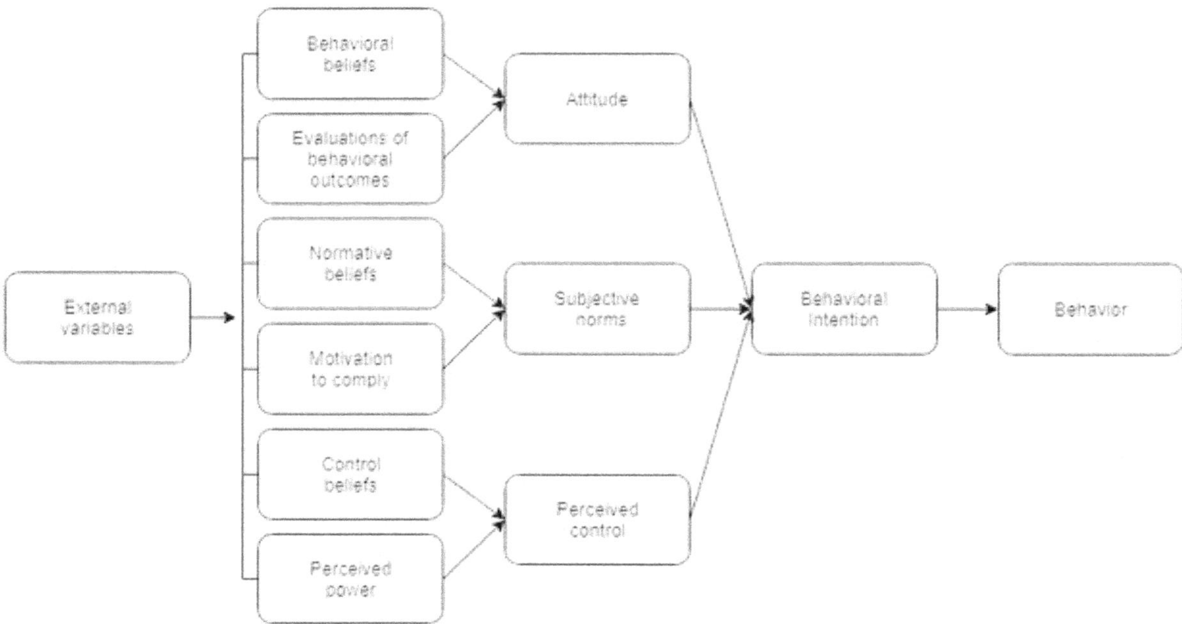

Perceived control is defined by control beliefs in connection with the presence or absence of barriers in the behavioral performance (this refers to the extent to which a person feels capable to perform a behavior), weighted by the perceived power (the impact of each control factor to facilitate or prevent behavior). The integration of the perceived control by Ajzen was based on the idea that the behavioral performance is defined by the motivations (intention) and the abilities (behavioral control). Fishbein and Ajzen (2010) proposed that perceived behavioral control and self-efficacy, as defined by Bandura (1997), constitute the same theoretical construct. Self-efficacy refers to judgments on how well one can perform actions required to handle future situations (Bandura, 1982). Self-efficacy has been linked to opportunity identification, risk-taking, and it has been found that it is positively related to global feasibility perceptions (Krueger, Reilly, and Carsrud, 2000). An individual's perception concerning control of the performance of the behavior, together with the intention, are expected to have direct impact on the behavior, especially when perceived control constitutes an accurate estimation of real behavioral control and when the volitional control is not high. In situations where volitional control is high, the impact of the perceived control is reduced and the intention is a sufficient behavior predicting factor (Madden, Ellen, and Ajzen, 1992).

While keeping the attitude and the subjective norms stable, the perception of an individual in connection with the ease or difficulty of behavioral performance will affect the behavior. TRA and TPB are a causal chain that connects behavioral beliefs, normative beliefs and control beliefs with the behavioral intention and subsequently, the behavior through attitudes, subjective norms and perceived control. One of the most important advantages of the TRA / TPB approach is the fact that proposed causal relationships are clearly defined and weighted (Fishbein & Ajzen, 2010). Other factors, like external factors (demographic, environmental etc), are deemed to function within the models and it is not believed that they contribute independently in the interpretation of the possibility that a behavior is conducted.

To sum up, TRA and TPB are focused on theoretical constructions that are related to individual motivational factors as determinants in respect of the possibility of conducting specific behaviors. TRA and TPB are based on a subjective hypothesis that the best predicting factor of behavior is intention, which is defined by the attitudes and subjective norms with regards to the behavior. Both provide a systematic method for identifying issues most important to decisions about performing specific behaviors. Finally, TPB (which is an extension of the TRA) includes an additional structure, the perceived control of the behavioral performance (Glanz et. al. 2015).

TPB /PARENTS OCCUPATION/ENTREPRENEURIAL INTENTION

An analysis of the relation of the TPB, entrepreneurial intention and Parents' Occupation is set out below. In addition to this analysis, the hypotheses are formed, which are considered the basis for this research.

Pursuant to the TPB model, an individual's intention to participate in the entrepreneurial process is positively formed by three main structures: their personal attitude towards a behavior (the extent to which the individual has positive or negative attitude concerning the adoption of the said behavior (of entrepreneurship)), the subjective norms (the social pressure perception to participate or not in this specific entrepreneurial behavior) and the perceived behavioral control (self-efficacy, that addresses the subjective perception of the feasibility of adopting an entrepreneurial behavior).

According to the above, personal attitude towards the behavior refers to the extent to which an individual assesses positively or negatively a specific behavior. The individuals form particular attitudes towards behaviors while connecting them to their possible results. If the results are desirable, the intention to perform a behavior is strong. On the other hand, if the results are not desirable, the intention to perform the behavior is weaker. In the case of creating a new business, the attitude towards the behavior may be assessed by evaluating the desire of the relevant results derived by creating the business. The perception of an individual concerning the positive and negative results of the creation of a new business, leads to the forming of their attitude towards the behavior. The extent to which the individual expects the outcomes of the creation of the new business to be positive ones, reveals their intention to create it (Glanz et. al. 2015, Krueger, 1993). As is apparent from the above mentioned, personal attitude is expected to relate with entrepreneurial intention.

H1: Personal attitude is related to entrepreneurial intention.

The second main construct of an individual's intention to participate in the entrepreneurial process are the subjective norms. Subjective norms refer to the belief that an important person or group of people will approve and support a particular behavior. These norms reflect the extent to which the said individuals approve or reject the performance of a given behavior and the power of an individual's motivations to comply with the desires of these individuals. In many cases, the result of supporting important individuals is a function of the general social support impact. In economies where entrepreneurship is not widely acceptable, it is expected that supporting the entrepreneurs is an important determinant for the entrepreneurial intention. If the individual has strong motivations to comply with the beliefs of important individuals, it is more likely to perform a behavior in line with these beliefs. In case the motivations are strong, and the important individuals approve of the behavior, it is more likely for the specific behavior to be implemented. The opposite happens in the inverse case. In case the individual has no motivation to comply with the important individuals, their intention to implement the behavior will not be affected. It is expected from the above that, subjective norms will relate to entrepreneurial intention.

H2: Subjective norms are related to entrepreneurial intention.

Perceived behavioral control (self-efficacy) (Ajzen, 1991, Bandura, 1977, Kreuger et al. 2000) refers to the perception of the ease or difficulty in the performance of a behavior and is deemed to include the expected barriers or the support that arises. (Ajzen,1991). Based on the TPB, it is proposed that self-efficacy is directly related to entrepreneurial intention. If the individual does not believe that they may successfully carry out their duties that are related to the beginning of a business, their intention to do it diminishes and vice versa (Glanz et. al. 2015). In line then with the above mentioned, perceived behavioral control is expected to relate positively with entrepreneurial intention.

H3: Perceived behavioral control is related with entrepreneurial intention.

The impact of family on entrepreneurial intentions of students is a very important factor. There are two models developed, addressing the importance of the family impact. The first is the parental role model, according to which the individuals with self-employed parents have greater chances to develop entrepreneurial activity, following the example of their parents (Osorio, Settles, and Shen, 2017, Laspita, et.al. 2012, Heck, et.al.2008). The second model is the family support model, which describes the usual phenomenon of economic and social support of the individuals who are doing business with the help of their families. The individuals, whose parents have their own small business, tend to develop entrepreneurial activities themselves, instead of choosing to work in a bigger enterprise (Wang, and Wong, 2004). The family is likely to provide advice, technical support and encouragement to younger members toward the direction of starting up a business. Parents offer their children experiences through family interaction and opportunities that support their learning (Bandura, 1977). Research shows that offspring of parents entrepreneurs or freelancers are likely to demonstrate higher levels of entrepreneurial intention (Sahinidis et al 2019; Bloemen-Bekx, Voordeckers, Remery, and Schippers, 2019; Liguori, Bendickson, and Mcdowell, 2017). Many studies propose that parents occupation is a key determinant of the action of new venture creation (Dioneo-Adetayo, 2006; Fayolle and Liñán, 2014; Krueger et al., 2000; Lanero et al., 2016).

H4: Offspring of entrepreneurs or freelancers are expected to demonstrate higher levels of entrepreneurial intention.

METHODS

After determining the initial aim and orientation of the proposed study and given its complexity, a questionnaire was used based on earlier studies to measure the concepts involved. There were overall 1244 questionnaires answered by students, who study in a Public Greek University based in Athens. The sample was a convenience one given that the resources available were limited, but we expect that the size of it allows us to proceed with reliable statistical analyses and produce valid conclusions. In order to determine the relationship between the variables stated in the hypotheses above and entrepreneurial intention, 19 questions were used (7-point Likert scale), in order to measure according to theory the elements of TPB (attitude, subjective norms, perceived behavioral control, intention). Subsequently, a multiple regression analysis was used, with Entrepreneurial Intention as a dependent variable and the other factors (attitude, subjective norms, perceived behavioral control) as independent variables. To examine the fourth hypothesis, 'H4: Offspring of entrepreneurs or freelancer parents are expected to demonstrate higher levels of entrepreneurial intention', we calculated the mean of entrepreneurial intention of offspring whose parents are entrepreneurs or freelancers in several combinations (1. Entrepreneurial intention of total sample, 2. Entrepreneurial intention of offspring whose parents are neither entrepreneurs nor freelancers, 3. Entrepreneurial intention of offspring whose mother is either entrepreneur or freelancer (but the father is not), 4. Entrepreneurial intention of offspring whose father is either entrepreneur or freelancer (but mother is not) and 5. Entrepreneurial intention of offspring whose both parents are either entrepreneurs or freelancers). The proposed hypotheses were empirically tested using the multiple regression analysis through the SPSS software version 24.

RESULTS AND FINDINGS

The overall regression model was significant, the value of R^2 is significantly greater than zero. That means that the independent variables are able to measure and predict the dependent variable of our sample. Figure 2 demonstrates the predictive power of the independent variables, in terms of entrepreneurial intention. The results have shown that 77.2% of the variance in the depended variable is explained by the independent variables (perceived behavioral control, subjective norms and attitude). Figure 4 shows the predictive ability of the three factors, concerning entrepreneurial intention and confirms our hypotheses. All the independent variables (perceived behavioral control, subjective norms and attitude) have positive relationship with entrepreneurial intention and have a statistically significant impact on the outcome variable (p values<0.05). The variable that affects entrepreneurial intention in the greatest extent is attitude.

Figure 2. Model summary

Model Summary

					Change Statistics				
Model	R	R Square	Adjusted R Square	Std. Error of the Estimate	R Square Change	F Change	df1	df2	Sig. F Change
1	.879[a]	.773	.772	.6497772392	.773	1405.927	3	1240	.000

a. Predictors: (Constant), Percieved behavioral control, Subjective norms, Attitude

The total sample of the study consist of (n=1244) students, 53% of the sample (n=660) consist of students whose parents are neither entrepreneurs nor freelancers, 6% of the sample (n=70) are students whose mother is either entrepreneur or freelancer, but the father is not, 29% of the sample (n=362) consist of students whose fathers are either entrepreneur or freelancer (but their mother is not) and 12% of the sample (n=152) are students whose both parents are either entrepreneurs or freelancers. The findings of this research confirm also the fourth hypothesis 'H4: Offspring of parents entrepreneurs or freelancers are expected to demonstrate higher levels of entrepreneurial intention'. From the results of the study and as shown in the diagram below, offspring of entrepreneur or freelancer parents demonstrate higher levels of entrepreneurial intention.

Figure 3. ANOVA

ANOVA[a]

Model		Sum of Squares	df	Mean Square	F	Sig.
1	Regression	1780.792	3	593.597	1405.927	.000[b]
	Residual	523.541	1240	.422		
	Total	2304.333	1243			

a. Dependent Variable: Intention

b. Predictors: (Constant), Percieved behavioral control, Subjective norms, Attitude

- The mean of entrepreneurial intention of the sample whose parents are neither entrepreneurs nor freelancers (n=660) is 4.5
- The mean of entrepreneurial intention of the total sample (n=1244) is 4.67
- The mean of entrepreneurial intention of the sample whose mother is either entrepreneur or freelancer (but the father is not) (n=70) is 4.75
- The mean of entrepreneurial intention of the sample whose father is either entrepreneur or freelancer (but mother is not) (n=362) is 4.84
- The mean of entrepreneurial intention of the sample whose both parents are either entrepreneurs or freelancers (n=152) is 4.91

Figure 4. Coefficients

Coefficients[a]

Model		Unstandardized Coefficients B	Unstandardized Coefficients Std. Error	Standardized Coefficients Beta	t	Sig.	95.0% Confidence Interval for B Lower Bound	95.0% Confidence Interval for B Upper Bound
1	(Constant)	-.768	.088		-8.713	.000	-.941	-.595
	Attitude	.586	.022	.521	26.708	.000	.543	.629
	Subjective norms	.189	.018	.181	10.518	.000	.154	.224
	Percieved behavioral control	.333	.019	.308	17.216	.000	.295	.371

a. Dependent Variable: Intention

Figure 5. Entrepreneurial intention mean

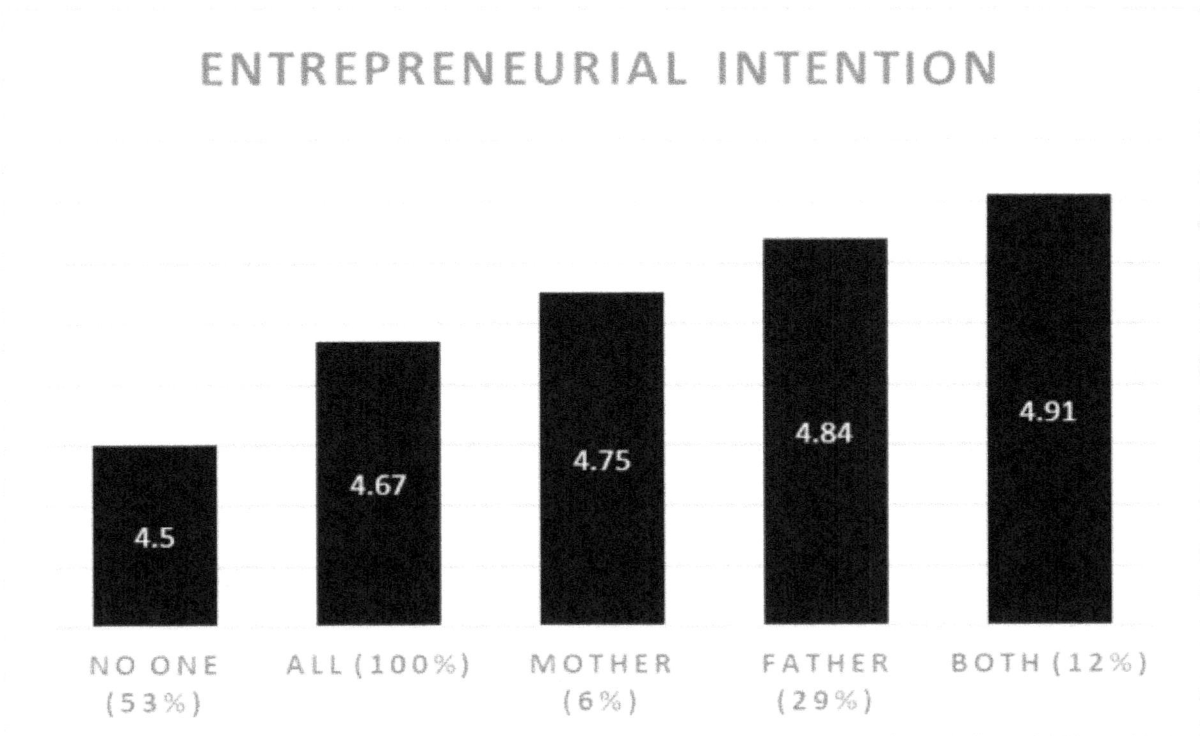

All findings are to some extent in line with those of the literature and support the proposed hypotheses. There is clear evidence of the relationship between entrepreneurial intention and Parental entrepreneurial activity. The relationship becomes more pronounced in the case where both parents are self-employed or entrepreneurs/freelancers. The father-entrepreneur relationship with entrepreneurial intention of children appears to be a stronger one than the corresponding relationship of the mother entrepreneur.

DISCUSSION

Understanding the process of becoming an entrepreneur is imperative in the study of entrepreneurship and management. Entrepreneurship has played a major role in encouraging economic development, reducing unemployment and helping social development. Researchers from many different countries have become increasingly interested in conducting more thorough studies about students' entrepreneurial intentions (Cao, and Ngo, 2019). Overall, this study examined the relationship between the three elements of TPB (personal attitude, subjective norms, perceived behavioral control) and entrepreneurial intention considering the influence of parent's occupation. The findings of this study support the hypotheses proposed above, based on the relevant literature. All of the variables examined here, have demonstrated a positive correlation with the entrepreneurial intention. Also, it has been proven that offspring of entrepreneurs or freelancers are expected to demonstrate higher levels of entrepreneurial intention. Children who grow up in entrepreneurs' families gain advantage in the development of entrepreneurial characteristics and tendencies (Zellweger, Sieger, and Halter, 2011).

This study, contributes to the literature regarding the factors influencing entrepreneurial intention, providing empirical evidence, to help formulate policies to encourage university students' entrepreneurship practices, attracting the interest of both educators and policy makers. The findings will become increasingly important, as research in the field of entrepreneurship continues to place models of entrepreneurial intentions at the center of our understanding of the entrepreneurial process (Butz, Hanson, Schultz, and Warzynski, 2018; Belias, 2019; Kavoura, and Koziol, 2017; Kavoura, and Andersson, 2016; Makarona, and Kavoura, 2019; Sahinidis, Vassiliou and Hyz 2014). Fostering entrepreneurship is one of the strategic goals of Greek government as it impacts economic development. Without entrepreneurs, entrepreneurship does not exist. Hopefully this research will improve the understanding of the psychological processes that precede a venture start-up, and turn the focus from the "dance" to the "dancer" (Jakopec, Krečar, and Sušanj, 2013).

Aside from the aforementioned contributions, this study also has a number of limitations that must be addressed. One limitation of this study is the fact that the findings are based on a setting of university students. The size of the sample in this study allows us to proceed with reasonable and reliable statistical analyses and produce valid conclusions, nevertheless university students of business studies are not representative of all students. A second limitation is that the sample comprises of Greek students. It would be most interesting to see if these relationships hold in more diverse settings and across different ethnic backgrounds (Maes, et.al., 2014). Finally, another limitation is the lack of addressing the gender issue, although a substantial number of studies has focused on that.

TPB has made a considerable contribution to the entrepreneurship literature, yet, there are many questions and gaps that remain unanswered and unfilled. Further, a certain level of caution should be observed as the mostly positive findings for the TPB may be due to current publishing standards, where only significant results make it to publication. Scholars should continue to grow this stream of the literature as significant contributions remain to be made (Lortie, and Castogiovanni, 2015). Future studies could investigate the validity of the findings reported here, in different contexts using more variables, not included in this study and inquire the potential existence of latent variables which may be confounding the relationships discussed above.

REFERENCES

Ajzen, I. (1991). The theory of planned behavior. *Organizational Behavior and Human Decision Processes, 50*(2), 179–211. doi:10.1016/0749-5978(91)90020-T

Ajzen, I. (2002). Perceived Behavioral Control, Self-Efficacy, Locus of Control, and the Theory of Planned Behavior1. *Journal of Applied Social Psychology, 32*(4), 665–683. doi:10.1111/j.1559-1816.2002.tb00236.x

Ajzen, I., & Fishbein, M. (1980). *Understanding attitudes and predicting social behavior*. Prentice-Hall.

Al-Jubari, I., Hassan, A., & Liñán, F. (2018). Entrepreneurial intention among University students in Malaysia: Integrating self-determination theory and the theory of planned behavior. *The International Entrepreneurship and Management Journal, 15*(4), 1323–1342. doi:10.100711365-018-0529-0

Armitage, C. J., & Conner, M. (2001). Efficacy of the Theory of Planned Behaviour: A meta-analytic review. *British Journal of Social Psychology*, *40*(4), 471–499. doi:10.1348/014466601164939 PMID:11795063

Autio, E., Keeley, R. H., Klofsten, M., Parker, G. G. C., & Hay, M. (2001). Entrepreneurial Intent among Students in Scandinavia and in the USA. *Enterprise and Innovation Management Studies*, *2*(2), 145–160. doi:10.1080/14632440110094632

Bandura, A. (1977). Self-efficacy: Toward a unifying theory of behavioral change. *Psychological Review*, *84*(2), 191–215. doi:10.1037/0033-295X.84.2.191 PMID:847061

Bandura, A. (1982). The assessment and predictive generality of self-percepts of efficacy. *Journal of Behavior Therapy and Experimental Psychiatry*, *13*(3), 195–199. doi:10.1016/0005-7916(82)90004-0 PMID:7142408

Bandura, A. (1997). *Self-efficacy: The exercise of control.* Freeman.

Baron, R. A., & Ensley, M. D. (2006). Opportunity Recognition as the Detection of Meaningful Patterns: Evidence from Comparisons of Novice and Experienced Entrepreneurs. *Management Science*, *52*(9), 1331–1344. doi:10.1287/mnsc.1060.0538

Belias, D. (2019). Entrepreneurship in the age of digital tourism; the future prospects from the use of robots. *Małopolska Journal, 42*(2), 89-99. doi:10.25944/znmwse.2019.02.8999

Bloemen-Bekx, M., Voordeckers, W., Remery, C., & Schippers, J. (2019). Following in parental footsteps? The influence of gender and learning experiences on entrepreneurial intentions. *International Small Business Journal: Researching Entrepreneurship*, *37*(6), 642–663. doi:10.1177/0266242619838936

Butz, N. T., Hanson, S., Schultz, P. L., & Warzynski, M. M. (2018). Beyond the Big Five: Does grit influence the entrepreneurial intent of university students in the US? *Journal of Global Entrepreneurship Research*, *8*(1), 15. Advance online publication. doi:10.118640497-018-0100-z

Cao, V. Q., & Ngo, T. T. T. (2019). Linking Entrepreneurial Intentions And Mindset Models: A Comparative Study Of Public And Private Universities In Vietnam. *Gadjah Mada International Journal of Business*, *21*(2), 115. doi:10.22146/gamaijb.34753

Dawson, C., & Henley, A. (2012). "Push" versus "pull" entrepreneurship: An ambiguous distinction? *International Journal of Entrepreneurial Behaviour & Research*, *18*(6), 697–719. doi:10.1108/13552551211268139

Decker, R., Haltiwanger, J., Jarmin, R., & Miranda, J. (2014). The Role of Entrepreneurship in US Job Creation and Economic Dynamism. *The Journal of Economic Perspectives*, *28*(3), 3–24. doi:10.1257/jep.28.3.3

Dioneo-Adetayo, E. A. (2006). Factors Influencing Attitude of Youth Towards Entrepreneurship. *International Journal of Adolescence and Youth*, *13*(1-2), 127–145. doi:10.1080/02673843.2006.9747970

Edwards, W. (1954). The theory of decision making. *Psychological Bulletin*, *51*(4), 380–417. doi:10.1037/h0053870 PMID:13177802

Esfandiar, K., Sharifi-Tehrani, M., Pratt, S., & Altinay, L. (2019). Understanding entrepreneurial intentions: A developed integrated structural model approach. *Journal of Business Research, 94*, 172–182. doi:10.1016/j.jbusres.2017.10.045

Fayolle, A., & Gailly, B. (2013). The Impact of Entrepreneurship Education on Entrepreneurial Attitudes and Intention: Hysteresis and Persistence. *Journal of Small Business Management, 53*(1), 75–93. doi:10.1111/jsbm.12065

Fayolle, A., & Liñán, F. (2014). The future of research on entrepreneurial intentions. *Journal of Business Research, 67*(5), 663–666. doi:10.1016/j.jbusres.2013.11.024

Fishbein, M., & Ajzen, I. (2010). *Predicting and changing behavior*. New York: Psychology Press.

Gieure, C., Benavides-Espinosa, M. D. M., & Roig-Dobón, S. (2019). Entrepreneurial intentions in an international university environment. *International Journal of Entrepreneurial Behaviour & Research, 25*(8), 1605–1620. doi:10.1108/IJEBR-12-2018-0810

Gird, A., & Bagraim, J. J. (2008). The Theory of Planned Behaviour as Predictor of Entrepreneurial Intent Amongst Final-Year University Students. *South African Journal of Psychology. Suid-Afrikaanse Tydskrif vir Sielkunde, 38*(4), 711–724. doi:10.1177/008124630803800410

Gird, A., & Bagraim, J. J. (2008). The Theory of Planned Behaviour as Predictor of Entrepreneurial Intent Amongst Final-Year University Students. *South African Journal of Psychology. Suid-Afrikaanse Tydskrif vir Sielkunde, 38*(4), 711–724. doi:10.1177/008124630803800410

Glanz, K., Rimer, B. K., & Viswanath, K. (2015). *Health behavior: theory, research, and practice*. Jossey-Bass.

González-González, J. M., Bretones, F. D., Zarco, V., & Rodríguez, A. (2011). Women, immigration and entrepreneurship in Spain: A confluence of debates in the face of a complex reality. *Women's Studies International Forum, 34*(5), 360–370. doi:10.1016/j.wsif.2011.05.007

Gorgievski, M. J., Stephan, U., Laguna, M., & Moriano, J. A. (2017). Predicting Entrepreneurial Career Intentions. *Journal of Career Assessment, 26*(3), 457–475. doi:10.1177/1069072717714541 PMID:30443149

Heck, R. K. Z., Hoy, F., Poutziouris, P. Z., & Steier, L. P. (2008). Emerging Paths of Family Entrepreneurship Research. *Journal of Small Business Management, 46*(3), 317–330. doi:10.1111/j.1540-627X.2008.00246.x

Hessels, J., Gelderen, M. V., & Thurik, R. (2008). Entrepreneurial aspirations, motivations, and their drivers. *Small Business Economics, 31*(3), 323–339. doi:10.100711187-008-9134-x

Jakopec, A., Krečar, I. M., & Sušanj, Z. (2013). Predictors Of Entrepreneurial Intentions Of Students Of Economics. *Studia Psychologica, 55*(4), 289–297. doi:10.21909p.2013.04.643

Kautonen, T., Gelderen, M. V., & Tornikoski, E. T. (2013). Predicting entrepreneurial behaviour: A test of the theory of planned behaviour. *Applied Economics, 45*(6), 697–707. doi:10.1080/00036846.2011.610750

Kavoura, A., & Andersson, T. (2016). Applying Delphi method for strategic design of social entrepreneurship. *Library Review*, *65*(3), 185–205. doi:10.1108/LR-06-2015-0062

Kavoura, A., & Koziol, L. (2017). *Polish Firms' Innovation Capability for Competitiveness via Information Technologies and Social Media Implementation.* In A. Vlachvei, O. Notta, K. Karantininis, & N. Tsountas (Eds.), *Factors Affecting Firm Competitiveness and Performance in the Modern Business World* (pp. 185–214). IGI Global.

Kristiansen, S., & Indarti, N. (2004). Entrepreneurial Intention Among Indonesian And Norwegian Students. *Journal of Enterprising Culture*, *12*(01), 55–78. doi:10.1142/S021849580400004X

Krueger, N. F., & Carsrud, A. L. (1993). Entrepreneurial intentions: Applying the theory of planned behaviour. *Entrepreneurship and Regional Development*, *5*(4), 315–330. doi:10.1080/08985629300000020

Krueger, N. F., & Day, M. (2010). Looking Forward, Looking Backward: From Entrepreneurial Cognition to Neuroentrepreneurship. Handbook of Entrepreneurship Research, 321–357. doi:10.1007/978-1-4419-1191-9_13

Krueger, N. F. Jr, Reilly, M. D., & Carsrud, A. L. (2000). Competing models of entrepreneurial intentions. *Journal of Business Venturing*, *15*(5-6), 411–432. doi:10.1016/S0883-9026(98)00033-0

Laguía, A., Moriano, J. A., & Gorgievski, M. J. (2019). A psychosocial study of self-perceived creativity and entrepreneurial intentions in a sample of university students. *Thinking Skills and Creativity*, *31*, 44–57. doi:10.1016/j.tsc.2018.11.004

Lanero, A., Vázquez, J.-L., & Aza, C. L. (2016). Social cognitive determinants of entrepreneurial career choice in university students. *International Small Business Journal: Researching Entrepreneurship*, *34*(8), 1053–1075. doi:10.1177/0266242615612882

Laspita, S., Breugst, N., Heblich, S., & Patzelt, H. (2012). Intergenerational transmission of entrepreneurial intentions. *Journal of Business Venturing*, *27*(4), 414–435. doi:10.1016/j.jbusvent.2011.11.006

Liguori, E. W., Bendickson, J. S., & Mcdowell, W. C. (2017). Revisiting entrepreneurial intentions: A social cognitive career theory approach. *The International Entrepreneurship and Management Journal*, *14*(1), 67–78. doi:10.100711365-017-0462-7

Liñán, F., & Chen, Y.-W. (2009). Development and Cross-Cultural Application of a Specific Instrument to Measure Entrepreneurial Intentions. *Entrepreneurship Theory and Practice*, *33*(3), 593–617. doi:10.1111/j.1540-6520.2009.00318.x

Liñán, F., & Santos, F. J. (2007). Does Social Capital Affect Entrepreneurial Intentions? *International Advances in Economic Research*, *13*(4), 443–453. doi:10.100711294-007-9109-8

Lortie, J., & Castogiovanni, G. (2015). The theory of planned behavior in entrepreneurship research: What we know and future directions. *The International Entrepreneurship and Management Journal*, *11*(4), 935–957. doi:10.100711365-015-0358-3

Madden, T. J., Ellen, P. S., & Ajzen, I. (1992). A comparison of the theory of planned behavior and the theory of reasoned action. *Personality and Social Psychology Bulletin*, *18*(1), 3–9. doi:10.1177/0146167292181001

Maes, J., Leroy, H., & Sels, L. (2014). Gender differences in entrepreneurial intentions: A TPB multigroup analysis at factor and indicator level. *European Management Journal*, *32*(5), 784–794. doi:10.1016/j.emj.2014.01.001

Makarona, E., & Kavoura, A. (2019). Redesigning the Ivory Tower: Academic entrepreneurship as a new calling supporting economic growth. *The Malopolska School of Economics in Tarnow Research Papers Collection*, *42*, 15–26. doi:10.25944/znmwse.2019.02.1526

Mwatsika, C. (2015). Entrepreneurship development and entrepreneurial orientation in rural areas in Malawi. *African Journal of Business Management*, *9*(9), 425–436. doi:10.5897/AJBM2014.7552

Mwatsika, C., Patrick, K., & Levison, C. (2018). Untangling the concept of entrepreneurship towards a common perspective. *African Journal of Business Management*, *12*(14), 451–470. doi:10.5897/AJBM2018.8587

Naushad, M. (2018). A study on the antecedents of entrepreneurial intentions among Saudi students. *Entrepreneurship and Sustainability Issues*, *5*(3), 600–617. doi:10.9770/jesi.2018.5.3(14)

Naushad, M., Faridi, M. R., & Syed, A. M. (2018). Economic development of community by entrepreneurship: An investigation of the entrepreneurial intent and the institutional support to the local community in Al-Kharj region. *Entrepreneurship and Sustainability Issues*, *5*(4), 899–913. doi:10.9770/jesi.2018.5.4(14)

Osorio, A. E., Settles, A., & Shen, T. (2017). The Influence of Support Factors on Entrepreneurial Attitudes and Intentions of College Students. *Academy of Management Proceedings*, *2017*(1), 10901. doi:10.5465/AMBPP.2017.10901abstract

Rosenberg, M. J. (1956). Cognitive structure and attitudinal affect. *Journal of Abnormal and Social Psychology*, *53*(3), 367–372. doi:10.1037/h0044579 PMID:13376244

Rotter, J. B. (1954). *Social learning and clinical psychology*. doi:10.1037/10788-000

Rueda, S., Moriano, J. A., & Liñán, F. (n.d.). Validating a theory of planned behavior questionnaire to measure entrepreneurial intentions. *Developing, Shaping and Growing Entrepreneurship*, 60–78. doi:10.4337/9781784713584.00010

Ruiz-Alba, J. L., Soares, A., Rodríguez-Molina, M. A., & Banoun, A. (2019). Gamification and entrepreneurial intentions. *Journal of Small Business and Enterprise Development*, *26*(5), 661–683. doi:10.1108/JSBED-09-2018-0266

Sahinidis, A., Polychronopoulos, G., & Kallivokas D. (2019). Entrepreneurship Education Impact on Entrepreneurial Intention Among Tourism Students: A Longitudinal Study. *Strategic Innovative Marketing and Tourism Springer Proceedings in Business and Economics*, 1245–1250. doi:10.1007/978-3-030-12453-3_142

Sahinidis, A., Stavroulakis, D., Kossieri, E., & Varelas, S. (2019). Entrepreneurial Intention Determinants Among Female Students. The Influence of Role Models, Parents' Occupation and Perceived Behavioral Control on Forming the Desire to Become a Business Owner. *Strategic Innovative Marketing and Tourism Springer Proceedings in Business and Economics,* 173–178. doi:10.1007/978-3030-12453-3_20

Sahinidis, A., Vassiliou, E. E., & Hyz, A. B. (2014). Factors Affecting Entrepreneurs' Intention to Start a New Venture: An Empirical Study. *International Journal on Strategic Innovative Marketing*, *1*, 148–162. doi:10.15556/ijsim.01.03.003

Santos, F. J., Roomi, M. A., & Liñán, F. (2014). About Gender Differences and the Social Environment in the Development of Entrepreneurial Intentions. *Journal of Small Business Management*, *54*(1), 49–66. doi:10.1111/jsbm.12129

Segal, G., Borgia, D., & Schoenfeld, J. (2005). The motivation to become an entrepreneur. *International Journal of Entrepreneurial Behaviour & Research*, *11*(1), 42–57. doi:10.1108/13552550510580834

Shapero, A. (1975). The displaced, uncomfortable entrepreneur. *Psychology Today*, *9*(November), 83–88, 133.

Shapero, A. (1984). *Why entrepreneurship?* Working paper, Babson College.

Sheppard, B. H., Hartwick, J., & Warshaw, P. R. (1988). The Theory of Reasoned Action: A Meta-Analysis of Past Research with Recommendations for Modifications and Future Research. *The Journal of Consumer Research*, *15*(3), 325. doi:10.1086/209170

Shook, C. L., & Bratianu, C. (2008). Entrepreneurial intent in a transitional economy: An application of the theory of planned behavior to Romanian students. *The International Entrepreneurship and Management Journal*, *6*(3), 231–247. doi:10.100711365-008-0091-2

Souitaris, V., Zerbinati, S., & Al-Laham, A. (2007). Do entrepreneurship programmes raise entrepreneurial intention of science and engineering students? The effect of learning, inspiration and resources. *Journal of Business Venturing*, *22*(4), 566–591. doi:10.1016/j.jbusvent.2006.05.002

Thurik, R., Verheul, I., Hessels, J., & Zwan, P. (2010). Factors Influencing the Entrepreneurial Engagement of Opportunity and Necessity Entrepreneurs. EIM Business and Policy Research. *Scales Research Reports.*, *6*. Advance online publication. doi:10.100740821-016-0065-1

Tkachev, A., & Kolvereid, L. (1999). Self-employment intentions among Russian students. *Entrepreneurship and Regional Development*, *11*(3), 269–280. doi:10.1080/089856299283209

Tsai, K.-H., Chang, H.-C., & Peng, C.-Y. (2014). Extending the link between entrepreneurial selfefficacy and intention: A moderated mediation model. *The International Entrepreneurship and Management Journal*, *12*(2), 445–463. doi:10.100711365-014-0351-2

Vaghely, I. P., & Julien, P.-A. (2010). Are opportunities recognized or constructed? *Journal of Business Venturing*, *25*(1), 73–86. doi:10.1016/j.jbusvent.2008.06.004

Veciana, J. M., Aponte, M., & Urbano, D. (2005). University Students' Attitudes Towards Entrepreneurship: A Two Countries Comparison. *The International Entrepreneurship and Management Journal*, *1*(2), 165–182. doi:10.100711365-005-1127-5

Vivarelli, M. (2004). Are All the Potential Entrepreneurs So Good? *Small Business Economics*, *23*(1), 41–49. doi:10.1023/B:SBEJ.0000026023.11752.a9

Wach, K., & Wojciechowski, L. (2016). Entrepreneurial Intentions of Students in Poland in the View of Ajzen's Theory of Planned Behaviour. *Entrepreneurial Business and Economics Review*, *4*(1), 83–94. doi:10.15678/EBER.2016.040106

Wang, C. K., & Wong, P.-K. (2004). Entrepreneurial interest of university students in Singapore. *Technovation*, *24*(2), 163–172. doi:10.1016/S0166-4972(02)00016-0

Zellweger, T., Sieger, P., & Halter, F. (2011). Should I stay or should I go? Career choice intentions of students with family business background. *Journal of Business Venturing*, *26*(5), 521–536. doi:10.1016/j.jbusvent.2010.04.001

KEY TERMS AND DEFINTIONS

Attitude: Individuals' beliefs about outcomes or attributes of performing the behavior, weighted by evaluations of those outcomes or attributes.

Entrepreneurial Intention: The recognized belief of a person who intends to undertake a new business venture.

Parents Occupation: A key determinant of the action of new venture creation.

Perceived Behavioral Control: People's perceptions of their ability to perform a given behavior.

Subjective Norms: Perceived social pressure from society as well as family and friends.

Theory of Planned Behavior (TPB): A framework which helps in the comprehension and study of entrepreneurial intentions.

Theory of Reasoned Action (TRA): A theory that aims to explain the relationship between attitudes and behaviours within human action.

Chapter 10
Orientation to Organizational Learning and Its Effects on Innovation and Performance:
The Colombian MSMEs Case

Fred Davinson Contreras Palacios
National Sports School, Colombia

Rafael Ignacio Perez-Uribe
https://orcid.org/0000-0001-9924-6657
EAN University, Colombia

Iván Rodrigo Vargas Ramírez
https://orcid.org/0000-0001-9037-0571
InvestprojectVR, Colombia

Carlos Salcedo-Perez
https://orcid.org/0000-0002-4433-5537
EAN University, Colombia

ABSTRACT

This research demonstrates how the orientation to organizational learning affects the innovation and performance of the Colombian micro, small, and medium (MSMEs) enterprises, based on a study with 403 Colombian MSMEs, pretending that the results allow the government sector and the academy to design strategies maintain or improve, as appropriate, innovative and learning practices within these organizations. Two hypotheses were raised: 1) learning orientation positively influences business performance and 2) learning orientation positively influences business innovation. The two hypotheses are demonstrated after performing a multiple regression analysis and a broadly significant relationship was evidenced both between the orientation to learning and innovation and in each of the dimensions that make it up: innovation in products/services, processes, and management.

DOI: 10.4018/978-1-7998-3648-3.ch010

INTRODUCTION

Worldwide, Micro, Small, and Medium Enterprises - MSMEs generate a high percentage of the jobs created, contribute considerably to production and trade, and they play a key role to achieve competitiveness; this is why their importance is recognized in most countries, and public and private sectors work together to strengthen them (Varela, 2011). In Colombia, data shows that they comprise 99,9% of all enterprises (96,4% micro and 3,5% small and medium), generating 63% of employment and contributing with 37,5% of the GDP (Confecamaras, 2016).

Makarona & Kavoura (2019) carry out studies in this regard, indicating the need to link the generation of wealth of this type of companies with innovation and academic activities that really strengthen the relationship between industry and academia.

In Latin America and Colombia, previous conditions that boosted interest to research MSMEs have not changed but increased, due to issues such as the development of new technologies, internationalization, business environment dynamics and complexity, and the economic crisis (Dini and Stumpo, 2019). The last one especially has affected their performance, as result of the conditions of the environment, and their endogenous competencies such as technology undertaking, workers' and entrepreneurs' qualification, people's knowledge, skills learning, management and productivity (Busłowska & Wiśniewska, 2017; CONPES, 2007).

Thoeni, Marshall & Campbell (2016) state that enterprises need to find management processes and techniques that allow them to achieve success, and different authors recognize that it is necessary to take adequate advantage of resources and capabilities available. How to get it and what to do to keep or increase a competitive position becomes a key topic for business management.

According to Vargo & Lusch (2014) and Sirvastava, Fahey & Christensen (2001), inimitability is higher in intangible than in tangible capabilities. In this sense, Slater & Narver (1995) consider innovation and organizational learning as capabilities that are difficult to imitate, besides, they are highlighted for their potential to generate other capabilities (Munuera *et al.*, 2007).

Innovation is considered a critical factor for enterprises' survival and success (Ramírez-Garzón and Pérez-Uribe, 2019; Formichella, 2005; Damanpour & Gopalakrishnan, 2001; Camelo, Romero and Valle, 2000; Rogers, 1983; Schumpeter, 1942), since innovative enterprises are more flexible, which allows them to learn and get better adapted to changes in the environment, to answer faster and better to changing needs of the society and therefore to get better results compared to those that are not (Miles & Snow, 1978; Drucker, 1985).

In the current changing business environment, to know more and quicker than the competitors may represent the difference between staying or getting out of business; in this sense, organizational learning is recognized as an essential organizational function (Yonso, Figueredo, Alvarado and Goyo, 2013). Orientation to learn refers to the director's attitude and commitment to incentive employees to get engaged to new ideas and knowledge, with an open attitude to experiment and to unlearn what was already learnt (Stary, 2016; Cardona and Calderón, 2006 ; Calantone, Cavusgil and Zhao, 2002); which is considered a long-term investment that may become a factor to survive (Vargas, 2018; Llonch, López and Eusebio, 2007). Different authors are showing a growing interest towards organizational learning, and particularly towards orientation to learning (Turi, Javed,, Bashir, Khaskhelly, Shaikh & Toheed, 2019).

Previous empirical studies show that innovation and organizational learning constitute distinctive capabilities and potential generators of competitive advantage for enterprises (Stable-Rodríguez, 2016); others state that learning and organizational knowledge precede innovation (Kavoura & Anderson, 2016;

Nonaka & Takeuchi, 1995; Hage, 1999); this means that it is necessary to learn in order to innovate (Rodríguez, Lozano and Hernández, 2011). In the same way, Kavoura & Koziol (2017) discusses cases in Poland and medium enterprises and found that social media and innovations are not be used so much by small and medium ones although this would benefit them.

Nevertheless, and even when there is literature that analyzes the relation between innovation, learning and organizational performance, there are few researches on this topic in Colombia and Latin America.

Aimed at filling this gap, the objective of this research is to analyze empirically the impact of the orientation to learning on the enterprises' innovation and performance. To do so, 403 Colombian MSMEs were analyzed to enrich similar researches, expecting that the results obtained will help the government and the academy to design strategies to keep and/or improve innovative and learning practices in MSMEs.

THEORETICAL FRAMEWORK

Theory of Resources and Capabilities

In the current competitive environment, characterized by open markets, globalization, economic crisis, development of new technologies, in which change is constant, in a knowledge society as Drucker (1993) states, in which nor capital neither natural resources but knowledge becomes the economical resource, enterprises need to manage processes and strategies that make them different from others and lead them to success.

Traditionally, the book Competitive Strategy, written by Porter, has been used by strategic management to explain competitive advantages; such book proposes a methodology based on the industries to which the enterprise belongs (Ynzunza and Izar, 2013). However, some researches evidenced the difficulties of such model to explain the origins of the competitive advantage, in which it was demonstrated that differences in results among sectors were less significant than differences inside the sectors themselves (Rumelt, 1991; Hansen and Wernerfelt, 1989). Then, in the 90's, researchers focused their attention on enterprises' internal factors to explain the results. Hence, the theory of resources and capabilities arises; it pretends to consider these internal aspects as the generators of competitive advantage for the enterprises. To do so, the enterprise is defined as a unique set of resources and capabilities that cannot be sold and bought in the market. The main mission of the researchers is the study of differences in the result, and their main premise is the presence of heterogeneity among the resources controlled by enterprises, which becomes the main factor that explains the difference of the results obtained among enterprises (Lippman and Rumelt, 1982; Rumelt, 1991; Barney, 1991).

Therefore, differences between the levels of success achieved by enterprises are explained more by resources and capabilities than by the structure of the industries to which they belong to (Barney, 1991; Ynzunza, *et al.*, 2013). Day (1994) states that the link between the enterprise's capabilities and its challenges is the most important factor to understand the success and failures of enterprises.

Therefore, key sources for MSMEs to achieve competitiveness are their own resources and capabilities as long as they adapt to the environment, being physical, technological, human and organizational resources are available and can be controlled by the enterprise; capabilities refer to the way in which the enterprise uses such resources (Salón 2018; Pulido, 2010; Munera and Rodríguez, 2007).

The enterprises' competitive advantages depend both on tangible and intangible assets. The latter, due to the difficulties encountered to imitate them, become key factors to compete nowadays (Munuera *et al.*, 2007). Hence, Srivastava et al (2001) states that inimitability is higher in intangible than in tangible capabilities. Cardona (2011) considers innovation and organizational learning as capabilities difficult to imitated and emphasizes on their potential to generate additional capabilities.

Learning

It is a complex concept that in which different fields of knowledge are used to explain it. Traditionally, psychologist and pedagogues who more frequently have studies this concept. Some of them link learning and change and others consider it a process. Conde, Correa and Delgado (2010) state that learning is a change relatively permanent of behavior. Del Rio and Santiesteban (2011) consider learning as a process by which knowledge is acquired through experience.

With a higher scope, some other authors link learning to change of behavior; they consider that this is the result of the interaction of the individual with his/her environment (Conde, et al, 2010). Nuñez (2004) cited by Contreras et al (2012) defines learning as the process by which the person assimilates the culture accumulated by others, as knowledge (conceptual, instrumental and operational) and as skills, emotions, feelings and values, generating his/her own.

Senge (2000) states that learning relates to the word "metanoia", understood as mental shift, change of approach or transit from one perspective to another. Therefore, he states that understanding the meaning of that word means understanding the most profound meaning of learning. In the same direction, Stable-Rodríguez (2016) refers to learning as those conscious processes that cause long-lasting mental shifts in individuals.

Therefore, innovation is considered a key factor for enterprises' survival (Ortiz and Arredondo, 2014), since innovative enterprises are more flexible, which allows them to analyze and adapt better to changes in the environment, to answer faster to changing needs of the society (Miles, *et al.*, 1978; Drucker, 1985), and to obtain better results than those that do not innovate. Therefore, organizational learning is recognized as a fundamental organizational function (Villegas, 2005), which is considered a long term investment, that may become a survival factor (Calantone, *et al.*, 2002); while others state that learning and organizational knowledge precede innovation (Nonaka *et al.*, 1995; Hage, 1999); meaning that learning is necessary in order to innovate (Rodríguez, *et al.*, 2011; Lado and Wilson, 1994).

Organizational Learning

Modern organizational theory states that organizations learn, since as they take their experiences into consideration, they modify their goals and daily procedures (Cyert and March, 1963). Drucker (1993) affirmed that around every century a significant transformation occurred in the Western civilization, indicating that we have gone from a "society of employees" and a "society of organizations" to a "knowledge society" and "knowledge workers". Knowledge will be the economic resource, nor the capital, neither natural resources.

Miller and Cangelloti (1965) cited by Realpe (2015) were the firsts who used the term Organizational Learning, in a publication in which they proposed a conceptual model of "adaptation-learning" based on the contingency theory. In the same direction, Levitt and March (1988) cited by Argote and Miron-Spektor (2011) consider learning as a dependent routine of the history of the organization, oriented to specific objectives that guide its behavior.

Argyris (1999) defines organizational learning as a process to discover and correct mistakes, indicating that the inability to detect mistakes and other facts arises from a defective learning in the organization. Such habits and attitudes allow an enterprise to hide its problems, leading it to rigidity and decline (Lozano and González, 2015; Basten and Haamann, 2018). Rowden (2011) considers the learning organization as model of strategic change, that helps the organization to plan and execute important institutional changes in an environment that quickly changes the conditions of enterprises.

Senge (1990) cited by Suddaby and Foster (2016) proposed five dimensions that he considers vital to create organizations with true capacity to learn, them being: systemic thought, personal control, mental models, build a shared vision and team learning.

Based on other authors, Garzon and Fischer (2008) cited by Galvez *et al.*, (2013), define organizational learning as the capacity that organizations have to create, organize and process information from their own sources in order to generate new individual, team, organizational and inter organizational learning, generating a culture that facilitates it, establishing the conditions that permit the development of new capabilities, the design of new products and service, the increase of the already existing offer and the improvement of long-lasting processes.

Within this organizational learning, different study trends for current administration are established, such as interest group theory (Freeman, 1984; Phillips, 2010) that seeks to identify the actors according to the degree of participation and interaction with the company, which allows you to learn to manage your relationships, on the other hand, there is the theory of the psychological contract (Máynes, Cavazos & Reyes, 2016; Huang, Niu, Pierce & Lee, 2015) that allows understanding the support learning mechanisms and complement to formal contracts, which generate a significant degree of expectations and promises for workers at the time of hiring (Vargas, 2020).

Organizational Learning Levels and Dimensions

Learning is considered a complex and dynamic topic. Some authors such as Simon (1991) cited by Paños, Ruiz, Sabater and Ruiz (2004) states that recent models consider that learning occurs at individual, group and organizational levels, therefore identifying the subjects that participate in the process: individual, group and organization.

Argyris (1999) identifies two types or learning in organizations: 1) one that tends to modify organizational routines, making it incremental and adaptive; 2) one that boosts practices that lead to the creation of new habits in a new learning environment.

Orientation to Organizational Learning

Orientation to learn can be conceptualized as a set of organizational values that influence the enterprise 1) to make it create and use knowledge (Sinkula, Baker and Noordewier, 1997); 2) in the degree in which the enterprise is satisfied with its own paradigms (Argyris and Schön, 1978); 3) in its mental models (Geus, 1988); and 4) in the predominant logics (Bettis and Prahalad, 1995).

In this sense, three organizational values that influence organizational to learn are usually being associated: commitment to learn, an open mind and a shared vision (Day 1991 and 1994; Senge 1990 and 1992; Tobin 1993; Sinkula et al, 1997). However, other authors consider four factors: commitment to learn, open mind, shared vision and knowledge exchange (Hurley and Hult, 1998; Hult and Ferrell, 1997; Hult, 1998).

Weerawardena, O´Cass and Julian (2006) identify three types of orientation to learn: orientation to learn from the market, relational orientation to learn, and internal orientation to learn.

In another approach, orientation to learn has been considered a dimension of organizational learning (Baker, *et al.,* 1999; Calantone *et al.,* 2002). Cardona *et al.,* (2006) identify it among the three dimensions that measure organizational learning: shared knowledge, knowledge recovery and orientation of learning. The latter is defined in three dimensions, being them: commitment to learn, openness and experimentation, and capacity to unlearn.

1) **Commitment to learn.** It is the degree at which an organization values and promoted learning (Sinkula, *et al.*, 1997), considering it as a long-term investment that becomes a surviving factor (Calantone *et al.*, 2002). This commitment and does not neccesarily mean forcing or imposing, since learning requires time and practice (Senge, 2000). Besides, learning also depends on the will, the advantage taken from the commitment, the imagination, enery and enthusiasm of people who work in the organization (Senge, 1990). Simon (1991) defends the approach that considers the learning process as exclusive of people or that at least starts from people. Paños et al, (2004) states that in order to boost the generation of new knowledge at individual level it is necessary, among other aspects, that organizations promote autonomy, creativity, motivation and improvement and in some cases they need to require employees to question constantly the norms that guide the organization (Day, 1991; Sinkula, 1994; Sinkula *et al.,* 1997). These considerations are fundamental since commitment and conviction from employees are the base of organizational learning (Cardona *et al.,* 2006).
2) **Unlearning.** Traditionally, enterprises and people insist on learning, however, one of the biggest obstacles to create new knowledge is unlearning what is already learnt; the latter understood as the process by which obsolete and deceiving knowledge is cast aside (Cegarra and Rodrigo, 2004). In addition, Huber (1998) states that one of the main factors that influence the success of organizational learning is the elimination of obsolete knowledge. This happens when the right conditions occur in the organization; to do so, top management needs to authorize them and conditions should not be blocked by norms or regulations (Nguyen, 2017). Therefore, an important factor to create organizational learning is to eliminate mental models that are implicit in the enterprises' structure, even if they were successful previously, since they affect negatively the rules that determine the behavior of individuals and groups throughout the (Grant, 1991). This way, organizations promote unlearning when they proactively question their routines and beliefs (Nguyen, 2017; Baker *et al.*, 1999).
3) **Openness and experimentation.** Weerawardena *et al.*, (2006) conceive orientation to internal learning as the capacity of an enterprise to develop knowledge through its internal resources, in which R&D plays a decisive role. Such learning disseminates, get rids of, or uses knowledge to bring about changes in the organization. Dixon (1992) and Huber (1998) consider that learning focused to the interior includes experiential learning (by trial and error) and experimental learning (development of new ways of doing things). Therefore, as time passes by, mental models become obsolete to face coming changes (Baker *et al.*, 1999), limiting the organization to habitual ways to think and act, unless there is an open mind that questions such ways (Porac and Thomas 1990; Senge 1992 and 1990). Hence, mind openness is linked to unlearning (Nystrom and Starbuck, 1984).

Innovation

There are different points of view about innovation; etymologically it comes from Latin *innovare*, that means to change or alter things by introducing novelties; the dictionary of the Royal Academy of Spanish provides a definition as the creation or modification of a product and its launch to the market (Ramírez-Salazar, Pérez-Uribe, Salcedo-Pérez and Juffington-Smith, 2019). In another definition, the Oslo Manual (OECD and EUROSTAT, 2005) states that it is the introduction of a new, or significantly improved product (good or service), process, new way to commercialize, new way to organize internal practices of an enterprise, the organization of the workplace or the relations with the outside of the organization.

Formicella (2005), in its research about the topic, states that the concept of innovation started to be appear in the writings of Adam Smith and David Ricardo, even though they did not mention it explicitly, being Joseph Schumpter the first top rated economist who broadly developed the concept of the innovation process, establishing the difference between invention, innovation and diffusion; from those first stages, studies on the topic have developed significantly.

From another perspective, Urrea and Mejia (2000) consider technological innovation as the socio-technical practice that creates new ways of doing things in different social environments. Such practices (the same authors affirm) transform into improvements, adaptations and modifications at different levels; besides they create tools, machines, products, and operational and organizational processes in the production of a good or service.

In such sense, innovation is the process of integration of existing technology and new inventions in order to create or improve a product, a process or a system. From an economic approach, innovation is the consolidation of a new product, process or improves system (Medina and Espinoza, 1994). Innovation is to produce, assimilate and take advantage of the novelty in economic and social environments (Perez-Uribe, Salcedo-Perez and Ocampo-Guzmán, 2018).

In the same direction, Ramírez-Salazar, *et al.,* (2019) state that once innovation is understood as a process of development and application, this would include both the idea of innovation from a technical perspective (technology, new products and services) and from an organizational perspective (procedures, policies and new organizational ways). Some studies have found that the implementation of managerial innovations tends to improve the competitiveness of enterprises (Ramírez-Salazar, Perez-Uribe and Salcedo-Perez, 2018).

Classification of Innovation

According to Cuevas and Roman (2008), innovation categories can be classified by using three basic criteria: the object, the degree of newness and the strategic aim of the innovation.

Schumpeter (1942) considered the introduction of a new good or type of goods to the market, the use of new sources of raw materials, the incorporation of a new method of production, and market innovation (open a new market in a different country or the implementation of a new market structure) as cases of innovation. The Asociación Española de Contabilidad y Administración de Empresas –Spanish Association of Accounting and Business Administration- (AECA, 1995), cited by Galvez (2014), states that there are three types of innovation: of products, processes and management. Product innovation materializes in the commercialization of a new product of the improving of an existing one; process innovation provides new equipment or production processes to the enterprise, tending to increase the productivity and reduce costs; management innovation gets the set of novelties and changes introduced in the organizational structure of the enterprise, in areas such as commercialization, financing, organization, etc. (Maldonado, Madrid, Martinez and Aguilera, 2009).

In this same sense, the Oslo Manual (OECD *et al.*, 2005) proposes four types of innovation; product, process, marketing and organizational:

1) **Innovation of product:** it is the launch of a new or significantly improved (regarding its characteristics or use) good or service; 2) **Innovation of process**: it is the introduction of a new or significantly improved method of production or distribution. This bring significant changes in techniques, materials and/or software; 3) **Innovation of marketing:** it is the application of a new method of commercialization that brings significant changes to a product design, package, positioning in the market or pricing; 4) **Organizational innovation**: it is the introduction of a new organizational method in the practices, workplace or external relations of the enterprise.

Depending on the degree of novelty, innovations can be classified into radical and incremental. Such distinction has an important economic impact (Freeman, 1987). Radical, also called basic, primary or total, innovations refer to totally new products or processes, since they present significant differences regarding their purpose, performance, characteristics, theoretical properties, raw materials or components used in their production. On the other side, incremental, also called partial, progressive or secondary innovations refer to improvements to already existing products or processes, bringing less novelty (INE, 2015).

Organizational Performance

Different methodologies and tools have been developed to measure the results of organizations, some of them being objective, meaning they take data, for example accounting and budgeting systems or the balance scorecard. The latter uses indicators such as: profitability, gross added value over payroll and sales over payroll (Jimenez and Sanz, 2006) return on investment, return on sales, increase in sales, and market share (Ma, Zhu and Hou, 2011); ROI and ROA (Pérez – Uribe, 2012, p. 54; Calantone *et al.*, 2002); relative changes in the market, success of new products (Baker *et al.*, 1999). Others are subjective, meaning they are obtained from the perception or points of view of those involved in the enterprise's processes or external observers; in such cases perceptions such as global profitability (Calantone *et al.*, 2002), global performance (Baker *et al.*, 1999); improvements in processes, in product quality, in tasks organization, increase in customer satisfaction, employees' motivation, increase in productivity, etc, are used (Quinn and Rohrbaugh, 1983).

This evidences that there is not agreement about a single general indicator to measure organizational performance so far. Performance measurement is considered one of the most relevant challenges faced by an enterprise, since it plays a key role in areas such as development of strategic plans, evaluation of goal achievements, assignation or incentives to top management, among others. Therefore, measuring organizational performance should not be limited to financial matters; it should also consider measurements of internal and external efficiency (Pérez – Uribe, 2012, pp. 53-55). Por ultimo, un studio realizado en Chipre, demuestra que para las pequeñas y medianas empresas jovenes

Table 1. Sample distribution by city

REGION	Number of companies
Centro (Bogotá, Bucaramanga)	133
Antioquia (Medellín)	89
Sur Occidente (Cali, Popayán, Pasto)	87
Norte (Barranquilla, Cartagena, Santa Martha)	70
Eje cafetero (Armenia, Manizales, Pereira)	24
Total	**403**

Source: self made

INVESTIGATION METHODOLOGY

This work is of a correlational type with a quantitative approach, since it aims to empirically measure the degree of relationship between learning orientation, innovation and organizational performance. The source of information used was primary, obtaining the data through a telephone survey. To test the hypotheses, a multivariate analysis was performed using multiple linear regressions. The different aspects of the methodology used for the research are described below:

The companies object of the study are formally constituted MSMEs, belonging to industry, construction, commerce and services; Located in different cities in Colombia, the sectors were chosen under an expert peer review exercise to establish those that would have more influence with development and competitiveness in the selected territory. A sample of 403 companies obtained by stratified sampling was used, taking into account the size of the company, sector of activity and city. Within each stratum, the selection was made by means of a simple random sampling with a sampling error of 4.9 points and a confidence level of 95% (tables 1 and 2)

Data collection was carried out during the months of June and July 2011, through a market research company; The instrument used was a structured survey, which was applied by telephone to the owners or managers of MSMEs.

HYPOTHESES AND MODEL OF ANALYSIS

Hypotheses

H1: Orientation to learn influences the performance of enterprises.
H2: The more the commitment to learn in the enterprise the easier to promote the innovation of products.

Table 2. Distribution of the sample by sector and size, and their respective estimation errors

SECTOR	Sample	Error (%)
Industry	198	6.9
Construction	21	21.3
Commerce	75	11.2
Services	109	9.4
SIZE		
5 a 10 workers	125	8.7
11 a 50 workers	196	7.0
51 a 250 workers	82	10.8
Total	**403**	**4.9**

Source: self made

Measurement of Variables

- **Orientation to organizational learning:** Even though there has been a crescent interest on organizational learning (Senge, 1990; Slater and Narver, 1994; Huber 1998), the different perspectives from which the concept has been studied have caused a confusion in the terminology (Jiménez *et al.*, 2006) and a disagreement on how to measure it; as a consequence, there is not agreement about which are the dimensions of organizational learning. Authors like Huber (1998) analyzed learning as stages of a process: acquisition, distribution, interpretation of knowledge and organizational memory; for Senge (1990 and 1992) and Varela (2011) organizational learning is a collective process that requires conditions such as personal control, mental models, shared vision, teamwork and systemic thinking, while for Sinkula et al (1997) orientation to learn can be conceptualized as a set of organizational values such as: commitment to learn, shared vision and open mind. In this research, after revising the tools used in other empirical studies (Nonaka *et al.*, 1995; Day, 1994; Sinkula *et al.*, 1997), and according to the goals of this research, the authors decided to use partially the scale developed Cardona et al (2006) to measure organizational learning, and which considers orientation to learn as one of the dimensions.
- **The Variable of Innovation:** There are two approaches to measure the degree of innovation of an enterprise (Zehira, Canb and Karabogac, 2015), 1) the objective approach that measures from quantitative data such as number of patents, or specific data of product innovation (number of new products) or processes (investment costs); 2) the subjective approach based on the perception of the manager or owner of the enterprise has about his/her innovative activities. The subjective approach is the most appropriated for SMEs, since the objective approach tends to underestimate the innovative activities of SMEs (Zehira, *et al.*, 2015). To work this factor in this research, the authors considered different concepts compiled in the bibliographical review, especially that of AECA (1995) which stated that innovation can be classified into technological and organizational. Technological innovations include significant novelties in products and processes while organizational innovations consider to changes introduced to the administrative structure of the enterprise, its commercialization and financing among others. The same classification has been used in dif-

ferent studies (Maldonado *et al.,* 2009; Van Auken, Madrid and García, 2008). A multi criteria measure with two or more items per innovation type was used to measure the degree of innovation in products (INNOVAPS), processes (INNOVAPC) and management (INNOVAMAN). A Likert scale of five answers was used. The variable that represents global innovation is calculated by using the arithmetic mean of the three innovation measures (also in a 1 to 5 scale).

- **Organizational performance:** The model of organizational performance developed by Quinn et al (1983) was used in this research; it is one of the most recognized methodologies worldwide to measure organizational performance. According to Rodríguez (2007) this methodology allows to analyze the enterprise's performance from a multidimensional perspective, from three dimensions: 1) the organizational approach, from an internal (based on a vision "micro" about the good personnel understanding and development to an external point of view (focused on the "macro" level of the enterprise's success); 2) regarding the organizational structure, focused on the enterprise's stability or flexibility; 3) related to the organizational means and goals. The following four models of performance arise from these three dimensions: 1) **Model of internal processes**: focused on control from an internal point of view, emphasizing especially on communication of information and aimed at control and stability; 2) **Model of open system:** focused on flexibility from an external point of view, contemplating growth, resource acquisition and external support as main objectives; 3) **Rational model:** directed towards control from an external point of view, emphasizing on efficiency and productivity; and 4) **Human relations model:** it focuses on flexibility from an internal point of view, considering the development of human resources as the main objective. Each one of these elements of performance was measured on a Likert scale of five possible answers going from very unsatisfied (1) to very satisfied (5).

Analytical Method

The multiple linear regression analysis was used to test the hypotheses. Independent variables are enterprises' age and size as control variables with one (Madura (Mature)) and two (Pequeña (Small) and Mediana (Mid)) categories respectively. Orientation to learn in each of its dimensions: directors and workers' commitment, openness and experimentation, and unlearning. Finally, as dependent variable, according to each model, the dimensions of the organizational performance were added: internal processes, human relations, rational and open system, and innovation in each of its dimensions: products/services, processes and management. This analytical model requires the compliance with a set of assumptions: linearity of the occurrence, constant variance, and independence and normal distribution of errors (Hair and fellows, 1999, mentioned by Contreras, *et al.,* 2012).

ANALYSIS OF RESULTS

Tables 3 and 4 show results obtained per sector, examining relations between orientation to global learning (OAGLOBAL), innovation and performance; they also show the control variables: age (D.Madura) and size (D.Pequeña, D.Mediana) of the enterprises.

Effect of Orientation to Learn on Innovation (per sector)

Results show a significant correlation between global orientation to learn (OAGLOBAL) in the manufacturing sector ($\beta = 0{,}340^c$) with an association of ($F = 5.367^c$) and in the services sector ($\beta = 0{,}544^c$) with a $F= 5.367^c$. However, the model does not explain the variability in the trade and construction sectors. It is then concluded that MSMEs of the manufacturing and services sectors show commitment to learn, experimentation and unlearning, therefore promoting product innovation, with size being a most influential factor in the manufacturing sector, more significant especially in small enterprises ($\beta = 0{,}365^c$).

Table 3 . Effect of orientation to learn on innovation (per sector)

Dependent Variable / Independent Variables	INNOVATION				
	SECTOR				Global
	Manufacturing	Services	Commerce	Construction	
Adjusted R^2	0,189	0.192	-0,039	0.705	0.119
Durwin-Watson	2.120	2.594	1.818	2.213	1.831
F	5.367^C	3.081^B	0.756	5.177	5.920^C
Higher VIF	1.931	2.077	1.342	2.523	1.709
OAGLOBAL: β t	$0{,}340^C$ 3.131	0.544^C 3.337	0.151 0.722	-0.500 -2.052	0.329^C 4.197
D.Madura β t	-0.094 -0.848	0.136 0.725	0.196 0.960	-1.035^b -3.311	-0.015 -0.185
D.Pequeña β t	0.365^b 2.619	0.156 0.808	-0.320 -1.422	1.379^b 4.227	0.185^a 1.911
D.Mediana β t	0.153 1.062	0.269 1.227	-0.084 -0.362	0.551 1.898	0.129 1.267

Significance level: ^{a} $p \leq 0{,}1$; ^{b} $p \leq 0{,}05$; ^{c} $p \leq 0{,}01$
Source: own elaboration

Effect of Orientation to Learn on Performance (per sector)

Contrary to innovation, results of the model show a significant relation between global orientation to learn (OAGLOBAL) and each of its different sectors: manufacturing ($F = 14.016^c$) with a significant regression coefficient ($\beta = 0{,}454^c$); services ($F = 12.460^c$) with a highly significant regression coefficient ($\beta = 0{,}546^c$); trade ($F = 5.977^c$) with a highly significant regression coefficient ($\beta = 0{,}445^c$); and construction ($F = 5.517^c$) with a highly significant regression coefficient ($\beta = 0{,}569^c$). In this model, the coefficient of the D.Madura variable is significantly negative, making evident that the orientation to learn in young enterprises has a higher effect on performance ($\beta = -0{,}447^b$); instead, in the manufacturing sector the orientation to learn is highly significant in mature enterprises, indicating that such enterprises promote and boost organizational learning through unlearning, commitment and experimentation, looking for internal and external efficiency.

Table 4. Effect of orientation to learn on performance (per sector)

Dependent Variable Independent Variables	PERFORMANCE				
	SECTOR				Global
	Manufacturing	Services	Commerce	Construction	
Adjusted R^2	0.209	0.30	0.212	0.475	0.238
Durwin-Watson	1.955	1.999	1.800	2.137	1.747
F	14.016[c]	12.460[c]	5.977[c]	5.517[c]	32.376[c]
Higher VIF	1.621	1.416	1.478	2.703	1.525
OAGLOBAL: β t	0.454[c] 6.919	0.546[c] 6.524	0.445[c] 3.987	0.569[c] 3.393	0.483[c] 10.694
D.Madura β t	0.125[a] 1.864	-0.077 -0.916	-0.168 -1.536	-0.447[b] -2.196	-0.031 -0.668
D.Pequeña β t	0.047 0.611	0.056 0.598	-0.048 -0.381	0.318 1.364	0.045 0.869
D.Mediana β t	-0.023 -0.289	0.028 0.292	0.078 0.634	0.437 1.640	0.037 0.696

Significance level: [a] $p \leq 0,1$; [b] $p \leq 0,05$; [c] $p \leq 0,01$
Source: own elaboration

CONCLUSION

Results show that a significant correlation between global learning (OAGLOBAL) in manufacturing and service sectors. However, the model does not explain the variability in trade and construction sectors. Then, it is concluded that MSMEs of the manufacturing and service sectors are committed to learn, experiment and unlearn, therefore promoting product innovation, with size being a more influential factor in the manufacturing sector, especially in small enterprises, confirming Hypothesis 2: "The more the commitment to learn in the enterprise the easier to promote the innovation of products" Abbas and Alireza, (2011) and Ma *et al.*, (2011) cited by Contreras *et al.*, (2012).

Contrary to innovation, results show a significant correlation between global learning (OAGLOBAL) and each of the economic sectors analyzed. The coefficient of the variable D.Madura is significantly negative, evidencing that orientation to learn in young enterprises has a higher effect on performance (Hypothesis 1). It is inverse in the manufacturing sector, meaning that orientation to learn is highly significant in mature enterprises, indicating that they promote and stimulate organizational learning through unlearning, commitment and experimentation, looking for internal and external efficiency (Hypothesis 2), coinciding with the results obtained by Contreras *et al.,* (2012), Calantone *et al.,* (2002) and Baker *et al.,* (1999).

LIMITATIONS AND FUTURE INVESTIGATIONS

This research has, among other limitations, the fact that it is based on cross-sectional data, which show how the orientation to learning is related to innovation and performance, and how significant this relationship is. Therefore, for future studies, an explanatory and longitudinal study is recommended, methodologically, to explain why this relationship occurs and under what conditions. Additionally, this research could be resumed to address elements that remain to be analyzed, such as the organizational culture, and the strategy in relation to its alignment with the learning process. Finally, for future relationships on the relationship orientation to learning, innovation and performance, the radical or incremental nature of the innovation should be taken into account.

REFERENCES

Argote, L. & Miron-Spektor, E. (2011). Organizational Learning: From Experience to Knowledge. *Organization Science*, *22*(5), 1123–1137. doi:10.1287/orsc.1100.0621

Argyris, C. (1999). *Conocimiento para la acción: Una guía para superar los obstáculos del cambio enla organización*. Granica.

Barney, J. B. (1991). Firm Resources and Sustained Competitive Advantage. *Journal of Management*, *17*(1), 99–120. doi:10.1177/014920639101700108

Basten, D., & Haamann, T. (2018). Approaches for Organizational Learning: A Literature Review. *SAGE Open - Literature Review*. Retrieved from https://journals.sagepub.com/doi/pdf/10.1177/2158244018794224

Bettis, R. A., & Prahalad, C. K. (1995). The Dominant Logic: Retrospective and Extension. *Strategic Management Journal*, *16*(1), 5–14. doi:10.1002mj.4250160104

Busłowska, A., & Wiśniewska, B. (2017). The bialystok functional area competency center as an example of development of human capital. *Ekonomia i Prawo*, *16*(4), 371–385. doi:10.12775/EiP.2017.026

Calantone, R., Cavusgil, T., & Zhao, Y. (2002). Learning Orientation, Firm Innovation Capability, and Firm Performance. *Industrial Marketing Management*, *31*(6), 515–524. doi:10.1016/S0019-8501(01)00203-6

Camelo, C., Romero, P., & Valle, R. (2000). Relación entre el tipo y el grado de innovación y el rendimiento de la empresa. *Economía Industrial*, *333*, 149–160.

Cardona, J., & Calderón, G. (2006, July). *El Impacto del Aprendizaje en el Rendimiento de las Organizaciones. Cuad. Adm.*

Cardona, R. A. (2011). Estrategia basada en los recursos y capacidades. Criterios de evaluación y el proceso de desarrollo. *Revista Electrónica Forum Doctoral*. Retrieved from www.eumed.net/tesis-doctorales/2012/zll/teorias-recursos-capacidades.html

Cegarra, J. G., & Rodrigo, B. (2004). Componentes de éxito del aprendizaje grupal en el capital intelectual. *Investigaciones Europeas de Dirección y Economía de la Empresa*, *10*(2), 75-92.

Conde, C. Y. A., Correa, C. Z., & Delgado, H. C. (2010). *Aprendizaje organizacional, una capacidad de los grupos de investigación en la universidad pública. Cuadernos de Administración, 44*. Retrieved from http://www.redalyc.org/pdf/2250/225017586002.pdf

Confecamaras. (2016). *Birth and survival of companies in Colombia.* Chambers of Commerce Network. Retrieved from: http://www.confecamaras.org.co/phocadownload/Cuadernos_de_analisis_economico/Cuaderno_de_An%D0%B0lisis_Economico_N_11.pdf

CONPES. (2007). Documento CONPES 3484. Consejo Nacional de Política Económica y Social. República de Colombia. Política nacional para la transformación productiva y la promoción de las micro, pequeñas y medianas empresas: Un esfuerzo público y privado. Bogotá.

Contreras, Gálvez, & González-Campo. (2012). Impacto de la orientación al aprendizaje en la innovación de las MIPYMES colombianas. *Cuadernos de Administración*, *28*(48).

Cuevas, J. J. G., and Román, J. A. M. (2008). Tipología de la innovación y perfiles empresariales: una aplicación empírica. *Economía industrial*, (368), 59-77.

Cyert, R., & March, J. (1963). *Teoría de las Decisiones Económicas en la Empresas*. Herrero Hermanos Sucesores, S.A Editores.

Damanpour, F., & Gopalakrishnan, S. (2001). The dynamics of the adoption of products and process innovations in organizations. *Journal of Management Studies*, *38*(1), 45–65. doi:10.1111/1467-6486.00227

Day, G. S. (1994). Continuous Learning about Markets. *Californian Management Review*, 9–31.

Day, S. (1991). *Learning About Markets*. Marketing Science Institute Report Number 91-117. Marketing Science Institute.

Del Río, C. J., & Santisteban, R. D. F. (2011, July-December). Perspectivas del aprendizaje organizacional como catalizador de escenarios competitivos. *Revista Ciencias Estratégicas*, *19*(26), 247–266.

Dickson, P. R. (1996). The Static and Dynamic Mechanics of Competition: A Comment on Hunt and Morgan's Comparative Advantage Theory. *Journal of Marketing*, *60*(October), 102–106. doi:10.2307/1251904

Dini, M., & Stumpo, G. (2019). *Mipymes en América Latina: un frágil desempeño y nuevos desafíos para las políticas de fomento. Síntesis.* Documentos de Proyectos (LC/TS.2019/20), Santiago, Comisión Económica para América Latina y el Caribe (CEPAL), 2019.

Drucker, P. (1985). *La Innovación y el empresario innovador*. Edhasa.

Drucker, P. (1993). *La sociedad post capitalista*. Editorial Deusto.

Formichella, M. (2005). *Evolución del concepto de innovación y su relación con el desarrollo.* Retrieved from https://core.ac.uk/download/pdf/48031881.pdf

Freeman, C. (1987). *Technology and Economic Performance: Lessons from Japan*. Pinter Publisher.

Gálvez, A. E. J. (2014). Tecnologías de información y comunicación, e innovación en las MIPYMES de Colombia. *Cuadernos de Administración*, *30*(51). Retrieved from http://www.scielo.org.co/pdf/cuadm/v30n51/v30n51a08.pdf

Geus, A. (1988). Plannig learning. *Harvard Business Review*, *66*(March-April), 70–74.

Grant, R. (1991). The Resource Base Theory of Competitive Advantage. *California Management Review*, *33*, 114–135. doi:10.2307/41166664

Hage, J. T. (1999). Organizational innovation and organizational change. *Annual Review of Sociology, 25*(1), 597–622. doi:10.1146/annurev.soc.25.1.597

Hair, J., Anderson, R., Tatham, R., & Black, W. (1999). *Análisis Multivariante* (5th ed.). Prentice Hall.

Hansen, G. S., & Wernerfelt, B. (1989). Determinants of Firm Perfomance: The Relative Importance of Economic and Organizational Factors. *Strategic Management Journal, 10*(5), 399–411. doi:10.1002mj.4250100502

Huber, G. (1998). Synergies Between Organizational Learning and Creativity & Innovation. *Creativity and Innovation Management, 7*(1), 3–8. doi:10.1111/1467-8691.00079

Hult, G. T. M. (1998). Managing the international strategic sourcing process as a market-driven organizational learning system. *Decision Sciences, 29*(1), 193–216. doi:10.1111/j.1540-5915.1998.tb01349.x

Hult, G. T. M., & Ferrell, O. C. (1997). A global learning organization structure and market information processing. *Journal of Business Research, 40*(2), 155–166. doi:10.1016/S0148-2963(97)00006-4

Hurley, R. F., & Hult, G. T. M. (1998). Innovation, market orientation, and organizational learning: An integration and empirical examination. *Journal of Marketing, 62*(3), 42–54. doi:10.1177/002224299806200303

INE. (2015). *Encuesta sobre Innovación Tecnológica en las empresas.* Madrid: Servicio de Publicaciones del Instituto de Estadìsticas. Retrieved from https://www.ine.es/prensa/np890.pdf

Jiménez, D., & Sanz, V. (2006). Innovación, aprendizaje organizacional y resultados empresariales: Un estudio empírico. *Cuadernos de Economía y Dirección de la Empresa.* Retrieved from www.redalyc.org/pdf/807/80702902.pdf

Kavoura, A., & Andersson, T. (2016). Applying Delphi method for strategic design of social entrepreneurship. *Library Review, 65*(3), 185–205. doi:10.1108/LR-06-2015-0062

Kavoura, A., & Koziol, L. (2017). *Polish Firms' Innovation Capability for Competitiveness via Information Technologies and Social Media Implementation.* In A. Vlachvei, O. Notta, K. Karantininis, & N. Tsountas (Eds.), *Factors Affecting Firm Competitiveness and Performance in the Modern Business World* (pp. 185–214). IGI Global.

Lado, A. A., & Wilson, M. C. (1994). Human resource systems and sustained competitive advantage: Toward a conceptual integration. *Journal of Management*, (18), 699–727.

Lippman, S. A., & Rumelt, R. P. (1982). Uncertain Imitability: An Analysis of Interfirm Differences in Efficiency under Competition. *The Bell Journal of Economics, 13*(2), 418–438. doi:10.2307/3003464

Llonch, A. J., López, B. M. P., & Eusebio, R. (2007). *Orientación al aprendizaje, Orientación al mercado, Resultados y el efecto moderador de la procedencia funcional del Director General. Cuadernos de Economía y Dirección de la Empresa, núm. 33, diciembre, 2007.* Asociación Científica de Economía y Dirección de Empresas Madrid.

Lozano, O. J., & González, C. C. H. (2015). Desarrollo de un modelo de gestión de la inteligencia organizacional para la compañía Gráficas Modernas S.A. *Universidad & Empresa, 17*(29), 2015. doi:10.12804/rev.univ.empresa.29.2015.03

Ma, W., Zhu, G., Hou, Y. (2011). Learning Orientation, Process Innovation, and Firm Performance in Manufacturing Industry. *Advances in information Sciences and Service Sciences, 3*(11).

Makarona, E., & Kavoura, A. (2019). Redesigning the Ivory Tower: Academic entrepreneurship as a new calling supporting economic growth. *The Malopolska School of Economics in Tarnow Research Papers Collection, 42*, 15–26. doi:10.25944/znmwse.2019.02.1526

Maldonado, G., Madrid, A., Martinez, M., & Aguilera, L. (2009). Los efectos de la innovación en el rendimiento de las MIPYMES de Aguasclientes: una evidencia empírica. *Revista economia.* Retrieved from http://www.revista.economia.uady.mx/2009/XXVI/73/02.pdf

Medina, C., & Espinoza, M. (1994). *La innovación en las organizaciones modernas.* Retrieved from http://www.azc.uam.mx/publicaciones/gestion/num5/doc06.htm

Miles, R., & Snow, C. (1978). *Organizational strategy, structure and process.* McGraw Hill.

Munuera, J. L., & Rodríguez, A. I. (2007). *Estrategias de marketing: Un enfoque basado en el proceso de dirección.* ESIC EDITOR.

Nguyen, N. (2017). *The journey of organizational unlearning: A conversation with William H. Starbuck.* Retrieved from https://www.researchgate.net/publication/313686391_The_journey_of_organizational_unlearning_a_conversation_with_William_H_Starbuck

Nonaka, H., & Takeuchi, H. (1995). *The knowledge-creating company. How Japanese companies create the dynamics of innovation.* Oxford University Press.

Nystrom, P. C., & Starbuck, W. (1984). To Avoid Organizational Crises, Unlearn. *Organizational Dynamics, 13*(Spring), 53–65. doi:10.1016/0090-2616(84)90011-1

Organización para la Cooperación y Desarrollo Económicos OECD y Oficina de Estadística de las Comunidades Europeas EUROSTAT. (2005). *Manual de Oslo.* Noruega. Retrieved from http://www.itq.edu.mx/convocatorias/manualdeoslo.pdf

Ortiz, P. C. F., & Arredondo, O. E. (2014). Competitividad y factores de éxito en empresas desarrolladoras de software. *Enl@ce: Revista Venezolana de Información, Tecnología y Conocimiento, 11*(3), 49-73. Retrieved from http://www.redalyc.org/pdf/823/82332932004.pdf

Paños A., Ruiz, C., Sabater, R., & Ruiz, J. (2004). *Modelo de Análisis del Aprendizaje Organizacional. Efecto en la Eficiencia Organizacional e Innovación.* 2o Congreso SOCOTE. Soporte del Conocimiento con la Tecnología, 5-21.

Pérez-Uribe, R. (2012). *El ambiente laboral y su incidencia en el desempeño de las organizaciones: estudio de las mejores empresas para trabajar en Colombia* (PhD dissertation). Universidad Antonio de Nebrija. Retrieved from http://edicionesean.ean.edu.co/index.php/es/productos-de-investigacion1/tesis-doctorales/23-publicaciones/192-el-ambiente-laboral-y-su-incidencia-en-el-desempeno-de-las-organizaciones-estudio-en-las-mejores-empresas-para-trabajar-en-colombia

Perez-Uribe, R., Salcedo-Perez, C., & Ocampo-Guzmán, D. (2018). *Handbook of Research on Intrapreneurship and Organizational Sustainability in SMEs.* IGI Global. https://www.igi-global.com/book/handbook-research-intrapreneurship-organizational-sustainability/181082

Porac, J. F., & Thomas, H. (1990). Taxonomic mental models in competitor definition. *Academy of Management Review*, *15*(2), 224–240. doi:10.5465/amr.1990.4308155

Pulido, B. (2010). *Teoría de los recursos y las capacidades: El foco estratégico centrado en el interior de la organización*. Retrieved from https://revistas.uexternado.edu.co/index.php/sotavento/article/download/1632/1471/

Quinn, R., & Rohrbaugh, J. (1983, March). A spatial model of effectiveness criteria: Towards a competing values approach to organizational analysis. *Management Science*, *29*(3), 363–377. doi:10.1287/mnsc.29.3.363

Ramírez-Garzón, M. T., & Pérez-Uribe, R. (2019). Componentes organizacionales que explican la rentabilidad en las pymes colombianas. *Revista Estudios en Ciencias Sociales y Administrativas de la Universidad de Celaya (ESCAUC)*, *9*(1), 7-19. Retrieved from http://ecsauc.udec.edu.mx/index.php/ECSAUC/issue/view/3/Vol.%209

Ramírez-Salazar, M. P., Perez-Uribe, R., & Salcedo-Perez, C. (2018). A Triple Helix Model Based on Open Collaborative Innovation in Colombia: A Proposal for Higher Education Institutions. In *Handbook of Research on Ethics, Entrepreneurship, and Governance in Higher Education*. https://www.igi-global.com/chapter/a-triple-helix-model-based-on-open-collaborative-innovation-in-colombia/212010

Ramírez-Salazar, M. P., Pérez-Uribe, R., Salcedo-Pérez, C., & Juffington-Smith, J. P. (2019). RISE Model: Its Application on Diving Enterprises Located in the San Andres Archipelago (Colombia). In *Studies on Entrepreneurship, Structural Change and Industrial Dynamics*. doi:10.1007/978-3-030-15526-1

Realpe, B. C. F. (2015). *Factores determinantes en las prácticas de aprendizaje organizacional en el marco de la relación Universidad-Empresa*. Universidad Icesi. Facultad de Ciencias Administrativas y Económicas. Programa de Economía y Negocios Internacionales. Retrieved from https://repository.icesi.edu.co/biblioteca_digital/bitstream/10906/80985/1/realpe_factores_determinantes_2015.pdf

Rodriguez, A. (2007). Transferencia de conocimiento en relaciones inter-organizacionales: su efecto sobre el desempeño de la firma receptora. *Estudios gerenciales*, *23*(103), 18-19.

Rodríguez, A., Lozano, G., & Hernández, M. (2011). *Aprendizaje como Antecedente de los Resultados de la Innovación y Análisis de Variables moderadoras*. Presentation. U. Externado.

Rogers, E. (1983). *Diffusion and Innovation*. Free Press.

Rowden, R. W. (2001). The Learning Organization and Strategic Change. *SAM Advanced Management Journal*, *66*(3), 11.

Rumelt, R. P. (1991): How much does Industry Matter? *Strategic Management Journal*, *12*(3), 167-185.

Salón, S. (2018). *Ventaja competitiva y posicionamiento de empresa: Claves de éxito*. Retrieved from https://es.semrush.com/blog/ventaja-competitiva-claves-exito/

Schumpeter, J. 1942). Capitalismo Socialismo y Democracia. New York: Harper and Row

Senge, P. (1990). *La Quinta Disciplina. El arte y la práctica de la organizacion abierta al aprendizaje*. Granica.

Senge, PM. (1992). Mental Models. *Plann Rev, 20,* 4– 10, 44.

Senge, P. M. (2000). *La danza del cambio: los retos de sostener el impulso en organizaciones abiertas al aprendizaje.* Ediciones Juan Granica S.A.

Simon, H. A. (1991). Bounded rationality and organizational learning. *Organization Science, 2*(1), 125–134. doi:10.1287/orsc.2.1.125

Sinkula, J., Baker, W., & Noordewier, T. (1997). A Framework for Market-Based Organizational Learning: Linking Values, Knowledge, and Behavior. *Journal of the Academy of Marketing Science.* Retrieved from https://link.springer.com/article/10.1177/0092070397254003

Slater, S. F., & Narver, J. C. (1995). Market Orientation and the Learning Organization. *Journal of Marketing, 59*(July), 63–74. doi:10.1177/002224299505900306

Srivastava, R. K., Fahey, L., & Christensen, H. K. (2001). The resource-based view and marketing: The role of market-based assets in gaining competitive advantage. *Journal of Management, 27*(6), 777–802. doi:10.1177/014920630102700610

Stable-Rodríguez, Y. (2016, January-April). Aprendizaje organizacional en organizaciones de ciencia tecnología e innovación. *Ingeniería Industrial, 37*(1), 78–90.

Stary, C. (2016). Open organizational learning: Stakeholder knowledge for process development. *Knowledge Management & E-Learning, 8*(1), 86. Retrieved from https://bdbiblioteca.universidadean.edu.co:2126/docview/1955093198?accountid=34925

Suddaby, R., & Foster, W. (2016). History and Organizational Change. *Journal of Management.* Advance online publication. doi:10.1177/0149206316675031

Thoeni, A. T., Marshall, G. W., & Campbell, S. M. (2016). A resource-advantage theory typology of strategic segmentation. *European Journal of Marketing, 50*(12), 2192–2215. doi:10.1108/EJM-08-2015-0585

Tobin, D. (1993). *Re-Educationg The Corporatión: Foundations for The Leraning Organizatión.* Oliver Wright.

Urrea Giraldo, F., & Mejía Sanabria, C. A. (2000). Innovación y cultura de las organizaciones en el Valle del Cauca. In F. Urrea Giraldo, C. A. Mejía Sanabria, L. G. Arango Gaviria, C. Dávila L. de Guevara, J. Parada Corrales, & C. E. Bernal Poveda (Eds.), Innovación y cultura de las organizaciones en tres regiones de Colombia (pp. 81-218). Corporación calidad.

Van Auken, H., & Madrid, A. (2008). Innovation and performance in Spanish manufacturing SMEs. *International Journal of Entrepreneurship and Innovation Management, 8*(1), 36–56. doi:10.1504/IJEIM.2008.018611

Varela, V. R. (2011). *Desarrollo, Innovación y Cultura Empresarial.* Centro de Desarrollo Empresarial y Universidad ICESI. Volume 1. Santiago de Cali. Retrieved from http://www.icesi.edu.co/images/Centros/cdee/informes/coleccion_dice/DICE1.pdf

Vargas Ramírez, I. (2018). *Gestión de conocimiento y liderazgo: perspectivas y relaciones. Tópicos gerenciales para la gestión de empresas: una mirada desde la investigación.* Universidad EAN.

Vargas Ramírez, I. (2020) El contrato psicológico y su relación con la teoría de los grupos de interés. Propuesta para el análisis en el desempeño administrativo de las gobernaciones en Colombia. Secretaria de Innovación, Ciencia y Educación Superior. Ideas Consyteg 15(246) México.

Vargo, S. L., & Lusch, R. F. (2014). Evolving to a new dominant logic for marketing. In *The Service-Dominant Logic of Marketing* (pp. 21–46). Routledge.

Villegas, G. (2005). Gestión por Factores Críticos de Éxito. *Revista EAFIT* - 105. Retrieved from: http://web.archive.org/web/20030205200444/www.eafit.edu.co/revista/105/villega.html

Weerawardena, J., O'Cass, A., & Julian, N. C. (2006). Does industry matter? Examining the role of industry structure and organizational learning in innovation and brand performance. *Journal of Business Research*, *59*(1), 37–45. doi:10.1016/j.jbusres.2005.02.004

Ynzunza, C. C. B., & Izar, L. J. M. (2013). Efecto de las estrategias competitivas y los recursos y capacidades orientados al mercado sobre el crecimiento de las organizaciones. *Contad. Adm*, *58*(1). Retrieved from: http://www.scielo.org.mx/scielo.php?script=sci_arttext&pid=S0186-04222013000100008

Yonso G., M., Figueredo Á., C.A., Alvarado, L., & Goyo A., A.Y. (2013). El aprendizaje organizacional en las empresas editoras de medios impresos. Caso: Empresa "Al día con la noticia C.A." *TEACS*, *6*(13).

Zehira, C., Canb, E., & Karabogac, T. (2015). Linking entrepreneurial orientation to firm performance: The role of differentiation strategy and innovation performance. 4th International Conference on Leadership, Technology, Innovation and Business Management. *Procedia: Social and Behavioral Sciences*, *210*, 358–367. doi:10.1016/j.sbspro.2015.11.381

KEY TERMS AND DEFINITIONS

Adjusted R^2: It is a measure of corrected goodness of fit (precision of the model) used for linear models. It identifies the percentage of variance in the objective filed that is explained by the entry or entries. It tends to estimate optimistically the adjustment of the linear regression.

D.Madura: Enterprise's age. Maturity dimension

D.Mediana: Enterprise's size. Medium dimension

D.Pequeña: Enterprise's size. Small dimension.

Durwin-Watson: In statistics, the Durbin-Watson statistic is a test statistic used to detect the presence of autocorrelation at lag 1 in the residuals (prediction errors) from a regression analysis. It is named after James Durbin and Geoffrey Watson.

INNOVAMAN: Degree of management innovation.

INNOVAPC: Degree of process innovation.

INNOVAPS: Degree of product innovation.

OAGLOBAL: Relations between the orientation to global learning.

ROA: Return on assets.

ROI: Return on investment.

Chapter 11
Re-Envisioning Formal and Informal Family Businesses in Nigeria:
The Evolution, Opportunities, Succession Model, and Sustainability Challenges

Lukman Raimi
https://orcid.org/0000-0002-5329-8715
American University of Nigeria, Nigeria

ABSTRACT

This chapter discusses the evolution, opportunities, succession model, and sustainability challenges of formal and informal family businesses in Nigeria. Using qualitative research method, while relying on content analysed secondary data, the chapter found that the family businesses that evolved in Nigeria laid the foundation for socio-economic development, and they contributed immensely to employment generation, stimulation of indigenous entrepreneurship, mobilization of idle savings, and growth of gross domestic product. Family businesses in Nigeria prefer relay succession planning for transferring control to family members. The major sustainability challenges include poor succession planning, harsh macro-economic environment, conflict of interest, emotional family problems, parochial family vision, absence of mentoring, competition from multinational corporation, poor access to funding, inadequate entrepreneurial knowledge, weak financial management, bad governance, and a host of others. The chapter concludes with research implications, limitations, and suggestions for further research.

DOI: 10.4018/978-1-7998-3648-3.ch011

INTRODUCTION

Family business as the oldest model of business throughout the world starts from corner shops with few employees to multinational corporations (MNCs) with thousands of employees. Examples of the world's largest family-run businesses are WALMART in the United States, Dangote Group of Companies in Nigeria, SAMSUNG in Korea, TATA in India, and FOXCONN in Taiwan (Raimi et al., 2016b). With specific reference to the United States of America, India, and Italy, family businesses played a very impressive role in the socio-economic development of these countries – a fact that has made them relevant and indispensable (Rome Business School, 2019). Similarly, family businesses in Nigeria have recorded a commendable level of growth, and they aim to grow aggressively at 25% over the next five years as against the global growth rate of 15% (PwC Nigeria (2017).

Before the independence and post-independence era, Nigeria experienced an explosive growth of formal and informal family businesses among the various ethnic groups in the country. The size of the family businesses and their geographical spread across the country suggest that they are viable and represent the preferred way of doing business (Joseph, 2014). Family businesses have for long flourished in both developed and developing economies, as they account for about 70 and 95% of all functional businesses contributing between 50-80% to national employment in most countries (European Family Business, 2012; Ogbechie and Anetor, 2015). Family businesses in Nigeria contribute approximately 47% of the nation's GDP (SMEDAN, 2012). Besides, family businesses also accounted for the largest percentage of businesses in contemporary times (Colli, 2003; Zahra and Sharma, 2004). As a distinct field of entrepreneurship, the family business has attracted a lot of attention in academic and policy circles because of its exploits across the globe. It is largely seen as a source of value addition, wealth creation and creation of job opportunities for family members and other people in the community. As a family asset, the management of a family business is sustained through the transfer of management and control from one family generation to the next generation (Shanker and Astrachan, 1996; Naseer et al., 2018).

In retrospect, family businesses perform wealth-creation, wealth reallocation and wealth-preservation roles thereby serving as intergenerational and geographical transmission mechanisms for owners' families (Carney, 2007). Other socio-economic roles of family businesses include stimulation of indigenous entrepreneurship (through the provision of goods and services) employment generation in the operating environment, wealth creation, embedding a culture of innovations and creativity, foreign exchange earnings, competing with large scale businesses including multinational companies (MNCs), mobilization of savings for production, and contribution to the GDP (Ogbechie and Anetor, 2015).

Despite the advantages inherent in modern shareholder-oriented businesses with heterogeneous owners, the family business model is still preferred and continued to be relevant in contemporary times because of several reasons. In family businesses, family members are passionate about keeping watch over the businesses with keen interest; they pay attention to details and minutest matters; and unlike outsiders, family members are committed to the continued survival and sustainability of the business (Ugoani, 2015). This argument finds justification because family businesses avoid the overlapping principal-agency problem in the Agency Theory of corporate governance. Agency theory explains the transactional contract between the principals (owners) and the agents (executive management) within an organization's corporate governance structure (Luhman and Cunliffe, 2013). The principals as owners engaged executive managers or agents with the promise to pay agreed remuneration on the condition that the latter protect the self-interests of the owners in the organizations (Laiho, 2011). Family businesses are protected from agency problem because the incentives for the principals and agents converge, that is, the owners are the executive managers running the organizations (Joshi and Akbar, 2012). Also, the governance of family businesses provides relative advantages in developing, sustaining, and appropriating value from a class of assets that are generic non-tradeable (GNTs), which are combined with tradable assets for maximum benefits (Gedajlovic and Carney, 2010).

From the foregoing explanations, agency theory suffers foundational problems because family businesses are run by the founder and family members, hence there is no need for executive managers to act as agents for the owners. Incidences in the corporate world have shown the limitation of agency theory. Scholars also explained that principal-agency relationship does not necessarily make corporate governance smooth, because sophisticated executive managers have failed woefully as agents to protect the interests of the owners – this breach of the agreement has resulted into bankruptcies (Arnold and De Lange, 2004; Jiraporn et al., 2008; Merino, Mayper and Tolleson, 2010). Therefore, family businesses require effective governance for survival because effective governance practices stimulate strategic planning and smooth succession in organizations (Neubauer and Lank, 2016).

Given the important socio-economic roles played by family businesses in Nigeria, it is pertinent to take a more in-depth look at the evolution, opportunities, governance, succession model and sustainability challenges facing the family businesses. For a country such as Nigeria rising poverty, crime and unemployment rates, the prospects and drawbacks of family businesses require wholesome research. Based on the foregoing, this chapter discusses the evolution, opportunities, succession model and sustainability challenges of formal and informal family businesses in Nigeria. There are five sections in this chapter. The first section discusses the overview of a family business as an evolving and distinct field of entrepreneurship. The second section focuses on the literature review. This section critically looked at the definitions of a family business, its evolution in Nigeria and the challenges facing family businesses in Nigeria and beyond. The third section discusses contingency leadership theory as a theoretical framework for the family business. The fourth section describes the methodology/approach used for chapter development with more details. The fifth part contextualized the evidence-based findings and insights that emerged from the chapter. The sixth section concludes with research implications (theoretical and managerial implications), limitations and suggestions for further research on the subject.

LITERATURE REVIEW AND THEORETICAL FRAMEWORK

Family Business Defined

The family business has been called different names such as family-owned business, family company and family entrepreneurship, hence there is a need to have it properly defined to avoid definitional ambiguity. The family business is a business entity where ownership and management including decision-making are influenced and concentrated in one or multiple generations of a family (De Massis, et al., 2014). The family business can also be defined as a business organization where the family owns the majority of the stock and by that exercise full managerial control over the management of the family business (Kampouri, Plakoyiannaki and Leppäaho, 2017). Most family businesses are established and managed by the family head as founder, and with time one or more members of the extended family are accommodated in the management of the businesses (Ugoani, 2015).

Similarly, Hall, Melin and Nordqvist (2001) define a family business as an organization started by a single founder, but progressively attract more family members who occupy leadership positions that are passed to the next generations of the family. A business can also be described as a family business when ownership, leadership and control; and decision-making are influenced by multiple generations of a family usually related by blood or marriage. This definition extends to a family-owned business, where a single person from a particular family is the controlling shareholder; that is, the person has enough shares to assume at least 20% of the voting rights and the highest percentage of voting rights in comparison to other shareholders (Raimi et al., 2016). Even in the organized private sector with several private limited and public limited companies, the family businesses still manifest. For instance, the active participation of more than one member of a family in the ownership and control of the company's total assets in the range of above 50% makes the business a family-owned business. This is done to ensure that the business ownership and management remain within the close control of family members over successive generations (Chua, Chrisman, & Sharma, 1999; Ayobami et al., 2018).

Concerning size, family businesses include small shops of sole proprietors, diverse models of partnerships, limited liability companies and multinational companies (Naseer, et al., 2018). Beyond mere nomenclature, a business qualifies to be called a family business if it manifests some unique characteristics, which shape the entrepreneurial attitude and impact on performance. The unique entrepreneurial characteristics of family businesses include: (a) ability to retains for a long time family board of directors, (2) ability to forge a close communication with employees, (3) high level of diversifications based on gender considerations, (4) possession of wealth of experience under the control more experienced older managers (Wilson et al., 2013; Naseer, et al., 2018). Other unique characteristics of family business include education, managerial acumen, personal involvement, community support/loyalty, size of the business, organization structure and degree of access to information (Detienne and Cardon, 2012; Hatak and Hyslop 2015; Naseer, et al., 2018). Family businesses are known to have the capacity to grow their revenues sustainably over a long period.

More importantly, family businesses operating in Nigeria could be classified into informal and informal typologies. The formal-informal paradigm is simply a continuum that explains the degree of sophistication of a business; and this changes as the size of the business grows at different phases of the growth process. At a point in time, to operate informally is appropriate, while at another phase of the growth process, formality becomes inevitable as operations become very complex, and it becomes necessary to manage labour matters and organizational policies more professionally (Marlow, Taylor & Thompson, 2010). Formality means operating based on legal contracts and explicit rules set by the government and other supervisory agencies in charge of the business. Most large businesses in embrace formality, whereas small businesses prefer to operate informally relying on traditional management systems built on social relationships and implicit norms (Lin, Lu, Li and Liu 2015; Raimi and Aslani, 2018). Some family businesses are informal because such businesses are owned and managed by a single owner lacking a professional understanding of how modern formalized management systems operate (Harney and Dundon, 2006). Besides, management systems in informal businesses are built on the personal idiosyncrasy of founders, informal practices, the domination of prerogative, adherence to normative prescriptions and policies and lack of respect for professional best practice (Raimi and Aslani, 2018). To wrap up this section, it is evident that, the owners of informal family businesses have to embrace formality when their business operations expand and management structures become more complex.

Evolution of Family Businesses in Nigeria

Nigeria's sound economic development in the areas of commerce, agriculture and industry were laid by ethnic entrepreneurs that operated several family businesses across the country at the pre and post-independence era. The owners of family businesses in Nigeria cut across the three major ethnic entrepreneurs, namely: Yorubas in western Nigeria, Igbo in eastern Nigeria and Hausa-Fulani in northern Nigeria. On the exploits of Yoruba-owned family businesses, it was reported that at least 200 years before independence, the Yoruba entrepreneurs from Oyo, Saki, Ogbomoso Ilorin, Igboho and other areas recorded landmark achievements in the establishment of several family businesses in their local communities and abroad, where they traded assorted clothes, hard wares, kola nuts, dried pepper, motorcycle or bicycle parts and locally manufactured equipment and household utensils (Olalere, 2013; Raimi et al., 2016a).

Igbo people are risk-takers and adventurists in the world of business. These unique entrepreneurial qualities have significantly assisted their family business accomplishments (Raimi et al., 2016a). Achebe (2012) noted that Igbos had a competitive edge in businesses because they could grab environmental opportunities that came their way. The Igbo-owned family businesses have a competitive edge in locations such as Lagos, Aba, Abuja, Onitsha, Nnewi, Kano, Kaduna, and Ibadan. Even outside the shores of Nigeria, the Igbos have established family businesses in places such as the US, Dubai, UK, Canada, China, Malaysia, Singapore, Canada, South Africa, Sierra Leone, Benin, Ghana, and African countries (Raimi and Aslani, 2019).

The Hausa-Fulani made a significant contribution to agricultural and commercial activities in the pre and post-independence era. As individuals and families, the Hausas traded in livestock, salts, leather products, and textiles at local and regional trade levels. Like the Yorubas, the Hausa traded in West Africa especially with the Ashante in Ghana, and Kankan in north-east Guinea. They are cultivators and livestock producers (Folami and Akoko, 2010). The exploits of Hausa-Fulani in business is largely shaped by their "cultural, attitudinal, and performative indicators" which are believed to have strengthened what has come to be known as Hausa-Fulani identity (Ochonu,2008; Raimi and Aslani, 2018).

SUCCESSION PLANNING OF FAMILY BUSINESSES

Succession planning and sustainability are two mutually reinforcing concepts with a cause-effect relationship. According to Luna (2012), the term succession planning refers to a systemic, long-term process of determining organizational goals, needs, and roles by preparing competent individuals and/or well-groomed employees to take-up tasks and responsibilities they are best suited for. Furthermore, succession planning is defined as a deliberate process by which individuals are vested with leadership positions with the intent of ensuring that business operations continue efficiently after the terminal exit of people holding key positions (Economic Times, 2019). Summing up the definitions above, succession planning is an ongoing process of identifying and developing internal people as new managers for the organizations to replace the former managers due to voluntary exit, retirement or death. The process of identifying and developing internal people entails an assessment of the right people, sustained training, mentoring and coaching, and delegation of duties.

Charan, Drotter and Noel, (2001) contrasted effective and ineffective succession. They posited that effective succession focuses on talent development to build an army of qualified people and groups in the entire leadership pipeline in the organization. It also extends to planning against the negative effects that the exit of key employees and/or founding CEO may have on the organization and its operations (Cosack, Guthridge and Lawson, 2010). The four phases of an effective succession planning process in any organization include transition (movement of new role), initiation, selection, and education (Economic Times, 2019).

In the developed economies with strong business culture, succession planning is taken very seriously by family businesses, however, the same is not the case in Nigeria. Consequently, family businesses in developing economies have a poor survival rate of 13 percent, which is of serious concern to policymakers considering the dominance of family businesses (Sharma et al, 1999). Akanazu (2016) discussed four (4) classic examples of family businesses that succeeded because of the founder's regards for a systematic exit strategy and a well-implemented succession plan. These four classic examples are here:

- Pascal Dozie, the founder of Diamond Bank PLC planned his exit/retirement and had long announced the intention to have a family member succeed him. With sustained effort, his first son, Uzoma Dozie took over the position of Group Managing Director of Diamond Bank and later emerged CEO.
- Otunba Subomi Balogun, the founder of First City Monument Bank initiated a systematic succession plan that led to his son Ladi Balogun taken over as the Group Managing Director.
- The Ibru family business dynasty under the hardworking businessman, Chief Michael Ibru followed the same pre-planned succession planning, which made the Ibru Croup one of the successful family businesses.
- Mulligan Murray-Bruce founded and managed Dominos Stores after he retired from the United African Company (UAC) many years ago. The Domino Stores as a family business still endues under the management of the founder's grandchildren, while his children, the Murray-Bruce brothers are serial entrepreneurs playing a leading role in the Nigerian entertainment industry.

Most family businesses across countries claim to have in place succession planning, but in reality this is often not the case. Consequently, some successful family businesses have gone into oblivion because of the issue of poor succession planning enunciated above. For instance, Ugoani (2015) reported that one of the critical sustainability challenges facing family businesses is lack of succession planning – a development that has led to the collapse of promising family businesses after the demise of the founder. He noted that, the succession plan becomes more complicated in a polygamous family characterized by the unhealthy struggle to take over the leadership of family businesses. Without deliberate succession planning through the early involvement of family members with the right entrepreneurial traits and competencies, the future of family business in Nigeria is bleak. For instance, the case of Odutola Business Empire built on the tall vision of two blood brothers: Alhaji Jimoh Odutola and Timothy Adeola Odutola is instructive. Both industrialists laid the foundation of commerce and industry in Nigeria, but on account of poor succession planning especially lack of interest in the family business by their children, their vast family business empire crumbled before their death. The same fate affected Ekene Dilichuku Transport, Henry Stephens Group with more than 20 companies; and Abiola's conglomerates such as Concord Group of Newspapers, Concord Airlines, Abiola Farms, and Wonder Loaf Bakery, Abiola Bookshops and Radio Communications Limited (Akanazu, 2016).

According to Proshare (2019), the 2018 Family Business Survey reported that 10% of family businesses interviewed said that they have a robust, documented and communicated succession plan, while 77% reported that they have plans to pass on ownership and management of their businesses to the next generation. The survey underscored the fact is that majority of Nigerian family businesses (77%) do not have appropriate structures for ensuring steady and hitch-free succession plans.

An earlier survey in Canada by the CIBC (2005) reported that contrary to presumption that organizations have succession planning, the survey found that 10% of the Small and medium-sized enterprises (SMEs) have formal and well-written succession plans; another 38% have informal/unwritten succession plans, and the remaining 52% of the SMEs do not have succession plans. Similarly, Waruiru and Kagiri (2015) found that 28% of the family businesses in Kenya had succession plans, 25% indicated that succession plan is still being developed, another 23% indicated that they just commenced the succession planning process, while the remaining 12% replied they were not sure there are succession plans for their organizations.

The implication of family businesses not having succession plans is grave; it is an indication that these businesses will be in crisis, if business assets change hands from present owners to their successors without a well-planned succession process. The next is to discuss the sustainability challenges of family businesses.

THEORETICAL FRAMEWORK

From the foregoing discourse, the contingency theory of leadership provides the theoretical underpinning for succession planning in family businesses. The contingency theory is predicated on the presumption that situation and context determine the right leadership, structure, processes, succession management and organization performance (Waruiru and Kagiri, 2015). Furthermore, Freeman (2015) posits that contingency theory explains the structure of organizations and how structure adjusts to external factors especially changing circumstances where uncertainty in decision-making is imperative. When linked to leadership, contingency theory asserts that the most appropriate leadership style depends on situational contingencies. The situational contingencies that determine the choice of leadership is predicated on the nature of the task, the degree of certainty or uncertainty of the task and profundity of decision making (Lorsch, 2010). Consequently, Rothwell (2010) explained that the best structure for organizations (otherwise Leader-Match Paradigm) depends largely on the extent to which the structure will meet future challenges in management. The Leader-Match paradigm emphasizes that under situational contingencies there is a need for organizations to match leaders to appropriate situations, and that performance of organizations depends on how well the leadership style of managers fits the context within which they operate. Extant literature identifies different types of leadership succession that fit different situations/ contexts (Whatley, 2011; Michel & Kammerlander, 2015).

Five succession planning models to be discussed include (1) Relay Succession/Crown Heir Succession, (2) Non-Relay Succession (Horse Race), (3) Outside Succession, (4) Coup d'état Succession, and (5) Boomerang Succession (Salleh and Rahman, 2017). Brief explanations of the five typologies of succession planning are discussed below.

1. **Relay Succession:** This is otherwise called 'Crown Heir Succession' in organizational leadership literature. It is a common pathway in leadership succession. It entails identifying a member of senior management as heir ahead of the actual transition. It is often practiced by organizations because it helps forestall the risk associated with selecting the wrong successor, and also it is preferred because it exploits maximally the successor's industry-based experience (Salleh and Rahman, 2017).

Furthermore, Santorin (2004) explains that a relay succession also occurs when the founding CEO of an organization transfers the reign of leadership to a successor over a long period. Before the transfer of leadership, the founder (mentor) is presumed to have trained and groomed the successor (mentee) by exposing the former to all aspects of the business including corporate challenges.

2. **Non-Relay Succession:** This type of succession as the name suggests is a 'Horse Race' competitive process of getting the right candidates to take over leadership of an organization. It entails several phases of screening, sifting and filtering prospective candidates based on several criteria developed by the top management including conducting a comprehensive background check on the professional competencies of the candidates (Salleh and Rahman, 2017).
3. **Outside Succession**: As the name indicates, it entails hiring external candidates or outsiders to occupy a leadership position in the organization, possibly in the absence of capable insiders with the right managerial and professional competencies to occupy the leadership positions. It is often adopted and preferred to ensure organizational stability and has been found to produce stronger performance results than relay succession (Gothard and Austin, 2012; Salleh and Rahman, 2017).
4. **Coup d'état Succession:** This has been described by scholars as a violent and unorganized succession. To preserve the fortunes of organizations in a period of instability, the stakeholders may decide to forces the succession through the process of power grab leading to the removal of the leadership (Salleh and Rahman, 2017).
5. **Boomerang Succession:** This type of succession entails bringing back the winning horse, that is, bringing back a former leader with outstanding records of performance to lead the organization in a period of turbulence. Organizations resort to Boomerang succession planning because there are no capable, strong and suitable candidates to occupy the sensitive leadership position at a critical phase in the organizational life. The often-cited example of boomerang succession is the case of Apple Computer Inc., which re-hired Steve Jobs during a period of bold turnaround plan in 1997 (Sharma and Grant, 2011; Salleh and Rahman, 2017).

The takeaway from the foregoing is that the situation and context determine the type of succession plans to be adopted by family businesses in their quest to transfer management and control to competent successors in the family.

METHODOLOGY AND APPROACH

A qualitative research method relying on desk research technique is used for this study because it is effective for exploring poorly researched and emerging phenomena in social and management research. To gain a deeper understanding, a review of relevant literature on family businesses, its evolution, opportunities, succession model and sustainability challenges were carried out. Guided by the desk research tradition, over 100 publications were sourced from the Goggle Scholar and internet resources, out of which a sample of 53 relevant publications on family businesses was selected using a purposive sampling technique. The sampled publications with heterogeneous findings were systematically reviewed and synthesized as integrated findings explaining the trends in financing programs for MSMEs in Nigeria. the extracted pieces of information sourced from scholarly articles and relevant internet resources on family businesses were synthesized and contextualized leveraging content analysis. The content analysis focuses on four thematic issues, namely: evolution of family businesses in Nigeria, inherent opportunities of family businesses, succession planning of family business and sustainability challenges of the family business. This approach aligns with several exploratory studies and best practices in management research (Mbow, et al, 2012; Gulaid & Kiragu, 2012; Hedger et al, 2008; Saunders et a, 2012). The essence of desk research is to systematically identify, assess and record the extent to which the phenomenon being investigated impacted and contributed to intended outcomes; it allows researchers to record lessons learned, report field challenges and highlight best practices. By-and large, desk research assists researchers to gain insights that can be applied when conducting an empirical investigation after the exploration.

FINDINGS AND DISCUSSIONS

After a modest review of the scholarly articles in this chapter, the following contextualized evidence-based findings emerged from the content analysis.

Evolution of Family Businesses in Nigeria

The family businesses evolved in Nigeria at pre and post-independence periods, and they laid the foundation for the country's economic development in the areas of commerce, agriculture and industry. The owners of family businesses in the country cut across the three major ethnic entrepreneurs, namely: Yorubas (Western Nigeria), Igbo (Eastern Nigeria) and Hausa-Fulani (Northern Nigeria). To these three ethnic entrepreneurs, presided over ownership, management and control their family businesses in a manner that could be described as a transition of leadership from one generation to another.

Inherent Opportunities of Family Businesses

Family businesses provide several opportunities for the national economy. The first opportunity is that they contribute to employment generation to the national economy of most countries, a fact that has made family businesses very relevant and indispensable. Related to that opportunity above is the opportunity of stimulation of indigenous entrepreneurship (through the provision of goods and services). Another opportunity provided by family businesses is mobilizing idle savings for production thereby contributing to the growth of the nation's growth of the gross domestic product (GDP) of the local economy.

Succession Planning of the family business in Nigeria

Reviewed literature established that family businesses in Nigeria manifested three types of attitudes towards succession planning. There are family businesses with formal and well-written succession plans; there are some with informal and unwritten succession plans, and there are others without succession plans. The three types of attitudes of family businesses towards succession planning are as depicted in Figure 1 below.

Figure 1.

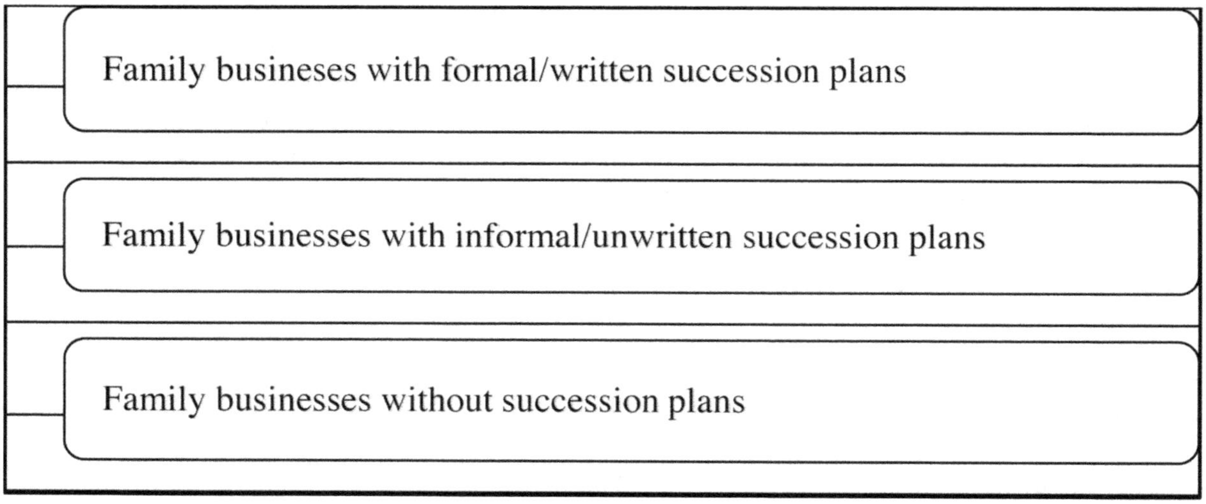

Moreover, it has been observed that family businesses in Nigeria mostly use relay succession planning in the process of transferring management and control of organizations to the next set of leaders. Contextually, the relay succession planning occurs when the founders/CEOs of family businesses transfer the reign of leadership, management and control to family members with the requisite qualities and competencies after a systematic exposure to all aspects of the business operations. To affirm the presumption above with regards to a preference for relay succession planning, Table 1 provides a tabular analysis of some family businesses in Nigeria and their succession planning typologies.

Sustainability Challenges of Family Businesses in Nigeria

Insights from the literature indicated that the main sustainability challenge facing family businesses include inadequate or outright lack of succession planning, conflict of interest, emotional family problems of divorce, separations/quarrels, a parochial family vision that precludes non-family members, absence of mentoring, lack of strategic planning, changing economic dynamics, financial limitation/paucity of funds for expansion, reckless business spending, corruption, lack of professionalism/business ethics, founder's fear of losing control, multiple taxations by government agencies, lack of antitrust laws and weak implementation of these laws to protect small family businesses, lack of advanced technologies, the unequal balance of power with MNCs, poor managerial knowledge, low international social networks, inadequate institutional support from the government and cultural determinants especially extended family system and inheritance laws. From the reviewed literature, the major sustainability challenging facing family businesses in Nigeria are depicted in Figure 2 below.

Table 1. Some family businesses in Nigeria and type of succession planning

SN	Name of Family Business	Founder	Type of Succession Planning and Sources
1	First City Monument Bank	Otunba Subomi Balogun	Relay succession planning was adopted: Ladi Balogun, son of the founder, took over as the Group Managing Director (Nawaeze, 2018)
2	Defunct Oceanic Bank Plc.	Chief Michael Ibru	Relay succession planning was adopted: His wife, Cecilia Ibru took over as CEO/Managing Director (McKinsey, 2012)
3	Diamond Bank Plc.	Pascal Dozie	Relay succession planning was adopted: His first son, Uzoma Dozie took over the position of Group Managing Director and later emerged as CEO (Nawaeze, 2018)
4	Ibru Group of Companies	Chief Michael Ibru	Relay succession planning was adopted: Family members, wife, children, and siblings; took leadership positions in all companies (Ekeh, 2016)
5	Dominos Stores	Mulligan Murray Bruce	Relay succession planning was adopted: The stores endue under the management of the founder's children and grandchildren (Emmanuel et. al., 2019)
6	Yinka Folawiyo & Sons Group of Companies	Late Alhaji (Dr.) Wahab, Iyanda Folawiyo CON	Relay succession planning was adopted: After the demise of the founder, the management of the Group of Companies was vested on founder's son, Tijani Babatunde Folawiyo as the Managing Director of Group with other family members working as professional managers (Nawaeze, 2018)
7	Globacom	Chief Michael Adenuga Snr,	Relay succession planning was adopted: The founder is the chairman, his first son, Paddy Adenuga Jnr., wield great influence as CEO at Globacom Limited, while the daughter, Mrs. Bella Disu was formerly an Executive Director, but is now the Executive Vice-Chairman (Technology Times, 2019)
8	Bola Ajibola & Co/ Crescent University	Prince Bola Ajibola	Relay succession planning was adopted: The management and control the law firm and university are under the founder and his children. Barrister Adesegun Mohammed Muruf Ajibola, SAN, is the Principal Partner of the firm after his father's exit. The founder is still the Proprietor of Crescent, while the Registrar is Barrister Z. A. Ajibola (Bola Ajibola & Co., 2019; Crescent University, 2019)
9	Dantata Organization	Alhaji Alhassan Dantata	Relay succession planning was adopted: The founder's son, Aminu Dantata took over the executive leadership of Alhassan Dantata and Sons in 1960 (Raimi et. al., 2016b)
10	Dangote Groups	Alhaji Aliko Dangote	Relay succession planning was adopted: The founder is still President & CEO but his children are wielding influence. Halima Aliko Dangote is the Executive Director of Aliko Danote Foundation and Dangote Industries Limited. She is also on the board of Dangote Group. Fatima Aliko Dangote is Director & Executive Director-Commercial at NASCON Allied Industries Plc. and a member of the board of Savannah Sugar Co Ltd., while Mariya Aliko-Dangote is a top manager in Dangote Group (Entsie, 2019; Italoye, 2019)

Source: Author's compilations from referenced materials

Figure 2. Sustainability challenges of family businesses

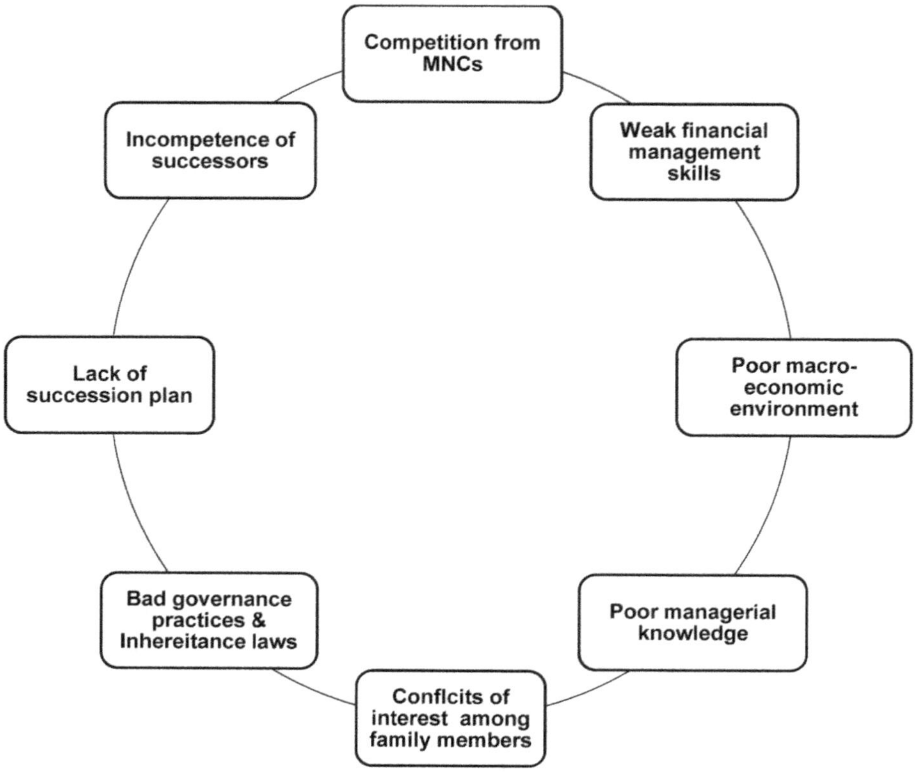

DISCUSSION

The first and second findings on family businesses are consistent with the view of Ogbechie and Anetor (2015a) that family businesses in Nigeria play critical roles in the economy through the creation of employment opportunities, maintenance of competition, stimulation of indigenous entrepreneurship, wealth creation, stimulation of innovations and creativity, generation of foreign exchange earnings, and mobilization of savings including contribution to the GDP. Family businesses in Nigeria cut across the three major ethnic entrepreneurs, namely: Yorubas in western Nigeria, Igbo in eastern Nigeria and Hausa-Fulani in northern Nigeria (Olalere, 2013; Raimi et al., 2016a). The third and fourth findings on succession planning of family businesses are also supported. According to Ogbechie and Anetor (2015a), most family-owned businesses in Nigeria do not have formal written succession plans and do not have formal criteria for choosing successors. The common success model is transferred from founders to family members because they are passionate at keeping watch over the businesses with keen interest; they pay attention to details and minutest matters; and unlike outsiders, family members are committed to the continued survival and sustainability of the business (Ugoani, 2015). Furthermore, Onuoha (2013) had earlier reported that almost 95% of family businesses in Nigeria do not have a succession plan. And where succession plans exist, not all the family members are aware of its existence because of the informality attached to succession planning by the founding owners of such businesses. Some of the sustainability challenges of family businesses have been reported in previous studies. Some of the reported sustainability challenges of family businesses include lack of enabling macro-economic environment, competition from a multinational corporation (MNCs), poor access to funding, poor succession planning, inadequate entrepreneurial knowledge and competencies, weak financial management skills, incorporation/registration bottlenecks, bad governance system and others (Onuoha, 2013; Proshare, 2019).

CONCLUSION, IMPLICATIONS, LIMITATIONS AND RECOMMENDATIONS

This study discusses the evolution, opportunities, succession model and sustainability challenges of formal and informal family businesses in Nigeria. After a critical review of the literature and other secondary materials. The chapter found that family businesses evolved in Nigeria at pre and post-independence periods, and they laid the foundation for the country's economic development in the areas of commerce, agriculture and industry. Secondly, it was established that family businesses contribute to employment generation, stimulate indigenous entrepreneurship (through the provision of goods and services, mobilize idle savings for production thereby contributing to the growth of the nation's growth of the gross domestic product (GDP) of the local economy. Thirdly, family businesses in Nigeria manifested three types of attitudes towards succession planning, viz: (a) family businesses with formal and well-written succession plans; (b) those with informal and unwritten succession plans; and (c) family businesses without succession plans.

With regards to succession planning, the insights from the literature indicated that family businesses in Nigeria mostly use relay succession in the process of transferring management and control of organizations to the next set of leaders. Functionally, the founders/CEOs transfer the reign of leadership, management and control to family members with the requisite qualities and competencies after a systematic exposure to all aspects of the business operations.

Some of the sustainability challenges of family businesses include lack of enabling macro-economic environment, competition from a multinational corporation (MNCs), poor access to funding, inadequate entrepreneurial knowledge and competencies, weak financial management skills, incorporation/registration bottlenecks, bad governance system, and others. The paper presents integrated findings largely hinged on theory and historical facts on the fortunes and misfortunes of informal and formal family businesses in Nigeria.

The implications of this research are diverse. From a theoretical standpoint, the chapter validates the contingency leadership theory as the most appropriate theory that explains the attitude, style and structure of family businesses in Nigeria. Specifically, relay succession planning is the most common succession model adopted by family businesses in Nigeria. From a managerial standpoint, the sustainability challenges facing family businesses have been critically discussed and affirmed on the strengths of several previous empirical studies. It is therefore instructive for the stakeholders to redress these sustainability challenges through the development of formal succession plan (founders/owners), modernization of traditional inheritance laws that favour mediocrity over merit including the formulation of succession planning policy by the regulatory agency to forestall the imposition of successors on family business where the founders died without formal succession plan (government).

This chapter contribution suffers empirical limitation as the qualitative findings are not based on the empirical investigation within a given time and space. For further study, an empirical study is suggested to strengthen and fortify the useful insights from the chapter. Despite the above-discussed limitation, this chapter is unique and distinct, as it opens the space further studies on this topical issue.

REFERENCES

Abouzaid, S. (2008). *IFC family business governance handbook*. Retrieved from http://www.ifc.org/wps/wcm/connect/159c9c0048582f6883f9ebfc046daa89/FB_English_final_2008.pdf?MOD=AJPERES

Achebe, C. (2012). Why Nigerians hate Igbos. *The Nation*. Available: http://thenationonlineng.net/new/why-nigerians-hate-igbos-by-chinua-achebe/

Akanazu, H. (2016). *Family Businesses in Nigeria and Inter-Generational Succession. Family-Owned Businesses Forum Nigeria*. Available: https://www.academia.edu/30992273/FAMILY-OWNED_BUSINESS_FORUM_NIGERIA.docx

Arnold, B., & De Lange, P. (2004). Enron: An examination of agency problems. *Critical Perspectives on Accounting*, *15*(6-7), 751–765. doi:10.1016/j.cpa.2003.08.005

Ayobami, A. O., Odey, O. D., Olanireti, A. M., & Babarinde, K. P. (2018). Family Business and Innovation in Nigeria: Problems and Prospects. *Covenant Journal of Entrepreneurship*, *2*(1), 26–33.

Bola Ajibola & Co. (2019). *Our Team Elements Presentation*. Available: http://www.bolaajibolaandco.com/?page_id=1600

Carney, M. (2007). Minority family business in emerging markets: Organization forms and competitive advantage. *Family Business Review*, *20*(4), 289–300. doi:10.1111/j.1741-6248.2007.00097.x

Charan, R., Drotter, S., & Noel, J. (2001). *The Leadership Pipeline: How to Build the Leadership-Powered Company*. John Wiley & Sons.

Chua, J. H., Chrisman, J. J., & Sharma, P. (1999). Defining the family business by behavior. *Entrepreneurship Theory and Practice*, *23*(4), 19–39. doi:10.1177/104225879902300402

CIBC. (2005). *Are Canadian Entrepreneurs Ready For Retirement?* CIBC World Markets Inc.

Colli, A. (2003). *The history of family business, 1850-2000* (Vol. 47). Cambridge University Press.

Cosack, S., Guthridge, M., & Lawson, E. (2010, August). Retaining key employees in times of change. *The McKinsey Quarterly*.

Crals, E., & Vereeck, L. (2004). *Sustainable entrepreneurship in SMEs: theory and practice*. In *3rd Global Conference in Environmental Justice and Global Citizenship*, Copenhagen, Denmark.

Crescent University. (2019). *The Management –Registrar.* Available: http://crescent-university.edu.ng/AboutUs.aspx

Dai, O., & Liu, X. (2009). Returning Entrepreneurs Vs Indigenous Entrepreneurs: An Investigation of High Technology SMEs in Emerging Markets. In K. Ibeh & S. Davies (Eds.), *Contemporary Challenges to International Business* (pp. 200–217). Palgrave MacMillan; doi:10.1057/9780230237322_12

De Massis, A., Kotlar, J., Chua, J. H., & Chrisman, J. J. (2014). Ability and willingness as sufficiency conditions for family-oriented particularistic behavior: Implications for theory and empirical studies. *Journal of Small Business Management*, *52*(2), 344–364. doi:10.1111/jsbm.12102

DeTienne, D. R., & Cardon, M. S. (2012). Impact of founder experience on exit intentions. *Small Business Economics, 38*(4), 351–374. doi:10.100711187-010-9284-5

Economic Times. (2019). *Definition of 'Succession Planning*. Bennett, Coleman & Co. Ltd. Available: https://economictimes.indiatimes.com/definition/succession-planning

Ekeh, P. (2016). *The age of Olorogun Michael Ibru Urhobo Perspectives on the Life and Times of Michael Christopher Onajirhevbe Ibru (1930-2016)*. Available: http://www.waado.org/Biographies/ibru_michael/THE_AGE_OF_MICHAEL_IBRU.pdf

Emmanuel, A. K., Peace, N. N., Ebele, O. M., Udeze, C. C., & Abiodun, O. A. (2019). Do Non-Family Member Managers Enhance Venture Performance of Family Businesses Evidence from Nigeria. *Academy of Entrepreneurship Journal, 25*(3). Available: https://www.abacademies.org/articles/do-nonfamily-member-managers-enhance-venture-performance-of-family-businesses-evidence-from-nigeria-8491.html

European Family Business. (2012). *Family business*. Retrieved from http://www.europeanfamilybusinesses.eu/uploads/Modules/Publications/family-business-statistics.pdf

Folami, O. M., & Akoko, A. (2010). *Climate Change and Inter-Ethnic Conflict Between Fulani Herdsmen and Host Communities in Nigeria. Ondo*. Adekunle Ajasin University.

Freeman, J. (2015). *Contingency theory*. Wiley Encyclopedia of Management; doi:10.1002/9781118785317.weom110129

Gedajlovic, E., & Carney, M. (2010). Markets, hierarchies, and families: Toward a transaction cost theory of the family firm. *Entrepreneurship Theory and Practice, 34*(6), 1145–1172. doi:10.1111/j.1540-6520.2010.00418.x

Gothard, S., & Austin, M. (2012). Leadership Succession Planning: Implications for Nonprofit Human Service Organizations. *Administration in Social Work, 37*(3), 272–285. doi:10.1080/03643107.2012.684741

Gulaid, L. A., & Kiragu, K. (2012). Lessons learnt from promising practices in community engagement for the elimination of new HIV infections in children by 2015 and keeping their mothers alive: Summary of a desk review. *Journal of the International AIDS Society, 15*, 17390.

Hall, A., Melin, L., & Nordqvist, M. (2001). Entrepreneurship as radical change in the family business: Exploring the role of cultural patterns. *Family Business Review, 14*(3), 193–208. doi:10.1111/j.1741-6248.2001.00193.x

Harney, B., & Dundon, T. (2006). Capturing complexity: Developing an integrated approach to analysing HRM in SMEs. *Human Resource Management Journal, 16*(1), 48–73. doi:10.1111/j.1748-8583.2006.00004.x

Hatak, I., & Hyslop, K. (2015). Cooperation between family businesses of different size: A case study. *Journal of Co-operative Organization and Management, 3*(2), 52–59. doi:10.1016/j.jcom.2015.11.003

Hedger, M. M., Mitchell, T., Leavy, J., Greeley, M., & Downie, A. (2008). *Desk review: evaluation of adaptation to climate change from a development perspective*. Available: http://citeseerx.ist.psu.edu/viewdoc/download?doi=10.1.1.575.1027&rep=rep1&type=pdf

Italoye, I. (2019). Mariya Dangote: Things You Don't Know About Dangote's Daughter. *Nigeria Infomedia*. Available: https://nigerianinfopedia.com.ng/mariya-dangote/

Jiraporn, P., Miller, G. A., Yoon, S. S., & Kim, Y. S. (2008). Is earnings management opportunistic or beneficial? An agency theory perspective. *International Review of Financial Analysis*, *17*(3), 622–634. doi:10.1016/j.irfa.2006.10.005

Joseph, A. (2014). Culture determinants and family business succession in Jos Metropolis, Plateau state Nigeria. *Journal of Emerging Trends in Economics and Management Science*, *5*(5), 379–390.

Joshi, M., & Akbar, M. (2012). Endogenous agency problems, their impact and mitigation in privately-held family firms for sustaining growth. *Amity Business Journal*, *1*(2), 1–22.

Kampouri, K., Plakoyiannaki, M. E., & Leppäaho, T. (2017). Family Business Internationalisation and Networks: Emerging Pathways. *Journal of Business and Industrial Marketing*, *32*(3), 1–38. doi:10.1108/JBIM-04-2015-0066

Laiho, T. (2011). *Agency theory and ownership Structure-Estimating the effect of ownership structure on firm performance* (Master's thesis). Department of Economics, Aalto University School of Economics.

Lin, D., Lu, J., Li, P. P., & Liu, X. (2015). Balancing Formality and Informality in Business Exchanges as a Duality: A Comparative Case Study of Returnee and Local Entrepreneurs in China. *Management and Organization Review*, *11*(2), 315–342. doi:10.1017/mor.2014.2

Lorsch, J. W. (2010). A Contingency Theory of Leadership. In N. Nohria & R. Khurana (Eds.), *Handbook of Leadership Theory and Practice*. Harvard Business Press.

Lucky, E. O. I., Minai, M. S., & Adebayo, O. I. (2011). A conceptual framework of family business succession: Bane of family business continuity. *International Journal of Business and Social Science*, *2*(18), 106–113.

Luhman, J. T., & Cunliffe, A. L. (2013). *Key concepts in organization theory*. SAGE Publications Ltd.; doi:10.4135/9781473914643

Malgwi, C. A., Owhoso, V., Gleason, K. C., & Mathur, I. (2006). Who invests in the least developed countries? An examination of US multinationals in Africa. *Journal of African Business*, *7*(1-2), 201–227. doi:10.1300/J156v07n01_10

Marlow, S., Taylor, S., & Thompson, A. (2010). Informality and formality in medium-sized companies: Contestation and synchronization. *British Journal of Management*, *21*(4), 954–966. doi:10.1111/j.1467-8551.2009.00635.x

Mbow, C., Skole, D., Dieng, M., Justice, C., Kwesha, D., Mane, L., & Virji, H. (2012). *Challenges and prospects for REDD+ in Africa: desk review of REDD+ implementation in Africa. Global Land Project Reports, 5. World Agroforestry Centre*. ICRAF.

McKinsey. (2012). Leading a developing-market bank: An interview with the CEO of Nigeria's Oceanic Bank. *McKinsey Quarterly*. Available: https://web.archive.org/web/20101202032653/http://www.mckinseyquarterly.com/Leading_a_developing-market_bank_An_interview_with_the_CEO_of_Nigerias_Oceanic_Bank_2395

Merino, B. D., Mayper, A. G., & Tolleson, T. D. (2010). Neoliberalism, deregulation and Sarbanes-Oxley: The legitimation of a failed corporate governance model. *Accounting, Auditing & Accountability Journal, 23*(6), 774–792. doi:10.1108/09513571011065871

Michel, A., & Kammerlander, N. (2015). Trusted advisors in a family business's succession-planning process—An agency perspective. *Journal of Family Business Strategy, 6*(1), 45–57. doi:10.1016/j.jfbs.2014.10.005

Naseer, M. S., Nazam, M., Randhawa, M. A., Ahamd, M., Maqbool, A., Khan, M. A., & Ayub, M. U. (2018). Exploring the determinants for a successful family entrepreneurship: Empirical evidences from Punjab Province. *African Journal of Business Management, 12*(22), 666–673. doi:10.5897/AJBM2018.8532

Neubauer, F., & Lank, A. G. (2016). *The family business: Its governance for sustainability*. Springer.

Nnabuife, E. K., & Okoli, I. E. (2017). Succession Planning and Sustainability of Selected Family Owned Businesses in Anambra State, Nigeria. *European Journal of Business and Management, 9*(34), 155–165.

Nwaeze, A. (2018). *4 Nigerian Companies Whose founders found the best CEOs in their sons*. Buzz Nigeria Publication. Available: https://buzznigeria.com/four-nigerian-companies-whose-founders-found-the-best-ceos-in-their-sons/

Ochonu, M. (2008). Colonialism within colonialism: The Hausa-Caliphate imaginary and the British colonial administration of the Nigerian Middle Belt. *African Studies Quarterly, 10*(2-3), 95–127.

Ogbechie, R., & Anetor, F. O. (2015a). An Appraisal of Succession Planning in Family-Owned Businesses in Lagos State, Nigeria. *European Journal of Business and Management, 7*(12), 1–5.

Ogbechie, R., & Anetor, F. O. (2015b). An Investigation into the Core Values That Drive Successful Family-Owned Businesses: A Case of Lagos State, Nigeria. *European Journal of Business and Management, 7*(17), 17–23.

Ogundele, O. J. K., Idris, A. A., & Ahmed-Ogundipe, K. A. (2012). Entrepreneurial succession problems in Nigeria's family businesses: A threat to sustainability. *European Scientific Journal, 8*(7).

Olalere, J. B. (2013). *Exploits of a migrants' community: Chronicles of Yorubas in Ghana*. Delight Communications West Africa Limited.

Onuoha, B. C. (2013). Poor Succession Planning by Entrepreneurs: The Bane of Generational Enterprises in South-East, Nigeria. *An International Journal of Arts and Humanities Bahir Dar, Ethiopia, 2*(2), 270–281.

Otika, U. S., Okocha, E. R., & Ejiofor, H. U. (2019). Inheritance Culture and Management Succession of Family-Owned Businesses in Nigeria: Am Empirical Study. *European Journal of Business and Innovation Research, 7*(3), 31–47.

Proshare. (2019). *Findings from Nigerian Family Business Report 2018*. Available: https://www.proshareng.com/news/Savings,-Thrift---Investment/Findings-From-Nigerian-Family-Business-R/43531

PwC Nigeria. (2017). *2014 Family Business Survey*. Available: http://www.pwc.com/ng/en/press-room/2014-family-business-survey.html

Raimi, L., & Aslani, B. (2019). Exploring the Contributions of Informal Ethnic Entrepreneurship to Economic Development in Nigeria. In V. Ramadani, L.-P. Dana, V. Ratten, & A. Bexheti (Eds.), *Informal Ethnic Entrepreneurship- Future Research Paradigms for Creating Innovative Business Activity* (pp. 179–194). Springer Nature; doi:10.1007/978-3-319-99064-4_12

Raimi, L., Moshood, A. B., Shokunbi, M. O., & Cole, B. M. (2016a). Indigenous entrepreneurs and battle for competitive edge with multinational corporations in Nigeria. *International Journal of Economic Behavior*, *6*(1), 85–96.

Raimi, L., Odebode, O. O., Salisu, O. O., & Oyewole, A. A. (2016b). Women Entrepreneurship. In *Fundamentals of Entrepreneurship Education*. Centre for Entrepreneurship Development, Yaba College of Technology.

Raimi, L., Peluola, S. B., Shokunbi, M. O., & Adebayo, M. S. (2016c). Women Entrepreneurship. In *Fundamentals of Entrepreneurship Education*. Centre for Entrepreneurship Development, Yaba College of Technology.

Rome Business School. (2019). *Family Business and Inter-Generational Succession*. Available: https://romebusinessschool.com/family-owned-businesses/

Rothwell, W. J. (2010). *Effective Succession Planning: Ensuring Leadership Continuity and Building Talent from Within* (4th ed.). American Management Association.

Ryan, L. V., & Schneider, M. (2003). Institutional Investor Power and Heterogeneity: Implications for Agency and Stakeholder Theories. *Business & Society*, *42*(4), 398–429. doi:10.1177/0007650303260450

Salleh, L. M., & Rahman, M. F. A. (2017). A comparative Study of Leadership Succession Models. Sci. *Int.(Lahore)*, *29*(4), 791–796.

Saunders, M. N., & Lewis, P. (2012). *Doing research in business & management: An essential guide to planning your project*. Pearson.

Shanker, M. C., & Astrachan, J. H. (1996). Myths and realities: Family businesses' contribution to the US economy. A framework for assessing family business statistics. *Family Business Review*, *9*(2), 107–123. doi:10.1111/j.1741-6248.1996.00107.x

Sharma, A., & Grant, D. (2011). Narrative, Drama and Charismatic Leadership: The Case of Apple's Steve Jobs. *Leadership*, *7*(1), 3–26. doi:10.1177/1742715010386777

SMEDAN & National Bureau of Statistics. (2012). *Survey Report on Micro, Small and Medium Enterprises in Nigeria: 2010 National MSME Collaborative Survey*. SMEDAN and National Bureau of Statistics.

Tilley, F., & Young, W. (2009). Sustainability Entrepreneurs - Could they be the True Wealth Generators of the Future? *Greener Management International*, *55*, 79–92.

Ugoani, J. N. N. (2015). Challenges of Succession on Family Business Success-Kitchen Model. *American Journal of Social Science Research*, *1*(3), 163–168.

Waruiru, W., & Kagiri, A. W. (2015). Effects of succession planning strategy on the performance of international non-governmental organizations in Kenya. *International Journal of Science and Research, 4*(5), 3147–3155.

Whatley, L. (2011). A New Model for Family Owned Business Succession. *Organization Development Journal, 29*(4), 21–32.

Wilson, N., Wright, M., & Scholes, L. (2013). Family business survival and the role of boards. *Entrepreneurship Theory and Practice, 37*(6), 1369–1389. doi:10.1111/etap.12071

Zahra, S. A., & Sharma, P. (2004). Family business research: A strategic reflection. *Family Business Review, 17*(4), 331–346. doi:10.1111/j.1741-6248.2004.00022.x

KEY TERMS AND DEFINITIONS

Boomerang Succession: This type of succession entails bringing back a former leader with outstanding records of performance to lead the organization in a period of turbulence.

Coup d'état Succession: This is a violent and unorganized succession that entails forcing candidates to occupy leadership position in the organization in order preserve the fortunes of organisations in a period of instability.

Family business: This is a business entity where ownership and management including decision-making are influenced and concentrated in one or multiple generations of a family.

Formality: This means operating based on legal contracts and explicit rules set by government and other supervisory agencies in charge of business.

Informality: This means operating based on traditional management system built on social relationships and implicit norms.

Non-Relay Succession: This type of succession involves getting the right candidates to take over leadership of an organisation.

Outside Succession: This type of succession entails hiring external candidates or outsiders to occupy leadership position in the organization, possibly in the absence of capable insiders with the right managerial and professional competencies to occupy the leadership positions.

Relay Succession: This is a common pathway in leadership succession that entails transferring the reign of leadership by the founder to a successor over a long period of time.

Sustainability: This refers to the enduring continuity and long-term commitment of businesses while operating to meeting the needs of both the present and future generations while contributing to socio-economic development.

Chapter 12
Performance Determinants in Family Business:
Linking Innovation and Internationalisation

Joana Costa
https://orcid.org/0000-0001-7514-9836
Universidade de Aveiro, Portugal

ABSTRACT

Family businesses (FBs) are central to economies: in Portugal the impact of these structures reaches 2/3 of the GDP, 1/2 of the labour force, and 4/5 of the firms in operation, most of them being SMEs. These organisations play a central role in terms of job creation, local development, knowledge transfer, and territorial cohesion. Innovative activities are key factors for competitive economies; yet innovation increases risk exposure and FBs are conservative and risk adverse, resisting change, relying on internal factors rather than opening to the external environment, consequently postponing innovation and thus pledging their future. Their embedded culture reduces innovative propensity; still, the existence loyalty trust and informal networks enhance individual or collective innovation processes. Using a dataset of 110 FBs innovation and internationalization along with other structural characteristics are connected to their economic performance, shedding light on the determinants FB economic efficiency. Given their importance, made-to-measure policy schemes should be designed.

INTRODUCTION

All over the world family businesses (FBs) play a central role in entrepreneurial dynamics. Despite the assortment of numbers concerning the proportion of FFs in business, research repeatedly reinforces the worldwide dominance of this type of organisations. According to the Family Firm Institute (2015), these businesses are the most important job creator as well as the most significant contributor to income generation, sources of regional and national growth, promoting job creation and inclusion, smoothing adverse phases of the business cycle. Given the singularities of their organisational structures they are a heterogeneous amalgamation (Chua et al., 2012).

DOI: 10.4018/978-1-7998-3648-3.ch012

Since Schumpeter's (1939 and 1942) seminal works, innovation has been considered to be the holy grail of firms' long-term success being therefore accepted as a critical success factor in globalised environments, empowering firm competition, promoting growth, and sustainable development. FBs are the most common form of business being considered as crucial for the economic progress and sustainability (Anderson and Reeb, 2003).

Developing innovative activities is central in a competitive economy; yet innovation exposes firms to additional risks due to the uncertainty concerning the outcomes; FBs are often classified as risk adverse, with conservative managerial styles, consequently resisting change. Additionally, very often, preferring the reliance on internal factors rather than opening to the external environment, which tend to postpone innovation risking the organisation survival (Kellermanns et al., 2012).

Two major branches of research can be identified when linking innovation with FBs. The first evidences that these firms have a reduced propensity to innovate due to their traditional culture; and the second points towards the existence of values such as loyalty trust and informal networks, which will raise the innovative dynamics based in both the individual or collective innovation cycles.

Relying on a dataset of 110 FBs (from a purposive survey) located in Portugal, the analysis of innovation and internationalisation as drivers of the firm performance were appraised, including a set of other controls (structural characteristics) usually connected to the firm efficiency literature. A multivariate analysis was run to identify the existing connections between those variables and performance. The importance of innovation was highlighted along with the existence of a solid human capital stock, and operations in external markets.

Despite the inexistent measurement of the differences between family and non-family firms, the literature evidences clear dissimilarities in terms of the innovative strategies of these organisations compared to others. Ignoring these specificities in the innovation policy may constitute a hindering factor for the extending innovation practices in these organisations. Existent analysis seems to be insufficient to draw a policy package devoted to FBs and theirs singularities, so it is aimed to shed some light on the inter-relation among factors as understanding the effective role of innovation, internationalisation and human capital om FBs performance will enhance their productive potential, success and survival.

Given the increased importance of these structures among the entrepreneurial fabric in an economic scenario urging for fast and sustainable recovery, designing measures to sustain and leverage their activities should grasp the attention of practitioners, the academia and policy makers.

BACKGROUND

In most countries FBs are the foundations of economic activity at the regional, sectoral and national level. In Portugal FBs are responsible for the generation of almost 2/3 of the Gross Domestic Product; generate half of the job opportunities, and, are 4/5 of the total numbers in terms of firms in operation (PWC, 2016). Despite most of them being small, there are also FBs quoted on the stock market (e.g. Sonae, Amorim, Jerónimo Martins). Due to their singularities, these forms promote local development, knowledge transfer and promote local cohesion.

The fact that the country is a Moderate Innovator (European Innovation Scoreboard, 2019), generates increased interest on its analysis as it needs a deeper effort for innovation practices to be disseminated among companies in operation being a generalised practise to leverage the overall performance of firms.

The plenty of FBs is perhaps the underlying reason for their heterogeneity. These businesses, according to the literature, present three peculiarities driving them away from other organisations: high management control, undisclosed wealth, non-financial achievements (de Massis, Frattini, and Lichtenthaler, 2013). Their contributions to the income generation are multidimensional as in one hand they are natural sources of income generation and value added, they create jobs for their entrepreneurs and for others, they promote and sustain technoogical takeoffs, they promote knowledge transfer and due to managerial styles, they promote proximity and empowerment of the human capital (Kraiczy, N., 2013).

All firms, and FBs are not exception, need to generate virtuous cycles of innovation, which will be retro feed, continuously improving its performance, the existence of new innovative activities will boost efficiency levels, employee productivity, cost reduction and therefore firm competitive advantages (Geroski et al., 1993); as a consequence innovative firms are expected to build advantages compared to their non-innovative counterparts. However, structural characteristics such as the sector may speed up or deter innovation achievements (Acs and Audretsch, 1987).

The present chapter will address the role of innovative strategies along with internationalisation in the economic performance of FBs, this phenomenon is somehow overlooked in the literature as in innovation studies the capital ownership dimension has not been separated from others. The objective is to appraise how far innovation can be a determinant of the firm success controlling for the other structural characteristics. The objective is twofold: promote the debate in terms of the desirability of innovation in managerial terms, and, reinforce the importance of disseminating innovation as a vector of policy support for this type of organisations.

This debate has more importance as it aim at producing clarification evidence in the context of a moderate innovator, as the literature is ambiguous. In one hand the arguments state that FBs are less prone to innovate given their governance, based on tradition and rigid cultural norms, and immutable values (de Clercq and Belausteguigoitia, 2015; de Massis, et al., 2016)), or more dynamic as they are more flexible, given the fact they belong to informal networks and establish proximity links which will enhance formal and informal knowledge transmission, reinforcing the innovation cycle (de Massis et al., 2013). The empirical evidence provided by the econometric estimation reinforces the importance of both innovation and internationalisation as enhancers of firm economic performance, and consequently, policy markers should take into consideration feeding the innovation strategies of these organisations.

This chapter provides an empirical analysis of a purposeful sample containing 110 firms which belong to different economic sectors (from the industrial sector mostly), therefore evidencing different technological intensities (according to the R&D expenditures and the SIC Codes) and dimensions. In order to appraise economic efficiency, the dependent variable was calculated considering Gross value added (GVA), divided by the total workforce, which leads to the GVA *per worker* ratio. By means of implementing this procedure, it is empirically proved that firms with better innovative performances or active internationalisation strategies are more economically efficient than their non-innovative or closed counterparts. Results also evidence the link of the economic performance to these vectors rather than conventional structural characteristics such as size, human capital or technological intensity.

Given the extant identification of the determinants of the economic efficiency, policy recommendations can be made, as all factors operating as barriers into these two dimensions should be removed to incentive profitability and as a consequence success and survival. Additionally, given the importance of these firms in number and turnover, along with their heterogeneity it is important to detail the innovation and export enhancers and design some fine tuning policy packages to meet those singularities and enhance the probability of these organisations to open their governance towards innovation and internationalisation.

The remainder of the chapter is organised as follows: section 2 presents the theoretical background of FBs innovation and internationalisation strategies, along with other structural traits. Section 3 presents the database, the methodology and the econometric model. In section 4 discusses the results from the econometric estimation; finally section 5 concludes and draws a policy package.

THEORETICAL BACKGROUND

The literature classifies FBs as the most heterogeneous, complex and challenging sectors to analyse both theoretical and empirically. This taxonomy includes all kinds of activities in terms of technological intensity, and all kinds of sectors. It also includes all firm dimensions from small to large firms, from regional to multinational markets in operation. Innovation is an underlying growth factor and as a consequence as expected enhancer of economic performance in FBs (Nieto et al. 2015; de Massis et al. 2015, Masouras, 2019). More than simply raising the short term economic performance innovation reinforces profitability, creating competitive advantages from competitors (de Massis et al., 2016). As a consequence and if the firm is able to feed the innovation cycle, it will reinforce its long term performance (Kellermanns et al., 2012). Academics have appraised the foundations of FBs innovation and enhanced several connections to the individuals, to the firms, and the environment. Notwithstanding, these factors are commonly addressed in a ceteris paribus analysis, still empirically, these factors are interconnected.

Family Business Definition

Portrayed as heterogeneous organisations, FBs are connected to stewardship and tradition, with immutable values and are unlikely to change established procedures (Werner et al., 2018). As innovation plays a central role in long-term success of firms, further comprehension of their innovative strategy is mandatory. Reinforced by its positive effect on firm survival, innovation is core for overpassing generations (Kim et al., 2008).

FBs are the most common business structure, being as a consequence considered essential for economic growth and sustainability (Anderson and Reeb, 2003). Even though, no universal definition of can be found in the literature (Miller, 2006, Siebels and Aufseß, 2012). Depicted as traditional organisations, FBs are difficult to change; hence, some of them are the most innovative firms worldwide due to their resilience. In general, innovation is extremely puzzling for these organizations due to their reliance on traditions and the concentration of the decision making process on the founder (Miller and Breton-Miller, 2014).

Despite the multiplicity of proposals, 2 definitions offer consensus among the academic community: the first relies on components-of-involvement approach classifying FBs according to the percentage of shares held by family members (Siebels and Aufseß, 2012); Chua et al. (2012) classify the firm as FB if the family owns most of the equity, it is noteworthy that presently in Europe, a firm is classified as FB if 25% or more of its shares are owned by the family. Additionally, they are wielded by family management, and some of the family members have positions in the company (Miller and Le Breton-Miller, 2014). The other classification relies on the essence approach model, demanding daily involvement in day-to-day operations, (Eddleston et al., 2012). As a consequence, a business can be considered FB if the family is involved in managerial decisions and discusses implementation of the firm strategy having daily involvement in activities and emotional attachment (Chua et al., 1999).

As authors draw upon the different conceptual frameworks, the empirical results may diverge (Chua et al., 2012). Frequently the accepted definition states that FBs are those firms in which equity is owned by the family whose members control the strategic and managerial decisions in a continuous perspective, playing active roles in operations and management. In practice, and based on the quantitative aspect, it is a firm as family in which the majority of equity owned by the family (Kontinen and Ojala, 2010; Swoboda and Olejnik, 2013; Piva et al., 2013).

Innovation in FBs

The discussion of the innovative strategies of family firms grasped the attention of researchers and policy makers, being quite curious that the empirical results are mismatched, and findings go in different directions. Still, successful firms, either FBs or not, are normally involved in innovative activities which improve their performance concerning cost reduction and the achievement of advantages compared to the competitors. Sectoral and firm characteristics are identified as determinants to generate tangible and intangible innovation (Acs and Audretsch 1987, 1988).

Leading countries have an entrepreneurial fabric which pursues innovation, yet innovation exposes firms to supplementary risks. In the innovation process, failure can be inevitable as the outcome of innovation projects is uncertain, thus risky. Internal or external investors are not sympathetic with risky activities, and, in some cases there is lack of external finance to support innovation, or it exists at a high cost. In other cases, it relies on internal finance. Consequently, the prize to be paid to investors must be higher independent on relying on internal or external sources (Hajivassiliou, and Savingnac, 2008). Very often, FBs are labelled as highly conservative, consequently less attracted to innovation, but neglecting the innovation may condemn FBs to failure (Canepa and Stoneman, 2002).

When launching innovation activities and despite the existence of forecasts, firms do not know if the project will succeed, how extensive will be the gain, and if hindering factors are about to emerge. When investment plans include innovative activities they are frequently unattractive to external investors due to moral hazard problems. Information asymmetries will disincentive venture capital due to the lack of warrantees, and frequently, intangible assets do not work as collaterals (Costa et al., 2018). As a consequence FBs may doubt on the desirability of innovation as they need to rely on internal finance which is naturally scant and in doing so they are exposing the organisation to increased risks (Claver, et al., 2008).

Academics are divided in what concerns the ownership effect in innovation (Anderson and Reeb, 2003). In some cases family values reinforce innovation culture (e.g. Kim et al., 2008; Llach and Nordqvist, 2010) in other cases, due to tradition, conservativeness and embeddedness, innovation is not accepted (e.g. Munari et al. 2010; Block, 2012). It is acceptable that the existing heterogeneity of FBs will produce a multiplicity of strategies concerning their innovation processes.

The success in the innovative projects is influenced by a multiplicity of factors such as: firm culture, experience in the field, managerial and operational skills connected to R&D, the validity of the innovation project, coherence of the project with the existent endowments of human capital and other factors, organisational flows, pricing strategies and market opportunity (van der Panne et al., 2003). Being normally associated with flexibility, plasticity and ability to reinvent the organisation, FBs may be more able to boost success.

It is certain that some firms may survive or even grow with no innovation due to product or context characteristics, indeed, not all sectors rely upon innovation, as a consequence, some FBs may opt not to innovate behaving as followers, simply imitating their competitors (Munari et al., 2010). However, the decision process of whether or not innovate must be free and conscientious and not constrained by hindering factors. In general, innovation is desirable, and as a consequence public policies should be encouraging innovative attitudes, providing FBs the accurate instruments in their innovation strategies allowing them to implement new ideas, to consolidate their position in the market.

Providing a detailed analysis of innovation inside these particular business structures is of central importance to policy makers given the number and importance of these organisations inside the industrial fabric of the country. FBs must be supported by the public policy given their importance in job market stabilisation, and smoothing the adversity of recessions. In the present context, in which very few is known about how long will it take for the economic rebirth, FBs will be central in the support of local communities, in the establishment of proximity ties and generate new economic dynamics

Internationalisation in FBs

Opening the operation to other markets may help firms in general; and FBs in particular in their long term success. Internationalisation provides the firm the opportunity to expand to new markets, and exploiting of economies of scale along with the access to diversified tangible and intangible assets, new consumers and preferences. Internationalization is a multidimensional process of cross-border flows and activities, this strategy can be classified as a growth strategy for companies. Therefore pursuing this action will lead to enlarged market opportunities, scale effects among others (Piva et al., 2013).

In an already globalised market, firms only have to decide if their internationalisation will be active or passive, if they are about to be movers or recipients. Actively taking part in the process requires flexibility and ability to observe and adapt as organisations need to meet the standards of the new markets either on the demand or the supply side. The process is hard and requires preparation nevertheless; the involvement, commitment and resilience of family members will soften the barriers; besides due to their commitment to stewardship and longevity, the likelihood of success will increase (Gallo and Sveen, 1991).

The presence in multiple markets, including the international reinforces economic performance, given the micro and macroeconomic advantages inherent to scalability and exposure to different business cycles (Kontinen and Ojala, 2010; Hagemejer and Kolasa, 2011; Swoboda and Olejnik, 2013; Piva et al., 2013). As a consequence, internationalisation process reinforces competitiveness despite requiring adaptive skills inside the organisational structure. Being emerged in multiple markets raises direct and indirect competition; as both internally and internationally the firm is pushed towards the constant seek for improvement and efficiency being otherwise stifled by worldwide competitors (Kafouros et al., 2008).

When fearing identity loss and control somehow inherent to this process, FBs may feel uncomfortable within internationalisation; nonetheless, identity preservation determines the success of this operation. Being unwilling to approach the new markets and build networked establishments will jeopardise the success of the operation (Gomez-Mejia et al., 2011; Pukall and Calabrò, 2014). It is therefore desirable that FBs bear in mind their values and tradition. Part of their unique identity to solidly approach the new markets consequently raising their probability to internationaly succeed.

Organisations which opt for closing their structures and focusing on a single market structure may lose competitiveness due to, in one hand, the obsolescence of their products concerning the dynamics of consumers' preferences, and on the other the presence of foreign alternatives on the domestic market

(Gallo, M. and Sveen, J., 1991; Pukall and Calabrò, 2014). As at present firms operate in unstable environments facing global threats and globalised competition standards, with shrinking product lifecycles and changing consumer preferences scaling production and minimising the risks connected to dependencies will reinforce performance.

Other Structural Characteristics

It is widely accepted that, at the macroeconomic level, education promotes growth (Ganotakis, 2012). When moving to the microeconomic domain, it is also proved a positive connection between human capital intensity and firm survival (e.g. Collier et al., 2011; Herstad et al. 2013). Innovation success depends on the endowments of resources such as human capital, technological accumulation, efficiency in the innovation process, the recognition of usability of external knowledge flows, its assimilation and internal transformation into commercial use (Cohen et al, 1990; Dosi, 1988; Lall, 1992).

Introducing new products and processes will boost the short run and long run productive potential, influencing performance in different dimensions (Lööf and Heshmati, 2006). Experience, and heritage enables the accumulation of learning-by-doing and learning-by-failing effects, as former success raises firm's R&D efficiency, and the second reinforces weaknesses and avoids the duplication of errors (Maidique and Zirger, 1985; Zirger, 1997 García-Vega and López, 2010).

Highly skilled human capital endowments will reinforce the ability to generate innovations as these staff members have an increased absorptive capacity which permits the utilisation of external knowledge flows in favour of the internal processes along with shared knowledge and simpler communication about innovation projects. Human resources by putting their skills at the service of the firm will allow a bifurcated innovation strategy: innovator or adopter. Due to their skills they will work as problem solvers in a daily basis, with intrapreneurial competences (Asonitou, S and Kavoura, A, 2019), raising the efficiency and timing of the innovation cycles. The availability of a higher quantity of educated workers will raise the productivity levels, internationalisation and innovation propensity and indirectly the propensity of the new products to be implemented and sold on the market which means that, human capital boosts economic performance (Asplund and Sandin, 1999).

The multiplicity of competences among the staff rises to propensity succeed of the manager (West and Noel, 2009), yet the success of R&D projects is strongly tied on the managers' competences (Chen et al., 2012). The formal education of person in charge is a good proxy for its vision and decision capacities (Sluis et al., 2008). Accordingly, skilled managers will make better decisions, consequently improving the performance of the firm. Managers must have multiple skills to grasp and increased ability to face the daily challenges and become efficient problem solvers (Koellinger, 2008).

When combining managerial skills with educated staff, firms will have an enhanced propensity to develop innovation related activities and absorb the existing knowledge reinforcing firm performance in multiple dimensions (Marrocu and Paci, 2012). Educated multidisciplinary stocks of human capital combined with accurate managerial skills will consolidate firm performance.

By nature, innovative activities are riskier than others; nevertheless they have high payoffs, despite the failure probability. Inside FBs due to the existence of strong values such as tradition and loyalty, along with family involvement, and commitment to survival, actions will be taken to accommodate market changeovers (van der Panne et al., 2003; Claver, et al., 2008).

According to the literature, on average, FBs present lower R&D levels when compared to other non-family firms with similar characteristics (Artz, et al., 2010), still it is not straightforward that they are less innovative, perhaps due to their specific characteristics, such as being more engaged with informal networks and knowledge flows along with multitasking, they are more efficient in innovation (Duran et al., 2016). R&D intensity and innovative output correlation is moderated by factors such as regional knowledge spillovers, demand-pull effects or differences in technological opportunity (Maidique and Zirger, 1985; Zirger, 1997 García-Vega and López, 2010). However, the effect is non-linear (Chen et al., 2012).

FBs operating in technological intensive sectors tend to be more dynamic, and more prone to develop innovation and internationalisation processes, as they present increased dynamism and possess the human capital stock to absorb the knowledge externalities which combined with the internal synergies will boost efficiency (Piva et al.,2013).

Table 1. Innovative strategies

Innovation Types	Innovative activities		Number of firms	TOTAL
Product Innovation	Single	n	2	69
		%	1,82%	
	Combined	n	67	
		%	60,90%	
Process Innovation	Single	n	3	68
		%	0,27%	
	Combined	n	65	
		%	59,09%	
Technological Innovation	Single	n	5	61
		%	4,55%	
	Combined	n	56	
		%	50,91%	
Organisational Innovation	Single	n	4	71
		%	3,64%	
	Combined	n	67	
		%	60,90%	
Marketing Innovation	Single	n	3	68
		%	2,73%	
	Combined	n	65	
		%	59,09%	

Firms with few years of activity and with few workers and the consequent exiguity in the stock of human capital that opt for pursuing innovation and internationalisation strategies, which are, by nature risky, may put themselves in danger, potentially facing severe financial constraints (Hadjimanolis, 1999). On the other side, larger firms may have alternative sources of finance, combined with an internal capability to take risks, being more capable to exploit new ideas, and to diffuse in the scale of production the sunk costs associated with innovation and internationalisation. Large organisations naturally have a higher endowment of workers with multiplicity of skills and are more prone to benefit from economies of scale; in a virtuous cycle, success will breed success and they will become more interested in innovation along with market expansion as it represents, for them a lower risk (Piva et al, 2013). The potential success of these endeavours is higher as the value of the stock of human capital is higher due to diversity (Giovannetti et al, 2013) moreover, the dimension of the organogram allow for concentrating in specific tasks rather than being compelled to multi task, which reinforces learning effects. Naturally, focusing on tasks will raise productivity due to repetition, which at the aggregate level boosts overall performance (Broekaert et al., 2016). Some hope is put on the flexibility effect over innovation, which is found very often in small FBs (Freel, 2000).

Understanding the enhancers of the economic performance of FBs is central as older literature has focused on the link between endowments of resources and performance, hence, more recent debates have emphasised the role of governance. As FBs have singularities in their governance (Siebels and Aufseß, 2012), which differ from other organisational structures. Analysis of the factors affecting economic performance of FBs can be divided into three branches: the first, tying performance to managerial competences relying on explicit and tacit competences. The second correlates economic performance with firm characteristics; and the third connecting firms' economic performance with the business environment. Here, the empirical relies on a combination among them, being closer to the second.

DATABASE AND EXPLORATORY RESULTS

Database

Empirical analysis will be performed based on a purposeful survey sent to Portuguese Family Businesses[1] included in the AICEP[2] database. The database includes firms operating in different economic sectors, with different dimensions sizes, belonging to heterogeneous technological regimes, and singular innovative and internationalisation strategies and other structural characteristics. The respondent sample includes 110 FBs operating in Portugal. Respondent firms provided information about structural characteristics, economic performance among other variables. Data will be statistically threated to highlight the role of innovation and internationalisation in the economic performance of FBs.

The following section provides a general overview of the respondent sample to appraise its composition concerning the structural characteristics in analysis. The database encompasses information concerning economic performance, innovation and internationalisation strategies, combined with a set of firm structural characteristics (firm size, SIC code, economic sector, technological intensity, education intensity, R&D intensity). This set of variables will be of use in a twofold appraisal: exploratory analysis and econometric estimations.

Exploratory Results

Concerning the variables in use to build the regression equation that is further explored in the econometric models, this section provides some exploratory results to characterise the 110 respondents in respect to their characteristics.

Size

The respondent sample includes mostly firms classified as being small; meaning that nearly three quarters of the respondents have a staff with less than 50 workers. The other quarter encompasses medium sized firms (ranging from 50 to 249 workers). No large firms are included on the sample. The distribution is to some extent similar to the Portuguese industrial fabric as most of the firms are small and medium sized.

Figure 1. Firms per size

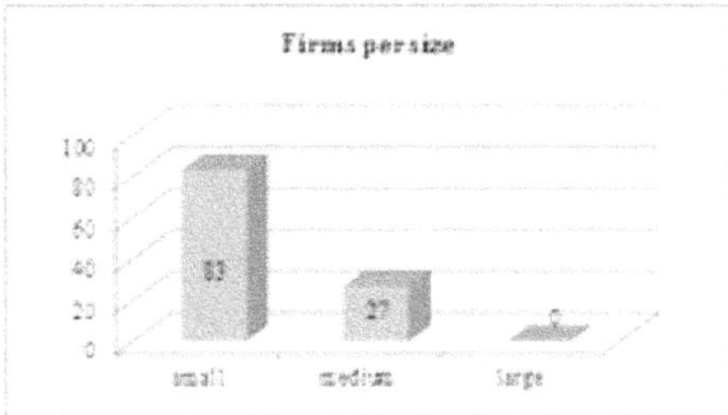

Economic Sector

The sample covers firms from the primary to the tertiary sector, as there are FBs operating in all kinds of activities. Nonetheless, manufacturing firms are the most important branch of activity, which is bonding to the research topic, as innovation and internationalisation strategies are more often studied in this sector. In that vein, firms with Industrial SIC Codes represent 48% of the sample.

Figure 2. Firms per Economic sector

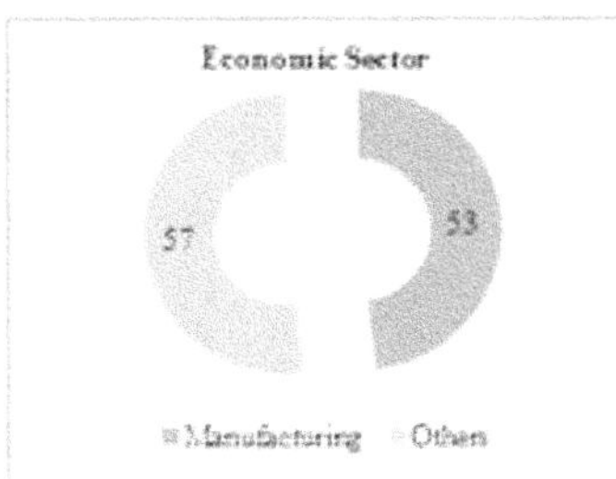

Manager Skills

Concerning the relevant skills of the manager, the literature has identified two major competences enhancing the innovative and internationalisation strategy: undergraduate in either engineering or economics. Results evidence half of the managers having an undergraduate in either engineering or economics.

Having this achievement proves that Portuguese FBs tend to have professional and qualified managers. Frequently the literature presents the lack of skills in the managerial structure as the explanation for poor organisational performance and aversion to innovate or internationalise.

Figure 3. Managers with and undergraduate in either engineering or economics

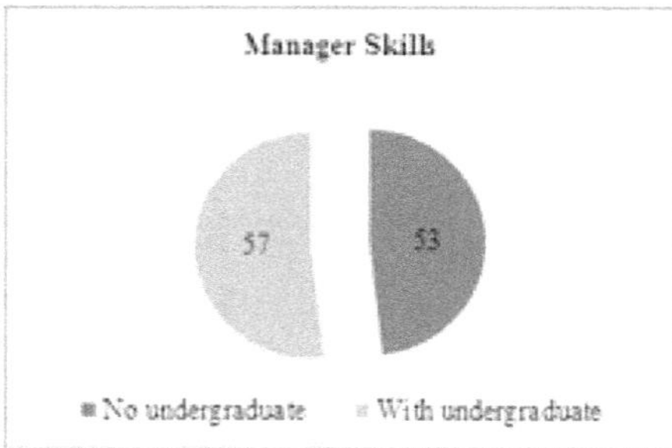

Technological Intensity

The respondent sample was segmented according to the classification proposed by Tidd et al., (2005)[3], as a consequence, the respondent sample was divided into five categories from the less intensive in technology to the most intensive in technology.

As a consequence, nearly 15% of the firms are included in low tech sectors (category 1); half of the sample operates in mid tech sectors (categories 2 and 3) and, the remaining sample 35% operates in high tech sectors.

Figure 4. Distribution according to technological intensity

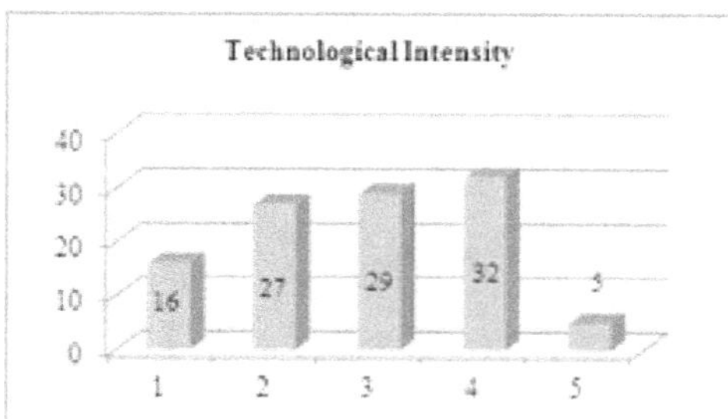

R&D Intensity

From the 110 respondents, only 43 did mention the existence of R&D expenditures, which is the same to say that 67 of them do not devote any kind of resource to innovation. Almost 60% of those making R&D expenditures devote 1-3% of the total turnover and the other 40% from 4-5% or 6-100% in equal proportions. This result deserves further analysis as it is of interest to understand the underlying reasons of this odd distribution.

Figure 5. Distribution according to R&D intensity

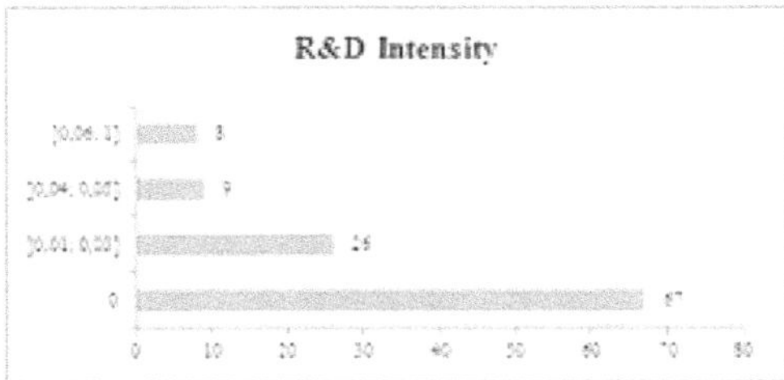

Skill Intensity

The literature strongly highlights the importance of the education levels of the staff. Organisations will raise efficiency and productivity when including members with formal education which helps them in their current tasks. Skilled workers are more able to absorb knowledge regardless its source and solve problems. The human component inside organisations is determinant for success, moreover when the aim is innovation.

Firms from the respondent sample are distributed as follows: 5% of the firms do not have any undergraduate in the staff; 60% have up to 25% of their workers with an undergraduate; and 6% of the firms had an entire staff with an undergraduate or more. Higher endowments of human capital inside FBs improve the ability to perform in different domains thus raising overall efficiency.

Figure 6. Distribution per skill intensity

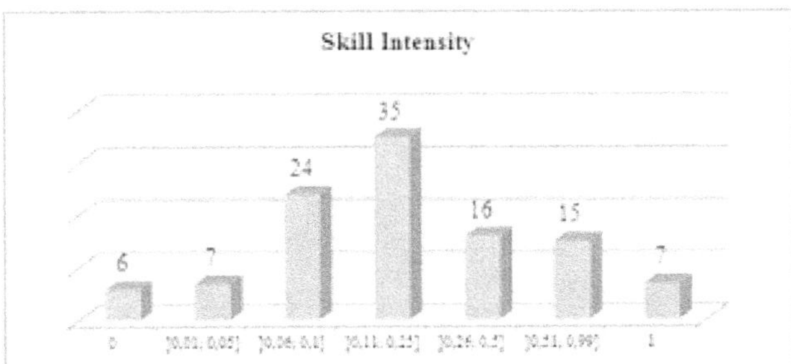

Export Intensity

As previously mentioned, internationalisation plays a central role in firm's efficiency due to spreading in operation risk. In the present analysis, internationalisation is proxied throughout export intensity (proportion of sales abroad to total sales).

The sample has an important proportion of FBs operating in foreign markets: one fifth of the firms sell their entire production abroad and 47% sell more than 25% of their products to foreign consumers. This is a solid proof of market dynamism, reinforcing the efforts to promote efficiency in a multimarket perspective.

Figure 7. Firm export intensity

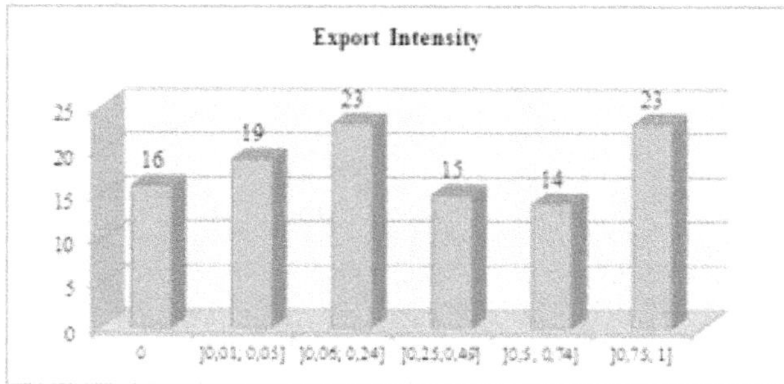

Productivity Per Worker

In terms of the proxy in use for productivity, the study relies on the yearly GVA *per worker* (in euros). This variable presents heterogeneous outcomes, the distribution ranges from *up to 1.000€,* to *more than 50.001€ per worker*. The most frequent achievement (53 firms) relies on the interval *from 10.001 to 30.000€.*

Figure 8. Firms per productivity level

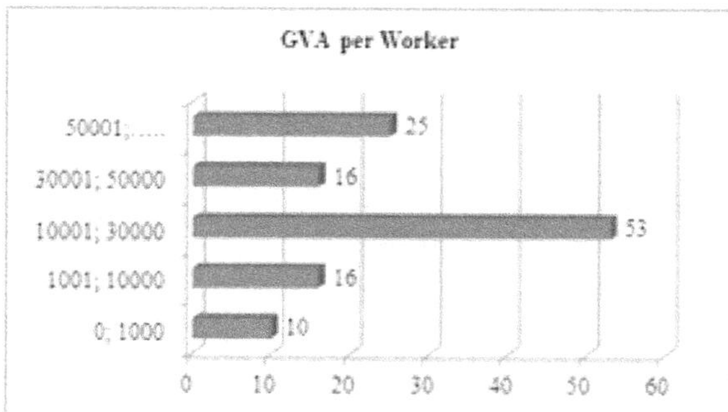

ECONOMETRIC RESULTS

Based on the theoretical arguments previously presented, this section will bring the estimation results. Summarising the previous debate, two hypotheses emerge from the literature. These empirical findings will be subsequently discussed.

Table 2. Hypothesis in test

Hypothesis	Description	Results
[H1]	Economic efficiency is positively influenced by the existence of innovative activities	Supported
[H2]	Economic efficiency is positively influenced by internationalisation	Supported

Model Specification

FBs economic efficiency will be appraised here by means of a multivariate regression. In doing so, its determinants will be identified in a ceteris paribus analysis. Models 1 and 2 will include explanatory variables relating to the hypotheses in analysis (innovation and internationalisation) added to five other controls relating to firm structural characteristics. Including controls is of major importance to avoid estimation biasedness caused by the omission of relevant variables, not directly linked to the research questions; dropping those controls will lead to the overestimation of the coefficients related to innovation and internationalisation.

Variables in Use

As previously mentioned, the dependent variable in economic performance, here it is proxied by the *Gross Value Added per Worker*, being continuous. To smooth the analysis, the logarithm of the gross value added per worker (euros per year) was considered.

To examine the determinants of economic performance at the firm level two explanatory variables were included: *Export_Intensity*, (proportion of Exports in the total revenue of the FB) and innovative performance (*Innovation*) throughout a count variable, ranging values from 0 to 4 depending on the number of innovation types performed by the firm (product, process, marketing, organisational).

The controls cover FBs structural characteristics including: technological intensity assessment in a twofold way: (*Technological_Intensity*), an increasing multinomial scale, from 1 to 5, according to the Tidd's taxonomy and (*R&D_Intensity*), ratio of R&D expenditures compared to total revenue. Then (*Managerial_Skills*), a binary variable taking the value 1 if the manager has an undergraduate in either engineering or economics; and *Human Capital_Intensity*, being the proportion of employees with at least an undergraduate degree over the total workforce and finally firm dimension (*Size*), which is the logarithm of the total workers.

Econometric Estimations

A multivariate model was used to assess the determinants of economic performance of FBs. Most of the variables are positively correlated with a moderate degree of significance. The economic performance of the firms will be approached by the explanatory variables and the structural characteristics.

Two alternative models were run (Model 1 and Model 2): the first addresses innovation and internationalisation strategies in separate, and the second include a linear combination of both to address eventual complementarities concerning the strategies. In both of the cases, the sample comprises 110 firms and models appear as statistically significant at the global level, and the Rsquared of approximately model 1 is 19,3%.

Whether or not to pursuit an innovative strategy is a firm strategical option, connected to a global entrepreneurial behaviour determinant of the firm present and determines the firm future. This means that it is part of the explanatory variables to long term success. FBs adoption innovative strategies independent of the innovation type are, accordingly to the literature more prone to present higher levels of economic efficiency. The relevance of innovation in FBs is assessed in the Next Generation family business (Deloitte University EMEA CVBA, 2017), and the majority of respondents reinforce the inclusion of innovation in their firm culture and mission statement. In model 1, innovation appears as statistically significant.

The persistent pursuit of innovation projects will reinforce the existence of comparative advantages and generate differentiation from the competitors. Innovators are able to operate from a monopolist position, and will improve their market share along with the profitability (Roberts, 1999).

Empirical evidence provided by Kim et al., (2008) and Llach and Nordqvist, (2010) and Werner et al. (2018) reinforce the increased propensity of FBs to be innovative, due to their organisational values, relying on the existence of formal and informal knowledge transfers supported by loyalty relationships, raising the efficiency levels and helping them surviving the long run. According to Model 1, each unitary increase in the collection of innovation types raises productivity by 26,6%, ceteris paribus. These results go along with the literature (Hua and Wemmerlöv, 2006; Artz et al., 2010 and Li et al., 2010) despite the difference in terms of the proxy in use. As a consequence, our hypothesis is supported by the evidence; moreover, the magnitude of the effect deserves the attention of practitioners and policy makers.

In what concerns export intensity, the empirical results reinforce the evidence from the literature; there is a positive effect of the export intensity in economic performance. A unitary change in export intensity, rises the GVA per worker by 166,7%. On average, the higher the export intensity, the higher the productivity levels. Again this result goes along with the evidence from previous works such Piva et al, (2013).

Moreover, according to Giovanetti et al. (2013) inputs to innovation are directly connected to the propensity to export, thus producing a double effect on efficiency. To address this finding Model 2 was run, to understand the eventual existence of these complementarities, notwithstanding, in our sample this combined effect fails to be statistically significant. In the respondent sample, innovation and internationalisation, when operated together fail to influence the economic efficiency.

Regarding R&D and technological intensity, no significant effect is found in the dependent variable. This result contradicts extant literature, as according to Artz et al. (2010) and Giovanetti et al. (2013) these variables improve the economic performance, as firms investing in R&D may benefit from increasing returns to scale, leveraging efficiency. Albeit, to Broekaert et al., (2016) FBs are less prone to make R&D expenditures compared to their non-family counterparts. Investments in R&D can be considered as an input to innovation, which combined with the technological regime, the availability of human capital and the managerial competences will boost economic performance throughout innovation success.

Managerial skills also fail to be statistically significant in our model. The effect of the CEO's undergraduate in Engineering or Economics does not affect the productivity levels. In the present case, education intensity of the manger does not affect performance.

Vis-à-vis human capital intensity, the effect is statistically significant; still it contradicts our previous epectation that the increase in the proportion of workers with an undergraduate should rise the GVA_*per_worker*. In model 2, this coefficient is also statistically significant and negative. This result is hardly explainable, even though, it may be linked to other structural characteristics or even the innovation strategy.

Relating to size, firms, independent of the capital ownership want to grow and succeed; nevertheless, size may generate handicaps mostly in what connected to efficiency and innovation based on the need for fast exploitation of market opportunities. Large firms are often slower and less plastic in their decision making processes, and that may hinder innovation and internationalisation, but for certain will have effects on economic efficiency. Small sized firms may accommodate market turbulence faster. However, they lack the financial and human resources to adopt innovation and internationalisation. In the present estimation, the elasticity of economic efficiency with respect to size fails to be statistically significant. So, despite the previous belief, dimension fails to affect firms' economic performance.

Table 3. Estimation results

Dependent variable: Productivity (gross value added per worker (ln))									
Variable	**Description**	**Estimate**	**SE**	**T-Statistic**	**P-value**	**Estimate**	**SE**	**T-Statistic**	**P-value**
Innovation	**Innovation types**	***0,266***	**0,144**	**1,854**	**0,067**				
Export_Intensity	**Exports to sales**	***1,667***	**0,580**	**2,875**	**0,005**				
Innov X Exp_Int	Combined strategy					0,326	0,196	1,661	0,100
Technological_Int	Sectoral intensity	-0,076	0,179	-0,423	0,673	-0,080	0,184	-0,435	0,665
Managerial_Skills	Education of Managers	0,385	0,440	0,876	0,383	0,398	0,461	0,863	0,390
R&D_ Intensity	R&D to sales	5,810	5,539	1,049	0,297	7,626	5,570	1,369	0,174
HC_Intensity	Proportion of undergraduates	-1,473	0,824	-1,788	0,077	-1,804	0,804	-2,245	0,027
Size	Workers (ln)	0,102	0,198	0,512	0,610	0,003	0,005	0,623	0,534
constant		8,247	0,977	8,437	0,000	9,474	0,681	13,906	0,000

CONCLUSION AND POLICY PACKAGE

With the present chapter authors aimed at empirically address productivity determinants in FBs, the emphasis was put on the role of innovation and internationalisation as enhancers of this performance. The empirical analysis encompasses a purposeful database of firms operating in the context of a moderate innovator, Portugal. The analysis of these organisations in this environment is of particular interest as most of the evidence is connected to innovation leaders, additionally, these organisations are the backbone of the Portuguese economy and mirror most of the entrepreneurial initiative; understanding their singularities will help policy makers in understanding the most important source of income and job creation.

FBs evidence the dynamism of the individual and collective entrepreneurial initiative, and their existence is more than ever determinant to the achievement of sustainability, avoid severe bumps over downturns in terms of job erosion and social exclusion. Regional cohesion is strongly connected by these firms due to the proximity effect they have in communities and staff, throughout informal networks. Given the classification of Portugal as a moderate innovator (EIS, 2019), expectably FBs will evidence a weak performance in terms of innovation and internationalisation despite the importance of these factors to firm success.

Firm dimension should positively affect innovative performance; empirical results do not sustain this theoretical proposal. Finding firm size irrelevant is important to rethink preconceived policy actions which positively discriminate large firms. So, they should not be the primary beneficiaries of public funds by means of subsidisation. This result is particularly interesting as policy makers argue in favour of these organisations and the collective benefit they generate, granting them fiscal benefits or subsidies due to their importance as innovation engines and vast job creators. It seems more efficient to encompass in the policy guidelines mandatory connections with the local community reinforcing the ties inside the ecosystem, cohesive territories support their citizens and prevent exclusion. In the present scenario, in which the future is an open question with uncertain answer, local communities are the epicentre of fast and sustainable recoveries.

Additionally, the irrelevance of technological intensity also deserves further analysis, as very often it works as a criterion to benefit from grants. In this vein, the recommendation is to support efficient firms rather than sectors of clusters regardless of their practices.

Inputs to innovation such as R&D expenditures fail to affect FBs performance; again preconceived ideas that work as guidelines for conventional policy making seem to be inaccurate. Perhaps due to their exiguous structure, firms in the sample need to find alternatives to boost productive potential due to potential difficulties in financing innovation. Once more, Governants should consider this result as a warning and approach Universities, Government Labs and Public institutes to this industrial fabric to help overcoming drawbacks, substituting internal sources of knowledge for external consequently generating open innovation spells.

The existence of a skilled labour force should raise the effectiveness of the innovative activities as well as the economic performance, but, in this case, is the opposite. This result potentially supports the trade-off between increased productivity and wage differentials. FBs not hiring qualified personnel will become more vulnerable to innovation and internationalisation failure. Again, policy actions should reinforce the role of the Academia as a supplier of undergraduates which are vehicles of knowledge transfer, whose capabilities should become valuable assets for FBs.

Policy packages must consider innovation as an engine of growth inside FBs, and diversity and multidimensional strategies continuously reinforce firm performance. In this vein, incentives to develop innovative strategies simultaneously including different innovation types are more efficient than singular strategies.

Given that internationalisation was proved to leverage efficiency, reinforcing the presence in foreign markets will push FBs to a highly competitive layer. FBs lacking some competences may fear internal constraints in both internationalisation and innovation strategy implementation aborting or postponing valuable projects, thus minimising risks. Once again, policy actions should mitigate this problem promoting the establishment of solid connections with the Academia and other firms, reinforcing the generation of common synergies.

Further analysis is required in terms of the theoretical complementarity of innovation and internationalisation. Future avenues of research need to deeply understand if there is bi-univocal connection between them, or if they are independent. Additionally, causality analysis should be performed, impossible to run in cross sectional samples such as the present, in doing so potential self-selection doubts in terms of economic efficiency will vanish.

Helix[4] reliance may be the cornerstone to overall improvement of FBs performance. Bearing in mind the recent health[5] problems with unprecedented economic consequences, concentrating on FBs to promote a sustainable and fast recovery is central. Policy actions should meet the specificities of these organisations and promote a model in which the economics of sharing solves most of the hinderers to FBs economic performance.

An inclusive multi-level policy strategy should be designed promoting local development, and FBs are in the foundations of inclusive communities. The future brings enormous challenges and trust must be reinforced to rebuild the economies and the entrepreneurial ecosystems; and it seems that the proximity structures are more engaging to individuals.

REFERENCES

Acs, Z., & Audretsch, D. (1987). Innovation, Market Structure, and Firm Size. *The Review of Economics and Statistics*, *69*(4), 567–575. doi:10.2307/1935950

Acs, Z., & Audretsch, D. (1988). Innovation in large and small firms: An empirical analysis. *The American Economic Review*, *78*, 680–681.

Anderson, R., & Reeb, D. (2003). Founding-Family Ownership and Firm Performance: Evidence from the S&P 500. *The Journal of Finance*, *58*(3), 1301–1328. doi:10.1111/1540-6261.00567

Artz, K. W., Norman, P. M., Hatfield, D. E., & Cardinal, L. B. (2010). A longitudinal study of the impact of R&D, patents, and product innovation on firm performance. *Journal of Product Innovation Management*, *27*(5), 725–740. doi:10.1111/j.1540-5885.2010.00747.x

Asonitou, S., & Kavoura, A. (2019). Accounting education, technology and entrepreneurship: Current trends and future outlook. *The Malopolska School of Economics in Tarnow Research Papers Collection*, *44*(4), 65–78.

Asplund, M., & Sandin, R. (1999). The survival of new products. *Review of Industrial Organization*, *15*(3), 219–237. doi:10.1023/A:1007708612713

Baldwin, J., & Lin, Z. (2002). Impediments to advanced technology adoption for Canadian manufacturers. *Research Policy*, *31*(1), 1–18. doi:10.1016/S0048-7333(01)00110-X

Bhattacharya, S., & Ritter, J. (1985). Innovation and communication: Signalling with partial disclosure. *The Review of Economic Studies*, *50*(2), 331–346. doi:10.2307/2297419

Block, J. (2012). R&D Investments in Family and Founder Firms: An Agency Perspective. *Journal of Business Venturing*, *27*(2), 248–265. doi:10.1016/j.jbusvent.2010.09.003

Broekaert, W., Andries, P., & Debackere, K. (2016). Innovation processes in family firms: The relevance of organizational flexibility. *Small Business Economics*, *47*(3), 771–785. doi:10.100711187-016-9760-7

Canepa, A., & Stoneman, P. (2002). *Financial constraints on innovations: A European cross-country study*. Working Paper no. 02–11, Kiel Institute of World Economics.

Chen, Y., Chang, K., & Chang, C. (2012). Nonlinear influence on R&D project performance. *Technological Forecasting and Social Change*, *79*(8), 1537–1547. doi:10.1016/j.techfore.2012.04.007

Chua, J., Chrisman, J., & Sharma, P. (1999). Defining the family business by behaviour. *Entrepreneurship Theory and Practice*, *23*(4), 19–39. doi:10.1177/104225879902300402

Chua, J., Chrisman, J., Steier, L., & Rau, S. (2012). Sources of Heterogeneity in Family Firms: An Introduction. *Entrepreneurship Theory and Practice*, *36*(6), 1103–1113. doi:10.1111/j.1540-6520.2012.00540.x

Claver, E., Rienda, L., & Quer, D. (2008). Family firms' risk perception: Empirical evidence on the internationalization process. *Journal of Small Business and Enterprise Development*, *15*(3), 457–471. doi:10.1108/14626000810892283

Collier, W., Green, F., Kim, Y.-B., & Peirson, J. (2011). Education, training and economic performance: Evidence from establishment survival data. *Journal of Labor Research*, *32*(4), 336–361. doi:10.100712122-011-9116-7

Costa, J., Botelho, A., & Matias, J. (2018). *Entrepreneurship along the Industry Life Cycle: The changing role of Entrepreneurial Activities and Knowledge Competencies* (S. Cubico, G. Favretto, J. Leitão, & U. Cantner, Eds.). Springer.

de Clercq, D., & Belausteguigoitia, I. (2015). Intergenerational Strategy Involvement and Family Firms' Innovation Pursuits: The Critical Roles of Conflict Management and Social Capital. *Journal of Family Business Strategy*, *6*(3), 178–189. doi:10.1016/j.jfbs.2015.04.003

de Massis, A., Frattini, F., Kotlar, J., Messeni-Petruzzelli, A., & Wright, M. (2016). Innovation through tradition: Lessons from innovative family businesses and directions for future research. *The Academy of Management Perspectives*, *30*(1), 93–116. doi:10.5465/amp.2015.0017

de Massis, A., Frattini, F., & Lichtenthaler, U. (2013). Research on Technological Innovation in Family Firms: Present Debates and Future Directions. *Family Business Review*, *26*(1), 10–31. doi:10.1177/0894486512466258

de Massis, A., Frattini, F., Pizzurno, E., & Cassia, L. (2015). Product innovation in family versus non family firms: An exploratory analysis. *Journal of Small Business Management*, *53*(1), 1–36. doi:10.1111/jsbm.12068

Deloitte University EMEA CVBA. (2017). *Next Generation family businesses. Leading a family business in a disruptive environment.* https://www2.deloitte.com/content/dam/Deloitte/ua/Documents/strategy/Next-generation-family-business.pdf

Eddleston, A., Rodrigo-Alarcón, J., Parra-Requena, G., García-Villaverde, P., Bolo, A., Muchemi, A., & Gomez-Mejia, L. (2012). The Succession Process from a Resource- and Knowledge-Based View of the Family Firm. *Family Business Review*, *2*(1), 328–353.

European Commission. (2019). *European Innovation Scoreboard.* Author.

Freel, M. (2000). Do Small Innovating Firms Outperform Non-innovators? *Small Business Economics*, *14*(3), 195–210. doi:10.1023/A:1008100206266

Gallo, M., & Sveen, J. (1991). Internationalizing the Family Business: Facilitating and Restraining Factors. *Family Business Review*, *4*(2), 181–190. doi:10.1111/j.1741-6248.1991.00181.x

Garcia, R., & Calantone, R. (2002). A critical look at technological innovation typology and innovativeness terminology: A literature review. *Journal of Product Innovation Management*, *19*(2), 110–132. doi:10.1111/1540-5885.1920110

Geroski, P., Machin, S., & van Reenen, J. (1993). The Profitability of Innovating Firms. *The RAND Journal of Economics*, *24*(2), 198–211. doi:10.2307/2555757

Geroski, P., van Reenen, J., & Walters, C. (1997). How persistently do firms innovate? *Research Policy*, *26*(1), 33–48. doi:10.1016/S0048-7333(96)00903-1

Giovannetti, G., Ricchiuti, G., & Velucchi, M. (2013). Location, internationalization and performance of firms in Italy: A multilevel approach. *Applied Economics*, *45*(18), 2665–2673. doi:10.1080/00036846.2012.665597

Gomez-Mejia, L., Cruz, C., Berrone, P., & de Castro, J. (2011). The Bind that ties: Socio-emotional wealth preservation in family firms. *The Academy of Management Annals*, *5*(1), 653–707. doi:10.5465/19416520.2011.593320

Hadjimanolis, A. (1999). Barriers to innovation for SMEs in a small less developed country (Cyprus). *Technovation*, *19*(9), 561–570. doi:10.1016/S0166-4972(99)00034-6

Hajivassiliou, V., & Savingnac, F. (2008). *Financing Constraints and a Firm's Decision and Ability to Innovate: Establishing Direct and Reverse Effects. Notes d'Études et de Recherche 202*. Banque de France.

Herstad, S., Sandven, T., & Solberg, E. (2013). Location, education and enterprise growth. *Applied Economics Letters*, *20*(10), 1019–1022. doi:10.1080/13504851.2013.772287

Heunks, F. (1998). Innovation, Creativity and Success. *Small Business Economics*, *10*(3), 263–272. doi:10.1023/A:1007968217565

Hua, S., & Wemmerlöv, U. (2006). Product change intensity, product advantage, and market performance: An empirical investigation of the PC industry. *Journal of Product Innovation Management*, *23*(4), 316–329. doi:10.1111/j.1540-5885.2006.00204.x

Kafouros, M., Buckley, P., Sharp, J., & Wang, C. (2008). The role of internacionalization in explaining innovation performance. *Technovation*, *28*(1-2), 63–74. doi:10.1016/j.technovation.2007.07.009

Kellermanns, F., Eddleston, K., Sarathy, R., & Murphy, F. (2012). Innovativeness in family firms: A family influence perspective. *Small Business Economics*, *38*(1), 85–101. doi:10.100711187-010-9268-5

Kim, H., Kim, H., & Lee, P. M. (2008). Ownership structure and the relationship between financial slack and R&D investments:dence from Korean firms. *Organization Science*, *19*(3), 404–418. doi:10.1287/orsc.1080.0360

Koellinger, P. (2008). Why are some entrepreneurs more innovative than others? *Small Business Economics*, *31*(1), 21–37. doi:10.100711187-008-9107-0

Kontinen, T., & Ojala, A. (2010). Internationalization pathways of family SMEs: Psychic distance as a focal point. *Journal of Small Business and Enterprise Development*, *17*(3), 437–454. doi:10.1108/14626001011068725

Kraiczy, N. (2013). *Innovations in Small and Medium-Sized Family Firms: An Analysis of Innovation Related Top Management Team Behaviors and Family Firm-Specific Characteristics*. Springer. doi:10.1007/978-3-658-00063-9

Li, Y., Su, Z., & Liu, Y. (2010). Can strategic flexibility help firms profit from product innovation? *Technovation*, *30*(5-6), 300–309. doi:10.1016/j.technovation.2009.07.007

Llach, J., & Nordqvist, M. (2010). Innovation in family and non-family businesses: A resource perspective. *International Journal of Entrepreneurial Venturing*, *2*(3), 381–399. doi:10.1504/IJEV.2010.037119

Lööf, H., & Heshmati, A. (2006). On the relationship between innovation and performance: A sensitivity analysis. *Economics of Innovation and New Technology*, *15*(4/5), 317–344. doi:10.1080/10438590500512810

Marrocu, E., & Paci, R. (2012). Education or creativity: What matters most for economic performance? *Economic Geography*, *88*(4), 369–401. doi:10.1111/j.1944-8287.2012.01161.x

Masouras, A. (2019). *Entrepreneurship in Small and Medium-Sized Enterprises.* Nova Publishers.

Miller, D. (2006). Technological diversity, related diversification, and firm performance. *Strategic Management Journal*, *27*(7), 601–619. doi:10.1002mj.533

Miller, D., & Le Breton-Miller, I. (2014). Deconstructing socioemotional wealth. *Entrepreneurship Theory and Practice*, *38*(4), 713–720. doi:10.1111/etap.12111

Mohnen, P., & Röller, L.-H. (2005). Complementarities in innovation policy. *European Economic Review*, *49*(6), 1431–1450. doi:10.1016/j.euroecorev.2003.12.003

Munari, F., Oriani, R., & Sobrero, M. (2010). The Effects of Owner Identity and External Governance Systems on R&D Investments: A Study of Western European Firms. *Research Policy*, *39*(8), 1093–1104. doi:10.1016/j.respol.2010.05.004

Nieto, M., Santamaria, L., & Fernandez, Z. (2015). Understanding the innovation behavior of family firms. *Journal of Small Business Management*, *53*(2), 382–399. doi:10.1111/jsbm.12075

Piva, E., Rossi-Lamastra, C., & De Massis, A. (2013). Family firms and internationalization: An exploratory study on high-tech entrepreneurial ventures. *Journal of International Entrepreneurship*, *10*(1), 109–129. doi:10.100710843-012-0100-y

Pizzurno, E., & Alberti, F. (2013). Technology innovation and performance in family firm. *International Journal of Entrepreneurship and Innovation Management*, *17*(1/2/3), 142–161. doi:10.1504/IJEIM.2013.055253

Price Waterhouse Coopers. (2016). *Inquérito Global sobre Empresas Familiares 2016*. Available at: https://www.pwc.pt/pt/publicacoes/family-business/pwc-family-business-2016.pdf

Pukall, T., & Calabrò, A. (2014). The Internationalization of Family Firms: A Critical Review and Integrative Model. *Family Business Review*, *27*(2), 103–125. doi:10.1177/0894486513491423

Schumpeter, J. (1934). Harvard Economic Studies: Vol. 46. *The theory of economic development: an inquiry into profits, capital, credit, interest and the business cycle*. Harvard College.

Schumpeter, J. (1942). Capitalism, Socialism and Democracy (3rd ed.). London: George Allen and Unwin.

Siebels, J.-F., & Aufseß, D. (2012). A Review of Theory in Family Business Research. *The Implications for Corporate Governance*, *14*, 280–304.

Sluis, J., Praag, M., & Vijverberg, W. (2008). Education and entrepreneurship selection and performance: A review of the empirical literature. *Journal of Economic Surveys*, *22*(5), 795–841. doi:10.1111/j.1467-6419.2008.00550.x

Souitaris, V. (2001). External communication determinants of innovation in the context of newly industrialised country: A comparison of objective and perceptual results from Greece. *Technovation*, *21*(1), 25–34. doi:10.1016/S0166-4972(00)00014-6

Swoboda, B., & Olejnik, E. (2013). A taxonomy of small and medium-sized international family firms. *Journal of International Entrepreneurship*, *10*(1), 130–157. doi:10.100710843-012-0101-x

Teece, D. (1996). Firm organization, industrial structure, and technological innovation. *Journal of Economic Behavior & Organization*, *31*(2), 193–224. doi:10.1016/S0167-2681(96)00895-5

van der Panne, G., van Beers, C., & Kleinknecht, A. (2003). Success and failure of innovation: A literature review. *International Journal of Innovation Management*, *7*(3), 1–30. doi:10.1142/S1363919603000830

Werner, Schroder, & Chlosta. (2018). Driving factors of innovation in family and non-family SMEs. *Small Business Economics, 50*(1), 201–218.

West, G. III, & Noel, T. (2009). The impact of knowledge resources on new venture performance. *Journal of Small Business Management*, *47*(1), 1–22. doi:10.1111/j.1540-627X.2008.00259.x

Zirger, B. (1997). The Influence of Development Experience and Product Innovativeness on Product Outcome. *Technology Analysis and Strategic Management*, *9*(3), 287–297. doi:10.1080/09537329708524285

ENDNOTES

1 An enlarged treatment of this data with diverse focus was made in a FEUP thesis from Pedro Oliveira (2011).

2 Agência para o Investimento e Comércio Externo de Portugal, E.P.E.

3 The taxonomy adopted follows Tidd, J., Bessant, J. and Pavitt, K. 2005. Managing innovation: Integrating technological, market and organizational change, 3rd edition. John Wiley & Sons.

4 Framework firstly proposed by Etzkowitz and Leydesdorff in the article:The dynamics of innovation: from National Systems and ''Mode 2'' to a Triple Helix of university–industry–government relations, with further developments to the Quadruple and the Quintuple.

5 In March 2020 the World was devastated by a pandemic crisis caused by a Corona Virus called COVID19.

Chapter 13
Local Authorities' Incubator as a Tool Supporting the Synergies Between Companies That Apply Corporate Social Responsibility and Social Enterprises

Anastasios K. Sepetis
University of West Attica, Greece

Marilena G. Sanida
University of Piraeus, Greece

George Pierrakos
University of West Attica, Greece

ABSTRACT

The local authorities' incubator for social enterprises should be supporting the connection of local companies that apply CSR with social enterprises that are trying to succeed social value. The research in this chapter relied on a systematic literature review. After reviewing the literature, a methodology has been developed that describes the process of designing and implementing a local authorities' incubator and the synergies with social enterprises and CSR. The benefit of a local authorities' incubator in the field of social entrepreneurship is the facilitation of new social enterprises to overcome knowledge barriers and implement best business practices. Finally, in this chapter, it is suggested that the cooperation between local companies that apply CSR and local social enterprises under the guidance and support of local authorities' incubator could create synergies and produce new local certified PGI (protected geographical indication) or PDO (protected designations of origin) social/ethical/green/fair-trade products and services and promote the local economy.

DOI: 10.4018/978-1-7998-3648-3.ch013

INTRODUCTION

The present chapter targets on how Local Authorities use Corporate Social Responsibility in order to reinforce Social Enterprises through the business tool of a Business Incubator. In a quickly transforming global economy, social enterprises are a steadily growing power for the enforcement of national economic development and employment. In the European level, the incubator is a common tool for economic strengthening and development of social enterprises. It is essential that Local authorities need to create and support social enterprises through incubators, especially in enterprises that focus on social innovation.

In the chapter entitled "The role of Local Authorities" is described how Local Authorities act as a coordinator between local stakeholders and businesses in order to contribute to supporting vulnerable social groups and aim to reduce unemployment through entrepreneurship. This particular role is not limited in providing subsidies but by making sensible use of Corporate Social Responsibility takes initiatives for the creation of a mutual support network between private and social businesses, aims at the development of social and economic environment. Within this framework, by taking advantage of financial subsidy tools and for the initial support of social businesses, Local Authorities create a supportive services network of social enterprises in their initial steps, which takes the form of an incubator. In the chapter entitled "Local Authorities Incubator" an extend reference is made in the incubator services and includes education, consulting, leadership and accounting support through concrete strategies. Part of the resources for the operation of the incubator comes from private local businesses in the framework of corporate social responsibility. Corporate Social Responsibility is an important part of businesses in their effort to gain an improved and better understanding of local society and their opinion for businesses that operate within their territory. See chapter Promotion of Synergies with Social Enterprises. It overcomes the plain term of corporate philanthropy and gets a business dimension in strengthening social capital that refers to social cohesion, social solidarity and social development. Supporting social entrepreneurship on behalf of businesses constitutes an important action of private businesses in the framework of corporate social responsibility.

This chapter has as a goal to: a) to support the necessity of corporate social responsibility that would work as a factor enhancing social capital of business organizations and entrepreneurship links with local society b) to highlight the role of local authorities as a regulator of the relationship between business action and social enterprises, c) the necessity to make good use of the incubator in supporting social entrepreneurship in its first steps, d) to promote actions for producing new local certified- PGI (Protected Geographical Indication) or P.D.O (Protected Designations of Origin) social/ ethical/green fair-trade products and services resulting from the cooperation and synergies of local businesses that apply CSR and local social enterprises in the context of the operation of Local Authorities Incubator.

BACKGROUND

During the last years, businesses regardless their shape, recognize the need to implement responsible business practices for protecting themselves from dangers that can affect their reputation. They realize they should stand on a responsible way towards their employees and the local society. In this framework, they adapt a new way of business trade beyond the classical approach of philanthropy. They add a new parameter in their business success, apart from the quality and the price of their products, which is their complete stance and contribution to the implementation of better working practices, they develop caring actions for Local Society and the protection of the environment. This consideration is well known as Corporate Social Responsibility (CSR) and has as its main target the reinforcement of Social Capital, namely special characteristics of the Local Society such as consent, trust, reciprocity, rules of social behavior and responsibility, cooperation, official and unofficial social network, access and information diffusion, social cohesion etc. Carrol (2015a) claims that nowadays, CSR is a global concept that has progressed from the interplay of thought and practice. CSR represents a language and a perspective that is known all over the world and has become increasingly vital as stakeholders have communicated that modern businesses are expected to do more than make money and obey the law (Carrol 2015a,b). Generally, CSR is a business concept according to which, companies, as well as organizations, incorporate in a voluntarily basis, social and environmental concerns in their entrepreneurial activities, as well as their contacts to other stakeholders. Basically, it concerns companies that have voluntarily decided to go beyond their legal obligations, having as their main goal to cope with the best possible way to social groups' needs (Carroll and Buchholtz 2015; Phillips 2019). Social entrepreneurship is another sector, which enforces social economy, which usually fills in the existing gaps in social services or special products in local level. Social Enterprises aim to the social and professional incorporation of disadvantaged people through the production process. From this point of view, training and employment are very important. Under the term 'Social Enterprise', their new productive role, their higher autonomy, their ability to create new employment positions and their contribution to local societies, are being underlined (Peredo and McLean 2006; Hastings and Weate, 2018). Social enterprises are included in the sector of social economy, are the result of citizens' initiatives, aim in making profit for the members of the society and show a limited interest in making profit. Their main characteristic is the participation of volunteers in the production of products and services, their autonomous function, the development of new flexible and alternative means of employment, the undertaking of financial risk and their continuous social and financial activity (Defourny and Nyssens, 2006; Saebi *et. al,* 2018).

The updated emphasis that is attributed to social entrepreneurship is based in the definition of the content, but also in the limits of defining "*Social Value*". Social value is the relationship and the contribution of companies to the society (Rispal and Bonler 2010). Mair and Marti (2006) claim that the creation of social value is very important to a Social Enterprise. It is also very important to understand the primary goal of Social Enterprise, which is the use of entrepreneurial and organizational abilities for the creation of social value through innovation. On the one side, according to Porter and Kramer (2006, 2011) the concept of corporate social responsibility practice of social value can be defined, as policies and operational practices, which strengthen a company's competition, while simultaneously upgrade the social and economic conditions in the communities, where social value is active.

Local Authorities should leverage the social value of local companies, somehow it connects to the inherent tendency of social enterprises, either to innovatively confront social or environmental problems with innovative ways or altering the old traditional ways (social innovation). As a result, regional and local companies' offer is enriched with new innovative products and services. Moreover, due to the geographical proximity between demand and supply, but also due to the knowledge of the local needs and markets, locating needs and providing customized services becomes easier and the flexibility of offer is improved, as well as the "evaluation" by the customers and consumers.

THE ROLE OF LOCAL AUTHORITIES

Local Authorities are usually composed of a deliberative or policy-making body (council or assembly) and an executive body (the Mayor or other executive officer), directly or indirectly elected or selected at local level. The term encompasses different tiers of government, e.g. villages, municipalities, districts, counties, provinces, regions, etc. Within this wide context, the focus of this Communication is however put on the municipal level, which is generally the lowest government tier of the public institutional system and the closest to citizens (Council of Europe, 2013).

In the business side, Corporate Social Responsibility (CSR) supports four strong trends which have firmed up its sustainable trajectory in the social issues conversation over the past several decades. These four trends have provided the impetus for CSR's solid position as the centerpiece for these contending and complimentary conceptions. The four trends include globalization of CSR practices, institutionalization of CSR within companies, strategic reconciliation with financial goals, and academic proliferation (Carroll 2015b). Skoloudis and Evangelinos (2012) reach the conclusion that CSR proves to have the biggest progress in North America and Western Europe, which makes trans-national comparisons difficult. They try to develop a national plan research on CSR. Based on previous theory and on excellent research methods that have been evolved in order to evaluate the multidimensional concept of CSR, they propose a research approach that can be implemented in every country, regardless the extent of the concept that has penetrated the domestic business sector. Sachinidis and Kavoura (2014) in a relevant research conducted in Greece, offer an approach for big Greek companies towards CSR and they prove the special importance that is given to specific sectors of CSR during the time of financial crisis. Considering the growing importance of CSR practices, based on the way entrepreneurship is conducted, the growing tense of adopting such practices and their communication with the participating stakeholders, they reach the result that the knowledge produced regarding corporate practices of CSR can assist in the creation and strengthening of good practices that can be promoted to the public, which resides in the country, where the enterprise is situated. Moreover, a significant research was conducted in Greece by Halkos and Sepetis (2007), which is relevant to how CSR (particularly environmental certificated companies), adds profit and financial value to its shareholders, in addition to its contribution to the social good of the society.

On the side of social enterprises, Bacq and Janssen (2011) define social entrepreneurship based on the following dimensions: "(1) social entrepreneurship is a process of entrepreneurial activities, which includes discovering, evaluating and pursuing opportunities that does not necessarily involve new venture creation; (2) social entrepreneurship includes formally constituted and informal organizations and activities initiated and launched by individuals; (3) social entrepreneurship principally aims to pursue a social goal". For the social entrepreneurship pursuing opportunities must not necessarily lead to the creation of a new venture. Further emphasis that this definition incorporates: "nonprofit, for-profit and hybrid forms of organizations, originating from the private, public or the third sectors without any restriction on their legal form, earning income strategies, scope of activities, or sector in which they operate" (Bacq and Janssen 2011). Social Enterprises tend to seek the creation of a more human, environmental friendlier, ethical society and choose this business function, which in long term will protect the interests of the local society (Rispal and Bonler 2010). Finally, according to Di Domenico, Haugh and Tracey (2014), social enterprise emphasizes on the importance of sustainable growth, as it provides solutions to various social and environmental challenges, through the use of economic methods for pertaining its central functions (Di Domenico et al., 2014).

Some authors consider CSR as a way to promote social entrepreneurship (Mitra and Borza 2010). This happens because the concepts of CSR and Social entrepreneurship both derived from the same context: 'sustainable development' (Seelos and Mair 2005). Respectively, Wei- Skillern *et al* (2007) suggest that there is a cross line between CSR profit and Social Enterprises profit with many common points such as: resource management, faith and trust to the company, strong networking. According to UNUNESCA the closer a social problem lies to a company that applies CSR, the greater is the chance the ways of cooperation with Social Enterprises to be controlled and the possibilities of social value to be developed, in order the society to be benefited (UNESCAP, 2010). Carolina and Silva (2015) support there are two alternate paths, that aim at the same ultimate goal, one is the Social Entrepreneurship which is intended to meet common needs resulting of the economic system and Corporate Social Responsibility, which it is the result of company ethical reflection based on interdependence and reciprocity of it to society, both paths are closely related to the creation of sustainable social value, but do not get in the same way, so it requires both (Carolina and Silva 2015).

Social entrepreneurs in rural and local areas, face many challenges including powerful resistance from time to time, while adopting new approaches to work for common and inclusive prosperity (Bornstein, 2007). Moreover, the researcher suggests that: "A social enterprise is also a business with primarily social objectives, whose surpluses are principally reinvested for that purpose in the business in the local community, rather than being driven by the need to maximize profit for shareholders and owners" (Borzaga et al., 2001). Social entrepreneurs lead villagers' cooperatives and rural communities towards a clear social mission so as to improve the living conditions of underprivileged people (Seelos and Mair, 2004). The outcome of this process of rural community development is largely dependent on the personal experiences of the social entrepreneur dealing with the challenges and obstacles (Yang and Li., 2008). The success of a social entrepreneur depends on his ability to attract resources (labor and capital) and innovative ways to create social value in a competitive environment in the local society (Cornwall, 1998). Governments' Social entrepreneurial policies play an important role in rural economic growth, which are dependent on allocation of research and development (R&D) resources and labor mobility by the government (Lan, 2014).

The connection between local companies that apply Corporate Social Responsibility and local Social Entrepreneurship is very crucial and Local Authorities can take the coordinative role by exploiting Corporate Social Responsibility of local companies. Moreover, special importance will be given in the disposal of financial resources and the time of employment employees spend in private businesses, according to the rules of Corporate Social Responsibility for the exchange of expertise in social entrepreneurship, which has a compensatory reinforcement profit for the local economy and market. Local Authorities take over a "political" role (referee, mediator, negotiator) and commit to the development of self- regulation models of the civil society (a network between social enterprises) (Totterman and Sten, 2005). Central goal is the decentralization of public services and the concession of particular activities in social entrepreneurships, leading Local Authorities to a strategically coordinated network center, which will consist of private businesses, profitable and non-profitable organizations and other civil service organizations, having as their main target the development of the local economy (Crouch et al., 2001). The above mentioned relations are possible to be implemented and reinforced through financing project models, which will be between the public sector and companies that can be represented by incubators. The profits from the creation of an incubator in the field of social entrepreneurship are making the overcoming of expertise obstacles easier and allow them to apply good practices within a safe business environment (Eshun, 2004). At the same time, local networking and efficient participation in the market competition create the preconditions, whereas in the end their social dimension is broadened by raising and maintaining work places (Jonsson, 2015).

The following question arises: why should local authorities invest to an incubator for connecting the CSR of companies with social enterprises? A short answer may be that: a) Social enterprises, by definition, use innovative approaches to solve social problems, b) Due to the fact that social enterprises attract financing from social responsibility investors, they have significantly more resources than traditional non-profits or NGOs. This allows them to leverage CSR money for much greater impact, c) More resources and a for-profit structure means the ability to pay better salaries, and attract the talent they want. They can also offer stock options, e) As social enterprises must have a revenue model, they have high potential for sustainability, which means that even after a CSR funding project finishes, the results and services continue to live on, f) The combination of a sustainable revenue model, more resources and focus on local talent and local innovation means that these organizations have the potential for scaling far greater than the traditional NGO/Non-profit model.

LOCAL AUTHORITIES' INCUBATOR

The definition and the term of incubator first appeared in 1959, when Batavia Company was established in New York (Allen 1987; McKee 1992). It started and it was mainly focused on public service, but it expanded in foundations that aimed in the creation of work places, or social care sector, focused on the quest for more employment chances for unemployed and minorities (Eshun, 2004). According to National Business Incubation Association, business incubation is a business support process that accelerates the successful development of start-up and fledgling companies by providing entrepreneurs with an array of targeted resources and services. These services are usually developed or orchestrated by incubator management and offer both in the business incubator and through its network of contacts. A business incubator's main goal is to produce successful firms that will leave the program financially viable and freestanding. These incubator graduates have the potential to create jobs, revitalize neighborhoods, commercialize new technologies, and strengthen local and national economies (NBIA, 2007). For the European Commission (EC, 2002), a business incubator is an organization that accelerates and systematizes the process of creating successful enterprises by providing them with a comprehensive and integrated range of support, including: Incubator space, business support services, and clustering and networking opportunities (EC, 2002). And for the United Nations Economic Commission for Europe (UN-ECE, 2010), an incubator is a place, where recently established companies are concentrated in a limited space. According to Sherman and Chappell (1998) business incubator is an economic development tool primarily designed to help create new businesses in a community. Business incubators help emerging businesses by providing various support services, such as assistance in developing business and marketing plans, building management teams, obtaining capital, and access to a range of more specialized professional services. They also provide flexible space, shared equipment, and administrative services. Aernoudt (2004) also suggests that an incubator is an interactive development process, where the aim is to encourage people to start their own business and to support start-up companies in the development of innovative products. Besides business spaces, an incubator should offer services, such as hands-on management, access to finance (mainly through links with seed capital funds or business angels), legal advice, operational know-how and access to new markets. Business incubators' role of networking can be identified from two perspectives; 'hubs position and a brokerage position (McAdam and Marlow,

2011). Moreover, Duff (2008) suggests that co-located entrepreneurial firms provide the possibility to generate a symbiotic environment, where entrepreneurs share resources and experiences, learn from one another, exchange business contacts and establish collaborative business relationships.

According to Sepetis, Amitsis and Sanida (2016), the relationship between Strategic Policies of the European Union regarding Social Enterprises has taken in the past several forms (Sepetis et al 2016, EC., 2013, 2014, 2019). Most of them can be mentioned below:

- ***Support strategy*:** This strategy is based in providing grants to private social services providers (ex. social enterprises, NGO's) with very few restrictions or conditions, as long as its use is socially oriented (ex. startup capitals for new social enterprises)
- ***Motivation strategy*:** In the framework of this strategy, public resources are allocated in private providers according to public policy targets. An example of this strategy is reducing the non-wage labor cost, which is being paid as a grant for the recruitment of disabled employees or socially excluded people
- ***Outsourcing strategy*:** In this case, public administration contracts with a private provider for the provision of certain services, according to the parameters of public administration. This is the most common and known practice, especially in the field of social services
- ***Coupon strategy*:** The users are entitled access to specific services with the financing provided from public administration. This strategy is used in several countries in order to satisfy the existing demand for the health care of children and home care.

The above mentioned European Union strategies that promote Social Enterprises do not have the same social value to public administration or to other cooperative companies, as these strategies do not have the economic value to be developed, in order the social cohesion and economic development to be benefited. Especially, the outsourcing strategies sometimes tend to limit innovation, as they focus on the provision of services, based on particular social parameters. The strategies of coupons and motives, on the other hand, allow more freedom for the creation of new types of services and new provision strategies, as they do not favor innovation and in some cases (ex. coupons do not entirely cover expenses) they draw money from their own private financing sources. As a result, these companies are economically only in short term (EC 2013, 2014, 2019; Sepetis, et al, 2016).

For the Local Authorities an incubator can possibly add social value to local companies and also economic value to social enterprises and the local society. A Local Authorities' incubator that connects CSR of local companies with local social enterprises should offer at least one of the following services: a) networking opportunities, b) management or technical assistance of the expertise, or/and a support network for the community, c) financing the various functioning stages of a company, d) relationship management with the customers (Rice, 1992). A Local Authorities' incubator consists of five dimensions: 1) Management of the enterprises, 2) Consultants, 3) Business cooperation/ networking, 4) Flexibility of Space, 5) common service. The Local Authorities' incubators manager and the rest of the management team members may take a very important role in providing help to their customers, in order to begin and develop their business activities (Smith και Zhang, 2012). Incubator consultants of the Local Authorities' incubators must be people that come from the business world, academic business schools, services providers, experienced business people and educated, who are willing to provide consulting and lead towards the development of those companies. Especially in Social enterprises, the role of Consultant refers to a better social behavior, reducing the effect of social or personal obstacles, by raising the ability and the self-confidence and the feeling of being accepted by the team (Wood, 2014). The psycho-social interferences could be effective not only for controlling situations and solving problems, but also for restoring the sense of self control, the personal efficiency and the active participation. The biggest emphasis is given to the creation of opportunities for local social entrepreneurs in order to create relations with local companies. One of the main targets of local social enterprises is to support local society or part of it as target group. In this framework, another main characteristic of social enterprises is integrated, which is the promotion of social responsibility of companies in local level. The incubator managers based on the previous factors, promote the social responsibility development networks without being limited to some particular sector of socioeconomic activity, but covering a broad spectrum of activities (Li Yunhe et al., 2015). The developmental profits of local social enterprise derive from relationships based on the exchange of knowledge, services and products, having as main target the successful use of the coordinated service of concrete needs of the society or special social groups. Space flexibility that is provided by the Local Authorities' incubators, comes from other incubators that offer small space leasing (ten square meters) usually with short term leasing. If the lessee fails, he/she shall leave immediately and with the less cost, and the incubator can host the next lessee. Nevertheless, the lessees have security while paying their rent. The dimension of common services refers to the incubator that provides concentrated equipment, services and facilities, such as a copier machine, a fax, customer service, mail management, meeting room, loading dock, etc. The newly born local social enterprises need these kind of services, but usually are too small to be able to justify the cost of such kind of services. The access of such kind of services through a Local Authorities' incubator means that social enterprises may invest their capitals in their missions, such as buying new products, while a new professional image for the business contacts and the clients is presented.

PROMOTION OF SYNERGIES WITH SOCIAL ENTERPRISES

The Local Authorities' Incubator and local companies have an important role to play in stakeholder networking, educating, and coaching, financing, social procurement, marketing and promoting for the new social enterprises. The important challenge in front of new social enterprises is to identify whom to contact, who are the key local stakeholders involved around the particular local social enterprise and what are their values. Among the highest needs they have, it is emphasized that they need to make contacts and be connected to the circles of both other social enterprises and related stakeholders. Meeting people, making contacts with them and working toward development of long-term relationships impacts social enterprises in a significant way. It is not seldom that social enterprises have no previous knowledge neither from the business side, nor from the societal one, and for those who have the background that is helpful in terms of establishing and developing social enterprise, there are still particularities that can be further explained. Teaching, coaching and knowledge from local companies' managers or local academic professors and sharing the new "Business idea", and the "business plan", and prompt the "business model" are the terms identified as being of concern, when it comes to motivation of social entrepreneurs to join the incubator programs. The coaching from the local manager or local academic professor under local authorities' incubator is different in comparison with the above presented teaching. In coaching, each of the new social enterprises has scheduled individual time to meet coaches, preferably specialized in their particular needs and should be addressed through the coaching instructions. Since it is individual, coaching, contrary to teaching, is tailored based on the needs of program participants, which is also important to be acknowledged, since social enterprises attending the program in one point of the time, might be in very different stages of their development. Moreover, the Local Authorities' incubator suggests and connects new social enterprises with local financial stakeholders under corporate social responsibility or EU-national funding programs and provide the sources of funding. To provide sources of funding is major concern for social enterprises. To make the contacts with different kind of investors is thus very important. This is recognized from the side of incubator programs that organize these kind of meetings through different events, study visits and workshops. Some of the meetings have as purpose just to connect social enterprises with investors, other to facilitate to entrepreneurs to present themselves and pitch their idea. Social enterprises have to collaborate with public sector, which is not only setting the rules and legislation but also represents the key customers of the social enterprise services. Social impact is an important feature for social enterprises. Local Authorities' incubator programs consider teaching regarding social impact, as one of the main themes on their lecture schedule. Social impact can be explained both as the consequence and the essential output of the activities that social enterprises undertake for helping their target group and improving the society as a whole. The Public social or green and sustainable procurement processes are related with public sector in local level and they present the processes that public institutions use to provide products and services for citizens. Process is conducted on the level of municipalities that represent the government entities responsible for the provision of numerous of local services. The European Commission intends to facilitate the uptake of socially-green and sustainable responsible criteria in public procurement and to promote their use across the EU. The EU Public authorities can engage in socially-responsible public procurement by buying ethical products and services, and by using public tenders to create job opportunities, decent work, social and professional inclusion and better conditions for disabled and disadvantaged people. Moreover, the EU Green Public Procurement (GPP) means that public authorities seek to purchase goods, services and works with a reduced environmental impact throughout their life-cycle compared to goods, services and works with the same primary function, which would otherwise be procured. The EU Sustainable Public Procurement (SPP) is a process by which public authorities seek to achieve the appropriate balance between the three pillars of sustainable development - economic, social and environmental - when procuring goods, services or works at all stages of the project (EU Social Procurement, Green and Sustainable 2019).

Furthermore the local authorities' incubator should be connected to local Social Enterprises with local companies that apply Corporate Social Responsibility and can take various forms, such as:

- ***Sponsorship*:** Companies provide financial support to Social Enterprises that may include cooperation in the promotion of the CSR program of companies to local society, as Social Enterprises have a thorough knowledge of the local societies' social and environmental problems
- ***Counseling*:** A company asks the advice of a Social Enterprise in issues regarding CSR, such as for a program that the company tends to elaborate regarding environmental protection or other social issues
- ***Cooperation in research*:** Both companies and Social Enterprises provide the necessary resources for social or environmental research programs. Companies through the CSR program can offer financing and Social Enterprises knowledge and executives
- ***Employee training in order to promote volunteering*:** Business executives that apply CSR are called to train Social Enterprises stuff
- ***Dialog Development*:** A company that applies CSR develops systematic dialog with Social Enterprises, such as conducting "round table" discussion for different CSR issues

- ***Elaborating common CSR programs*:** The cooperative company that applies CSR participates in common actions and implements common social or environmental programs with Social Enterprises
- ***Strategic Partnerships*:** Long term cooperation between a Social Enterprise and a company that applies CSR can take the form of a written agreement, ex the provision of a common service or a new products/services
- ***Mediation*:** Social Enterprises and their networks are responsible for motivating other entities or local social enterprises in poor or less developed countries in order to cooperate with companies in the implementation of CSR programs
- ***Shareholder Activism and Stakeholder Advocate*:** Many Social Enterprises and companies that apply CSR are participating in social funds that have adopted "Shareholder Activism and Stakeholder Advocate". They buy a package of shares from non-ethical enterprises and as they have minority interests in the general meetings of shareholders, they condemn potential infringement of business ethics in those companies in social and environmental issues and they suggest substantive changes in corporate policy.
- ***Commercial Network of consumer products and supplies*:** Many social enterprises act while having as a target the consumer protection and they promote fair trade and certified social or environmentally friendly products. Moreover, companies that apply CSR produce products and services which are named social/green/ethical etc. In those local commercial networks, companies, which apply CSR could cooperate with social enterprises networks and could create new local social, ethical, sustainable fair-trade products etc, under Local Authorities Certification and be certified as P.D.O (Protected Designations of Origin).

According to the above, a Local Authorities' incubator for cooperation between local companies that apply CSR and local Social Enterprises will add new business strategies and new innovation practices in the local society. It will also promote economic and social value and will create a new local-national and international market with new social-green or sustainable certificate products and services.

A short analysis for new business strategy and innovation practices in the Local Authorities' incubator for social enterprises is the following:

- **Innovation development**: According to our vision, Corporate Social Responsibility and Social Enterprise together should incorporate social mission and management in their operation and respond to new local market priorities, with new innovative business practices and local products in order to succeed profitability.
- **Promoting CSR and social economy in the education**. Since the middle of 2000 field studies have proved the increasing desire of students and the demand in incorporating CSR and social economy studies in the local educational process, besides traditional Schools, such as Economics and Business Administration (Sepetis and Rizos 2011, Moon and Orlitzky 2011). Many researchers have stated that in order such educational programs to be promoted, a higher demand by the enterprises and the public is needed, in order Moral Conscious in Education and Market to be developed. Many Universities (Kavoura and Andersson 2016), local administration entities and businesses express their interest for cooperation between CSR issues and social economy on several ways, which can be included as following: a) in the development of local university education and research for CSR and social economy to students, to employees and local society, b) in the

cooperation with businesses in matters of internships of students and education of employees in matters of CSR and social economy, c) in the development of educational tools for LLL, d) in the development of business tools in teaching CSR and social economy in the local community, e) in the education of students, regarding the principles of CSR and social economy for a fairer and more moral consumer market, f) in the implementation of common educational programs of CSR of the Universities with the local administration, in order to strengthen social enterprises. The success of CSR and of social enterprises derives from EU funding, such as the strengthening of education and the employment of local workforce.

- **Financial risk and improvement of the relationships with investors and financial market.** Local Financial stakeholders that apply CSR and investors, who actively participate in a dialogue and in a cooperation with businesses that apply CSR and with social enterprises, have a better view of the potential risks that they face and the capability to manage a potential crisis better and exit faster and with less losses of it. Despite the fact that financial stakeholders and investors are usually not interested in the non-financial sides of social enterprises, the positively proven relationship between CSR and economic performance of businesses is not less interesting to them. For this reason, nowadays, a new financial market service has been created, which entirely finances companies that apply CSR and social enterprises. There is also a number of financial indexes that are used as a benchmark in order to compare the efficiency of companies and companies that apply CSR.
- **Corporate reputation improvement and development of new local markets.** The improvement of reputation and of the concept of a commercial label of social enterprises and of companies that apply CSR derives from recognizing the improved quality of the local product, also on behalf of the consumer and of the investor that derives from issues that regard employees and from the sensitivity for social and environmental and ethical issues.
- **Corporate reputation of new social enterprises that is based on trust and appreciation for the local authorities would be trust for local stakeholders and local market.** Many companies that apply CSR practices and many Social Enterprises should be certificated with the equivalent certification of business management (ISO etc) and with PGI (Protected Geographical Indication) or P.D.O (Protected Designations of Origin), in order to declare their uniqueness from other similar products and be recognized in the certified products and services market.

In this chapter, we suggest that certified commercial products and services, which have been promoted by local authorities' incubators and were created in cooperation with companies that apply CSR and SE, will lead in these new markets. These new products and services that have social and economic value, will incorporate the competitive advantage and the business skills of the companies that apply CSR and will also promote the competitive advantage and the social network of social enterprises, so that a Win-Win situation will be developed.

CONCLUSION

The profits from creating an incubator in social entrepreneurship are helping new social enterprises to overcome any expertise barriers and allow them to apply good practices in a safely business environment. The cooperation between social enterprises that will develop in the framework of a Local Authorities' incubator, will provide the perspective of creating a symbiotic environment, where social entrepreneurs share their resources and their experiences and learn from them, while at the same time contribute to raising social capital. Very important element for the Local Authorities' incubator is the existence and function of organized consultancy services and psycho-social strengthening. The role of the Consultant refers to a better way of social behavior, by reducing the effect of social and personal obstacles, by raising the capability and the self-confidence and the feeling of acceptance by the team. The psycho-social interferences could be effective, not only for controlling the situations and solving the problems, but also for restoring the self-control feeling in personal efficiency and active participation. The pioneer dynamic of social entrepreneurship in the protected environment of a Local Authorities' incubator is broadened with the efforts of its members to reassure sufficient resources and follow proved and correctly efficient practices. In this way, the long term sustainability of Social Enterprise is reassured, as the success of its financial activity and the efforts that the members and/or the employees make, are based on a concrete plan. As the networking of local companies that apply CSR and local Social Enterprises is concerned, the support and the service of Local Society is incorporated in the promotion strategy of social responsibility and social value in local level. This happens through the sufficient utilization of cooperative cooperation between local companies that apply CSR and local Social Enterprises and Universities (Makarona and Kavoura A 2019) that cover a wider range of activities and through the exchange of knowledge, services and products they accelerate the raise of productivity and their survival in the competitive environment. Finally, the new local pioneer 'certified products of social and economic value", such as for example the social or ethical or green certified products or PGI (Protected Geographical Indication) or P.D.O (Protected Designations of Origin) that will be derived from a local cooperation between local companies that apply CSR and local Social Enterprises, will have access to a different market in the local society and in the international market of fair trade and of certified products.

REFERENCES

Aernoudt, R. (2004). Incubators: Tool for Entrepreneurship? *Small Business Economics*, *23*(2), 127–135. doi:10.1023/B:SBEJ.0000027665.54173.23

Bacq, S., & Janssen, F. (2011). The multiple faces of social entrepreneurship: A review of definitional issues based on geographical and thematic criteria. *Entrepreneurship and Regional Development*, *23*(5-6), 373–403. doi:10.1080/08985626.2011.577242

Bornstein, D. (2007). *How to Change the World: Social Entrepreneurs and the Power of New Ideas.* Oxford University Press.

Borzaga, C., & Defourny, J. (Eds.). (2001). *The Emergence of Social Enterprise*. Routledge. doi:10.4324/9780203164679

Carolina, A., & Silva, N. (2015). Social Entrepreneurship and Corporate Social Responsibility: Differences and Points in Common *Journal of Business &. Economic Policy*, *2*(2), 85–93.

Carroll, A. B. (2015a). Corporate social responsibility: The centerpiece of competing and complementary frameworks. *Organizational Dynamics*, *44*(2), 87–96. doi:10.1016/j.orgdyn.2015.02.002

Carroll, A. B. (2015b). Corporate Social Responsibility (CSR) is on a Sustainable Trajectory. *Journal of Defense Management*, *5*, 132. doi:10.4172/2167-0374.1000132

Carroll, A. B., & Buchholtz, A. K. (2015). Business and Society: Ethics, Sustainability, and Stakeholder Management (9th ed.). Cengage Learning.

Cornwall, J. R. (1998). The entrepreneur as a building block for community. *Journal of Developmental Entrepreneurship*, *3*, 141–148.

Council of Europe. (2013). *Structure and operation of local and regional democracy Greece Situation in 2012 this report has been prepared and elaborated by the Ministry of Interior of the Hellenic Republic.* Directorate of Democratic Institutions Directorate General of Democracy and Political Affairs. https://www.eetaa.gr/en_pages/Structure_and_operation_Greece_2012.pdf

Crouch, C., Le Galès, P., Trigilia, C., & Voelzkow, H. (2001). *Local Production Systems in Europe. Rise or demise?* Oxford University Press.

Defourny, J., & Nyssens, M. (2006). Defining Social Enterprise. In M. Nyssens (Ed.), *Social Enterprise: At the crossroads of market, public policies and civil society*. Routledge.

Di Domenico, M., Haugh, H., & Tracey, P. (2010). Social Bricolage: Theorizing Social Value Creation in Social Enterprises. *Entrepreneurship Theory and Practice*, *34*(4), 681–703. doi:10.1111/j.1540-6520.2010.00370.x

Duff, A. (1994). *Best practice in business incubator management*. Booragon, Australia: AUSTEP Strategic Partnering Pty.

EC. (2002). *Benchmarking of Business Incubators*. Final Report. Brussels: EC.

Eshun, J. P. (2004). *Where Do Business Incubators Came From? The Origins, Evolutions, and Institutionalization of Business Incubators: Evaluating Performance and Assessing Outcome* (Unpublished doctoral dissertation). Columbia University.

European Commission. (2013). *Social economy and social entrepreneurship Social Europe guide*. Author.

European Commission. (2014). *A map of social enterprises and their eco-systems in Europe*. Author.

European Commission. (2019). *Social enterprises and their ecosystems in Europe. Updated country report: Greece*. Luxembourg: Publications Office of the European Union. Available at https://europa.eu/!Qq64ny

Halkos, G., & Sepetis, A. (2007). Can capital markets respond to environmental policy of firms? Evidence from Greece. *Ecological Economics*, *63*(2-3), 578–587. doi:10.1016/j.ecolecon.2006.12.015

Hastings, C., & Weate, J. (2018). Local Governments and Social Enterprise: Meeting Community Challenges Together? In Social Capital and Enterprise in the Modern State, (pp.117-146). Academic Press.

Jonsson, S. (2015). Entrepreneurs' network evolution – the relevance of cognitive social capital. *International Journal of Entrepreneurial Behaviour & Research*, *21*(2), 197–223. doi:10.1108/IJEBR-09-2013-0147

Kavoura, A., & Andersson, T. (2016). Applying Delphi method for strategic design of social entrepreneurship. *Library Review*, *65*(3), 185–205. doi:10.1108/LR-06-2015-0062

Lan, H., Zhu, Y., Ness, D., Xing, K., & Schneider, K. (2014). The role and characteristics of social entrepreneurs in contemporary rural cooperative development in China: Case studies of rural social entrepreneurship. *Asia Pacific Business Review*, *20*(3), 379–400. doi:10.1080/13602381.2014.929300

Li, Y., Tang, L., & Lio, Z. (2015). Research about the Effection of Incubated Enterprises Business Network on the Enterprise Performance. *2nd International Conference on Education Reform and Modern Management (ERMM),* 382-285.

Mair, J., & Marti, I. (2006). Social Entrepreneurship Research: A Source of Explanation, Prediction, and Delight. *Journal of World Business*, *41*(1), 36–44. doi:10.1016/j.jwb.2005.09.002

Makarona, E., & Kavoura, A. (2019). Redesigning the Ivory Tower: Academic entrepreneurship as a new calling supporting economic growth. *The Malopolska School of Economics in Tarnow Research Papers Collection*, *42*, 15–26.

McAdam, M., & McAdam, R. (2008). High tech start-ups in University Science Park incubators: The relationship between the start-up's lifecycle progression and use of the incubator's resources. *Technovation*, *28*(5), 277–290. doi:10.1016/j.technovation.2007.07.012

McKee, B. (1992). A boost for start-ups. *Nation's Business*, 40–42.

Mitra, C., & Borza, A. (2010). The role of corporate social responsibility in social entrepreneurship. Management and Marketing Challenges for knowledge. *Society*, *5*(2), 63–76.

Moon, J. & Orlitzky, M., (2011). Corporate social responsibility and sustainability education: a trans-Atlantic comparison. *Journal of Management & Organization, 17*, 583-563.

National Business Incubation Association. (1990). *The State of The Business Incubation Industry*. NBIA.

NBIA. (2011). *Business incubation FAQ*. NBIA.

OECD. (2010). *High-Growth Enterprises—What Governments Can Do to Make a Difference*. OECD Publishing.

Peredo, C., & McLean, A. (2006). Social Entrepreneurship: A Critical Review of the Concept. *Journal of World Business*, *41*(1), 56–65. doi:10.1016/j.jwb.2005.10.007

Phillips, R., Schrempf-Stirling, J., & Stutz, C. (2019). The Past, History, and Corporate Social Responsibility. *Journal of Business Ethics*. Advance online publication. doi:10.100710551-019-04319-0

Porter, M., & Kramer, M. R. (2011). Creating shared value: How to reinvent capitalism and unleash a wave of innovation and growth. *Harvard Business Review*, *12*(4), 1–17.

Porter, M. E., & Kramer, M. R. (2006). Strategy and society: The link between competitive advantage and corporate social responsibility. *Harvard Business Review*, 1–13. PMID:17183795

Rice, M. P. (1992). *Intervention mechanisms used to influence the critical success factors of new ventures: An exploratory study*. Centre for Entrepreneurship of New Technological Ventures, Rensselaer Polytechnic Institute.

Rispal, H. H., & Bonler, J. (2010). Social entrepreneurship in France: Organizational and relational issues. In A. Fayolle & H. Matlay (Eds.), *Handbook of research on social entrepreneurship*. Edward Elgar Publishing Ltd.

Saebi T, Foss J N., & Linder S. (2018). Social Entrepreneurship Research: Past Achievements and Future Promises Volume. *Journal of Management, 45*(1), 70-95.

Sahinidis, A., & Kavoura, A. (2014). Exploring Corporate Social Responsibility practices of Greek companies. *The Małopolska School of Economics in Tarnów Research Papers Collection*, *25*(2), 186–193.

Seelos, C., & Mair, J. (2005). Social entrepreneurship: Creating new business models to serve the poor. *Business Horizons*, *48*(3), 241–246. doi:10.1016/j.bushor.2004.11.006

Sepetis A., Amitsis G. & Sanida M. (2016). Connecting Corporate Social Responsibility Strategies with Social Enterprises Policies in the concept of the European Union Policies for Sustainable Development. *Journal of Regional & Socio- Economic Issues*, *6*(2), 2049-1395.

Sepetis, A., & Rizos, F. (2011). Sustainable Development and Corporate Social Responsibility in Higher Education: Some Evidence from Greece. *International Conference on Integrated Information Kos*.

Sherman, H., & Chappell, D. S. (1998). Methodological challenges in evaluating busi- ness incubator outcomes. *Economic Development Quarterly*, *12*(4), 313–321. doi:10.1177/089124249801200403

Skouloudis, A., & Evangelinos, K. (2012). A research design for mapping national CSR terrains International. *Journal of Sustainable Development & World Ecology*, *19*(2), 130–143. doi:10.1080/13504509.2011.606338

Smith, D., & Zhang, J. (2012). Michael Introduction: The evolution of the incubator concept. *International Journal of Entrepreneurship and Innovation*, *13*(4), 227–234. doi:10.5367/ijei.2012.0096

Totterman, H., & Sten, J. (2005). Start-ups: Business Incubation and Social Capital. *International Small Business Journal*, *23*(5), 487–511. doi:10.1177/0266242605055909

United Nations Economic and Social Commission for Asia and Pacific (UNESCAP). (2010). Creating business and social value: The Asian way to integrate CSR into business strategies. Studies in Trade and Investments # 68. New York: United Nations.

Wei-Skillern, J. C., Austin, J. E., Leonard, H. B., & Stevenson, H. H. (2007). *Entrepreneurship in the Social Sector*. Sage Publications.

Wood, M. W. (2014). *Addressing Sustainability in an Entrepreneurship Ecosystem: A Case Study of a Social Incubator in Mexico* (Unpublished doctoral dissertation). Arizona State University.

Yang, J. Y., & Li, J. (2008). The development of entrepreneurship in China. *Asia Pacific Journal of Management*, *25*(2), 335–359. doi:10.100710490-007-9078-8

ADDITIONAL READING

Carroll, A. B. (1979). A three-dimensional conceptual model of corporate social performance. *Academy of Management Review*, *4*(4), 497–505. doi:10.5465/amr.1979.4498296

Carroll, A. B. (2016). Carroll's pyramid of CSR: Taking another look. *Int J Corporate Soc Responsibility*, *1*(1), 3. doi:10.118640991-016-0004-6

Chell (2007). Social Enterprise and Entrepreneurship Towards a Convergent Theory of the Entrepreneurial Process. *International Small Business Journal 25(1)*

Elkington, J. (1997). *Cannibals With Forks: The Triple Bottom Line of 21st Century Business*. Capstone Publishing Limited.

Friedman, M. (1970). The social responsibility of business is to increase its profits. New York Times Magazine 13, September: 33ff.

KEY TERMS AND DEFINITIONS

Business Incubator: Facility established to nurture young (startup) firms during their early months or years. It usually provides affordable space, shared offices and services, hand-on management training, marketing support and, often, access to some form of financing.

Corporate Social Responsibility: A company's sense of responsibility towards the stakeholders, the community, and the environment (both ecological and social) in which it operates.

Local Authorities: The organizations which is responsible for the government of a local area.

PDO (Protected Designation of Origin): Mark identifies a product originating in a specific place, region or country, whose quality or characteristics are essentially or exclusively due to a particular geographical environment with its inherent natural (raw materials, environmental characteristics, location) and human (traditional and artisanal production) factors the production, processing and preparation steps of which all take place in the defined geographical area and in line with the strict production regulations established.

PGI (Protected Geographical Indication): Mark designates a product originating in a specific place, region or country whose given quality, reputation or other characteristic is essentially attributable to its geographical origin and at least one of the production steps of which takes place in the defined geographical area.

Social Enterprise: A social enterprise is defined as a business that has specific social objectives that serve its primary purpose. Social enterprises seek to maximize profits while maximizing benefits to society and the environment.

Social Value: Social value is the relationship and the contribution of companies to the society as well as is larger concept which includes social capital and the subjective aspects of the citizens' well-being, such as their ability to participate in making decisions that affect them.

Chapter 14
The Effective Use of Digital Technology by SMEs

Antonios Georgios Zairis
Neapolis University, Cyprus

ABSTRACT

Most researches emphasize the importance of small and medium-sized enterprises (SMEs) as main contributors to economic growth and their role in the global economy. The purpose of this study is to provide information on the implementation of digital technology in SMEs and the challenges they face. It seems that the evolution of internet technology and communication platforms has been largely adopted in the corporate environment and constitutes an important component of competitive advantage for large corporations. But the same does not exactly apply for SMEs as they come up against numerous issues. The chapter also focuses on the digital state of Greek SMEs and attempts to identify the main problems and opportunities for promoting their development through digital technology, as they appear to be weak in this field especially when comparing to the majority of European countries. These findings enrich the literature on Greek SMEs and their future capabilities.

INTRODUCTION

Although the subject of digitalization in SMEs is not new, it is a very much alive issue and its analysis remains highly topical. Digital technology is an integral part of the future industry, and it is no secret that it is reshaping the world economy. Its use can enhance the performance of SMEs and offer them more opportunities in order to compete with their larger competitors (Cenamor et al., 2019). It is also well known that innovation and the use of new digital technologies is the key to a company's survival in today's competitive business environment (Kavoura and Andersson, 2016; Kavoura and Koziol, 2017; Makarona and Kavoura, 2019). And innovation it does not always mean complicated and costly processes (Masouras, 2019).

New technologies have emerged, such as cloud computing, communication platforms, data analytics, big data, automation, robotics, artificial intelligence, machine learning, virtual reality and even 3D printing that offer new opportunities for small enterprises (Ulas, 2019). However, up taking new digital

DOI: 10.4018/978-1-7998-3648-3.ch014

technologies proves to be uneven and depends on many factors such as the size of the company or the country's level of economic development, and also politics and regulations (Chakravorti et al., 2017). It seems that one of the inherent advantages that larger companies have (over the smaller ones) is their ability to adopt digital technologies more easily, as they have the capital and human resources to do so. In Europe, larger corporations employ more IT/ICT specialists and use data sharing infrastructure (e.g. ERP) and cloud computing more often than smaller companies. On the other side, almost half of European SMEs (44%) use social media to promote their business. Regarding the use of mobile internet by SMEs, there has been an increase from 20% to 29% (2012-2016) while it remains stable (64%) for the bigger firms (European Commission, 2017).

This article aims to provide an overview on the use of digital technology by SMEs specifically in Greece. It analyses the concept and importance of SMEs in the country's economy and focuses on their course over the last eight years. This is followed by a description of the country's digital status and the use of digital tools by Greek SMEs. The final section contains the concluding remarks.

BACKGROUND

The Concept of SMEs

Before we begin our analysis it is important to highlight what determines an SME and what distinguishes it from a larger corporation.The concept of SMEs is designated with distinct terminology, depending on the country or the institution that reports their statistics (for example the World Bank or the United Nations Development Programme-UNDP) and no widely accepted definition exists (Gibson and Van der Vaart, 2008). The quantitative criteria that constitute a micro, small or medium sized company, vary according to a country's economy and the characteristics of its corporate sector. The common element in most economies is the number of employees, which is usually combined with other determinants (such as the company's assets or revenues). These standards are modified infrequently (ESCAP, 2009). The upper and lower range limit of the "employee" factor may differ to such an extent that a country may regard an SME, as a company occupying fewer than 300 employees (for example Vietnam), while another (for example Egypt) as an enterprise having 50 employees (Ayyagari et al.,2003;Gibson and Van der Vaart, 2008). For the purposes of this paper the definition of SMEs according to the European Union (EU) is used.

Based on the Commission Recommendation 2003/361/EC (European Commission, 2003), which updated the 96/280/EC Recommendation of 1996, the three criteria that determine the maximum values of SMEs are: the number of employees, the company's turnover and the balance sheet total. *Medium* sized companies occupy fewer than 250 employees, have an annual turnover that does not exceed 50 million euro, and their annual balance sheet total does not surpass 43 million euro. In the second article it is specified that within the broad category, a *Small* company is described as an enterprise that employs fewer than 50 people, and whose annual turnover and balance sheet total does not exceed 10 million euro. In the *Micro* category companies have fewer than 10 employees, while their annual turnover and balance sheet total does not exceed 2 million euro. As is appreciated, SMEs are a very heterogeneous group of companies, covering a broad spectrum of business activities, and operate in multiple markets. Furthermore, they feature many different types of organizational culture, entrepreneurial orientation, growth skills, labour force and capital. It should also be mentioned that in many economies, a substantial number of small and micro enterprises are part of the informal sector or the shadow economy (OECD, 2004). Although large firms have a commanding influence on aggregate economic activity, and each small company does not add considerably as a unit, SMEs impact as a group is extremely important (Cull et al., 2006; OECD, 2014). More specifically, although data may differ across countries, SMEs dominance in numbers is indisputable: they account for more than 95% of global enterprises and represent approximately 60% of employment in the private sector. In 2014 SMEs accounted for 99,8% of all companies (in the non financial business sector) and 66,8% of the total employment (88,8 million people) in the European Union (EU28). At the same time, the amount of value added that was generated by SMEs was calculated at 58,1% representing approximately 28% of the EU GDP (Muller et al., 2014). Three years later (SBA, 2018) the number of companies remained at the same level but a slight decrease was observed in the number of people employed (66,4%) and the value added (56,8%).

SMEs are also considered the key components of economic growth, income generation, export revenues and employment creation in developing, transitional and high income countries (Tewari et al., 2013). According to Hallberg (2000) the importance of such companies differs across countries, and even varies in the different stages of development of the same country. Moreover, their contribution to GDP depends on each economy: for the low income countries it has been estimated at about 16% of GDP (the phenomenon of large number of companies that belong to the informal sector occurs) and for high income countries it has been reckoned at 51% of GDP (Edinburgh Group, 2012). These companies strongly promote entrepreneurship, which is a fundamental element of economic growth and job creation (ESCAP, 2009). More specifically, they constitute the most crucial source of new employment positions in Europe, since over four million jobs per year are created in the sector (European Commission, 2013a). The SMEs community is considered to be more competitive, innovative and dynamic (especially start-ups) in relation to larger firms. They are also considered to be more adaptable, resilient, and flexible in terms of reducing cost. Many corporations, selling new products (such as high technology commodities) or services, have their origin in the specific sector, which is regarded as a ‘nursery’ for talented young entrepreneurs, and also as a ‘bridge’ between the informal (for example a small family company) and the formal corporate sector. Almost all large corporations began as SMEs (Lukacs, 2005). They can therefore, enhance the transformation of developing countries in many ways (such as moving up the value chain). SMEs are equally important for promoting the work of women, young people and minorities. In addition, these companies strengthen a country’s regional competitiveness, as they mainly use local resources and their profits remain in the region. If they succeed in exporting their products to foreign markets, they become sources of foreign exchange earnings and their contribution to the home country increases (Ayyagari et al., 2011; Robu, 2013; ESCAP, 2014). Furthermore, the strong presence of micro and small enterprises reduces the creation of monopolistic or oligopolistic economies and prevents the larger companies from dominating the market (Savlovschi and Robu, 2011). On the other hand, SMEs are criticised for low survival rates, as many are led to bankruptcy after a short period of time. This is attributed to the fact that some of these companies offer low value added products, poor quality service or short life goods (Hobohm, 2001). But according to Kok et al. (2011) the employment positions that are created by new entrants in the sector are more than the job losses caused by the death of SMEs. Based on Peters et al. (2014) SMEs are more vulnerable to the business cycle than larger companies. It should also be noted that the presence of SMEs in a country does not automatically lead to growth or poverty alleviation. Other factors should also be met in order for economic development to occur (ESCAP, 2009).

The Course of SMEs in Greece (2010 – 2018)

According to the European Commissions' SBA Fact Sheet (2010-2018) SMEs account for a lion's share of the enterprises operating in the Greek economy, especially in the sectors of construction, industry, distributive trades and services. Their dominance is evident in terms of value added, employment and number of enterprises. The basic figures are presented in Tables 1, 2 and 3. More specifically, Greece has a very high share of SMEs, with large enterprises representing only 0,1% of all businesses. In 2017 SMEs generated 63,6% of value added and 85,2% of employment (overcoming the EU average of 56,8% and 66,4% respectively) with micro firms being considered as the backbone of the economy, since they correspond to six out of ten jobs. Due to this higher proportion, SMEs in Greece are smaller as they employ 2,4 people averagely, compared to the average of 3,9 people in the rest of the EU. Nonetheless, in 2017, the vastly fewer large companies managed to create 36,4% of value added compared to the 22,7% of the micro enterprises, suggesting that the productivity of the later was quite low. The data highlight their central role at such level that when one describes the Greek private sector usually refers to small-scale companies that often include self-employment or family-owned firms and businesses units with fewer than five employees. Thus, Greek SMEs have to face a series of barriers, such as lack of financial resources and traditional management methods (Labrianidis and Vogiatzis, 2013).

In the last few years, SMEs in Greece were hit extremely hard by the economic crisis and they still haven't fully recovered. The adverse effects had become felt across all the three indicators presented in the graphs 1, 2 and 3. It appears that Greek SMEs had suffered a dramatic decrease. Based on the 2012 SBA report, the total number had drastically fallen since 2003, as there were nearly 90.000 fewer companies in 2011 than in 2008, which was the last year of the pre-crisis period. In terms of employment, that was reflected in the loss of more than 200.000 jobs and that negative development also applied for the value added data. Numbers continued to decline in the next year's report as well. This was mainly attributed to the austerity measures that were implemented (increased taxes, reduction in salaries/pensions) that reduced the purchasing power of consumers, and increased both the financial and tax obligations of the Greek companies. In 2013, there were some signs that the economy was recovering (after the prolonged recession), with the downward trend to slowing down and even showing some positive signs. In 2015, the recession had turned into stagnation. Value added in 2016 remained at roughly the same level as in 2013 (after the five previous years in which both value added and employment dropped). But still, added value was 35% and employment 23% below the respective levels of 2008. On the other hand, employment rose almost 40% since 2012 mostly thanks to the considerable performance of micro firms. Two years after the imposition of capital controls it appears that important progress has been made in rebounding from the recession.

The issue of financial recourses was never an easy case for SMEs. In 2010, a high share of unsuccessful loan applications (36%) combined with an intense reduction in the number of loans being offered by banks weakened the position of Greek SME managers. Furthermore, the venture capital market investment was also more limited. Consequently, there were excessive payment delays which further increased the cost of doing business in the country. In an attempt to compensate this situation, the government provided micro and small companies with low interest loans in order to cope with tax and insurance liabilities, as well as other state debt. In 2011, they launched a program that financed enterprises with investment in venture capital, provided risk-sharing loans at reduced rates and guarantees for loans (SBA Fact Sheet, 2011). In the following report, evidence showed that unsuccessful loan applications dropped to 29%, as banks were extremely reluctant to grant loans (SBA Fact Sheet, 2012). This was an extremely awful development considering that almost 96% of Greek SMEs relied on bank loans as an external source of financing (European Commission 2013a). In 2013, although the government continued to support SMEs, all financing indicators had deteriorated and were below the EU average (SBA Fact Sheet, 2013). The sovereign debt crisis had left no instrument of financial support intact, and that definitely undermined all efforts for Greek SMEs to continue their activity (GSEVEE, 2014). According to Tzakou-Lambropoulou (2014) almost 42% of SMEs in Greece could not receive financing and some were unwilling to even attempt it. The critical support of European funds should also be mentioned, such as the 1.6 billion Euros that were used for Financial Engineering Instruments between 2007-2013 (Reichenbach, 2014). In 2013 all financing indicators in the SBA report (with the exception of interest rates for small and large loans) were below the EU average proving that the situation had deteriorated (SBA Fact Sheet, 2014). For example, one in three loan applications would either be rejected or receive an offer with unbearable terms. In addition, the days for an entrepreneur to get paid were almost 96 compared to 50 in other Member States. It should also be pointed that the government continued to provide incentives and implementing measures in order to improve liquidity. Despite the fact that signs of improvement were apparent, Greece continued to score below the EU average for most indicators of the 2018 SBA report. As it is shown in Table 4, the amount of days that took a company to get paid was about 65, which is approximately a month longer that it took the average European firm. Although bank lending remained a significant barrier, banks seemed more willing to lend than they were in 2015 and access to public financial support had improved.

MAIN FOCUS OF THE CHAPTER

The Digital Footprint of Greek SMEs

Prior to the analysis of evidence relating to SMEs it was considered appropriate to present certain facts concerning the development of the digital economy in Greece and how the country is doing in the digital world in general. Regarding its position in the digital map Greece was ranked 26th out of the 28 EU members in the European Commission Digital Economy and Society Index (DESI, 2019). Based on the data presented the country had slightly improved its position, mainly in the factors of human capital (since the number of ICT specialists as a percentage in total employment increased, and so did the number of graduates) and the supply side of digital public services. But despite those improvements it remained behind the EU average. Specifically, the digital skills of the population group over the age of 55, which forms the majority of 30% of the population either had never used the Internet or was significantly deficient in digital skills compared to the EU corresponding average. In the field of connectivity, the transition to fast and ultrafast broadband was also moving slower compared to the rest of Europe. This was attributed to the considerable delays in project implementation and the low absorption rate of the funds allocated. On the positive side, the number of internet users was improving in individual activities (such as access to information, entertainment, social networks, games), and the use of Internet for communication purposes, but the country was significantly below the EU average in the areas of electronic trading, online shopping and pay-TV. It was also lagging behind in broadband speeds, penetration and cost of fixed and mobile broadband connections and coverage of next generation networks. With regard to businesses using digital technology, the percentage of sales through e-commerce was small, electronic documents had limited penetration and only few enterprises used modern technologies of production organization. Furthermore, the ICT industry contributed very little to the country's economy and to employment while its outward orientation was very limited. It should also be pointed that the progress with integrating digital technology into the business environment remained slow except for the use of Big Data which is higher than the EU average (DESI, 2019). In the last few years specific reference is made to the phenomenon of Big Data which refers to a huge amount of data (i.e. information) that cannot be analysed using traditional computing methods and tools. From a business prospective this means that organizations today (more than ever before) have access to consumer information and potential insight, but in most cases they cannot seem to get value out of it (Zikopoulos et al., 2012). This means that the difference between data quantity and the percentage of their usage is becoming bigger, and the actual data processed and analyzed by organizations are in constant decline (Krasavac et al.,2016). On average, across the EU, Big Data analysis is adopted by 33% of large firms, 19% of medium-size and 10% of small enterprises (Eurostat, 2019). It should also be mentioned that differences in the adoption gaps are observed across countries, between small and large companies and according to Bianchini and Michalkova (2019) Greece is amongst the countries with the smallest divides (12% vs. 20%).

Piperopoulos (2007) concluded that the factors constraining innovation performance of SMEs in Greece were the lack of financial support (mainly from the government) and the country's bureaucratic structure. Other barriers that prevented the innovative process were the use of old management techniques and the lack of cooperation between the economic academic institutions and the business environment.

According to Mylonas and Tzakou-Lampropoulou (2016) 66% of SMEs in Greece used at least one type of digital tool. They separated these enterprises into two main categories: a) the vast majority that used some kind of digital tool (which was usually acquired or upgraded in the previous five years) and b) the corresponding 'digital' percentage that simply had a website or a rudimentary presence on social networks. Regarding the use by sector, IT, transport and heavy manufacturing were the most advanced industries, while food manufacturing, construction, small chemical industries and the small tourism businesses (which are extremely important for the Greek economy) seemed a bit behind in the digital world. As to their internal operations, Greek SMEs were characterised as digitally immature. That was reflected in the fact that even those companies handling a digital tool, had not proceeded to the creation of a substantially advanced system. The most common specialized management software (such as inventories or accounts) were used by 12% of SMEs, less than 10% owned ERP or CRM, and an even a lower proportion (6% of SMEs) used data analytics. Corporate-size discrepancies were significant, with most small businesses having almost no digital internal operations tool, as opposed to the 16% of the larger ones. Their digital image seemed more improved regarding the adoption of communication tools, with 58% having a website or at least a relevant presence on social networks in order to share or exchange information with their clients. That high percentage (that showed signs of digital familiarity), was regarded as encouraging for the use of more sophisticated digital tools in the future. However, the use of more advanced tools was limited (only 18% offered the option of e-shopping either directly or through a provider and 19% used digital marketing). Consequently, the digital immaturity of Greek SMEs was evident at this factor as well, since 85% of those who actually benefited from a digital communication tool did not use a wider digital toolset. Here too, the divergences between the very small and the larger SMEs were limited to simple client tools (such as a web site), but were apparent in the more sophisticated formats. For example, e-commerce accounted for 15% of very small SMEs, versus 28% of other types of SMEs. Since most sectors show significant differences in terms of operation (e.g. manufacturing makes more use of digital tools for internal processes while hotels benefit from e-commerce tools) it is worth mentioning some data per industry. As far as e-commerce is concerned, the trade sector was considered the most dynamic one. On the other hand, despite the relatively high use of e-commerce, the hotel industry appeared below its potential. In terms of how digital technologies were acquired, in-house tools seem to be acquired mainly through outsourcing and secondarily developed within the company itself. However, it is noteworthy that one in four companies using digital tools had already switched to the innovative cloud technology. In contrast, digital communication tools with customers were mainly developed within the company (as they are largely related to website creation). It should also be noted that 75%-85% of companies stated that the digital upgrade had increased their profit, regardless of the type of digital tool or how it was acquired. The only exceptions were in-house development and outsourcing of digital in-house tools for small businesses. For these companies, cloud solutions seemed to improve their profitability even more. Consequently, improving the digital footprint of a small or medium sized business can provide competitive advantages both in terms of profitability and sales. Finally, regarding the adequacy parameter, the researchers noted that 19% of SMEs stated that the digital tools they used for internal operations were sufficient and twice as many (38%) stated that the digital communication tools were adequate. The SMEs future investment was also in the right direction to fill the digital gap with Europe. They concluded that at least in the year that their study was conducted the digital profile of Greek SMEs was still in its infancy.

In a more recent research study Giotopoulos et. al. (2017) focused on the ICT adoption in terms of implementation, infrastructure, internet integration, e-sales and e-procurement. It appears that SMEs associated with research and development or other innovative activities in general, were more likely to adopt ICTs. Another crucial factor was the technological skills and scientific background of the workforce which mainly affected ICT related intentions and not so much the e-commerce activities. The results indicated that in order to assimilate new technologies and to increase the usage of e-commerce applications more advanced ICT skills were necessary. On the issue of organization, the presence of inspiring and insightful combined with a decentralized structure of the company's decision-making process were important elements of ICT implementation. In relation to the divergences between the micro and the slightly larger firms is that the majority of the first do not have the skills, the resources, or the time to implement more advanced technological strategies in their operation. Furthermore, the recruitment of skilled personnel or the training of the human capital is considered a luxury for their financial position.

In 2017, Greece's overall performance in respect to the integration of digital technology was still characterised as inadequate, but some progress had been made. The number of SMEs using social media platforms and digital sales channels had increased and the average turnover from online sales had grew significantly (from 1,2% in 2015 to 5,9% in 2016). But the percentage of firms using electronic invoices or cloud computing services was still very low (3% and 5% respectively). It was also pointed that the country's level in terms of maturity and readiness for adopting the digital transformation was lower than the EU average (Nikolaidis et. al., 2017).

Another survey series that was carried out in two consecutive years investigated the challenges that SMEs face in Greece, but also the affect of online presence and the use of digital technology in their daily operation. Based on the results, approximately three in four companies have established their web presence, as they understand the need to adopt new technologies and follow the global trend towards digitalization. Companies that follow this practice believe that it has improved their competitive advantage, the efficiency and speed of business processes, the company's image, the collaboration with corporate partners and the overall customer service to a significant extent (ELTRUN, 2018).

CONCLUSION

As mentioned in the analysis of the country's digital situation, Greek SMEs have been left behind in terms of adopting digital tools compared to the corresponding European data. Although steps have been made towards the right direction, it is clear that the difficulties they faced in the last eight years (with the prolonged recession and the challenging economic climate) have been an almost insurmountable barrier to their digital growth. But since digitalization improves and stimulates a firm's productivity and innovative procedures, provides access to new markets, increases the purchasing audience and ultimately improves its competitiveness, it is imperative to systematically encourage SMEs to technologically upgrade and transform their operations. Although these decisions are not simple and depend on many factors their growth and even their survival cannot be achieved without the use of advanced digital technology. Therefore, both government and European policy makers should provide support and create the appropriate conditions in order for SMEs to benefit from these crucial opportunities.

REFERENCES

Ayyagari, M., Beck, T., & Demirguc-Kunt, A. (2003). Small and Medium Enterprises across the globe: A new database. *World Bank Policy Research Working Paper, 3127*, 3–34. doi:10.1596/1813-9450-3127

Ayyagari, M., Demirguc-Kunt, A., & Maksimovic, V. (2011). Small vs. young firms across the world: Contribution to employment, job creation, and growth. *World Bank Policy Research Working Paper, 5631*, 2–41. doi:10.1596/1813-9450-5631

Bianchini, M., & Michalkova, V. (2019). *Data Analytics in SMEs:Trends and Policies*. OECD SME and Entrepreneurship Papers No. 15. Retrieved from https://www.oecd-ilibrary.org/economics/data-analytics-in-smes_1de6c6a7-en

Cenamor, J., Paridab, V., & Wincent, J. (2019). How entrepreneurial SMEs compete through digital platforms: The roles of digital platform capability, network capability and ambidexterity. *Journal of Business Research, 100*, 196–206. doi:10.1016/j.jbusres.2019.03.035

Chakravorti, B., Bhalla, A., & Chaturvedi, R. S. (2017). *60 Countries' Digital Competitiveness, Indexed*. Retrieved from https://hbr.org/2017/07/60-countries-digital-competitiveness-indexed

Cull, R., Davis, L. E., Lamoreaux, N. M., & Rosenthal, J. (2006). Historical financing of Smalland Medium-size Enterprises. *Journal of Banking & Finance, 30*(11), 3017–3042. doi:10.1016/j.jbankfin.2006.05.005

DESI - Digital Economy and Society Index (DESI). (2019). *Country Report – Greece*. Retrieved from https://ec.europa.eu/digital-single-market/en/scoreboard/greece

Edinburgh Group. (2012). *Growing the global economy through SMEs*. Retrieved from http://www.edinburgh-group.org/activities/papers.aspx

ELTRUN. (2018). *Greek SMEs - Challenges and Opportunities*. Retrieved from https://www.douleutaras.gr/ereuna-gia-mikromesaies-epixeiriseis/en/

ESCAP-The United Nations Economic and Social Commission for Asia and the Pacific. (2009). *Globalization of production and the competitiveness of Small and Medium-sized Enterprises in Asia and the Pacific: Trends and prospects, studies in trade and investment No. 65*. Retrieved from https://www.unescap.org/resources/globalization-production-and-competitiveness-small-and-medium-sized-enterprises-asia-and

ESCAP. (2014). *Policy Guidebook for SME development in Asia and the Pacific*. Retrieved from https://www.unescap.org/sites/default/files/0%20-%20Full%20Report_7.pdf

European Commission. (2003). Commission Recommendation 2003/361/EC - The Definition of Micro, Small and Medium-sized enterprises. *Official Journal of the European Union*. Retrieved from https://eurlex.europa.eu/LexUriServ/LexUriServ.do?uri=OJ:L:2003:124:0036:0041:en

European Commission. (2013a). *2020 Action Plan - Reigniting the Entrepreneurial Spirit in Europe*. Retrieved from https://eur-lex.europa.eu/legal-content/EN/TXT/?uri=celex:52012DC0795

European Commission. (2017). *Integration of Digital Technology*. Retrieved from file:///C:/Users/pvelo/Downloads/EuropesDigitalProgressReportIntegration ofDigitalTechnologyChapter%20(2).pdf

Gibson, T., & Van der Vaart, H. J. (2008). Defining SMEs: A Less Imperfect Way of Defining Small and Medium Enterprises in Developing Countries. *Brookings Global-Economy and Development*. Retrieved from https://www.brookings.edu/~/media/research/files/papers/2008/9/development%20gibson/09_development_gibson.pdf

Giotopoulos, I., Kontolaimou, A., Korra, E., & Tsakanikas, A. (2017). What drives ICT adoption by SMEs? Evidence from a large-scale survey in Greece. *Journal of Business Research, 81*, 60–69. doi:10.1016/j.jbusres.2017.08.007

GSEVEE - Hellenic Confederation of Professionals, Craftsmen & Merchants. (2014). *The Development of SMEs in Greece*. Retrieved from https://www.gsevee.gr/press/mme_eng.pdf

Hallberg, K. (2000). A Market-oriented strategy for Small and Medium Scale Enterprises. *International Finance Corporation Discussion Paper - The World Bank*. Retrieved from http://documents.worldbank.org/curated/en/2000/04/693275/market-oriented-strategy-small-medium-scale-enterprises

Hobohm, S. (2001). Small and Medium-sized Enterprises in economic development: the UNIDO experience. *Journal of Economic Cooperation Among Islamic Countries, 22*(1), 1-42.

Kavoura, A., & Andersson, T. (2016). Applying Delphi method for strategic design of social entrepreneurship. *Library Review, 65*(3), 185–205. doi:10.1108/LR-06-2015-0062

Kavoura, A., & Koziol, L. (2017). Polish Firms' Innovation Capability for Competitiveness via Information Technologies and Social Media Implementation. In A. Vlachvei, O. Notta, K. Karantininis, & N. Tsountas (Eds.), *Factors Affecting Firm Competitiveness and Performance in the Modern Business World* (pp. 185–214). IGI Global. doi:10.4018/978-1-5225-0843-4.ch007

Kok, J., Vroonhof, P., Verhoeven, W., Timmermans, N., Kwaak, T., Snijders, J., & Westhof, F. (2011). Do SMEs create more and better jobs? *Report of the EIM Business & Policy Research*. Retrieved from https://ec.europa.eu/enterprise/policies/sme/facts-figures-analysis/performance-review/files/supporting-documents/2012/methodological-report_en.pdf

Krasavac, K. C., Biljana Soldic, A., & Jasna Petkovic, G. (2016). The big data phenomenon: The business and public impact. *Industrija, 44*(2), 117–144. doi:10.5937/industrija44-10036

Labrianidis, L., & Vogiatzis, N. (2013). *Restructuring in SMEs: Greece*. Retrieved from: https://www.eurofound.europa.eu/mk/publications/report/2013/greece/labour-market-business/restructuring-in-smes-greece

Lukacs, E. (2005). The economic role of SMEs in world economy, especially in Europe. *European Integration Studies, 1*(4), 3–12.

Makarona, E., & Kavoura, A. (2019). Redesigning the Ivory Tower: Academic entrepreneurship as a new calling supporting economic growth. *The Malopolska School of Economics in Tarnow Research Papers Collection, 42*, 15–26.

Masouras, A. (2019). Young entrepreneurship in Cyprus: An institutional analysis. *The Małopolska School of Economics in Tarnów Research Papers Collection, 42*(2), 27–42.

Muller, P., Gagliardi, D., Caliandro, C., Bohn, N.U., & Klitou, D. (2014). *SME Performance Review 2013/2014 - A partial and fragile recovery*. European Commission Annual -Report on European SMEs, 2013/2014 – A, 1-124.

Nikolaidis, P., Michalopoulos, N., Kokkalas, C., Pateli, K., Anastopoulou, I., Vrettaros, Y., Panopoulos, D., Papoulia, K., Sirros, Y., & Achilleopoulos, N. (n.d.). *Enhasing Digital Skills in Greece - National Action plan (2017-2020) for Digital Skills and Jobs*. Retrieved from http://elke.eap.gr/wp-content/uploads/2018/07/dsgr_action_plan_eng_subm4_no-memo.pdf

Organization for Economic Co-Operation and Development - OECD. (2004). *Promoting SMEs for Development: The enabling environment and trade and investment capacity building*. Paper presented in the 2nd OECD Conference of Ministers responsible for SMEs, Istanbul, Turkey.

OECD. (2014). Small and Medium-sized enterprises. In *OECD Factbook 2014: Economic, Environmental and Social Statistics*. OECD Publishing. doi:10.1787/factbook-2014-20-

Peters, B., Dachs, B., Dunser, M., Hud, M., Kohler, C., & Rammer, C. (2014). *Firm growth, innovation and the business cycle*. Background Report for the 2014 Competitiveness Report. Retrieved from ftp://ftp.zew.de/pub/zew-docs/gutachten/CR2014_BackgroundStudy.pdf>

Piperopoulos, P. (2007). Barriers to innovation for SMEs: Empirical evidence from Greece. *International Journal of Business Innovation and Research, 1*(4), 365–386. doi:10.1504/IJBIR.2007.013725

Robu, M. (2013). The dynamic and importance of SMEs in economy. The USV Annals of Economics and Public Administration, 13(1-17), 84-89.

Small Business Act (SBA) Fact Sheet. (n.d.a). *Annual Report 2010-2011*. Retrieved from https://ec.europa.eu/enterprise/policies/sme/facts-figures-analysis/performance-review/files/countries-sheets/2010-2011/greece_en.pdf

Small Business Act (SBA) Fact Sheet. (n.d.b). *Annual Report 2012*. Retrieved from https://ec.europa.eu/enterprise/policies/sme/facts-figures-analysis/performance-review/files/supporting-documents/2012/annual-report_en.pdf

Small Business Act (SBA). (n.d.a). *Annual Report 2013*. Retrieved from https://ec.europa.eu/enterprise/policies/sme/facts-figures-analysis/performance-review/files/supporting-documents/2013/annual-report-smes-2013_en.pdf

Small Business Act (SBA). (n.d.b). *Annual Report 2014*. Retrieved from https://ec.europa.eu/enterprise/policies/sme/facts-figures-analysis/performance-review/files/supporting-documents/2014/annual-report-smes-2014_en.pdf

Small Business Act (SBA). (n.d.c). *Annual Report 2015*. Retrieved from http://www.heliachamber.gr/iliaimages/greece_en_F19573.pdf

Small Business Act (SBA). (n.d.d). *Annual Report 2016*. Retrieved from https://www.ggb.gr/sites/default/files/basic-page-files/Greece%202016%20SBA%20Fact%20Sheet.pdf

Small Business Act (SBA). (n.d.e). *Annual Report 2017*. Retrieved from https://ec.europa.eu/docsroom/documents/29489/attachments/13/translations/en/renditions/pdf

Small Business Act (SBA). (n.d.f). *Annual Report 2018*. Retrieved from https://ec.europa.eu/growth/smes/business-friendly-environment/performance-review_en

Tewari, P., Skilling, D., Kumar, P., & Zack, W. (2013). Competitive Small and Medium Enterprises: A diagnostic to help design smart SME policy. World Bank, 82516, 1-35.

Tzakou-Lambropoulou, N. 2014. *Restoring the competitiveness of the SME sector in Greece. GR for Growth: Funding SMEs*. Retrieved from http://www.helex.gr/documents/10180/2084352/Session2_Nelly_Tzakou_Labropoulou_Presentation.pdf/422e0a8d-6d29-4961-9ecd-8d43d182c74d

Ulas, D. (2019). Digital Transformation Process and SMEs. *Procedia Computer Science*, *158*, 662–671. doi:10.1016/j.procs.2019.09.101

Zikopoulos, P. C., Eaton, C., de Roos, D., Deutch, T., & Lapis, G. (2012). *Understanding Big Data, Analytics for Enterprice Class Hadoop and Streaming Data*. McGraw Hill.

KEY TERMS AND DEFINITIONS

Big Data: A large amount of information about an organization (both structured and unstructured) that cannot be analysed using traditional computing methods.

Communication Platforms: Digital media (e.g. Facebook, Instagram and Twitter) that are used as means of communication. In marketing, they provide information and awareness about a specific product or brand.

Digital Economy: An economy that is based on digital technologies and the Internet.

Digital Footprint: The information left behind as a result of digital activities and communications stated on the Internet.

Digital Skills: A range of technical skills and abilities associated with understanding and using communication applications, networks and digital devices in order to access and manage information.

Digitalization: The use of digital technologies and digitized data in the way companies operate and communicate with their customers.

Family-Owned Firms: A type of business organization in which two or more family members are involved in the management and the majority of ownership or company control lies within the same family.

ICT: An umbrella term that refers to Information and communications technology.

SME: A micro, small or medium sized company.

Compilation of References

Abeysekera, I. (2006). Issues relating to designing a work-integrated learning program in an undergraduate accounting degree program and its implications for the curriculum. *Asia Pacific Journal of Cooperative Education*, *7*(1), 7–15.

AboutUs. (2020). Retrieved from https://www.tuktukhop.com/about

Abouzaid, S. (2008). *IFC family business governance handbook*. Retrieved from http://www.ifc.org/wps/wcm/connect/159c9c0048582f6883f9ebfc046daa89/FB_English_final_2008.pdf?MOD=AJPERES

Achebe, C. (2012). Why Nigerians hate Igbos. *The Nation*. Available: http://thenationonlineng.net/new/why-nigerians-hate-igbos-by-chinua-achebe/

Acs, Z. J., Estrin, S., Mickiewicz, T., & Szerb, L. (2018). Entrepreneurship, institutional economics, and economic growth: An ecosystem perspective. *Small Business Economics*, *51*(5), 1–14. doi:10.100711187-018-0013-9

Acs, Z., & Audretsch, D. (1987). Innovation, Market Structure, and Firm Size. *The Review of Economics and Statistics*, *69*(4), 567–575. doi:10.2307/1935950

Acs, Z., & Audretsch, D. (1988). Innovation in large and small firms: An empirical analysis. *The American Economic Review*, *78*, 680–681.

Adejimola, A. S. (2008). Language, communication and information flow in entrepreneurship. *African Journal of Business Management*, *2*, 201–208.

Aernoudt, R. (2004). Incubators: Tool for Entrepreneurship? *Small Business Economics*, *23*(2), 127–135. doi:10.1023/B:SBEJ.0000027665.54173.23

Ajzen, I. (1991). The theory of planned behavior. *Organizational Behavior and Human Decision Processes*, *50*(2), 179–211. doi:10.1016/0749-5978(91)90020-T

Ajzen, I. (2002). Perceived Behavioral Control, Self-Efficacy, Locus of Control, and the Theory of Planned Behavior1. *Journal of Applied Social Psychology*, *32*(4), 665–683. doi:10.1111/j.1559-1816.2002.tb00236.x

Ajzen, I., & Fishein, M. (1969). The Prediction of Behavioral Intentions in a Choice Situation. *Journal of Experimental Social Psychology*, *5*(4), 400–416. doi:10.1016/0022-1031(69)90033-X

Ajzen, I., & Fishein, M. (1980). *Understanding attitudes and predicting social behavior*. Prentice-Hall.

Akanazu, H. (2016). *Family Businesses in Nigeria and Inter-Generational Succession. Family-Owned Businesses Forum Nigeria*. Available: https://www.academia.edu/30992273/FAMILY-OWNED_BUSINESS_FORUM_NIGERIA.docx

Al-adawi, Z., Yousafzai, Z., & Pallister, J. (2005, September). Conceptual Model of citizen adoption of e-government. *Second International Conference on Innovations in Information Technology*.

Al-Jubari, I., Hassan, A., & Liñán, F. (2018). Entrepreneurial intention among University students in Malaysia: Integrating self-determination theory and the theory of planned behavior. *The International Entrepreneurship and Management Journal*, *15*(4), 1323–1342. doi:10.100711365-018-0529-0

Almunia, M., Bénétrix, A., Eichengreen, B., O'Rourke, K., & Rua, G. (2009). *From Great Depression to Great Credit Crisis: Similarities, Differences and Lessons*. NBER Working Paper 15524.

Alsos, G. A., Eide, D., & Madsen, E. L. (2014). Introduction: Innovation in tourism industries. In *Handbook of research on innovation in tourism industries*. Edward Elgar Publishing. doi:10.4337/9781782548416.00006

Altinay, L., Madanoglu, M., Daniele, R., & Lashley, C. (2012). The influence of family tradition and psychological traits on entrepreneurial intention. *International Journal of Hospitality Management*, *31*(2), 489–499. doi:10.1016/j.ijhm.2011.07.007

Ambec, S., Cohen, M., Elgie, S., & Lanoie, P. (2013). The Porter Hypothesis at 20: Can Environmental Regulation Enhance Innovation and Competitiveness? *Review of Environmental Economics and Policy*, *7*(1), 2–22. doi:10.1093/reep/res016

Amit, R., & Zott, C. (2012). Creating Value Through Business Model Innovation. *MIT Sloan Management Review*. http://sloanreview.mit.edu/article/creating-value-through-business-model-innovation/

Ammenberg, J., Börjesson, B., & Hjelm, O. (2017). Joint EMS and group certification: a cost-effective route for SMEs to achieve ISO 14001. In *ISO 14001* (pp. 58–66). Routledge. doi:10.4324/9781351282765-6

Anderson, R., & Reeb, D. (2003). Founding-Family Ownership and Firm Performance: Evidence from the S&P 500. *The Journal of Finance*, *58*(3), 1301–1328. doi:10.1111/1540-6261.00567

Antoniadis, I., & Charmantzi, A. (2016). Social network analysis and social capital in marketing: Theory and practical implementation. *International Journal of Technology Marketing*, *11*(3), 344–359. doi:10.1504/IJTMKT.2016.077387

Antoniadis, I., Tsiakiris, T., & Tsopogloy, S. (2015). Business Intelligence during times of crisis: Adoption and usage of ERP systems by SMEs. *Procedia: Social and Behavioral Sciences*, *175*, 299–307. doi:10.1016/j.sbspro.2015.01.1204

Antonio, N., de Almeida, A., & Nunes, L. (2019). Hotel booking demand datasets. *Data in Brief*, *22*, 41–49. doi:10.1016/j.dib.2018.11.126 PMID:30581903

Archibugi, D., Filippetti, A., & Frenz, M. (2013). Economic crisis and innovation: Is destruction prevailing over accumulation? *Research Policy*, *42*(2), 303–314. doi:10.1016/j.respol.2012.07.002

Argote, L. & Miron-Spektor, E. (2011). Organizational Learning: From Experience to Knowledge. *Organization Science*, *22*(5), 1123–1137. doi:10.1287/orsc.1100.0621

Argyris, C. (1999). *Conocimiento para la acción: Una guía para superar los obstáculos del cambio enla organización*. Granica.

Armitage, C. J., & Conner, M. (2001). Efficacy of the Theory of Planned Behaviour: A meta-analytic review. *British Journal of Social Psychology*, *40*(4), 471–499. doi:10.1348/014466601164939 PMID:11795063

Arnold, B., & De Lange, P. (2004). Enron: An examination of agency problems. *Critical Perspectives on Accounting*, *15*(6-7), 751–765. doi:10.1016/j.cpa.2003.08.005

Arora, R. (2015). *Why India Is the Land of Rising Entrepreneurship*. Retrieved 7 April 2020, from https://www.inc.com/rohit-arora/why-india-is-the-land-of-rising-entrepreneurship.html

Arrowsmith, S. (2001). E-Commerce Policy and the EC Procurement Rules. The Clash between Rhetoric and Reality. *Common Market Law Review*, *38*(6), 1447–1477. doi:10.1023/A:1013990310541

Artz, K. W., Norman, P. M., Hatfield, D. E., & Cardinal, L. B. (2010). A longitudinal study of the impact of R&D, patents, and product innovation on firm performance. *Journal of Product Innovation Management*, *27*(5), 725–740. doi:10.1111/j.1540-5885.2010.00747.x

Asonitou, S., & Kavoura, A. (2019). Accounting education, technology and entrepreneurship: Current trends and future outlook. *The Malopolska School of Economics in Tarnow Research Papers Collection*, *44*(4), 65–78.

Asplund, M., & Sandin, R. (1999). The survival of new products. *Review of Industrial Organization*, *15*(3), 219–237. doi:10.1023/A:1007708612713

Atalatti, A., Lanham, E., & Coldwell-Neilson, J. (2015). Usability in mLearning. In *Proceedings of the 7th International Conference on Computer Supported Education* (pp. 213-219). Lisbon, Portugal: SCITEPRESS.

Ateljevic, J., & Li, L. (2009). Tourism entrepreneurship–concepts and issues. In J. Ateljevic & S. J. Page (Eds.), *Tourism and entrepreneurship: International perspectives* (pp. 9–32). Butterworth-Heinemann. doi:10.1016/B978-0-7506-8635-8.00002-2

Aulet, B. (2013). *Disciplined Entrepreneurship, 24 Steps to a Successful Start Up*. John Wiley & Sons, Inc.

Au, N., Ngai, W., & Cheng, T. (2008). Extending the understanding of end user information systems satisfaction formation: An equitable needs fulfillment model approach. *Management Information Systems Quarterly*, *32*(1), 43–66. doi:10.2307/25148828

Autio, E., Keeley, R. H., Klofsten, M., Parker, G. G. C., & Hay, M. (2001). Entrepreneurial Intent among Students in Scandinavia and in the USA. *Enterprise and Innovation Management Studies*, *2*(2), 145–160. doi:10.1080/14632440110094632

Autry, C., Grawe, S., Daugherty, P., & Richey, G. (2010). The effects of technological turbulence and breadth on supply chain technology acceptance and adoption. *Journal of Operations Management*, *28*(6), 522–536. doi:10.1016/j.jom.2010.03.001

Ayobami, A. O., Odey, O. D., Olanireti, A. M., & Babarinde, K. P. (2018). Family Business and Innovation in Nigeria: Problems and Prospects. *Covenant Journal of Entrepreneurship*, *2*(1), 26–33.

Ayres, N., & Maglaras, L. A. (2016). Cyberterrorism targeting the general public through social media. *Security and Communication Networks*, *9*(15), 2864–2875. doi:10.1002ec.1568

Ayyagari, M., Beck, T., & Demirguc-Kunt, A. (2003). Small and Medium Enterprises across the globe: A new database. *World Bank Policy Research Working Paper*, *3127*, 3–34. doi:10.1596/1813-9450-3127

Ayyagari, M., Demirguc-Kunt, A., & Maksimovic, V. (2011). Small vs. young firms across the world: Contribution to employment, job creation, and growth. *World Bank Policy Research Working Paper*, *5631*, 2–41. doi:10.1596/1813-9450-5631

Babbie, E. (2010). *The Basis of Social Research*. Wadsworth Cengage Learning Publisher.

Bacq, S., & Janssen, F. (2011). The multiple faces of social entrepreneurship: A review of definitional issues based on geographical and thematic criteria. *Entrepreneurship and Regional Development*, *23*(5-6), 373–403. doi:10.1080/08985626.2011.577242

Bagozzi, R., Davis, F., & Warshaw, P. (1992). Development and Test of a Theory of Technological Learning and Usage. *Human Relations*, *45*(7), 659–686. doi:10.1177/001872679204500702

Bagozzi, R., & Yi, Y. (1988). On the Evaluation of Structural Equation Models. *Journal of the Academy of Marketing Science*, *16*(1), 74–94. doi:10.1007/BF02723327

Baldwin, J., & Lin, Z. (2002). Impediments to advanced technology adoption for Canadian manufacturers. *Research Policy*, *31*(1), 1–18. doi:10.1016/S0048-7333(01)00110-X

Balea, J. (2016). *Thailand plans $570m venture fund for startups.* Retrieved from https://www.techinasia.com/thailand-fund-startups

Bandura, A. (1977). Self-efficacy: Toward a unifying theory of behavioral change. *Psychological Review*, *84*(2), 191–215. doi:10.1037/0033-295X.84.2.191 PMID:847061

Bandura, A. (1982). The assessment and predictive generality of self-percepts of efficacy. *Journal of Behavior Therapy and Experimental Psychiatry*, *13*(3), 195–199. doi:10.1016/0005-7916(82)90004-0 PMID:7142408

Bandura, A. (1997). *Self-efficacy: The exercise of control.* Freeman.

Bangkok Post. (2019a). *Record 38.27m tourists in 2018; 41m expected in 2019.* Retrieved from https://www.bangkokpost.com/business/1619182/record-38-27m-tourists-in-2018-41m-expected-in-2019

Bangkok Post. (2019b). *Airbnb, state agencies aid homestay operators.* Retrieved from https://www.bangkokpost.com/business/1776619/airbnb-state-agencies-aid-homestay-operators

Banwell, C., Dixon, J., Seubsman, S., Pangsap, S., Kelly, M., & Sleigh, A. (2013). Evolving food retail environments in Thailand and implications for the health and nutrition transition. *Public Health Nutrition*, *16*(4), 608–615. doi:10.1017/S1368980012004223 PMID:23021291

Barney, J. B. (1991). Firm Resources and Sustained Competitive Advantage. *Journal of Management*, *17*(1), 99–120. doi:10.1177/014920639101700108

Baron, R. A., & Ensley, M. D. (2006). Opportunity Recognition as the Detection of Meaningful Patterns: Evidence from Comparisons of Novice and Experienced Entrepreneurs. *Management Science*, *52*(9), 1331–1344. doi:10.1287/mnsc.1060.0538

Baron, R., & Markman, G. (2000). Beyond social capital: How social skills can enhance entrepreneurs' success. *The Academy of Management Executive*, *14*(1), 106–116. doi:10.5465/ame.2000.2909843

Baruch, Y., & Holtom, B. C. (2008). Survey response rate levels and trends in organizational research. *Human Relations*, *61*(8), 1139–1160. doi:10.1177/0018726708094863

Basten, D., & Haamann, T. (2018). Approaches for Organizational Learning: A Literature Review. *SAGE Open - Literature Review.* Retrieved from https://journals.sagepub.com/doi/pdf/10.1177/2158244018794224

Beckwith, L., Sorte, S., Burnett, M., Wiedenbeck, S., Chintakovid, T., & Cook, C. (2005). Designing Features for Both Genders in End-User Programming Environments. In *Proceedings of the 2005 I.E. Symposium on Visual Languages and Human-Centric Computing* (pp. 153-160). Washington, DC: IEEE Computer Society. 10.1109/VLHCC.2005.31

Belias, D. (2019). Entrepreneurship in the age of digital tourism; the future prospects from the use of robots. *Małopolska Journal, 42*(2), 89-99. doi:10.25944/znmwse.2019.02.8999

Belleau, B. D., Summers, T. A., Xu, Y., & Pinel, R. (2007). Theory of reasoned action: Purchase intention of young consumers. *Clothing & Textiles Research Journal*, *25*(3), 244–257. doi:10.1177/0887302X07302768

Benzing, C., Chu, H. M., & Kara, O. (2009). Entrepreneurs in Turkey: A factor analysis of motivations, success factors, and problems. *Journal of Small Business Management*, *47*(1), 58–91. doi:10.1111/j.1540-627X.2008.00262.x

Bettis, R. A., & Prahalad, C. K. (1995). The Dominant Logic: Retrospective and Extension. *Strategic Management Journal*, *16*(1), 5–14. doi:10.1002mj.4250160104

Bhattacharya, S., & Ritter, J. (1985). Innovation and communication: Signalling with partial disclosure. *The Review of Economic Studies*, *50*(2), 331–346. doi:10.2307/2297419

Bhattacherjee, A., Davis, C. J., Connolly, A. J., & Hikmet, N. (2017). User response to mandatory IT use: A Coping Theory perspective. *European Journal of Information Systems*, 1–21. doi:10.105741303-017-0047-0

Bianchini, M., & Michalkova, V. (2019). *Data Analytics in SMEs:Trends and Policies*. OECD SME and Entrepreneurship Papers No. 15. Retrieved from https://www.oecd-ilibrary.org/economics/data-analytics-in-smes_1de6c6a7-en

Bias, R. G., & Mayhew, D. J. (2005). *Cost-Justifying Usability: An Update for an Internet Age*. Morgan Kaufman. doi:10.1016/B978-012095811-5/50001-8

Blal, I., & Sturman, M. C. (2014). The differential effects of the quality and quantity of online reviews on hotel room sales. *Cornell Hospitality Quarterly*, *55*(4), 365–375. doi:10.1177/1938965514533419

Block, J. (2012). R&D Investments in Family and Founder Firms: An Agency Perspective. *Journal of Business Venturing*, *27*(2), 248–265. doi:10.1016/j.jbusvent.2010.09.003

Bloemen-Bekx, M., Voordeckers, W., Remery, C., & Schippers, J. (2019). Following in parental footsteps? The influence of gender and learning experiences on entrepreneurial intentions. *International Small Business Journal: Researching Entrepreneurship*, *37*(6), 642–663. doi:10.1177/0266242619838936

Bogoudinova, R. Z., & Kazakova, W. A. (2018) Engineering pedagogy in the system of formation of professional engineering competences. *Engineering Education*, *24*, 45-50.

Bola Ajibola & Co. (2019). *Our Team Elements Presentation*. Available: http://www.bolaajibolaandco.com/?page_id=1600

Bookis, A. (2016). *Managing Innovation within Organizations*. Doi:10.4018/978-1-4666-9607-5.ch012

Bornstein, D. (2007). *How to Change the World: Social Entrepreneurs and the Power of New Ideas*. Oxford University Press.

Borzaga, C., & Defourny, J. (Eds.). (2001). *The Emergence of Social Enterprise*. Routledge. doi:10.4324/9780203164679

Bosma, N., & Kelley, D. (2019). *Global Entrepreneurship Monitor 2018/2019 Global Report*. Retrieved from: https://www.gemconsortium.org/report/gem-2018-2019-global-report

Brandon-Jones, A., & Kauppi, K. (2018). Examining the antecedents of the technology acceptance model within e-procurement. *International Journal of Operations & Production Management*, *38*(1), 22–42. doi:10.1108/IJOPM-06-2015-0346

Branstad, P., Jackson, B., & Banerji, S. (2009). *Rethink Your Strategy An Urgent Memo To the CEO*. Booz & Company Inc.

Braun, M. T. (2013). Obstacles to social networking website use among older adults. *Computers in Human Behavior*, *29*(3), 673–680. doi:10.1016/j.chb.2012.12.004

Briciu, V.-A, Briciu, A., & Nechita, F. (2018). Content Analysis Made Simple for Students. An Interactive Online Application Solution. *Cognitive Science – New Media – Education, 5*(2), 77-91.

Briciu, V.-A., Briciu, A., & Găitan, Ș.-M. (2019). New Media and Organizational Communication. A Multiple Analysis of Romanian Bank Online Environment. In *6th International Multidisciplinary Scientific Conference on Social Sciences and Arts SGEM 2019, Conference Proceedings* (pp. 41-52). Sofia: STEF92 Technology Ltd. 10.5593gemsocial2019V/6.1/S07.006

Briciu, V.-A., Briciu, A., & Găitan, Ș.-M. (2019). The Image Management Strategy through Social Networks. An Analysis of the Banking Environment in Romania. In V. Bevanda (Ed.), *International Scientific Conference EMAN – Economics & Management: How to Cope with Disrupted Times - Conference Proceedings* (pp. 583-588). Belgrade: All in One Print Center Publisher. 10.31410/EMAN.2019.583

Briciu, A., & Briciu, V.-A. (2020). Participatory Culture and Tourist Experience: Promoting Destinations Through YouTube. In A. Kavoura, E. Kefallonitis, & P. Theodoridis (Eds.), *Strategic Innovative Marketing and Tourism. Springer Proceedings in Business and Economics* (pp. 425–433). Springer. doi:10.1007/978-3-030-36126-6_47

Briciu, V.-A., Briciu, A., & Găitan, Ș.-M. (2020). Impression Management Through Websites: An Analysis of the Romanian Banking Industry. In A. Kavoura, E. Kefallonitis, & P. Theodoridis (Eds.), *Strategic Innovative Marketing and Tourism. Springer Proceedings in Business and Economics* (pp. 417–424). Springer. doi:10.1007/978-3-030-36126-6_46

Broekaert, W., Andries, P., & Debackere, K. (2016). Innovation processes in family firms: The relevance of organizational flexibility. *Small Business Economics*, *47*(3), 771–785. doi:10.100711187-016-9760-7

Brown, S., Massey, A., Montoya-weiss, M., & Burkman, J. R. (2002). Do I really have to? User acceptance of mandated technology. *European Journal of Information Systems*, *11*(4), 283–295. doi:10.1057/palgrave.ejis.3000438

Budget Direct. (2020). *Singapore Tourism Statistics 2020*. Retrieved from https://www.budgetdirect.com.sg/travel-insurance/research/singapore-tourism-statistics

Busenitz, L. W., Gómez, C., & Spencer, J. W. (2000). Country institutional profiles: Unlocking entrepreneurial phenomena. *Academy of Management Journal*, *43*(5), 994–1003. doi:10.2307/1556423

Busłowska, A., & Wiśniewska, B. (2017). The bialystok functional area competency center as an example of development of human capital. *Ekonomia i Prawo*, *16*(4), 371–385. doi:10.12775/EiP.2017.026

Buttle, F., & Bok, B. (1996). Hotel marketing strategy and the theory of reasoned action. *International Journal of Contemporary Hospitality Management*, *8*(3), 5–10. doi:10.1108/09596119610115943

Butz, N. T., Hanson, S., Schultz, P. L., & Warzynski, M. M. (2018). Beyond the Big Five: Does grit influence the entrepreneurial intent of university students in the US? *Journal of Global Entrepreneurship Research*, *8*(1), 15. Advance online publication. doi:10.118640497-018-0100-z

Çakmak, E., Lie, R., & Selwyn, T. (2019). Informal tourism entrepreneurs' capital usage and conversion. *Current Issues in Tourism*, *22*(18), 2250–2265. doi:10.1080/13683500.2018.1448763

Calantone, R., Cavusgil, T., & Zhao, Y. (2002). Learning Orientation, Firm Innovation Capability, and Firm Performance. *Industrial Marketing Management*, *31*(6), 515–524. doi:10.1016/S0019-8501(01)00203-6

Calloway, L. J., & Keen, P. G. W. (1996). Organizing for crisis response. *Journal of Information Technology*, *11*(1), 13–27. doi:10.1177/026839629601100102

Camelo, C., Romero, P., & Valle, R. (2000). Relación entre el tipo y el grado de innovación y el rendimiento de la empresa. *Economía Industrial*, *333*, 149–160.

Canepa, A., & Stoneman, P. (2002). *Financial constraints on innovations: A European cross-country study*. Working Paper no. 02–11, Kiel Institute of World Economics.

Cao, V. Q., & Ngo, T. T. T. (2019). Linking Entrepreneurial Intentions And Mindset Models: A Comparative Study Of Public And Private Universities In Vietnam. *Gadjah Mada International Journal of Business*, *21*(2), 115. doi:10.22146/gamaijb.34753

Carayannis, E., Samara, E., & Bakouros, Y. (2014). *Innovation and Entrepreneurship -"Theory, Policy and Practice.* Springer.

Cardona, R. A. (2011). Estrategia basada en los recursos y capacidades. Criterios de evaluación y el proceso de desarrollo. *Revista Electrónica Forum Doctoral.* Retrieved from www.eumed.net/tesis-doctorales/2012/zll/teorias-recursos-capacidades.html

Cardona, J., & Calderón, G. (2006, July). *El Impacto del Aprendizaje en el Rendimiento de las Organizaciones. Cuad. Adm.*

Carlisle, S., Kunc, M., Jones, E., & Tiffin, S. (2013). Supporting innovation for tourism development through multi-stakeholder approaches: Experiences from Africa. *Tourism Management, 35,* 59–69. doi:10.1016/j.tourman.2012.05.010

Carney, M. (2007). Minority family business in emerging markets: Organization forms and competitive advantage. *Family Business Review, 20*(4), 289–300. doi:10.1111/j.1741-6248.2007.00097.x

Carolina, A., & Silva, N. (2015). Social Entrepreneurship and Corporate Social Responsibility: Differences and Points in Common *Journal of Business &. Economic Policy, 2*(2), 85–93.

Carroll, A. B., & Buchholtz, A. K. (2015). Business and Society: Ethics, Sustainability, and Stakeholder Management (9th ed.). Cengage Learning.

Carroll, A. B. (2015a). Corporate social responsibility: The centerpiece of competing and complementary frameworks. *Organizational Dynamics, 44*(2), 87–96. doi:10.1016/j.orgdyn.2015.02.002

Carroll, A. B. (2015b). Corporate Social Responsibility (CSR) is on a Sustainable Trajectory. *Journal of Defense Management, 5,* 132. doi:10.4172/2167-0374.1000132

Carter, L., & Belanger, F. (2005). The Utilization of E-Government Services: Citizen Trust, Innovation and Acceptance Factors. *Information Systems Journal, 15*(1), 5–25. doi:10.1111/j.1365-2575.2005.00183.x

Cegarra, J. G., & Rodrigo, B. (2004). Componentes de éxito del aprendizaje grupal en el capital intelectual. *Investigaciones Europeas de Dirección y Economía de la Empresa, 10*(2), 75-92.

Cegarra-Navarra, J., Reverte, C., Gómez-Melero, E., & Wensley, K. P. (2016). Linking social and economic responsibilities with financial performance: The role of innovation. *European Management Journal, 34*(5), 530–539. doi:10.1016/j.emj.2016.02.006

Cenamor, J., Paridab, V., & Wincent, J. (2019). How entrepreneurial SMEs compete through digital platforms: The roles of digital platform capability, network capability and ambidexterity. *Journal of Business Research, 100,* 196–206. doi:10.1016/j.jbusres.2019.03.035

Chakravorti, B., Bhalla, A., & Chaturvedi, R. S. (2017). *60 Countries' Digital Competitiveness, Indexed.* Retrieved from https://hbr.org/2017/07/60-countries-digital-competitiveness-indexed

Chandy, R. K., & Tellis, G. J. (2000). The incumbent's curse? Incumbency, size, and radical product innovation. *Journal of Marketing, 64*(3), 1–17. doi:10.1509/jmkg.64.3.1.18033

Chang, J. (2011). Introduction: Entrepreneurship in tourism and hospitality: The role of SMEs. *Asia Pacific Journal of Tourism Research, 16*(5), 467–469. doi:10.1080/10941665.2011.597572

Chan, I. C. C., Lam, L. W., Chow, C. W. C., Fong, L. H. N., & Law, R. (2017). The effect of online reviews on hotel booking intention: The role of reader-reviewer similarity. *International Journal of Hospitality Management, 66,* 54–65. doi:10.1016/j.ijhm.2017.06.007

Channel News Asia. (2017). *Funding Possibilities for Start-ups in Thailand.* Retrieved from https://www.channelnewsasia.com/news/startup/articles/money-matters/funding-possibilities-for-start-ups-in-thailand-8875136

Charan, R., Drotter, S., & Noel, J. (2001). *The Leadership Pipeline: How to Build the Leadership-Powered Company.* John Wiley & Sons.

Chatzinikolaou, D. (2002). Statistics for Economists. Academic Press.

Chelcea, S. (2001). Tehnici de cercetare sociologică. Academic Press.

Chen, L., & Aklikokou, A. K. (2019). Determinants of Egovernment Adoption: Testing the Mediating Effects of Perceived Usefulness and Perceived Ease of Use. *International Journal of Public Administration*, 1–16. Advance online publication. doi:10.1080/01900692.2019.1660989

Chen, T. B., & Chai, L. T. (2010). Attitude towards the environment and green products: Consumers' perspective. *Management Science and Engineering*, *4*(2), 27.

Chen, Y. (2008). Herd behavior in purchasing books online. *Computers in Human Behavior*, *24*(5), 1977–1992. doi:10.1016/j.chb.2007.08.004

Chen, Y., Chang, K., & Chang, C. (2012). Nonlinear influence on R&D project performance. *Technological Forecasting and Social Change*, *79*(8), 1537–1547. doi:10.1016/j.techfore.2012.04.007

Cheung, C. M., Lee, M. K., & Rabjohn, N. (2008). The impact of electronic word-of-mouth: The adoption of online opinions in online customer communities. *Internet Research*, *18*(3), 229–247. doi:10.1108/10662240810883290

Cheung, R. (2014). The influence of electronic word-of-mouth on information adoption in online customer communities. *Global Economic Review*, *43*(1), 42–57. doi:10.1080/1226508X.2014.884048

Chevalier, J. A., & Mayzlin, D. (2006). The Effect of Word of Mouth on Sales Online Book Reviews. *JMR, Journal of Marketing Research*, *43*(3), 345–354. doi:10.1509/jmkr.43.3.345

Chiru, I. (2003). *Comunicarea interpersonală.* Tritonic Publishing House.

Christensen, C. M. (1997). *The Innovator's Dilemma- When New Technologies Cause Great Firms to Fail.* Harvard Business School Press.

Chua, J. H., Chrisman, J. J., & Sharma, P. (1999). Defining the family business by behavior. *Entrepreneurship Theory and Practice*, *23*(4), 19–39. doi:10.1177/104225879902300402

Chua, J., Chrisman, J., Steier, L., & Rau, S. (2012). Sources of Heterogeneity in Family Firms: An Introduction. *Entrepreneurship Theory and Practice*, *36*(6), 1103–1113. doi:10.1111/j.1540-6520.2012.00540.x

CIBC. (2005). *Are Canadian Entrepreneurs Ready For Retirement?* CIBC World Markets Inc.

Claver, E., Rienda, L., & Quer, D. (2008). Family firms' risk perception: Empirical evidence on the internationalization process. *Journal of Small Business and Enterprise Development*, *15*(3), 457–471. doi:10.1108/14626000810892283

CMS. (2019). *E-public procurement.* CMS Public Procurement Group. Retrieved from: https://cms.law/en/int/publication/e-public-procurement

Colesca, S. E., & Dobrica, L. (2008). Adoption and use of e-government services: The case of Romania. *Journal of Applied Research and Technology*, *6*(3), 204–217. doi:10.22201/icat.16656423.2008.6.03.526

Coletta, M., & Kapoor, C. (2019). The State of Travel Start Ups Interactive Database. *Phocuswright.* Retrieved from https://www.phocuswright.com/Travel-Research/Technology-Innovation/The-State-of-Travel-Startups-Interactive-Database

Colli, A. (2003). *The history of family business, 1850-2000* (Vol. 47). Cambridge University Press.

Collier, W., Green, F., Kim, Y.-B., & Peirson, J. (2011). Education, training and economic performance: Evidence from establishment survival data. *Journal of Labor Research*, *32*(4), 336–361. doi:10.100712122-011-9116-7

Colombo, M. G., & Piva, E. (2008). Strengths and weaknesses of academic startups: A conceptual model. *Engineering Management. IEEE Transactions on*, *55*(1), 37–49.

Concha, G., Astudillo, H., Porrúa, M., & Pimenta, C. (2012). E-Government procurement observatory, maturity model and early measurements. *Government Information Quarterly*, *29*(1), S43–S50. doi:10.1016/j.giq.2011.08.005

Concha, G., Porrúa, M., & Pimenta, C. (2010). E-government procurement observatory model, design and pilot testing. In *Proceedings of the 4th International Conference on Theory and Practice of Electronic Governance ICEGOV '10* (pp. 195–201). New York: ACM. 10.1145/1930321.1930362

Conde, C. Y. A., Correa, C. Z., & Delgado, H. C. (2010). *Aprendizaje organizacional, una capacidad de los grupos de investigación en la universidad pública. Cuadernos de Administración, 44.* Retrieved from http://www.redalyc.org/pdf/2250/225017586002.pdf

Confecamaras. (2016). *Birth and survival of companies in Colombia.* Chambers of Commerce Network. Retrieved from: http://www.confecamaras.org.co/phocadownload/Cuadernos_de_analisis_economico/Cuaderno_de_An%D0%B0lisis_Economico_N_11.pdf

CONPES. (2007). Documento CONPES 3484. Consejo Nacional de Política Económica y Social. República de Colombia. Política nacional para la transformación productiva y la promoción de las micro, pequeñas y medianas empresas: Un esfuerzo público y privado. Bogotá.

Constantin, F., & Kavoura, A. (2019). Entrepreneur without Intention with Websites as a Communication Tool. Current Trends in Romania. In A. Kavoura, E. Kefallonitis, & A. Giovanis (Eds.), *Strategic Innovative Marketing and Tourism* (pp. 1093–1101). Springer. doi:10.1007/978-3-030-12453-3_126

Contreras, Gálvez, & González-Campo. (2012). Impacto de la orientación al aprendizaje en la innovación de las MIPYMES colombianas. *Cuadernos de Administración*, *28*(48).

Cook, A. J., Janicke, H., Maglaras, L., & Smith, R. (2017). An assessment of the application of IT security mechanisms to industrial control systems. *International Journal of Internet Technology and Secured Transactions*, *7*(2), 144–174. doi:10.1504/IJITST.2017.087163

Cornwall, J. R. (1998). The entrepreneur as a building block for community. *Journal of Developmental Entrepreneurship*, *3*, 141–148.

Corsi, M. (2006). *Good Governance for Development in Arab Countries Initiative E-Procurement Overview*. Retrieved from: OECD, http://unpan1.un.org/intradoc/groups/public/ documents/caimed/unpan024302.pdf

Cosack, S., Guthridge, M., & Lawson, E. (2010, August). Retaining key employees in times of change. *The McKinsey Quarterly*.

Costa, J., Botelho, A., & Matias, J. (2018). *Entrepreneurship along the Industry Life Cycle: The changing role of Entrepreneurial Activities and Knowledge Competencies* (S. Cubico, G. Favretto, J. Leitão, & U. Cantner, Eds.). Springer.

Council of Europe. (2013). *Structure and operation of local and regional democracy Greece Situation in 2012 this report has been prepared and elaborated by the Ministry of Interior of the Hellenic Republic.* Directorate of Democratic Institutions Directorate General of Democracy and Political Affairs. https://www.eetaa.gr/en_pages/Structure_and_operation_Greece_2012.pdf

Cowling, M., Liu, W., & Ledger, A. (2012). Small business financing in the UK before and during the current financial crisis. *International Small Business Journal*, *30*(7), 778–800. doi:10.1177/0266242611435516

Cozzolino A., Verona G., Rothaermel F. (2018). Unpacking the Disruption Process: New Technology, Business Models, and Incumbent Adaptation. *Journal Of Management Studies*. doi:10.1111/joms.12352

Craig, B. (2017). *84 Percent of People Trust Online Reviews As Much As Friends. Here's How to Manage What They See*. Retrieved from https://www.inc.com/craig-bloem/84-percent-of-people-trust-online-reviews-as-much-.html

Crals, E., & Vereeck, L. (2004). *Sustainable entrepreneurship in SMEs: theory and practice*. In *3rd Global Conference in Environmental Justice and Global Citizenship*, Copenhagen, Denmark.

Crals, E., & Vereeck, L. (2005). The affordability of sustainable entrepreneurship certification for SMEs. *International Journal of Sustainable Development and World Ecology*, *12*(2), 173–183. doi:10.1080/13504500509469628

Craven, M. (2016). *For hotels, online reviews really matter to the bottom line*. Retrieved from https://www.wsj.com/articles/for-hotels-online-reviews-really-matter-to-the-bottom-line-1479477602

Crescent University. (2019). *The Management –Registrar.* Available: http://crescent-university.edu.ng/AboutUs.aspx

Croom, S., & Johnston, R. (2003). Examining the contribution of internal customer service to improved e-procurement performance: A Case Study investigation. In *Proceedings of* 3rd *International Conference on Electronic Business (ICEB 2003)*. National University of Singapore. Retrieved from: http://iceb.johogo.com/proceedings/2003/

Crouch, C., Le Galès, P., Trigilia, C., & Voelzkow, H. (2001). *Local Production Systems in Europe. Rise or demise?* Oxford University Press.

Cuevas, J. J. G., and Román, J. A. M. (2008). Tipología de la innovación y perfiles empresariales: una aplicación empírica. *Economía industrial*, (368), 59-77.

Cull, R., Davis, L. E., Lamoreaux, N. M., & Rosenthal, J. (2006). Historical financing of Smalland Medium-size Enterprises. *Journal of Banking & Finance*, *30*(11), 3017–3042. doi:10.1016/j.jbankfin.2006.05.005

Cyert, R., & March, J. (1963). *Teoría de las Decisiones Económicas en la Empresas*. Herrero Hermanos Sucesores, S.A Editores.

Dai, O., & Liu, X. (2009). Returning Entrepreneurs Vs Indigenous Entrepreneurs: An Investigation of High Technology SMEs in Emerging Markets. In K. Ibeh & S. Davies (Eds.), *Contemporary Challenges to International Business* (pp. 200–217). Palgrave MacMillan; doi:10.1057/9780230237322_12

Damanpour, F. (1992). Organizational size and innovation. *Organization Studies*, *13*(3), 375–402. doi:10.1177/017084069201300304

Damanpour, F., & Gopalakrishnan, S. (2001). The dynamics of the adoption of products and process innovations in organizations. *Journal of Management Studies*, *38*(1), 45–65. doi:10.1111/1467-6486.00227

Das, K. (2019). Vietnam's Tourism Industry Continues its. *Growth, 2018*. https://www.vietnam-briefing.com/news/vietnams-tourism-industry-continues-growth-2018.html/

Davis, F. (1980). Perceived Usefulness, Perceived Ease of Use, and User Acceptance of Information Technology. *Management Information Systems Quarterly*, *13*(3), 318–341.

Davis, F., Bagozzi, R., & Warshaw, P. (1989). User Acceptance of Computer Technology: A Comparison of Two Theoretical Models. *Management Science*, *35*(8), 982–1003. doi:10.1287/mnsc.35.8.982

Dawson, C., & Henley, A. (2012). “Push” versus “pull” entrepreneurship: An ambiguous distinction? *International Journal of Entrepreneurial Behaviour & Research*, *18*(6), 697–719. doi:10.1108/13552551211268139

Day, G. S. (1994). Continuous Learning about Markets. *Californian Management Review*, 9–31.

Day, S. (1991). *Learning About Markets*. Marketing Science Institute Report Number 91-117. Marketing Science Institute.

de Clercq, D., & Belausteguigoitia, I. (2015). Intergenerational Strategy Involvement and Family Firms’ Innovation Pursuits: The Critical Roles of Conflict Management and Social Capital. *Journal of Family Business Strategy*, *6*(3), 178–189. doi:10.1016/j.jfbs.2015.04.003

de Massis, A., Frattini, F., Kotlar, J., Messeni-Petruzzelli, A., & Wright, M. (2016). Innovation through tradition: Lessons from innovative family businesses and directions for future research. *The Academy of Management Perspectives*, *30*(1), 93–116. doi:10.5465/amp.2015.0017

de Massis, A., Frattini, F., & Lichtenthaler, U. (2013). Research on Technological Innovation in Family Firms: Present Debates and Future Directions. *Family Business Review*, *26*(1), 10–31. doi:10.1177/0894486512466258

de Massis, A., Frattini, F., Pizzurno, E., & Cassia, L. (2015). Product innovation in family versus non family firms: An exploratory analysis. *Journal of Small Business Management*, *53*(1), 1–36. doi:10.1111/jsbm.12068

De Massis, A., Kotlar, J., Chua, J. H., & Chrisman, J. J. (2014). Ability and willingness as sufficiency conditions for family-oriented particularistic behavior: Implications for theory and empirical studies. *Journal of Small Business Management*, *52*(2), 344–364. doi:10.1111/jsbm.12102

De Pelsmacker, P., van Tilburg, S., & Holthof, C. (2018). Digital marketing strategies, online reviews and hotel performance. *International Journal of Hospitality Management*, *72*, 47–55. doi:10.1016/j.ijhm.2018.01.003

Decker, R., Haltiwanger, J., Jarmin, R., & Miranda, J. (2014). The Role of Entrepreneurship in US Job Creation and Economic Dynamism. *The Journal of Economic Perspectives*, *28*(3), 3–24. doi:10.1257/jep.28.3.3

Defourny, J., & Nyssens, M. (2006). Defining Social Enterprise. In M. Nyssens (Ed.), *Social Enterprise: At the crossroads of market, public policies and civil society*. Routledge.

Del Río, C. J., & Santisteban, R. D. F. (2011, July-December). Perspectivas del aprendizaje organizacional como catalizador de escenarios competitivos. *Revista Ciencias Estratégicas*, *19*(26), 247–266.

Deloitte University EMEA CVBA. (2017). *Next Generation family businesses. Leading a family business in a disruptive environment*. https://www2.deloitte.com/content/dam/Deloitte/ua/Documents/strategy/Next-generation-family-business.pdf

DESI - Digital Economy and Society Index (DESI). (2019). *Country Report – Greece*. Retrieved from https://ec.europa.eu/digital-single-market/en/scoreboard/greece

DeTienne, D. R., & Cardon, M. S. (2012). Impact of founder experience on exit intentions. *Small Business Economics*, *38*(4), 351–374. doi:10.100711187-010-9284-5

Devang, A., Kruse, C., Parker, A., & Siren, P. (2017). The next wave of business models in asia. *MIT Sloan Management Review*, *58*(2), 35–39.

Di Domenico, M., Haugh, H., & Tracey, P. (2010). Social Bricolage: Theorizing Social Value Creation in Social Enterprises. *Entrepreneurship Theory and Practice*, *34*(4), 681–703. doi:10.1111/j.1540-6520.2010.00370.x

Dickson, P. R. (1996). The Static and Dynamic Mechanics of Competition: A Comment on Hunt and Morgan’s Comparative Advantage Theory. *Journal of Marketing*, *60*(October), 102–106. doi:10.2307/1251904

Dini, M., & Stumpo, G. (2019). *Mipymes en América Latina: un frágil desempeño y nuevos desafíos para las políticas de fomento. Síntesis.* Documentos de Proyectos (LC/TS.2019/20), Santiago, Comisión Económica para América Latina y el Caribe (CEPAL), 2019.

Dioneo-Adetayo, E. A. (2006). Factors Influencing Attitude of Youth Towards Entrepreneurship. *International Journal of Adolescence and Youth, 13*(1-2), 127–145. doi:10.1080/02673843.2006.9747970

Djankov, S., Qian, Y., Roland, G., & Zhuravskaya, E. (2006). Entrepreneurship in China and Russia compared. *Journal of the European Economic Association, 4*(2/3), 352–365. doi:10.1162/jeea.2006.4.2-3.352

Doan, E. Z. (2020) Number of International Tourist Arrivals (ITA) in Vietnam 2019. *Statista.* Retrieved from https://www.statista.com/statistics/981987/vietnam-number-international-tourist-arrivals/

Dong, P. T. (2019). *Rào cản nào trong tiếp cận vốn tín dụng của Doanh nghiệp nhỏ và vừa ở Việt Nam?* [What barrier small & medium enterprises face when accessing financial credit?]. Retrieved from https://nhadautu.vn/rao-can-nao-trong-tiep-can-von-tin-dung-cua-doanh-nghiep-nho-va-vua-o-viet-nam-d21068.html

Drucker, P. (1985). *La Innovación y el empresario innovador.* Edhasa.

Drucker, P. (1993). *Innovation and Entrepreneurship: Practice and Principle.* HarperBusiness.

Drucker, P. (1993). *La sociedad post capitalista.* Editorial Deusto.

Duff, A. (1994). *Best practice in business incubator management.* Booragon, Australia: AUSTEP Strategic Partnering Pty.

Dung, V. (2019). *Từ 01/7/2019, doanh nghiệp nhỏ và vừa được vay vốn tối đa 7 năm* [From 1st July 2019, small and medium enterprises can apply for financial credit for maximum 07 years]. Retrieved from http://tapchitaichinh.vn/co-che-chinh-sach/tu-0172019-doanh-nghiep-nho-va-vua-duoc-vay-von-toi-da-7-nam-306978.html

EC. (2002). *Benchmarking of Business Incubators.* Final Report. Brussels: EC.

Economic Times. (2019). *Definition of 'Succession Planning.* Bennett, Coleman & Co. Ltd. Available: https://economictimes.indiatimes.com/definition/succession-planning

Eddleston, A., Rodrigo-Alarcón, J., Parra-Requena, G., García-Villaverde, P., Bolo, A., Muchemi, A., & Gomez-Mejia, L. (2012). The Succession Process from a Resource- and Knowledge-Based View of the Family Firm. *Family Business Review, 2*(1), 328–353.

Edinburgh Group. (2012). *Growing the global economy through SMEs.* Retrieved from http://www.edinburgh-group.org/activities/papers.aspx

Edwards, W. (1954). The theory of decision making. *Psychological Bulletin, 51*(4), 380–417. doi:10.1037/h0053870 PMID:13177802

EHL Education Group. (2020). *Singapore Startup Ecosystem: An Entreprenuers' Paradise?* Retrieved from https://hospitalityinsights.ehl.edu/bridging-valley-death-singapore

Eijdenberg, E.L., Isaga, N.M., Paas, L.J., & Masurel, E. (2020). Fluid entrepreneurial motivations in Tanzania. *Journal of African Business.* doi:10.1080/15228916.2019.1695191

Eijdenberg, E. L., Thompson, N. A., Verduijn, K., & Essers, C. (2019). Entrepreneurial activities in a developing country: An institutional theory perspective. *International Journal of Entrepreneurial Behaviour & Research, 25*(3), 414–432. doi:10.1108/IJEBR-12-2016-0418

Ekeh, P. (2016). *The age of Olorogun Michael Ibru Urhobo Perspectives on the Life and Times of Michael Christopher Onajirhevbe Ibru (1930-2016).* Available: http://www.waado.org/Biographies/ibru_michael/THE_AGE_OF_MICHAEL_IBRU.pdf

ELTRUN. (2018). *Greek SMEs - Challenges and Opportunities.* Retrieved from https://www.douleutaras.gr/ereuna-gia-mikromesaies-epixeiriseis/en/

Emmanuel, A. K., Peace, N. N., Ebele, O. M., Udeze, C. C., & Abiodun, O. A. (2019). Do Non-Family Member Managers Enhance Venture Performance of Family Businesses Evidence from Nigeria. *Academy of Entrepreneurship Journal, 25*(3). Available: https://www.abacademies.org/articles/do-nonfamily-member-managers-enhance-venture-performance-of-family-businesses-evidence-from-nigeria-8491.html

Enuoh, R. O., & Inyang, B. J. (2009). Entrepreneurial Competencies: The Missing Links to Successful Entrepreneurship in Nigeria. *International Business Research, 2*(2), 62–71.

ESCAP. (2014). *Policy Guidebook for SME development in Asia and the Pacific.* Retrieved from https://www.unescap.org/sites/default/files/0%20-%20Full%20Report_7.pdf

ESCAP-The United Nations Economic and Social Commission for Asia and the Pacific. (2009). *Globalization of production and the competitiveness of Small and Medium-sized Enterprises in Asia and the Pacific: Trends and prospects, studies in trade and investment No. 65.* Retrieved from https://www.unescap.org/resources/globalization-production-and-competitiveness-small-and-medium-sized-enterprises-asia-and

Esfandiar, K., Sharifi-Tehrani, M., Pratt, S., & Altinay, L. (2019). Understanding entrepreneurial intentions: A developed integrated structural model approach. *Journal of Business Research, 94*, 172–182. doi:10.1016/j.jbusres.2017.10.045

Eshun, J. P. (2004). *Where Do Business Incubators Came From? The Origins, Evolutions, and Institutionalization of Business Incubators: Evaluating Performance and Assessing Outcome* (Unpublished doctoral dissertation). Columbia University.

Estrin, S., Mickiewicz, T., Stephan, U., & Wright, M. (2018). Entrepreneurship in emerging markets. In R. Grosse & K. Meyer (Eds.), *The Oxford handbook of management in emerging markets.* Oxford University Press.

European Commission. (2003). Commission Recommendation 2003/361/EC - The Definition of Micro, Small and Medium-sized enterprises. *Official Journal of the European Union.* Retrieved from https://eurlex.europa.eu/LexUriServ/LexUriServ.do?uri=OJ:L:2003:124:0036:0041:en

European Commission. (2013). *Social economy and social entrepreneurship Social Europe guide.* Author.

European Commission. (2013a). *2020 Action Plan - Reigniting the Entrepreneurial Spirit in Europe.* Retrieved from https://eur-lex.europa.eu/legal-content/EN/TXT/?uri=celex:52012DC0795

European Commission. (2014). *A map of social enterprises and their eco-systems in Europe.* Author.

European Commission. (2014). *Report from the Commission to the Council and the European Parliament - EU Anti-Corruption Report.* Retrieved from: https://ec.europa.eu/dgs/home-affairs /e-library/documents/policies/ organized-crime-and-humantrafficking/ corruption/docs/acr_2014_en.pdf

European Commission. (2016). *Public procurement – Study on administrative capacity in the EU Greece Country Profile.* Retrieved from: https://ec.europa.eu/ regional_policy/sources/ policy/how/improving-investment/ public-procurement/study/ country_profile/el.pdf

European Commission. (2017). *Digital agenda scoreboard 2017.* Author.

European Commission. (2017). *Integration of Digital Technology.* Retrieved from file:///C:/Users/pvelo/Downloads/EuropesDigitalProgressReportIntegration ofDigitalTechnologyChapter%20(2).pdf

European Commission. (2019). *European Innovation Scoreboard.* Author.

European Commission. (2019). *Social enterprises and their ecosystems in Europe. Updated country report: Greece.* Luxembourg: Publications Office of the European Union. Available at https://europa.eu/!Qq64ny

European Court of Auditors. (2018). *Public Procurement in Western Balkans.* Retrieved from: https://www.eca.europa.eu/ other%20publications/synthesis _w_balkans/synthesis_w_balkans_en.pdf

European Family Business. (2012). *Family business.* Retrieved from http://www.europeanfamilybusinesses.eu/uploads/Modules/Publications/family-business-statistics.pdf

European Institute of Technology (EIT) Digital - Start-Ups in Greece 2018. (2018). *A maturing ecosystem points to a brighter future EIT Digital in partnership with Velocity Partners.* Author.

European Union. (2019). *Public Procurement.* Retrieved from: https://ec.europa.eu/growth/single-market/public-procurement_en

Evans, M. H., He, Y., Maglaras, L., & Janicke, H. (2019). Heart-is: A novel technique for evaluating human error-related information security incidents. *Computers & Security, 80*, 74–89. doi:10.1016/j.cose.2018.09.002

Fayolle, A., & Gailly, B. (2013). The Impact of Entrepreneurship Education on Entrepreneurial Attitudes and Intention: Hysteresis and Persistence. *Journal of Small Business Management, 53*(1), 75–93. doi:10.1111/jsbm.12065

Fayolle, A., & Liñán, F. (2014). The future of research on entrepreneurial intentions. *Journal of Business Research, 67*(5), 663–666. doi:10.1016/j.jbusres.2013.11.024

Federal Law of July 24, 2007 N° 209-FZ On the development of small and medium entrepreneurship in the Russian Federation. Retrieved from: https://fzrf.su/zakon/maloe-i-srednee-predprinimatelstvo-209-fz/

Federal State Statistics Service of the Russian Federation. (2019). *Maloe i srednee predprinimatelstvo v Rossii 2019* [Small and medium-sized entrepreneurship in Russia 2019]. Retrieved from: https://gks.ru/storage/mediabank/Mal-pred_2019.pdf

Fedko, V. T., & Dolgun, B. G. (2004) Experience in implementing the integrated training system "HTEI-plant". *Engineering Education, 2*, 146-155.

Ferrag, M. A. (2018). *Authentication schemes for Smart Mobile Devices: Threat Models, Countermeasures, and Open Research Issues.* arXiv preprint, arXiv:1803.10281

Ferrand, A. (2019). *e-Procurement: lessons from interventions and approaches from Emerging Economies of Eastern Europe and Western Balkans K4D Helpdesk Report.* Brighton, UK: Institute of Development Studies. Retrieved from: https://assets.publishing.service.gov.uk/ media/5dcd797ce5274a07 aad0a54b670_eProcurement_lessons_from_interventions_ and_approaches_from_Emerging _Economies_of_Eastern_Europe_ and_Western_Balkans.pdf

Finch, W. H., & French, B. F. (2015). *Latent Variable Modeling with R.* Routledge. doi:10.4324/9781315869797

Fishbein, M., & Ajzen, I. (2010). *Predicting and changing behavior.* New York: Psychology Press.

Folami, O. M., & Akoko, A. (2010). *Climate Change and Inter-Ethnic Conflict Between Fulani Herdsmen and Host Communities in Nigeria. Ondo.* Adekunle Ajasin University.

Formichella, M. (2005). *Evolución del concepto de innovación y su relación con el desarrollo.* Retrieved from https://core.ac.uk/download/pdf/48031881.pdf

Fornell, C., & Larcker, D. F. (1981). Evaluating structural equation models with unbearable and measurement error. *JMR, Journal of Marketing Research*, *18*(1), 39–50. doi:10.1177/002224378101800104

Foroudi, P. (2019). Influence of brand signature, brand awareness, brand attitude, brand reputation on hotel industry's brand performance. *International Journal of Hospitality Management*, *76*, 271–285. doi:10.1016/j.ijhm.2018.05.016

Freel, M. (2000). Do Small Innovating Firms Outperform Non-innovators? *Small Business Economics*, *14*(3), 195–210. doi:10.1023/A:1008100206266

Freeman, C. (1987). *Technology and Economic Performance: Lessons from Japan*. Pinter Publisher.

Freeman, J. (2015). *Contingency theory*. Wiley Encyclopedia of Management; doi:10.1002/9781118785317.weom110129

Fulton, B. R. (2018). Organizations and survey research: Implementing response enhancing strategies and conducting nonresponse analyses. *Sociological Methods & Research*, *47*(2), 240–276. doi:10.1177/0049124115626169

Fyall, A., Buhalis, D., & Parra López, E. (2009). Entrepreneurship and innovation in tourism. *Pasos: Revista De Turismo y Patrimonio Cultural*, *7*(3), 355–357. doi:10.25145/j.pasos.2009.07.024

Gallo, M., & Sveen, J. (1991). Internationalizing the Family Business: Facilitating and Restraining Factors. *Family Business Review*, *4*(2), 181–190. doi:10.1111/j.1741-6248.1991.00181.x

Gálvez, A. E. J. (2014). Tecnologías de información y comunicación, e innovación en las MIPYMES de Colombia. *Cuadernos de Administración*, *30*(51). Retrieved from http://www.scielo.org.co/pdf/cuadm/v30n51/v30n51a08.pdf

Gamble, N., Patrick, C. J., & Peach, D. (2010). Internationalising work-integrated learning: Creating global citizens to meet the economic crisis and the skills shortage. *Higher Education Research & Development*, *29*(5), 535–546. doi:10.1080/07294360.2010.502287

Gao, L., & Bai, X. (2014). A unified perspective on the factors influencing consumer acceptance of internet of things technology. *Asia Pacific Journal of Marketing and Logistics*, *26*(2), 211–231. doi:10.1108/APJML-06-2013-0061

Garcia, R., & Calantone, R. (2002). A critical look at technological innovation typology and innovativeness terminology: A literature review. *Journal of Product Innovation Management: An International Publication of the Product Development & Management Association*, *19*(2), 110–132. doi:10.1111/1540-5885.1920110

Gavilan, D., Avello, M., & Martinez-Navarro, G. (2018). The influence of online ratings and reviews on hotel booking consideration. *Tourism Management*, *66*, 53–61. doi:10.1016/j.tourman.2017.10.018

Gedajlovic, E., & Carney, M. (2010). Markets, hierarchies, and families: Toward a transaction cost theory of the family firm. *Entrepreneurship Theory and Practice*, *34*(6), 1145–1172. doi:10.1111/j.1540-6520.2010.00418.x

Gelderen, M.V., Thurik, R., & Niels Bosma, N. (2003). *Success and Risk factors in the Pre-Start-Up Phase*. EIM – Business & Policy Research, SCALES Scientific Analysis of Entrepreneurship and SMEs – Paper N200314

Geroski, P., Machin, S., & van Reenen, J. (1993). The Profitability of Innovating Firms. *The RAND Journal of Economics*, *24*(2), 198–211. doi:10.2307/2555757

Geroski, P., van Reenen, J., & Walters, C. (1997). How persistently do firms innovate? *Research Policy*, *26*(1), 33–48. doi:10.1016/S0048-7333(96)00903-1

Getz, D., & Petersen, T. (2005). Growth and profit-oriented entrepreneurship among family business owners in the tourism and hospitality industry. *International Journal of Hospitality Management*, *24*(2), 219–242. doi:10.1016/j.ijhm.2004.06.007

Geus, A. (1988). Plannig learning. *Harvard Business Review*, *66*(March-April), 70–74.

Ghotbabadi, A. L., Feiz, S., & Baharun, R. (2016). The Relationship of Customer Perceived Risk and Customer Satisfaction. *Mediterranean Journal of Social Sciences*, *7*(1), S1. doi:10.5901/mjss.2016.v7n1s1p161

Gibson, T., & Van der Vaart, H. J. (2008). Defining SMEs: A Less Imperfect Way of Defining Small and Medium Enterprises in Developing Countries. *Brookings Global-Economy and Development*. Retrieved from https://www.brookings.edu/~/media/research/files/papers/2008/9/development%20gibson/09_development_gibson.pdf

Gieure, C., Benavides-Espinosa, M. D. M., & Roig-Dobón, S. (2019). Entrepreneurial intentions in an international university environment. *International Journal of Entrepreneurial Behaviour & Research*, *25*(8), 1605–1620. doi:10.1108/IJEBR-12-2018-0810

Gillen, J. (2010). Tourism and Entrepreneurialism in Southeast Asian cities. *Geography Compass*, *4*(4), 370–382. doi:10.1111/j.1749-8198.2010.00322.x

Giotopoulos, I., Kontolaimou, A., Korra, E., & Tsakanikas, A. (2017). What drives ICT adoption by SMEs? Evidence from a large-scale survey in Greece. *Journal of Business Research*, *81*, 60–69. doi:10.1016/j.jbusres.2017.08.007

Giovannetti, G., Ricchiuti, G., & Velucchi, M. (2013). Location, internationalization and performance of firms in Italy: A multilevel approach. *Applied Economics*, *45*(18), 2665–2673. doi:10.1080/00036846.2012.665597

Gird, A., & Bagraim, J. J. (2008). The Theory of Planned Behaviour as Predictor of Entrepreneurial Intent Amongst Final-Year University Students. *South African Journal of Psychology. Suid-Afrikaanse Tydskrif vir Sielkunde*, *38*(4), 711–724. doi:10.1177/008124630803800410

Girotra, K., & Netessine, S. (2014, July). Four Paths to Business Model Innovation. *Harvard Business Review*. https://hbr.org/2014/07/four-paths-to-business-model-innovation

GKToday. (2019). *India in the Travel & Tourism Competitiveness Index 2019*. Retrieved from https://www.gktoday.in/current-affairs/india-in-the-travel-tourism-competitiveness-index-2019/

Glanz, K., Rimer, B. K., & Viswanath, K. (2015). *Health behavior: theory, research, and practice*. Jossey-Bass.

Godes, D., & Mayzlin, D. (2004). Using online conversations to study word-of-mouth communication. *Marketing Science*, *23*(4), 545–560. doi:10.1287/mksc.1040.0071

Gomez-Mejia, L., Cruz, C., Berrone, P., & de Castro, J. (2011). The Bind that ties: Socio-emotional wealth preservation in family firms. *The Academy of Management Annals*, *5*(1), 653–707. doi:10.5465/19416520.2011.593320

González-González, J. M., Bretones, F. D., Zarco, V., & Rodríguez, A. (2011). Women, immigration and entrepreneurship in Spain: A confluence of debates in the face of a complex reality. *Women's Studies International Forum*, *34*(5), 360–370. doi:10.1016/j.wsif.2011.05.007

Gorges, J., Schwinger, M., & Kandler, C. (2013). Linking University Students' Willingness to Learn to Their Recollections of Motivation at Secondary School. *Europe's Journal of Psychology*, *9*(4), 764–782. doi:10.5964/ejop.v9i4.638

Gorgievski, M. J., Stephan, U., Laguna, M., & Moriano, J. A. (2017). Predicting Entrepreneurial Career Intentions. *Journal of Career Assessment*, *26*(3), 457–475. doi:10.1177/1069072717714541 PMID:30443149

Gothard, S., & Austin, M. (2012). Leadership Succession Planning: Implications for Nonprofit Human Service Organizations. *Administration in Social Work*, *37*(3), 272–285. doi:10.1080/03643107.2012.684741

Goulas, A., Blanas, G., & Gomes, E. (2008). The Formation of Strategic Groups in the Athens Stock Exchange. *MIBES Transactions*, *2*(1), 60–77.

Gozzi, R. (2000). The Trojan horse metaphor. *ETC: A Review of General Semantics*, *57*(1), 80-84.

Grant, R. (1991). The Resource Base Theory of Competitive Advantage. *California Management Review*, *33*, 114–135. doi:10.2307/41166664

Gray, C., & Mabey, C. (2005). Management development: Key differences between small and large businesses in Europe. *International Small Business Journal*, *23*(5), 467–485. doi:10.1177/0266242605055908

Gregoire, Y., & Fisher, R. J. (2008). Customer betrayal and retaliation: When your best customers become your worst enemies. *Journal of the Academy of Marketing Science*, *36*(2), 247–261. doi:10.100711747-007-0054-0

Gregori, P., Wdowiak, M. A., Schwarz, E. J., & Holzmann, P. (2019). Exploring Value Creation in Sustainable Entrepreneurship: Insights from the Institutional Logics Perspective and the Business Model Lens. *Sustainability*, *11*(9), 2505. doi:10.3390u11092505

Griffin, P., & Care, E. (2015). The ATC21S method. In P. Griffin & E. Care (Eds.), *Assessment and teaching of 21st century skills: Methods and approaches* (pp. 3–33). Springer.

Grosse, R., & Kujawa, D. (1995). *International Business, Theory and Management Applications* (3rd ed.). Irwin.

GSEVEE - Hellenic Confederation of Professionals, Craftsmen & Merchants. (2014). *The Development of SMEs in Greece*. Retrieved from https://www.gsevee.gr/press/mme_eng.pdf

Gudov, A. (2013). Combining formal and informal financial sources. *Journal of Chinese Entrepreneurship*, *5*(1), 39–60. doi:10.1108/17561391311297879

Guelich, U. (2018). GEM Thailand Report 2017/2018. *Bangkok University & Global Entrepreneurship Monitor*. Retrieved from https://www.researchgate.net/publication/330105669_2017-18_GEM_Thailand_Report

Gulaid, L. A., & Kiragu, K. (2012). Lessons learnt from promising practices in community engagement for the elimination of new HIV infections in children by 2015 and keeping their mothers alive: Summary of a desk review. *Journal of the International AIDS Society*, *15*, 17390.

Gulati, R., Nohria, N., & Wohlgezogen, F. (2010). Roaring out of recession. *Harvard Business Review*, *88*(3), 62–69.

Gunasekarana, A., & Ngai, E. (2008). Adoption of e-procurement in Hong Kong: An empirical research. *International Journal of Production Economics*, *113*(1), 159–175. doi:10.1016/j.ijpe.2007.04.012

Gurel, E., Altinay, L., & Daniele, R. (2010). Tourism students' entrepreneurial intentions. *Annals of Tourism Research*, *37*(3), 646–669. doi:10.1016/j.annals.2009.12.003

Hadjimanolis, A. (1999). Barriers to innovation for SMEs in a small less developed country (Cyprus). *Technovation*, *19*(9), 561–570. doi:10.1016/S0166-4972(99)00034-6

Hage, J. T. (1999). Organizational innovation and organizational change. *Annual Review of Sociology*, *25*(1), 597–622. doi:10.1146/annurev.soc.25.1.597

Hair, F. Jr, Anderson, R. E., Tatham, R. L., & Black, W. C. (1998). *Multivariate data analysis* (5th ed.). Prentice Hall.

Hair, J., Anderson, R., Tatham, R., & Black, W. (1999). *Análisis Multivariante* (5th ed.). Prentice Hall.

Hajivassiliou, V., & Savingnac, F. (2008). *Financing Constraints and a Firm's Decision and Ability to Innovate: Establishing Direct and Reverse Effects. Notes d'Études et de Recherche 202*. Banque de France.

Halkias, D., Nwajiuba, C., Harkiolakis, N., Clayton, G., Akrivos, P. D., & Caracatsanis, S. (2009). Characteristics and business profiles of immigrant-owned small firms: The case of African immigrant entrepreneurs in Greece. *International Journal of Business Innovation and Research*, *3*(4), 382–401. doi:10.1504/IJBIR.2009.027104

Halkos, G., & Sepetis, A. (2007). Can capital markets respond to environmental policy of firms? Evidence from Greece. *Ecological Economics*, *63*(2-3), 578–587. doi:10.1016/j.ecolecon.2006.12.015

Hall, A., Melin, L., & Nordqvist, M. (2001). Entrepreneurship as radical change in the family business: Exploring the role of cultural patterns. *Family Business Review*, *14*(3), 193–208. doi:10.1111/j.1741-6248.2001.00193.x

Hallak, R., Assaker, G., & Lee, C. (2015). Tourism entrepreneurship performance: The effects of place identity, self-efficacy, and gender. *Journal of Travel Research*, *54*(1), 36–51. doi:10.1177/0047287513513170

Hallam, C., Novick, D., Gilbert, D. J., Frankwick, G. L., Wenker, O., & Zanella, G. (2017). Academic Entrepreneurship and the Entrepreneurial Ecosystem: The UT transform project. *Academy of Entrepreneurship Journal*, *23*(1), 2017.

Hallaq, B. N. (2018). CYRAN: a hybrid cyber range for testing security on ICS/SCADA systems. In Cyber Security and Threats: Concepts, Methodologies, Tools, and Applications (pp. 622-637). IGI.

Hallberg, K. (2000). A Market-oriented strategy for Small and Medium Scale Enterprises. *International Finance Corporation Discussion Paper - The World Bank*. Retrieved from http://documents.worldbank.org/curated/en/2000/04/693275/market-oriented-strategy-small-medium-scale-enterprises

Hancock, G. R., & Mueller, R. O. (Eds.). (2012). *Structural Equation Modeling: A Second Course* (2nd ed.). IAP.

Handfield, R., Jeong, S., & Choi, T. (2018). Emerging procurement technology: Data analytics and cognitive analytics. *International Journal of Operations & Production Management*, *38*(1), 22–42.

Han, L., & Jin, Y. (2009). A Review of Technology Acceptance Model in the E-commerce Environment. In *Proceedings of the 2009 International Conference on Management of e-Commerce and e-Government* (pp. 28- 31) IEEE. 10.1109/ICMeCG.2009.64

Hansen, G. S., & Wernerfelt, B. (1989). Determinants of Firm Perfomance: The Relative Importance of Economic and Organizational Factors. *Strategic Management Journal*, *10*(5), 399–411. doi:10.1002mj.4250100502

Hansen, T., Møller Jensen, J., & Stubbe Solgaard, H. (2004). Predicting online grocery buying intention: A comparison of the theory of reasoned action and the theory of planned behavior. *International Journal of Information Management*, *24*(6), 539–550. doi:10.1016/j.ijinfomgt.2004.08.004

Harney, B., & Dundon, T. (2006). Capturing complexity: Developing an integrated approach to analysing HRM in SMEs. *Human Resource Management Journal*, *16*(1), 48–73. doi:10.1111/j.1748-8583.2006.00004.x

Hastings, C., & Weate, J. (2018). Local Governments and Social Enterprise: Meeting Community Challenges Together? In Social Capital and Enterprise in the Modern State, (pp.117-146). Academic Press.

Hatak, I., & Hyslop, K. (2015). Cooperation between family businesses of different size: A case study. *Journal of Co-operative Organization and Management*, *3*(2), 52–59. doi:10.1016/j.jcom.2015.11.003

Hausman, A., & Johnston, W. J. (2014). The role of innovation in driving the economy: Lessons from the global financial crisis. *Journal of Business Research*, *67*(1), 2720–2726. doi:10.1016/j.jbusres.2013.03.021

Heck, R. K. Z., Hoy, F., Poutziouris, P. Z., & Steier, L. P. (2008). Emerging Paths of Family Entrepreneurship Research. *Journal of Small Business Management*, *46*(3), 317–330. doi:10.1111/j.1540-627X.2008.00246.x

Hedger, M. M., Mitchell, T., Leavy, J., Greeley, M., & Downie, A. (2008). *Desk review: evaluation of adaptation to climate change from a development perspective*. Available: http://citeseerx.ist.psu.edu/viewdoc/download?doi=10.1.1.575.1027&rep=rep1&type=pdf

Hellenic Republic. (2018). *Greece: A growth strategy for the future.* Retrieved from: http://www.mindev.gov.gr/wp-content/uploads/2018/09/Growth-Strategy.pdf

Henderson, R. M., & Clark, K. B. (1990). Architectural innovation: The reconfiguration of existing. *Administrative Science Quarterly*, *35*(1), 9–30. doi:10.2307/2393549

Hennig-Thurau, T., Gwinner, K. P., Walsh, G., & Gremler, D. D. (2004). Electronic word-of-mouth via consumer-opinion platforms: What motivates consumers to articulate themselves on the internet? *Journal of Interactive Marketing*, *18*(1), 38–52. doi:10.1002/dir.10073

Herstad, S., Sandven, T., & Solberg, E. (2013). Location, education and enterprise growth. *Applied Economics Letters*, *20*(10), 1019–1022. doi:10.1080/13504851.2013.772287

Hessels, J., Gelderen, M. V., & Thurik, R. (2008). Entrepreneurial aspirations, motivations, and their drivers. *Small Business Economics*, *31*(3), 323–339. doi:10.100711187-008-9134-x

Heunks, F. (1998). Innovation, Creativity and Success. *Small Business Economics*, *10*(3), 263–272. doi:10.1023/A:1007968217565

Hobohm, S. (2001). Small and Medium-sized Enterprises in economic development: the UNIDO experience. *Journal of Economic Cooperation Among Islamic Countries, 22*(1), 1-42.

Hommen, L., & Rolfstam, M. (2009). Public procurement and innovation: Towards a taxonomy. *Journal of Public Procurement*, *9*(1), 17–56.

Hormiga, E., & Batista-Canino, R.M., & Sánchez-Medina, A. (2010). The role of intellectual capital in the success of new ventures. *Journal of International Enterpreneuship Management.*

Hua, S., & Wemmerlöv, U. (2006). Product change intensity, product advantage, and market performance: An empirical investigation of the PC industry. *Journal of Product Innovation Management*, *23*(4), 316–329. doi:10.1111/j.1540-5885.2006.00204.x

Huber, G. (1998). Synergies Between Organizational Learning and Creativity & Innovation. *Creativity and Innovation Management*, *7*(1), 3–8. doi:10.1111/1467-8691.00079

Hult, G. T. M. (1998). Managing the international strategic sourcing process as a market-driven organizational learning system. *Decision Sciences*, *29*(1), 193–216. doi:10.1111/j.1540-5915.1998.tb01349.x

Hult, G. T. M., & Ferrell, O. C. (1997). A global learning organization structure and market information processing. *Journal of Business Research*, *40*(2), 155–166. doi:10.1016/S0148-2963(97)00006-4

Hurley, R. F., & Hult, G. T. M. (1998). Innovation, market orientation, and organizational learning: An integration and empirical examination. *Journal of Marketing*, *62*(3), 42–54. doi:10.1177/002224299806200303

Hyytinen, A., & Toivanen, O. (2005). Do financial constraints hold back innovation and growth?: Evidence on the role of public policy. *Research Policy*, *34*(9), 1385–1403. doi:10.1016/j.respol.2005.06.004

IBEF. (2020). *ITourism & Hospitality Industry in India*. Retrieved from https://www.ibef.org/industry/tourism-hospitality-india.aspx

IMF. (2011a). *World Economic Outlook: Slowing Growth, Rising Risks*. IMF.

IMF. (2011b). *Global Financial Stability Report*. IMF.

Indian Brand Equity Foundation. (2020). *Indian Tourism and Hospitality Industry Analysis*. Retrieved from https://www.ibef.org/industry/indian-tourism-and-hospitality-industry-analysis-presentation

INE. (2015). *Encuesta sobre Innovación Tecnológica en las empresas*. Madrid: Servicio de Publicaciones del Instituto de Estadìsticas. Retrieved from https://www.ine.es/prensa/np890.pdf

Isotalo, J. (2014). *Basics of Statistics*. Available at: http://www.mv.helsinki.fi/home/jmisotal/BoS.pdf

Istudor, L. G. (2019). Innovation and entrepreneurship in tourism. *Cactus*, *1*(1), 6–11.

Italoye, I. (2019). Mariya Dangote: Things You Don't Know About Dangote's Daughter. *Nigeria Infomedia*. Available: https://nigerianinfopedia.com.ng/mariya-dangote/

Jackson, D. (2015). Employability skill development in work-integrated learning: Barriers and best practice. *Studies in Higher Education*, *40*(2), 350–367. doi:10.1080/03075079.2013.842221

Jacob, M. (2017). Entrepreneurship and Startup Programs: Opportunities in Travel and Tourism. Atna. *Journal of Tourism Studies*, *12*(2), 51–65. doi:10.12727/ajts.18.3

Jagongo, A., & Kinyua, C. (2013). The Social Media and Entrepreneurship Growth (A New Business Communication Paradigm among SMEs in Nairobi). *International Journal of Humanities and Social Science*, *3*(10), 213–227.

Jakopec, A., Krečar, I. M., & Sušanj, Z. (2013). Predictors Of Entrepreneurial Intentions Of Students Of Economics. *Studia Psychologica*, *55*(4), 289–297. doi:10.21909p.2013.04.643

Jiménez, D., & Sanz, V. (2006). Innovación, aprendizaje organizacional y resultados empresariales: Un estudio empírico. *Cuadernos de Economía y Dirección de la Empresa*. Retrieved from www.redalyc.org/pdf/807/80702902.pdf

Jiraporn, P., Miller, G. A., Yoon, S. S., & Kim, Y. S. (2008). Is earnings management opportunistic or beneficial? An agency theory perspective. *International Review of Financial Analysis*, *17*(3), 622–634. doi:10.1016/j.irfa.2006.10.005

Johnson, R. (1997). Negotiating the start-up obstacle course, Mastering Enterprise. *Financial Times Management*, 126-129.

Jonsson, S. (2015). Entrepreneurs' network evolution – the relevance of cognitive social capital. *International Journal of Entrepreneurial Behaviour & Research*, *21*(2), 197–223. doi:10.1108/IJEBR-09-2013-0147

Joseph, A. (2014). Culture determinants and family business succession in Jos Metropolis, Plateau state Nigeria. *Journal of Emerging Trends in Economics and Management Science*, *5*(5), 379–390.

Joshi, M., & Akbar, M. (2012). Endogenous agency problems, their impact and mitigation in privately-held family firms for sustaining growth. *Amity Business Journal*, *1*(2), 1–22.

Juntunen, M., Ahonkangas, P., & Nguyen, A. (2018). Business Model Scalability in the cloud business context. *Journal of Business Models*, *6*(1), 19–39.

Kafouros, M., Buckley, P., Sharp, J., & Wang, C. (2008). The role of internacionalization in explaining innovation performance. *Technovation*, *28*(1-2), 63–74. doi:10.1016/j.technovation.2007.07.009

Kamble, Z., Namnuad, S., Phuong, N. H., Tuan, N. D., & Hanh, N. H. (2020). Review of Social Media's Influence on Airbnb Accommodation's Booking Intention. In A. Kavoura, E. Kefallonitis, & P. Theodoridis (Eds.), *Strategic Innovative Marketing and Tourism. Springer Proceedings in Business and Economics*. Springer. doi:10.1007/978-3-030-36126-6_79

Kampouri, K., Plakoyiannaki, M. E., & Leppäaho, T. (2017). Family Business Internationalisation and Networks: Emerging Pathways. *Journal of Business and Industrial Marketing*, *32*(3), 1–38. doi:10.1108/JBIM-04-2015-0066

Karafoti, D. (2013). *Bureaucracy and corruption in public administration* (Master thesis). University of Peloponnese. (in Greek)

Karamanos, A. (2016). Effects of a firm's and their partners' alliance ego–network structure on its innovation output in an era of ferment. *R & D Management*, *46*(S1), 261–276. doi:10.1111/radm.12163

Karavasilis, I., Vrana, V., & Zafiropoulos, K. (2016). An Extended Model of E-Government Adoption by Civil Servants in Greece. *International Journal of Electronic Government Research*, *12*(1), 1–23. doi:10.4018/IJEGR.2016010101

Kassim, E. S., Jailani, S. F. A. K., Hairuddin, H., & Zamzuri, H. N. (2011). Information System Acceptance and User Satisfaction: The Mediating Role of Trust. *Procedia: Social and Behavioral Sciences*, *57*(9), 412–418.

Kastaniotia, C., Kontodimopoulos, N., Stasinopoulos, D., Kapetaneas, N., & Polyzos, N. (2013). Public procurement of health technologies in Greece in an era of economic crisis. *Health Policy (Amsterdam)*, *109*(1), 7–13. doi:10.1016/j.healthpol.2012.03.015 PMID:22502936

Kautonen, T., Gelderen, M. V., & Tornikoski, E. T. (2013). Predicting entrepreneurial behaviour: A test of the theory of planned behaviour. *Applied Economics*, *45*(6), 697–707. doi:10.1080/00036846.2011.610750

Kavoura, A. a. (2017). Polish Firms' Innovation Capability for Competitiveness via Information Technologies and Social Media Implementation. Factors Affecting Firm Competitiveness and Performance in the Modern Business World. In A. N. Vlachvei (Ed.), Factors Affecting Firm Competitiveness and Performance in the Modern Business World. Academic Press.

Kavoura, A., & Andersson, T. (2016). Applying Delphi method for strategic design of social entrepreneurship. *Library Review*, *65*(3), 185–205. doi:10.1108/LR-06-2015-0062

Kavoura, A., & Koziol, L. (2017). *Polish Firms' Innovation Capability for Competitiveness via Information Technologies and Social Media Implementation.* In A. Vlachvei, O. Notta, K. Karantininis, & N. Tsountas (Eds.), *Factors Affecting Firm Competitiveness and Performance in the Modern Business World* (pp. 185–214). IGI Global.

Kavoura, A., & Koziol, L. (2017). Polish Firms' Innovation Capability for Competitiveness via Information Technologies and Social Media Implementation. In A. Vlachvei, O. Notta, K. Karantininis, & N. Tsountas (Eds.), *Factors Affecting Firm Competitiveness and Performance in the Modern Business World* (pp. 185–214). IGI Global. doi:10.4018/978-1-5225-0843-4.ch007

Kellermanns, F., Eddleston, K., Sarathy, R., & Murphy, F. (2012). Innovativeness in family firms: A family influence perspective. *Small Business Economics*, *38*(1), 85–101. doi:10.100711187-010-9268-5

Kenkre, P. S. (2014). Taxonomy and survey of collaborative intrusion detection. *ACM Computing Surveys, 47*(4), 55.

Kenkre, P. S. (2014). Real time intrusion detection and prevention system. In *3rd International Conference on Frontiers of Intelligent Computing: Theory and Applications (FICTA)* (pp. 405-411). Springer International Publishing.

Ketchen, D. J. Jr, & Shook, C. L. (1996). The application of cluster analysis in strategic management research: An analysis and critique. *Strategic Management Journal*, *17*(6), 441–458. doi:10.1002/(SICI)1097-0266(199606)17:6<441::AID-SMJ819>3.0.CO;2-G

Khang, D. (2018*). Vietnam named Asia's leading destination at World Travel Awards*. Retrieved from https://tuoitrenews.vn/news/business/20180905/vietnam-named-asias-leading-destination-at-world-travel-awards/47032.html

Khanka, S. S. (2006). *Entrepreneurial development* (Vol. S). Chand Publishing.

Khodaei, H., & Ortt, R. (2019). Capturing Dynamics in Business Model Frameworks, Journal of Open Innovation: Technology. *Market and Complexity*, *5*, 8. doi:10.3390/joitmc5010008

Khokhlov, N. G. (1994). Directions and forms of integration of education, science and production. *Higher Education in Russia*, 3, 108-112.

Kim, H., Kim, H., & Lee, P. M. (2008). Ownership structure and the relationship between financial slack and R&D investments:dence from Korean firms. *Organization Science*, *19*(3), 404–418. doi:10.1287/orsc.1080.0360

Kipkorir, R. N., & Omwenga, J. Q. (2015). Factors Contributing to Adoption of E-Procurement in County Governments: A Case Study of County Government of Bomet. *International Journal of Academic Research in Business and Social Sciences*, *5*. Advance online publication. doi:10.6007/IJARBSS/v5-i10/1871

Klabi, H., Mellouli, S., & Rekik, M. (2018). A reputation based electronic government procurement model. *Government Information Quarterly*, *35*(4), 543–553. doi:10.1016/j.giq.2016.01.001

Knoema. (2020). *Singapore – Contribution of Travel and Tourism to Employment*. Retrieved from https://knoema.com/atlas/Singapore/topics/Tourism/Travel-and-Tourism-Total-Contribution-to-Employment/Contribution-of-travel-and-tourism-to-employment

Kochanova, A., Hasnain, Z., & Larson, B. (2016). *Does e-Government improve government capacity? Evidence from Tax Administration and Public Procurement*. Background Paper to the 2016 World Development Report. Retrieved from: http://documents.worldbank.org/curated/en/334481468193734893/pdf/WPS7657.pdf

Koellinger, P. (2008). Why are some entrepreneurs more innovative than others? *Small Business Economics*, *31*(1), 21–37. doi:10.100711187-008-9107-0

Koh, C. E., Prybutok, V. R., Ryan, S. D., & Wu, Y. (2010). A model for mandatory use of software technologies: An integrative approach by applying multiple levels of abstraction. *Informing Science: the International Journal of an Emerging Transdiscipline*, *13*, 177–203. doi:10.28945/1326

Kok, J., Vroonhof, P., Verhoeven, W., Timmermans, N., Kwaak, T., Snijders, J., & Westhof, F. (2011). Do SMEs create more and better jobs? *Report of the EIM Business & Policy Research*. Retrieved from https://ec.europa.eu/enterprise/policies/sme/facts-figures-analysis/performance-review/files/supporting-documents/2012/methodological-report_en.pdf

Konig, A. (1997). A business plan to entice backers, Mastering Enterprise. *Financial Times Management*, 116-119.

Kontinen, T., & Ojala, A. (2010). Internationalization pathways of family SMEs: Psychic distance as a focal point. *Journal of Small Business and Enterprise Development*, *17*(3), 437–454. doi:10.1108/14626001011068725

Koutsouris, D., & Maglavera, S. (2006). *Public procurement in Healthcare*. Retrieved from: http://www.ebusinessforum.gr/ engine/index.php?op=modload& modname=Downloads& action=downloadsviewfile &ctn=1078&language=el

Kraiczy, N. (2013). *Innovations in Small and Medium-Sized Family Firms: An Analysis of Innovation Related Top Management Team Behaviors and Family Firm-Specific Characteristics*. Springer. doi:10.1007/978-3-658-00063-9

Krasavac, K. C., Biljana Soldic, A., & Jasna Petkovic, G. (2016). The big data phenomenon: The business and public impact. *Industrija*, *44*(2), 117–144. doi:10.5937/industrija44-10036

Kristiansen, S., & Indarti, N. (2004). Entrepreneurial Intention Among Indonesian And Norwegian Students. *Journal of Enterprising Culture*, *12*(01), 55–78. doi:10.1142/S021849580400004X

Krueger, N. F., & Day, M. (2010). Looking Forward, Looking Backward: From Entrepreneurial Cognition to Neuroentrepreneurship. Handbook of Entrepreneurship Research, 321–357. doi:10.1007/978-1-4419-1191-9_13

Krueger, N. F., & Carsrud, A. L. (1993). Entrepreneurial intentions: Applying the theory of planned behaviour. *Entrepreneurship and Regional Development*, *5*(4), 315–330. doi:10.1080/08985629300000020

Krueger, N. F. Jr, Reilly, M. D., & Carsrud, A. L. (2000). Competing models of entrepreneurial intentions. *Journal of Business Venturing*, *15*(5-6), 411–432. doi:10.1016/S0883-9026(98)00033-0

Kumar, A. (2013). Thrillophilia: Chitra & Abhishek Daga's Rs 2.8 crore travel company. *The Economic Times*. Retrieved on 30 January 2019 from https://economictimes.indiatimes.com/small-biz/entrepreneurship/thrillophilia-chitra-abhishek-dagas-rs-2-8-crore-travel-company/articleshow/25892583.cms?from=mdr

Labrianidis, L., & Vogiatzis, N. (2013). *Restructuring in SMEs: Greece*. Retrieved from: https://www.eurofound.europa.eu/mk/publications/report/2013/greece/labour-market-business/restructuring-in-smes-greece

Lado, A. A., & Wilson, M. C. (1994). Human resource systems and sustained competitive advantage: Toward a conceptual integration. *Journal of Management*, (18), 699–727.

Laguía, A., Moriano, J. A., & Gorgievski, M. J. (2019). A psychosocial study of self-perceived creativity and entrepreneurial intentions in a sample of university students. *Thinking Skills and Creativity*, *31*, 44–57. doi:10.1016/j.tsc.2018.11.004

Laiho, T. (2011). *Agency theory and ownership Structure-Estimating the effect of ownership structure on firm performance* (Master's thesis). Department of Economics, Aalto University School of Economics.

Lanero, A., Vázquez, J.-L., & Aza, C. L. (2016). Social cognitive determinants of entrepreneurial career choice in university students. *International Small Business Journal: Researching Entrepreneurship*, *34*(8), 1053–1075. doi:10.1177/0266242615612882

Lan, H., Zhu, Y., Ness, D., Xing, K., & Schneider, K. (2014). The role and characteristics of social entrepreneurs in contemporary rural cooperative development in China: Case studies of rural social entrepreneurship. *Asia Pacific Business Review*, *20*(3), 379–400. doi:10.1080/13602381.2014.929300

Laspita, S., Breugst, N., Heblich, S., & Patzelt, H. (2012). Intergenerational transmission of entrepreneurial intentions. *Journal of Business Venturing*, *27*(4), 414–435. doi:10.1016/j.jbusvent.2011.11.006

Lau, J. (2019). Entrepreneur's out-of-the-box idea for shipping-container hotel in Singapore. *The Straits Times*. Retrieved from https://www.straitstimes.com/singapore/entrepreneurs-out-of-the-box-idea-for-shipping-container-hotel

Leask, G., & Parker, D. (2006). Strategic group theory: Review, examination, and application in the UK pharmaceutical industry. *Journal of Management Development*, *25*(4), 386–408. doi:10.1108/02621710610655846

Lee, J., Park, D., & Han, I. (2008). The effect of negative online consumer reviews on product attitude: An information processing view. *Electronic Commerce Research and Applications*, *7*(3), 341–352. doi:10.1016/j.elerap.2007.05.004

Leisure hospitality startup 'V resorts' raises $10M in fresh series A funding. (2019). *Business World*. Retrieved from https://search-proquest-com.elibrary.jcu.edu.au/docview/2205290384?accountid=16285

Lesenciuc, A. (2017). Teorii ale comunicării. Braşov: Academia Forţelor Aeriene „Henri Coandă" Publishing House.

Li, Y., Tang, L., & Lio, Z. (2015). Research about the Effection of Incubated Enterprises Business Network on the Enterprise Performance. *2nd International Conference on Education Reform and Modern Management (ERMM)*, 382-285.

Licenji, A. (2015). Standards and challenges of public procurement. *European Scientific Journal*, *11*(25), 229–240.

Liguori, E. W., Bendickson, J. S., & Mcdowell, W. C. (2017). Revisiting entrepreneurial intentions: A social cognitive career theory approach. *The International Entrepreneurship and Management Journal*, *14*(1), 67–78. doi:10.100711365-017-0462-7

Liñán, F., & Chen, Y.-W. (2009). Development and Cross-Cultural Application of a Specific Instrument to Measure Entrepreneurial Intentions. *Entrepreneurship Theory and Practice*, *33*(3), 593–617. doi:10.1111/j.1540-6520.2009.00318.x

Liñán, F., & Santos, F. J. (2007). Does Social Capital Affect Entrepreneurial Intentions? *International Advances in Economic Research, 13*(4), 443–453. doi:10.100711294-007-9109-8

Lin, D., Lu, J., Li, P. P., & Liu, X. (2015). Balancing Formality and Informality in Business Exchanges as a Duality: A Comparative Case Study of Returnee and Local Entrepreneurs in China. *Management and Organization Review, 11*(2), 315–342. doi:10.1017/mor.2014.2

Lippman, S. A., & Rumelt, R. P. (1982). Uncertain Imitability: An Analysis of Interfirm Differences in Efficiency under Competition. *The Bell Journal of Economics, 13*(2), 418–438. doi:10.2307/3003464

Litvin, S. W., Goldsmith, R. E., & Pan, B. (2008). Electronic word-of-mouth in hospitality and tourism management. *Tourism Management, 29*(3), 458–468. doi:10.1016/j.tourman.2007.05.011

Liu, C. S., & Fang, Y. (2016). Night markets: Entrepreneurship and achieving competitive advantage. *International Journal of Contemporary Hospitality Management, 28*(11), 2374–2398. doi:10.1108/IJCHM-03-2015-0114

Li, X., Pan, B., Zhang, L., & Smith, W. W. (2009). The effect of online information search on image development: Insights from a mixed-methods study. *Journal of Travel Research, 48*(1), 45–57. doi:10.1177/0047287508328659

Li, Y., Su, Z., & Liu, Y. (2010). Can strategic flexibility help firms profit from product innovation? *Technovation, 30*(5-6), 300–309. doi:10.1016/j.technovation.2009.07.007

Llach, J., & Nordqvist, M. (2010). Innovation in family and non-family businesses: A resource perspective. *International Journal of Entrepreneurial Venturing, 2*(3), 381–399. doi:10.1504/IJEV.2010.037119

Llonch, A. J., López, B. M. P., & Eusebio, R. (2007). *Orientación al aprendizaje, Orientación al mercado, Resultados y el efecto moderador de la procedencia funcional del Director General. Cuadernos de Economía y Dirección de la Empresa, núm. 33, diciembre, 2007.* Asociación Científica de Economía y Dirección de Empresas Madrid.

Loan, D. (2019). *Int'l tourists to Vietnam up 39% y-o-y in Nov.* Retrieved from https://en.thesaigontimes.vn/tinbaichitiet/73166/

Lööf, H., & Heshmati, A. (2006). On the relationship between innovation and performance: A sensitivity analysis. *Economics of Innovation and New Technology, 15*(4/5), 317–344. doi:10.1080/10438590500512810

Lordkipanidze, M., Brezet, H., & Backman, M. (2005). The entrepreneurship factor in sustainable tourism development. *Journal of Cleaner Production, 13*(8), 787–798. doi:10.1016/j.jclepro.2004.02.043

Lorsch, J. W. (2010). A Contingency Theory of Leadership. In N. Nohria & R. Khurana (Eds.), *Handbook of Leadership Theory and Practice.* Harvard Business Press.

Lortie, J., & Castogiovanni, G. (2015). The theory of planned behavior in entrepreneurship research: What we know and future directions. *The International Entrepreneurship and Management Journal, 11*(4), 935–957. doi:10.100711365-015-0358-3

Lozano, O. J., & González, C. C. H. (2015). Desarrollo de un modelo de gestión de la inteligencia organizacional para la compañía Gráficas Modernas S.A. *Universidad & Empresa, 17*(29), 2015. doi:10.12804/rev.univ.empresa.29.2015.03

Lucky, E. O. I., Minai, M. S., & Adebayo, O. I. (2011). A conceptual framework of family business succession: Bane of family business continuity. *International Journal of Business and Social Science, 2*(18), 106–113.

Luhman, J. T., & Cunliffe, A. L. (2013). *Key concepts in organization theory.* SAGE Publications Ltd.; doi:10.4135/9781473914643

Lukacs, E. (2005). The economic role of SMEs in world economy, especially in Europe. *European Integration Studies, 1*(4), 3–12.

Ma, W., Zhu, G., Hou, Y. (2011). Learning Orientation, Process Innovation, and Firm Performance in Manufacturing Industry. *Advances in information Sciences and Service Sciences, 3*(11).

Madden, T. J., Ellen, P. S., & Ajzen, I. (1992). A comparison of the theory of planned behavior and the theory of reasoned action. *Personality and Social Psychology Bulletin, 18*(1), 3–9. doi:10.1177/0146167292181001

Maes, J., Leroy, H., & Sels, L. (2014). Gender differences in entrepreneurial intentions: A TPB multigroup analysis at factor and indicator level. *European Management Journal, 32*(5), 784–794. doi:10.1016/j.emj.2014.01.001

Maglaras, L. A., Kim, K.-H., Janicke, H., Ferrag, M. A., Rallis, S., Fragkou, P., Maglaras, A., & Cruz, T. J. (2018). Cyber security of critical infrastructures. *ICT Express, 4*(1), 42–45. doi:10.1016/j.icte.2018.02.001

Mair, J., & Marti, I. (2006). Social Entrepreneurship Research: A Source of Explanation, Prediction, and Delight. *Journal of World Business, 41*(1), 36–44. doi:10.1016/j.jwb.2005.09.002

Makarona, E. K. A. (2019). Redesigning the Ivory Tower: Academic entrepreneurship as a new calling supporting economic growth, The Malopolska School of Economics. *Tarnow Research Papers Collection, 42*, 15–26.

Makarona, E., & Kavoura, A. (2019). Redesigning the Ivory Tower: Academic entrepreneurship as a new calling supporting economic growth. *Tarnów Research Papers Collection, 42*(2), 15–26.

Makarona, E., & Kavoura, A. (2019). Redesigning the Ivory Tower: Academic entrepreneurship as a new calling supporting economic growth. *The Malopolska School of Economics in Tarnow Research Papers Collection, 42*(2), 15–26.

Makarona, E., & Kavoura, A. (2019). Redesigning the Ivory Tower: Academic entrepreneurship as a new calling supporting economic growth. *The Malopolska School of Economics in Tarnow Research Papers Collection, 42*, 15–26. doi:10.25944/znmwse.2019.02.1526

Makkonen, H., Pohjola, M., Olkkonen, R., & Koponen, A. (2014). Dynamic capabilities and firm performance in a financial crisis. *Journal of Business Research, 67*(1), 2707–2719. doi:10.1016/j.jbusres.2013.03.020

Maldonado, G., Madrid, A., Martinez, M., & Aguilera, L. (2009). Los efectos de la innovación en el rendimiento de las MIPYMES de Aguasclientes: una evidencia empírica. *Revista economia.* Retrieved from http://www.revista.economia.uady.mx/2009/XXVI/73/02.pdf

Malgwi, C. A., Owhoso, V., Gleason, K. C., & Mathur, I. (2006). Who invests in the least developed countries? An examination of US multinationals in Africa. *Journal of African Business, 7*(1-2), 201–227. doi:10.1300/J156v07n01_10

Marchese, M., Giuliani, E., Salazar-Elena, J. C., & Stone, I. (2019). *Enhancing SME productivity: Policy highlights on the role of managerial skills, workforce skills and business linkages. OECD SME and Entrepreneurship Papers, No16.* Paris: OECD Publishing; doi:10.1787/825bd8a8-

Marketer. (2019). *Thailand lacks 'travel tech', pushing tourism not to end, Tourism Authority of Thailand to solve games, focusing on creating people for innovation.* Retrieved from https://marketeeronline.co/archives/104901

Marlow, S., Taylor, S., & Thompson, A. (2010). Informality and formality in medium-sized companies: Contestation and synchronization. *British Journal of Management, 21*(4), 954–966. doi:10.1111/j.1467-8551.2009.00635.x

Marrocu, E., & Paci, R. (2012). Education or creativity: What matters most for economic performance? *Economic Geography, 88*(4), 369–401. doi:10.1111/j.1944-8287.2012.01161.x

Martin, C., & Iucu, R. (2013). Teaching entrepreneurship to educational sciences students. *Procedia: Social and Behavioral Sciences*, *116*, 4397–4400. doi:10.1016/j.sbspro.2014.01.954

Masika, D. (2013). *Challenges and Prospects for using ICT in public procurement in Tanzania. The case of Maryland global initiative Tanzania–head Office* (Master thesis). Mzumbe University

Masouras, A. (2019). Young entrepreneurship in Cyprus: An institutional analysis. *Tarnów Research Papers Collection*, *42*(2), 27–42.

Masouras, A. (2019). Young entrepreneurship in Cyprus: An institutional analysis. *The Małopolska School of Economics in Tarnów Research Papers Collection*, *42*(2), 27–42.

Masouras, A. (2019a). Young entrepreneurship in Cyprus. *The Małopolska School of Economics in Tarnów Research Papers Collection*, *42*, 2.

Masouras, A. (2019b). *Entrepreneurship in Small and Medium-Sized Enterprises*. Nova Science Publishers.

Masouras, A., & Papademetriou, C. (2018). Digital Consumer Behaviour in Cyprus: From Uses and Gratifications Theory to 4C's Online Shopping Approach. *Journal of Advertising and Public Relations*, *1*(1), 1–11.

Masouras, A., Siakalli, M., & Papademetriou, C. (2016). *E-marketing in the Hotel Industry: Marketing Mix Strategies*. Springer International Publishing.

Mas-Ruiz, F. J., Ruiz-Moreno, F., & Ladrón de Guevara Martínez, A. (2014). Asymmetric rivalry within and between strategic groups. *Strategic Management Journal*, *35*(3), 419–439. doi:10.1002mj.2102

Massa, S., & Testa, S. (2008). Innovation and SMEs: Misaligned perspectives and goals among entrepreneurs, academics, and policy makers. *Technovation*, *28*(7), 393–407. doi:10.1016/j.technovation.2008.01.002

Mather, D., Caputi, P., & Jayasuriya, R. (2002). Is the technology acceptance model a valid model of user satisfaction of information technology in environments where usage is mandatory? In A. Wenn, M. McGrath, & F. Burstein (Eds.), *Enabling organisations and society through information systems* (pp. 1241–1250). Victoria University.

Mathieson, K. (1991). Predicting User Intentions: Comparing the Technology Acceptance Model with the Theory of Planned Behavior. *Information Systems Research*, *2*(3), 173–191. doi:10.1287/isre.2.3.173

Mazzarol, T. (2015). SMEs engagement with e-commerce, e-business and e-marketing. *Small Enterprise Research*, *22*(1), 79–90. doi:10.1080/13215906.2015.1018400

Mbow, C., Skole, D., Dieng, M., Justice, C., Kwesha, D., Mane, L., & Virji, H. (2012). *Challenges and prospects for REDD+ in Africa: desk review of REDD+ implementation in Africa. Global Land Project Reports, 5. World Agroforestry Centre*. ICRAF.

McAdam, M., & McAdam, R. (2008). High tech start-ups in University Science Park incubators: The relationship between the start-up's lifecycle progression and use of the incubator's resources. *Technovation*, *28*(5), 277–290. doi:10.1016/j.technovation.2007.07.012

McKee, B. (1992). A boost for start-ups. *Nation's Business*, 40–42.

McKinsey. (2012). Leading a developing-market bank: An interview with the CEO of Nigeria's Oceanic Bank. *McKinsey Quarterly*. Available: https://web.archive.org/web/20101202032653/http://www.mckinseyquarterly.com/Leading_a_developing-market_bank_An_interview_with_the_CEO_of_Nigerias_Oceanic_Bank_2395

Medina, C., & Espinoza, M. (1994). *La innovación en las organizaciones modernas.* Retrieved from http://www.azc.uam.mx/publicaciones/gestion/num5/doc06.htm

Merino, B. D., Mayper, A. G., & Tolleson, T. D. (2010). Neoliberalism, deregulation and Sarbanes-Oxley: The legitimation of a failed corporate governance model. *Accounting, Auditing & Accountability Journal, 23*(6), 774–792. doi:10.1108/09513571011065871

Meyers, P. W., & Tucker, F. G. (1989). Defining roles for logistics during routine and radical technological innovation. *Journal of the Academy of Marketing Science, 17*(1), 73–82. doi:10.1007/BF02726356

Michel, A., & Kammerlander, N. (2015). Trusted advisors in a family business's succession-planning process—An agency perspective. *Journal of Family Business Strategy, 6*(1), 45–57. doi:10.1016/j.jfbs.2014.10.005

Miles, R., & Snow, C. (1978). *Organizational strategy, structure and process.* McGraw Hill.

Miller, D. (2006). Technological diversity, related diversification, and firm performance. *Strategic Management Journal, 27*(7), 601–619. doi:10.1002mj.533

Miller, D., & Le Breton-Miller, I. (2014). Deconstructing socioemotional wealth. *Entrepreneurship Theory and Practice, 38*(4), 713–720. doi:10.1111/etap.12111

Ministry of Development and Investments. (2019). *ESIDIS 2018. Annual Report on statistics of National electronic Public Procurement System.* Retrieved from http://www.eprocurement.gov.gr/ webcenter/files/statistics/yearly/ 2018_%CE%95%CF%84%CE% AE%CF%83%CE%B9%CE%BF% CE%94%CE%B5%CE%BB%CF%84%CE%AF%CE%BF%CE%95%CE% A3%CE%97%CE%94% CE%97%CE%A3.pdf

Ministry of Tourism. (2019). India Tourism Statistics at a Glance – 2019. *Government of India.* Retrieved from http://tourism.gov.in/sites/default/files/Other/India%20Tourism%20Statistics%20at%20a%20Glance%202019.pdf

Ministry of Tourism. (2020). Human Resource Development. *Government of India.* Retrieved from http://tourism.gov.in/human-resource-development

Mitra, C., & Borza, A. (2010). The role of corporate social responsibility in social entrepreneurship. Management and Marketing Challenges for knowledge. *Society, 5*(2), 63–76.

Mohnen, P., & Röller, L.-H. (2005). Complementarities in innovation policy. *European Economic Review, 49*(6), 1431–1450. doi:10.1016/j.euroecorev.2003.12.003

Mok, K. H. (2005). Fostering entrepreneurship: Changing role of government and higher education governance in Hong Kong. *Research Policy, 34*(4), 537–554. doi:10.1016/j.respol.2005.03.003

Monsuwe, T. P., Dellaert, B. G., & Ruyter, K. D. (2004). What drives consumers to shop online? A literature review. *International Journal of Service Industry Management, 15*(1), 102–121. doi:10.1108/09564230410523358

Moon, J. & Orlitzky, M., (2011). Corporate social responsibility and sustainability education: a trans- Atlantic comparison. *Journal of Management & Organization, 17*, 583-563.

Morozova, M. V., & Suzdalova, M. A. (2014). Bachelor's programs in technical colleges inn Russia and abroad (empirical research). *Professional Education in Russia and Abroad, 2*(14), 84-88.

Mufutau, G. O., & Ajetomobi, O. S. (2016). Procurement Functions as Tools for Entrepreneurial Success. *IOSR Journal of Business and Management, 18*(1), 1–8.

Muller, P., Gagliardi, D., Caliandro, C., Bohn, N.U., & Klitou, D. (2014). *SME Performance Review 2013/2014 - A partial and fragile recovery.* European Commission Annual -Report on European SMEs, 2013/2014 – A, 1-124.

Munari, F., Oriani, R., & Sobrero, M. (2010). The Effects of Owner Identity and External Governance Systems on R&D Investments: A Study of Western European Firms. *Research Policy, 39*(8), 1093–1104. doi:10.1016/j.respol.2010.05.004

Munuera, J. L., & Rodríguez, A. I. (2007). *Estrategias de marketing: Un enfoque basado en el proceso de dirección*. ESIC EDITOR.

Mustapha, M., & Subramaniam, P. (2015). Challenges and Success Factors of Female Entrepreneurs: Evidence from a Developing Country. *International Review of Management and Marketing*.

Muzyca, D. (1997). Spotting the Market Opportunity, Mastering Enterprise. *Financial Times Management*, 28-31.

Mwatsika, C. (2015). Entrepreneurship development and entrepreneurial orientation in rural areas in Malawi. *African Journal of Business Management*, *9*(9), 425–436. doi:10.5897/AJBM2014.7552

Mwatsika, C., Patrick, K., & Levison, C. (2018). Untangling the concept of entrepreneurship towards a common perspective. *African Journal of Business Management*, *12*(14), 451–470. doi:10.5897/AJBM2018.8587

Napsah, M. (2016). *The Adoption of E-procurement in the Indonesian Public Sector* (Ph.d Thesis). School of Built Environment Department of Construction Management, Curtin University.

Naseer, M. S., Nazam, M., Randhawa, M. A., Ahamd, M., Maqbool, A., Khan, M. A., & Ayub, M. U. (2018). Exploring the determinants for a successful family entrepreneurship: Empirical evidences from Punjab Province. *African Journal of Business Management*, *12*(22), 666–673. doi:10.5897/AJBM2018.8532

National Business Incubation Association. (1990). *The State of The Business Incubation Industry*. NBIA.

National Electronic Public Procurement System. (2019). *National Electronic Public Procurement System. Supplies and Services*. Retrieved from: http://www.eprocurement.gov.gr/ webcenter/faces/oracle/webcenter/page/ scopedMD/sd0cb90ef _26cf_4703_99d5_1561 ceff660f/Page120. jspx?_afrLoop= 17663529742836374

Naushad, M. (2018). A study on the antecedents of entrepreneurial intentions among Saudi students. *Entrepreneurship and Sustainability Issues*, *5*(3), 600–617. doi:10.9770/jesi.2018.5.3(14)

Naushad, M., Faridi, M. R., & Syed, A. M. (2018). Economic development of community by entrepreneurship: An investigation of the entrepreneurial intent and the institutional support to the local community in Al-Kharj region. *Entrepreneurship and Sustainability Issues*, *5*(4), 899–913. doi:10.9770/jesi.2018.5.4(14)

NBIA. (2011). *Business incubation FAQ*. NBIA.

Nelson, R. R. (2009). *An evolutionary theory of economic change*. Harvard University Press.

Neubauer, F., & Lank, A. G. (2016). *The family business: Its governance for sustainability*. Springer.

Neupane, A., Soar, J., Vaidya, K., & Yong, J. (2012). Role of public e-procurment technology to reduce corruption in Government Procurement. In *Proceedings of the International Public Procurement Conference* (pp. 304-334). IPPC.

Ngoasong, M. Z., & Kimbu, A. N. (2016). Informal microfinance institutions and development-led tourism entrepreneurship. *Tourism Management*, *52*, 430–439. doi:10.1016/j.tourman.2015.07.012

Nguyen, N. (2017). *The journey of organizational unlearning: A conversation with William H. Starbuck*. Retrieved from https://www.researchgate.net/publication/313686391_The_journey_of_organizational_unlearning_a_conversation_with_William_H_Starbuck

Nhan Dan Online. (2018). *Innovating thinking in tourism*. Retrieved from https://en.nhandan.com.vn/travel/item/6479102-innovating-thinking-in-tourism.html

Nhan Dan Online. (2019a). *World Bank sees Vietnam's economy grow 6.8% in 2019*. Retrieved from https://en.nhandan.org.vn/business/item/8236002-world-bank-sees-vietnam%E2%80%99s-economy-grow-6-8-in-2019.html

Nhan Dan Online. (2019b). *Young tourism start-up provides exciting experience for visitors to Ben Tre*. Retrieved from https://en.nhandan.com.vn/travel/item/8113102-young-tourism-start-up-provides-exciting-experience-for-visitors-to-ben-tre.html)

Nieto, M., Santamaria, L., & Fernandez, Z. (2015). Understanding the innovation behavior of family firms. *Journal of Small Business Management*, *53*(2), 382–399. doi:10.1111/jsbm.12075

Nikolaidis, P., Michalopoulos, N., Kokkalas, C., Pateli, K., Anastopoulou, I., Vrettaros, Y., Panopoulos, D., Papoulia, K., Sirros, Y., & Achilleopoulos, N. (n.d.). *Enhasing Digital Skills in Greece - National Action plan (2017-2020) for Digital Skills and Jobs*. Retrieved from http://elke.eap.gr/wp-content/uploads/2018/07/dsgr_action_plan_eng_subm4_no-memo.pdf

Nistor, C. (2010). *Comunicare şi negociere în afaceri*. Europlus Publishing House.

Nnabuife, E. K., & Okoli, I. E. (2017). Succession Planning and Sustainability of Selected Family Owned Businesses in Anambra State, Nigeria. *European Journal of Business and Management*, *9*(34), 155–165.

Nonaka, H., & Takeuchi, H. (1995). *The knowledge-creating company. How Japanese companies create the dynamics of innovation*. Oxford University Press.

Notta, O., & Vlachvei, A. (2014). The impact of Financial Crisis on firm performance in case of Greek food manufacturing firms. *Procedia Economics and Finance*, *14*, 454–460. doi:10.1016/S2212-5671(14)00734-5

Notta, O., & Vlachvei, A. (2015). Marketing responses of Greek food manufacturing firms due to economic crisis. *Procedia: Social and Behavioral Sciences*, *175*, 350–357. doi:10.1016/j.sbspro.2015.01.1210

Ntshangase, S. D., & Ezeuduji, I. O. (2019). The attributes of successful tourism-related entrepreneurs: A case from south africa. *Euroeconomica*, *38*(2), 296–313.

Nwaeze, A. (2018). *4 Nigerian Companies Whose founders found the best CEOs in their sons*. Buzz Nigeria Publication. Available: https://buzznigeria.com/four-nigerian-companies-whose-founders-found-the-best-ceos-in-their-sons/

Nystrom, P. C., & Starbuck, W. (1984). To Avoid Organizational Crises, Unlearn. *Organizational Dynamics*, *13*(Spring), 53–65. doi:10.1016/0090-2616(84)90011-1

Ochonu, M. (2008). Colonialism within colonialism: The Hausa-Caliphate imaginary and the British colonial administration of the Nigerian Middle Belt. *African Studies Quarterly*, *10*(2-3), 95–127.

OECD. (2005). *Annual Report 2005*. OECD.

OECD. (2010). *High-Growth Enterprises—What Governments Can Do to Make a Difference*. OECD Publishing.

OECD. (2014). Small and Medium-sized enterprises. In *OECD Factbook 2014: Economic, Environmental and Social Statistics*. OECD Publishing. doi:10.1787/factbook-2014-20-

OECD. (2016). *Preventing Corruption in Public Procurement*. Retrieved from: http://www.oecd.org/gov/ethics/Corruption-Public-Procurement-Brochure.pdf

OECD. (2019a). *Is there a role for blockchain in responsible supply chains?* Retrieved from: https://mneguidelines.oecd.org/Is-there-a-role-for-blockchain-in-responsible-supply-chains.pdf

OECD. (2019b). *Productivity in Public Procurement. A case study of Finland: Measuring the effiency and effectiveness of Public Procurement*. Retrieved from: https://www.oecd.org/gov/public-procurement/ publications/productivity-public-procurement.pdf

Ogbechie, R., & Anetor, F. O. (2015a). An Appraisal of Succession Planning in Family-Owned Businesses in Lagos State, Nigeria. *European Journal of Business and Management*, *7*(12), 1–5.

Ogbechie, R., & Anetor, F. O. (2015b). An Investigation into the Core Values That Drive Successful Family-Owned Businesses: A Case of Lagos State, Nigeria. *European Journal of Business and Management*, *7*(17), 17–23.

Ogundele, O. J. K., Idris, A. A., & Ahmed-Ogundipe, K. A. (2012). Entrepreneurial succession problems in Nigeria's family businesses: A threat to sustainability. *European Scientific Journal*, *8*(7).

Olalere, J. B. (2013). *Exploits of a migrants' community: Chronicles of Yorubas in Ghana*. Delight Communications West Africa Limited.

Onetti, A., Zucchella, A., Jones, M. V., & McDougall-Covin, P. P. (2010). Internationalization, innovation and entrepreneurship: Business models for new technology-based firms. *The Journal of Management and Governance*, *16*(3), 337–368. doi:10.100710997-010-9154-1

Onuoha, B. C. (2013). Poor Succession Planning by Entrepreneurs: The Bane of Generational Enterprises in South-East, Nigeria. *An International Journal of Arts and Humanities Bahir Dar, Ethiopia*, *2*(2), 270–281.

Openbusiness.ru: Encyclopedia of Russian business. Available from: https://www.openbusiness.ru/

Organización para la Cooperación y Desarrollo Económicos OECD y Oficina de Estadística de las Comunidades Europeas EUROSTAT. (2005). *Manual de Oslo*. Noruega. Retrieved from http://www.itq.edu.mx/convocatorias/manualdeoslo.pdf

Organization for Economic Co-Operation and Development - OECD. (2004). *Promoting SMEs for Development: The enabling environment and trade and investment capacity building*. Paper presented in the 2nd OECD Conference of Ministers responsible for SMEs, Istanbul, Turkey.

Orman, H. (2003). The Morris worm: A fifteen-year perspective. *IEEE Security and Privacy*, *1*(5), 35–43. doi:10.1109/MSECP.2003.1236233

Orrell, J. (2011). *ALTC good practice report: Work-integrated learning*. Australian Learning and Teaching Council.

Ortiz, P. C. F., & Arredondo, O. E. (2014). Competitividad y factores de éxito en empresas desarrolladoras de software. *Enl@ce: Revista Venezolana de Información, Tecnología y Conocimiento*, *11*(3), 49-73. Retrieved from http://www.redalyc.org/pdf/823/82332932004.pdf

Osipov, V., Skryl, T. (2016). The strategic decisions of the modern Russian economic development. *International Business Management, 10*(6), 710-717.

Osorio, A. E., Settles, A., & Shen, T. (2017). The Influence of Support Factors on Entrepreneurial Attitudes and Intentions of College Students. *Academy of Management Proceedings*, *2017*(1), 10901. doi:10.5465/AMBPP.2017.10901abstract

Otika, U. S., Okocha, E. R., & Ejiofor, H. U. (2019). Inheritance Culture and Management Succession of Family-Owned Businesses in Nigeria: Am Empirical Study. *European Journal of Business and Innovation Research*, *7*(3), 31–47.

Oustapassidis, K. (1998). Performance of strategic groups in the Greek dairy industry. *European Journal of Marketing*, *32*(11/12), 962–973. doi:10.1108/03090569810243578

Padilla-Meléndez, A., & Garrido-Moreno, A. (2012). Open innovation in universities: What motivates researchers to engage in knowledge transfer exchanges? *International Journal of Entrepreneurial Behaviour & Research*, *18*(4), 417–439. doi:10.1108/13552551211239474

Panagiotidou, E., & Intzesiloglou, N. (2016). The 'morality' of Practices in Public Procurement. Economic and Social Development: Book of Proceedings, 306-316.

Panayides, P. M. (2002). Identification of strategic groups using relationship marketing criteria: A cluster analytic approach in professional services. *Service Industries Journal, 22*(2), 149–166. doi:10.1080/714005071

Panayiotou, N. A., Gayialis, S. P., & Tatsiopoulos, I. P. (2004). An e-procurement system for governmental purchasing. *International Journal of Production Economics, 90*(1), 79–102. doi:10.1016/S0925-5273(03)00103-8

Paños A., Ruiz, C., Sabater, R., & Ruiz, J. (2004). *Modelo de Análisis del Aprendizaje Organizacional. Efecto en la Eficiencia Organizacional e Innovación.* 2o Congreso SOCOTE. Soporte del Conocimiento con la Tecnología, 5-21.

Papademetriou, C., Masouras, A., & Ioannou, A. (2020) Social Networking Sites: The New Era of Effective Online Marketing and Advertising. In A. Kavoura, E. Kefallonitis & P. Theodoridis (Eds.), Strategic Innovative Marketing and Tourism. Springer Proceedings in Business and Economics (pp. 443-448). Cham: Springer.

Parikka, J. (2007). *Digital contagions: A media archaeology of computer viruses.* Peter Lang.

Park, C., & Lee, T. M. (2009). Information direction, website reputation and eWOM effect: A moderating role of product type. *Journal of Business Research, 62*(1), 61–67. doi:10.1016/j.jbusres.2007.11.017

Park, D.-H., Lee, J., & Han, I. (2007). The effect of on-line consumer reviews on consumer purchasing intention: The moderating role of involvement. *International Journal of Electronic Commerce, 11*(4), 125–148. doi:10.2753/JEC1086-4415110405

Park, H. S. (2000). Relationships among attitudes and subjective norms: Testing the theory of reasoned action across cultures. *Communication Studies, 51*(2), 162–175. doi:10.1080/10510970009388516

Pay, T. M's journey now a case study at Harvard. (2017). Retrieved from https://www.business-standard.com/article/news-ians/paytm-s-journey-now-a-case-study-at-harvard-117013000774_1.html

Peredo, C., & McLean, A. (2006). Social Entrepreneurship: A Critical Review of the Concept. *Journal of World Business, 41*(1), 56–65. doi:10.1016/j.jwb.2005.10.007

Perez, K. T., & Bui, T. L. H. (2010). Closing Doors And Opening Windows: Opportunities For Entrepreneurship In An Emerging Asian Country For A Seasoned Woman Professional. *International Journal of Entrepreneurship, 14*, 45–49. https://search-proquest-com.elibrary.jcu.edu.au/docview/885013588?accountid=16285

Pérez-Uribe, R. (2012). *El ambiente laboral y su incidencia en el desempeño de las organizaciones: estudio de las mejores empresas para trabajar en Colombia* (PhD dissertation). Universidad Antonio de Nebrija. Retrieved from http://edicionesean.ean.edu.co/index.php/es/productos-de-investigacion1/tesis-doctorales/23-publicaciones/192-el-ambiente-laboral-y-su-incidencia-en-el-desempeno-de-las-organizaciones-estudio-en-las-mejores-empresas-para-trabajar-en-colombia

Perez-Uribe, R., Salcedo-Perez, C., & Ocampo-Guzmán, D. (2018). *Handbook of Research on Intrapreneurship and Organizational Sustainability in SMEs.* IGI Global. https://www.igi-global.com/book/handbook-research-intrapreneurship-organizational-sustainability/181082

Peris-Ortiz, M., Fuster-Estruch, V., & Devece-Carañana, C. (2014). Entrepreneurship and Innovation in a Context of Crisis. In *Entrepreneurship, Innovation and Economic Crisis* (pp. 1–10). Springer. doi:10.1007/978-3-319-02384-7_1

Person, G., & Van Beek, H. H. (1998). Uninvited Guests: Tourists and Environment in Siberut. In V. King (Ed.), *Environmental Challenges in Southeast Asia* (pp. 317–341). Routledge.

Peters, B., Dachs, B., Dunser, M., Hud, M., Kohler, C., & Rammer, C. (2014). *Firm growth, innovation and the business cycle.* Background Report for the 2014 Competitiveness Report. Retrieved from ftp://ftp.zew.de/pub/zew-docs/gutachten/CR2014_BackgroundStudy.pdf>

Peters, M., Frehse, J., & Buhalis, D. (2009). The importance of lifestyle entrepreneurship: A conceptual study of the tourism industry. *Pasos (El Sauzal)*, *7*(2), 393–405. doi:10.25145/j.pasos.2009.07.028

Petrof, J. V. (1980). Entrepreneurial profile: A discriminant analysis. *Journal of Small Business Management, 18*(4), 13.

Petrov, N. A., Abramov, D. V., & Michailov, A. M. (2018). Modern state of the institutional environment of the region as a factor influencing the outcome foreign investments. *RUDN* Journal of Economics, 26(2), 283–295

Phillips, L., & Oliveros, J. (2018). Open innovation as means of building social capital. globalization for traditional SMEs. Journal of Strategic Innovation and Sustainability, 13(3), 115-126.

Phillips, P., Barnes, S., Zigan, K., & Schegg, R. (2017). Understanding the impact of online reviews on hotel performance: An empirical analysis. *Journal of Travel Research*, *56*(2), 235–249. doi:10.1177/0047287516636481

Phillips, R., Schrempf-Stirling, J., & Stutz, C. (2019). The Past, History, and Corporate Social Responsibility. *Journal of Business Ethics*. Advance online publication. doi:10.100710551-019-04319-0

Pietraru, R. N., Banu, A., Mocanu, Ș., & Saru, D. (2018). Low cost technologies for awarness and early warning in conditions of severe weather. *The International Scientific Conference eLearning and Software for Education, 2*, 349-354.

Pilcher, J., & Bedford, L. (2011). Willingness and Preferences of Nurses Related to Learning With Technology. *Journal for Nurses in Staff Development*, *27*(3), E10–E16. doi:10.1097/NND.0b013e318217b447 PMID:21602623

Piperopoulos, P. (2007). Barriers to innovation for SMEs: Empirical evidence from Greece. *International Journal of Business Innovation and Research*, *1*(4), 365–386. doi:10.1504/IJBIR.2007.013725

Piva, E., Rossi-Lamastra, C., & De Massis, A. (2013). Family firms and internationalization: An exploratory study on high-tech entrepreneurial ventures. *Journal of International Entrepreneurship*, *10*(1), 109–129. doi:10.100710843-012-0100-y

Pizzurno, E., & Alberti, F. (2013). Technology innovation and performance in family firm. *International Journal of Entrepreneurship and Innovation Management*, *17*(1/2/3), 142–161. doi:10.1504/IJEIM.2013.055253

Platis, C., Karafyllis, I., & Kaoura, G. (2019). E-Procurement in Public Hospitals in Greece. In Strategic Innovative Marketing and Tourism. Springer doi:10.1007/978-3-030-12453-3_134

Political bureau decree. (2017, January 16). *Nghị Quyết Của Bộ Chính Trị Về Phát Triển Du Lịch Trở Thành Ngành Kinh Tế Mũi Nhọn* [Political bureau: to make tourism industry a top industry to develop]. Retrieved from https://thuvienphapluat.vn/van-ban/thuong-mai/Nghi-quyet-so-08-NQ-TW-phat-trien-du-lich-tro-thanh-nganh-kinh-te-mui-nhon-2017-338542.aspx

Popescu, D. (2003). Comunicarea managerială, strategii și tehnici de negociere. Academic Press.

Porac, J. F., & Thomas, H. (1990). Taxonomic mental models in competitor definition. *Academy of Management Review*, *15*(2), 224–240. doi:10.5465/amr.1990.4308155

Porter, M. E. (1980). *Competitive strategy*. Free Press.

Porter, M. E., & Kramer, M. R. (2006). Strategy and society: The link between competitive advantage and corporate social responsibility. *Harvard Business Review*, 1–13. PMID:17183795

Porter, M., & Kramer, M. R. (2011). Creating shared value: How to reinvent capitalism and unleash a wave of innovation and growth. *Harvard Business Review*, *12*(4), 1–17.

Praveen, N., & Khaliq, M. (2018). A General Study for Role of the Quality in the E-Procurement Process. *International Journal of Scientific Research in Computer Science. Engineering and Information Technology*, *3*(1), 102–106.

Price Waterhouse Coopers. (2016). *Inquérito Global sobre Empresas Familiares 2016*. Available at: https://www.pwc.pt/pt/publicacoes/family-business/pwc-family-business-2016.pdf

Proshare. (2019). *Findings from Nigerian Family Business Report 2018*. Available: https://www.proshareng.com/news/Savings,-Thrift---Investment/Findings-From-Nigerian-Family-Business-R/43531

Puffer, S. M., McCarthy, D. J. (2015). Institution building and institutional voids: Can Poland's experience inform Russia and Brazil? *International Journal of Emerging Markets, 11*(1), 18-41.

Pukall, T., & Calabrò, A. (2014). The Internationalization of Family Firms: A Critical Review and Integrative Model. *Family Business Review*, *27*(2), 103–125. doi:10.1177/0894486513491423

Pulido, B. (2010). *Teoría de los recursos y las capacidades: El foco estratégico centrado en el interior de la organización*. Retrieved from https://revistas.uexternado.edu.co/index.php/sotavento/article/download/1632/1471/

PwC Nigeria. (2017). *2014 Family Business Survey*. Available: http://www.pwc.com/ng/en/press-room/2014-family-business-survey.html

Quah, J. L., Yap, S., Cheah, S. O., Ng, Y. Y., Goh, E. S., Doctor, N., Leong, B. S.-H., Tiah, L., Chia, M. Y. C., & Ong, M. E. H. (2014). Knowledge of signs and symptoms of heart attack and stroke among Singapore residents. *BioMed Research International*, *2014*, 1–8. doi:10.1155/2014/572425 PMID:24812623

Quinn, R., & Rohrbaugh, J. (1983, March). A spatial model of effectiveness criteria: Towards a competing values approach to organizational analysis. *Management Science*, *29*(3), 363–377. doi:10.1287/mnsc.29.3.363

Qureshi, D., & Ahmed, M. L. (2012). Strengthening women entrepreneurs through tourism employment and entrepreneurship of the rural women in aurangabad. *Johar*, *7*(1), 54–66.

Raimi, L., & Aslani, B. (2019). Exploring the Contributions of Informal Ethnic Entrepreneurship to Economic Development in Nigeria. In V. Ramadani, L.-P. Dana, V. Ratten, & A. Bexheti (Eds.), *Informal Ethnic Entrepreneurship- Future Research Paradigms for Creating Innovative Business Activity* (pp. 179–194). Springer Nature; doi:10.1007/978-3-319-99064-4_12

Raimi, L., Moshood, A. B., Shokunbi, M. O., & Cole, B. M. (2016a). Indigenous entrepreneurs and battle for competitive edge with multinational corporations in Nigeria. *International Journal of Economic Behavior*, *6*(1), 85–96.

Raimi, L., Odebode, O. O., Salisu, O. O., & Oyewole, A. A. (2016b). Women Entrepreneurship. In *Fundamentals of Entrepreneurship Education*. Centre for Entrepreneurship Development, Yaba College of Technology.

Ramalingegowda, C., & Khare, S. (2014). *Indian Government Entrepreneurship Programs*. Retrieved 23 December 2019, from https://yourstory.com/2014/08/indian-government-entrepreneurship-programs?utm_pageloadtype=scroll

Rambler Group. (2019). Sekret firmy [Company's secret: online business magazine]. Available from: https://secretmag.ru/

Ramírez-Garzón, M. T., & Pérez-Uribe, R. (2019). Componentes organizacionales que explican la rentabilidad en las pymes colombianas. *Revista Estudios en Ciencias Sociales y Administrativas de la Universidad de Celaya (ESCAUC), 9*(1), 7-19. Retrieved from http://ecsauc.udec.edu.mx/index.php/ECSAUC/issue/view/3/Vol.%209

Ramírez-Salazar, M. P., Perez-Uribe, R., & Salcedo-Perez, C. (2018). A Triple Helix Model Based on Open Collaborative Innovation in Colombia: A Proposal for Higher Education Institutions. In *Handbook of Research on Ethics, Entrepreneurship, and Governance in Higher Education*. https://www.igi-global.com/chapter/a-triple-helix-model-based-on-open-collaborative-innovation-in-colombia/212010

Ramírez-Salazar, M. P., Pérez-Uribe, R., Salcedo-Pérez, C., & Juffington-Smith, J. P. (2019). RISE Model: Its Application on Diving Enterprises Located in the San Andres Archipelago (Colombia). In *Studies on Entrepreneurship, Structural Change and Industrial Dynamics*. doi:10.1007/978-3-030-15526-1

Realpe, B. C. F. (2015). *Factores determinantes en las prácticas de aprendizaje organizacional en el marco de la relación Universidad-Empresa*. Universidad Icesi. Facultad de Ciencias Administrativas y Económicas. Programa de Economía y Negocios Internacionales. Retrieved from https://repository.icesi.edu.co/biblioteca_digital/bitstream/10906/80985/1/realpe_factores_determinantes_2015.pdf

Reinhart, C., & Rogoff, K. (2009). *This Time is Different*. Princeton University Press.

Reinhart, V. (2011). A year of living dangerously: The management of the financial crisis in 2008. *The Journal of Economic Perspectives*, *25*(1), 71–90. doi:10.1257/jep.25.1.71

Rezaei, S., & Amin, M. (2013). Exploring online repurchase behavioural intention of university students in Malaysia. *Journal of Global Business Advancement*, *6*(2), 92–119. doi:10.1504/JGBA.2013.053561

Rice, M. P. (1992). *Intervention mechanisms used to influence the critical success factors of new ventures: An exploratory study*. Centre for Entrepreneurship of New Technological Ventures, Rensselaer Polytechnic Institute.

Riegelsberger, J., Sasse, M. A., & McCarthy, J. D. (2005). The mechanics of trust: A framework for research and design. *International Journal of Human-Computer Studies*, *62*(3), 381–422. doi:10.1016/j.ijhcs.2005.01.001

Ries, E. (2011). *The Lean Start Up*. Crown Publishing Group.

Rispal, H. H., & Bonler, J. (2010). Social entrepreneurship in France: Organizational and relational issues. In A. Fayolle & H. Matlay (Eds.), *Handbook of research on social entrepreneurship*. Edward Elgar Publishing Ltd.

Roberts, E.B., Murray, F., & Kim, J.D. (2015). *Entrepreneurship and innovation at MIT, Continuing Global Growth and Impact*. Martin Trust Center for MIT Entrepreneurship, MIT.

Robu, M. (2013). The dynamic and importance of SMEs in economy. The USV Annals of Economics and Public Administration, 13(1-17), 84-89.

Rodriguez, A. (2007). Transferencia de conocimiento en relaciones inter-organizacionales: su efecto sobre el desempeño de la firma receptora. *Estudios gerenciales, 23*(103), 18-19.

Rodríguez, A., Lozano, G., & Hernández, M. (2011). *Aprendizaje como Antecedente de los Resultados de la Innovación y Análisis de Variables moderadoras*. Presentation. U. Externado.

Rogers, E. (1983). *Diffusion and Innovation*. Free Press.

Rome Business School. (2019). *Family Business and Inter-Generational Succession*. Available: https://romebusinessschool.com/family-owned-businesses/

Rosenberg, M. J. (1956). Cognitive structure and attitudinal affect. *Journal of Abnormal and Social Psychology*, *53*(3), 367–372. doi:10.1037/h0044579 PMID:13376244

Rosseel, Y. (2012). lavaan: An R Package for Structural Equation Modeling. *Journal of Statistical Software*, *48*(2), 1–36. doi:10.18637/jss.v048.i02

Rothwell, W. J. (2010). *Effective Succession Planning: Ensuring Leadership Continuity and Building Talent from Within* (4th ed.). American Management Association.

Rotich, G. K., & Okello, B. (2015). Analysis and use of e-procurement on performance of the procurement functions of Country governments in Kenya. *International Journal of Economics. Commerce and Management, 3*(6), 1381–1396.

Rotsios, K., Sklavounos, N., & Hajidimitriou, Y. (2019). (in press). Successful Knowledge Transfer in International Joint Ventures: The Role of Trust, Partner Compatibility and Expected Benefits. *European Journal of International Management*. Advance online publication. doi:10.1504/EJIM.2019.10017016

Rotter, J. B. (1954). *Social learning and clinical psychology*. doi:10.1037/10788-000

Rowden, R. W. (2001). The Learning Organization and Strategic Change. *SAM Advanced Management Journal, 66*(3), 11.

Rowe, W. D. (1977). *An Anatomy of Risk*. John Wiley & Sons.

Roy R. (2019). For Innovations That Have no Precedent in Human History It's Time to Ask Disruptive Questions. *Performance Improvement, 58*(6). Doi:10.1002/pfi.21879

Rrustemi, V., & Jashari, F. (2018). Impact of online reviews in online booking – case study capital city of kosovo. *Euro-Economica, 37*(1) Retrieved from https://search-proquest-com.elibrary.jcu.edu.au/docview/2118384814?accountid=16285

Rueda, S., Moriano, J. A., & Liñán, F. (n.d.). Validating a theory of planned behavior questionnaire to measure entrepreneurial intentions. *Developing, Shaping and Growing Entrepreneurship*, 60–78. doi:10.4337/9781784713584.00010

Ruiz-Alba, J. L., Soares, A., Rodríguez-Molina, M. A., & Banoun, A. (2019). Gamification and entrepreneurial intentions. *Journal of Small Business and Enterprise Development, 26*(5), 661–683. doi:10.1108/JSBED-09-2018-0266

Rumelt, R. P. (1991): How much does Industry Matter? *Strategic Management Journal, 12*(3), 167-185.

Ryan, L. V., & Schneider, M. (2003). Institutional Investor Power and Heterogeneity: Implications for Agency and Stakeholder Theories. *Business & Society, 42*(4), 398–429. doi:10.1177/0007650303260450

Sadeghi, A. R. (2015). Security and privacy challenges in industrial internet of things. In *52nd Annual Design Automation Conference* (p. 52). ACM. 10.1145/2744769.2747942

Saebi T, Foss J N., & Linder S. (2018). Social Entrepreneurship Research: Past Achievements and Future Promises Volume. *Journal of Management, 45*(1), 70-95.

Sahinidis, A., Polychronopoulos, G., & Kallivokas D. (2019). Entrepreneurship Education Impact on Entrepreneurial Intention Among Tourism Students: A Longitudinal Study. *Strategic Innovative Marketing and Tourism Springer Proceedings in Business and Economics*, 1245–1250. doi:10.1007/978-3-030-12453-3_142

Sahinidis, A., Stavroulakis, D., Kossieri, E., & Varelas, S. (2019). Entrepreneurial Intention Determinants Among Female Students. The Influence of Role Models, Parents' Occupation and Perceived Behavioral Control on Forming the Desire to Become a Business Owner. *Strategic Innovative Marketing and Tourism Springer Proceedings in Business and Economics,* 173–178. doi:10.1007/978-3030-12453-3_20

Sahinidis, A., & Kavoura, A. (2014). Exploring Corporate Social Responsibility practices of Greek companies. *The Małopolska School of Economics in Tarnów Research Papers Collection, 25*(2), 186–193.

Sahinidis, A., Stavroulakis, D., Kossieri, E., & Varelas, S. (2019). Entrepreneurial Intention Determinants Among Female Students. The Influence of Role Models, Parents' Occupation and Perceived Behavioral Control on Forming the Desire to Become a Business Owner. In A. Kavoura, E. Kefallonitis, & A. Geovanis (Eds.), *Strategic Innovative Marketing and Tourism. Springer Proceedings in Business and Economics* (pp. 173–178). Springer. doi:10.1007/978-3-030-12453-3_20

Sahinidis, A., Vassiliou, E. E., & Hyz, A. B. (2014). Factors Affecting Entrepreneurs' Intention to Start a New Venture: An Empirical Study. *International Journal on Strategic Innovative Marketing, 1*, 148–162. doi:10.15556/ijsim.01.03.003

Salleh, L. M., & Rahman, M. F. A. (2017). A comparative Study of Leadership Succession Models. Sci. *Int.(Lahore), 29*(4), 791–796.

Salón, S. (2018). *Ventaja competitiva y posicionamiento de empresa: Claves de éxito.* Retrieved from https://es.semrush.com/blog/ventaja-competitiva-claves-exito/

Samara, E., Galanakis, K., Bakouros, I., & Platias, S. (2010). The spin-off chain. *Journal of Technology Management & Innovation, 5*(3), 51–68.

Samara, E., Galanakis, K., Bakouros, I., & Skalkos, D. (2018). Effectiveness of Regional Innovation Actions: Cases from Small, Low-Innovative Regions. *Journal of the Knowledge Economy*, •••, 1–34. doi:10.100713132-018-0518-0

Santisteban J., Mauricio D. (2017). Systematic Literature Review of Critical Success Factors of Information Technology Startups. *Academy of Entrepreneurial Journal, 23*(2).

Santos, F. J., Roomi, M. A., & Liñán, F. (2014). About Gender Differences and the Social Environment in the Development of Entrepreneurial Intentions. *Journal of Small Business Management, 54*(1), 49–66. doi:10.1111/jsbm.12129

Santos, G., Mendes, F., & Barbosa, J. (2011). Certification and integration of management systems: The experience of Portuguese small and medium enterprises. *Journal of Cleaner Production, 19*(17-18), 1965–1974. doi:10.1016/j.jclepro.2011.06.017

Saunders, M. N., & Lewis, P. (2012). *Doing research in business & management: An essential guide to planning your project.* Pearson.

Savvas, A. (2018). *Public Procurement Suplies and services, Use of ESHDHS* (Master Thesis). Technological Education Institute of Epirous.

Schillewaert, N., Ahearne, M., Frambachc, R., & Moenaert, R. (2005). The adoption of information technology in the sales force. *Industrial Marketing Management, 34*(4), 323–336. doi:10.1016/j.indmarman.2004.09.013

Schumpeter, J. (1942). Capitalism, Socialism and Democracy (3rd ed.). London: George Allen and Unwin.

Schumpeter, J. 1942). Capitalismo Socialismo y Democracia. New York: Harper and Row

Schumpeter, J. (1934). Harvard Economic Studies: Vol. 46. *The theory of economic development: an inquiry into profits, capital, credit, interest and the business cycle.* Harvard College.

Schumpeter, J. A. (1983). *The Theory of Economic Development.* Transaction Publishers.

Seelos, C., & Mair, J. (2005). Social entrepreneurship: Creating new business models to serve the poor. *Business Horizons, 48*(3), 241–246. doi:10.1016/j.bushor.2004.11.006

Segal, G., Borgia, D., & Schoenfeld, J. (2005). The motivation to become an entrepreneur. *International Journal of Entrepreneurial Behaviour & Research, 11*(1), 42–57. doi:10.1108/13552550510580834

Senge, PM. (1992). Mental Models. *Plann Rev, 20,* 4– 10, 44.

Senge, P. (1990). *La Quinta Disciplina. El arte y la práctica de la organizacion abierta al aprendizaje.* Granica.

Senge, P. M. (2000). *La danza del cambio: los retos de sostener el impulso en organizaciones abiertas al aprendizaje.* Ediciones Juan Granica S.A.

Sepetis A., Amitsis G. & Sanida M. (2016). Connecting Corporate Social Responsibility Strategies with Social Enterprises Policies in the concept of the European Union Policies for Sustainable Development. *Journal of Regional & Socio- Economic Issues, 6*(2), 2049-1395.

Sepetis, A., & Rizos, F. (2011). Sustainable Development and Corporate Social Responsibility in Higher Education: Some Evidence from Greece. *International Conference on Integrated Information Kos*.

Serdaris, P., Antoniadis, I., & Tomlekova, N. (2014). Supply chain management: A view of the distribution channel. *Bulgarian Journal of Agricultural Science*, *20*(2), 480–486.

Shankar, V., & Krisnamurti, L. (1999). What are the Options for Later Entrants? Mastering Marketing. *Financial Times*, 172-178.

Shanker, M. C., & Astrachan, J. H. (1996). Myths and realities: Family businesses' contribution to the US economy. A framework for assessing family business statistics. *Family Business Review*, *9*(2), 107–123. doi:10.1111/j.1741-6248.1996.00107.x

Shan, Y. (2016). How credible are online product reviews? The effects of self-generated and system-generated cues on source credibility evaluation. *Computers in Human Behavior*, *55*, 633–641. doi:10.1016/j.chb.2015.10.013

Shapero, A. (1984). *Why entrepreneurship?* Working paper, Babson College.

Shapero, A. (1975). The displaced, uncomfortable entrepreneur. *Psychology Today*, *9*(November), 83–88, 133.

Sharabati, M. M. N., Sulaiman, A., & Salleh, M. N. A. (2015). End User Satisfaction and Individual Performance Assessments in e-Procurement Systems. *International Journal of Computer Theory and Engineering*, *7*(6), 503–509. doi:10.7763/IJCTE.2015.V7.1010

Sharma, Y. (2019). *Number of Startups in India grew 7X to 50K in a decade: KPMG report*. Retrieved from https://entrackr.com/2019/02/startups-india-grew-50k-2019/

Sharma, A., & Grant, D. (2011). Narrative, Drama and Charismatic Leadership: The Case of Apple's Steve Jobs. *Leadership*, *7*(1), 3–26. doi:10.1177/1742715010386777

Shaw, G., & Williams, A. M. (2013). From lifestyle consumption to lifestyle production: Changing patterns of tourism entrepreneurship. In *Small firms in tourism* (pp. 109–124). Routledge.

Sheppard, B. H., Hartwick, J., & Warshaw, P. R. (1988). The Theory of Reasoned Action: A MetaAnalysis of Past Research with Recommendations for Modifications and Future Research. *The Journal of Consumer Research*, *15*(3), 325. doi:10.1086/209170

Sherman, H., & Chappell, D. S. (1998). Methodological challenges in evaluating busi- ness incubator outcomes. *Economic Development Quarterly*, *12*(4), 313–321. doi:10.1177/089124249801200403

Shinde, K. A. (2010). Entrepreneurship and indigenous entrepreneurs in religious tourism in india. *International Journal of Tourism Research*, *12*(5), 523–535. doi:10.1002/jtr.771

Shook, C. L., & Bratianu, C. (2008). Entrepreneurial intent in a transitional economy: An application of the theory of planned behavior to Romanian students. *The International Entrepreneurship and Management Journal*, *6*(3), 231–247. doi:10.100711365-008-0091-2

Siakalli, M., & Masouras, A. (2020). Factors That Influence Tourist Satisfaction: An Empirical Study in Pafos. In *Strategic Innovative Marketing and Tourism* (pp. 459–466). Springer. doi:10.1007/978-3-030-36126-6_51

Siam Commercial Bank. (2016). *Insight: Thai Tourism: Sustaining Success*. Retrieved from https://www.scbeic.com/en/detail/file/product/2953/ekn1rppsq7/EIC_Insight_ENG_Tourism_2016.pdf/preview

Siebels, J.-F., & Aufseß, D. (2012). A Review of Theory in Family Business Research. *The Implications for Corporate Governance*, *14*, 280–304.

Siegel, J. A. (2019). Future City newsletter: Struggles at SoftBank's $10B hospitality startup, the death of CediFi & more. *The Real Deal New York Estate News*. Retrieved from https://therealdeal.com/2019/12/27/future-city-newsletter-struggles-at-softbanks-10b-hospitality-startup-the-death-of-credifi-more/

Simon, H. A. (1991). Bounded rationality and organizational learning. *Organization Science*, *2*(1), 125–134. doi:10.1287/orsc.2.1.125

Singapore Tourism Board. (2011). *Fact Sheet: Tourism Perfomance for Jan-Dec 2010*. Retrieved from https://www.stb.gov.sg/content/dam/stb/documents/statistics-marketing-insights/Quarterly-Tourism-Performance-Report/stb-monthly-factsheet-jan-to-dec-2010.pdf

Singapore Tourism Board. (2020a). *Singapore Tourism Accelerator*. Retrieved from https://www.stb.gov.sg/content/stb/en/trade-events-and-resources/Singapore-Tourism-Accelerator.html

Singapore Tourism Board. (2020b). *Grants Overview*. Retrieved from https://www.stb.gov.sg/content/stb/en/assistance-and-licensing/grants-overview.html#

Singapore Tourism Board. (2020c). *Tourism Sector Performance Q4 2019 Report*. Retrieved from https://www.stb.gov.sg/content/dam/stb/documents/statistics-marketing-insights/Quarterly-Tourism-Performance-Report/STB%20Q4%20 2019_Final.pdf

Sinkovics, R. R., Bell, J., & Deans, K. R. (2004). Using Information Communication Technology to Develop International Entrepreneurship Competencies. *Journal of International Entrepreneurship*, *2*(1/2), 125–137. doi:10.1023/B:JIEN.0000026909.49686.a5

Sinkula, J., Baker, W., & Noordewier, T. (1997). A Framework for Market-Based Organizational Learning: Linking Values, Knowledge, and Behavior. *Journal of the Academy of Marketing Science*. Retrieved from https://link.springer.com/article/10.1177/0092070397254003

Skouloudis, A., & Evangelinos, K. (2012). A research design for mapping national CSR terrains International. *Journal of Sustainable Development & World Ecology*, *19*(2), 130–143. doi:10.1080/13504509.2011.606338

Slater, S. F., & Narver, J. C. (1995). Market Orientation and the Learning Organization. *Journal of Marketing*, *59*(July), 63–74. doi:10.1177/002224299505900306

Sluis, J., Praag, M., & Vijverberg, W. (2008). Education and entrepreneurship selection and performance: A review of the empirical literature. *Journal of Economic Surveys*, *22*(5), 795–841. doi:10.1111/j.1467-6419.2008.00550.x

Small Business Act (SBA) Fact Sheet. (n.d.a). *Annual Report 2010-2011*. Retrieved from https://ec.europa.eu/enterprise/policies/sme/facts-figures-analysis/performance-review/files/countries-sheets/2010-2011/greece_en.pdf

Small Business Act (SBA) Fact Sheet. (n.d.b). *Annual Report 2012*. Retrieved from https://ec.europa.eu/enterprise/policies/sme/facts-figures-analysis/performance-review/files/supporting-documents/2012/annual-report_en.pdf

Small Business Act (SBA). (n.d.a). *Annual Report 2013*. Retrieved from https://ec.europa.eu/enterprise/policies/sme/facts-figures-analysis/performance-review/files/supporting-documents/2013/annual-report-smes-2013_en.pdf

Small Business Act (SBA). (n.d.b). *Annual Report 2014*. Retrieved from https://ec.europa.eu/enterprise/policies/sme/facts-figures-analysis/performance-review/files/supporting-documents/2014/annual-report-smes-2014_en.pdf

Small Business Act (SBA). (n.d.c). *Annual Report 2015*. Retrieved from http://www.heliachamber.gr/iliaimages/greece_en_F19573.pdf

Small Business Act (SBA). (n.d.d). *Annual Report 2016.* Retrieved from https://www.ggb.gr/sites/default/files/basic-page-files/Greece%202016%20SBA%20Fact%20Sheet.pdf

Small Business Act (SBA). (n.d.e). *Annual Report 2017.* Retrieved from https://ec.europa.eu/docsroom/documents/29489/attachments/13/translations/en/renditions/pdf

Small Business Act (SBA). (n.d.f). *Annual Report 2018.* Retrieved from https://ec.europa.eu/growth/smes/business-friendly-environment/performance-review_en

SMEDAN & National Bureau of Statistics. (2012). *Survey Report on Micro, Small and Medium Enterprises in Nigeria: 2010 National MSME Collaborative Survey.* SMEDAN and National Bureau of Statistics.

Smith, D., & Zhang, J. (2012). Michael Introduction: The evolution of the incubator concept. *International Journal of Entrepreneurship and Innovation, 13*(4), 227–234. doi:10.5367/ijei.2012.0096

Soininen, J., Puumalainen, K., Sjögrén, H., & Syrjä, P. (2012). The impact of global economic crisis on SMEs: Does entrepreneurial orientation matter? *Management Research Review, 35*(10), 927–944. doi:10.1108/01409171211272660

Solomon, M. R. (2009). *Consumer behavior: Buying, having, and being* (8th ed.). Pearson Prentice Hall.

Solvoll, S., Alsos, G. A., & Bulanova, O. (2015). Tourism entrepreneurship - review and future directions. *Scandinavian Journal of Hospitality and Tourism, 15*(sup1), 120-137. doi:10.1080/15022250.2015.1065592

Sood, A. K., & Enbody, R. J. (2011). Malvertising–exploiting web advertising. *Computer Fraud & Security, 2011*(4), 11–16. doi:10.1016/S1361-3723(11)70041-0

Souitaris, V. (2001). External communication determinants of innovation in the context of newly industrialised country: A comparison of objective and perceptual results from Greece. *Technovation, 21*(1), 25–34. doi:10.1016/S0166-4972(00)00014-6

Souitaris, V., Zerbinati, S., & Al-Laham, A. (2007). Do entrepreneurship programmes raise entrepreneurial intention of science and engineering students? The effect of learning, inspiration and resources. *Journal of Business Venturing, 22*(4), 566–591. doi:10.1016/j.jbusvent.2006.05.002

Sparks, B. A., & Browning, V. (2011). The impact of online reviews on hotel booking intentions and perception of trust. *Tourism Management, 32*(6), 1310–1323. doi:10.1016/j.tourman.2010.12.011

Springer, K. (2019). *Best places to visit for the ultimate Asia experience.* Retrieved from https://edition.cnn.com/travel/article/asia-best-places-to-visit/index.html

Spyropoulos, T. (in press a). Start-Ups Ecosystems Comparison: MIT and Greece Experiences. *The Małopolska School of Economics in Tarnów Research Papers Collection.*

Spyropoulos, T. (in press b). MIT Start-Ups Ecosystems and Greek Start-Up Reality – an Ecosystem Comparison. In A. Kavoura, E. Kefallonitis, & P. Theodoridis (Eds.), *Strategic Innovative Marketing and Tourism.* Springer Cham. doi:10.1007/978-3-030-36126-6_102

Srivastava, R. K., Fahey, L., & Christensen, H. K. (2001). The resource-based view and marketing: The role of market-based assets in gaining competitive advantage. *Journal of Management, 27*(6), 777–802. doi:10.1177/014920630102700610

Stable-Rodríguez, Y. (2016, January-April). Aprendizaje organizacional en organizaciones de ciencia tecnología e innovación. *Ingeniería Industrial, 37*(1), 78–90.

Stary, C. (2016). Open organizational learning: Stakeholder knowledge for process development. *Knowledge Management & E-Learning, 8*(1), 86. Retrieved from https://bdbiblioteca.universidadean.edu.co:2126/docview/1955093198?accountid=34925

Stojanović, S. (2018). Entrepreneurship innovations in tourism. *Industrija, 46*(4), 69–83. doi:10.5937/industrija46-18741

Stott, R.N., Stone, M., & Fae, J. (2016). Business models in the business-to-business and business-to-consumer worlds – what can each world learn from the other? *Journal of Business & Industrial Marketing, 31*(8), 943–954. DOI doi:10.1108/JBIM-10-2016-267

Straub, D., & Welke, R. (1998). Coping With Systems Risk: Security Planning Models for Management Decision Making. *Management Information Systems Quarterly, 22*(4), 441–469. doi:10.2307/249551

Subramanya, S. R., & Lakshminarasimhan, N. (2001). Computer viruses. *IEEE Potentials, 20*(4), 16–19. doi:10.1109/45.969588

Suddaby, R., & Foster, W. (2016). History and Organizational Change. *Journal of Management.* Advance online publication. doi:10.1177/0149206316675031

Sundbo, J., Orfila-Sintes, F., & Sørensen, F. (2007). The innovative behaviour of tourism firms—Comparative studies of Denmark and Spain. *Research Policy, 36*(1), 88–106. doi:10.1016/j.respol.2006.08.004

Sun, X., & Xu, H. (2017). Lifestyle tourism entrepreneurs' mobility motivations: A case study on Dali and Lijiang, China. *Tourism Management Perspectives, 24*, 64–71. doi:10.1016/j.tmp.2017.06.004

Swoboda, B., & Olejnik, E. (2013). A taxonomy of small and medium-sized international family firms. *Journal of International Entrepreneurship, 10*(1), 130–157. doi:10.100710843-012-0101-x

Tahinakis, P., Mylonakis, J., & Protogeros, N. (2006). The contribution of e-government to the modernization of the Hellenic taxation system. *Electronic Government, an International Journal, 3*(2), 139-157.

Tajeddini, K., Ratten, V., & Denisa, M. (2017). Female tourism entrepreneurs in bali, indonesia. *Journal of Hospitality and Tourism Management, 31*, 52–58. doi:10.1016/j.jhtm.2016.10.004

Tang, C. F., & Tan, E. C. (2013). How stable is the tourism-led growth hypothesis in Malaysia? Evidence from disaggregated tourism markets. *Tourism Management, 37*, 52–57. doi:10.1016/j.tourman.2012.12.014

Tanner, Wölfle, & Quade, (2006). *The role of information technology in procurement in the Top 200 companies in Switzerland.* Basel: Competence Center E-Business Basel at the University of Applied Sciences Northwestern Switzerland – FHNW.

TASS Russian News Agency. (2019*). Natsionalnyj proekt "Maloe i srednee predprinimatelstvo i podderzhka predprinimatelskoj initsiativy" [Medium and small entrepreneurship: National project information* [PDF document]. Retrieved from: https://cdn.tass.ru/data/files/ru/maloe-i-srednee-predprinimatelstvo.pdf

Teece, D. (1996). Firm organization, industrial structure, and technological innovation. *Journal of Economic Behavior & Organization, 31*(2), 193–224. doi:10.1016/S0167-2681(96)00895-5

Teo, T., Srivastava, S., & Jiang, L. (2009). Trust and Electronic Government Success: An Empirical Study. *Journal of Management Information Systems, 25*(3), 99–131. doi:10.2753/MIS0742-1222250303

Tewari, P., Skilling, D., Kumar, P., & Zack, W. (2013). Competitive Small and Medium Enterprises: A diagnostic to help design smart SME policy. World Bank, 82516, 1-35.

Thai, K. V. (2009). *International Handbook of Public Procurement: Public Administration and Public Policy.* CRC Press.

Thaivest. (2018). *Even More Thailand 2018 Tourism Awards Have the Country Hit High Spot*. Retrieved from https://www.thaivest.com/thailand-2018-tourism-awards

Thapphila, S. (2019, March 13). เอ็นไอเอดัน'ทราเวลเทค' ผสานท่องเที่ยว-นวัตกรรม [NIA pushes 'Traveltech' to combine tourism – innovation]. Retrieved from https://www.bangkokbiznews.com/news/detail/828393

Thoeni, A. T., Marshall, G. W., & Campbell, S. M. (2016). A resource-advantage theory typology of strategic segmentation. *European Journal of Marketing*, *50*(12), 2192–2215. doi:10.1108/EJM-08-2015-0585

Thurik, R., Verheul, I., Hessels, J., & Zwan, P. (2010). Factors Influencing the Entrepreneurial Engagement of Opportunity and Necessity Entrepreneurs. EIM Business and Policy Research. *Scales Research Reports.*, *6*. Advance online publication. doi:10.100740821-016-0065-1

Tilley, F., & Young, W. (2009). Sustainability Entrepreneurs - Could they be the True Wealth Generators of the Future? *Greener Management International*, *55*, 79–92.

Tkachev, A., & Kolvereid, L. (1999). Self-employment intentions among Russian students. *Entrepreneurship and Regional Development*, *11*(3), 269–280. doi:10.1080/089856299283209

Tobin, D. (1993). *Re-Educationg The Corporatión: Foundations for The Leraning Organizatión*. Oliver Wright.

Tödtling, F., & Kaufmann, A. (2001). The role of the region for innovation activities of SMEs. *European Urban and Regional Studies*, *8*(3), 203–215. doi:10.1177/096977640100800303

Togni, M., Cubico, S., & Favretto, G. (2010). Owners and managers in an economic crisis: How to exploit the differences. *Procedia: Social and Behavioral Sciences*, *5*, 1312–1316. doi:10.1016/j.sbspro.2010.07.281

Totskaya, N. (2015). Relational ties in emerging markets: What is their contribution to SME growth? *New England Journal of Entrepreneurship*, *18*(2), 47–60. doi:10.1108/NEJE-18-02-2015-B004

Totterman, H., & Sten, J. (2005). Start-ups: Business Incubation and Social Capital. *International Small Business Journal*, *23*(5), 487–511. doi:10.1177/0266242605055909

Trading Economics. (2020). *Thailand GDP*. Retrieved from https://tradingeconomics.com/thailand/gdp

TripAdvisor. (2018). *How Does TripAdvisor Catch Fake Reviews?* Retrieved from https://www.tripadvisor.com/TripAdvisorInsights/w3688

Truong, V. D., & Le, A. (2017). The Evolution of Tourism Policy in Vietnam: 1960-2015. In The Routledge Handbook of Tourism in Asia (pp. 191-204). New York: Routledge.

Tsagkaris, A., Tzouros, Th., Patelis, A., & Tolis, D. (2010). *The Logistics Operation at the Hellenic Public Hospital*. Myth or Reality; 1st Olympus Internation Conference on Supply Chains, Katerini, Greece. (in Greek)

Tsai, K.-H., Chang, H.-C., & Peng, C.-Y. (2014). Extending the link between entrepreneurial selfefficacy and intention: A moderated mediation model. *The International Entrepreneurship and Management Journal*, *12*(2), 445–463. doi:10.100711365-014-0351-2

Tsai, P., Yen, Y., Huang, L. C., & Huang, I. C. (2007). A study on motivating employees' learning commitment in the post-downsizing era: Job satisfaction perspective. *Journal of World Business*, *42*(2), 157–169. doi:10.1016/j.jwb.2007.02.002

Tsang, A., & Prendergast, G. (2009). Is a "star" worth a thousand words? *European Journal of Marketing*, *43*(11/12), 1269–1280. doi:10.1108/03090560910989876

Tsao, W., Hsieh, M., Shih, L., & Lin, T. M. Y. (2015). Compliance with eWOM: The influence of hotel reviews on booking intention from the perspective of consumer conformity. *International Journal of Hospitality Management*, *46*, 99–111. doi:10.1016/j.ijhm.2015.01.008

Tsourgiannis, L., Errington, A., Eddison, J., Mattas, K. and Tsakiridou, E. (2005). Marketing strategies of agricultural producers in objective one Greek region: the factors affecting the selection of marketing channels of sheep and goat producers. *Cahiers Options Méditerranéennes*, (64), 307-320.

Tu, C. C., Fang, K., & Lin, C. Y. (2012). Perceived Ease of Use, Trust, and Satisfaction as Determinants of Loyalty in e-Auction Marketplace. *Journal of Computers*, *7*(3), 645–652. doi:10.4304/jcp.7.3.645-652

Tzafilkou, K., Protogeros, N., Karagiannidis, C., & Koumpis, A. (2017). Gender-based behavioral analysis for end-user development and the 'RULES' attributes. *Education and Information Technologies*, *22*(4), 1853–1894. doi:10.100710639-016-9519-4

Tzakou-Lambropoulou, N. 2014. *Restoring the competitiveness of the SME sector in Greece. GR for Growth: Funding SMEs*. Retrieved from http://www.helex.gr/documents/10180/2084352/Session2_Nelly_Tzakou_Labropoulou_Presentation.pdf/422e0a8d-6d29-4961-9ecd-8d43d182c74d

Ugoani, J. N. N. (2015). Challenges of Succession on Family Business Success-Kitchen Model. *American Journal of Social Science Research*, *1*(3), 163–168.

Ulas, D. (2019). Digital Transformation Process and SMEs. *Procedia Computer Science*, *158*, 662–671. doi:10.1016/j.procs.2019.09.101

Ulrich, S., Rogovsky, N., & Lamotte, D. (2009). *Promoting Responsible and Sustainable Enterprise-Level Practices at Times of Crisis: A Guide for Policy-Makers 105 and Social Partners*. International Labour Organization. available at: http://www.ilo.org/empent/Publications/WCMS_108420/lang--en/index.htm

UN. (2005). Entrepreneurship and economic development: the empretec showcase. In *United nations conference on trade and Development*. Retrieved from: https://unctad.org/en/Docs/webiteteb20043_en.pdf

United Nations Economic and Social Commission for Asia and Pacific (UNESCAP). (2010). Creating business and social value: The Asian way to integrate CSR into business strategies. Studies in Trade and Investments # 68. New York: United Nations.

UNWTO. (2018). *UNWTO partners with IE Business School to promote tourism innovation and entrepreneurship*. Retrieved from https://www.unwto.org/global/press-release/2018-06-29/unwto-partners-ie-business-school-promote-tourism-innovation-and-entreprene

Urrea Giraldo, F., & Mejía Sanabria, C. A. (2000). Innovación y cultura de las organizaciones en el Valle del Cauca. In F. Urrea Giraldo, C. A. Mejía Sanabria, L. G. Arango Gaviria, C. Dávila L. de Guevara, J. Parada Corrales, & C. E. Bernal Poveda (Eds.), Innovación y cultura de las organizaciones en tres regiones de Colombia (pp. 81-218). Corporación calidad.

Usman, M., & Vanhaverbeke, W. (2017). How start-ups successfully organize and manage open innovation with large companies. *European Journal of Innovation Management*, *20*(1), 171–186. doi:10.1108/EJIM-07-2016-0066

Vaghely, I. P., & Julien, P.-A. (2010). Are opportunities recognized or constructed? *Journal of Business Venturing*, *25*(1), 73–86. doi:10.1016/j.jbusvent.2008.06.004

Vaidya, K., Sajeev, A. S. M., & Callender, G. (2006). Critical Factors that Influence E Procurement Implementation Success in the Public Sector. *Journal of Public Procurement*, *6*(1), 70–99. doi:10.1108/JOPP-06-01-02-2006-B004

Vaidyanathan, G., & Devaraj, S. (2008). The role of quality in e-procurement performance: An empirical analysis. *Journal of Operations Management, 26*(3), 407–425. doi:10.1016/j.jom.2007.08.004

Van Auken, H., & Madrid, A. (2008). Innovation and performance in Spanish manufacturing SMEs. *International Journal of Entrepreneurship and Innovation Management, 8*(1), 36–56. doi:10.1504/IJEIM.2008.018611

van der Panne, G., van Beers, C., & Kleinknecht, A. (2003). Success and failure of innovation: A literature review. *International Journal of Innovation Management, 7*(3), 1–30. doi:10.1142/S1363919603000830

Varela, V. R. (2011). *Desarrollo, Innovación y Cultura Empresarial.* Centro de Desarrollo Empresarial y Universidad ICESI. Volume 1. Santiago de Cali. Retrieved from http://www.icesi.edu.co/images/Centros/cdee/informes/coleccion_dice/DICE1.pdf

Vargas Ramírez, I. (2020) El contrato psicológico y su relación con la teoría de los grupos de interés. Propuesta para el análisis en el desempeño administrativo de las gobernaciones en Colombia. Secretaria de Innovación, Ciencia y Educación Superior. Ideas Consyteg 15(246) México.

Vargas Ramírez, I. (2018). *Gestión de conocimiento y liderazgo: perspectivas y relaciones. Tópicos gerenciales para la gestión de empresas: una mirada desde la investigación.* Universidad EAN.

Vargo, S. L., & Lusch, R. F. (2014). Evolving to a new dominant logic for marketing. In *The Service-Dominant Logic of Marketing* (pp. 21–46). Routledge.

Veciana, J. M., Aponte, M., & Urbano, D. (2005). University Students' Attitudes Towards Entrepreneurship: A Two Countries Comparison. *The International Entrepreneurship and Management Journal, 1*(2), 165–182. doi:10.100711365-005-1127-5

Vermeulen, I. E., & Seegers, D. (2009). Tried and tested: The impact of online hotel reviews on consumer consideration. *Tourism Management, 30*(1), 123–127. doi:10.1016/j.tourman.2008.04.008

Verreynne, M., Williams, A. M., Ritchie, B. W., Gronum, S., & Betts, K. S. (2019). Innovation diversity and uncertainty in small and medium sized tourism firms. *Tourism Management, 72*, 257–269. doi:10.1016/j.tourman.2018.11.019

Villegas, G. (2005). Gestión por Factores Críticos de Éxito. *Revista EAFIT* - 105. Retrieved from: http://web.archive.org/web/20030205200444/www.eafit.edu.co/revista/105/villega.html

Vivarelli, M. (2004). Are All the Potential Entrepreneurs So Good? *Small Business Economics, 23*(1), 41–49. doi:10.1023/B:SBEJ.0000026023.11752.a9

Wach, K., & Wojciechowski, L. (2016). Entrepreneurial Intentions of Students in Poland in the View of Ajzen's Theory of Planned Behaviour. *Entrepreneurial Business and Economics Review, 4*(1), 83–94. doi:10.15678/EBER.2016.040106

Wales, W. J., Shirokova, G., Sokolova, L., & Stein, C. (2016). Entrepreneurial orientation in the emerging Russian regulatory context: The criticality of interpersonal relationships. *European* Journal of International Management, 10(3), 359–382.

Wang, C. K., & Wong, P.-K. (2004). Entrepreneurial interest of university students in Singapore. *Technovation, 24*(2), 163–172. doi:10.1016/S0166-4972(02)00016-0

Waruiru, W., & Kagiri, A. W. (2015). Effects of succession planning strategy on the performance of international non-governmental organizations in Kenya. *International Journal of Science and Research, 4*(5), 3147–3155.

Webster, C., & Ivanov, S. (2014). Transforming competitiveness into economic benefits: Does tourism stimulate economic growth in more competitive destinations? *Tourism Management, 40*, 137–140. doi:10.1016/j.tourman.2013.06.003

Weerakkody, V., Irani, Z., Lee, H., Hindi, N., & Osman, I. (2014). A Review of the Factors Affecting User Satisfaction in Electronic Government Services. *International Journal of Electronic Government Research, 10*(4), 21–56. doi:10.4018/ijegr.2014100102

Weerawardena, J., O'Cass, A., & Julian, N. C. (2006). Does industry matter? Examining the role of industry structure and organizational learning in innovation and brand performance. *Journal of Business Research, 59*(1), 37–45. doi:10.1016/j.jbusres.2005.02.004

Wei-Skillern, J. C., Austin, J. E., Leonard, H. B., & Stevenson, H. H. (2007). *Entrepreneurship in the Social Sector.* Sage Publications.

Wei, Y., & Guo, W. (2010). Construction of the Entrepreneurship Education Teachers Based on the Characteristics of Business Education Level. *International Education Studies, 3*(2), 91–96. doi:10.5539/ies.v3n2p91

Werner, Schroder, & Chlosta. (2018). Driving factors of innovation in family and non-family SMEs. *Small Business Economics, 50*(1), 201–218.

West, G. III, & Noel, T. (2009). The impact of knowledge resources on new venture performance. *Journal of Small Business Management, 47*(1), 1–22. doi:10.1111/j.1540-627X.2008.00259.x

Whatley, L. (2011). A New Model for Family Owned Business Succession. *Organization Development Journal, 29*(4), 21–32.

Widing, R. E. (2003). *Customer behaviour: Consumer behaviour and beyond.* Thomson Learning.

Wilson, N., Wright, M., & Scholes, L. (2013). Family business survival and the role of boards. *Entrepreneurship Theory and Practice, 37*(6), 1369–1389. doi:10.1111/etap.12071

Wood, M. W. (2014). *Addressing Sustainability in an Entrepreneurship Ecosystem: A Case Study of a Social Incubator in Mexico* (Unpublished doctoral dissertation). Arizona State University.

Woo, P. S. (2015). *Towards Cyber Security Risks Assessment in Electric Utility SCADA Systems. Electrical Engineering and Technology, 10*(3), 888–894.

Workman, J. P. Jr. (1993). Marketing's limited role in new product development in one computer systems firm. *JMR, Journal of Marketing Research, 30*(4), 405–421. doi:10.1177/002224379303000402

World Bank Group. (2019a) *Doing business 2019. A World Bank flagship report.* Retrieved from: https://www.doingbusiness.org/content/dam/doingBusiness/media/Annual-Reports/English/DB2019-report_web-version.pdf

World Bank Group. (2019b). *Enterprise surveys data for the Russian* Federation. Available from: https://www.enterprisesurveys.org/en/data/exploreeconomies/2019/russia

World Bank Group. (2019c). *Enterprise surveys: what businesses experience. Russian Federation 2019 Country Profile* [PDF document]. Retrieved from: https://www.enterprisesurveys.org/content/dam/enterprisesurveys/documents/country/Russian-Fedaration-2019.pdf

World Bank Group. (2019d) *World Bank Group support for small and medium enterprises: A synthesis of evaluative findings.* Retrieved from: https://ieg.worldbankgroup.org/evaluations/world-bank-group-support-small-and-medium-enterprises-smes

World Tourism Organisation. (2020). International Tourism, Number of arrivals. *The World Bank.* Retrieved from https://data.worldbank.org/indicator/ST.INT.ARVL?end=2018&locations=TH&start=2016

WorldAtlas. (2020). *The Economies of Southeast Asian Nations*. Retrieved from https://www.worldatlas.com/articles/the-economy-of-the-southeast-asian-nations.html

Xu, Y., Summers, T., & Belleau, B. (2004). Who buys American alligator? Predicting purchase intention of a controversial product. *Journal of Business Research*, *57*(10), 1189–1198. doi:10.1016/S0148-2963(02)00327-2

Xu, Z. (2015). Online comment-based hotel quality automatic assessment using improved fuzzy comprehensive evaluation and fuzzy cognitive map. *IEEE Transactions on Fuzzy Systems*, *23*(1), 72–84. doi:10.1109/TFUZZ.2015.2390226

Yang, C. (2019). *Is there a role for blockchain for enhancing public Procurement integrity? 2019 OECD Anti-corruption and integrity forum*. Retrieved from: http://www.oecd.org/corruption/integrity-forum/academic-papers/Chan-Yang-blockchain-public-procurement-integrity.pdf

Yang, J. Y., & Li, J. (2008). The development of entrepreneurship in China. *Asia Pacific Journal of Management*, *25*(2), 335–359. doi:10.100710490-007-9078-8

Yang, L., & Wall, G. (2008). Ethnic tourism and entrepreneurship: Xishuangbanna, Yunnan, China. *Tourism Geographies*, *10*(4), 522–544. doi:10.1080/14616680802434130

Ye, Q., Law, R., & Gu, B. (2009). The impact of online user reviews on hotel room sales. *International Journal of Hospitality Management*, *28*(1), 180–182. doi:10.1016/j.ijhm.2008.06.011

Yeung, H. W. (2002). *Entrepreneurship and the internationalisation of asian firms: An institutional perspective*. Edward Elgar Pub. doi:10.4337/9781843765516

Ynzunza, C. C. B., & Izar, L. J. M. (2013). Efecto de las estrategias competitivas y los recursos y capacidades orientados al mercado sobre el crecimiento de las organizaciones. *Contad. Adm*, *58*(1). Retrieved from: http://www.scielo.org.mx/scielo.php?script=sci_arttext&pid=S0186-04222013000100008

Yonso G., M., Figueredo Á., C.A., Alvarado, L., & Goyo A., A.Y. (2013). El aprendizaje organizacional en las empresas editoras de medios impresos. Caso: Empresa "Al día con la noticia C.A." *TEACS*, *6*(13).

Yousafzai, S. Y., Foxall, G. R., & Pallister, J. G. (2010). Explaining internet banking behavior: Theory of reasoned action, theory of planned behavior, or technology acceptance model? *Journal of Applied Social Psychology*, *40*(5), 1172–1202. doi:10.1111/j.1559-1816.2010.00615.x

Yusuf, L. (2014). Entrepreneurship, tourism and Malaysian economy. *Journal of Asia Entrepreneurship and Sustainability*, *10*(1), 49–67.

Zafiropoulos, K., Karavasilis, I., & Vrana, V. (2014). Exploring e-governance acceptance by primary and secondary education teachers in Greece. *International Journal of Information Technology and Management*, *13*(4), 285–304. doi:10.1504/IJITM.2014.065629

Zahra, S. A., & Sharma, P. (2004). Family business research: A strategic reflection. *Family Business Review*, *17*(4), 331–346. doi:10.1111/j.1741-6248.2004.00022.x

Zamberi, A. S., & Xavier, S. (2012). Entrepreneurial environments and growth: Evidence from Malaysia GEM data. *Journal of Chinese Entrepreneurship*, *4*(1), 50–69. doi:10.1108/17561391211200939

Zamhury, N. (2015). The praxis of langkawi's sustainable regeneration strategy through eco-tourism. *Procedia: Social and Behavioral Sciences*, *170*, 49–57. doi:10.1016/j.sbspro.2015.01.014

Zehira, C., Canb, E., & Karabogac, T. (2015). Linking entrepreneurial orientation to firm performance: The role of differentiation strategy and innovation performance. 4th International Conference on Leadership, Technology, Innovation and Business Management. *Procedia: Social and Behavioral Sciences*, *210*, 358–367. doi:10.1016/j.sbspro.2015.11.381

Zellweger, T., Sieger, P., & Halter, F. (2011). Should I stay or should I go? Career choice intentions of students with family business background. *Journal of Business Venturing*, *26*(5), 521–536. doi:10.1016/j.jbusvent.2010.04.001

Zhang, K. Z. K., Xu, H., Zhao, S., & Yu, Y. (2018). Online reviews and impulse buying behavior: The role of browsing and impulsiveness. *Internet Research*, *28*(3), 522–543. doi:10.1108/IntR-12-2016-0377

Zhang, X. L., Liu, S., Chen, X., Wang, L., Gao, B., & Zhu, Q. (2018). Health information privacy concerns, antecedents, and information disclosure intention in online health communities. *Information & Management*, *55*(4), 482–493. doi:10.1016/j.im.2017.11.003

Zhao, X., Wang, L., Guo, X., & Law, R. (2015). The influence of online reviews to online hotel booking intentions. *International Journal of Contemporary Hospitality Management*, *27*(6), 1343–1364. doi:10.1108/IJCHM-12-2013-0542

Zikopoulos, P. C., Eaton, C., de Roos, D., Deutch, T., & Lapis, G. (2012). *Understanding Big Data, Analytics for Enterprice Class Hadoop and Streaming Data*. McGraw Hill.

Zirger, B. (1997). The Influence of Development Experience and Product Innovativeness on Product Outcome. *Technology Analysis and Strategic Management*, *9*(3), 287–297. doi:10.1080/09537329708524285

About the Contributors

Andreas Masouras is an Assistant Professor at Neapolis University in Pafos in the fields of marketing management, entrepreneurship and innovation. He holds a PhD (Honors) from the Department of Political Science and International Relations of the University of the Peloponnese. The title of his doctoral dissertation is: "Entrepreneurship and Competitiveness through the lens of the Institutional Analysis: The Case of Cyprus". Also, he holds a Professional Doctorate in Management (D.Mgt.) from Monarch Business School (Switzerland) and MPhil from Brighton University (Media Management). Andreas has been a Visiting Research Fellow at Antwerp University in Belgium, at the Central European University in Hungary and at Fordham University, NY. He is a visiting researcher at several other universities. Main researcher of the Centre of International & European Political Economy & Governance – CIEPEG of the University of Peloponnese. Member of the Scientific Council, as an external visitor, of the Centre of the Study of Media and Culture in Small Nations of the University of South Wales.

Georgios Maris is Associate Professor at the Department of Mediterranean Studies at the University of the Aegean. He was Lecturer at the University of Neapolis Pafos and Special Scientist at the Department of Social Sciences and Political Sciences and the Department of Economics (University of Cyprus). His academic research focuses on Political Economy, European Studies and International and European Political Economy. He was a Visiting Fellow at the Department of Politics and International Relations, Center for International Studies (University of Oxford) and he has already completed post-doctoral research at the Department of Political Science and Public Administration (National and Kapodistrian University of Athens) and at the Department of Political Science and International Relations (University of the Peloponnese). He received his doctorate in Political Science and International Relations from the University of Peloponnese with excellent. He holds a MA in European Studies from King's College London, MSc in Political, Economic and International Relations in the Mediterranean from the University of the Aegean and a Bachelor Degree in Public Administration from the Panteion University (Athens).

Androniki Kavoura has a Communication and Culture specialization and her PhD has been funded by the Greek States Scholarships Foundation. Her research interests include social media, branding, tourism marketing and culture. She is editor in chief of the International Conference on Strategic Innovative Marketing and Tourism (ICSIMAT) that is under the auspices of more than 50 universities worldwide Her scientific achievements include participation in the editorial board of international journals, over 1200 citations in scientific publications, co-chairing and participation in scientific committees of international conferences and journals. She is coordinating Interinstitutional cooperations with many universities globally under ERASMUS+ and represents her University in research projects.

* * *

Muhammad Mashhood Ahmed received the BSc (hons) degree in software engineering from the Beaconhouse National University, Pakistan, in 2015 and the MSc degree in cyber security from the De Montfort University, United Kingdom, in 2019. He is a managing director and co-founder at ADSS cyber security limited. He has experience in the IT security field.

Sahinidis Alexandros is a Professor in the Department of Business Administration at the University of West Attica, Athens, Greece. He studied in the USA, where he earned his BBA from Baruch College of the City University of New York, his MBA from Long Island University (New York), and completed the coursework of the Ph. D program of Rutgers University (Newark, New Jersey). He received his Doctoral Degree from University of Pireaus (Greece). His research interests include Motivation, Leadership, Organizational Change, Organizational Culture, Entrepreneurship, Corporate Social Responsibility etc. He published in international and local refereed journals and presented his work in a number of conferences. He has additionally taught, in several occasions in Greece and abroad, in seminars for executives as well as lower employees of numerous companies, private and public ones.

Ioannis Antoniadis has received an MSc Degree in Marketing from Reading University, UK and a PhD Degree in Corporate Governance from the Aristotle University of Thessaloniki, Greece. His research interests focus on corporate strategy, and governance, finance, and marketing. He has participated in international conferences and has published various papers in international journals and book chapters. He is currently an Assistant Professor of Corporate Strategy at the University of Western Macedonia in the Dept. of Regional and Cross-Border Studies.

Nikolaos G. Bitzidis holds a bachelor's degree in Business Administration from the Hellenic Open University and a Master's Degree in Public Administration from International Hellenic University. His thesis entitled "Public Administration and e-Governance" evaluates National Electronic Public Procurement System (ESIDIS/ΕΣΗΔΗΣ). He is currently a municipal employee, Head of the Procurement Department of Serres Municipality, responsible for the design of online contests for public supplies and services via ESIDIS.

Arabela Briciu is a Lecturer at the Department of Social Studies and Communication, Faculty of Sociology and Communication, Transilvania University of Braşov, Romania. She has a PhD in Communication and her research and teaching interests are oriented towards social media, political communication, electoral debates, brand management and corporate identity.

Victor-Alexandru Briciu is a Lecturer at the Department of Social Studies and Communication, Faculty of Sociology and Communication, Transilvania University of Braşov, Romania. He has a PhD in Communication and his research and teaching interests are oriented towards communication, public relations campaigns and strategies, branding, online branding strategies.

Fred Contreras Palacios is a research professor, Faculty of Administration, National Sports School, Cali-Colombia. Candidate for a doctorate in administration, Universidad del Valle, Cali-Colombia.

Joana Costa is a Professor at the Economics, Management, Industrial Engineering and Tourism Department (DEGEIT), University of Aveiro, whose professional activities are Managing Innovation, Structural Change and Innovation, Innovation and Technology, and Econometrics. She is also a researcher in GOVCOPP mostly interested in Innovation Policy, Economic Growth, Sustainable Innovation and Innovation dynamics. Joana Costa held a PhD in Public Policy – Economics of Innovation from the DCSPT, University of Aveiro and attended the Master in Economics at FEP, Universidade do Porto. Also has a Degree in Economics from EEG, Universidade do Minho.

Sotirios Dimitriadis received his Diploma in Mechanical Engineering and Ph.D. in Industrial Management, from the Aristotle University of Thessaloniki. He is currently a Professor at the Department of Business Administration of the International Hellenic University, Greece. His research interests lie in the areas of operations management, production scheduling, optimisation and simulation. His work has been published in refereed international scientific journals and conference proceedings. He is the co-author of a book in operations management (in Greek). He has in the past worked as Industrial Management Consultant for multinational and domestic companies and has served as a member of research project teams in the Greek public sector.

Mohamed Amine Ferrag received the bachelor's, master's, and Ph.D. degrees from Badji Mokhtar–Annaba University, Algeria, in 2008, 2010, and 2014, respectively, all in computer science. Since 2014, he has been an Assistant Professor with the Department of Computer Science, Guelma University, Algeria. He has edited the book Security Solutions and Applied Cryptography in Smart Grid Communications (IGI Global). His research interests include wireless network security, network coding security, and applied cryptography. He is currently serving in various editorial positions such as Editorial Board Member with Computer Security Journals like the International Journal of Information Security and Privacy (IGI Global), the International Journal of Internet Technology and Secured Transactions (Inderscience Publishers), and the EAI Endorsed Transactions on Security and Safety (EAI). He has served as an Organizing Committee Member (the Track Chair, the Co-Chair, the Publicty Chair, the Proceedings Editor, and the Web Chair) in numerous international conferences.

Thirumaran K., PhD, is an academic at James Cook University Singapore. His research interests are in luxury, heritage and cultural tourism. With over a decade of industry experience, he is very much committed to share and prepare the next generation of young people to drive the tourism economy.

Zilmiyah Kamble is working with James Cook University, Singapore as a lecturer in Hospitality and Tourism. Her work experience that spans over 14 years across five different countries (UK, Seychelles, India, Malaysia and currently Singapore). Her academic experience has been in the areas of Tourism, Events and Hospitality management courses at both Undergraduate and Post-graduate levels. Apart from teaching, she has led curriculum development teams and as well as been a member of the board of studies in approving and developing tourism and hospitality courses at different levels. She is also actively involved with leading journals as a reviewer of research papers and gained experience through membership of the scientific committees for conferences. Dr. Zilmiyah has consulted for the Seychelles Ministry of Tourism, and published research pertaining to tourism impacts, tourism development and policy reviews of tourism development post-war in Sri Lanka.

Thomai Karamitsou graduated from the department of Computer Engineering, Technological Educational Institute of Epirus. She has received an MSc degree in Business Administration from Technological Educational Institute of Western Macedonia - National Economic University of Ternopil. She is working as Research Associate, at the University of Western Macedonia in research projects since 2012. Her research interests include management of innovation, marketing, wireless sensor networks, IoT, and smart farming.

George Karavasilis received his BSc in Mathematics from the University of Ioannina, Greece. He holds a Ph.D. in Stochastic Point Processes from the Polytechnic School of Democritus University of Thrace and MEd from the Hellenic Open University. His research interests include time series analysis, statistical software and educational assessment. His work has been published in refereed international scientific journals and conference proceedings. He is currently an education consultant and adjunct professor at the Business Administration Department of International Hellenic University.

Evangelos Kehris holds a bachelor's degree in mathematics from Aristotle University of Thessaloniki (Greece), an MSc in Operational Research from LSE (UK) and a Ph.D. in Computer Simulation from Lancaster University (UK). Dr. Kehris has been employed as a research associate in research centers and universities in the UK and Greece. Currently, he is a professor at the Dept. of Business Administration at the Hellenic Open University, Greece. His research interests include modeling, decision making, and information technologies.

Leandros Maglaras received the B.Sc. degree from Aristotle University of Thessaloniki, Greece in 1998, M.Sc. in Industrial Production and Management from University of Thessaly in 2004 and M.Sc. and PhD degrees in Electrical & Computer Engineering from University of Volos, in 2008 and 2014 respectively. He is currently a Lecturer in the School of Computer Science and Informatics at the De Montfort University, U.K. He has participated in various research programs investigating vehicular and ICT technologies (C4C-project.eu, reduction-project.eu), sustainable development (islepact.eu, Smile-gov), cyber security (cockpitci.eu, fastpass-project.eu) and optimization and prediction of the dielectric behavior of air gaps (optithesi.webs.com). He is general (co-)Chair of INISCOM 2016, a new, annual, EAI and Springer sponsored conference on industrial networks and intelligent systems. He is an author of more than 65 papers in scientific magazines and conferences and is a senior member of IEEE.

Dam Xuan Minh has a Master of International Tourism and Hospitality Management from James Cook University Singapore, is working in the Consular section in the Royal Embassy of Saudi Arabia in Hanoi. He has a research interest in tourism and hospitality. He has more than 5 years of professional experience in luxury hotels holding various positions related to Sales and Marketing.

Ioana-Alexandra Mircea is a master student in Management of Image Campaigns, second year, Faculty of Sociology and Communication, Transilvania University of Brașov. In 2018, she graduated the Bachelor program of Communication and Public Relations in the same faculty. Over the years she has been involved in various projects, such as researching in evolution of inter-human communication process in virtual world and promoting an institution using a video material, participating in various sessions of scientific and voluntary student communication sessions. She worked as a social journalist and editor in chief. Currently, she is working in marketing and PR field and she is the PR of the biggest organisation of business people from Braşov, Romania. She is interested, from a professional point of view, in the development of etiquette in business, international relation, cultural communication and short film directing.

Nguyen Hoai Nam is a postgraduate student in Tourism and Hospitality Management (MITHM) from James Cook University, Singapore. He is interested in tourism and hospitality and marketing.

Rafael Pérez-Uribe has a PhD in Managerial Sciences, Nebrija University. Diploma of Advanced Studies in Applied Economics, Nebrija University. Master in Management of Organizations, EAN University. Maître es Sciences, University of Quebec a Chicoutimi. Specialist in Evaluation y Creation of Managerial Indicators for Tertiary Education, Business Administration School. Graduate studies as Kenkyusei (Assigned researcher) in Total Quality Control and Quality Circles, Fukushima University, Japan. Business Administrator, Jorge Tadeo Lozano University. Director of the research group in Management of Large, Medium and Small companies (G3pymes) and Professor assigned at the Research and Knowledge Management Division EAN University.

George Pierrakos is Professor (Organisation and Management of Primary Healthcare Services) in the Department of Business Administration and director of Social Policy Division at the Athens University of West Attica Greece. He is also visiting professor at Leeds Beckett University. He holds Ph.D from the Faculty of Political Science & Public Administration of the Kapodestrian University of Athens. He holds also a MSc from the Faculty of Political Science & Public Administration of the Kapodestrian University of Athens and BSc from Nursing department of the Kapodestrian University of Athens. He has participated in several Research Programs of the European Union as a member or coordinator of various research teams such as Central Support Mechanism of the development and promotion of Social Coopeative Enterprises Ministry of Labour and Social Insurance, and Primary Health Care Services evaluation in local community Ministry of Education, Lifelong Learning and Religious Affairs and Development of a Total Quality Model in the Health Education concerning Cancer rehabilitation and palliative care Ministry of health. He has substantial teaching experience in the topics of Health Systems Organization, Health Management, and Health Economics in Postgraduate programs and has been the author and co-author of several publications.

Yash Bhushan Prabhugaonkar is a graduate with a Master of Business Administration and International Tourism and Hospitality Management from James Cook University, Singapore. His primary areas of research are experience economy, sharing economy, service quality, MICE tourism and destination marketing.

Sapon Pruhtpaon is a graduate with Bachelor in Chemical Engineering from King Mongkut's University of Technology Thonburi, Thailand. He has a research interest in Business Operations and Management.

Mohit Raghav is a graduate with a Bachelor of Business from James Cook University, Singapore. He currently works for World Lifestyle in India. His primary area of research is in Luxury tourism, Luxury & Lifestyle Marketing, Service Experiences, and Destination Marketing. With strong industry connections, he hopes to inspire the next generation in Hospitality & Tourism.

Lukman Raimi is an Assistant Professor of Entrepreneurship at the American University of Nigeria. Previously, he was a Principal Lecturer/Coordinator of Training & Part-Time Programme at the Centre for Entrepreneurship Development (CED), Yaba College of Technology, Lagos. His research interests include: Entrepreneurship, Development Economics, Corporate Social Responsibility, General Management and Human Resources Management. Raimi is an alumnus of both Cumberland Lodge, Windsor, United Kingdom and Entrepreneurship Development Institute (EDI), Ahmedabad, India. He had undergone special training in Enterprise Education for Employability facilitated by the Oxford Brookes University and the Pan African University Nigeria under the British Council's sponsorship. University Degree: Ph.D., De Montfort University, Leicester (UK); M.Sc., Industrial Relations & Personnel Management, University of Lagos (Nigeria); M.Sc.., Economics, University of Lagos (Nigeria); B.Sc., Economics, Obafemi Awolowo University (Nigeria); and Certificate; Small Business Promotion, Entrepreneurship Development Institute (India).

Elpida Samara graduated from the department of Mechanical Engineering, Aristotle University of Thessaloniki. She holds her PhD with subject "National Innovation Systems, an innovation model using System Dynamics", at the Department of Mechanical Engineering, University of Western Macedonia. Furthermore, she is working as a project manager with the UOWM in many EU projects. She has a teaching experience at the University of Western Macedonia and at the Technological Education Institute of Kozani where she is working as a Scientific Collaborator with full qualifications since 2004. Her research interests include modelling of innovation systems and technological innovation, management of innovation and technology and technology transfer, entrepreneurship.

Marilena Sanida holds a Degree in International and European Studies from Panteion University of Social and Political Sciences and a MA in European Studies from the University of Hamburg. She has worked in different countries in International Institutions, Consultancies and as a Political Advisor in different Ministries. She is currently a PhD candidate at the University of Piraeus, department of Maritime Studies in the field of CSR in ports.

Anastasios Sepetis, PhD., MA and BA, is a member of Social Management Research Hub at University of West Attica. He has undertaken research and teaching since 2003 in various Universities in Greece and abroad in areas Sustainable Development and Strategies of Corporate Environmental and Social Policy relating to International, European and comparative, management, finance, Health, and Social security, Social enterprises and Social economy, Circular economy.

Karen Sim holds a Master of Business Administration from University of Western Australia, and a Bachelor of Science (Cum Laude) in Hotel Management with University of Nevada, Las Vegas. She is an adjunct lecturer at James Cook University, Singapore. A result-oriented professional with an engaging personality and known for her ability to build high-profile global brands, she eagerly shares with students her more than 25 years of experience in the Hospitality and Tourism, Financial and Technology industries across Asia-Pacific and Middle East.

Theocharis Stylianos Spyropoulos combines professional expertise and academic experience; he has more than 20 years international experience as a senior Marketing & Business Development professional in I.T. sector, and as a senior manager & advisor for Greek and international companies. Mr Spyropoulos has accumulated experience in innovation management, business development, e-business, entrepreneurship and start-ups. Mr. Spyropoulos is also a part-time lecturer at Perrotis College of the American Farm School of Thessaloniki for the courses of Entrepreneurship and e-Commerce, and a member of European Institute of Technology (EIT) Food Council. Mr. Spyropoulos holds an MBA (Marketing) from Sheffield University Management School, and his research focuses on innovation management. Mr. Spyropoulos can be contacted at info@exoha.biz and hspyro@afs.edu.gr.

Doan Toan recently graduated with a Masters in Tourism and Hospitality Management (MITHM) from James Cook University, Singapore. He is keen marketing management aspects of the hotel industry. He is currently based in Vietnam and works with Trip.com, Vietnam.

Natalya Totskaya received her PhD in Management from Concordia University (Montréal, Canada) and is currently an Associate Professor at the Faculty of Management, Laurentian University of Sudbury. She teaches Strategic Management and Global Management at the undergraduate and graduate levels. Her research interests are the areas of entrepreneurship and SME development in emerging markets.

Panagiotis Tsaknis is a PhD student in the Department of Business Administration at the University of West Attica, Athens, Greece.

Vasiliki Vrana is a Professor at the Department of Business Administration, the International Hellenic University and adjunct academic staff at Hellenic Open University. She holds a BA in Mathematics, an MS in Information Systems from the Hellenic Open University and a Ph.D. in Computer Science from the Aristotle University of Thessaloniki. She was an Education Consultant at secondary education for three years. She has published two books and more than 100 papers in international journals and proceedings that have attracted more than 800 citations. Currently, she is doing research on Web 2.0 applications and Social Network Analysis.

Antonis Zairis was born in Piraeus. He studied Political Science and holds an MBA. His doctoral dissertation was on Consumer Behavior, specializing in Retail. He has 32 years of experience as General Manager in various Multinational and Greek Companies while serving Public Management through various positions. He has taught at the Athens University of Economics and Business, at the Democritus University of Thrace as well as at the Universities of Tirana and Prague. He has participated in many international conferences and has had several academic publications with the peer review system. He has authored 17 books, 3 of them in English, on Business Administration, Marketing, Sales and Business Communication. From 2019 serves as Assistant Professor of Public Administration at Neapolis University, Pafos, Cyprus.

Zeng Zeqi undertakes a Master's in Business Administration from James Cook University, Singapore. He is interested in media and marketing.

Liao Zihui undertakes a Master's in Business Administration from James Cook University, Singapore. She is interested in marketing management.

Index

G

H

I

L

M

N

O

P

R

S

www.ingramcontent.com/pod-product-compliance
Lightning Source LLC
LaVergne TN
LVHW062143300926
849161LV00010B/2612
9781799836483